The Constitution and Campaign Finance Reform

An Anthology

Edited by
Frederick G. Slabach

CAROLINA ACADEMIC PRESS
Durham, North Carolina

The following articles in this book are reprinted with the permission of the law reviews and authors listed below. These organizations and individuals retain the copyright in the articles referred to.

Richard Briffault, *Campaign Finance, the Parties and the Court: A Comment on Colorado Republican Federal Campaign Committee v. FEC*, 14 CONST. COMMENTARY 91 (1997); Thomas F. Burke, *The Concept of Corruption in Campaign Finance Reform Law*, 14 CONST. COMMENTARY 127 (1997); David L. Boren, *A Recipe for the Reform of Congress*, 21 OKLA. CITY U. L. REV. 1 (1996); Richard L. Hasen, *Clipping Coupons for Democracy: An Egalitarian/Public Choice Defense of Campaign Finance Vouchers*, 84 CALIF. L. REV. 1 (1996); Peter M. Shane, *Back to the Future of the American State: Overruling Buckley v. Valeo and Other Madisonian Steps*, 57 U. PITT. L. REV. 443 (1996); Bradley A. Smith, *Faulty Assumptions and Undemocratic Consequences of Campaign Finance Reform*, 105 YALE L.J. 1049 (1996); Fred Wertheimer and Susan Weiss Manes, *Campaign Finance Reform: A Key to Restoring the Health of Our Democracy*, 94 COLUM. L. REV. 1126 (1996); Vincent Blasi, *Free Speech and the Widening Gyre of Fundraising*, 94 COLUM. L. REV. 1281 (1994); David A. Strauss, *Corruption, Equality and Campaign Finance Reform*, 94 COLUM. L. REV. 1369 (1994); Cass R. Sunstein, *Political Equality and Unintended Consequences*, 94 COLUM. L. REV. 1390 (1994); Timothy J. Moran, *Format Restrictions on Televised Political Advertising: Elevating Political Debate Without Supressing Free Speech*, 67 IND. L.J. 663 (1992); Jill E. Fisch, *Frankenstein's Monster Hits the Camlpaign Trail: An Approach to Regulation of Corporate Political Expenditures*, 32 WM. & MARY L. REV. 587 (1991); Daniel Hays Lowenstein, *On Campaign Finance Reform: The Root of All Evil is Deeply Rooted*, 18 HOFSTRA L. REV. 301 (1989); Lillian R. BeVier, *Money and Politics: A Perspective on the First Amendment and Campaign Finance Reform*, 73 CALIF. L. REV. 1045 (1985); J. Skelly Wright, *Politics and the Constitution: Is Money Speech?*, 85 YALE L.J. 1001 (1976).

**Library of Congress Cataloging-in-Publication Data
will be found at the end of this book.**

CAROLINA ACADEMIC PRESS
700 Kent Street, Durham, North Carolina 27701
Telephone (919) 489-7486 / Facsimile (919) 493-5668
www.cap-press.com

Printed in the United States of America

For Melany

Contents

Section IV — Alternative Methods of Regulation

Epilogue

Table of Cases

Acknowledgments

This book would not have been completed without the extraordinary efforts of Siobhan Groleau (class of 1998) who served as my research assistant at Whittier Law School. For her dedication and perseverance in completing this overwhelming and complicated task, I will be forever grateful. John A. FitzRandolph, Dean of Whittier Law School, provided the financial resources for my research assistant and the valuable computer support of Mary James and Maria Harris. I am also grateful to Mary Ellen Gale who reviewed earlier drafts of portions of this book, and to other members of the faculty at Whittier Law School who listened patiently to a colloquia presentation of this material and engaged in provocative discussion. I would also like to thank Keith Sipe, Russ Bahorsky, Greta Strittmatter, Kathy Kay and the dedicated band of scholar/publishers at Carolina Academic Press for their confidence in and expert handling of this material.

Finally, I would like to thank the editors of the law reviews and authors whose work appears in these pages. I owe a special debt of gratitude to James Skelly Wright, Jr. and Mrs. J. Skelly Wright who kindly gave me permission to reprint Judge Wright's indispensible comments on *Buckley v. Valeo*.

Frederick G. Slabach
Long Beach, California

Note on Editing

Articles contained in this anthology originally appeared in print over a period of twenty-two years. Every effort was made to conform the editorial style of each article to the Sixteenth Edition of the Harvard Uniform System of Citation. Space limitations precluded reprinting each article in its entirety. Where material is deleted, three asterisks [***] appear. Cass R. Sunstein's article contains several minor changes in the text and in the footnote order to accommodate format restrictions of the book.

Preface

Introduction to Campaign Finance Law and Organization of Materials

During the last several years, campaign finance reform has been a topic of considerable debate.[1] Campaign finance reform supporters and opponents alike have invoked the U.S. Constitution in support of their positions. The purpose of this anthology is to make a sampling of some of the most stimulating critical thinking on the subject of the U.S. Constitution and campaign finance reform accessible to students of the law.

Introduction to Campaign Finance Law

In 1974, Congress passed the Federal Election Campaign Act Amendments [hereinafter FECA] in response to the elections scandals uncovered during the Watergate investigation. The FECA provided five major reforms:

1. Contribution limits to candidates for federal office:
   a. Individuals could give a maximum of $1,000 per candidate per election and $25,000 per year overall.
   b. Multi candidate political committees could give a maximum of $5,000 per candidate per election.
2. Expenditure limits by candidates for federal office:
   a. Independent Expenditures - Individuals could make a maximum $1,000 independent expenditure to support a "clearly identified" candidate.

---

1. The U.S. Senate recently debated the so-called McCain-Feingold bill. This legislation would attempt to ban "soft money," limit "issue advocacy" which benefits a candidate, and condition certain government benefits on voluntary spending limits. *See* S. 25 (version 3), 105 Cong. Other reform proposals recently debated in the U.S. Congress as well as in the states have included some version of overall caps on the amount of money candidates for federal office may spend in an election cycle, aggregate limits on the amount of PAC contributions a campaign could accept, elimination of PACs or further reductions in the amount PACs could contribute to federal campaigns. In the November 4, 1996 elections, ballot initiatives to limit individual and corporate campaign contributions were adopted in Arkansas, California, Colorado, Maine, Montana and Nevada. *See* Judith Havemann, *Coloradans Reject Parental Rights Issue*, WASHINGTON POST, Nov. 7, 1996, at A41.

    b. Personal Funds—A candidate for President or Vice President could spend a maximum of $50,000 of the candidate's own money and candidates for the Senate and House could spend a maximum of $25,000; and a candidate for the House could spend $25,000.

    c. Total campaign Expenditures—Presidential nomination expenditures were limited to $10 million; Presidential general election expenditures were limited to $20 million; expenditure limits for candidates to other federal offices varied with the size of the voting age population adjusted yearly to reflect inflation.

3. Record keeping—Required record keeping and disclosure on the part of candidates, their committees, and those individuals who make independent expenditures advocating the election or defeat of identified candidates.

4. Public financing of both Presidential primary and general elections and of party nominating conventions for candidates who agreed to limit campaign expenditures.

5. A Federal Elections Commission was established to oversee the administration of the law.[2]

In *Buckley v. Valeo*,[3] the Supreme Court struck down the expenditure limitations,[4] except those tied to the acceptance of public financing in presidential elections,[5] but upheld the contribution limits.[6] The Court held that money spent in connection with political campaigns is essential to political speech and that limits on the amount of money spent affect First Amendment rights. Such limits are subject to strict scrutiny.[7]

The Court considered and rejected the argument that giving and spending money is conduct which only incidentally affects speech without restricting the content of speech and thus can be regulated without violating the First Amendment as in *U.S. v. O'Brien*.[8] According to the *Buckley* court, contributing or spending money is not conduct. It is speech. And for this reason strict scrutiny must be given to any regulation of money contributed or spent in the political arena.[9]

---

2. Federal Election Campaign Act Amendments, Pub. L. No. 93-443, 88 STAT. 1263 (1974).

3. 424 U.S. 1 (1976).

4. *Id.* at 39-59.

5. *Id.* at 85-109.

6. *Id.* at 23-38.

7. *Id.* at 12-23.

8. 391 U.S. 367 (1968).

9. Buckley v. Valeo, 424 U.S. 1, 14-23 (1976).

Likewise, the Court also rejected the notion that restrictions on campaign finance are permissible time, place and manner limitations on conduct which only incidentally burden speech. According to the Court, the government was interested in regulating campaign expenditures because too much speech during the conduct of a campaign is harmful. The Court found that the law, though ideologically neutral, was aimed at the harmful content of the political communication: too much speech. In this sense the law was content based and subject to strict scrutiny.[10]

Many commentators have criticized this basic holding in *Buckley*. Political contributions and expenditures are not pure speech. It is speech related conduct.[11] Money is not speech. It is a medium of exchange which facilitates speech. Giving or spending money is a physical act similar to burning a draft card or broadcasting from a sound truck.

Using this analogy, the Court should apply an intermediate level of scrutiny. The regulation of money would be constitutional if (1) it is justified by an important governmental interest, (2) that interest in unrelated to suppression of speech, and (3) the incidental restriction on alleged First Amendment freedom is no greater than is essential to the furtherance of that governmental interest.[12] Under this analysis, both contribution and expenditure limits would survive constitutional challenge. Expenditure limits as well as contribution limits were designed to avoid the reality and appearance of corruption as well as other important governmental interests and had no impact on the content of the speech.

This is the analysis used in the sound truck cases. In *Kovacs v. Cooper*,[13] and *Grayned v. City of Rockford*,[14] the Court upheld antinoise ordinances which prohibited loud and raucous sound trucks. The important government interest was the nuisance to residents of loud noise. Limiting the volume level of the sound trucks was unrelated to the suppression of the speech emanating from the trucks. And the incidental restriction on alleged First Amendment rights—the volume penetration of the message—was not greater than was essential to prevent the nuisance. In *Grayned*, the Court stated flatly, "[i]f overamplified loud speakers assault the citizenry, government may turn them down."[15] If a local government may constitutionally limit the volume (the electrical juice) of a

---

10. *Id.* at 18.

11. *See, e.g.*, J. Skelly Wright, *Politics and the Constitution: Is Money Speech*, 85 Yale L. J. 1001, 1006 (1976).

12. United States v. O'Brien, 391 U.S. 367, 377 (1968). *See* J. Skelly Wright, *Politics and the Constitution: Is Money Speech*, 85 Yale L. J. 1001, 1006 (1976).

13. 336 U.S. 77 (1949).

14. 408 U.S. 104 (1972).

15. *Id.* at 116.

sound truck to avoid the nuisance of waking residents from their sound slumber, *Buckley* critics argue that Congress may regulate the financial juice of campaign conduct to avoid the important governmental interest in avoiding the appearance of political corruption and to promote equality of opportunity in a representative democracy.

Although the *Buckley* Court applied strict scrutiny, it also discerned a difference in the relative value of speech represented by contributions and that represented by expenditures. The *Buckley* per curiam concluded that a contribution is only a generalized expression of support for a candidate, not a communication of the reasons for the support. As a result, "the size of the contribution provides a very rough index of the intensity of the contributors' support for the candidate."[16] It is the fact of the contribution, not its size, that is speech. Thus, a limit on the amount of a contribution does not limit speech. The size of an expenditure for campaign speech, however, directly affects the quantity and quality of the debate. Therefore, a limit on the amount of an expenditure does limit speech. So, while limits on both contributions and expenditures warrant strict scrutiny, limiting the size of contributions is an incidental burden on speech. Such an incidental burden can be justified by the government's compelling interest in prohibiting the appearance and reality of corruption resulting from contributions. Limiting the size of an expenditure, however, is a direct burden on speech and is not justified by the government's anti corruption interests.[17]

Since *Buckley* was decided in 1976, the Court has rendered several decisions relating to the constitutionality of state and federal campaign finance regulations. Although the Court has not revisited its basic holding that money is essential to political speech, it has struggled to apply the contribution/expenditure dichotomy of *Buckley*. Commentators have noted that what is an expenditure to one may be a contribution to another. For example, independent expenditures by an individual or political action committee on behalf of a candidate can be just as ripe for quid pro quo corruption as a contribution to a candidate. And the size of a contribution to a political action committee has just as much of an effect on the quantity and quality of debate about the issues as the amount of that committee's expenditures, since without the contribution, it can make no expenditures.[18]

The Court has also struggled with the concept of corruption which may serve as a compelling governmental interest. Three post-*Buckley* cases,

---

16. Buckley v. Valeo, 424 U.S. 1, 21 (1976).

17. *Id.* at 14-38.

18. Richard Briffault, *Campaign Finance, the Parties and the Court: A Comment on Colorado Republican Federal Campaign Committee v. Federal Election Commission*, 14 CONST. COMMENTARY 91 (1997).

FEC v. National Right to Work Committee,[19] *FEC v. Massachusetts Citizens for Life,*[20] and *Austin v. Michigan State Chamber of Commerce,*[21] support the proposition that corruption may mean more than quid pro quo bribery. In these cases the Court recognized the government's compelling interest in preventing the threat of political corruption resulting from huge corporate treasuries accumulated with the help of the state conferred corporate structure which could distort the political process and *influence unfairly the outcome of elections.* As the Court noted in *National Right to Work Committee,* the government has a compelling interest in limiting such contributions and expenditures to ensure that substantial aggregations of wealth amassed by the special advantages which go with the corporate form of organization not be converted into political "war chests" which could be used to incur political debts from legislators who are aided by the contributions.[22]

This compelling governmental interest justified a complete ban on for profit corporate contributions *and* expenditures. Because the *Buckley* court found quid pro quo corruption could not justify a ban on individual and political committee expenditures, one could argue the aggregation of wealth and its unfair influence on elections is a more compelling governmental interest that quid pro quo corruption. If Congress could determine that other "special advantages" granted by the state lead to the aggregation of wealth, perhaps it could use these cases to support expenditure limits.

For example, if certain tax advantages such as estate and gift tax exemptions, capital gains treatment or other government bestowed advantages lead to the aggregation of wealth by an individual which could be converted into political a "war chest," could not Congress limit the amount of money that individual could spend on his own candidacy for President? Similarly, if the solicitation rules for PACs which are established by Congress and the FEC, allow PACs to aggregate large war chests which could be used to incur political debts, could not Congress limit independent expenditures by PACs?

Organization and Summary of Materials

Because of *Buckley,* every proposal to regulate spending relating to political campaigns must be reviewed under strict scrutiny. The articles in

---

19. 459 U.S. 197 (1982).
20. 479 U.S. 238 (1986).
21. 494 U.S. 652 (1990).
22. *Id.*

this anthology have been arranged to follow the structural organization of the *Buckley* opinion. Section I contains two articles that provide a historical overview of campaign finance reform and the *Buckley* decision. Section II contains two essays discussing the concept of money as speech. Section III contains seven excerpts articulating various views on possible compelling governmental interests to justify the regulation of campaign finance. And Section IV contains six articles discussing alternative methods of regulating campaign finance and the Constitutional issues in each case. The Epilogue contains comments on the constitutionality of several provisions of the so-called McCain-Feingold reform legislation considered by the U.S. Senate in 1997 and again in 1998.

Section I — Overview

A. A Recipe for the Reform of Congress

Former U.S. Senator David L. Boren led the effort to reform campaign finance laws in the U.S. Senate for more than ten years before he left Congress to become President of the University of Oklahoma in 1994. His article describes the skyrocketing costs of running for federal office and cites this trend as a major contributing cause of voter cynicism, political upheaval and perhaps the imminent demise of the two-party U.S. political system. Senator Boren chronicles the recent Congressional efforts to make legislative changes in campaign finance law, briefly identifies the major constitutional problems raised by such efforts, and suggests potential solutions.

B. Campaign Finance, The Parties and The Court: A Comment on Colorado Republican Federal Campaign Committee v. Federal Elections Commission

Law professor Richard Briffault utilizes the Supreme Court's multiple opinions in *Colorado Republican Federal Campaign Committee v. Federal Election Commission*[23] to illustrate the difficulty of applying *Buckley's* analysis and of justifying its theoretical underpinnings. It is reprinted in its entirety to provide an immersion into the *Buckley* analysis through the lens of the most recent Supreme Court decision and to provide an overview of current constitutional battles. Briffault utilizes the

---

23. 116 S. Ct. 2309 (1996).

eight major Court decisions following *Buckley* to argue the Court has run into three problems in applying the *Buckley* framework to new campaign finance cases: (1) applying the contribution/expenditure distinction; (2) determining the meaning of corruption; and (3) deciding the degree of deference to be accorded to Congress or state officials in determining whether the kinds of dangers which the Court has indicated may be the justification of regulation actually exist in a particular case. Briffault notes that all three problems are present in the FECA's limits on party spending coordinated with candidates at issue in *Colorado Republican*. And he explains how each opinion in the case dealt with these problems.

Section II — Is Money Speech?

Buckley[24] held that the contribution and expenditure of money in political campaigns is essential to speech and is protected by the First Amendment. The Court found that effective communication of ideas requires the expenditure of money. Regulating money, therefore, regulates speech.

> A restriction on the amount of money a person or group can spend on political communication during a campaign necessarily reduces the quantity of expression by restricting the number of issues discussed, the depth of their exploration, and the size of the audience reached.[25]

This conclusion has been roundly criticized by commentators.[26] The Court, however, has not reexamined the issue since *Buckley*.

A. Politics and the Constitution: Is Money Speech?

Section II begins with the classic commentary on *Buckley* by the late D.C. Circuit Court of Appeals Judge, J. Skelly Wright which remains remarkably relevant more than twenty years after it first appeared in print. Wright argues that money is not speech. The *Buckley* Court's decision was based, according to Wright, upon a pluralist view of politics, which,

---

24. 424 U.S. 1 (1976).

25. *Id.* at 19.

26. *See, e.g.,* Cass R. Sunstein, *Political Equality and Unintended Consequences,* 94 COLUM. L. REV. 1390, 1394 (1994)(*Buckley* one of most vilified Supreme Court decisions of post-World War II era).

though a powerful and dominant theory, is not compelled by the core notion of the First Amendment. Wright argues that nothing in the First Amendment prohibits the creation of a process in which ideas and candidates prevail, not because wealthy and organized interest groups support them, but because of their inherent worth. According to Wright, ideas not intensities, form the core concept of the First Amendment. Money may measure intensity, but it does not communicate ideas. He rejects strict scrutiny of government limits on contributions and expenditures and proposes an intermediate level of scrutiny appropriate for reviewing all government regulation of conduct—such as picketing or a sound truck—which facilitates pure speech. Such regulation would be constitutional if it serves an important government interest which is unrelated to suppression of speech. Using this analysis, the government may limit both contributions and expenditures in a content neutral manner.

B. Money and Politics: A Perspective on the First Amendment and Campaign Finance Reform

Law professor Lillian R. BeVier argues that the Court was correct in concluding that limitations of election campaign contributions and expenditures impinge significantly on core First Amendment rights and require application of strict scrutiny. She laments, however, that the Court did not better articulate its rationale. She also criticizes the Court's distinction between contributions and expenditures.

BeVier's starting point is that the U.S. Constitution establishes a representative democracy and that freedom of expression is fundamental to the well functioning of such a political system. She then advances the notion that spending money for political activity is at the very heart of activities protected by the First Amendment. She rejects the argument that spending money is conduct which may be regulated under the Court's analysis in *United States v. O'Brien* by dismissing that case and its attempt to establish an artificial distinction between speech and non speech elements of conduct. She also argues that campaign finance reform by its nature cannot be content neutral because every change in the legal context of political activity redistributes political power.

Professor BeVier parts company with the *Buckley* analysis by arguing that government regulation of campaign contributions requires the same strict scrutiny as regulation of expenditures. Contribution limitations will limit the same political activity as expenditure limitations. Moreover, she rejects the Court's characterization of contributions as "proxy speech," i.e. speech by someone other than the contributor. There is no distinction, according to BeVier, between proxy speech and real speech since all campaign money, whether a contribution or an expenditure, must be turned over to someone else before it becomes speech.

Section III — Compelling Government Interests in Regulating Campaign Finance

Because of the Court's conclusion that political money is speech, campaign finance regulation is subject to strict scrutiny, and it must be justified by compelling governmental interests. In *Buckley*, the Court considered two possible governmental interests.

The government argued in *Buckley* that it had a compelling interest in equalizing the ability of individuals and groups to exercise electoral influence. The Court dismissed this argument without analysis.

> [T]he concept that government may restrict the speech of some elements of our society in order to enhance the relative voice of others is wholly foreign to the First Amendment, which was designed to secure the widest possible dissemination of information. The First Amendment's protection against governmental abridgment of free expression cannot properly be made to depend on a person's financial ability to engage in public discussion.[27]

According to the Court, the goal of political equality cannot be invoked to stop a person from spending money on her own campaign or on candidates of her choice.

The government also argued in *Buckley* that it had a compelling interest in combating both the appearance and reality of corruption. The Court held this was a sufficiently compelling governmental interest to justify the contribution limitations. The Court deferred to Congress' judgment that large contributions were often given to candidates to secure political favors and it should be allowed to limit the opportunity for political quid pro quos. The Court gave no such deference to Congress' determination that expenditures by the candidate or by supporters on behalf of the candidate presented opportunities for corruption. Since expenditures (whether by the candidate, the candidate's campaign, or by an individual spending money independently to support a candidate) are not given to the candidate, there can be no quid pro quo corruption. Without this compelling government interest the Court struck down the expenditure limits.

---

27. Buckley v. Valeo, 424 U.S. 1, 48-49 (1976).

A. Campaign Finance Reform: A Key to Restoring the Health of Our Democracy

Many legal commentators have argued that the compelling governmental interest in avoiding corruption and the appearance of corruption should encompass campaign money influence in pubic policy debate. If that form of corruption is recognized, former Common Cause officials, Fred Wertheimer and Susan Weiss Manes lay out the factual basis for limitation of campaign contributions as well as expenditures. In the first excerpt from their article, they chronicle the increase in the cost of federal campaigns and detail the composition of those contributions (and thus the source of the expenditures) as flowing from organized interest groups and lobbyists with an interest in matters before Congress to incumbent members of Congress. Utilizing Federal Election Commission records, Wertheimer and Manes argue that this money has bought influence in Congress and they use the savings and loan scandal of the 1980s as an example.

B. Faulty Assumptions and Undemocratic Consequences of Campaign Finance Reform

The first excerpt from Bradley A. Smith's article disputes the major assumption of reformers such as Wertheimer and Manes that the amount of money in elections and its influence in the legislative process constitutes a compelling governmental interest justifying limits on constitutionally protected speech. He argues that reformers rely upon four faulty assumptions about the cause and effect of political corruption: (1) that too much money is spent on election campaigns (he asks whether too little is spent); (2) that campaigns funded with small contributions are more democratic (he argues that ideological fringe candidates, e.g., Goldwater, McGovern, and North, finance their campaigns with small contributions); (3) that money buys elections (he notes that candidates who spend more than their opponents often lose); and (4) that money is a corrupting influence on candidates (he argues there is little data showing that money has influence).

Not only does he reject these assumptions as faulty, he argues limits on campaign spending have undemocratic consequences. Among these consequences are: (1) entrenching the status quo by hindering the ability of challengers to compete with those in power; (2) the promotion of influence peddling through special interest legislative strategies (as opposed to electoral strategies); (3) favoring non-monetary elites such as Hollywood celebrities, academics, labor organizers, and media editors rather than those with money, (4) the favoring of millionaire candidates whose spending cannot be constitutionally limited; and (5) the favoring of organized special interests over volunteer grassroots activity.

C. On Campaign Finance Reform: The Root of All Evil Is Deeply Rooted

In the first excerpt from his article, Daniel Hays Lowenstein argues that the payment of money to bias the judgment or sway the loyalty of persons holding positions of public trust is a practice condemned throughout history. This condemnation, coupled with the recognition that money has the power to tempt one away from one's ethical responsibilities and highest interests, leads society to the conclusion that the influence of money in politics is corrupting, whether such influence expresses itself as a quid pro quo or not. He contends that contributors seek and receive influence which, as a result of traditional notions of conflict of interest, has a measurable effect on legislators' actions. Although some scholars question this premise, Lowenstein determines that the current campaign finance system is corrupt.

D. Corruption, Equality, and Campaign Finance Reform

David Strauss argues that defining corruption is not as easy as it seems. While both corruption and equality are identified as separate governmental interests by reformers of campaign finance, corruption is actually derivative of inequality and the nature of democratic politics. For if equality in campaign spending were achieved, there would be little concern about corruption. The extent to which corruption would still be a problem would be a result of the tendency in representative democracy for politics to become a struggle among interest groups. Strauss admits that corruption in campaign finance is a concern, not because it constitutes conventional quid pro quo bribery, but because of the concerns of inequality and the dangers of interest group politics. He also argues that corruption in the campaign finance system is objectionable because of the danger of coercion of (rather than by) contributors.

E. The Concept of Corruption in Campaign Finance Law

Political Science professor Thomas F. Burke explores the concept of corruption by asking this question: On what basis can we say that public officials influenced by contributions are corrupt? Because this question is not answered by the Court, he asserts that we must consider political theory to answer it. He rejects Lowenstein's argument that the payment of money to bias the judgment of public officials is corrupt simply because of a strong cultural norm that money in the form of personal gifts or campaign contributions should not influence public action. Only a theoretical argument, not merely public opinion or even statutory bans, can answer the question.

Burke addresses the pluralist and deliberative theories of representative democracy. Under the deliberative theory, representation involves deliberation about the public good and contributions which influence representatives are a corruption of the democratic process. The pluralistic theory, on the other hand, describes politics as a market of interests and politicians as retailers of those interests. Under such a theory, contributions that influence representatives are not a corruption of the democratic process, but rather are necessary and even laudable components of that process.

Burke concludes that the deliberative theory of representative democracy should be adopted since it was embraced by the framers of the constitution and should illuminate the Court's decisions on the constitutionality of campaign finance regulation. If the government's regulations can be justified by this monetary influence concept of corruption, they should be sustained.

F. Free Speech and the Widening Gyre of Fund-Raising: Why Campaign Spending Limits May Not Violate the First Amendment After All

Law professor Vincent Blasi argues that candidates for office spend too much time raising money at the expense of the quality of representation. He contends that if a candidate or federal office holder is not substantially free to spend time representing her constituents, the electoral process falls short of the constitutional norm embodied in Article One, the Republican Form of Government Clause, and the Seventeenth Amendment guarantee to the People of the United States that they shall be governed by representatives. As a result, Blasi argues that the constitutionally recognized value of representation will justify limits on overall campaign spending. Adoption of this approach, he contends, deviates from the dispute over the appropriate theory of democratic representation. Regardless of whether one espouses the deliberative republican or pluralist theories, representatives can neither deliberate nor attend their parochial interests if their schedules are consumed by fundraising.

G. Back to the Future of the American State: Overruling Buckley v. Valeo and Other Madisonian Steps

University of Pittsburgh School of Law Dean, Peter M. Shane, argues that the conclusion in *Buckley* that only corruption and the appearance of corruption can justify regulation of campaign finance should and can be overruled. Shane argues that the Madisonian concept of a deliberative process of representative democracy through which the common good of society as a whole is pursued without interference from narrow special interests is a compelling governmental interest which will justify government regulation of campaign finance. He argues that a return to this Madisonian constitutionalism will not require a paradigm shift since normal principles of *stare decisis* would allow the Court to overrule *Buckley*. According to Shane, the Court has customarily asked the following questions in considering whether to overrule a precedent: (1) whether the original holding was wrong from the start; (2) whether the basis for the decision has eroded over time; (3) whether the Court has had difficulty applying the holding; (4) whether later opinions are in tension with it; (5) whether the holding is practically workable; and (6) whether there has been the kind of reliance on the decision that would create special hardships if it is overruled. The answers to these questions, according to Shane, lead to the conclusion that *Buckley* should be overruled.

Section IV—Alternative Methods of Regulation

Immediately following the *Buckley* decision, numerous proposals were presented in Congress which would have created publicly funded campaigns coupled with voluntary overall spending caps for the U.S. House and Senate based on the Presidential campaign model upheld in *Buckley.*[28]

As an alternative to the total public financing of Congressional elections, reformers began to propose partial federal funding and other incentives to induce candidates to voluntarily limit campaign spending. These proposals include reduced mailing and broadcast advertising rates and triggering mechanisms that would grant public funds to complying candidates if their opponents decided not to voluntarily cap spending or received the benefit of an independent expenditure.[29]

---

28. *See,* David L. Boren, *A Recipe for Reform of Congress,* 21 OKLAHOMA CITY UNIV. L. REV. 1 (1996).

29. *See,* S. 25 (version 1), 105 Cong.

A. Campaign Finance Reform: A Key to Restoring the Health of Our Democracy

In the second excerpt from their article, Wertheimer and Manes propose a reform of the federal campaign finance system through public financing based on the Presidential model contained in the 1974 FECA. They argue that the initial experience under the Presidential system shows it could be an effective means for curbing special-interest influence in Congressional elections. They contend, however, that "soft money" contributions threaten the Presidential system, and that the FEC has failed to enforce the laws already on the books. Wertheimer and Manes argue that a comprehensive reform should include public financing based upon the presidential system coupled with a ban on soft money contributions and an overhaul of the enforcement structure of the FEC.

B. Political Equality and Unintended Consequences

Law professor Cass R. Sunstein notes that command and control government regulations often have unintended negative consequences. This is true, according to Sunstein, in the area of campaign finance regulations. Each command and control regulation has a consequence. For example, campaign finance limits may entrench incumbents, limits on individual contributions will produce more (and more influential) political action committees, and limits on "hard money" encourage a shift to "soft money." As an alternative to traditional command and control regulations, Sunstein suggests incentive based campaign finance strategies. For example, public financing conditioned upon voluntary spending limits and funding campaigns through voter vouchers.

C. Format Restrictions on Televised Political Advertising: Elevating Political Debate Without Suppressing Free Speech

Timothy Moran suggests that government not only can, but should take affirmative steps to improve the level of public debate during elections through television advertisement format restrictions. He believes, however, that strict scrutiny and the doctrine of unconstitutional conditions limit the range of format restrictions available to the government. Moran analyzes four proposals: (1) candidate personal appearance in any advertisement that attacks another candidate; (2) "talking heads" format for all political advertising; (3) strengthening disclosure and identification requirements; and (4) free advertising to candidates conditioned on a "talking heads" format with a minimum length suitable to the development and discussion of issues. He concludes that the first and second proposals are unconstitutional because they substantially curtail political speech, but that the third and fourth proposals are constitutional if narrowly tailored because they do not curtail candidate speech and, in the case of free air time, may in fact increase it.

D. Frankenstein's Monster Hits the Campaign Trail: An Approach to Regulation of Corporate Political Expenditures

Law professor Jill E. Fisch suggests an alternative method of regulating corporate political speech through common law corporate concepts and state corporations laws. In *Austin v. Michigan Chamber of Commerce*, the Supreme Court upheld a state statute prohibiting independent expenditures by corporations. Professor Fisch questions both the asserted compelling governmental interest in regulating corporate speech and whether such prohibitions are narrowly tailored to serve that interest. She asserts that the real concern regarding corporate political expenditures is not the large war chests, but the possibility that corporate management may make such expenditures when not in the corporation's (and therefore the shareholders') best interests.

Fisch first outlines two existing limits on the ability of corporate management: (1) shareholder actions against management under the common law concepts of self-dealing and waste if management spends corporate funds on political issues that further its political objectives rather than those of the corporation; and (2) fear of being voted out of office if management does not pursue the achievement of corporate profits. Although she recognizes that shareholder action to discipline management is largely ineffective, Fisch suggests that amendment of the Securities and Exchange Act to require disclosure of all corporate political expenditures would strengthen shareholder discipline. Such a reform is much more closely tied to the specific danger of corporate political speech: the separation of ownership and management.

A second alternative more narrowly tailored to the alleged harm of corporate political speech, according to Fisch, is amendment of state corporation statutes to limit or even ban corporate political speech. However, she recognizes that states are unlikely to utilize these statutes as a check on corporate political speech. Finally, Fisch suggests that state corporation statutes could require corporations to address the political expenditure issues explicitly in their charters. If the charter expressly authorized how much and under what circumstances a corporation could make political expenditures, the danger arising from the separation of ownership and control would be resolved without mandatory government imposed limits on protected speech.

E. Clipping Coupons for Democracy: An Egalitarian / Public Choice Defense of Campaign Vouchers

Law professor Richard L. Hasen proposes a mandatory voucher plan to fund political campaigns. All voters would be given vouchers worth $100 to contribute to candidates for federal office. Only vouchers could be spent to support or oppose candidates for federal office. Using the methodology of public choice theory coupled with the goal of promoting an egalitarian pluralist political market, Hasen argues that such a plan would minimize the impact of wealth on the political system, empower those who currently lack political capital and promote a fairer legislative process. He also defends its constitutionality.

F. On Campaign Finance Reform: The Root of All Evil Is Deeply Rooted

The second excerpt from Daniel Hays Lowenstein's article proposes public funding of political campaigns allocated by legislative party leadership to candidates. Rather than fully fund each federal candidate's campaign, Lowenstein's proposal reduces the amount of public funds to less than $100 million per fiscal year. The legislative leadership within each party would determine which campaigns were competitive and which were not and allocate their finite resources accordingly. Additional funds would be allocated for generic party advertising. He would also place $100 limits on individual contributions and aggregate limits on contributions from political action committees. Finally, he would provide matching public funds to a candidate whose opponent benefits from independent expenditures.

The Constitution and
Campaign Finance Reform

Section I

Overview

A Recipe for the Reform of Congress

David L. Boren

The next decade is likely to produce more political change in this country than any period since the Civil War. The reason for the coming upheaval is a stunning lack of public confidence in our federal government. All of the data indicates it. A public opinion poll taken in 1964 found that 76% of the American people trusted their government to do what is right most or all of the time.[1] Thirty years later, in 1994, the same poll reported only 21% of the public having the same level of faith in Washington's decisions—the lowest reflection of confidence in the history of the study.[2] In fact, a different survey in the summer of 1995 showed that 76% of the people do not trust the federal government to do the right thing.[3] According to yet another 1995 poll, nearly half of those questioned believe the federal government in Washington is controlled by lobbyists and special interests.[4] An August 1995 survey taken by CNN, USA Today, and the Gallup organization, indicated that Americans are not likely to tolerate the status quo much longer, as 62% of those polled felt the need for a third political party.[5] Some observers read the elections of 1994 as a mandate for a new Republican majority. Less than a year later it appears that Americans are dissatisfied with both parties and are not convinced that either party really wants the kind of fundamental change desired and demanded by the public.

---

1. CENTER FOR POLITICAL STUDIES, UNIV. OF MICH., AMERICAN NATIONAL ELECTION STUDIES 26 (1952–1994). Every two years since 1964, the study has included a survey in which respondents are asked: "How much of the time do you think you can trust the government in Washington to do what is right—just about always, most of the time, or only some of the time?" *Id.*

2. *Id.*

3. *Americans Talk Issues Foundation Survey, Master Questionnaire No. 28,* U.S. NAT'L SURVEY (conducted June 21-28, 1995).

4. Campaign for America Project, Press Release, *Nearly 50% of Americans Believe Lobbyists & Special Interests Control Washington; Former Rep. Synar Sends Letter to Perot Outlining New Poll* 1 (Aug. 10, 1995) (on file with the Oklahoma City University Law Review).

5. Richard Benedetto, *Voters Want Independent in Race,* USA TODAY, Aug. 11, 1995, at 1A.

Added to the disillusionment of the voters is the belief held by a huge majority of the population that office holders are not going to change those elements of the political system that give a substantial advantage to incumbents and make the Washington establishment unreachable by outsiders. Genuine congressional reform can help prevent a major political upheaval and the possible demise, or temporary suspension, of the two-party system as we have known it. Congressional reform is not an abstract issue of interest only to academics; it is central to the reversal of the current sour political climate.

Fortunately, those who would seek to truly reform Congress do not have to start from ground zero. Reform-minded members in the 103rd Congress and earlier sessions from both political parties advanced several thoughtful initiatives dealing with the ailments that plague Capitol Hill. Specifically, legislation was advanced to reform the campaign fundraising system,[6] change the internal rules under which Congress operates,[7] close the "revolving door" through which members of Congress and their staffs easily pass from government service to private lobbying,[8] remove congressional exemptions from major laws imposed on the private sector,[9] and streamline the internal workings of Capitol Hill.[10] Each of these bills has undergone extensive hearings and revisions. Most of these proposals were bipartisan in origin and remain so to this day. In fact, the 104th Congress has already passed a modest number of the proposed internal changes as well as legislation applying certain laws to Congress.[11] However, much remains to be done if we are to truly bring needed change to Capitol Hill. The blueprint is in place, but it has not been implemented.

This article will serve as a broad overview of these initiatives and briefly identify the constitutional, legal, or public policy questions they raise. Many of these proposals are reviewed in greater detail elsewhere in this volume. Extra attention will be given to campaign finance reform, which is arguably the topic most relevant to both the concerns of the public and the future of our representative democracy, but has undoubtedly sparked the greatest constitutional and political debate.

---

6. *See* discussion *infra* part I.

7. *See* discussion *infra* part III.

8. *See* discussion *infra* part II.

9. *See infra* part III.B.4 and notes 133-37 and accompanying text.

10. *See* discussion *infra* part III.

11. *See* discussion *infra* part III.C.

I. Campaign Finance Reform

A. Background and *Buckley v. Valeo*[12]

After the Watergate scandal exposed grave abuses of then existing federal election law, Congress responded by passing the Federal Election Campaign Act Amendments of 1974 (1974 Act).[13] Among the many provisions of the 1974 Act were new limits on both campaign contributions and expenditures. Specifically, the new law limited the amount an individual could give to a campaign to $ 1000 per election.[14] Other provisions limited the amount an individual could independently spend on behalf of a "clearly identified" candidate to $ 1000 per election[15] and limited the amount the candidate could spend from his own pockets depending on the office sought.[16] The Act also limited the total amount a campaign could spend.[17] Finally, the Act established the publicly-financed Presidential matching fund system, including voluntary spending limits, which remains in effect today.[18]

In its 1976 decision in *Buckley v. Valeo,*[19] the Supreme Court held the $1000 limitation on independent expenditures, the limits on a candidate's expenditures from personal funds, and the overall spending limits for congressional races violated the First Amendment's right to free speech.[20] Reasoning that the 1974 Act's limitations dealt with pure political speech at the heart of the First Amendment's protection, the Court subjected these provisions to a strict scrutiny test requiring a compelling govern-

---

12. 424 U.S. 1 (1976).

13. Pub. L. No. 93-443, 88 Stat. 1263 (1974) (amended 1976, 1980, & 1986) (amending the Federal Election Campaign Act of 1971, Pub. L. No. 92-225, 86 Stat. 11 (1972)) (codified as amended in scattered sections of 2 U.S.C., 18 U.S.C., and 26 U.S.C.).

14. *Id.* § 101(a), 88 Stat. 1263 (originally codified at 18 U.S.C. § 608(b)(1) (Supp. 1974)), repealed by Federal Election Campaign Act Amendments of 1976, § 201(a), 90 Stat. 496, re-enacted by Federal Election Campaign Act Amendments of 1976, § 112(2), 90 Stat. 487, renumbered by Federal Election Campaign Act Amendments of 1979, § 105(5), 93 Stat. 1354 (codified at 2 U.S.C. § 441a(a)(1)(A) (1994)).

15. *Id.* § 101(a), 88 Stat. 1265 (codified at 18 U.S.C. § 608(e)(1)-(2) (Supp. 1974)).

16. *Id.* § 101(b)(1), 88 Stat. at 1266 (codified at 18 U.S.C. § 608(a)(1)-(4) (Supp. 1974)).

17. *Id.,* 88 Stat. at 1264-65 (codified at 18 U.S.C. § 608(c)(1)-(4) (Supp. 1974)).

18. *Id.* §§ 403-08, 88 Stat. 1291-1303 (codified at 26 U.S.C. §§ 9001-13, 9031-42 (1994)).

19. 424 U.S. 1 (1976).

20. *Id.* at 12-59.

mental interest for any infringement.[21] Specifically, the Court found the main purported purpose of the limitations—the reduction of corruption and the appearance of corruption—inadequate to justify the intrusions caused by the ceilings on independent expenditures, personal expenditures by the candidate, and overall campaign spending.[22] However, the Court did find this purpose to be adequately compelling and tailored to the $ 1000 individual contribution limit, and consequently, this provision was upheld.[23] This differential treatment of contributions and expenditures seems largely to stem from the Court's view of corruption only as a classic quid pro quo—a legislative favor in exchange for a sizeable campaign contribution.[24] Finally, in contrast to the mandatory overall spending limits set for congressional races, the Court upheld the Presidential election system wherein voluntary spending limits are accepted as a condition of the receipt of massive public funds.[25]

B. The Modern Money Chase

Since the *Buckley* decision literally blew the lid off the amount of money that can be spent in a congressional race, campaign spending has continually skyrocketed. For example, the average cost of winning a U.S. Senate seat increased from $610,026 in 1976 to $ 3.8 million in 1992.[26] Members have become part-time legislators and full-time fundraisers as the average senator must now raise $ 12,000 per week to run for reelection.

Worse yet, with the $ 1000 individual contribution limit still intact, fundraising has become tremendously lopsided toward Washington-based political action committees (PACs), which can give $ 5000 per election.[27] PACs often represent a single industry, company, or other special interest

---

21. *Id.* at 25.

22. *Id.*

23. *Id.* at 26.

24. The *Buckley* Court repeatedly used this type of example in its analysis. *See id.* at 26, 27, 47.

25. *Id.* at 85-109.

26. Fred Wertheimer & Susan W. Manes, *Campaign Finance Reform: A Key to Restoring the Health of Our Democracy*, 94 Colum. L. Rev. 1126, 1132 (1994); *see also* Common Cause, Press Release, *1994 Incumbent Reelection Rate Tops 90 Percent; In a Year of Turnover, Campaign Money Advantage Played Key Role in Incumbent Wins, According to Common Cause Analysis of November 8 Elections* 4 (Nov. 10, 1994) [hereinafter Common Cause] (on file with Oklahoma City University Law Review).

27. *See* 2 U.S.C. § 441a(a)(2)(a)(1994).

group. Between the passage of 1974 Act and the 1992 elections, the number of PACs grew roughly eightfold to over 4,600.[28] Further, the amount PACs contribute to congressional races has exploded. In 1974, PACs gave $ 12.5 million to congressional candidates; by the 1990 elections, PAC contributions totalled $ 150.6 million—an increase of over 500% after adjusting for inflation![29]

More alarming is the pattern of PAC giving. PAC contributions seem to have little to do with a candidate's ideas or qualifications. Former Senator Rudy Boschwitz (R-MN) described the motivation behind PAC contributions this way:

> Our [Republican-leaning] political action committees, those who tend to look at our side, look at the whole political process as horse trading. They do not have a philosophy they want to present. They do not have a philosophy they want to defend. They do not have a philosophy they want to further. Their philosophy is winning, to get on the horse that you think will win so that you will have access when he or she does indeed win. That is really the goal of their giving.[30]

Thus, the money flows to incumbents, who are usually the winners. PAC contributions to challengers in 1994 House races totaled $ 7.3 million[31]—the same amount given in 1980. During the same period (1980 to 1994), House incumbents enjoyed a 360% increase in PAC receipts, from $ 25 million to $ 88.3 million.[32] About 85% of PAC money now goes to incumbents.[33] The average amount of PAC donations received by 1994 House incumbents was $ 230,441 compared to only $ 21,697 for challengers—over a 10 to 1 advantage.[34] This fundraising advantage has enabled incumbents to consistently outspend and defeat their challengers. In 1994, incumbent senators outspent challengers in 22 of 26 contests and 24 won reelection.[35] In the House, 378 of 383 incumbents outspent their challengers, with 349 being reelected—a reelection rate of 91%.[36] Interestingly, there is evidence that as the Senate and House majorities

---

28. Gary S. Stein, *The First Amendment and Campaign Finance Reform: A Timely Reconciliation*, 44 Rutgers L. Rev. 743, 758 (1992).

29. S. Rep. No. 41, 25-26 (1993) [hereinafter Senate Report on S. 3].

30. 134 Cong. Rec. S1107 (daily ed. Feb. 23, 1988) (statement of Senator Boschwitz).

31. Common Cause *supra* note 26, at 5.

32. *Id.*

33. Senate Report on S. 3, *supra* note 29, at 26.

34. *Id.* at 22.

35. Common Cause, *supra* note 26, at 3.

36. *Id.*

switched from Democrat to Republican in 1994, so too has the bulk of the PAC money switched to the Republican direction.[37]

Because of this trend, many members focus their fundraising primarily in Washington, not in their home states or districts, and this practice has led to the perception that our elected officials are more responsive to these special interest groups than they are to the voters.[38] Instead of singling out any one group or contributor, voters feel disenfranchised by a system they feel is corrupt in the aggregate. A study by the Kettering Foundation based on citizen interviews across the country summarized this feeling and the effect it is having on our democracy:

> People believe two forces have corrupted democracy. The first is that lobbyists have replaced representatives as the primary political actors. The other force, seen as more pernicious, is that campaign contributions seem to determine political outcomes more than voting. No accusation cuts deeper because when money and privilege replace votes, the social contract underlying the political system is abrogated. Influenced by this widespread perception, people decide that voting doesn't really count any more — so why bother?[39]

A more recent public opinion poll reveals that more than two out of three Americans believe interest group campaign contributions "affect the member of Congress' vote a lot."[40]

Further, the mere existence of huge campaign "war chests" given by PACs to incumbents discourage grassroots challengers with valuable experience and new ideas from becoming candidates. In this way, current campaign law encourages practices that actually squelch political discourse. In the 1994 elections, 160 House members (over one third of the House) ran either unopposed or "financially unopposed" because they faced challengers with less than $ 25,000 to spend — all won reelection.[41] Another 163 incumbents ran with at least double the campaign funds available to their challengers — 150, or 92%, were victors.[42] In a year that supposedly witnessed a revolution in the House of Representatives, three quarters of the seats were decided in financially noncompetitive races or with no race

---

37. Thomas B. Edsall, *Capital Drama: As the PACs Turn; Campaign Cash Flow Shifts Direction Toward New GOP Majority,* WASH. POST, July 23, 1995, at A8.

38. Senate Report on S. 3, *supra* note 29, at 26.

39. David Matthews, *Forward* to KETTERING FOUNDATION, CITIZENS AND POLITICS: A VIEW FROM MAIN STREET AMERICA at v (1991).

40. Campaign for America Project, *supra* note 4, at 4.

41. Common Cause, *supra* note 26, at 2.

42. *Id.*

at all. It is no wonder the public has turned to drastic measures like term limits to oust incumbents.[43]

C. The Campaign Reform Proposal

Given the problems caused by runaway campaign spending, the proliferation of PAC giving, and the practice of building war chests, any meaningful campaign reform must include both overall spending caps and an aggregate limit on PAC contributions—a ceiling, expressed as a percentage, on the proportion of a candidate's campaign funds that can come from PACs. Aggregate PAC limits without overall spending ceilings, however, would fail to slow the money chase since PACs could increase their contributions to the maximum and more PACs could be formed. Since mandatory limits have been rejected by the Court, congressional reformers have pushed voluntary spending limits, grounding their argument in a footnote from *Buckley* in which the Court stated:

> Congress may engage in public financing of election campaigns and may condition acceptance of public funds on an agreement by the candidate to abide by specified expenditure limitations. Just as a candidate may voluntarily limit the size of the contributions he chooses to accept, he may decide to forgo private fundraising and accept public funding.[44]

In the late 1980's, congressional reformers put forth legislative proposals based largely on the Presidential system under which candidates agree to abide by spending limits in exchange for public financing.[45] Because of concern over the cost of the proposals and disagreement over the policy of total public financing in congressional races, the initiatives were revised to use a combination of incentives short of total public financing in order to encourage candidates to comply with spending limits.[46]

---

43. *See* Paul M. Barrett & Gerald F. Seib, *Term Limits Are Set Back By High Court,* WALL ST. J., May 23, 1995, at A3 (stating that *U.S. Term Limits v. Thornton,* 115 S. Ct. 1842 (1995), effectively struck down laws in 23 states that had independently limited the number of times a person can run for Congress).

44. *Buckley,* 424 U.S. at 57 n.65.

45. *See generally The Federal Page—Campaign Finance: The Senators and Their Money,* WASH. POST, June 24, 1987, at A23 (providing excerpts from Senators regarding the proposed Senatorial Election Campaign Act of 1987, numbered S. 2).

46. *See generally* Helen Dewar, *Senate GOP Makes Counteroffer on Campaign Finance Reform,* WASH. POST, July 26, 1990, at A7; Helen Dewar, *Parties Split on Campaign Finance Bill; Dole-Mitchell Deal Called Key to Passage,* WASH. POST, Apr. 22, 1990, at A6; Helen Dewar, *Campaign Finance Bill Loses Again in Senate; GOP Blocks Vote on Limited Spending,* WASH. POST, Feb. 27, 1988, at A4.

Under the major campaign reform bill in the 103rd Congress, candidates who agreed to abide by the spending ceilings automatically received lower mailing and broadcast rates as well as an exemption from having their campaigns taxed as corporations.[47] Other benefits were triggered by the actions of opposing candidates. A complying candidate attacked by an "independent expenditure" (an ad or mailing paid for by an outside group instead of one's opponent) in excess of $ 10,000 would receive public benefits to respond to the effort.[48] Additionally, a complying candidate would receive public funds if his opponent surpassed the spending cap. The corresponding benefits would be given in stages: the more the opponent spends over the cap, the more benefits the complying candidate would receive.[49] The proposal also placed aggregate limits on the amount campaigns could accept from PACs to the smaller of 20% of the spending limit or $ 825,000.[50] Similar legislation by the House capped PAC contributions at 33% of the spending limit.[51]

Unfortunately, campaign finance reform efforts in the 103rd Congress failed when Senate proponents were unable to break a Republican filibuster on the S. 3 conference report.[52] However, a bipartisan bill containing a system of voluntary spending limits, as well as similar incentives for compliance, has been introduced in the 104th Congress.[53]

---

47. S. 3, 103rd Cong. (1993). The bill established voluntary spending limits for Senate races based upon the voting age population of the state represented. *Id.* § 101. A candidate that agrees to the spending limit and raises a threshold amount of private funds would be eligible for half-priced television broadcast rates during the last 30 days of a primary election and the last 60 days of a general election. *Id.* They would also receive discounted mailing rates for one piece of mail for every eligible voter. *Id.* As amended on the Senate floor, the bill also defined campaigns as corporations for tax purposes and then exempted the campaigns of candidates who agree to the spending limits. *See* 139 CONG. REC. S7358-64 (daily ed. June 16, 1993).

48. S. 3 § 101. The United States Supreme Court in *Buckley* overturned the 1974 Act's statutory limit on outside expenditures. 424 U.S. at 45. Congressional reformers, therefore, proposed matching the money spent by outside groups by giving publicly financed broadcast vouchers to the attacked candidate.

49. S. 3 § 101. For example, when the noncomplying candidate exceeded the spending limit, the complying candidate would receive broadcast vouchers equal to one-third of the relevant spending limit. If the noncomplying candidate exceeded the limit by a third, the complying candidate would receive vouchers equal to an additional third, and so on.

50. Senate Report on S. 3, *supra* note 29, at 26.

51. *See* H.R. Rep. No. 375, pt. 1 (1993). For an excellent side-by-side analysis of the House and Senate campaign reform bills of the 103rd Congress as they passed each chamber, *see Campaign Finance Bills Compared,* CONG. Q., Feb. 5, 1994, at 262-69.

52. *See* 140 CONG. REC. S13,760 (daily ed. Sept. 30, 1994).

53. S. 1219, 104th Cong. (1995).

D. First Amendment Issues

If a system of voluntary spending limits like those in S. 3 were to become law, it would be immediately challenged and a largely different Supreme Court[54] would have the opportunity to reexamine the logic of *Buckley* and its consequences. Two separate constitutional questions would have to be addressed.

1. Is Money Speech?

Judge Skelly Wright, a member of the appellate court panel that upheld the provisions of the 1974 Act,[55] was among the first to see the miscalculation of the Supreme Court's ruling that spending money equates to political speech.[56] Wright and his colleagues viewed political giving not as pure speech, but as speech-related conduct, similar to the burning of a draft card in *United States v. O'Brien*[57] and therefore more easily regulated.[58] In an article published just months after the Supreme Court's decision, Judge Wright said:

> The real question in the case was: Can the use of money be regulated, by analogy to conduct such as draft-card burning, where there is an undoubted incidental effect on speech? However, what the Court asked was whether pure speech can be regulated where there is some incidental effect on money. Naturally the answer to the Court's question was "No." But this left untouched the real question in the case. The Court riveted its attention on what the money could buy — be it communication or communication, mixed with conduct. Yet the campaign reform law did not dictate what could be bought. It focused exclusively on the giving and spending itself.[59]

Evidence from modern campaigns suggests Wright has the better argument. An incredible amount of campaign funds are spent on items other than speech, including overhead costs, polling, and opposition research. Campaign funds are used to send flowers, purchase plane tickets, and make gifts to charity.

A still better reason not to treat money as political speech is the very real, chilling effect which incumbents' war chests have on spirited, con-

---

54. Chief Justice Rehnquist and Justice Stevens are the only current members of the Court who served on the Court in 1976.

55. Buckley v. Valeo, 519 F.2d 821, 840-41 (D.C. Cir. 1975), aff'd in part and rev'd in part, 424 U.S. 1 (1976).

56. *See* J. Skelly Wright, *Politics and the Constitution: Is Money Speech?*, 85 YALE L.J. 1001 (1976).

57. 391 U.S. 367 (1968).

58. Wright, *supra* note 56, at 1005-10.

59. *Id.* at 1007-08 (citation omitted).

tested elections and real political speech and debate. As discussed above,[60] mammoth campaign treasuries scare off even the most qualified challengers. As a result, voters are given no real option since many members of Congress face little or no opposition. The practical effect of the *Buckley* view is to give constitutional protection of the highest order to incumbency. The Court should welcome the opportunity to correct this very real, however unintended, consequence of its nearly twenty year old decision.

2. Voluntary Spending Limits as Unconstitutional Conditions?

If the Court refused to reopen the "speech vs. conduct" debate, any voluntary spending limit plan passed by Congress would certainly be reviewed under strict scrutiny under both traditional First Amendment analysis and the doctrine prohibiting unconstitutional conditions. Under the latter approach, strict judicial scrutiny is applied when the government coercively pressures one to forfeit his constitutional liberties.[61] Assuming for the sake of argument that the Court finds the triggered benefits to be coercive, a voluntary spending limit proposal like that contained in S. 3 could receive favorable consideration without wholly reversing course from *Buckley*.

To survive strict scrutiny, the coercive legislation should be narrowly tailored to further a compelling state interest.[62] The key consideration is the clear articulation of the updated government interests that would be served by voluntary spending limits. As noted above,[63] the only governmental interest weighed in *Buckley* was quite narrow — the elimination of the perception of the classic quid pro quo practice of influence peddling.[64] But as has been demonstrated, the *Buckley* decision helped spawn a system that has given rise to a wider range of blights on our democracy. The republic's interest in reversing these trends must be laid before the Court so a proper balancing of all relevant competing interests can be made. I

---

60. *See supra* notes 30-43 and accompanying text.

61. For a discussion of the importance of finding "coercion" in modern unconstitutional condition analysis, *see* Kenneth J. Levit, *Campaign Finance Reform and the Return of* Buckley v. Valeo, 103 YALE L. J. 469, 483-84 (1993). Levit concludes that the triggered benefits contained in S. 3 are coercive and therefore require strict judicial scrutiny. *Id.* at 492-98.

62. *See* Adarand Constructors, Inc. v. Pena, 115 S. Ct. 2097, 2113 (1995) (stating that for statutes to pass the strict scrutiny test, they must be "narrowly tailored...to further compelling governmental interests").

63. *See supra* text accompanying note 22.

64. *Buckley*, 424 U.S. at 25.

* * *

and others have attempted to spell out these interests. A revised, nonexclusive suggested list includes:

1) eliminating the perception of corruption in the aggregate that has alienated voters from Congress as an institution;
2) restoring competition to elections so qualifications and ideas will matter more than fundraising ability;
3) enabling members of Congress to devote more time to the nation's business and less time to raising money.

With these goals as well as extensive evidence of the consequences of the *Buckley* decision before the Court, it is possible that effective, voluntary spending limits could be upheld and meaningful campaign finance reform enforced. The effort must be made. The public has waited twenty years, and the results have been disastrous for America's democracy. No other initiative deserves more attention from the new Congress.

* * *

Conclusion

Despite the fanfare surrounding the recent change in the leadership of the Congress, a deep underlying sense of cynicism and helplessness still pervades the public's view of our nation's lawmaking process. Voters view Capitol Hill as a closed society where their concerns take a backseat to those of well-financed, well-connected interests that know how to manipulate a complicated maze of rules. A comprehensive reform agenda is needed to help restore public faith in Congress as an institution. Cosmetic changes will not satisfy a public that has become increasingly well informed on issues like the role of lobbyists and the influence of political action committees. The new Congress has not yet fully acted upon the recipe for reform that already exists. Thoughtful, refined, constitutional proposals to curb the role of money in elections, clean up the lobbying process, and improve the way Congress conducts its business are ready and waiting for consideration. It is now up to the members of the new Congress, especially the new leadership of both chambers, as the trustees of that institution to enact these proposals into law in order to restore the health of our democracy. The polling data shows that Americans are angry; however, they are not angry because they hate their country or their government. Americans are frustrated because they love their country and want it to be all that it can become. These strong feelings can lead to either constructive or destructive results. What happens in the fight for congressional reform will have a great impact on our political future.

Campaign Finance, the Parties and the Court: A Comment on *Colorado Republican Federal Campaign Committee v. Federal Elections Commission*

Richard Briffault

Last Term, in *Colorado Republican Federal Campaign Committee v. Federal Election Commission,*[1] the Supreme Court considered a direct attack on the constitutionality of the Federal Election Campaign Act's ("FECA") limits on political party expenditures. *Colorado Republican* was the Court's first campaign finance case in six years and the first in which the four Justices appointed by Presidents Bush and Clinton had an opportunity to participate. *Colorado Republican* was also the first case in the twenty-year regime of *Buckley v. Valeo*[2] concerned with the constitutionality of restrictions on parties.[3] Coming at a time of rising public concern, increased legislative activity, and continued academic ferment over

---

1. 116 S. Ct. 2309 (1996).

2. 2 424 U.S. 1 (1976).

3. *Buckley* addressed only one issue concerning parties—the claim that FECA discriminated, in violation of the Fifth Amendment's Due Process Clause, against independent candidates and parties without national committees because the Act authorized additional spending for political party national committees. The Court determined that, as a portion of the *Buckley* decision invalidated the limits on aggregate campaign expenditures and independent expenditures, it had eliminated the basis for the discrimination claim. 424 U.S. at 58–59 and nn.66, 67. The Court did not consider any First Amendment challenge to limits on party spending.

In *Federal Elections Commission v. Democratic Senatorial Campaign Committee*, 454 U.S. 27, 28–29 (1981), the Court considered the statutory question of whether FECA barred an "agency agreement," that is, a state party's designation of a national party committee as the state party's agent for making expenditures allowed by the Act. In *Brown v. Socialist Workers '74 Campaign Committee*, 459 U.S. 87, 88 (1982), the Court consid-

campaign finance, *Colorado Republican* offered the promise of clarifying the current Court's approach to campaign finance regulation, marking out the contours of the rights of parties in the campaign finance context, and assessing the implications of judicial doctrine for potential legislative changes.

The Court, however, failed to resolve the central issue in the case. Instead, it fragmented into four opinions, none of which commanded the votes of more than three Justices.[4] A seven-member majority rejected the effort of the Federal Elections Commission ("FEC") to enforce FECA in the case before it, but the three Justices who joined the pivotal opinion authored by Justice Breyer limited their views — and, thus, the holding of the Court — to the facts of the case and declined to reach the broader issue of the constitutionality of limits on party involvement in campaign finance. The six Justices who did reach the issue were sharply divided. Moreover, one Justice directly, and two others implicitly, challenged *Buckley v. Valeo's* basic approach to campaign finance regulation — although their different opinions embraced decidedly different perspectives.

Colorado Republican illustrates nicely the conceptual difficulties built into the Court's campaign finance doctrine. *Buckley's* central concerns have proven difficult to apply in practice or justify in theory, and the Court has vacillated with respect to the degree of deference to be given to the judgment of the political branches concerning whether campaign practices present dangers that may be the basis for regulation.

Moreover, political party spending is particularly difficult to fit into the Court's conceptual framework because party activities bridge *Buckley's* basic doctrinal categories. Many academics have urged a more party-centered approach to campaign finance — the Committee for Party Renewal filed an amicus brief in the case — claiming it would reduce the influence of special interests on the political process. However, so long as parties themselves receive their funds from private individuals and organizations, it is questionable whether a party-centered system would do much to ameliorate special interest influence. Moreover, judicial establishment of an unlimited party spending right could have broader effects on the campaign finance laws.

Part I of this comment briefly summarizes the facts, statutory framework, and procedural history of *Colorado Republican*. Part II reviews the *Buckley* doctrine. Parts III and IV examine and appraise the Court's multiple opinions. Finally, Parts V and VI consider the implications of consti-

---

ered the constitutionality of the application of disclosure requirements to a minor party that had been subject to government harassment.

4. In a sense there were five opinions, since Justice Thomas's opinion was joined in part, but only in part, by two other Justices.

tutional protection of party spending for the campaign finance laws, and the implications of *Colorado Republican* for the future of campaign finance doctrine.

I. Background: The Facts, the Statute, and the Procedural History

Colorado Republican was ten years in the making. In January 1986, then-Representative Tim Wirth declared his candidacy for the Democratic nomination for the Senate seat being vacated by Gary Hart that fall.[5] Shortly thereafter, Wirth began to run ads outlining his position on a number of issues. In April and May 1986, the Colorado Republican Party paid for three radio ads and two pamphlets criticizing Wirth's voting record, mentioning that he was running for the Senate, and charging Wirth with misrepresenting his record in his ads. The anti-Wirth radio ad which became the subject of the FEC's enforcement action against the Colorado Republican Party included the following statements:

"I just saw some ads where Tim Wirth said he's for a strong defense and a balanced budget. But according to his record, Tim Wirth voted against every major new weapon system in the last five years. And he voted against the balanced budget amendment."

"Tim Wirth has a right to run for the Senate, but he doesn't have a right to change the facts."[6]

The state party committee paid $15,000 to run the ad. At the time it was aired, three Republicans were seeking their party's nomination, although two withdrew before the Republican state convention in June. Wirth and his Republican opponent, Rep. Ken Kramer, were not officially nominated until their party primaries in August.

In June 1986, the Colorado Democratic Party filed a complaint with the FEC alleging that the Republican anti-Wirth expenditures violated the spending limits FECA imposes on party committees.[7] In January 1989, the FEC determined there was probable cause to believe the Republicans had violated FECA and, when settlement negotiations failed, instituted a

---

5. Wirth won the election, served out his six-year term, and declined to seek another term, all before the district court in this case reached a decision. The case then took three more years to wind its way to the Supreme Court.

6. FEC v. Colorado Republican Fed. Campaign Comm., 59 F.3d 1015, 1018 n.1 (10th Cir. 1995).

7. The Democrats also alleged that the Republicans violated FECA's reporting requirements in listing the costs of the anti-Wirth program as operating expenses and not as expenditures with respect to an election for federal office.

civil enforcement action. The Republicans responded by arguing that the expenditures in question were not subject to the FECA limits, and that the FECA limits are unconstitutional.

FECA provides two avenues for parties to spend money on behalf of candidates for federal office. First, parties, like all other political committees, may contribute up to $5000 to a candidate "with respect to any election for Federal office."[8] Second, parties may make "coordinated expenditures" on behalf of their candidates. FECA ordinarily treats expenditures made "in cooperation, consultation, or concert, with" a candidate as contributions subject to contribution limits even if the "donor" did not actually give the money *to* a candidate.[9] FECA, however, provides a special exception for party committee spending "in connection with the general election campaign of candidates"[10] for Congress. In a Senate election, a party committee may spend up to two cents times the voting age population of the state in which the race occurs, or $20,000 adjusted for inflation from a 1974 base, in coordination with the party's Senate candidate's campaign.[11]

On the other hand, the FEC has determined that parties may not make "independent expenditures," that is, expenditures not in "cooperation, consultation, or concert" with a candidate. FECA, as amended in 1974, had imposed dollar ceilings on independent expenditures by individuals and political committees, but the Supreme Court in *Buckley* held such limits unconstitutional. The FEC subsequently deemed parties incapable of making expenditures truly independent of their own candidates' campaigns,[12] and adopted a regulation forbidding national and state party committees from making "independent expenditures in connection with the general election campaign[s]" for federal office.[13]

At the time of the 1986 election, the limit on coordinated party spending for the Senate race in Colorado was $103,000, which would have been more than enough to cover the anti-Wirth ad. However, the Colorado state party, like most state Republican parties, had assigned to

---

8. 2 U.S.C. § 441a(a)(2)(A) (1994).

9. 2 U.S.C. § 441a(a)(7)(B)(i) (1994).

10. 2 U.S.C. § 441a(d)(1) (1994).

11. 2 U.S.C. § 441a(d)(3)(A) (1994). This limit also applies to House of Representatives races in any state entitled to only one Representative. For other elections to the House, the ceiling is $10,000 adjusted for inflation from a 1974 base. 2 U.S.C. § 441a(d)(3)(B) (1994).

12. *See* FEC Adv. Op'n 1985–14, 2 FED. ELEC. CAMP. FIN. GUIDE (CCH) 5819 at 11,185 n.4 (5/30/85); FEC Adv. Op'n 1984–15, 1 FED. ELEC. CAMP. FIN. GUIDE (CCH) 5766 at 11,070 n. 2 (5/31/84).

13. 11 C.F.R. § 110.7(b)(4) (1996).

the National Republican Senatorial Committee ("NRSC") its coordinated spending authority. As a result, the anti-Wirth ad violated FECA—if the spending limit applied, and was constitutional.

In the lower courts, much of the *Colorado Republican* litigation focused on the question of the applicability of the FECA limits to the anti-Wirth ad. FECA's coordinated spending ceiling and reporting requirements apply only to expenditures "in connection with" a federal election. But the notion of spending "in connection with" an election campaign is inherently fuzzy and potentially sweeping. Communications concerning the performance of public officials or the wisdom of pending legislation can certainly affect the electoral fortunes of candidates, so campaign finance regulations could logically apply to a wide range of communications concerning politics and government. Such a broad reading could chill free and unfettered discussion of public issues. The Supreme Court thus determined that the First Amendment requires statutes regulating spending "in connection with" elections to be read narrowly and limited to spending expressly advocating the election or defeat of a clearly identified candidate.[14]

Although the Colorado Republicans' ad clearly identified Tim Wirth, it did not literally urge Wirth's defeat or the election of a Republican. The district court concluded that the ad "[a]t best...contains an indirect plea for action" which fell short of the "express advocacy" required to avoid infringing on constitutionally protected discussion of public issues.[15] The FECA limit thus did not apply to the anti-Wirth ad, and the court dismissed the FEC's suit.

The Tenth Circuit Court of Appeals reversed. The appellate court agreed with the district court that the anti-Wirth ad was not express advocacy "within the narrow definition" of prior Supreme Court cases.[16] But, after extended analysis,[17] the court deferred to the FEC's determination that limits on coordinated party spending could be constitutionally applied to spending with an "electioneering message" concerning a clearly identified candidate. The court found that the Republican ad did have an

---

14. *See, e.g., Buckley v. Valeo,* 424 U.S. 1, 42–43 (1976); FEC v. Massachusetts Citizens for Life ("*MCFL*"), 479 U.S. 238, 248–50. The discussion in *Buckley* concerned a provision of FECA that *Buckley* ultimately invalidated. *MCFL* considered the restriction on expenditures by corporations and unions. Neither case directly addressed the meaning of the "in connection with" language in the context of party coordinated spending.

15. FEC v. Colorado Republican Fed. Camp. Comm., 839 F. Supp. 1448, 1455–56 (D. Colo. 1993).

16. FEC v. Colorado Republican Fed. Camp. Comm., 59 F.3d 1015, 1023 n.10 (10th Cir. 1995).

17. *Id.* at 1019–23.

electioneering message with respect to Wirth and, thus, that the FECA limit applied. Since the state Republicans had transferred their statutory spending authority to the NRSC, their expenditures violated the FECA ceiling on coordinated party spending. The court then briefly considered and rejected the Republican claim that the FECA limit was unconstitutional.

II. The *Buckley* Doctrine and Party Spending

A. Basic Elements Of *Buckley*

In both the Tenth Circuit and the Supreme Court, the analysis of the constitutionality of the FECA spending limits was framed by *Buckley v. Valeo*. Although "one of the most vilified Supreme Court decisions of the post-World War II era,"[18] *Buckley* has for two decades dominated judicial review of campaign finance regulations.

Buckley has three major elements. First, the Court determined that campaign finance regulations impinge on the core First Amendment concerns of political expression and association. Without quite concluding that "money is speech," the Court found that money is essential for the dissemination of political messages and that contributing money "enables like-minded persons to pool their resources in furtherance of common political goals."[19] As a result, government regulation of campaign finances would be subject to "the exacting scrutiny required by the First Amendment."[20]

Second, and more controversially, the Court determined that the sole justification for limiting political spending is the prevention of corruption and the appearance of corruption. The Court rejected the argument that restrictions could be used to promote equality of political influence among individuals or groups or to equalize candidates' resources.[21] As the Court "famously or notoriously"[22] asserted: "the concept that government may restrict the speech of some elements of our society in order to enhance the relative voice of others is wholly foreign to the First Amendment."[23]

18. Cass R. Sunstein, *Political Equality and Unintended Consequences*, 94 COLUM. L. REV. 1390, 1394 (1994).

19. 424 U.S. at 22. *See also id.* at 65–66.

20. *Id.* at 16.

21. *Id.* at 48–49, 56–57. The Court also rejected the argument that the government could restrict spending in order to limit the cost of political campaigns. *Id.* at 57.

22. David A. Strauss, *Corruption, Equality, and Campaign Finance Reform*, 94 COLUM. L. REV. 1369, 1369 (1994).

23. 424 U.S. at 48–49.

Third, the Court drew an operational distinction between expenditures—that is, spending by candidates, organizations and individuals on direct communications with voters—and contributions—that is, payments by an individual or group *to* a candidate, which the candidate uses to fund political communication with the voters. Expenditures were held to be core political speech and not to raise a danger of the corruption of candidates. As a result, *Buckley* invalidated FECA's restrictions on expenditures by candidates and independent committees.

Contributions, by contrast, were given less protection. Unlike an expenditure, a contribution does not entail an expression of political views: "A contribution serves as a general expression of support for the candidate and his views, but does not communicate the underlying basis for the support." The expressive component of a contribution "rests solely on the undifferentiated, symbolic act of contributing." In contrast, the *size* of the contribution "does not increase perceptibly" the quantity of the contributor's communication. "While contributions may result in political expression if spent by a candidate or an association to present views to the voters, the transformation of contributions into political debate involves speech by someone other than the contributor."[24]

Moreover, contributions do raise the spectre of corruption: "To the extent that large contributions are given to secure a political *quid pro quo* from current and potential officeholders, the integrity of our system of representative government is undermined."[25] Congress—and state and local governments regulating campaigns for state and local offices—could thus impose dollar limits on the size of contributions.

B. Problems With Applying *Buckley*

Although the *Buckley* framework appears straightforward, the Court has had great difficulty with campaign finance cases.[26] The Court has run

---

24. *Id.* at 21.

25. *Id.* at 26–27.

26. The *Buckley* decision commanded a 6–2 majority, although three members of the court dissented from portions of the per curiam opinion. The next major campaign finance case, *First Nat'l Bank of Boston v. Bellotti*, 435 U.S. 765 (1978) drew four dissents. The critical opinion in *California Med. Ass'n v. FEC*, 453 U.S. 182 (1981) was joined only by a plurality. *Citizens Against Rent Control v. City of Berkeley*, 454 U.S. 290 (1981) drew one dissent and three concurring Justices who endorsed a narrower rationale than Chief Justice Burger's opinion for the Court. *FEC v. National Conservative Political Action Committee*, 470 U.S. 480 (1984) drew two dissents. *FEC v. Massachusetts Citizens for Life,* 479 U.S. 238 (1986) and *Austin v. Michigan State Chamber of Commerce*, 494 U.S. 652 (1990) were marked by 5–4 and 6–3 splits and multiple opinions. Of the

into three problems: (i) applying the contribution/expenditure distinction; (ii) determining the meaning of corruption; and (iii) deciding the degree of deference to be accorded to Congress or state and local elected officials — and the extent of consideration given to empirical evidence presented by litigants defending campaign finance restrictions—in determining whether the kinds of dangers which the Court has indicated may be the basis of regulation actually exist in a particular case.

(1) Drawing the Contribution/Expenditure Line: The contribution/expenditure distinction so central to the analysis in *Buckley* and later cases has proven difficult to apply. Some campaign practices—a candidate's donation of personal funds to her own campaign, or expenditures by groups not connected with a candidate expressly advocating the election or defeat of a clearly identified candidate—are arguably both contributions and expenditures. The candidate's donation to her own campaign is in form a contribution, yet it funds the candidate's own speech so it resembles an expenditure.[27] Independent expenditures are formally expenditures but raise the possibility that a candidate who benefits from an independent committee's support will feel an obligation to the spender comparable to that created by a contribution.[28]

Other practices—such as a contribution to a political organization or intermediary for election-related purposes—are arguably neither contributions nor expenditures within the *Buckley* analysis. A contribution to an intermediary is plainly not an expenditure, but, given the lack of a direct tie between donor and candidate, it may not present the vice *Buckley* found in contributions.[29]

And proposals to impose limits on the total amount of contributions candidates can receive from particular categories of donors, such as polit-

---

major constitutional cases, only *FEC v. National Right to Work Committee*, 459 U.S. 197 (1982) produced a unanimous Court.

27. *Buckley* treated a candidate's contribution of personal funds to her own campaign as an expenditure for First Amendment purposes. 424 U.S. at 51–54. Justice Marshall, who joined all other aspects of *Buckley*, dissented from this point. *Id.* at 286–87.

28. The Court has held that independent expenditures undertaken without "pre-arrangement and coordination" with a candidate are to be treated as expenditures for First Amendment purposes. *Id.* at 39–51. *Accord, National Conservative PAC*, 470 U.S. at 497–501. *But see id.* at 502, 510–11 (White, J., dissenting); 518–21 (Marshall, J., dissenting). *But cf. Austin*, 494 U.S. at 668–69 (upholding prohibition on spending by corporations).

29. *See, e.g.,* California Med. Ass'n v. FEC, 453 U.S. 182 (1981); Citizens Against Rent Control v. City of Berkeley, 454 U.S. 290 (1981); FEC v. Nat'l Right to Work Committee, 459 U.S. 197 (1982).

ical action committees,[30] or to impose very low contribution limits,[31] point up the constitutionally troublesome fact that all expenditures, except those funded by a candidate's personal wealth, ultimately derive from contributions.

The difficulty of applying the contribution/expenditure distinction is closely connected to the distinction's shaky justification. It might be easier to draw the line if the Court had been more persuasive in explaining why the line ought to be drawn. The Court's effort to establish that contributions are a lower order of speech than expenditures (assuming that both are constitutionally protected speech) seems increasingly tenuous. For candidates, in the absence of public funding, contribution limits necessarily curtail the expenditures of all but the wealthiest, self-funding candidates, or force them to shift their activities from actually communicating with voters to prospecting among donors for funds,[32] thus reducing the amount of public political speech. For donors, a contribution is a device for pooling individual views and enabling them to be amplified by a candidate—who can be a "great communicator"—thus providing more effective dissemination of those views than if the donor had spent an identical sum on expenditures to speak to the voters directly.

Contribution limits are particularly problematic from the perspective of freedom of association. Contributions may be only indirect speech— "speech by proxy"[33]—but they are a direct form of association. If speech is infringed by spending limits, then freedom of association ought to be comparably infringed by contribution ceilings that limit the amount of support an individual can give to a campaign. Indeed, in cases since *Buckley* the Court has given greater weight to freedom of association in reviewing campaign regulations.[34] Increasingly, the justification for the contribution limits, and for the contribution/expenditure distinction, ap-

---

30. *Cf.* Gard v. Wisconsin State Elec. Bd., 456 N.W.2d 809, 812, 829 (Wis.), *cert. den.* 498 U.S. 982 (1990) (sustaining absolute dollar cap on funding a candidate may receive from all committees, including PACs and party committees).

31. *See, e.g.,* Carver v. Nixon, 72 F.3d 633 (8th Cir. 1995) (invalidating low contribution limit); National Black Police Ass'n v. D.C. Bd. of Elec. and Ethics, 924 F. Supp. 270 (D.D.C. 1996)(same).

32. For a forceful argument concerning the constitutional significance of the diversion of officeholders' time to fundraising, *see* Vincent Blasi, *Free Speech and the Widening Gyre of Fund-Raising: Why Campaign Spending Limits May Not Violate the First Amendment After All*, 94 COLUM. L. REV. 1281 (1994).

33. Cal. Med. Ass'n v. FEC, 453 U.S. 182, 196 (1981) (plurality opinion).

34. *See, e.g., Citizens Against Rent Control,* 454 U.S. at 295–99; FEC v. Massachusetts Citizens for Life, 479 U.S. 238, 251–56 (plurality opinion); *id.* at 265–66 (O'Connor, J., concurring).

pears to rely less on the lower status of contributions than on the greater dangers contributions are said to pose for the political process.

(2) The Meaning of Corruption: Preventing corruption and the appearance of corruption "are the only legitimate and compelling government interests thus far identified for restricting campaign finances."[35] The Court, however, has never actually defined what it means by "corruption or the appearance of corruption." "Corruption" is sometimes equated with "improper influence" or "undue influence" over officeholders—without analysis of the distinction between proper and improper influences. Typically, the Court has given the notion of corruption a narrow reading, akin to bribery. As then-Justice Rehnquist asserted in *FEC v. National Conservative Political Action Committee ("NCPAC")*, "[t]he hallmark of corruption is the financial *quid pro quo:* dollars for political favors."[36] In this vision, the corruption concern is triggered only by the exchange of favors or the possibility of (and the appearance of the possibility of) the exchange of favors between donors and elected officials.

If corruption means exchange of favors, then the contribution/expenditure distinction may be sound in principle—contributions raise the possibility of the exchange of favors, whereas direct communications to the voters by candidates or interest groups do not involve such exchanges. But gross inequalities in spending by candidates, interest groups, or other political organizations that do not involve quid pro quos are not considered corrupting and thus cannot be barred by restrictions on spending. With corruption as quid pro quo, moreover, some hard cases, such as the issue of a candidate's use of personal wealth, become easy since the candidate cannot corrupt herself.

On other occasions, however, the Court has suggested that "corruption" may be read more broadly to include the spending of large sums of money that have an "undue influence on the outcome" of an election and thereby undermine "the confidence of the people in the democratic process and the integrity of government."[37] If corruption includes the influence that large sums of money can have on the outcome of an election—whether because such influence is itself corrupting[38] or because

---

35. *National Conservative PAC*, 470 U.S. at 496–97.

36. *Id.* at 497.

37. *See* First Nat'l Bank of Boston v. Bellotti, 435 U.S. 765, 789 (1978). *See also* Citizens Against Rent Control v. City of Berkeley, 454 U.S. 290, 301 (1981) (Marshall, J., concurring); *id* at 302–03 (Blackmun, J., and O'Connor, J., concurring).

38. *Cf.* Austin v. Michigan Chamber of Commerce, 494 U.S. 652, 659–60 (1990) (referring to the "corrosive and distorting effects of immense aggregations of wealth" and asserting that "[c]orporate wealth can unfairly influence elections when it is deployed in the form of independent expenditures, just as it can when it assumes the guise of political contributions").

it jeopardizes "voter confidence in government"[39]—then expenditures can be as corrupting as contributions and expenditures could be limited in the name of preventing corruption and the appearance of corruption.

Prior to 1990 the Court had never found evidence that the potential to engage in unlimited spending posed a threat to voter confidence in government adequate to justify a spending restriction, but in that year *Austin v. Michigan Chamber of Commerce*[40] upheld a state law restricting corporate political expenditures by finding that the state could justify the law as necessary to control "the corrosive and distorting effects of immense aggregations of wealth" which could "unfairly influence elections when... deployed in the form of independent expenditures."[41] If undue influence on the electoral process—and not just undue influence over elected officials, which is the sole focus of the quid pro quo model—could become a basis for campaign finance restrictions, then both the practical ability and the normative rationale for distinguishing between contributions and expenditures for First Amendment purposes would be substantially eroded.

To be sure, central to *Austin* and other cases dealing with limits on corporate political activity was the Court's assertion that corporations pose a unique danger of corruption. Corporations enjoy a "unique state-conferred corporate structure"[42] that enables them to accumulate large sums of money. These financial resources reflect the success of the corporation's commercial activities and not the extent of support for its political ideas. Limits on corporations are justifiable "to ensure that substantial aggregations of wealth amassed by the special advantages which go with the corporate form of organization...[are] not converted into political 'war chests'."[43]

Austin's attempt to limit its concern with large campaign war chests to corporations is unpersuasive. In *First National Bank of Boston v. Bellotti*,[44] its first case dealing with corporate political spending, the Court emphasized that the touchstone for analysis was "[t]he inherent worth of the speech in terms of its capacity for informing the public...not...the identity of its source, whether corporation, association, union, or individual."[45] The corporate status of the speaker, then, ought to be irrelevant to

39. *Citizens Against Rent Control*, 454 U.S. at 302 (Blackmun, J., and O'Connor, J., concurring).

40. 494 U.S. 652 (1990).

41. *Id.* at 660.

42. *Id.* at 659–60.

43. FEC v. Nat'l Right to Work Comm., 459 U.S. 197, 207 (1982).

44. 435 U.S. 765 (1978)

45. *Id.* at 777. *Bellotti* differed from *Austin* in one important respect. *Bellotti* involved corporate spending in a referendum election, whereas *Austin* addressed independent corporate spending in a candidate election. That difference would have significance if "cor-

an assessment of the basis for regulating the speech. It is hard to see why state-granted advantages make corporate speech more corrupting. Moreover, as Justice Scalia pointed out in his *Austin* dissent, corporations are not alone in receiving special advantages from the state.[46] Nor are corporations unique in their capacity to divert wealth obtained in the economic marketplace to political purposes. Other business associations — as well as billionaire individuals who benefit from inheritance laws or obtain their wealth from investments in corporations — may build up campaign war chests "that have little or no correlation to the public's support for the[ir] ... political ideas."[47]

Nonetheless, whatever the logical difficulties of limiting *Austin's* more expansive notion of "corruption" to corporations, that is what the Court asserted it did. As a result, "quid pro quo" remains the dominant model of "corruption," and the "undue influence over electoral outcomes" definition of corruption has been limited to cases involving corporations. Still, *Austin*—the last campaign finance case prior to *Colorado Republican*— opened up the possibility of a broader meaning of corruption, including a concern with the kinds of inequalities *Buckley* dismissed. And, as Archibald Cox observed, "[o]nce loosed, the idea of Equality is not easily cabined."[48]

(3) Degree of Deference to Elected Decisionmakers: The constitutionality of the regulation of independent expenditures is an empirical question as well as a normative one. Even if the meaning of corruption were clear, and even if it were limited to the quid pro quo model, it would still be debatable whether the danger of corruption is present in a particular setting.

Thus, a legislature might conclude that expenditures by independent committees supporting or opposing particular candidates might raise the prospect of quid pro quo corruption. Similarly, even if an individual's contribution to a political action committee or other political organization raises no question of the individual corrupting the organization, a legislature might conclude that there was sufficient danger that donors might use such intermediaries as conduits for the exchange of favors with the

---

ruption" were limited to the danger of quid pro quos, since the Court has determined that referenda and other ballot questions do not present the danger of an exchange of favors between special interests and officeholders. *Id.* at 790. However, *Austin's* expansion of "corruption" to include "undue influence" over election outcomes eliminates the significance of that difference. If *Austin* really is a "corporations" case, it is in direct tension with *Bellotti*.

46. *Austin*, 494 U.S. at 680.

47. *Id.* at 652. *See* Gerald E. Ashdown, *Controlling Campaign Spending and the 'New Corruption': Waiting for the Court*, 44 VAND. L. REV. 767, 783–84 (1991).

48. Archibald Cox, *Foreword: Constitutional Adjudication and the Promotion of Human Rights*, 80 HARV. L. REV. 91, 91 (1966).

candidates who receive contributions from the intermediary, so that contributions by individuals to political organizations that do not run candidates for office ought to be regulated. In addition, a legislature has to make the very basic decision of how large (or, perhaps, how small) a contribution raises the danger of corruption.

The Court thus has to decide how much deference to give to the elected decisionmakers in determining whether a particular campaign practice presents a danger of corruption. But the Court's standard of deference has ranged widely. In *Buckley* the Court deferred to Congress concerning the level of limits on individual donations to candidates, and the overall limit on individual contributions to political committees in a calendar year. Sustaining FECA's low reporting and recordkeeping thresholds, *Buckley* stated "we cannot require Congress to establish that it has chosen the highest reasonable threshold." That "line" was "best left to congressional discretion" and was upheld because it was not "wholly without rationality"[49] — a remarkably relaxed standard given the Court's finding that the reporting and disclosure rules implicate fundamental rights and are subject to "exacting scrutiny."[50] Similarly, the Court has also deferred to a Congressional judgment that contributions to intermediary organizations could be regulated because of the danger that those organizations might serve as conduits linking their donors to candidates.[51]

On the other hand, the Court has repeatedly rejected Congressional judgments that expenditures by independent committees raise dangers of corruption. Relying on its own armchair empiricism, *Buckley* found that because of the "absence of prearrangement and coordination," such expenditures "may well provide little assistance" to a candidate's campaign and, thus, alleviate the danger of a quid pro quo. A decade later *NCPAC* reaffirmed this position, notwithstanding evidence that independent committees had played an important role in the 1980 presidential race, largely in support of Ronald Reagan.

Critics of independent spending had urged that candidates and independent committees had found ways to use the independent committees to bolster candidates even in the absence of formal "prearrangement and coordination," and that organizers of the pro-Reagan independent committees had received appointments in the Reagan Administration.[52] But *NCPAC* found that on the record before it "an exchange of political favors for uncoordinated expenditures remains a hypothetical possibility

---

49. 424 U.S. at 83.

50. *Id.* at 64.

51. California Med. Ass'n v. FEC, 453 U.S. 182, 197–98, 201 (1981).

52. *See, e.g.,* ELIZABETH DREW, POLITICS AND MONEY 136–41 (Macmillan, 1983); HERBERT E. ALEXANDER, FINANCING THE 1980 ELECTION 142 (Lexington Books, 1983).

and nothing more,"[53] even though the trial court excluded most of the evidence of corruption proffered by the FEC—a decision which the Supreme Court sustained.[54] Thus, a strong evidentiary burden is placed on those who would regulate independent expenditures—with the Court unwilling to look at much of the evidence.

In the corporations cases the Court's vacillation has been acute. In different cases, it has dismissed out of hand the argument that corporations present any danger of undue influence;[55] deferred to a Congressional or state legislative judgment that corporations in general present unique dangers, without requiring that regulation be limited to corporations that actually amass the wealth necessary to fund a war chest that poses a danger of undue influence;[56] and upheld regulation in principle but required Congress to target only those corporations whose war chests are divorced from political support.[57]

Outside the corporate context, the Court's rule appears to be: As contributions in general raise the danger of corruption, Congress may regulate them without showing that a particular type of contribution raises any danger, but as expenditures in general raise little danger of corruption, Congress must meet an exacting burden of demonstrating that a particular expenditure raises the danger of corruption. The stringency of review thus seems to turn on the Court's own antecedent judgment of the relative degree of danger a practice presents, even though legislative findings or empirical evidence are supposed to be the *basis* of the Court's determination of whether a danger justifying regulation is present.

C. Implications For FECA Limits On Party Spending

The FECA limit on party spending potentially raises—and intertwines—all three questions that have plagued the application of *Buckley*. Party spending blurs the expenditure/contribution distinction. It is formally an expenditure, but given the close ties between parties and their candidates, party spending could plausibly be treated as a contribution. FECA and the FEC treat party spending like contributions and impose dollar limits. Should the judgment of the political branches receive deference, or should the Court engage in its own non-deferential assessment of the dangers posed by party spending?

---

53. 470 U.S. at 498.
54. *Id.* at 499–500.
55. *See, e.g., Bellotti*, 435 U.S. at 789.
56. FEC v. Nat'l Right to Work Comm., 459 U.S. 197, 210 (1982).
57. *See, e.g.,* FEC v. Massachusetts Citizens for Life, Inc., 479 U.S. 238 (1986).

Does party committee spending pose a danger of the corruption of candidates? Does the close relationship between a party and its candidate that makes the contribution/expenditure distinction so difficult to apply undermine the concern with party corruption of a candidate—or does it just make the concern stronger? What would corruption mean in this context? Can party committee spending be regulated because of the danger that the party will be a conduit for interest group or wealthy individual donations? Can party spending committees be regulated to prevent one party from having an undue influence over the election? What weight should be given to the judgment of Congress or the FEC that party spending presents some danger of corruption?

The *Colorado Republican* Court failed to reach a consensus on any of these issues, leaving the extent of deference to Congress, the categorization of party-spending within the *Buckley* framework, the meaning of corruption in the party-candidate context, and the constitutionality of the regulation of party spending outside the particular facts of the anti-Wirth ad, unresolved.

III. The Fragmented *Colorado Republican* Court

Colorado Republican produced four opinions, none of which garnered the support of more than three Justices. Four Justices, in two opinions joined by three Justices apiece—with two Justices joining both opinions—were willing to strike down FECA's limits on party spending coordinated with candidates. Two Justices voted to validate FECA's limits and to enforce the FEC's suit against the Colorado Republican Party. Three Justices determined that the FECA restriction could not be constitutionally applied against the anti-Wirth ad campaign but declined to consider the broader question of the constitutionality of limits on party spending. Moreover, none of the opinions considered the question that had divided the lower courts in this and other cases—whether FECA's limits can be applied to speech that falls short of express advocacy but contains an "electioneering message."

A. The Plurality Opinion

Justice Breyer, joined by Justices O'Connor and Souter, determined that the FECA limit on coordinated expenditures could not be applied to the anti-Wirth ad because the Colorado Republican Party had not, in fact, coordinated the ads with any Republican candidate. The Colorado Republican spending was, thus, truly independent spending and, like the independent spending of "individuals, candidates and ordinary political committees" could not be subject to limitation.[58]

First, the plurality found that the anti-Wirth spending was not in fact coordinated with any Republican candidate. The ads were aired at a time when there were three Republicans contending for the Senate nomination so there was no general election candidate. Moreover, the impetus for the ad had come from the state party chairman, who had "arranged for the development of the script at his own initiative." Work on the script was limited to state party staff; the senate contenders and their staffs were not involved.[59]

Second, the plurality rejected the FEC's argument that party committees are incapable of making expenditures independent of their party's candidates, since the FEC failed to provide any empirical support, either in its advisory opinions or in its arguments before the Court, for this assertion.[60] Moreover, the statute itself did not clearly preclude a finding that some party spending could be independent.

Finally, Justice Breyer concluded that the government presented no evidence that independent spending by parties presents any greater dangers of corruption than the independent spending of other political committees or individuals. Once again, "the absence of prearrangement and coordination" was said to "alleviate" the danger of a quid pro quo.[61] Comparing independent spending by party committees and individuals, "the constitutionally significant fact, present equally in both instances, is the lack of coordination between the candidate and the source of the expenditure."[62]

Having determined that FECA's limits on coordinated expenditures could not constitutionally be applied to an expenditure that was independent-in-fact, the plurality declined to reach the general question of the constitutionality of FECA's limits on party spending. Indeed, the plurality avoided any statement that parties enjoy a constitutionally preferred position with respect to campaign finance. The plurality rejected the argument, embraced by one of the concurrences, that "a party and its candidate are identical,"[63] and, in stressing the significance of the independence of the anti-Wirth spending in avoiding the danger of corruption, it implicitly rejected the contention of the other concurrence that parties are inca-

---

58. Colorado Republican Fed. Campaign Comm. v. FEC, 116 S. Ct. 2309, 2317 (1996).

59. *Id.* at 2315.

60. *Id.* at 2318.

61. *Id.* at 2316.

62. *Id.* at 2317.

63. *Id.* at 2319.

pable of corrupting their candidates.[64] Indeed, the plurality commented that parties "share relevant features with many PACs."[65]

The Breyer opinion managed to block the application of the FECA limit to the anti-Wirth ad while doing minimal damage to the overall structure of FECA and avoiding the tensions in the *Buckley* framework. The plurality minimized the significance of its lack of deference to the political branches by noting that the FEC had failed to do the homework necessary to prove that "independent" party spending is impossible in fact, and that Congress's authorization of party coordinated expenditures up to a statutory ceiling did not preclude a finding that some party expenditures could be truly independent.

Thus, although the idea of "independent" party spending creates a hole in FECA it appears to reflect the plurality's effort to adhere to *Buckley's* contribution/expenditure distinction. Party committees were presumed to be like other political committees—some party spending might be coordinated with candidates and some might be independent. Indeed, noting that coordinated party expenditures "share some of the constitutionally relevant features" of both expenditures and contributions, the plurality gave the very inability of party spending to fit neatly into *Buckley's* conceptual boxes as a reason for not addressing the Republicans' broader challenge to the constitutionality of the limits on party spending.[66]

B. The Concurring Opinions

Four Justices in two overlapping groups of three concurred in the judgment but dissented from the plurality's reasoning: they would have completely invalidated FECA's ceiling on coordinated party spending. Justice Kennedy's opinion rejected the idea of party independence from candidates, but concluded that, whether or not coordinated with their candidates, party spending ought to be treated as constitutionally protected expenditures. Justice Thomas's opinion urged that since party spending presents only a minimal danger of corruption there is no constitutional basis for its limitation.

Justice Kennedy's opinion explicitly rejected the plurality's emphasis on the independence of the Colorado Republicans' spending. Instead, joined by Chief Justice Rehnquist and Justice Scalia, Justice Kennedy stressed the "practical identity of interests between the two entities [parties and their

---

64. *Id.* at 2316.
65. *Id.* at 2320.
66. *Id.*

candidates] during an election" and the "tradition of political parties and their candidates engaging in joint First Amendment activity."[67] Rather than look to independence-in-fact of a particular expenditure, he concluded that a party's "fate in an election is inextricably intertwined with that of its candidates."[68]

Justice Kennedy acknowledged that party spending would generally function as a contribution to a candidate, but found that such spending also represents the party's speech on its own behalf since "in the context of particular elections, candidates are necessary to make the party's message known and effective, and vice versa."[69] As the political speech of a political association, party spending, even spending coordinated with the candidate a party supports, could not constitutionally be limited.

Justice Thomas's opinion, also joined by Chief Justice Rehnquist and Justice Scalia, took a slightly different tack. Justice Thomas ridiculed the assertion that there was any danger of corruption in a party supporting its own candidate. Justice Thomas considered two possible sources of corruption: the influence of the party itself on the candidate, and the influence of a party's donors. Justice Thomas denied that party influence per se could ever be considered corruptive. "The very aim of a political party is to influence its candidate's stance on issues." If a party succeeds "that is not corruption; that is successful advocacy of ideas in the political marketplace and representative government in a party system."[70]

As for any danger that coordinated party spending might provide an opportunity for donors to the party to exert undue influence over the party's nominee, Justice Thomas noted that the "numerous members with a wide variety of interests" found in parties makes it unlikely that any one person or interest group could use a party to exact a quid pro quo from a candidate. The influence of particular interests would be "significantly diffused" by other interests. Further, there is "little risk" that a party could be used by wealthy donors as a conduit for corrupting candidates so long as the Court "continues to permit Congress to subject individuals to limits on the amount they can give to parties"[71]—although in another part of his opinion, not joined by any other Justice, Justice Thomas urged that contribution caps be held unconstitutional.[72]

---

67. *Id.* at 2323.
68. *Id.*
69. *Id.* at 2322.
70. *Id.* at 2331.
71. *Id.*
72. *Id.* at 2329.

C. The Dissent

Justice Stevens, joined by Justice Ginsburg, dissented in a brief opinion.[73] The dissent agreed with Justice Kennedy that a party and its candidate have "a unique relationship" which precludes Justice Breyer's finding of independence. The dissenting Justices, however, concluded that Congress could constitutionally limit party spending.

Disagreeing with Justice Thomas, Justice Stevens found that party coordinated spending could be corrupting—or, rather, that Congress could find it so—first, because it could give a party, "or the persons who control the party" influence "over the candidate by virtue of its power to spend," and, second, because of the danger of conduit corruption.[74]

In addition, Justice Stevens asserted that limits on party spending were justified by the government's "important interest in levelling the electoral playing field by constraining the cost of federal campaigns."[75]

IV. Analysis: Placing Parties in the *Buckley* Framework

A. Independence-in-fact?

Despite its clever use of the idea of independence-in-fact to avoid addressing the constitutional challenge raised by the Colorado Republican Party, the plurality opinion causes considerable problems on its own. First, it is highly fact-dependent, without making clear exactly the facts on which it depends. The anti-Wirth ad campaign occurred before the party had nominated a candidate, indeed, while the nomination was still contested by several candidates. Is that essential, or can a party engage in independent spending on behalf of the likely nominee—including an incumbent—or even for the actual nominee, provided that formal contact between the candidate and the party committee is avoided?

And exactly what formal contact has to be avoided? Justice Breyer's opinion emphasized the lack of coordination with respect to the advertising campaign itself.[76] Can a party committee that provides a candidate with computer services, polling data, assistance in training staff, fundrais-

---

73. *Id.* at 2332.
74. *Id.*
75. *Id.*
76. *Id.* at 2315.

ing and even funds,[77] engage in an "independent" media campaign on the candidate's behalf if it avoids direct contact with the candidate and the candidate's committee with respect to advertising strategy?

Second, to the extent that party committees take care to minimize their actual cooperation with candidates, the plurality opinion could have the potentially perverse consequence — perverse, that is, from the perspective of those who have called for a more party-centered campaign finance system as a way of promoting party accountability in government — of driving parties away from their candidates. The modern trend in Congressional campaigns has been for party committees, especially the Republican and Democratic campaign committees, to take a greater role in recruiting candidates, assisting candidates with their campaigns, and, especially, helping candidates with communications, including the development of issue positions and the actual production of advertising.[78] One result has been a "greater nationalization of campaign themes,"[79] which may be a step toward greater party cohesion with respect to major issues.

The plurality's approach could force parties to choose between providing financial support to their candidates and working with those candidates on their campaign agendas. Thus, greater independent party spending might actually reinforce, rather than undermine, the candidate-centered campaigns that party government advocates have criticized.

Third, *Colorado Republican* will make it difficult for the FEC to enforce the ceiling on coordinated expenditures that the plurality was careful to avoid upsetting. As journalists and scholars who have examined "independent" spending by non-party political committees have observed, "[t]here are all manners of ways in which people running 'independent' campaigns can run them in tandem with the candidates" without formal consultation."[80] The prospects for tacit cooperation are far greater in the candidate-party context given the likelihood of ongoing ties between parties and their candidates, the involvement of many candidates in their parties, and the stakes parties have in the success of their candidates. The FEC, which has never been known for its timely or vigorous

---

77. For a description of the kinds of services party committees now provide their candidates, *see* LARRY J. SABATO, THE PARTY'S JUST BEGUN: SHAPING POLITICAL PARTIES FOR AMERICA'S FUTURE 75–81 (Scott, Foresman, 1988); PAUL S. HERRNSON, PARTY CAMPAIGNING IN THE 1980s 47–83 (Harvard U. Press, 1988).

78. *See, e.g.,* HERRNSON, *supra* note 77, at 60–65.

79. *Id.* at 64.

80. *See* DREW, *supra* note 52, at 136–41; ALEXANDER, *supra* note 52, at 142.

enforcement of the campaign finance laws,[81] is poorly situated to police the relationships between candidates and committees, or to carry the heavy burden of proving that independence-in-fact has been compromised in a particular case.

Although the FEC may have erred in concluding that independence-in-fact is never possible, it seems likely that it is relatively rare. The presumption of coordination may have been an administratively useful prophylactic rule for enforcing the statutory ban on coordinated expenditures.[82] By forcing the FEC to make the case not simply that party spending occurred but that the party committee actually cooperated with a candidate, the plurality may have invalidated the FECA limit in practice even as it strained to avoid doing so in theory.

Finally, the whole notion of party "independent" spending seems formalistic and naive. Seeing the trees but not the forest, the plurality's tight focus on the absence of party-candidate discussion of a particular ad misses the web of relationships that link parties to their candidates' campaigns. Parties back candidates and provide them with financial and logistical support. Candidates run on party lines, belong to parties, are often active in party organizations, and are frequently identified in terms of their party affiliation. Party committees, in turn, define their mission as the election of candidates bearing the party label. The protection of independent spending enables groups or individuals with independent agendas—that is, concerns other than the outcome of elections—to communicate their views with respect to elections to the voters. But the principal agenda of a political party committee is the election of the party's candidates.[83] The Colorado Republican Party's ad campaign was intended to weaken Tim Wirth and to elect a Republican—any Republican who might be nominated—not to further nonpartisan ideological or economic goals.

---

81. At least part of the FEC's difficulties derive from the weak institutional structure imposed by Congress, *see* BROOKS JACKSON, BROKEN PROMISE: WHY THE FEDERAL ELECTION COMMISSION FAILED (Priority Press, 1990).

82. The plurality in *Colorado Republican* noted that "[t]he Commission has not claimed…that, administratively speaking, it is more difficult to separate a political party's 'independent' from its 'coordinated' expenditures than, say, those of a PAC," 116 S. Ct. at 2318, but as the Colorado Republican Party had not argued that its spending was "independent" and not "coordinated" spending, it is not clear why the FEC would have thought it necessary to defend its position that all party spending is coordinated spending.

83. *See, e.g.,* GERALD M. POMPER, PASSIONS AND INTERESTS: POLITICAL PARTY CONCEPTS OF AMERICAN DEMOCRACY 3–4 (U. Press of Kansas, 1992) ("Parties are unique in their nominal unity and electoral focus.").

In finding that parties could engage in independent spending, Justice Breyer sought to assure parties parity with PACs, other political committees, and individuals. But given their ongoing ties to candidates, and their focus on electing candidates, parties are not quite comparable to these other participants in the political process. That does not mean that they should receive less constitutional protection or more protection; it means simply that the effort to treat parties just like these other political actors is unpersuasive.

As the other *Colorado Republican* opinions demonstrate, however, it is not easy to determine exactly what rights parties ought to enjoy, or to situate that determination within the *Buckley* doctrine.

B. Party–Candidate Identity?

Central to Justice Kennedy's opinion is the claim that parties have a distinctive relationship with candidates which provides parties with a constitutional right to engage in unlimited campaign spending. Although the notion of a distinctive relationship seems right—and the failure to acknowledge that relationship is the Achilles' heel of the plurality opinion—it is not obvious why the result is unlimited party spending.

Initially, Justice Kennedy's opinion somewhat exaggerates the distinction between party committees and other political committees in terms of the relationship between committees and candidates. As the rise of "generic" party advertising indicates, parties are not entirely dependent on candidate campaigns to get their message across. Parties can and do spend money to voice party positions apart from urging the election or defeat of specific candidates. On the other hand, non-party committees might believe that the most effective way to get their message across is by supporting the campaign of a particular candidate. Certainly, if a candidate has embraced a controversial position on a particular issue—such as gun control, health care, or abortion—organizations sharing that issue position might assert "a practical identity of interests" between themselves and the candidate during the pendency of the campaign.

The real difference between parties and other committees is the structural inability of parties to pursue their goals with respect to candidate elections independently of their candidates' campaigns. Other political committees can mount independent campaigns. Given the web of ties between candidates and parties, it would be "impractical and imprudent," if not impossible, for parties to mount independent campaigns.[84]

But that does not mean that limits on coordinated spending "stifle" a party's voice. If, as Justice Kennedy contends, there is a "practical iden-

---

84. 116 S. Ct. at 2323.

tity" between party and candidate, then presumably the party's message is being advanced by its nominee. As long as the party's candidate—its designated representative in the election—has a right of unlimited spending, then the FECA limits on coordinated spending cannot limit the communication of the party's message, since the candidate's spending will convey that message to the voters.

Ironically, the real problem with the FECA limits may derive not from party-candidate identity but from the existence of some differences between party and candidate interests. Party committees have such a major stake in the electoral success of their nominees that true independence is extremely unlikely, yet party committees may also have their own distinctive interests—such as the concern of party bureaucrats and professionals in maintaining the party as an organization—not represented by the candidate. Restrictions on party coordinated spending may limit the ability of party committees to advance those particular interests.

The constitutionality of the FECA limits then turns on the central *Buckley* questions of whether coordinated party spending presents dangers of corruption or the appearance of corruption—which also entails consideration of the degree of deference due to the political branches in making that judgment. Justice Kennedy's opinion failed to address the question of corruption. Whether party spending can corrupt was, however, the focus of the Justice Thomas' concurrence and Justice Stevens's dissent.

C. Party–Candidate Corruption?

(1) Conduit Corruption:[85] Justice Thomas appears to be on shaky ground in his quick dismissal of the dangers of conduit corruption. Clever party manipulation of the provision added to FECA in 1979 exempting money for state and local level volunteer activity and voter registration and get-out-the-vote drives from the Act's contribution and expenditure limitations[86]—so-called "soft money"—has eroded the significance of

---

85. After the submission of this Comment, a major campaign finance scandal involving the activities of the Democratic National Committee surfaced during the final weeks of the 1996 presidential campaign. This scandal confirms the significance of the conduit corruption concern raised in this section. Although the discussion in text gives more attention to the activities of the Republican National Committee, the activities of DNC fundraisers in 1996 amply demonstrates that conduit corruption is a serious danger for both parties. Further analysis of the fundraising activities of the major parties in the 1996 election is beyond the scope of this Comment.

86. See 2 U.S.C. § 431(8)(B)(v), (x), (xi), (xii) (1994); 2 U.S.C. § 431(9)(B)(iv), (viii), (ix) (1994).

FECA's limits on donations to party committees.[87] Although the law permitting soft money contributions restricts their use, the funds support party-building activities and free up federally regulated contributions for use in candidates' campaigns.[88] Thus, both candidates and parties benefit from large soft money contributions.

A relatively small number of "high rollers" play an important role in party fund-raising. More than sixty contributors gave the Republican National Committee at least $100,000 apiece in soft money in the 1991–92 campaign, while the Democrats received gifts of more than $100,000 from 72 donors, including nearly $400,000 from the steelworkers union and nearly $350,000 from the National Education Association.[89] Some interests loom large in the financing of particular parties. For example, between January 1, 1995 and June 30, 1996 — that is, well before the peak months of the 1996 presidential campaign — national Republican committees received $1.6 million from Philip Morris Co., $970,000 from RJR Nabisco, $448,000 from US Tobacco, $400,000 from Brown & Williamson Tobacco Co., and $300,000 from the Tobacco Institute.[90] These are pretty large sums to be "diffused" — and there is at least anecdotal evidence of national Republican officials seeking to make state officeholders more attentive to the tobacco industry's interests.[91] Moreover, the parties have taken steps to promote direct contact, at meals, private meetings, and policy retreats, between their major financial backers and elected officeholders.[92]

As the soft money gifts suggest, a broad-based party can serve as a conduit for more narrow interests. Like Justice Thomas, many advocates of a more party-centered campaign finance system have argued that an ex-

---

87. The literature on "soft money" is legion. For a description of the history of soft money and its role in the 1992 election, *see* HERBERT E. ALEXANDER AND ANTHONY CORRADO, FINANCING THE 1992 ELECTION 147–75 (M.E. Sharpe, 1995).

88. BROOKS JACKSON, HONEST GRAFT: BIG MONEY AND THE AMERICAN POLITICAL PROCESS 146 (Knopf, 1988).

89. *See* ALEXANDER AND CORRADO, *supra* note 87, at 153–56.

90. *Top "Soft Money" Contributors to Republican Party Committees,* WASH. POST, Aug. 14, 1996, at A19.

91. *See, e.g.,* Timothy Noah, *GOP's Chief Pushed Pro-tobacco Bill at State Level, Arizona Lawmaker Says,* WALL ST. J., Feb. 20, 1996, at A20 (RNC National Chairman Haley Barbour phoned the Speaker of the Arizona House of Representatives to pressure him into supporting a pro-tobacco bill); *Tobacco Ties,* WALL ST. J., March 1, 1996, at A1 (reporting that Haley Barbour called Texas Governor Bush's office to check on status of bill to restrict city anti-smoking ordinances).

92. *See* JACKSON, *supra* note 88, at 9–10, 98–99; SABATO, *supra* note 77, at 77; HERRNSON, *supra* note 77, at 35–36.

panded party role would dilute the influence of big special interest donors.[93] The growing role of special interest contributions in party finances, however, casts doubt on this sunny scenario. Removing limits on party spending without providing for public funding would almost certainly increase the parties' incentives to pursue large contributions, and concomitantly increase the prospects of special interests pursuing their agendas, and securing quid pro quos, through donations to the parties.[94] Conduit corruption is at heart an issue with a strong empirical component, but Justice Thomas's opinion reflects more armchair political science theorizing than any familiarity with campaign finance data. On the other hand, Justice Stevens' opinion does little more than state that the possibility of conduit corruption is enough to justify the FECA limits. If, as the *Buckley* doctrine provides, party contributions are a form of constitutionally protected speech, then there ought to be at least some assessment of the seriousness of the corruption danger as a part of the determination whether constitutionally protected speech may be curtailed. Even deference to Congress is not the same as abdication.

The conduit corruption issue nicely displays the importance of questions about deference and empirical justification when courts consider the constitutionality of campaign finance limits. The gap between Justice Thomas and Justice Stevens demonstrates anew how the Court has been unable to resolve this central question. Unfortunately, the Court's difficulties seem to stem not from reasonable disagreements about how to assess disputed evidence but from an apparent unwillingness to deal seriously with empirical evidence and legislative justifications at all. As the Thomas and Stevens opinions reveal, the Court's two principal approaches have been either to disregard empirical evidence or not to require any. Surely, there is a middle position between complete dismissal of Congress' judgment[95] and evidence that might support its action, and failure even to require that evidence be presented and defended.

---

93. *See, e.g.,* Kirk J. Nahra, *Political Parties and the Campaign Finance Laws: Dilemmas, Concerns, and Opportunities,* 56 FORDHAM L. REV. 53 (1987); Clarisa Long, *Shouting Down the Voice of the People: Political Parties, Powerful PACs, and Concerns About Corruption,* 46 STAN. L. REV. 1161 (1994).

94. Brooks Jackson contended that Rep. Tony Coelho's efforts to strengthen Congressional Democrats' finances in the 1980s "actually encouraged House Democrats to become more reliant on special interest money. The [Democratic Congressional] campaign committee gets its own funds increasingly from lobbyists, PACs, and businessmen...." JACKSON, *supra* note 88, at 296.

95. According to Justice Thomas, "[t]here is good reason to think that campaign reform is an especially inappropriate area for judicial deference to legislative judgment." 116 S. Ct. at 2330 n.9.

(2) Party Influence Corruption: Justice Thomas's denial that party influence per se can be corrupting would appear to have a more substantial foundation than his summary rejection of conduit corruption. Party committee spending on behalf of candidates is far more likely to be an instance of money used to advance shared candidate-donor interests in order to persuade voters than of money to influence a candidate to adopt or change a position.

Nevertheless, candidate and party committee interests can diverge. In those circumstances, Justice Stevens may well be correct in asserting that "by virtue of its power to spend" the party may be able to exert "influence over the candidate."[96] The Progressive Era laws that shifted control over nominations from party committees and conventions to primaries constituted an effort to reduce the influence of party organizations over party candidates, presumably reflecting the notion that candidates (and elected officials) would embrace different positions on issues of public importance if they were less beholden to party officials.[97] Moreover, there is also evidence that contemporary party committees may attempt to leverage their control over coordinated spending to influence candidates—for example, to "persuade" candidates to hire the committees' preferred consultants or accept the committees' strategic advice with respect to their campaigns.[98]

Still, the preeminent goal of party committees is the election of party candidates, rather than influencing the issue positions of elected officials. Party committees will back only their own party's candidates, whereas many other political committees, particularly non-ideological political committees, will often offer some support to both major party candidates in a race, as a means of ensuring an opportunity to influence whoever wins the election.

Moreover, even if Justice Stevens is right that unlimited coordinated spending would provide the opportunity for greater party influence over candidates, influence is not the same as corruption. The real question is whether such party influence would be "improper" or "undue." As the cases from *Buckley* to *Austin* demonstrate, the Court has never determined what makes influence undue, other than to indicate that large sums of money given to a candidate or spent in coordination with the candidate can be a source of improper influence. But the distinction between money

---

96. 116 S. Ct. at 2332.

97. *See, e.g.,* Jo Freeman, *Political Party Contributions and Expenditures Under the Federal Election Campaign Act: Anomalies and Unfinished Business,* 4 PACE L. REV. 267, 290 (1984) ("Historically, there certainly has been a belief that parties were capable of corruption. Most of the state laws regulating parties passed at the turn of the century were intended to eliminate perceived corruption.").

98. *See* HERRNSON, *supra* note 77 at 57, 59.

given to influence a candidate and money given to help a candidate who is receptive to the donor's views or is otherwise politically aligned with the donor is often elusive.

Underlying Justice Thomas's concurrence is the assumption that a party cannot "unduly" influence its candidates. Apparently the more influence a party has over its candidates the better. That is also the position embraced by the party-responsibility school. The more influence a party committee has over its candidates, presumably, the greater cohesion there will be among the party's officeholders, the more the party label will mean something in government and to the electorate, and the more the voters can look to party as a means of establishing government accountability. There is considerable scholarly support for a party-centered campaign finance system as a step toward creating a more "responsible" two-party system, with attendant benefits for government performance and responsiveness.[99]

But despite Justice Thomas's reference to "representative government in a party system," the United States has a long tradition of candidate-centered elections coexisting with its party system.[100] Parties are nowhere mentioned in the constitution. For most of this century, party committees have not controlled party nominations. Candidates have historically organized, conducted, and financed their own campaigns. Candidates' campaigns often emphasize a candidate's independence from party offices and even from other elected officials of their own party. The limit on party co-ordinated spending grows out of and is consistent with this tradition.

In essence, the question of whether party committee coordinated spending raises a danger of parties corrupting candidates is really a question of how much or how little potential for influence parties ought to be allowed to have over their candidates' campaigns—and whether Congress or the Court should decide this. Certainly, elected officials seem to be in a much better position to consider and combine the multiple and often conflicting values of candidate autonomy, party responsibility, voter participation, and the potential for parties to serve as conduits for special interest influence. Elected officials are more likely to understand the impact of the campaign finance laws on the political process and the interaction of party spending with other campaign finance laws and governance generally.[101]

---

99. *See, e.g.,* SABATO, *supra* note 77, at 185–88, 212–23.

100. *See, e.g.,* LEON EPSTEIN, POLITICAL PARTIES IN THE AMERICAN MOLD 5 (U. of Wisconsin Press, 1986) (American "political culture" is one "in which voters choose individuals, not merely parties, to represent them in executive and legislative offices").

101. This includes the balance of political forces between the parties. Given the Republicans' traditionally greater success in raising funds, any change in the rules governing the party role has partisan implications as well. From a partisan perspective, *Colorado Republican* is a victory for Republicans in general, as well as for the Colorado Republican

Certainly there is no reason to believe that elected officials are likely to be hostile to party interests. Some independent committees may be composed of political outsiders, but party committees are the ultimate political insiders. The vast majority of elected federal and state officials are elected on party lines and nearly all carry major party labels. All of the members of the extremely important national party congressional campaign finance committees are members of Congress,[102] and Congress has deliberated various bills that would expand the parties' role. As Republican party committees have generally outpaced their Democratic counterparts in raising money,[103] Republicans in Congress have tended to make lifting the limits on donations to parties and spending by parties a component of their campaign finance legislative agenda.[104]

Party committees have not done badly under FECA. The Act allows individuals to give national party committees $20,000 in a calendar year, and it allows political committees to give national party committees $15,000 per year, whereas the limits on individual and committee donations to candidates are $1,000, and $5,000, respectively, per candidate per election.[105] The soft money exemption added in 1979 has enabled the parties to raise tens of millions of dollars for party-building activities.[106] Most scholars of the political parties have determined that the national parties have enjoyed greater influence with respect to the finances of their candidates' congressional campaigns since FECA's enactment than at any other time in their history.[107] Given the existence of campaign finance

Party. Of course, had either of the concurring opinions won the approval of a majority of the Court, the Republicans' victory would have been even more substantial.

102. HERRNSON, *supra* note 77, at 40; DAVID B. MAGLEBY AND CANDICE J. NELSON, THE MONEY CHASE: CONGRESSIONAL CAMPAIGN FINANCE REFORM 100–01 (Brookings Institution, 1990).

103. *See, e.g.,* JOHN H. ALDRICH, WHY PARTIES? THE ORIGIN AND TRANSFORMATION OF POLITICAL PARTIES IN AMERICA 256–58 (U. of Chicago Press, 1995); EPSTEIN, *supra* note 100, at 216–23; MAGLEBY AND NELSON, *supra* note 102, at 102–12; SABATO, *supra* note 77 at 75–81.

104. *See, e.g.,* HERBERT E. ALEXANDER AND MONICA BAUER, FINANCING THE 1988 ELECTION 117–18 (Westview Press, 1991) (discussing Republican campaign finance reform proposals); *see also id.* at 136 (noting partisan effects of Democratic proposals to tighten up on soft money).

105. 2 U.S.C. § 441a(a) (1994).

106. *See, e.g.,* ALEXANDER AND CORRADO, *supra* note 87 at 158 (noting that "both parties appear to be increasingly incorporating soft money into their overall financial schemes"). Early estimates indicate that the Democratic and Republican party committees each raised about $100 million in soft money in the 1995–96 election cycle. *See* Peter H. Stone, *The Green Wave*, 28 NAT'L JOURNAL 2410 (Nov. 9, 1996).

107. *See, e.g.,* EPSTEIN, *supra* note 100, at 217–18.

laws that limit both donations to candidates and the financial activities of non-party political committees, the concurring Justices' determination that parties have an unlimited right to engage in coordinated spending could, if embraced by a Court majority, provide an impetus for a more party-centered campaign finance system. This might, as party-responsibility advocates contend, promote party cohesion and government accountability. A party-centered system might very well be a good idea. But it would be a major departure from past and present practice. And it is hard to believe that the decision whether to have a party-centered or candidate-centered system is a question of constitutional law, to be decided by the Supreme Court, rather than a preeminently political question to be decided by Congress.

V. Implications of a Right of Unlimited Party Coordinated Spending for the Campaign Finance Laws

Colorado Republican came within one vote of eliminating limits on party spending in connection with congressional campaigns. The plurality's focus on the asserted independence-in-fact of the anti-Wirth ad campaign is unlikely to provide a stable resolution of the question of party spending, and the question of the constitutionality of limits on party spending is likely to recur. Moreover, that question has broad implications for the overall structure of campaign finance regulation as well as for proposed reforms.

Striking the limits on party spending may be like pulling on a loose thread and causing a whole sleeve to unravel. Justice Thomas's presumption that parties are incapable of corrupting their candidates would appear to eliminate the basis for restrictions on party contributions to candidates. Justice Kennedy's opinion sought to leave open the constitutionality of restrictions on "undifferentiated political party contributions,"[108] but his notion of the "practical identity" of party and candidate implicitly invalidates restrictions on party contributions to candidates, too—assuming parties would still want to make contributions if they enjoyed the right of unlimited coordinated expenditure. Thus, under either approach, invalidating the limit on coordinated spending is likely to result in the elimination of any limits on party financial support for candidates.

Further, Justice Thomas's opinion suggests the basis for an attack on the limits on contributions to parties. In cases dealing with contributions

---

108. 116 S. Ct. at 2323.

to political committees, the Court has given great weight to the corruptive potential of contributions *by* an organization in order to justify restrictions on contributions *to* the organization. Thus, *Citizens Against Rent Control v. City of Berkeley*[109] invalidated an ordinance restricting contributions to committees that support or oppose ballot measures, reasoning that since spending by a ballot measure committee raises no possibility of corruption (since there were no candidates to corrupt) there was no constitutional basis for limiting contributions to the committee. But in *California Medical Ass'n v. FEC,* and *FEC v. National Right to Work Committee* the Court relied on the anti-corruption rationale to uphold limits on contributions to PACs that gave funds to candidates.[110]

Given Justice Thomas's reliance on the statutory limits on contributions to parties to rebut the argument that party expenditures raise the risk of conduit corruption, my argument that the logic of Thomas's position would undermine the limits on donations to parties may be something of a speculative stretch. Nevertheless, if the Court were to buy the argument that there is nothing corrupting in a party's influence over its candidates and that party size and diversity mitigate the danger of conduit corruption, then the anti-corruption rationale for limiting contributions to parties would be discredited. Although the growth of soft money has eroded the effect of FECA's limits on donations to parties, acceptance of Justice Thomas's argument might make it impossible to close the soft money loophole, and would also, of course, have implications for state laws that impose limits on contributions to state parties in connection with state campaigns.

A right of unlimited party spending could also knock out the spending limits in the presidential public funding system, and, similarly, jeopardize state public funding laws for state elections and proposals to use public funds to limit the use of private funds. *Buckley* invalidated limits on campaign expenditures but held that Congress could condition the grant of public funds on a candidate's acceptance of spending limits.[111] The limit on publicly-funded candidate spending has also applied to spending by the candidate's party. The rise of soft money has dramatically expanded the amount of private funds available to publicly-funded presidential candidates. Nevertheless, the statutory restrictions on party spending in support of presidential candidates make presidential elections primarily publicly funded and assure a measure of parity between the major party candidates.

---

109. 454 U.S. 290, 297 (1981).

110. *See Cal Med,* 453 U.S. at 197–99, 201; *NRWC,* 459 U.S. at 207–10.

111. 424 U.S. at 57 n.65. *See also* Republican Nat'l Comm. v. Fed. Election Comm'n, 487 F. Supp. 280 (S.D.N.Y. 1980), *aff'd* 445 U.S. 955 (1980).

Could those restrictions survive a holding that party expenditures are constitutionally protected? If, as Justice Kennedy contends, "candidates are necessary to make the party's message known and effective" and limits on party spending "constrain [ ] the party in advocating its most essential positions and pursuing its most basic goals,"[112] then how can party spending on behalf of its leading speaker—its presidential candidate—be limited?[113] Under *Buckley* a presidential candidate can waive his or her own right to unlimited spending in order to receive party funds, but would a candidate's waiver bind party committees?

In *NCPAC*, the Court held that a candidate's acceptance of spending limits as a condition for public funding did not bind independent committees, which remain entitled to spend unlimited sums in support of that candidate. Notwithstanding Justice Kennedy's rhetoric about the "practical identity" of candidates and parties, presidential candidates do not control their party committees—certainly not the state committees or the congressional finance committees which might want to spend in support of the presidential candidate in order to have an effect on the fortunes of party candidates further down the ballot. If, as Justice Kennedy put it, parties "exist to advance their members' shared political beliefs,"[114] it may not be possible for one candidate to waive the speech rights of the many people affiliated with the party.

A right of unlimited party coordinated spending thus might make it impossible to limit candidate spending even as a condition for the receipt of public funds. It is possible that only parties could waive party spending rights. This might mean that any attempt to use the public funding system to enforce spending limits might require offering public funding to the parties rather than (or in addition to) the candidates. This would certainly serve to promote greater party responsibility in government, and might even be a good idea, but it would be a sharp departure from existing practice if public funding of parties were to become necessary to impose spending limits on candidates.[115]

---

112. 116 S. Ct. at 2322–23.

113. Indeed, even the plurality threatens public funding since party committees, such as state party committees, that avoid direct contact with the presidential candidates could be "independent-in-fact" and presumably could engage in unlimited spending on behalf of the party's presidential candidate. Under the concurrences, party committees might be able to work with their presidential candidate directly.

114. *Id.* at 2322.

115. It is possible that in the existing presidential public funding system, the provision of public funds for the national party conventions could provide the basis for the party waiver of the right of unlimited coordinated spending. However, if the parties were able to raise and spend unlimited amounts of money in the presidential election they might choose to forgo public funds for the convention. Despite the public funding law, large

VI. Implications of *Colorado Republican* for *Buckley v. Valeo*

Colorado Republican was a hard case, as the multiple opinions suggest. The Court's difficulty may have been attributable in part to the constitutionally ambiguous status of parties. In other cases, the Court has treated parties both as quasi-state actors, subject to constitutional requirements, and as the epitome of the private political associations shielded by the First Amendment from state regulation. Indeed, earlier this past Term, the Court fragmented along lines similar to those in *Colorado Republican* when it considered whether the Voting Rights Act could be applied to a change in a state party's convention rules.[116]

Moreover, party spending poses a particularly hard issue for the *Buckley* framework. *Buckley's* contribution/expenditure distinction and its concern with corruption implicitly assume a separation between candidates and their financial backers, and the possibility that financial support will be a source of improper influence on candidates. But parties are composed of both candidates and contributors to their campaigns. Party committees support candidates primarily to advance their shared interests rather than to influence them. Parties thus straddle the candidate-contributor gap intrinsic to the *Buckley* model.

Colorado Republican may also be indicative of deeper difficulties in the Court's approach to campaign finance regulation. *Buckley's* assumes a distinction between expressions of support for political ideas and positions and efforts to influence candidates — the former are treated as constitutionally protected from restriction while the latter are treated as problematic and subject to regulation. Yet the distinction between support for ideas and efforts to influence candidates is often elusive. Money given to support a candidate who shares the donor's beliefs or issue-positions may influence the candidate to continue to adhere to that position, while

---

donors currently play a significant role in financing the party conventions. *See* Phil Kuntz and Michael K. Frisby, *For Big Contributors, Convention's Business Isn't at the Podium*, WALL ST. J., Aug. 13, 1996 at A1. Nor, given the traditionally decentralized structure of the major parties, is it clear that the party national committee's agreement to limit spending in exchange for convention funds would bind state party committees.

116. *See* Morse v. Republican Party of Virginia, 116 S. Ct. 1186 (1996). As in *Colorado Republican,* the principal groupings on the Court were Justices Stevens and Ginsburg in an opinion by Justice Stevens; Justices Breyer, O'Connor and Souter in an opinion by Justice Breyer; and Justices Kennedy, Thomas and Scalia, and Chief Justice Rehnquist in multiple overlapping opinions.

money given to influence a candidate usually goes to candidates who have signaled at least some openness to supporting the donor's position.

Moreover, *Buckley* is focused entirely on the question of the influence of campaign money on candidates and officeholders; the Court firmly ruled out consideration of the influence of campaign money or of disparities in resources available for political activity on the conduct or outcomes of elections as a factor in constitutional analysis. Concerns about the influence of money, and especially of unequal sums of money, on election outcomes has been a prime factor driving campaign finance regulation. Even the Court, *Buckley* notwithstanding, has not been entirely immune to these concerns, as *Austin's* focus on corporate campaign war chests demonstrates—although *Austin* wrapped its concern over unequal spending in the open-ended language of corruption.

Dissatisfaction with *Buckley* led one *Colorado Republican* Justice explicitly and two others implicitly to break away from the *Buckley* framework. Justice Thomas, in the portion of his opinion not joined by any other Justice, rejected the contribution/expenditure distinction, and urged that restrictions on contributions, as well as limitations on expenditures, be subject to strict scrutiny. In his view, bribery laws and disclosure requirements are adequate to prevent corruption.[117] Conversely, one of the reasons Justice Stevens, joined by Justice Ginsburg, gave for sustaining the FECA limits is the government's "important interest in leveling the electoral playing field by constraining the cost of federal campaigns."[118] This is flatly inconsistent with *Buckley's* rejection of any government interest in limiting the cost of campaigns as a justification for limiting campaign finances.[119] Moreover, the dissent's citation to Justice White's *Buckley* dissent, its skepticism that increased campaign spending necessarily promotes the "informed debate protected by the First Amendment," and its willingness to "accord special deference" to Congress's "wisdom and experience" concerning campaign finance suggest that Justices Stevens and Ginsburg may have rejected the *Buckley* doctrine generally.

Colorado Republican's difficulties in applying the *Buckley* framework and the rejection of the *Buckley* approach by three members of the Court indicate the troubled state of the current doctrinal approach to campaign

---

117. 116 S. Ct. at 2325–29.

118. 116 S. Ct. at 2332.

119. Indeed, one of the reasons the plurality rejected the danger of corruption as a basis for restricting party independent spending is its determination that Congress adopted the FECA ceiling not to control corruption "but rather for the constitutionally insufficient purpose of reducing what it saw as wasteful and excessive campaign spending." 116 S. Ct. at 2317.

finance regulation. Nonetheless, it may be a little premature to toll *Buckley's* death knell. Chief Justice Burger and Justice White dissented from basic elements of *Buckley* twenty years ago and Justice Marshall subsequently came to reject the contribution/expenditure distinction[120] so the doctrine has survived the opposition of three sitting Justices before.

Moreover, given the different directions in which the Thomas and Stevens opinions pull, the Court seems far from a consensus on a model that would replace *Buckley*. *Austin* hinted at a greater acceptance of egalitarian arguments for campaign limits, but with the replacement of *Austin's* author, Justice Marshall, by Justice Thomas, *Austin* itself may be hanging by a thread and may be more of a special "corporations" case now than ever before.[121] At the same time, no other member of the *Colorado Republican* Court endorsed Justice Thomas's extreme hostility to campaign finance regulation. The plurality's fact-specific decision may indicate a concern by those three Justices to minimize judicial disruption of Congress' campaign finance handiwork. Judicially mandated deregulation of campaign finance seems even less probable than judicial endorsement of egalitarian restrictions.

For all its problems, then, *Buckley* continues to shape judicial consideration of campaign finance regulation. *Buckley's* internal tensions will make the doctrine difficult to apply and the evolution of case law difficult to predict. Campaign finance cases are likely to remain an arena of conflict within the Court, much as *Buckley's* limited focus on quid pro quo corruption will continue to be a source of conflict between the Court and campaign finance reformers.

---

120. *National Conservative PAC*, 470 U.S. at 518.

121. *Austin* was decided by a vote of 6–3. The six Justices in the majority were Justice Marshall, Chief Justice Rehnquist, and Justices Brennan, White, Blackmun and Stevens. Justices Kennedy, O'Connor and Scalia dissented. The replacement of Justice Marshall by Justice Thomas reduces support for *Austin's* broad reading of corruption from six to five. Chief Justice Rehnquist has consistently supported the *Buckley* framework, but has equally consistently made a special exception to permit restrictions on corporations. There is no evidence that any of the *Austin* dissenters have become more receptive to arguments that governments may justify spending restrictions to limit the impact of campaign war chests on the electorate.

Section II

Is Money Speech?

Politics and the Constitution: Is Money Speech?

J. Skelly Wright

Lawyers are often surprised to learn that Alexander Meiklejohn, whose name is so often invoked in epic battles over the meaning of the First Amendment, was not a lawyer. He was a philosopher and educator of the first rank. Perhaps this background positioned him to discern, as he did with unique clarity, the central meaning of freedom of speech under our Constitution. In all events it made him especially sensitive to the Supreme Court's role as teacher to the nation. "[T]he court," he wrote,

> holds a unique place in the cultivating of our national intelligence. Other institutions may be more direct in their teaching influence. But no other institution is more deeply decisive in its effect upon our understanding of ourselves and our government.[1]

In this spirit I wish to examine this Term's most important First Amendment decision, *Buckley v. Valeo*.[2] For I am concerned lest the Court's teaching in that case distort our understanding of ourselves and our government.

I. *Buckley v. Valeo*: Campaign Financing and the First Amendment

Under review in the *Buckley* case was the complex law passed in 1974 to reform the way we finance our federal election campaigns.[3] I focus here

---

1. ALEXANDER MEIKLEJOHN, POLITICAL FREEDOM: THE CONSTITUTIONAL POWERS OF THE PEOPLE 32 (1960).

2. 424 U.S. 1 (1976).

3. Federal Election Campaign Act Amendments of 1974, Pub. L. No. 93-443, 88 Stat. 1263 (1974) U.S. CODE CONG. & AD. NEWS 1436 (amending Federal Election Campaign Act of 1971, Pub. L. No. 92-225, 86 Stat. 3 (1972)) [hereinafter cited without cross-reference as 1974 Act]. §§ 101–302 of the 1974 Act dealt with private financing of federal election campaigns. §§ 403–408 made changes in the scheme of public financing of presidential elections. Further amendments were made in 1976. Federal Election Campaign Act Amendments of 1976, Pub. L. No. 94-283, (1976) U.S. CODE CONG. & AD. NEWS (90 Stat. 475) [hereinafter cited without cross-reference as 1976 Act].

on only one part of that reform-the limits placed on campaign contributions and campaign expenditures.[4] Congress imposed rather strict ceilings on contributions to candidates for federal office in order to prevent large contributions from, in effect, buying favorable governmental decisions. Individuals cannot give more than $1,000 to a candidate per election,[5] nor can they give more than $25,000 overall.[6]

Congress also imposed restrictions on campaign expenditures. It limited to $1,000 the independent expenditures an individual or organization could make in support of a "clearly identified" candidate.[7] The term "independent expenditures" means expenditures undertaken without the cooperation or control of the candidate.[8] It was Congress's judgment that large independent outlays might circumvent the contribution limitations

---

4. There were three other major portions of the 1974 law. One portion set new requirements for recordkeeping and disclosure on the part of candidates, their committees, and those individuals who make independent expenditures advocating the election or defeat of identified candidates. 2 U.S.C. §§ 431–437b (Supp. IV 1974) (modified 1976). Another provided for the public financing of both presidential primary and general elections and of party nominating conventions. I.R.C. §§ 9001–9042 (amended 1976). A third part established a Federal Elections Commission to oversee the administration of the law. 2 U.S.C. §§ 437c-438 (Supp. IV 1974) (modified 1976).

The Supreme Court upheld the disclosure requirements and the public financing provisions, but it ruled that the appointment of some of the members of the Commission by congressional leaders violated the separation-of-powers principle of U.S. CONST. art. II, § 2, which authorizes the President to appoint "Officers of the United States." 424 U.S. at 84, 108, 140. This defect was remedied by the 1976 Act § 101(a)(1), 2 U.S.C.A. § 437c(a)(1) (Sept. 1976 Pamphlet).

5. 18 U.S.C. § 608(b)(1) (Supp. IV 1974) (modified 1976; to be recodified at 2 U.S.C. § 441a).

6. 18 U.S.C. § 608(b)(3) (Supp. IV 1974) (modified 1976; to be recodified at 2 U.S.C. § 441a). Contributions by political committees were also restricted under the 1974 law. 18 U.S.C. § 608(b)(2) (Supp. IV 1974) (modified 1976; to be recodified at 2 U.S.C. § 441a) (limiting political committees, as defined therein and in 18 U.S.C. § 591(d) (Supp. IV 1974), to a contribution ceiling of $5,000 per candidate per election).

7. 18 U.S.C. § 608(e) (Supp IV 1974) (repealed 1976).

8. Expenditures "authorized or requested by the candidate, an authorized committee of the candidate, or an agent of the candidate," id. at § 608(c)(2)(B)(ii) (modified 1976; to be recodified at 2 U.S.C. § 441a), were regarded as expenditures by the candidate, 18 U.S.C. § 608(c)(2)(A),(B)(ii) (Supp. IV 1974) (modified 1976; to be recodified at 2 U.S.C. § 441a), and as contributions by the individual or group that made the actual expenditure. 424 U.S. at 46–47 & n.53.

and themselves result in a form of political bribery.[9] Congress also placed certain higher limits on how deeply a candidate could dig into his own pocket to finance his campaign.[10] And finally, Congress enacted overall ceilings on the total amount a candidate and his committees could spend in advancing his candidacy.[11]

Congress passed these provisions in response to political abuses which culminated in the 1972 presidential campaign and its aftermath, com-

---

9. *See* S. REP. No. 93-689, 93rd Cong. 18–19, *reprinted in* 1974 U.S. CODE CONG. & AD. NEWS 5587, 5604–05.

10. In campaigns during a calendar year, a candidate for federal office could not make use of his personal funds or those of his immediate family in excess of the following limits: $50,000 for presidential and vice presidential candidates; $35,000 for senatorial candidates; and $25,000 for candidates for United States Representative, 18 U.S.C. § 608(a) (Supp. IV 1974) (repealed 1976). If the individual were a candidate for United States Representative from a state that is only entitled to one Representative, the relevant limit was $35,000. *Id. at* § 608(a)(1)(B) (repealed 1976).

11. The expendiute limits were $10 million for a candidate for the presidential nomination of a political party and $ 20 million for a candidate for election to the office of the President. *Id.* at § 608(c)(1) (repealed 1976). Expenditures on behalf of a candidate nominated by a political party for the office of Vice President of the United States were counted toward the $20 million limit for the presidential candidate. *Id.* at § 608(c)(2)(A) (repealed 1976). The total expenditure limits for candidates to other federal offices generally varied with the size of the voting age population of the relevant jurisdiction. *Id.* at § 608(c)(1)(C)-(F) (repealed 1976). Expenditure limits were to be adjusted yearly to reflect rising prices. *Id.* at § 608(d) (repealed 1976).

The 1976 amendments removed all the major contribution and expenditure provisions from Title 18 and placed them, in slightly modified form, in Title 2 of the United States Code. 1976 Act §§ 112, 201. In response to the Supreme Court's *Buckley* decision, however, Congress did make one major modification in these provisions. The expenditure ceilings, which the Court declared unconstitutional, were omitted from 2 U.S.C.A. § 441a (Sept. 1976 Pamphlet), the section that replaces 18 U.S.C. § 608 (Supp. IV 1974)-with one significant exception that corresponds to a curious wrinkle in the *Buckley* decision.

Without even discussing possible problems under the doctrine of unconstitutional conditions, *see generally* William W. Van Alstyne, *The Demise of the Right-Privilege Distinction in Constitutional Law*, 81 HARV. L. REV. 1439 (1968), the Supreme Court left standing the requirement in the 1974 Act § 404(a), 408(c), I.R.C. §§ 9004, 9035 (amended 1976), that presidential candidates who voluntarily accept public funding must agree to abide by the ceilings on total campaign outlays. 424 U.S. at 108–09. These voluntary expenditure ceilings continue under the 1976 Act § 1122 U.S.C.A. § 441a(b) (Sept. 1976 Pamphlet), and have been broadened to require that presidential candidates accepting public funding agree to limit spending from personal funds to $50,000 in both the primary campaign and the general election. 18 U.S.C. §§ 301(a), 305(a) (Supp. IV 1974) (to be codified at I.R.C. §§ 9004, 9035).

monly called Watergate.[12] Congress found that these excesses were fueled by money collected for political purposes.[13] There can be no question that under the Constitution Congress properly assumed responsibility for combating federal election abuses. Repeatedly the courts have recognized that Congress maintains a strong, vital interest in protecting the political process from distortion and corruption.[14]

Congress, of course, knew there were difficult First Amendment questions involved in limiting campaign contributions and expenditures.[15] Money does facilitate communication of political preferences and prejudices. It is also clear that money influences the outcome of elections. Generally speaking, the more money spent in behalf of a candidate, the better the candidate's chances of winning. Indeed, a veteran of political campaigns has declared that money is the mother's milk of politics.[16]

But the real questions are these: To what extent does this kind of mother's milk poison the political process? To what extent does it distort, the truth-seeking process that lies at the heart of the First Amendment conception?[17] And most importantly, what may the people, acting through Congress, do about it?

The Supreme Court answered these questions by saying that Congress, in passing the campaign reform law, tried to do too much. The Justices left the statute's contribution limits in place, but they struck down all the spending ceilings-on independent expenditures in behalf of a candidate, on personal funds spent by a candidate in his own campaign, and on total

---

12. For a detailed account of these abuses, *see, e.g.,* FINAL REPORT OF THE SENATE SELECT COMM. ON PRESIDENTIAL CAMPAIGN ACTIVITIES OF THE U.S. SENTATE, S. REP. No. 93-981, 93d Cong. (1974) [hereinafter cited as FINAL REPORT]. A comprehensive "Bibliography of Watergate Source Materials" may be found in WATERGATE SPECIAL PROSECUTION FORCE, REPORT 265–73 (1975).

13. *See, e.g.,* FINAL REPORT, *supra* note 12, at 212.

14. *See, e.g.,* United States v. Classic, 313 U.S. 299, 317–20 (1941); Burroughs v. United States, 290 U.S. 534, 545 (1934); *Ex parte* Yarbrough, 110 U.S. 651, 657–67 (1884).

15. *See, e.g.,* FINAL REPORT, *supra* note 12, at 571.

16. TIME, Jan. 5, 1968, at 44 (statement of Jesse Unruh, former Speaker of the California Assembly, now California State Treasurer).

17. The First Amendment conception of which I speak is perhaps best stated by Justice Holmes, dissenting in Abrams v. United States, 250 U.S. 616, 630 (1919):

[W]hen men have realized that time has upset many fighting faiths, they may come to believe even more than they believe the very foundations of their own conduct that the ultimate good desired is better reached by free trade in ideas-that the best test of truth is the power of the thought to get itself accepted in the competition of the market, and that truth is the only ground upon which their wishes safely can be carried out. That at any rate is the theory of our Constitution. It is an experiment, as all life is an experiment.

outlays by the candidate. Asserting that today "virtually every means" for effectively communicating ideas requires the expenditure of money,[18] the Court found that these provisions placed substantial, direct restrictions on the ability of individuals to engage in protected political expression.[19] The Court concluded that, unlike the contribution limitations, the expenditure ceilings failed sufficiently to serve the governmental interest in preventing corruption,[20] therefore, the burden they placed on "core First Amendment expression" was unconstitutional.[21]

I take issue with the Court's answers, but not primarily because of the result reached in this particular case. Rather, I am deeply concerned with the lesson the Court taught in the course of reaching its result. Throughout its discussion of contributions and expenditures, the Court persisted in treating the regulation of campaign monies as tantamount to regulation of political expression. The Court told us, in effect, that money is speech.

This, in my view, misconceives the First Amendment. It accepts far too narrow a conception of political dynamics in our society. It accepts without question elaborate mass media campaigns that have made political communication expensive, but at the same time remote, disembodied, occasionally even manipulative. Nothing in the First Amendment prevents us, as a political community, from making certain modest but important changes in the kind of process we want for selecting our political leaders. Nothing bars us from choosing, as I am convinced the 1974 legislation did choose, to move closer to the kind of community process that lies at the heart of the First Amendment conception-a process wherein ideas and candidates prevail because of their inherent worth, not because prestigious or wealthy people line up in favor, and not because one side puts on the more elaborate show of support. Nothing in the First Amendment

18. 424 U.S. at 19.

19. *Id.* at 58–59.

20. Proponents of the expenditure limitations had argued that the ceilings also served to equalize the abilities of individuals and groups to influence the outcome of elections and the abilities of candidates to bring their messages before the public. The Court rejected these objectives as constitutionally illegitimate and unlikely to be achieved by the expenditure limitations. *Id.* at 48–49, 54, 56–57.

21. *Id.* at 47–51, 53–54, 55–59. The Court was also careful to note that the Act had to be tested against the First Amendment's guarantee of freedom of association. *See, e.g., id.* at 15, 22–23, 24–49. The only extended discussion of this First Amendment right, however, appears in the Court's discussion of contribution limitations. *Id.* at 24–29. The right of free association played only a limited role in the Court's consideration of the three types of expenditure ceilings and in its decision to strike them down. *Id.* at 22–23. The dispositive factor was the Court's view that expenditure ceilings abridge the right of free expression. *See id.* at 39, 47–51, 52–53, 55, 58–59.

bars us from those steps, for nothing in the First Amendment commits us to the dogma that money is speech.

II. Money as Speech: The Legal Argument

A. The Court's Precedents

No one disputes that the money regulated by the campaign reform legislation is closely related to political expression. And no one disputes that the First Amendment applies with special force to the political arena.[22] The legal question is thus not whether the restrictions on giving and spending are subject to First Amendment scrutiny at all. The question is what degree of scrutiny should apply. There are basically two choices[23]-and I am painting here with a very broad brush. The first is to treat campaign contributions and expenditures as equivalent to pure speech. If this approach is proper, then the giving and spending restrictions enacted in 1974 should be treated in the same way as laws imposing a prior restraint on speech or censoring particular points of view. Such laws are subject to the most rigorous scrutiny known to constitutional law, and rightly so.[24] Nothing distorts the truth-seeking process so much as prior restraint or government censorship. Even ideas utterly false serve the purpose of testing and strengthening views with a better claim to the truth.[25] For this reason only the most intensely compelling governmental interests can sustain such restrictions.

The second legal alternative is to treat political giving and spending as a form of conduct related to speech-something roughly equivalent to the physical act of picketing or to the use of a soundtruck.[26] Alert and careful judicial scrutiny is still warranted, for an ostensibly neutral regulation of

---

22. *See, e.g.,* Monitor Patriot Co. v. Roy, 401 U.S. 265, 272 (1971); Mills v. Alabama, 384 U.S. 214, 218–19 (1966); Garrison v. Louisiana, 379 U.S. 64, 74–75 (1964).

23. *See* 424 U.S. at 15.

24. *See, e.g.,* New York Times Co. v. United States, 403 U.S. 713, 714 (1971); Organization for a Better Austin v. Keefe, 402 U.S. 415, 419 (1971); Freedman v. Maryland, 380 U.S. 51, 57 (1965); Bantam Books, Inc. v. Sullivan, 372 U.S. 58, 70 (1963); Thomas v. Collins, 323 U.S. 516, 530 (1945); Near v. Minnesota, 283 U.S. 697, 713–16 (1931). *See generally* Emerson, *The Doctrine of Prior Restraint,* 20 LAW & CONTEMP. PROB. 648 (1955).

25. *See* JOHN STUART MILL, *Essay on Liberty, in* ON LIBERTY AND CONSIDERATION ON REPRESENTATIVE GOVERNMENT 1, 15–21 (B. Blackwell ed. 1946); Walter Bagehot, *The Metaphysical Basis of Toleration, in* 2 THE WORKS OF WALTER BAGEHOT 339, 343, 350 (Forrest Morgan ed. 1891).

26. *See, e.g.,* Grayned v. City of Rockford, 408 U.S. 104 (1972); Cameron v. Johnson, 390 U.S. 611 (1968); Adderley v. Florida, 385 U.S. 39 (1966); Cox v. Louisiana 379 U.S.

conduct may merely disguise an attempt at silencing a particular view-point. Nevertheless, a carefully tailored regulation of the nonspeech element-the picketing or the soundtruck-can survive without being required to pass the rigorous test applied to restrictions on pure speech. The regulation is constitutional if it serves an important governmental interest and if that interest is unrelated to suppression of speech.[27]

When the campaign finance reform law came before the United States Court of Appeals for the District of Columbia Circuit-the court on which I serve-we found the second approach to be the proper one. We held[28] that political giving and spending were not pure speech, that they should be treated as speech-related conduct under principles announced in the leading case of *United States v. O'Brien.*[29] And we found the contribution and expenditure limits constitutional.[30] The law, we thought, was carefully tailored to serve the government's undeniably important interest in purifying elections.[31]

In the *O'Brien* case the Supreme Court approved the conviction of a war protester under a statute that banned the burning of draft cards. O'Brien claimed that in publicly burning his draft card he was merely exercising his right to free expression against the Vietnam War. But the Court held that his act was not pure speech; that an important governmental interest was served by preservation of draft cards; and that his expression-related conduct in burning the draft card was subject to the restrictions Congress had enacted.[32]

O'Brien used the burning of his draft card as a vehicle for expressing his political convictions. So too the use of money in political campaigns serves as nothing more than a vehicle for political expression. It may not have the same overt physical quality that burning a draft card or picketing at the statehouse has, but it remains a mere vehicle. Restrictions on the use of money should be judged by the tests employed for vehicles-for speech-related conduct-and not by the tests developed for pure speech. Our court therefore held that campaign giving and spending, like draft-card burning, were speech-related conduct.

---

559 (1965); Kovacs v. Cooper, 336 U.S. 77 (1949). *See generally* Schneider v. State, 308 U.S. 147, 160 (1939).

27. *See* United States v. O'Brien, 391 U.S. 367, 376–77 (1968).

28. Buckley v. Valeo, 519 F.2d 821, 840–41 (D.C. Cir. 1975), *aff'd in part and rev'd in part,* 424 U.S. 1 (1976).

29. 391 U.S. 367 (1968).

30. 519 F.2d at 843–44, 851–60.

31. *See id.* at 842–44. The Supreme Court has emphasized the importance of the governmental interest in maintaining federal elections free from corruption. *See, e.g.,* Burroughs v. United States, 290 U.S. 534, 545 (1934); *Ex parte* Yarbrough, 110 U.S. 651, 666–67 (1884).

32. 391 U.S. at 382.

The Supreme Court disagreed. "The expenditure of money," it wrote,

> simply cannot be equated with such conduct as destruction of a draft card. Some forms of communication made possible by the giving and spending of money involve speech alone, some involve conduct primarily, and some involve a combination of the two. Yet this Court has never suggested that the dependence of a communication on the expenditure of money operates itself to introduce a nonspeech element or to reduce the exacting scrutiny required by the First Amendment.[33]

I am bound to say that this passage performs a judicial sleight of hand. The real question in the case was: Can the use of *money* be regulated, by analogy to conduct such as draft-card burning, where there is an undoubted incidental effect on *speech?* However, what the Court asked was whether *pure speech* can be regulated where there is some incidental effect on *money*. Naturally the answer to the Court's question was "No." But this left untouched the real question in the case. The Court riveted its attention on what the money could buy-be it communication, or communication mixed with conduct. Yet the campaign reform law did not dictate what could be bought. It focused exclusively on the giving and spending itself.[34] In short, the Court turned the congressional telescope around and looked through the wrong end.

Perhaps I can clarify the difference by an example. Suppose a state enacts a law banning all political advertisements in newspapers during the week preceding an election. Such a law targets the communication itself. It should be subject to rigorous scrutiny. And it should be struck down.[35] If the state attorney general were to argue that the law is justified on the ground that there is a nonspeech element present, simply because somebody has to spend money to place a political advertisement, he would of course lose.

But such a statute is not comparable to the campaign finance law at issue in *Buckley*. The 1974 law targeted the money itself, utterly divorced from the kind of communication-or other campaign services-the money would buy. Congress was not trying to justify suppression of pure speech by seizing on money as a nonspeech element. It was trying to justify a straightforward regulation of the excessive use of money as a blight on the political process. Like draft-card burning, however speech-related, this was a vice Congress had authority to control.[36]

---

33. 424 U.S. at 16.

34. Justice White was able to see the distinction clearly. *Id.* at 259–64 (White, J., dissenting in relevant part).

35. *Cf.* Mills v. Alabama, 384 U.S. 214 (1966) (Alabama statute banning publication on election day of editorial supporting candidate violates First Amendment).

36. After rejecting *O'Brien's* applicability to the *Buckley* case on the ground that campaign contributions and expenditures are speech, not conduct, the Supreme Court went

Let me approach the question from another angle. The main evil against which rigorous First Amendment scrutiny is designed to guard is content discrimination-discrimination based on the message itself. As the Supreme Court held in unmistakable terms in 1972:

> [A]bove all else, the First Amendment means that government has no power to restrict expression because of its message, its ideas, its subject matter, or its content.... [O]ur people are guaranteed the right to express any thought, free from government censorship. The essence of this forbidden censorship is content control.[37]

There has been no showing that the 1974 ceilings on contributions and expenditures discriminate against certain viewpoints.[38] In fact, one could

---

on to contend that even if they were speech-related conduct, their regulation by the 1974 law was unconstitutional under *O'Brien*. 424 U.S. at 17. *O'Brien* required that a regulation of speech-related conduct not be aimed at "the suppression of free expression." 391 U.S. at 377. The *Buckley* Court held that the 1974 law was aimed at suppressing communication because Congress meant it, in part, to reduce the quantity of speech on the part of wealthy individuals and interest groups. 424 U.S. at 17.

This rather mechanical application of the *O'Brien* test is unsatisfactory. Congress meant the statute to reduce the quantity of *spending* on the part of wealthy individuals and candidates, but it was unconcerned with the type or quantity of *speech* that might result when people operated within the new limits. More importantly, the "suppressing communication" test is concerned primarily with statutes that are aimed at suppressing a particular viewpoint-statutes which discriminate on the basis of content. *O'Brien* itself makes this interpretation clear. In explaining the test, the *O'Brien* Court took as its example the case of Stromberg v. California, 283 U.S. 359 (1931). 391 U.S. at 382. The California statute in *Stromberg* ostensibly regulated conduct-the use, in certain circumstances, of "any flag, badge, banner, or device," 283 U.S. at 361-but it did not do so evenhandedly. It denied the use of any flag or device to those who intended thereby to demonstrate their "opposition to organized government." *Id.* Demonstrators not opposing organized government could use any flag or banner they wished. *See id.* at 369–70.

Statutes of this type are invalid because they use the regulation of conduct as a subterfuge for suppressing a certain message. *O'Brien* condemns statutes which are, *in this sense,* aimed at suppressing communication. *See* 391 U.S. at 382. The 1974 law thus did not run afoul of *O'Brien*. As the *Buckley* Court itself recognized, the campaign reform statute did "not focus on the ideas expressed" by those subject to its limits. 424 U.S. at 17. It was content-neutral and, properly understood, did not aim at suppressing communication.

37. Police Dep't v. Mosley, 408 U.S. 92, 95–96 (1972). For a recent discussion of content discrimination, *see* Kenneth L. Karst, *Equality as a Central Principle in the First Amendment,* 43 U. Chi. L. Rev. 20 (1975). *See also* Thomas Irwin Emerson, The System of Freedom of Expression 633–34 (1970).

38. The plaintiffs in *Buckley* argued that candidates who challenge incumbents are uniquely burdened by the contribution and expenditure limits. Brief of the Plaintiffs at 149–61, 175–83, Buckley v. Valeo, 519 F.2d 821 (D.C. Cir. 1975). Even if true, this is not

argue that money limitations, if properly drafted and administered, are uniquely manageable as content-neutral controls on political abuses.[39]

Let me reiterate, however, one important qualification. I am not saying that Congress has a free hand so long as it targets money. There are delicate links between political giving and spending, on the one hand, and political speech, on the other. Every regulatory scheme concerning campaign finances requires careful judicial review to make sure that Congress maintains a close relation between the important ends sought and the precise means chosen. Some measures may be more clearly justified than others. For example, a far more compelling case can be made for contribution limitations than for the overall candidate spending ceilings, since the former are more closely tied to the paramount goal of preventing political corruption.[40] Thus, I am not suggesting that courts, when faced with regu-

---

quite the same as discrimination based on content of ideas; not all challengers, by any means, represent one particular viewpoint. In any event, the evidence of such a burden is far from conclusive. *See* 424 U.S. at 33–34 (no such showing in record relative to contribution limits of $1,000). *But see id.* at 31 n.33 (suggesting possibility of more serious problem when contribution limits are combined with 1974 Act's limitations on expenditures by groups and individuals, on candidate's use of personal and family resources, and on overall campaign expenditures, but not resolving question).

39. The capacity for abuse is directly related to the size of the contribution or expenditure. Thus ceilings operate in a straightforward manner to curb the capacity for abuse; they are tailored rather precisely to the problem Congress sought to remedy. At the same time, all candidates-popular and unpopular, majority and minority-use money in roughly the same way. It is, to say the least, not immediately apparent how ceilings-so long as they apply evenly across the board-could be designed so as to cast a disproportionate burden on minority or disfavored points of view. Money restrictions, therefore, contrast sharply with laws which seem evenhanded but which in reality make things especially hard for the weak and unpopular-for example, laws banning leafletting, laws curtailing speaking in public places, or indeed, to borrow Anatole France's classic example, laws prohibiting rich and poor alike from sleeping under bridges. ANATOLE FRANCE, THE RED LILY 91 (W. Stephens trans. 1894). *See* Harry Kalven, Jr., *The Concept of the Public Forum:* Cox v. Louisiana, 1965 SUP. CT. REV. 1, 30.

40. This of course was not the only goal of the 1974 law. In some contexts other goals were equally compelling. For example, as Mr. Justice Marshall eloquently demonstrates in his partial dissent, the limits on spending by a candidate from his personal funds, 18 U.S.C. § 608(a) (Supp. IV 1974) (repealed 1976), were tailored to serve the nation's vital interest in "promoting the reality and appearance of equal access to the political arena," 424 U.S. at 287–90. I agree fully with Mr. Justice Marshall that § 608(a)'s limits should have been conceived as limits on the *contribution* a candidate may make to his own campaign, *id.* at 286–87, and therefore are justified on much the same grounds as those the Court found persuasive with respect to the general contribution limits.

As I shall discuss more fully below, another important objective of the campaign financing reform was to stimulate more direct, personal forms of political speech. Indeed,

lations like these, be less than vigilant. But the sensitive judicial task is not aided by a blunderbuss formula that equates money and speech.[41]

---

that those nearing their contribution limits could still engage in more direct communications efforts was an important factor in the Court's decision to uphold the contribution ceilings. I pause here only to ask why that same logic could not have been taken one small step further, with the result that the ceiling on independent expenditures would also have been recognized as constitutional.

The court upheld the contribution limits because, the opinion explains, those limits constitute only a *"marginal restriction* upon the contributor's ability to engage in free communication." *Id.* at 20–21 (emphasis added). This is so because people who would otherwise give amounts greater than the statutory limits are hardly bottled up once they reach the ceiling. Many avenues of communication remain open to them since, the Court states, they can "expend such funds on *direct political expression." Id.* at 21–22 (emphasis added). In other words, the spender could buy the newspaper ad or TV commercial or handbills directly, instead of giving the money to the candidate for the candidate to choose how to spend it. If he avoided collaboration with the candidate, his spending in this fashion would not count as a contribution. *Id.* at 46–47 & n.53. There would be no limits on his spending to advocate the candidate's election, because the Court struck down the limits on independent expenditures.

But exactly parallel reasoning should have led the Court to sustain the limits on independent expenditures. Properly viewed, those limits constitute nothing but a "marginal restriction." They do nothing but push the spender a little closer still to "direct political expression." Under the statutory provisions for ceilings on independent expenditures, one who has spent his limit-and $1,000 is a generous limit-hardly has his free expression bottled up. Nothing prevents him from devoting future efforts to volunteer activity, door-to-door canvassing, or organizing meetings. And what is this if it is not *direct political expression?* It may not be the form of political expression which the Supreme Court had in mind-expensive things like TV commercials and newspaper ads. But it is no less a real outlet for political expression simply because it is *more* direct.

41. The *Buckley* defendants also contended that the money restrictions were valid under a line of cases permitting government regulation of the time, place, and manner of speaking. *See, e.g.,* Adderley v. Florida, 385 U.S. 39 (1966); Cox v. Louisiana, 379 U.S. 559 (1965); Kovacs v. Cooper, 336 U.S. 77 (1949). The Court rejected this argument. 424 U.S. at 17–18. The logic of the Court's position, however, is not immediately apparent, for the 1974 law does, on its face, look like a regulation of the manner of speech. The statute says, in effect, speak in a frugal rather than lavish manner.

But the Court did not see the limits in this way: "The critical difference between this case and those time, place, and manner cases is that the present Act's contribution and expenditure limitations impose *direct quantity restrictions* on political communication and association...." *Id.* at 18 (emphasis added). The Court went on in a footnote to emphasize the difference it perceived between the campaign law's money limits and the decibel limits imposed on a soundtruck operator and upheld in *Kovacs*: "The decibel restriction upheld in *Kovacs* limited the *manner* of operating a soundtruck, but not the *extent* of its proper use." *Id.* at 18–19 n.17 (emphasis in original).

The Court, in other words, erected a new distinction between statutes that regulate

B. The Court's Premise

The premise apparently underlying the Court's treatment of money restrictions as restraints on free expression was that "in today's mass society" the use of money is essential for "effective political speech."[42] But does the First Amendment condemn us to accept helplessly all the implications of the so-called "mass society"? Must we adopt the mass society's definitions of effectiveness? I think not.

Consider this: A half-minute spot commercial can reach into thousands of homes, although with a cursory message. This is the essence of effectiveness in the mass society. And it costs money-lots of it. A lesser amount of money, however, might suffice to purchase the paid staff and supplies necessary to sustain a small army of volunteer canvassers,[43] perhaps enough to reach all the same homes on a meaningful, personal basis.

Which is truly more effective, the spot commercial or the volunteer activity? It depends on whose standards one uses: those implicit in the mass society, or those implicit in the First Amendment. It is certainly possible to

---

manner of speech and those that may be said to regulate quantity of speech. Statutes of the former type are permissible; statutes of the latter type are, at a minimum, subject to the most stringent scrutiny.

But the distinction simply does not bear up under analysis. The time, place, and manner cases dealt with restrictions that can just as easily be read as quantity restrictions. In *Kovacs*, for example, the soundtruck operator was surely faced with a quantity restriction. Operating at an unrestricted decibel level, he might have been able to reach all the citizens of his target area by, say, driving down every third street. Operating within the ordinance at a lower volume might have required driving down every street. The quantity of his speech, if one chooses to view it in that fashion, has been reduced by two-thirds. He can reach only a third of the people he could otherwise reach in a given amount of time. Regulations of time and place of expression can generally be seen as working similar quantity restrictions. The Court's rationale for distinguishing the time, place, and manner cases is unconvincing.

42. 424 U.S. at 19.

43. The 1974 law is structured so as to provide added inducements for volunteer activity. An individual who devotes his time without pay is not required to place a monetary value on that time in order to count it against any contribution or independent expenditure ceiling. In other words, a person can volunteer his time without limit. 18 U.S.C. § 591(e)(5)(A) (Supp. IV 1974). Moreover, the first $500 of expenses incidental to such volunteer activity is also exempt from the ceilings. *Id.* at § 591(e)(5)(B)-(D), (f)(4)(D),(f)(4)(E). The Court expressly approved these inducements, noting "Congress' valid interest in encouraging citizen participation in political campaigns." 424 U.S. at 36–37.

argue that the volunteer, face-to-face communication is more effective in a sense highly relevant to the First Amendment: it promotes real interchange among citizens concerning the issues and candidates about which they must make a choice.

The Supreme Court seemed to recognize that "effective political speech" is a multi-dimensional concept. It depends, the Court suggested, on "the number of issues discussed, the depth of their exploration, and the size of the audience reached."[44] Viewed in this light, the effectiveness of political speakers is not necessarily diminished by reasonable contribution and expenditure ceilings. The giving and spending restrictions may cause candidates and other individuals to rely more on less expensive means of communication. But there is no reason to believe that such a shift in means reduces the number of issues discussed in a campaign. And, by forcing candidates to put more emphasis on local organizing or leafletting or door-to-door canvassing[45] and less on full-page ads and television spot commercials, the restrictions may well generate deeper exploration of the issues raised. Finally, even to the extent that smaller audiences result from diminished use of the most expensive and pervasive media-and the campaigning so far gives no substantial indication that this happens-the effectiveness of a given speaker does not decline in relation to that of his

---

44. 424 U.S. at 19 (footnote omitted).

45. Because these activities require a large amount of volunteer effort, some commentators have suggested that contribution and expenditure ceilings discriminate unfairly in favor of those who have a lot of free time. *See, e.g.,* Winter, *Money, Politics and the First Amendment, in* H. PENNIMAN & R. WINTER, CAMPAIGN FINANCES: TWO VIEWS OF THE POLITICAL IMPLICATIONS 57–58 (1971). This strikes me as a particularly weak claim of discrimination.

In a system dominated by contributions of money, rather than of free time, all but the fabulously wealthy must make hard choices about how they will apply limited financial resources. For most people, making a large contribution means foregoing or postponing something else-an expensive vacation, perhaps, or a new car. In a system where contributions of free time are more important, people are still faced with choices about the application of a limited resource, a temporal resource. A person *can,* if the candidate's success is important enough to him, forego or postpone or rearrange business commitments or outside activities that consume time in order to volunteer for the campaign. I see no reason why the temporal choice should be considered inequitable when the financial choice is not.

If the concern is for those at the margin who really cannot squeeze out additional free time-those who must work long hours simply to provide food and shelter for their families-I would only observe that such people are hardly disadvantaged by contribution and expenditure ceilings. They surely are not the ones whose political spending is cut short by the 1974 law.

opponents. All similarly situated competitors face the same constraints. Within those limits effectiveness still depends on the creativity of the speaker-and on the soundness of his ideas.

If there is a problem latent in expenditure ceilings, it stems not from any disparities in effectiveness among rival campaigns, but from the fact that there are, of course, no dollar limitations on nonpolitical speech. If campaign money ceilings were so low that political speech really were in danger of being drowned out by commercial or other apolitical speech, then those ceilings might well be unconstitutional. But no one has claimed, and no one could credibly claim, that the reasonable ceilings enacted in 1974 pose such a threat.[46] There will be time enough to remedy the problem if at some point the political dialogue truly becomes submerged.[47] In the meantime, we would do well to focus our concern on the danger that certain individual candidates will find *their* speech drowned out by well-heeled opponents who can vastly outdistance them in the spending race-exactly the danger that the overall expenditure limits were meant to minimize.

III. Money as Speech: The Pluralist Underpinnings

Though the equation of money and speech is supported by neither the precedents nor the premise relied on by the Court, the notion may well derive from a more basic source. If so, it is important that we explore it. We can, I believe, identify this source by analyzing carefully the position of the *Buckley* plaintiffs, the opponents of the 1974 law, in order to discern the image of the political process that underlay their opposition to limitations on giving and spending. The image they embraced makes it natural to conclude that money is speech, but I think we shall see that it differs significantly from the image of the political process the First Amendment bids us to accept.

In their brief before the court of appeals, the plaintiffs argued strongly that money is essential to effectiveness in the political contest.[48] Again and again they asserted their central theme:

> It is...too crabbed a notion of the political process to restrain people from demonstrating the intensity of their convictions on particular issues. Indeed,

---

46. *See, e.g.,* 424 U.S. at 21–22 (no such problem in connection with contribution limits of $1,000).

47. The Court has shown its readiness to act when reductions in degree result in differences in kind. *Compare* Kusper v. Pontikes, 414 U.S. 51, 59–61 (1973) *with* Rosario v. Rockefeller, 410 U.S. 752 (1973). *See* 424 U.S. at 30.

48. Brief of the Plaintiffs, *supra* note 38, at 102.

> it is hard to see how a democratic nation can have a stable government if it does not permit intensity of feeling as well as numbers of adherents to be reflected in the political process.... Campaign contributions represent a means by which intensity can be shown....
>
> Of course, those who contribute money to a candidate hope to further their political, social and economic views....[49]

Now it is true that a government which hopes to maintain stability must preserve for its citizens some means of demonstrating intensity of feeling. The plaintiffs, however, evidently interpret intensity not from the standpoint of the potential contributor, but from the standpoint of the candidate or official who is the target of the intensity. I say this because it is brutally obvious that the size of a contribution provides a hopelessly inadequate measure of intensity as felt by the giver. Consider the wealthy man who regularly contributes $5,000 to a particular incumbent, simply to keep open his channels of communication. Compare him to the student who scrapes together $100 for a candidate in whom she passionately believes. Intensity is all with the student, but if one looks only at the dollar totals, this fact is completely obscured. The contribution ceiling in the 1974 law in no way prevents the student from demonstrating her genuine intensity of feeling.

Thus, when the plaintiffs complain that a $1,000 contribution limit thwarts the expression of intensity, they must be viewing intensity from the standpoint of the recipient-the candidate. *He* certainly will feel the heat more intensely from a $5,000 contributor than from a $100 contributor, whatever the subjective feelings of the two contributors themselves. And, the plaintiffs argue, the First Amendment requires that Congress not impede contributors from making candidates feel this kind of intensity.

Consider, then, the picture the plaintiffs' brief paints for us of the way political decisions are made. Campaign monies should be unrestricted because they are a means by which people intensify the pressure to get governmental decisions to come out their way. There is competition among various viewpoints, and candidates and others who want to see certain governmental policies adopted roll up their sleeves and plunge into the competition with all the resources at their command. The prospect of large contributions may, for example, influence a legislator to vote a particular way. Or sizeable media expenditures may swing an important electoral race through advanced techniques of salesmanship. People band together and pool their funds in order to bring pressure on the

---

49. *Id.* at 105. Obviously the plaintiffs' observation is not limited to contributions; it extends to expenditures as well: "[T]hose making the expenditures seek to communicate with the public to promote views they think should become governmental policy or for persons whom they believe will, as public officials, share those views." *Id.* at 100.

decisionmakers or to elect different decisionmakers in their place. The key to effectiveness is not the soundness of the program advocated, or even the number of voters who support the program, but rather the intensity of the pressure imposed. This picture of the political process that emerges from the plaintiffs' arguments corresponds closely to a picture familiar to political science as the special interest or pluralist model.[50] This correspondence should not be surprising, even though it has received relatively little attention. Pluralist thinking has dominated political science for years,[51] and it traces its roots to Tocqueville,[52] and even back to Madison's

---

50. Some writers have made even more explicit the pluralist underpinnings of their attack on campaign finance reform laws. *See, e.g.,* Sterling, *Public Financing of Campaigns: Equality Against Freedom,* 62 A.B.A.J. 197, 200 (1976); Sterling, *Control of Campaign Spending: The Reformers' Paradox,* 59 A.B.A.J. 1148, 1153 (1973). *See also* Joel L. Fleishman, *Freedom of Speech and Equality of Political Opportunity: The Constitutionality of the Federal Election Campaign Act of 1971,* 51 N.C. L. Rev. 389, 462 (1973) ("The fact that people vote with dollars as well as ballots is to be celebrated in a democracy rather than bemoaned.") Compare the unrestrained enthusiasm of one early writer, quoted prominently, with minor, inadvertent alterations, in an important pluralist textbook, Wilfred Ellsworth Binkley & Malcolm C. Moos, A Grammar of American Politics: The National Government 2(3d ed 1958):

> [M]en and women who touch practical politics...know that men and women now may have as many votes in government as they have interests for which they are willing to sacrifice time and thought and money. The ruling classes are those who use their craft societies, medical associations, farm bureaus, labor unions, bankers' associations, women's leagues and the like to influence government. Of course, it takes time and intelligence and a little money, but not much. For fifty dollars a year [membership dues] the average family ought to be able to buy half a dozen powerful votes in government, each vote ten times as powerful as the vote guaranteed by the Constitution.

William Allen White, Politics: The Citizen's Business 15, 16–17 (1924). For a dramatically contrasting view, albeit one with serious problems of implementation and limitations, *see* Marlene Arnold Nicholson, *Campaign Financing and Equal Protection,* 26 Stan. L. Rev. 815, 821, 825–36, 853–54 (1974) (giving of large contributions is form of multiple voting invalid under "one person, one vote" doctrine; courts could, regardless of statutory limits, hold unconstitutional any financing system permitting large contributions).

51. *See, e.g.,* Arthur Fisher Bentley, The Process of Government (1908); Robert Dahl, A Preface to Democratic Theory (1956), Robert Dahl, Who Governs? (1961); Edward Herring, Group Representation Before Congress (1929); Earl Latham, The Group Basis of Politics (1952); Charles Edward Lindblom, The Intelligence of Democracy (1956); Arnold Marshall Rose, The Power Structure (1967); David Truman, The Governmental Process (2d ed. 1971).

52. *See* Alexander de Tocqueville, Decocracy in America 174–80 (J. Mayer & M. Lerner eds. 1966).

Celebrated *Federalist No. 10*.[53] The pluralist view is a powerful conception, and it explains much about how our government works. I do not demean its value when I say nonetheless that it has certain shortcomings. Let me set forth the pluralist outlook in its strongest form, so that we may clearly see the problems.

To the pluralist, the political process consists precisely of the pulling and hauling of various competing interest groups. Organized groups, not individuals, constitute the only relevant political units.[54] They rise and decline, coalesce and fragment, confront countervailing groups and aid complementary groups. Through lobbying, publicity, campaign contributions, independent expenditures, and other methods-all of which cost money-they bring pressures to bear which ultimately determine the outcome of governmental decisions. They thereby achieve a form of "functional representation," based upon intersecting economic and social groupings, which cuts across our usual conception of political representation based upon "one person-one vote."[55]

The pluralist model tends to be a highly mechanistic conception. The clash of competing groups comes to be seen as the only factor of importance in politics. Force collides with counterforce, pressure meets counterpressure, and the strongest force or the most intense pressure determines the outcome of the governmental process. Some pluralist writers even talk wistfully about the possibility of reducing the political process to a mathematical chart. If only our techniques were sophisticated enough, they suggest, groups pursuing interests could all be measured and then graphed as vectors. And trends in public policy could then be predicted because they automatically conform to the resultant, the mathematical sum of all the private vectors.[56]

Other pluralists go so far as to equate this resultant vector with the "public interest." The very term, they imply, has no meaning apart from the outcome of the pressure group process. Individual assertions as to where the public interest lies are all inherently suspect. Only the group process can be relied upon as 'the practical test of what constitutes the public interest.'"[57]

---

53. THE FEDERALIST NO. 10, at 57 (J. Cooke ed. 1961). *See* TRUMAN, *supra* note 51, at 4–7. *But see* note 72 *infra.*

54. *See, e.g.,* BENTLEY, *supra* note 51, at 208; HERRING, *supra* note 51, at 5–6. *See generally* Myron Q. Hale, *The Cosmology of Arthur F. Bentley, in* THE BIAS OF PLURALISM 35–50 (William E. Connolly ed. 1969).

55. *See generally* HERRING, *supra* note 51, at 8–12.

56. BINKLEY & MOOS, *supra* note 50, at 6 (quoting Childs, *Pressure Groups and Propaganda, in* THE AMERICAN POLITICAL SCENE 205, 225 (E. Logan ed. 1936)).

57. BINKLEY & MOOS, *supra* note 50, at 7. *See* Stoke, *The Paradox of Representative Government, in* ESSAYS IN POLITICAL SCIENCE 77, 80–83 (John Mabry Mathews &

By this pluralist line of reasoning, the First Amendment's highest function is to let group pressure run its course unimpeded,[58] lest we skew the process that determines for us the public interest. Giving and spending money are important ways for groups to bring pressure-to magnify intensity-and thereby to make the process work. Restrictions on giving and spending can be nothing but unwarranted impediments in the path of the process. It follows, in the pluralist view, that all such restrictions are unconstitutional.

Such is the theory. But time has eroded at least the more exuberant forms of pluralist thinking. Recent years have seen scores of books and articles questioning the theory's assumptions or its application.[59] Two major critiques deserve emphasis.

First, pluralists countenance a system which gives undeserved weight to highly organized and wealthy groups.[60] For the pluralist, this imbalance is a virtue to be embraced, not a flaw to be redressed. Under an unrestrained pluralist system, a clustering of people with common interests, even if it is a majority, cannot prevail if it is without organization and without significant funds.[61] And of course we know of instances in our current system where the popular will is thus thwarted-where public opinion polls tell us that a majority prefers a certain policy, and yet that majority seems unable to carry out its wishes against the opposition of a highly organized, narrowly based group able to spend its money freely. Gun control provides an obvious example.[62]

James Hart eds. 1937); Wilson, *The Pragmatic Electorate*, 24 AMER. POL. SCI. REV. 16, 33 (1930).

58. *See* Brief of the Plaintiffs, *supra* note 38, at 101–02.

59. For a sampling of the most penetrating critiques of the pluralist viewpoint, *see* HENRY S. KARIEL, THE DECLINE OF AMERICAN PLURALISM (1961); THEODORE LOWI, THE END OF LIBERALISM (1969); GRANT MCCONNELL, PRIVATE POWER AND AMERICAN DEMOCRACY (1966); William E. Connolly, *The Challenge to Pluralist Theory, in* THE BIAS OF PLURALISM, *supra* note 54, at 3. *See also* SIMON LAZARUS, THE GENTEEL POPULISTS 167–89 (1964).

60. I have pursued this line of criticism elsewhere in a somewhat different context. J. Skelly Wright, *Professor Bickel, The Scholarly Tradition, and the Supreme Court*, 84 HARV. L. REV. 769, 789 (1971).

61. *See* Note, *The New Public Interest Lawyers*, 79 YALE L.J. 1069, 1070–71 n.3 (1970). Indeed, some critics argue forcefully that the system may prevent such diffuse groups even from achieving effective articulation of their grievances. Their grievances will be seen not as potential issues for the public but merely as troubles afflicting private individuals. *See* Connolly, *supra* note 59, at 14.

62. *See* N.Y. TIMES, June 5, 1975, at 20 (67% of those polled favored registration of all firearms; results consistent with surveys over three decades showing steady support for such gun control legislation); M. HINDELAND, C. DUNN, A. AUMICK & L. SUTTON, SOURCEBOOK OF CRIMINAL JUSTICE STATISTICS—1974 183–88 (1975) (summaries of

A number of encouraging reform efforts of recent years may be seen as attempts to rectify this systemic imbalance.[63] The public interest law movement, for example, often sees itself as a means for giving diffuse but significant groups a more effective voice.[64] The flowering of so-called citizens' or public interest lobbies is part of the same development. And the campaign reform legislation reviewed in the *Buckley* case can also be seen in this light. In a sense, it *is* an attempt to expand participation in the pluralist pulling and hauling. The well-organized are deprived of certain financial advantages. The decisionmakers are then better able to respond to the interests of the under-organized, free from imperative obligations to special interest money-providers.

There is a second and more basic critique of the pluralists' view. Their mechanistic conception tends to drain politics of its moral and intellectual content.[65] Rather than seeing the political process as a battle of ideas, informed by values-as the means by which the citizens apply their intelligence to the making of hard public choices[66]-pluralists tend to view politics as a mere clash of forces, a battle of competing intensities, a universe of vectors.

Forces can be measured by science; resultant vectors can be computed by mathematics. Alexander Meiklejohn diagnosed the shortcomings of this kind of thinking with his usual penetrating insight. He wrote:

> In the understanding of a free society, scientific thinking has an essential part to play. But it is a secondary part. We shall not understand the Constitution of the United States if we think of men only as pushed around by forces. We must see them also as governing themselves.[67]

The First Amendment sees people in this way. Although our political practice may often fall woefully short, the First Amendment is founded on a certain model of how self-governing people-both citizens and their representatives-make their decisions.[68] It is a model that restores considera-

---

polls showing similar strong support for gun control and detailing response to particular gun control proposals).

63. *See* Lazarus, *supra* note 59, at 267–74.

64. *See* Note, *supra* note 61, at 1070–71 n.3.

65. *See* Lowi, *supra* note 59, at 46–54, 57–58, 68–72, 155–56, 281–82.

66. *See* Meiklejohn, *supra* note 1, at 75, 109.

67. *Id.* at 12–13. Meiklejohn has made explicit his critique of pluralist thinking elsewhere. *Id.* at 162–63. *See also id.* at 73–75.

68. *See generally* Whitney v. California, 274 U.S. 357, 375–78 (1927) (Brandies, J., concurring), *overruled by* Brandenburg v. Ohio, 395 U.S. 444 (1969); Abrams v. United States, 250 U.S. 616, 630 (1919) (Holmes, J., dissenting). "The purpose of constitutional protection of speech is to foster peaceful interchange of all manner of thoughts, information, and ideas. Its policy is rooted in faith in the force of reason." Kunz v. New York, 340 U.S. 290, 302 (1951) (Jackson, J., dissenting).

tions of justice and morality to the political process-considerations absent from the pluralist approach.[69]

Self-governing people do not simply let the organized groups of the day play out their battle of influence and then vote the way of the prevailing forces. They are more responsible, more independent than that. Instead, they see the group process as a way of calling forth the various positions. They listen to all-the weak and timid voice of the under-organized as well as the sometimes bombastic, sometimes sophisticated, but always elaborated communication of the affluent highly-organized. They do their best to filter out the decibels so that they may penetrate to the merits of the arguments. They retire and consider the positions. And then they choose the course which seems wisest. It may be the course of the noisy or the course of the quiet. At times it may be the course advocated by an apparent minority. But it is a course chosen on the merits.

Thus, what the pluralist rhetoric obscures is that *ideas*, and not intensities, form the heart of the expression which the First Amendment is designed to protect.[70] Money may register intensities, in one limited sense of the word, but money by itself communicates no ideas. Money, in other words, may be related to speech, but *money itself is not speech*. Courts ought to judge restrictions on giving and spending accordingly.

The 1974 campaign reform law moves us closer, even if but a small distance, toward the idealized First Amendment model of self-government sketched out above. Herein lies the key to the statute's importance. Here is why, far from stifling First Amendment values, it actually promotes them. The ceilings on giving and spending take from wealthy citizens, candidates, and organizations only certain limited political advantages totally unrelated to the merits of their arguments-advantages which all too frequently *obscure* the merits of the arguments. In place of unlimited spending, the law encourages all to emphasize less expensive face-to-face communica-

---

69. *See* LOWI, *supra* note 59, at 289–91.

70. *Cf.* Paul A. Freund, *Commentary, in* ALBERT ROSENTHAL, FEDERAL REGULATIONS OF CAMPAIGN FINANCE: SOME CONSTITUTIONAL QUESTIONS 72, 74 (Citizens' Research Found. 1972):

> The right to speak is, I submit, more central to the values envisaged by the First Amendment than the right to spend. We are dealing here not so much with the right of personal expression or even association, but with dollars and decibels. And just as the volume of sound may be limited by law, so the volume of dollars may be limited, without violating the First Amendment.... [Large contributors] are operating vicariously through the power of their purse, rather than through the power of their ideas, and again I would scale that relatively lower in the hierarchy of First Amendment values.

tions efforts,[71] exactly the kinds of activities that promote real dialogue on the merits and leave much less room for manipulation and avoidance of the issues.

I can hear the pluralists' rejoinder. You are deeply unrealistic, they might charge. You swallow an 18th-century idealized vision of a process and ignore the play of organized groups and private interests. And indeed if they are right that the "public interest" is nothing more than the outcome of the group process, then we should release our grasp on the First Amendment ideal and let the pulling and hauling proceed without hindrance.

But we need not accept the pluralists' proposition. We simply are not so helpless that we must blindly equate the outcome of the group pressure process with the public interest.[72] To return to our gun control example, it is certainly possible to assert—indeed, the case is compelling—that the pluralist process has thwarted the public interest for years.

---

71. *See* note 43 *supra.*

72. For a thorough development of this point, *see* Brian Barry, *The Public Interest, in* THE BIAS OF PLURALISM, *supra* note 54, at 159.

Some of the pluralist writers who have equated the public interest with the outcome of the group process are listed in note 57 *supra.* Even so perceptive a pluralist writer as Robert Dahl, although he avoids the simple equation of the earlier writers, joins with other pluralists in concluding, based on his relentlessly empirical approach, that the concept "public interest" is fundamentally meaningless. *See* ROBERT DAHL, A PREFACE TO DEMOCRATIC THEORY, 25–27, 69 n.5 (1956). *Cf.* TRUMAN, *supra* note 51, at 50–51 (a totally "inclusive interest" within a nation does not exist).

Dahl elaborates these views in the course of analyzing Madison's famous definition of "faction," which is set forth in *The Federalist No. 10.* Madison's essay is often regarded as a precursor of pluralist thinking, but the passage containing the definition makes it clear that Madison did not regard the "public interest" concept as meaningless, nor did he regard the essentially moral quest for its attainment as an unworthy or futile enterprise. Moreover, the passage suggests-and the full essay makes clear-that he considered interest group competition as an evil to be rendered tolerable, not as a democratic safeguard to be embraced:

> By a faction I understand a number of citizens, whether amounting to a majority or minority of the whole, who are united and actuated by some common impulse of passion, or of interest, *adverse to the rights of other citizens, or to the permanent and aggregate interests of the community.*

THE FEDERALIST NO. 10, *supra* note 53 at 57 (J. Cooke ed. 1961) (emphasis added).

Lowi demonstrates that the moral dimension of Madison's definition is often lost when pluralists invoke Madison as a spiritual forebear. David Truman, he points out, quotes the definitional passage but leaves off the crucial italicized clause, thereby removing from "faction" the pejorative connotation Madison intended and incidentally obscuring Madison's moral concern. LOWI, *supra* note 59, at 296 (discussing TRUMAN, *supra* at 4).

Realism consists in acknowledging the group process and allowing for it. Group activity is an essential and desirable part of the American system, and indeed the First Amendment recognizes this: it protects the right of assembly and the right of association. But it is simply not true that the play of influence, of competing intensities, is *all there is* to politics. The play of ideas, the sifting of good ideas from bad, of truth from falsehood, of justice from injustice-all these are essential parts of our system as well. One cannot deny this without denying the very essence of the First Amendment. One cannot deny this without letting realism descend to cynicism.

The Framers were not so cynically realistic when they established our form of government. Had they been, we might not have had a First Amendment. A government dedicated to liberty was more a visionary than a realistic enterprise in those days. The world had scarcely known such a creature. But the Framers persevered. And the power of that vision of self-government which they wrote into the Constitution and the Bill of Rights has earned the respect even of realists. As Meiklejohn put it: "[T]he adoption of the principle of self-government...set loose upon us and upon the world at large an idea which is still transforming men's conceptions of what they are and how they may best be governed."[73] "No institution," Charles Black has written, "can be as perfect, in men or work, as its ideal model, [but] the very mark of the truly living institution is that it has an ideal model which is always there nudging its elbow."[74] The 1974 law, in its own modest way, escalated the nudge to a gentle shove.[75] If we are realistic, and not cynical, we will hold fast to such fragments of progress toward the ideal the Framers held out to us.

---

73. Alexander Meiklejohn, *The First Amendment is an Absolute*, 1961 SUP. CT. REV. 245, 264.

74. CHARLES BLACK, THE PEOPLE AND THE COURT 50 (1960).

75. The court of appeals opinion in the *Buckley* case came to a close on a similar note:
    [T]hese latest efforts on the part of our government to cleanse its democratic processes should at least be given a chance to prove themselves. Certainly they should not be rejected because they might have some incidental, not clearly defined, effect on First Amendment freedoms. To do so might be Aesopian in the sense of the dog losing his bone going after its deceptively larger reflection in the water.

519 F.2d at 897–98.

Money and Politics: A Perspective on the First Amendment and Campaign Finance Reform

Lillian R. BeVier

* * *

The First Amendment Stakes

This Part will argue that limitations of election campaign contributions and expenditures impinge significantly on core first amendment rights. It is important to consider this seemingly familiar issue for a number of reasons. First, the Court has been surprisingly cryptic in announcing its rationale for strict scrutiny of campaign reform legislation. In addition, arguments supporting judicial deference in this area continue to depend heavily, if implicitly, upon the premise that such laws simply do not implicate significant first amendment rights. Finally, an intelligible analysis of the important first amendment enforcement issues that are intrinsic to judicial review of election reform laws requires that certain fundamental assumptions about the amendment be made explicit at the outset.

This Part will begin by describing and defending the Court's decision in *Buckley* to engage in careful scrutiny of the FECA Amendments of 1974. It will then consider the first amendment interest in political contributions, an issue that has become more sharply focused in the reform debate following *Buckley*.

A. *Buckley v. Valeo*

1. The First Amendment Vision

The precise issues raised by the 1974 amendments were so novel that it was not at all clear what level of scrutiny the Court would apply to them. Never before had Congress undertaken such an ambitious effort to reform the electoral process. Moreover, those subjected to the campaign finance restrictions that were in effect prior to enactment of the FECA had lacked the incentive to press their constitutional claims, since the restrictions either could be readily avoided or had been emasculated by courts.[43]

Despite the novelty of the precise issues, however, the Court surprised no one when it observed "that a major purpose of [the First] Amendment was to protect the free discussion of governmental affairs,"[44] and asserted that contribution and expenditure limitations "operate in an area of the most fundamental First Amendment activities."[45] Giving money to political campaigns, after all, long had been a customary and peaceful way of expressing political preferences and thereby of participating in the free discussion of governmental affairs.

The first amendment protects the free discussion of governmental affairs because the "Constitution establishes a representative democracy,"[46] which is a "form of government that would be meaningless without free-

---

43. For a useful summary of the political and judicial history of pre-FECA regulatory efforts aimed at corporations and labor unions, *see* John R. Bolton, *Constitutional Limitations on Restricting Corporate and Union Political Speech*, 22 ARIZ. L. REV. 373, 374–402 (1980); *see also* Robert M. Cohan, *Of Politics, Pipefitters, and Section 610: Union Political Contributions in Modern Context*, 51 Tex. L. Rev. 936 (1973) (history of union political activity, regulation thereof, and combination of evasion and judicial emasculation of the regulations).

44. Buckley v. Valeo, 424 U.S. 1, 14 (1976) (per curiam) (quoting Mills v. Alabama, 384 U.S. 214, 218 (1966)).

45. *Id.*

46. Lillian R. BeVier, *The First Amendment and Political Speech: An Inquiry into the Substance and Limits of Principle*, 30 STAN. L. REV. 229, 308 (1978). Reasoning from the constitutional establishment of representative democracy is a familiar means of generating conclusions about the categories of speech that are most clearly within the first amendment's ambit. *See, e.g.*, Robert H. Bork, *Neutral Principles and Some First Amendment Problems*, 47 IND. L. J. 1 (1971) (because Constitution establishes representative democracy, first amendment must protect political speech, but no other category of speech is protected in principle). Such reasoning however has been used less often in considering the function of freedom of speech in our political system and whether there are occasions when courts ought to defer to legislative decisions to encroach upon it.

dom to discuss government and its policies."[47] In terms of the function that freedom of speech plays in our system, the constitutional establishment of a representative democracy is significant because it assures that victory at the polls carries with it the right to govern.[48] Freedom of speech helps citizens to become informed so that they can vote intelligently for those who will represent them.[49] Free discussion functions also to permit citizens to persuade one another. Moreover, it allows them to communicate with their representatives at the same time that it allows candidates and their backers to garner the electorate's support. In other words, free discussion is critically important for affecting political outcomes and achieving political victory. This, in turn, is the first step to securing the adoption of desired governmental policies.[50]

This discussion of the function of freedom of speech in a representative democracy suggests that the Court in *Buckley* correctly asserted that limitations on political campaign giving and spending involve "the most fun-

---

47. Bork, *supra* note 46, at 23.

48. Given the complexity of the task of governing, it would undoubtedly be more accurate to say that victory at the polls carries with it the right, temporary and subject among other important constraints to accountability at the next election, to exercise somewhat more actual governing authority than does loss at the polls.

49. The "informing function" of free political speech has received elaborate if ambiguous rhetorical embellishment in recent Supreme Court opinions.

> Our precedents have focused not only on the role of the First Amendment in fostering individual self-expression but also on its role in affording the public access to discussion, debate, and the dissemination of information and ideas.... And we have recognized that the State may not, consistently with the spirit of the First Amendment, contract the spectrum of available knowledge.

Bd. of Educ. v. Pico, 457 U.S. 853, 866 (1982) (quoting First Nat'l Bank v. Bellotti, 435 U.S. 765, 783 (1978), and Griswold v. Connecticut, 381 U.S. 479, 482 (1965), respectively).

50. *But cf.* Edwin Baker, *Realizing Self-Realization: Corporate Political Expenditures and Redish's the Value of Free Speech*, 130 U. Pa. Rev. 646, 674 (1982) ("[N]othing about the political context requires that political contributions or the candidate's personal expenditures be designed only to purchase winning speech, as opposed to speech that promotes their views or values."). Professor Baker may be correct that the political context does not necessarily require individuals to purchase speech. It is hard to see, however, why someone committed to a set of "views and values" would not—given a context in which winning is possible—prefer winning to losing. In his analysis of the political context, moreover, Professor Baker seems to ignore the complex and often powerful effects that minor parties and other sure losers can in fact exert upon political outcomes. *See generally* Steven J. Rosentone, Roy L. Behr, & Edward H. Lagarus, Third Parties in America 8 (1984) (arguing that third parties "affect the content and range of political discourse, and ultimately public policy, by raising issues and options that the two major parties have ignored").

damental First Amendment activities."[51] Those who give to and spend on election campaigns are intrinsically legitimate participants in the ongoing process of representative democracy at least insofar as they wish, like other participants, to "see [their] views become public policy."[52] The Court must carefully police legislative attempts to limit such activities because the activities themselves are constitutionally valuable.

2. Doctrinal Maneuvers and *United States v. O'Brien*

The advocates in *Buckley* who defended judicial deference to the contribution and expenditure limitations acknowledged that the limitations involved first amendment concerns. However, they refused to accept the corollary proposition that strict first amendment scrutiny was appropriate. They attempted to deprecate the first amendment arguments of those who challenged the limitations by invoking a series of doctrines whose central import is to reduce the level of judicial scrutiny.

The defenders of judicial deference made two primary arguments. First, they argued that the limitations imposed by the FECA did not involve central first amendment issues because the limitations "deal[t] only with conduct, [or] with the transfer or use of money and other material resources"[53] and not "with speech directly."[54] Second, they argued that the restrictions were content-neutral. Consequently, the restrictions allegedly did not seriously threaten first amendment values. Indeed, advocates of this position analogized the restrictions to genuine time, place, and manner regulations, which, like decibel restrictions on sound trucks, seem designed to regulate evils quite divorced from communicative significance.[55]

---

51. *Buckley*, 424 U.S. at 14; *see also* Note, *Regulation of Campaign Contributions: Maintaining the Integrity of the Political Process Through an Appearance of Fairness*, 56 S. Cal. L. Rev. 669, 677-81 (1983).

52. Brief of the Appellant at 48-49, Buckley v. Valeo, 424 U.S. 1 (1976) (per curiam).

Of course, those who contribute money to a candidate hope to further their political, social and economic views—just as those who engage in demonstrations and rallies, write books on political issues, organize like-minded citizens, draft and circulate petitions, buy advertisements, publish periodicals or newspapers, make speeches, sponsor seminars or teach-ins, or engage in litigation hope to further their political, social and economic views. Such activities are the hallmark—as well as the indispensable precondition—of a free society.

Id. at 50-51.

53. Brief of Senators Hugh Scott and Edward M. Kennedy, Amici Curiae, at 24, Buckley v. Valeo, 424 U.S. 1 (1976) (per curiam).

54. *Id.* at 26.

55. *Id.* at 30.

Proponents of deference in *Buckley* relied heavily on *United States v. O'Brien*,[56] the draft-card burning case. The Court there held that "when 'speech' and 'nonspeech' elements are combined in the same course of conduct, a sufficiently important governmental interest in regulating the nonspeech element can justify incidental limitations on First Amendment freedoms."[57] It then announced a comparatively undemanding test for determining when a government regulation of the 'nonspeech element' is 'sufficiently justified.' The test implied that lenient review was appropriate if the governmental interest in regulating the nonspeech element "is unrelated to the suppression of free expression."[58]

a. Speech vs. Nonspeech and Campaign Contributions

In *Buckley*, the Court rejected the draft-card burning analogy. The Court asserted that "[t]he expenditure of money simply cannot be equated with such conduct as destruction of a draft card."[59] Unfortunately, the Court failed to articulate its rationale for this conclusion.

In *O'Brien*, two purported characteristics of the draft-card burning statute influenced the Court to apply a lenient standard of review. First, the Court indicated, the statute's operative effects could be analytically carved up and its impact upon the nonspeech element of *O'Brien's* behavior considered separately from its impact upon the speech element. Second, the statute's purpose in regulating the nonspeech element could plausibly be regarded as "unrelated to the suppression of expression."[60] For the Court's refusal in *Buckley* to follow *O'Brien* to be justifiable, therefore, the spending and contribution limitations of the FECA must possess one or the other of these characteristics.

A conceptual problem immediately arises. The supposed distinction between the speech and nonspeech elements—of either draft-card burning or political spending—lacks analytic utility. The Court has long been unable to render a coherent account of the implications of the first amendment's textual limitation to abridgements of speech.[61] On the one hand, the Court has refrained from extending the amendment's ambit to cover

---

56. 391 U.S. 367 (1968).

57. *Id.* at 376.

58. *Id.* at 377.

59. *Buckley*, 424 U.S. at 16.

60. *Cf.* Dean Alfange, Jr., *Free Speech and Symbolic Conduct: The Draft-Card Burning Case*, 1968 Sup. Ct. Rev. 1, 17. Alfange argues that even though the Court begged the speech-conduct question, the result in *O'Brien* is defensible because of the nature of the governmental interest promoted by the statute.

61. *See generally* Fred Schauer, *Speech and 'Speech'—Obscenity and 'Obscenity': An Exercise in the Interpretation of Constitutional Language*, 67 Geo. L. J. 899 (1979).

everything the dictionary might define as speech.[62] On the other hand, the Court has also extended first amendment protection to expressive activities other than speaking.[63] In these cases, the Court may have been influenced by a conception, albeit a not fully articulated one, of what the amendment was designed to protect.[64] Whatever the conceptual motivation, however, the Court often has extended first amendment protection to activities that seem at first glance quite unspeech-like.

In *O'Brien*, the Court avoided confronting these parallel but conflicting lines of authority. The Court, claiming to synthesize past cases, developed a doctrinal formulation that purported to preserve intensive review for regulations of "pure" speech and to reserve more relaxed scrutiny for rules directed at nonspeech. Reaching a rare consensus, commentators agreed that there was a fatal flaw in the new test: the "speech" and the "conduct" that the Court purported to distinguish were in fact "an undifferentiated whole."[65] Thus, the distinction between the speech and non-

---

62. *See* Fred Schauer, *Categories and the First Amendment: A Play in Three Acts*, 34 VAND. L. REV. 265, 267-82 (1981) ("Not every case is a first amendment case."). Accordingly, the Court has occasionally construed first amendment speech not to include verbal behavior that would certainly seem to be speech in any ordinary meaning of the term. *See* Chaplinsky v. New Hampshire, 315 U.S. 568, 571-72 (1942) ("There are certain well-defined and narrowly limited classes of speech, the prevention and punishment of which have never been thought to raise any Constitutional problem. These include the lewd and obscene, the profane, the libelous, and the insulting or 'fighting' words....") (footnote omitted).

63. *See, e.g.*, Brown v. Louisiana, 383 U.S. 131 (1966) (silent standing in library); West Va. State Bd. of Educ. v. Barnette, 319 U.S. 624 (1943) (refusal to salute flag); Stromberg v. California, 283 U.S. 359 (1931) (display of red flag).

64. Unfortunately, the Court has not been scrupulous to explain why these activities could claim freedom from regulation by the terms of a constitutional provision protecting speech. In other cases the textual limitation to speech appeared as a convenient device for reining in the amendment's coverage. The Court simply labeled some forms of nonverbal communicative activity 'conduct,' thus rendering a superficially plausible account of its decision to permit particular inhibitions. *See, e.g.*, Cox v. Louisiana, 379 U.S. 559, 563 (1965). The Court in *Cox* held that a statute governing the conduct of picketing and parading did not infringe free speech.

> The examples are many of the application by this Court of the principle that certain forms of conduct mixed with speech may be regulated or prohibited.... The most stringent protection of free speech would not protect a man in falsely shouting fire in a theatre and causing a panic. A man may be punished for encouraging the commission of a crime, or for uttering fighting words, this principle has been applied to picketing and parading in labor disputes.

Id. at 563 (citations omitted).

65. John Hart Ely, *Flag Desecration: A Case Study in the Roles of Categorization and Balancing in First Amendment Analysis*, 88 HARV. L. REV. 1482, 1496 (1975). To gener-

speech elements of conduct does not genuinely serve to indicate the appropriate intensity of first amendment concern.[66]

The Court's assertion in *Buckley* that "[t]he expenditure of money simply cannot be equated with such conduct as destruction of a draft card"[67] is flawed because it rests upon a specious distinction between conduct and speech. As was true with the draft-card burning in *O'Brien*, the speech and conduct involved in campaign contributions and expenditures represent an undifferentiated whole. Not only does money permit the purchase of communication, but — more importantly for purposes of this part of the analysis — political giving and spending are themselves communicative acts. Their message of support (presumably their speech element) is quite inseparable from "the transfer or use of money" (presumably their conduct element). Thus, in *Buckley*, the attempt to separate conduct from speech is neither more nor less arbitrary than was the similar attempt in *O'Brien*. The purported distinction simply does not reflect a useful predicate for reasoning about the appropriate intensity of first amendment scrutiny. Therefore, another approach is necessary.

b. *Government Interests Unrelated to the Suppression of Free Expression*

John Hart Ely once offered a convincing way out of the conceptual black box into which laws that regulate speech and conduct seem to fall. One of the *O'Brien* conditions for lenient scrutiny of regulations of communicative conduct was that the governmental interest served be "unrelated to the suppression of free expression." Ely translates this to mean

---

alize from that insight, "[a] constitutional distinction between speech and nonspeech has no content. A constitutional distinction between speech and conduct is specious. Speech is conduct, and actions speak." Louis Henkin, *Foreword: On Drawing Lines*, 82 Harv. L. Rev. 63, 79 (1968); *see also* Lawrence Tribe, American Constitutional Law § 12-7, at 599 (1978) ("The trouble with the distinction between speech and conduct is that it has no real content."); Melville B. Nimmer, *The Meaning of Symbolic Speech Under the First Amendment*, 21 UCLA L. Rev. 29, 33 (1973) ("Any attempt to disentangle 'speech' from conduct which is itself communicative will not withstand analysis.").

66. The Court ought to be concerned whenever legislation inhibits conduct or applies in contexts that, according to any intelligible conception of the first amendment's purposes, ought to be kept relatively free from regulation. The speciousness of the distinction between speech and conduct combines with its false clarity and its aura of determinacy to deflect inquiry from the most difficult but only important questions: whether, pursuant to the first amendment and in this context, regulations of this conduct ought to be strictly scrutinized by the Court, and with what conception of the amendment's essential function would strict scrutiny in this case be consistent. *Cf.* Henkin, *supra* note 65, at 77 (arguing that the Court has never done what it ought to do, namely relate the distinction between speech and conduct to the language and purposes of the first amendment).

67. *Buckley*, 424 U.S. at 16.

that deference is warranted only if "the harm that the state is seeking to avert is one that...would arise even if the defendant's conduct had no communicative significance whatsoever."[68]

Tested by this formulation, neither of the two principal purposes proffered in *Buckley* to support the contribution and expenditure limitations of the FECA Amendments could be deemed "unrelated to the suppression of free expression." The regulations sought to prevent harms that would only arise if giving and spending money has communicative significance.[69] They therefore required strict scrutiny.

The first purpose advanced in support of the FECA contribution and expenditure limitations was preventing political corruption. Campaign contributions can be the effective equivalent of bribery and thus be considered corrupt when they are given not as a signal of support "but in expectation of influencing or changing [candidates'] positions" on specific issues.[70] When this is the case, they harm the political process because they distort the motivations of public decision-makers in determinate and improper ways. "To the extent that large contributions are given to secure political quid pro quos from current and potential office holders, the integrity of our system of representative democracy is undermined."[71]

The systemic harm that stems from political quid pro quos would never eventuate if the payment of money had no communicative significance. Not only does the payment identify the terms of the arrangement but also it indicates that at least one party believes that the deal itself will be or has been made. Without this communicative effect, it could neither harm our system of representative democracy nor undermine the integrity of an officeholder's public decisionmaking. Thus, insofar as the harm prevented by the regulation of campaign giving and spending is corruption, it is a harm that arises only because the regulated behavior has communicative significance. To this extent, therefore, the regulation is not "unrelated to the suppression of free expression."

The second purpose of the FECA, conceptually distinct from corruption prevention, was to equalize the relative ability of individuals and groups to influence election outcomes. The harm to be prevented by equalizing regulations is also systemic, but more broadly so, for the tar-

---

68. Ely, *supra* note 65, at 1497; *cf.* TRIBE, *supra* note 65, § 12-7, at 601 ("For whatever reason the distinction [between speech and conduct] survives, it may be taken at most as shorthand for an inquiry into the aim of the government's regulation.").

69. *But see* Archibald Cox, *The Supreme Court, 1979 Term—Foreward: Freedom of Expression in the Burger Court*, 94 HARV. L. REV. 1, 59 (1980).

70. HERBERT E. ALEXANDER, FINANCING POLITICS — MONEY, ELECTIONS AND POLITICAL REFORM 79 (2d ed. 1980).

71. *Buckley*, 424 U.S. at 26-27.

gets of such regulations are not merely officeholders or voters, but the entire political system. This equalization goal is more ambitious than just preventing specific instances or opportunities for abuse of the public trust by public officials. It is to reallocate political power throughout the entire electoral system. Rather than seeking to prevent corrupt political deals, legislation that pursues an equalization goal seeks to shift political outcomes away from those favored by persons who presently have "too much" political power and toward those favored by persons whose present share of political power is deemed "too little."

The harm prevented by such legislation—the exercise or possession of "too much" political power by some individuals or groups—could not arise unless the giving and spending of money has communicative significance. The whole point of giving and spending money in election campaigns is to communicate: to signal support, to persuade (or purchase the means of persuasion), to participate in the effort to get a message to elected officials or to the voting public, and thereby to affect political outcomes. Moreover, only if money has communicative significance can individuals or groups achieve "too much" political influence simply by spending it on or contributing it to election campaigns.

The conclusion that "money talks" thus seems inescapable. That it talks not too loudly but too well[72] explains why reformers want to regulate its giving and spending in political contexts. It also explains why laws that limit political giving and spending raise serious free speech issues.

c. Content Neutrality

Even when the defenders of deference in *Buckley* acknowledge the communicative significance of contributions and expenditures, they insist that strict scrutiny is unnecessary because the FECA's limitations upon these activities are "content neutral" and thus benign in first amendment terms. "The FECA," they argued, "is not concerned with what is said, how often it is said, or who speaks...The evils which Congress addressed are the corrosive influence of large contributions and expenditures of money—dangers in nowise resulting from the ideas expressed or the vol-

---

72. A favorite analogy of reformers is between contribution or spending limitations and decibel limits. *See, e.g.,* Paul A. Freund, *Commentary, in* FEDERAL REGULATION OF CAMPAIGN FINANCE: SOME CONSTITUTIONAL QUESTIONS 72-73 (Albert J. Rosenthal ed. 1972) ("[J]ust as the volume of sound may be limited by law, so the volume of dollars may be limited without violating the First Amendment."). The analogy is flawed because the evil created by too much sound is noise in a strictly physical sense, whereas that thought to be created by too many dollars is noise only in a normative sense—namely that, in the view of the person drawing the analogy, too many dollars permit certain messages to be heard too much.

ume of expression."[73] Justice White, dissenting from the Court's invalidation of the expenditure limitations, similarly concluded that "the contribution and expenditure limitations are neutral as to the content of speech and are not motivated by fear of the consequences of the political speech of particular candidates or of political speech in general..."[74]

Defenders of deference note that contribution and expenditure limitations on their face are not directed toward any specific candidates; rather they apply across the board to the speech of all political candidates. Facial neutrality, however, does not alone justify judicial deference to such limitations.

In the first place, the FECA's facially neutral terms cannot without more establish a completely convincing case for content neutrality. Although the doctrine of content neutrality has not been applied consistently,[75] scholars generally agree that viewpoint discrimination is the principal first amendment evil to be prevented.[76] When the issue is viewpoint neutrality of laws that regulate speech and conduct, as do expenditure and contribution limitations, courts confront a difficult dilemma. They have tried to develop doctrinal tools capable of rooting out the evil of viewpoint discrimination in literally neutral statutes without requiring in every case full-blown inquiries into either discriminatory legislative motives or uneven regulatory effects.[77] Therefore, to suggest that a statute's literally content-neutral terms are always a trustworthy proxy for actual

---

73. Brief of Senators Hugh Scott and Edward M. Kennedy, Amici Curiae, at 28-29, Buckley v. Valeo, 424 U.S. 1 (1976) (per curiam).

74. *Buckley*, 424 U.S. at 259-60 (White, J., concurring and dissenting). Professor Tribe also confesses that "limitations on campaign contributions and expenditures...seem entirely content-neutral; they do not pass judgment on or inhibit any particular political message or even any identifiable kind of message." TRIBE, *supra* note 65, § 13-27, at 800-01; *see also* J. Skelly Wright, *Politics and the Constitution: Is Money Speech?*, 85 YALE L.J. 1001, 1009 (1976) ("[M]oney limitations, if properly drafted and administered, are uniquely manageable as content-neutral.").

75. *See generally* Daniel A. Farber, *Content Regulation and the First Amendment: A Revisionist View*, 68 GEO. L. J. 727 (1980); Martin H. Redish, *The Content Distinction in First Amendment Analysis*, 34 STAN. L. REV. 113 (1981); Paul B. Stephan, III., *The First Amendment and Content Discrimination*, 68 VA. L. REV. 203 (1982); Geoffrey Stone, *Content Regulation and the First Amendment*, 25 WM. & MARY L. REV. 189 (1983) [hereinafter cited as Stone, *Content Regulation*]; Geoffrey Stone, *Restrictions of Speech Because of its Content: The Peculiar Case of Subject-Matter Restrictions*, 46 U. CHI. L. REV. 81 (1978) [hereinafter cited as Stone, *Restrictions of Speech*].

76. *See, e.g.*, Farber, *supra* note 75, at 735; Redish, *supra* note 75, at 117; Stone, *Restrictions of Speech*, *supra* note 75, at 108; Wright, *supra* note 74, at 1009.

77. For a useful and perceptive analysis of this very puzzling "jurisprudential conflict between precision of analysis and clarity of doctrine," see Stone, *Content Regulation*, *supra* note 75, at 251-52 (footnote omitted). *See also* Schauer, *supra* note 62, at 280-81.

viewpoint neutrality is at best to oversimplify this complex doctrinal issue.[78]

Secondly, contribution and expenditure limitations operate explicitly within the political arena, where the concern that government not engage in viewpoint discrimination ought to be most acute. Within this traditional first amendment protectorate, limitations on giving and spending burden certain forms of political participation rather than regulating the entire range of political activities.[79] The political realities of campaign finance reform, moreover, suggest that these activities are the target of regulation at least in part because they are closely tied to political agendas that reformers oppose.[80]

Finally, changing the legal context of political activity inevitably redistributes political power. "Reform is not neutral. When the rules of the game are changed, advantages shift and institutions change...."[81] At the very least, whatever the motivations of their political sponsors, laws directly regulating explicitly political behavior can never have a neutral im-

---

78. *Cf.* TRIBE, *supra* note 65, § 12-6, at 598 (when the government's goal is to suppress particular ideas, even content-neutral regulations require closer scrutiny).

79. *But cf.* Stone, *Restrictions of Speech, supra* note 75, at 109-15 (suggesting that "subject-matter restrictions" on speech, such as those at issue in *Buckley*, carry exaggerated risks of viewpoint discrimination only when they restrict speech about a specific issue or cluster of issues, and thus only then should they be strictly scrutinized.). In this respect, the Court's more deferential review of legislation restricting the political activities of certain government employees is perhaps explicable. *See, e.g.*, United States Civil Serv. Comm'n v. Nat'l Ass'n of Letter Carriers, 413 U.S. 548 (1973); United Public Workers v. Mitchell, 330 U.S. 75 (1947).

80. Sanford Levinson, *Book Review*, 96 HARV. L. REV. 1466, 1478 (1983) (reviewing THE POLITICS OF LAW: A PROGRESSIVE CRITIQUE (David Kairys ed. 1982)). *See also* the candid assessment of Professor Karst, who worried that while regulation of campaign finance is "motivated by egalitarian goals of the highest order...at least some of the laws involve what can only be called discrimination based on speech content." Kenneth L. Karst, *Equality as a Central Principal of the First Amendment*, 43 U. CHI. L. REV. 20, 64 (1975). Judge Wright professes to see the matter quite differently: "It is, to say the least, not immediately apparent how [contribution or expenditure] ceilings—so long as they apply evenly across the board—could be designed so as to cast a disproportionate burden on minority or disfavored points of view." Wright, *supra* note 74, at 1009 n.39.

81. ALEXANDER, *supra* note 70, at 15; *see also* M. JOHNSTON, POLITICAL CORRUPTION AND PUBLIC POLICY IN AMERICA 144 (1982) ("A...basic problem with structural reform is that...governmental structures...are almost never neutral in their impact.... [D]ecisions about institutional reform are still decisions about what kind of politics and policy we want, whether we realize it or not. People who do realize this have at times used reform as camouflage for their own political agenda."); *cf.* William Patton & Randall Bartlett, *Corporate 'Persons' and Freedom of Speech: The Political Impact of Legal Mythology*, 1981 WIS. L. REV. 494, 510 (Law is "not given the luxury of adopting a position which has no political consequences.").

pact. In no case will the effects upon individuals, interest groups, and other political actors be precisely evenhanded.[82] Indeed, it is ironic that the most forceful argument supporting campaign finance legislation praises the FECA for depriving the wealthy of the advantage of their position.[83] The argument implies that the chief virtue of reform measures is their lack of neutrality of impact.[84] Statutes that are supported precisely because they deprive a particular group of its ability to engage relatively effectively in politics, therefore, may not be as "entirely content neutral" as they seem.[85]

B. "Proxy Speech"

In *Buckley* the Court distinguished between limits on contributions of money to politicians or their campaigns and limits on expenditures by citizens or candidates.[86] A contribution limit, the Court said, "entails only a marginal restriction upon the contributor's ability to engage in free communication"[87] because "the transformation of contributions into political debate involves speech by someone other than the contributor."[88]

---

82. *Cf.* Ralph K. Winter, *Changing Concepts of Equality: From Equality Before the Law to the Welfare State*, 1979 WASH. U. L. Q. 741, 752 ("[I]t is naive to believe that such regulation can ever be evenhanded.").

83. TRIBE, *supra* note 65, § 13-27, at 800-03. *See generally* J. Skelly Wright, *Money And The Pollution Of Politics: Is The First Amendment An Obstacle To Political Equality?*, 82 COLUM L. REV. 609 (1982).

84. *Cf.* David Adamany, *Money, Politics, and Democracy: A Review Essay*, 71 AM. POL. SCI. REV. 289, 296 (1977) ("If recent writing is the measure, the analysis of political finance often turns on the author's ideological perspective."). Because political reforms cannot be neutral, to claim that spurious assertions of neutrality ought not deflect first amendment strict scrutiny is not to make any statement whatsoever about whether the particular nonneutrality itself violates or is permissible under the first amendment. The Court in *Buckley*, of course, held both that the contribution and spending limitations were not neutral and that the nonneutral purpose of equalizing political power was "wholly foreign to the First Amendment." *Buckley*, 424 U.S. at 49.

85. *Cf., e.g.*, Irving Ferman, *Congressional Controls on Campaign Financing: An Expansion or Contraction of the First Amendment?*, 22 AM. U. L. REV. 1 (1972) (attempt to limit influence of wealth on campaigns is equivalent to content discrimination).

86. *Buckley*, 424 U.S. at 19-21. *See generally* Eric L. Richards, *The Rise and Fall of the Contribution/Expenditure Distinction: Redefining the Acceptable Range of Campaign Finance Reforms*, 18 NEW ENG. L. REV. 367 (1983).

87. *Buckley*, 424 U.S. at 20-21.

88. *Id.* at 21.

Expenditure limits, on the other hand, "represent substantial rather than merely theoretical restraints on the quantity and diversity of political speech."[89]

Several members of the Court have used this distinction to justify less intense scrutiny where a campaign finance regulation purportedly governs contributions. In *California Medical Association v. Federal Election Commission*,[90] for example, the Court sustained FECA limits upon the amount an unincorporated association (CMA) was permitted to give to a multicandidate political committee (CALPAC). The challengers argued that the restriction was "akin to an unconstitutional expenditure limitation because it restricts the ability of CMA to engage in political speech through a political committee, CALPAC."[91] The plurality was unpersuaded: "The type of expenditures that this Court in *Buckley* considered constitutionally protected were those made independently by a candidate, individual or group in order to engage directly in political speech."[92] What CMA wanted to do, by contrast, was to engage in "speech by proxy," a form of political advocacy "not...entitled to full First Amendment protection."[93]

The distinction between expenditures and contributions has been so severely criticized that it may no longer support a different level of scrutiny for contribution than for expenditure limitations.[94] In his separate opinion in *Buckley*, Chief Justice Burger initiated the criticism by calling the distinction a word game.[95] For him, the distinction is not a reliable barometer of the relative significance of the first amendment values at stake.[96] Moreover, he noted, the distinction is so inherently meaningless that "the

---

89. *Id.* at 19.

90. 453 U.S. 182 (1981).

91. *Id.*

92. *Id.* (emphasis in original).

93. *Id.* at 196.

94. Indeed, the distinction has been abandoned by Justice Marshall, one of its adherents on the Court. *See* Federal Election Comm'n v. Nat'l Conservative Political Action Comm., 105 S. Ct. 1459, 1481 (1985) (Marshall, J., dissenting) ("I now believe that the distinction has no constitutional significance."). For Justice Marshall, however, abandoning the distinction does not mean that both expenditure and contribution limitations will be subjected to more intensive scrutiny formerly deemed appropriate only for the former. Rather it means that both forms of limitation can be more readily justified.

95. *Buckley*, 424 U.S. at 244 (Burger, C.J., concurring in part and dissenting in part).

96. "[P]eople—candidates and contributors—spend money on political activity because they wish to communicate ideas, and their constitutional interest in doing so is precisely the same whether they or someone else utter the words." *Id.*

contribution limitations will, in specific instances, limit exactly the same political activity that the expenditure ceilings limit, and at least one of the 'expenditure' limitations the Court finds objectionable operates precisely like the 'contribution' limitations."[97]

Professor Powe has persuasively made a similar point. He observes that regulations of "proxy speech" (i.e., contributions) supposedly differ from regulations of "real speech" (i.e., expenditures) in that "proxy speech is speech by another." The difference, however, is largely chimerical.

> All of the campaign finance cases involve speech by another. In some circumstances an individual gives to a committee which in turn gives to a professional or to a campaign treasury. In other cases a campaign treasury turns money over to a professional.... An individual choice to have a message with which he agrees prepared by professionals is no less speech. Proxy speech is simply a pejorative name for a political commercial. It is still speech.[98]

---

97. *Id.* at 243-44. *But see* Note, *The Unconstitutionality of Limitations on Contributions to Political Committees in the 1976 Federal Election Campaign Act Amendments*, 86 YALE L.J. 953, 957–61 (1977), which argues that gifts to political committees, denoted "contributions" by the FECA, are not genuinely analogous either to candidate contributions or to independent expenditures as defined in *Buckley*, and therefore should be given a different label and subjected to a different first amendment analysis.

98. L.A.Powe, Jr., *Mass Speech and the Newer First Amendment*, 1982 SUP. CT. REV. 243, 258–59 (emphasis added). Professor Cox, discussing 26 U.S.C. § 9012(f) (1982), disagrees:

> Organized fundraising, purchase of television time, and other political advertising by a political committee are clearly types of conduct affecting speech and entitled to some degree of first amendment protection. It can be argued, however, that these activities are not speech itself, and therefore do not merit the full shelter of the first amendment. The argument is given point by asking whose right of speech is abridged by the restriction. Those who give the money are not engaging in communication. As in the case of a contribution directly to a candidate, there is "only a marginal restriction upon the contributor's ability to engage in free communication" because "the transformation of contributions into political debate involves speech by someone other than the contributor." Those who constitute the committee to raise and spend the money do not engage in speech; their concern is to provide the money. Having combined contributions into a pool, the committee will simply turn it over to one or more advertising agencies to conduct an advertising campaign through the mass media. The space advertising will present the picture and slogans of the candidate. The television spots will present the visage and voice of the candidate taken from newscasts and previous television appearances. It would not be surprising to find an independent committee simply buying additional time to rerun the candidate's own spots. In short, the committee's activities are much more like the contributions held subject to regulation in *Buckley* than like the

In addition to the arbitrariness necessarily entailed in implementing a distinction without a difference, a rule that accords less first amendment protection to contributions than to expenditures severely infringes upon the right of association.[99] Contributions by individual citizens to candidates might be thought merely to signal the contributor's support. Contributions by individuals to groups or to political committees, however, permit the pooling of resources. This amplifies the contributors' individual voices. In *NAACP v. Alabama*,[100] when the Court for the first time gave explicit first amendment protection to freedom of association,[101] it recognized that "[e]ffective advocacy of both public and private points of view, particularly controversial ones, is undeniably enhanced by group association."[102] Limits on political contributions obviously constrain the efforts of groups of individuals to increase the effectiveness of their advocacy. The limits also limit the ability of citizens to choose for themselves the scope and extent of their political participation.

Since the legitimacy of the constitutional status of the right of political association is not in doubt, the burden of justifying judicial deference to limits upon its exercise rests with those who argue that such deference is

---

individual expenditures held immune. Furthermore, individual speech is in no sense involved because section 9012(f) applies only to the expenditures of an organized political committee.

Cox, *supra* note 69, at 62-63. For an argument along lines similar to those endorsed by Professor Cox, *see* Anne V. Simonett, *The Constitutionality of Regulating Independent Expenditure Committees in Publicly Funded Presidential Campaigns,* 18 HARV. J. ON LEGIS. 679, 688-94 (1981).

99. *See generally* Young & Herbert, *Political Association Under the Burger Court: Fading Protection,* 15 U.C.D. L. REV. 53 (1981) (review of Burger Court decisions on freedom of association cases).

100. 357 U.S. 449 (1958).

101. The fact that the right of association is only implicitly protected by the first amendment is not necessarily relevant to the question of the appropriate degree of its protection. Freedom of political association seems a wholly appropriate inference to draw from the text, structure, and history of the Constitution. *Cf.* Fellman, *Constitutional Rights of Association,* 1961 SUP. CT. REV. 74, 104-08, 133-34 ("The rights of association are central to any serious conception of constitutional democracy." *Id.* at 133.) It is fully consistent both with the normative vision of the first amendment in terms of which the protection of contributions and expenditures is justified and with the Court's stated assumptions about what the first amendment necessarily implies. *See, e.g.,* Roberts v. United States Jaycees, 104 S. Ct. 3244, 3252 (1984) ("[W]e have long understood as implicit in the right to engage in activities protected by the First Amendment a corresponding right to associate with others in pursuit of a wide variety of political, social, economic, educational, religious, and cultural ends.").

102. *NAACP v. Alabama,* 357 U.S. at 460.

warranted. Apart from specious distinctions between the first amendment values of contributions and expenditures, or between "proxy speech" and "real speech," the burden has yet to be borne.[103]

* * *

---

103. In his analysis of *Buckley v. Valeo*, Professor Polsby made an important effort to justify the distinction between contributions and expenditures. His basic conclusion was that, insofar as there was a genuine difference, it was not a first amendment difference but rather a difference in the governmental interests supporting regulation. Daniel D. Polsby, Buckley v. Valeo: *The Special Nature of Political Speech*, 1976 Sup. Ct. Rev. 1, 21–25. The latter kind of difference might support different results in contribution from those in expenditure regulation cases, but it would not in principle support a lower level of judicial deference for one than the other. *See supra* notes 95-102 and accompanying text.

* * *

Section III

Compelling Government Interests in Regulating Campaign Finance

Campaign Finance Reform: A Key to Restoring the Health of Our Democracy

[Excerpt One]

Fred Wertheimer
Susan Weiss Manes

> One of the first tasks today is to cope with the prevailing cynicism—and that cannot be done unless we learn to hold our top leaders to account. The simple rule is: Hold power accountable. That means, among other things, that we can no longer tolerate a system of campaign financing that makes our leaders accountable to donors rather than voters, that makes it possible for money to buy political outcomes, to buy politicians. Until that change is made the relentless power players who control Washington will continue to rule silently. And, as usual, when their work is done there will be no fingerprints on the butchered corpse of the nation's public interest.

John Gardner, in a February 17, 1993 speech entitled "Rebirth of a Nation"[1]

Introduction

Our democracy is founded on the concept of representation. Citizens elect leaders who are entrusted to weigh the competing interests that reflect our diversity, and to decide what, in their best judgment, will serve the interests of the citizenry. We believe that our best chance at governing ourselves lies in obtaining the best judgments of those we elect to represent us.

---

1. John Gardner, Address at the Forum Club of Houston (Feb. 17, 1993) (transcript on file with the *Columbia Law Review*).

Increasingly, our campaign finance system is undermining this system of self-government. People engaged in the business of influencing government decisions provide large amounts of money to the elected officials who make those decisions. The huge economic stakes involved in government decisions and the ever-increasing amounts necessary to run political campaigns have combined to make influence-seeking money a pervasive force today in the nation's capital. Our nation's campaign finance laws have legalized the use of campaign contributions to secure access to and influence over the legislative process. Our elected representatives are so indebted to the special-interest donors on whom they depend for their political existence that they are losing their ability to provide their best judgment in representing the citizens who elected them.

As former Senator Barry Goldwater (R-Ariz.) wrote almost a decade ago:

> The fact that liberty depended on honest elections was of the utmost importance to the patriots who founded our nation and wrote the Constitution. They knew that corruption destroyed the prime requisite of constitutional liberty, an independent legislature free from any influence other than that of the people. Applying these principles to modern times, we can make the following conclusions. To be successful, representative government assumes that elections will be controlled by the citizenry at large, not by those who give the most money. Electors must believe their vote counts. Elected officials must owe their allegiance to the people, not to their own wealth or to the wealth of interest groups who speak only for the selfish fringes of the whole community[2]

The pervasive dependence of elected officials on special-interest money is central to the crisis in public confidence that faces our government today. The public's belief that its interests are not being served in Washington is a direct reflection of the way in which monied interests and the pursuit of political-influence money by elected officials have become dominant forces in our political life. The extraordinary public cynicism we see today profoundly threatens our democracy.

The present campaign finance system also has played a central role in shaping an electoral landscape that is grossly unfair to challengers. Democracy depends for its survival on having real elections with real choices if the people are truly to have the power to elect representatives that can be held accountable. Congressional incumbents now have such an extraordinary advantage over their challengers in raising campaign contributions that we are losing the ability to hold real elections for Congress. The current congressional campaign finance system, and the ab-

---

2. Barry Goldwater, The Road to Anarchy—Excessive Campaign Spending, Statement Before the Commission on National Elections 6 (Sept. 17, 1985) (transcript on file with the *Columbia Law Review*).

sence of competition it has engendered, have helped to create an absence of accountability for elected officials that is a fundamental problem for our political system today.

This Article examines the problems in the current campaign finance system and proposes steps necessary to achieve real reform of the system. These include the following:

(1) substantial public campaign resources and reasonable spending limits for congressional races to allow candidates to run for office without being dependent on special-interest campaign contributions and to provide challengers with a fair chance to compete;

(2) dramatic reductions in the flow of political action committee (PAC) contributions and other special-interest political money to free legislators to represent their constituents without the corrupting influence of these contributions;

(3) measures to effectively close the bundling loophole used by PACs, lobbyists, and others to evade the federal contribution limits and channel thousands of dollars above and beyond these limits to Members of Congress;

(4) provisions to close the "soft money" loophole that has been opened in the presidential campaign financing system, which allows corporations, labor unions, and wealthy individuals to make large donations in contravention of present law; and

(5) an overhaul of the Federal Election Commission to provide effective oversight and enforcement of the federal campaign finance laws.

I. The Dangers of Private Influence Money

There is an inherent problem with a system in which individuals and groups with an interest in government decisions can give substantial sums of money to elected officials who have the power to make those decisions. The Supreme Court recognized this when it upheld the constitutionality of campaign finance contribution limits in *Buckley v. Valeo*:[3]

> It is unnecessary to look beyond the Act's primary purpose—to limit the actuality and appearance of corruption resulting from large individual financial contributions—in order to find a constitutionally sufficient justification for the $ 1,000 contribution limitation.... To the extent that large contributions are given to secure political quid pro quos from current and potential office holders, the integrity of our system of representative democracy is undermined. Although the scope of such pernicious practices can never be reliably ascertained, the deeply disturbing examples surfacing after the 1972 election demonstrate that the problem is not an illusory one.

---

3. 424 U.S. 1 (1976).

> Of almost equal concern as the danger of actual quid pro quo arrangements is the impact of the appearance of corruption stemming from public awareness of the opportunities for abuse inherent in a regime of large individual financial contributions.[4]

A growing number of our elected representatives recognize that the role of PACs, lobbyists, and other influence seekers in financing congressional elections has fundamentally compromised the decision-making process in Congress. As Senator Robert Byrd (D-W. Va.), the Senate's president pro tempore, said, "Money talks, and the perception is that money will talk here in this Senate. Money will open the door. Money will hold the balance of power."[5] Another senior Member of Congress, Senator Dale Bumpers (D-Ark.), spoke even more bluntly about the problem: "Every Senator knows I speak the truth when I say bill after bill after bill has been defeated in this body because of campaign money."[6] "As far as the general public is concerned," observed former Senator Goldwater (R-Ariz.) in 1986, "it is not 'We the People,' but political action committees and monied interests who are setting the nation's political agenda and are influencing the position of candidates on the important issues of the day."[7]

The late Senator Paul Douglas (D-Ill.), a widely respected Senator in the 1940s and 1950s, described the effect of favors and benefits provided to elected officials:

> What happens is a gradual shifting of a man's loyalties from the community to those who have been doing him favors. His final decisions are, therefore, made in response to his private friendships and loyalties rather than to the public good. Throughout this whole process, the official will claim—and may indeed believe—that there is no causal connection between the favors he has received and the decisions which he makes. He will assert that the favors were given and received on the basis of pure friendship unsullied by worldly considerations. He will claim that the decisions, on the other hand, will have been made on the basis of the justice and equity of the particular case. The two series of acts will be alleged to be as separate as the east is from the west. Moreover, the whole process may be so subtle as not to be detected by the official himself.[8]

The testimony of these observers attests to the power of special interest political contributions to distort and to influence improperly the decisions

---

4. *Id.* at 26–27.

5. 134 CONG. REC. S1534 (daily ed. Feb. 26, 1988) (statement of Sen. Byrd).

6. 139 CONG. REC. S7187 (daily ed. June 15, 1993) (statement of Sen. Bumpers).

7. *Senate Comm. on Rules and Administration*, 99 Cong. 1 (1986) (statement of Sen. Goldwater).

8. PAUL H. DOUGLAS, ETHICS IN GOVERNMENT 44 (1952).

being made in the nation's capital. The hundreds of millions of dollars in campaign contributions from PACs and other influence seekers exert a major impact on the way our national government works.

These contributions also have had a powerful effect on the profound disaffection with which citizens view the nation's capital. Public opinion polls document the public's deep distrust of their elected leaders: A May 1992 Gordon S. Black poll found that 74% of registered likely voters agreed that "Congress is largely owned by the special interest groups," 83% agreed that "the special interest groups that give campaign contributions to candidates have more influence over the government than the voters," and 85% agreed that "special interest money buys the loyalty of candidates."[9] Just before Election Day in 1992, 75% of voters polled by The Washington Post and ABC News said that they worried either "a great deal" or a "good amount" that "special interest groups have too much influence over elected officials."[10] A February 1993 Washington Post/ABC News poll found that "only 21 percent of those interviewed said they trusted government in Washington to do what was right "OK all' or "most of the time.'"[11] A 1991 study by the Harwood Group for the Kettering Foundation, entitled Citizens and Politics: A View from Main Street America, concluded:

> People believe two forces have corrupted democracy. The first is that lobbyists have replaced representatives as the primary political actors. The other force, seen as more pernicious, is that campaign contributions seem to determine political outcomes more than voting. No accusation cuts deeper because when money and privilege replace votes, the social contract underlying the political system is abrogated.[12]

A similar conclusion was reached by political analysts Doug Bailey and Peter D. Hart in their 1991 study People Versus Politics. They wrote "many Americans…believe that 'the squeaky wheel gets the grease,' and that their government has been hijacked by powerful interests ordinary people cannot begin to compete with or hold in check."[13] According to Bailey and Hart:

---

9. Gordon S. Black Corp., The Politics of American Discontent, at Table 3 (public opinion poll released on June 3, 1992).

10. Dan Balz & Richard Morin, *Voters Voice Hope, Discontent- and Sense of Involvement*, WASH. POST, Nov. 3, 1992, at A1.

11. Dan Balz & Richard Morin, *Clinton Plan Enjoys Strong Public Support: Polls Find Anti-Washington Mood Remains*, WASH. POST, Mar. 2, 1993, at A8.

12. Richard C. Harwood, Kettering Foundation, *Citizens and Politics: A View from Main Street America*, at v (1991).

13. Doug Bailey & Peter D. Hart, Centel Public Accountability Project, People Versus Politics: Citizens Discuss Politicians, Campaigns, and Political Reform 2 (1991) (on file with the *Columbia Law Review*).

People across the United States increasingly have come to doubt whether our political system works, either as a vehicle for expressing their will or as an effective mechanism for confronting the nation's problems. Many citizens, even those who still vote, have concluded that they do not exercise real authority over the political system. Americans desperately want to believe that theirs is a government of, by, and for the people; deep down, however, very few think we have that today.[14]

The current campaign finance system lies at the heart of the public's disillusionment. As Senate Majority Leader George Mitchell (D-Me.), a long-time leader of the campaign finance reform fight, said in 1991 as the Senate was considering comprehensive reform legislation:

Increasingly, the American people have come to see their Federal Government as no longer responsive to their needs. They believe Congress acts to fulfill commitments to campaign contributors, rather than to serve the interests of the people...It is understandable that many Americans do not have a favorable impression of this body or of the means which its Members are elected. They see a campaign finance system that places tremendous money demands on those who run for the Senate, a system that overwhelmingly benefits incumbents, and a system dominated by negative campaigns.[15]

In America today, far too many people believe that the system in Washington is fixed and that political-influence money is doing the fixing at the expense of the average citizen. This public mistrust of government discourages citizen participation and leads individuals to believe they have no voice in government.

II. Congressional Elections: Uncontrolled Spending and the Absence of Public Campaign Resources

A. The Current System

Congress in 1974 passed legislation directed at limiting the impact of special-interest money on congressional election campaigns. The legisla-

---

14. *Id.* at 1.
15. *See* 137 CONG. REC. S5879 (daily ed. May 15, 1991) (statement of Sen. Mitchell).

tion imposed limits on both campaign contributions from donors and campaign expenditures by candidates. The legislation did not, however, provide for public financing of congressional elections.[16]

In *Buckley v. Valeo*, the Supreme Court upheld the contribution limits, but struck down the mandatory congressional spending limits on First Amendment grounds.[17] As a result, while there are now limits on the amounts that individuals and groups may contribute to congressional campaigns, there are no limits on the amounts candidates may spend to run for office. And since the 1974 act did not provide for any public financing, there are no public campaign resources to provide an alternative to dependence on special-interest money.

From 1974 to 1990, the Democratically-controlled House successfully bottled up all legislative efforts to create a system of spending limits and public financing for House races. Sixteen years passed during which comprehensive reform legislation was kept off the House floor. In the Senate during this time, periodic efforts were mounted to enact a system of spending limits and public financing for congressional campaigns, but they were blocked by Republican filibusters until 1991. The next year, Congress finally passed comprehensive campaign finance reform legislation,[18] but it was vetoed by President George Bush.

In 1993, both the House and Senate again passed campaign finance reform bills.[19] Although both bills contain spending limits, only the House bill would establish direct public financing.[20] The Senate bill instead provides candidates who agree to abide by spending limits with substantial television discounts, as well as back-up public financing for candidates whose opponents exceed the voluntary spending limits.[21]

Since 1974, spending for congressional campaigns has soared and the absence of public campaign resources has fueled an enormous demand for special-interest campaign contributions. The result has been to push congressional office out of the reach of most challengers. Spending in

---

16. *See* Federal Election Campaign Act Amendments of 1974, Pub. L. No. 93-443, 103, 88 Stat. 1267, 1272 (1974).

17. *See* Buckley v. Valeo, 424 U.S. 1, 29, 51 (1976). The Court also found that spending limits to which candidates voluntarily agree in return for receiving public funds were constitutional.

18. *See* S. 3, 102nd Cong. (1991).

19. *See* H.R. 3, 103rd Cong. (1993); S. 3, 103rd Cong. (1993). The House and Senate had not reached agreement on a final bill when this Article was written.

20. *See* H.R. 3, 103rd Cong. 1211–23, 1000 (1993).

21. *See* S. 3, 103rd Cong. 101 (1993).

Senate races has increased more than five-fold, from a total of $ 38.1 million in the 1976 election cycle[22] to a total of $ 210.8 million in the 1992 elections.[23] In the 1976 election cycle, Senate winners spent an average of $ 610,026.[24] By 1992, the average cost of winning a Senate seat had climbed to $ 3.8 million-or an average of $ 12,000 in contributions each week for every week of a six-year Senate term.[25] Similarly, spending in House races has skyrocketed from a total of $ 60.9 million in the 1976 election cycle[26] to a total of $ 326.9 million in the 1992 election cycle.[27] In the 1976 election cycle, House winners spent an average of $ 87,280,[28] while in the 1992 election cycle, the average winning House candidate spent $ 549,571, more than a six-fold increase.[29] Fifty House candidates spent more than $ 1 million each for their 1992 campaigns.[30]

Under the current system of unlimited spending, there are no constraints on how much money candidates raise. An arms race mentality takes over and candidates raise and spend escalating amounts, in order to stay one step ahead of any possible opponent and to deal with any possi-

---

22. *See* FED. ELECTION COMM'N, FEC DISCLOSURE SERIES NO. 6: 1976 SENATORIAL CAMPAIGNS RECEIPTS AND EXPENDITURES 3, (1977).

23. *See 1992 Senate Campaign Financing*, PRESS RELEASE (Common Cause, Washington, D.C., Spring 1993), at Chart 1 [hereinafter *1992 Senate Campaign Financing*] (on file with the *Columbia Law Review*).

24. *See* FED. ELECTION COMM'N, FEC DISCLOSURE SERIES NO. 6: 1976 SENATORIAL CAMPAIGNS RECEIPTS AND EXPENDITURES 6 (1977).

25. *See 1992 Senate Campaign Financing, supra* note 23, at Chart 1. In the most expensive Senate races, the sums of political money involved are huge. Thirteen Senate candidates raised more than $ 5 million each during the 1992 election cycle. For example, incumbent Senator Alfonse D'Amato (R-N.Y.) raised over $ 11.2 million in his successful bid to retain his Senate seat. *See id.* at 3. Senator Arlen Specter (R-Pa.), another incumbent, raised over $ 10.4 million in his winning reelection campaign. *See id.* Senator Bob Packwood (R-Or.), also an incumbent, raised over $ 8.2 million to hold onto his seat. *See id.* Each of these incumbents raised at least $ 4 million more than their challengers. Senator Barbara Boxer (D-Ca.), running in an open seat race, raised almost $ 10.4 million in her successful bid for the Senate. *See id.*

26. *See* FED. ELECTION COMM'N, FEC DISCLOSURE SERIES NO. 9: 1976 HOUSE OF REPRESENTATIVES CAMPAIGNS RECEIPTS AND EXPENDITURES 4 (1977).

27. *See 1992 House Campaign Financing*, PRESS RELEASE (Common Cause, Washington, D.C.), Spring 1993, at Chart 1 [hereinafter *1992 House Campaign Financing*] (on file with the *Columbia Law Review*).

28. *See* FED. ELECTION COMM'N, FEC DISCLOSURE SERIES NO. 9: 1976 HOUSE OF REPRESENTATIVES CAMPAIGNS RECEIPTS AND EXPENDITURES 11 (1977).

29. *See 1992 House Campaign Financing, supra* note 27, at Chart 1.

30. *See id.* at 56.

ble contingency. Incumbents also stockpile large campaign war chests to discourage serious challengers from entering the race.[31]

Raising campaign contributions, particularly in the Senate with its state-wide election contests, commands an enormous commitment of a candidate's time and attention, and candidates have become consumed with raising money. "As soon as a Senator is elected here, that Senator better start raising money for the next election 6 years down the pike," Senator Tom Harkin (D-Iowa) has said. "Everyone here does it, and to deny that is to deny the obvious and to deny what is also on the record."[32] For incumbent Members of Congress, the money chase has become a way of life. As Senator Byrd (D-W. Va.) has observed, "To raise the money, Senators start hosting fund-raisers years before they next will be in an election. They all too often become fund-raisers first, and legislators second."[33]

Not only has the total amount of campaign money being raised and spent increased during the past two decades, but so has the gap between the resources available to incumbents and challengers. Unable to compete with the ability of incumbent officeholders to raise huge sums of money from PACs, lobbyists, and other givers interested in government decisions, challengers have fallen further and further behind. In 1976, for example, House incumbents on average outspent challengers by a ratio of 1.5 to 1, or $ 79,252 to $ 49,207.[34] By 1992, House incumbents were outspending their challengers on average by a ratio of almost 4 to 1, or $ 582,330 to $ 154,607.[35]

Some argue that public disclosure of campaign contributions, already required under federal law, provides an adequate solution to deal with the problems of the current influence-money system because disclosure gives voters the information they need to make an informed choice and the option to vote against candidates they believe are too tied to special-interest money. But the reality is that the current congressional campaign finance system, with the enormous fund-raising edge it gives to incumbents, has created an electoral system so stacked against challengers that in many elections voters have no real choices—and therefore no effective tool for

---

31. *See The Task Force on Campaign Finance Reform of the House Comm. on House Administration*, 102nd Cong. 56 (1991) (statement of Fred Wertheimer, President, Common Cause).

32. 134 CONG. REC. S1053 (daily ed. Feb. 22, 1988) (statement of Sen. Harkin).

33. 138 CONG. REC. S115 (daily ed. Jan. 6, 1987) (statement of Sen. Byrd).

34. *See* FED. ELECTION COMM'N, FEC DISCLOSURE SERIES NO. 9: 1976 HOUSE OF REPRESENTATIVES CAMPAIGNS RECEIPTS AND EXPENDITURES 11 (1977).

35. *See 1992 House Campaign Financing, supra* note 27, at Chart 1.

holding incumbent officeholders accountable. As Senator David Boren (D-Okla.), a key leader in the fight to reform the current campaign finance system, has said:

> When we see the influence of money itself on the system, and we realize that more and more people are being elected not on the basis of their qualifications, not upon the strength of their character, not based upon the ideas they have to confront America's needs, but based upon which one can raise the most money, we know that something is wrong...[36]

The House and Senate increasingly are becoming exclusive clubs whose price of admission includes the ability to obtain access to very large sums of private money. "Our nation is facing a crisis of liberty if we do not control campaign expenditures," former Senator Barry Goldwater (R-Ariz.) observed in the mid-1980s.[37] "Unlimited campaign spending eats at the heart of the democratic process."[38] As Senator Goldwater asked, "What are we doing? Are we saying that only the rich have brains in this country? Or only the people who have influential friends who have money can be in the Senate?"[39]

B. The Incumbents' Edge: A System Grossly Unfair to Challengers

The extraordinary campaign finance advantage that House incumbents had over their challengers in the 1992 elections dramatically illustrates the unfairness of the current system. A few key facts highlight the problem:

(1) House incumbents had over $ 248 million in total available campaign funds. This is five times more than the approximate sum of $ 49 million their challengers had.[40]

(2) House incumbents had ten times more PAC money than challengers.[41]

(3) House incumbents spent almost four times more than challengers.[42]

(4) 279 of the 349 House incumbents, or 80% of those who sought reelection, ran unopposed (26), ran financially unopposed with

---

36. 137 CONG. REC. S.5876 (daily ed. May 15, 1991) (statement of Sen. Boren).

37. *Senate Comm. on Rules*, 98th Cong. 7 (1983) (statement of Sen. Goldwater).

38. *Id.* at 2.

39. *Senate Comm. on Rules and Administration*, 100th Cong. 6 (1987) (Sen. Goldwater quoted in testimony of Fred Wertheimer, President, Common Cause).

40. *See 1992 House Campaign Financing, supra* note 27, at Chart 1.

41. *See id.*

42. *See id.* at 1.

challengers who raised less than $ 25,000 (86), or ran financially noncompetitive races against challengers who raised less than half of the amount that incumbents raised (167).[43]

(5) Of these, 274 of the 279 incumbents, or 98%, won.[44]

(6) Only seven House challengers outspent their incumbent opponents in 1992.[45]

(7) Overall, 325 of the 349 House incumbents seeking reelection, or 93%, won.[46]

These findings were even starker for the 1990 House elections when 369 of 406-or 91%-of House incumbents seeking reelection were unopposed (79), financially unopposed (158), or in financially noncompetitive races (132). Of these, 365 of the 369 incumbents, or 99%, won. Overall, 391 of the 406 incumbents who sought reelection, or 96%, won in 1990.[47]

In the Senate, incumbents also have enjoyed a massive financial advantage over their challengers. In 1992, while the average Senate incumbent spent almost $ 4.2 million for their campaign, the average challenger could only counter with approximately $ 1.7 million.[48] In 1992, Senate incumbents outspent their challengers in 27 out of 28 races.[49] Only four of these incumbents lost.[50] The numbers in 1990 showed a similar tilt toward Senate incumbents. The average Senate incumbent spent $ 4 million, compared to only $ 1.7 million spent by the average challenger.[51] Senate incumbents outspent their challengers in 26 out of 28 races, and only one Senate incumbent lost to a challenger.[52]

PACs have played a pivotal role in providing incumbents with their huge financial advantage over challengers. Because PAC money is gener-

---

43. *See id.*

44. *See id.*

45. *See id.* at app. These seven were Janos Horvath (R-Ind.); Susan Stokes (R-Ky.); Linda Bean (R-Me.); Dick Chrysler (R-Mi.); James Talent (R-Mo.); Paul Kilker (D-Pa.); and Edward Blum (R-Tex.).

46. *See id.* at 1.

47. *See Home Field Advantage,* COMMON CAUSE NEWS (Common Cause, Washington, D.C.), Mar. 26, 1991, at 34 (on file with the *Columbia Law Review*).

48. *See 1992 Senate Campaign Financing, supra* note 23, at Chart 1.

49. *See id.* at 1.

50. *See id.* These four were John Seymour (R-Ca.); Wyche Fowler (D- Ga.); Terry Sanford (D-N.C.); and Robert Kasten (R-Wis.).

51. *See Nearly Half of Senate Incumbents Seeking Election in 1990 Were Unopposed or Financially Unopposed,* COMMON CAUSE NEWS (Common Cause, Washington, D.C.), Feb. 28, 1991, at 12 (on file with the *Columbia Law Review*).

52. *See id.* at app. III. The one losing Senate incumbent was Rudy Boschwitz (R-Minn.).

ally an investment in the decision-making process in Congress, it flows overwhelmingly to incumbent Members of Congress who, unlike challengers, are in a position to make decisions affecting the PAC's interests. For most PACs, contributions to challengers are seen as a waste of money. Moreover, few PACs are willing to run the risk of antagonizing an incumbent Member of Congress by contributing to his or her opponent. The contribution patterns of PACs strongly reflect this preference for incumbents. For example, in 1992, House incumbents received $ 91.4 million from PACs, while challengers received only $ 8.7 million-a 10.5 to 1 PAC fund-raising advantage for House incumbents.[53] Senate incumbents in the 1992 elections raised more than $ 38 million from special-interest PACs-six times the $ 6.37 million raised by their challengers.[54]

Because the congressional campaign finance system so favors incumbents, challengers, regardless of party affiliation, are all but locked out of the competition. This lack of competition occurred even in 1992, a year when the voters' revolt and the impact of reapportionment were expected to produce far more incumbent defeats than in fact occurred. The issue involved here is not one of electing challengers or defeating incumbents but rather the basic question of whether the present system is providing American voters with real choices in real elections on Election Day. What is at stake is the fairness of the electoral process itself and the ability of citizens to hold their elected representatives accountable.

C. Dependence on Special-Interest PAC Money

Special-interest PAC contributions have become a dominant force in the financing of congressional campaigns, particularly in the House of Representatives. The dependence of Members of Congress on special-interest PAC contributions has seriously compromised the integrity and public credibility of the congressional decision-making process.

Contrary to myth, and contrary to the assertions of those who oppose campaign finance reform, PACs did not spring from the reforms initiated by the 1974 amendments to the Federal Election Campaign Act. PACs have existed since the 1950s, and were recognized as problematic in the early 1970s. However, instead of solving this problem, Congress bowed to business and labor pressure and, in 1974, changed the law specifically to authorize for the first time the establishment and operation of PACs by those with government contracts.[55] This provision opened the door to

---

53. *See 1992 House Campaign Financing, supra* note 27, at Chart 1.

54. *See 1992 Senate Campaign Financing, supra* note 23, at Chart 1.

55. *See* Robert Mutch, Campaigns, Congress and Courts 164–65 (1988); Federal Election Campaign Act Amendments of 1974, Pub. L. No. 93-443, 103, 88 Stat.

tremendous growth in the number of PACs, since many businesses and some labor unions had contracts with the government.[56]

The inclusion of this pro-PAC measure in the 1974 post-Watergate reform legislation has given rise to the erroneous claim that PACs were "created" as a result of "reform." In fact, the 1974 repeal of the ban on government contractors' PACs was designed by special interests to protect PACs and to enhance the role of PACs and was not proposed or enacted as a reform.[57] There was nothing unintended about the resulting explosion in PACs.[58] By its actions, Congress opened the door to the explosive growth that has occurred in the number of PACs from approximately six hundred in 1974 to more than four thousand today.[59] At the same time in 1974 that Congress ended the ban on government contractor PACs, it paved the way for PACs and other private-influence seekers to play an ever-increasing role in financing congressional elections by rejecting public financing for congressional races while establishing public financing for

---

1267, 1272 (1974). This pro-PAC provision was an amendment to an existing general ban on contributions from government contractors. The amendment allows such contributions from "separate segregated" funds of such contractors. The general ban itself was later repealed entirely in 1976. See 18 U.S.C. § 611 (1988). Common Cause strongly opposed the pro- PAC measure, and a number of newspapers editorialized against it at the time. The Washington Post, for example, wrote: "This, in short, is an odd time to open still another loophole to more "corruption in American politics' and the House should waste no time in knocking the effort on the head." Battle Over PAC Money Looms as Campaign Finance Reform Issue Moves to House, EDITORIAL MEMORANDUM (Common Cause, Washington, D.C.), June 1991, at 56 (on file with the Columbia Law Review). Despite public opposition, the provision sailed through the House Administration Committee, which held no public hearings on the bill and adopted it unanimously. See 28 CONG. Q. ALMANAC 724 (1972). The bill was then quickly adopted by the full House in the fall of 1972. See id. Although Senators William Proxmire (D-Wis.) and Robert Stafford (R-Vt.) initially managed to block the bill in the Senate in 1972, the pro-PAC provision was subsequently attached to a 1973 Senate campaign finance bill. S. 372, 93rd Cong. (1973). An amendment by Senator Proxmire to delete the provision from the bill was defeated on the Senate floor. See 119 CONG. REC. S14845 (1973). The 1973 bill eventually was folded into the 1974 Watergate reform legislation. See Federal Election Campaign Act Amendments of 1974, Pub. L. No. 93-443, 103, 88 Stat. 1267, 1272 (1974).

56. See Hearings on the Federal Election Campaign Act Before the Senate Comm. on Rules and Administration, 99th Cong. 24 (1986) (testimony of Archibald Cox, Chairman, Common Cause and Fred Wertheimer, President, Common Cause).

57. See id. at 34.

58. See id. at 24.

59. See FEC Releases 1993 Mid-Year PAC Count, PRESS RELEASE (Fed. Election Comm'n, Washington, D.C.), Aug. 2, 1993.

presidential elections. In creating two systems for federal elections, one public and the other private, Congress all but guaranteed that private-influence money would come to dominate congressional races. These actions by Congress in 1974 set the stage for the enormous PAC growth and involvement in congressional races that has occurred.

The dependence of House incumbents on PAC contributions has increased dramatically, from 28% of total contributions in 1976[60] to 47% in 1992.[61] In the 1992 elections, 26 House candidates, all incumbents, raised over $ 500,000 each from PACs.[62] Two House members raised more than $ 1 million each from PACs.[63] PACs have also played an increasing role in the financing of senatorial campaigns. In the Senate, 24 incumbents raised more than $ 1 million each from PACs during the 1992 election cycle.[64] On average, incumbent Senators raised approximately $ 1.4 million from PACs in the 1992 elections.[65]

PAC contributions have a special quality. PACs are almost always affiliated with organizations that are engaged in organized, ongoing lobbying activities to influence government decisions, and PAC contributions are an integral part of concerted efforts to influence Congress. As former Senator Rudy Boschwitz (R-Minn.) has said about PACs:

> Our political action committees, those who tend to look at our [Republican] side, look at the whole political process as horse trading. They do not have a philosophy they want to present. They do not have a philosophy they want to defend. They do not have a philosophy they want to further. Their philosophy is winning, to get on the horse that you think will win so that you will have access when he or she does indeed win. That is really the goal of their giving.[66]

While individual contributions, also pose problems as a vehicle for obtaining undue influence, individual contributions, unlike PAC contributions, may or may not come from a contributor who is involved in trying to influence government decisions. This difference is illustrated by the sharp variations in contribution patterns of PACs and individuals. PACs gave to House incumbents over challengers in the 1992 elections, for ex-

---

60. *See* FED. ELECTION COMM'N, FEC DISCLOSURE SERIES NO. 9: 1976 HOUSE OF REPRESENTATIVES CAMPAIGNS RECEIPTS AND EXPENDITURES 8 (1977).

61. *See 1992 House Campaign Financing, supra* note 27, at Chart 1.

62. *See id.* at 45.

63. *See id.* at 1.

64. *See 1992 Senate Campaign Financing, supra* note 23, at 34.

65. *See id.* at Chart 1.

66. 134 CONG. REC. S1132 (daily ed. Feb. 23, 1988) (statement of Sen. Boschwitz).

ample, by a margin of 10.5 to 1,[67] while individual contributions went to House incumbents over challengers by 2.7 to 1.[68]

As mentioned above, PAC contributions flow overwhelmingly to incumbents because they are used to secure access and influence with elected representatives who are currently in a position to make decisions about government policy. Senator George Mitchell (D-Me.) has said:

> Under the current system, incumbents have an overwhelming advantage in raising campaign funds over their challengers. And I say that as an incumbent who is now engaged in that very process. Every political action committee can attest to that. They simply will not give contributions to challengers to run against an incumbent who votes almost every day on legislation affecting the interests of that political action committee.[69]

PAC officials also have acknowledged their preference for incumbents. "Gone were our free-spending days when we poured money into a black hole called 'challenger candidates,'" said Doug Thompson, a former vice president of the National Association of Realtors, which operates one of the largest PACs. "Our marching orders on PAC contributions were very clear: Stop wasting money on losers."[70] The late John Sloan, Jr., when he was president of the National Federation of Independent Business, criticized leaders of some business PACs as "corporate technocrats concerned only about access to a sitting politician and their own short-term bottom line."[71]

The pressures exerted by PAC contributions are magnified when PACs of similar interests join in giving to a candidate. Through their aggregate contributions, PACs are able to bring considerably more pressure on the decision-making process. As former Senator Warren Rudman (R-N.H.) observed when he served in the Senate:

> If we really want to have reform around here, we ought to get the special interests. I call them wolf packs. Sure, the PAC's can only give x amount of dollars, but you can take 10 PAC's who are interested in defense or 10 PAC's interested in energy or 10 PAC's interested in agriculture or 10 PAC's

---

67. *See supra* note 53.

68. *See 1992 Congressional Election Spending Jumps 52% to $ 678 Million*, PRESS RELEASE (Fed. Election Comm'n), Mar. 4, 1993, at 7.

69. 134 CONG. REC. S815 (daily ed. Feb. 17, 1988) (statement of Sen. Mitchell).

70. Richard L. Berke, *PAC's Hear, and Make, Calls for Their Abolition*, N.Y. TIMES, Nov. 21, 1988, at B17 (quoting Doug Thompson).

71. Dale Russakoff, *The Fickle Affections of PACs*, WASH. POST, Jan. 5, 1989, at A23 (quoting John Sloan, Jr.).

interested in trade issues, and put them together and you have $ 100,000 between the primary and the general election.[72]

The savings and loan (S&L) scandal provides a stark example of the price citizens pay for the access and influence that political-influence money buys in Congress.[73] During the 1980s, when savings and loan institutions were engaged in the activities that ultimately led to the biggest American financial scandal since Teapot Dome, S&L interests poured at least $ 11,699,499 in campaign contributions to congressional candidates and political party committees, including $ 6.3 million through PAC's.[74] Despite mounting evidence that the S&L industry was risking billions of dollars in federally insured deposits through questionable business practices, Congress during this period helped to protect the S&L industry from the kind of regulatory control that was needed to safeguard the interests of the American taxpayer.[75] In the end, the American taxpayer had to bail out the S&L industry to the tune of $ 150 billion to $200 billion.[76] During a 1993 debate on the Senate floor over legislation to reform the campaign finance system, Senator John Kerry (D-Mass.) pointed to the S&L debacle in exhorting his colleagues to face up to the urgent need for reform:

> We give away billions of dollars in Washington to people who stand in the corridors outside the Ways and Means Committee and the Finance Committee and work their way. You can go back and look at the savings and loan crisis and see what a Congressman from Rhode Island did in the dead of night, taking $ 40,000 up to $ 100,000, [increasing the amount of deposits federally guaranteed] just to make a few bankers very happy. And now we have the savings and loan crisis for $ 150 billion plus as a consequence...Dark of night; favored legislation; billions of dollars lost to this country because of money, money and politics.[77]

Tony Coelho (D-Cal.), a former Member of Congress who was a major fund-raiser for congressional Democrats in the 1980s and also served as House majority whip, described how PAC contributions affect decision-making in Congress:

---

72. 134 CONG. REC. S1347 (daily ed. Feb. 23, 1988) (statement of Sen. Rudman).

73. *See* 1990 CONG. Q. ALMANAC 7897 (1990).

74. *See It's A Wonderful Life*, COMMON CAUSE NEWS (Common Cause, Washington, D.C.), June 29, 1990, at 1 (on file with the *Columbia Law Review*).

75. *See* Helen Dewar, *Stalemate of Survival*, WASH. POST, Aug. 6, 1992, at A1 (describing the "Keating Five" scandal).

76. *See* Jerry Knight, *$ 45 Billion Sought for Thrift Cleanup*, WASH. POST, Mar. 17, 1993, at C1; *Last Installment for the S&Ls*, WASH. POST, June 28, 1993, at A18.

77. 139 CONG. REC. S6678 (statement of Sen. Kerry).

Take anything. Take housing. Take anything you want. If you are spending all your time calling up different people that you're involved with, that are friends of yours, that you have to raise $ 50,000, you all of a sudden, in your mind, you're in effect saying, "I'm not going to go out and develop this new housing bill that may get the Realtors or may get the builders or may get the unions upset. You know, I've got to raise the $ 50,000; I've got to do that."[78]

Former Senator Proxmire (D-Wis.) made the point that PAC influence does not simply come in terms of votes; it takes more subtle forms as well:

It may not come in a vote. It may come in a speech not delivered. The PAC payoff may come in a colleague not influenced. It may come in a calling off of a meeting that otherwise would result in advancing legislation. It may come in a minor change in one paragraph in a 240-page bill. It may come in a witness, not invited to testify before a committee. It may come in hiring a key staff member for a committee who is sympathetic to the PAC. Or it may come in laying off or transferring a staff member who is unsympathetic to a PAC.[79]

PAC contributions do not guarantee outcomes. PACs do not always win their legislative battles. But it is quite clear that the hundreds of millions of dollars in PAC contributions given to incumbent members of Congress have left their mark on the legislative process and on public confidence in government. PAC contributions are giving special interests undue influence over Congress and fundamentally compromising the credibility of the congressional decision-making process.

D. The Bundling Loophole

These dangers posed by political-influence contributions are magnified by a loophole in the law through which PACs and others with an interest in government decisions have been able to provide contributions to candidates in amounts that greatly exceed the current contribution limits. The loophole, called bundling, works in the following way: a PAC, for example, solicits contributions from its members made out to a particular candidate and then turns over these contributions or otherwise arranges for them to be channeled to that candidate. Because the contributions technically originate with the person who signs the contribution check, the contributions involved do not count toward the $ 5,000 limit[80] on the

---

78. *Senate Comm. on Rules and Administration*, 100th Cong. 12 (1987) (former Rep. Coelho quoted in testimony of Fred Wertheimer, President, Common Cause).

79. 132 CONG. REC. S11, 163 (daily ed. Aug. 11, 1986) (statement of Sen. Proxmire).

80. *See* 2 U.S.C. 441a(a)(2)(A) (1988).

amount the PAC can contribute to a candidate. The PAC, however, gets the credit-and the influence that flows from it-for giving the total amount of bundled contributions to the candidate. Bundling thereby effectively allows the PAC to evade its contribution limits.[81]

The successful use of the bundling loophole by PACs and other political committees has led to blatant evasion of the contribution limits. In one well-known bundling case in the 1980s, the National Republican Senatorial Committee (NRSC) circumvented the limit on contributions by the NRSC to Senate candidates by claiming that the monies it received from donors were "earmarked" for specific candidates. The NRSC made this claim even in cases where the donors' checks were made out to the NRSC and not to any specific candidate, and even though individual donors in later interviews denied having earmarked their checks. By the month before the 1986 elections, the NRSC had provided a total of more than $ 6 million to 1986 candidates in bundled contributions.[82] Defense-related PACs and arms control groups have both used the bundling loophole to deliver-and to get political credit for-contributions far in excess of their PAC contribution limit.[83] So too have groups that focus on women's issues. EMILY's List, for example, a PAC that contributes to pro-choice Democratic women, used the bundling loophole to become the largest House and Senate PAC contributor in 1992, reportedly bundling some $ 6 million to congressional candidates.[84]

Bundling by PACs is a relatively new phenomenon that did not become a serious problem until the 1980s. Because much of the bundling that occurs is undisclosed and hidden from public view, it is difficult to provide reliable statistics on the amount of money being turned over to candidates in bundled contributions. It is clear, however, from both published newspaper reports and disclosure by some PACs, that bundling has become an increasingly widespread practice by both PACs and lobbyists.[85] The bundling loophole poses a serious threat to the integrity of existing federal

---

81. In the mid-1980s, for example, an insurance PAC made a $ 1000 contribution to a Member of Congress. It also provided the Member with $ 215,000 in bundled contributions raised by the PAC that did not count against the PAC's $ 5000 per election contribution limit. *See* Brooks Jackson, *Insurance Industry Boosts Political Contributions as Congress Takes Up Cherished Tax Preferences*, WALL ST. J., Oct. 10, 1985, at 64.

82. *See* Thomas B. Edsall, *Campaign Skirts Rules By "Bundling' Contributions*, WASH. POST, Oct. 20, 1986, at A8.

83. *See* Top Guns, COMMON CAUSE NEWS (Common Cause, Washington, D.C.), Aug. 29, 1987, at 34 (on file with the *Columbia Law Review*); Maxwell Glenn, *Focus on Fund Raising*, NAT'L J., at 2799 (1985).

84. *See* Helen Dewar, *EMILY's List Falls Prey to PAC Hunt*, WASH. POST, Mar. 7, 1993, at C1.

85. *See* Helen Dewar, *Stalemate of Survival*, WASH. POST, Aug. 6, 1992, at A1.

contribution limits and the ability of these limits to protect the political system from potential corruption as a result of large political contributions.

Faulty Assumptions and Undemocratic Consequences of Campaign Finance Reform

Bradley A. Smith

Very few aspects of American politics fit the metaphor of Plato's cave better than the realities of American campaign finance.[1]

I. Introduction

Over the past twenty-five years, efforts to reform the campaign finance system have been exceptionally popular with both the general public[2] and legal academics,[3] and few commentators have argued against the need for some kind of reform. Most reformers have attempted to limit alleged political "corruption" and to promote a brand of political equality. Taking an instrumentalist view of the First Amendment, they have chafed at the

---

1. Frank J. Sorauf, Inside Campaign Finance 26 (1992).

2. For examples of reform advocacy outside legal circles, see Elizabeth Drew, Politics and Money: The New Road to Corruption (1983); Philip M. Stern, The Best Congress Money Can Buy (1988). Over 400 newspapers editorialized in favor of campaign finance reform in 1988. Herbert E. Alexander & Monica Bauer, Financing the 1988 Election 113 (1991). In the 1994 elections, Missouri, Montana, and Oregon passed referenda limiting contributions in support of state legislative candidates to just $ 100. A similar measure passed in Washington, D.C., in 1992. See Alversie Mitchell & Doug Funderburk, We Must Finish Campaign Finance Overhaul, Kansas City Star, Apr. 14, 1995, at C7. However, voters in Colorado defeated a similar proposal. See id.

3. See, e.g., Daniel H. Lowenstein, On Campaign Finance Reform: The Root of All Evil Is Deeply Rooted, 18 Hofstra L. Rev. 301, 348-60 (1989); Marlene A. Nicholson, Continuing the Dialogue on Campaign Finance Reform: A Response to Roy Schotland, 21 Cap. U. L. Rev. 463, 471-82 (1992); Fred Wertheimer & Randy Huwa, Campaign Finance Reforms: Past Accomplishments, Future Challenges, 10 N.Y.U. Rev. L. & Soc. Change 43 (1980-81); Fred Wertheimer & Susan W. Manes, Campaign Finance Reform: A Key to Restoring the Health of Our Democracy, 94 Colum. L. Rev. 1126, 1149-57 (1994). This is but the tip of an enormous iceberg of legal literature urging restrictions on campaign spending, contributions, or both.

more libertarian First Amendment approach to campaign finance taken by the Supreme Court in Buckley v. Valeo.[4]

This Essay argues that reform scholarship has erred in its assumptions about the causes and effects of political corruption. It challenges the basic assumptions of campaign finance reform advocates, rather than the mechanics or structure of regulation. Further, this Essay argues that it is actually campaign finance regulation that is in conflict with accepted notions of equality, so much so as to be broadly characterized as undemocratic. Regulatory reform efforts thus fail to accomplish even those goals that, under the reformers' instrumentalist First Amendment theory, justify limitations on speech. Beyond asserting the failure of the reformers' program on their own terms, this Essay argues that First Amendment protection, applied unflinchingly to political activity such as campaign contributions and spending, is not a barrier to greater political equality or to the rooting out of corruption, but is a considered instrumentalist response to these problems.

The longstanding agenda of the campaign finance reform movement has been to lower the cost of campaigning, reduce the influence of special interests in both elections and the legislative process, and open up the political system to change.[5] Reformers have sought to accomplish this primarily through campaign contribution and expenditure limits and, ultimately, through public funding of political campaigns. In 1974, the reform movement seemed to achieve its greatest victory with the passage of major amendments to the Federal Elections Campaign Act (FECA).[6] Many FECA provisions were soon echoed in state legislation around much of the nation.[7] Yet the reformist agenda remained unfulfilled. Between 1977 and 1992, congressional campaign spending increased by

---

4. 424 U.S. 1 (1976) (per curiam). For examples of this instrumentalist view, *see, e.g.,* J. Skelly Wright, *Money and the Pollution of Politics: Is the First Amendment an Obstacle to Political Equality?*, 82 COLUM. L. REV. 609, 625-42 (1982). For an example of a broader instrumentalist view, *see* Owen M. Fiss, *Free Speech and Social Structure*, 71 IOWA L. REV. 1405 (1986).

5. Frank J. Sorauf, *Politics, Experience, and the First Amendment: The Case of American Campaign Finance*, 94 COLUM. L. REV. 1348, 1357 (1994); Wertheimer & Huwa, *supra* note 3, at 45.

6. Wertheimer & Huwa, *supra* note 3, at 45.

7. Many of FECA's provisions, however, were quickly declared unconstitutional by the Supreme Court in *Buckley v. Valeo*, 424 U.S. 1 (1976) (per curiam). *See infra* notes 45-46 and accompanying text. Reform advocates have, with some justification, argued that *Buckley's* elimination of some of FECA's most important provisions explains the apparent failure of reform efforts. I will attempt to show that, even apart from the *Buckley* Court's holding, FECA was inherently flawed.

347%.[8] Congressional election contributions by political action committees (PACs) increased from $ 20.5 million in 1976[9] to $ 189 million in
1994.[10] Since 1974, the number of federal PACs has increased from 608[11]
to over 4500.[12] House incumbents, who in 1976 outspent challengers by a
ratio of 1.5 to 1, in 1992 outspent challengers by almost 4 to 1.[13]
Meanwhile, incumbent reelection rates reached record highs in the House
in 1984 and 1988, before declining slightly in the 1990s.[14]

Despite the apparent failings of the 1974 FECA amendments, critics of
reform measures have generally accepted, at least on a theoretical level,
that reform can accomplish its goals.[15] Rather, their objections to reform
have focused either on the First Amendment,[16] or on the difficulty of controlling for "unintended consequences."[17]

---

8. *Spending Explodes Since Reform*, CAMPAIGNS & ELECTIONS, June-July 1993, at
1, 1. However, spending did level off, and even declined in terms of inflation-adjusted dollars, in the late 1980s. *See* David S. Broder, *Campaign Finance Farce*, WASH. POST, May
3, 1992, at C7.

9. Frank J. Sorauf, *Political Parties and Political Action Committees: Two Life
Cycles*, 22 ARIZ. L. REV. 445, 451 (1980).

10. *Final Tabulations: PACs Contributed $ 189.4 Million to Congressional Candi-
dates During 1993-94 Election Cycle*, POL. FIN. & LOBBY REP., Apr. 12, 1995, at 1,1.

11. Wertheimer & Huwa, *supra* note 3, at 48.

12. A. Martin Willis, *Penniless PACs: Why Do They Bother to Exist?*, POL. FIN. &
LOBBY REP., Nov. 9, 1994, at 1, 3 (indicating number of PACs filing Federal Election
Commission (FEC) reports in first 18 months of election cycle).

13. Wertheimer & Manes, *supra* note 3, at 1133.

14. Cass R. Sunstein, *Political Equality and Unintended Consequences*, 94 COLUM.
L. REV. 1390, 1402 tbl. 2 (1994).

15. *See, e.g.*, Lillian R. BeVier, *Money and Politics: A Perspective on the First Amendment and Campaign Finance Reform*, 73 CAL. L. REV. 1045 (1985). Professor BeVier
finds reformists' legal arguments lacking under traditional First Amendment analysis.
However, BeVier admits that she "has deliberately not addressed what is of course the
most profound issue: whether political freedom as we have known it can in principle be
reconciled with active legislative pursuit of equality of political influence." *Id.* at 1090.

16. *See, e.g.*, BeVier, *supra* note 15; Richard A. Epstein, *Property, Speech, and the Politics of Distrust*, *in* THE BILL OF RIGHTS IN THE MODERN STATE 41 (Geoffrey R. Stone et
al. eds., 1992) (invoking concepts of natural rights and property rights as well as speech
rights in opposition to regulation of campaign finance); Daniel D. Polsby, Buckley v.
Valeo: *The Special Nature of Political Speech*, 1976 SUP. CT. REV. 1 (arguing that campaign contributions should be considered speech entitled to full First Amendment protection).

17. *See, e.g.*, Michael J. Malbin, *Looking Back at the Future of Campaign Finance
Reform: Interest Groups and American Elections*, *in* MONEY AND POLITICS IN THE UNIT-
ED STATES: FINANCING ELECTIONS IN THE 1980s 232, 232 (Michael J. Malbin ed., 1984);
Roy A. Schotland, *Proposals for Campaign Finance Reform: An Article Dedicated to*

However, the problem with campaign finance reform is not merely unanticipated consequences; rather, at their core, reform efforts are based on faulty assumptions and are, in fact, irretrievably flawed.[18] Reform proposals inherently favor certain political elites, support the status quo, and discourage grassroots political activity. Even if these proposals worked as intended, they would have an undemocratic effect on American elections.

* * *

III. Faulty Assumptions of Campaign Finance Reformers

Four general assumptions underlie the arguments made in favor of campaign finance regulation: First, there is too much money being spent in political campaigns;[58] second, campaigns based on small contributions are, in some sense, more democratic, more in touch with the "people," than campaigns financed through large contributions;[59] third, money buys elections, presumably in a manner detrimental to the public good;[60] and fourth, money is a corrupting influence on the legislature.[61] Given these assumptions, it is believed that the end result of an unregulated finance

---

Being Less Dull Than Its Title, 21 CAP. U. L. REV. 429, 436-37 (1992); Sunstein, *supra* note 14, at 1390. Schotland and Sunstein generally support reform efforts, but argue that reformers have not been sensitive enough to manipulation of reform by incumbents, *see* Schotland, *supra,* at 443; Sunstein, *supra* note 14, at 1400, and the possibility that campaign finance laws might be circumvented, *see id.* at 1403-11. Stephen Gottlieb, whose critique comes closest to my own, expresses broad concern that reformers have promoted major changes in our democratic processes without a solid understanding of the empirical results of proposed reforms. *See* Stephen E. Gottlieb, *The Dilemma of Election Campaign Finance Reform,* 18 HOFSTRA L. REV. 213, 213-14 (1989). He suggests that there is simply no way to define in advance the resources that any group deserves, and that all proposals to limit spending and contributions will therefore produce unintended consequences that are often detrimental, "both to the goals of the reformers and the values traditionally cherished in first amendment jurisprudence." *Id.* at 214-16.

18. This Essay will focus primarily on the regulation of federal campaigns, recognizing that many states have adopted similar regulatory schemes with similar negative effects. These state laws share the assumptions and basic structure of the federal regime. For a brief summary of state regulation, *see* FRANK SORAUF, MONEY IN AMERICAN ELECTIONS 285-90 (1988).
    * * *
58. *See* JOHN W. GARDNER, IN COMMON CAUSE 38, 56 (1972).
59. *See id.* at 55.
60. *Cf. id.* at 38-39 (arguing that candidates must appeal to monied interests).
61. *See id.* at 41-42.

system will be a political process increasingly dominated by wealthy individuals whose interests are at odds with those of ordinary citizens.[62] But are these assumptions warranted? This part of the Essay will examine each of them in turn and conclude that each one is seriously flawed.

A. Assumption One: Too Much Money is Spent on Campaigns

One often hears that too much money is spent on political campaigns.[63] The language in which campaigns are described in the general

---

62. See DREW, *supra* note 2, at 5; Sunstein, *supra* note 14, at 1392-93; Wertheimer & Manes, *supra* note 3, at 1126-27.

63. *See, e.g.,* Schotland, *supra* note 17, at 443. This view is certainly popular among the general public. One recent poll found that 90% of respondents agreed with the proposition that "'there's way too much money in politics.'" Terry Ganey, *To Campaign Finance Reform Advocates, the Webster Scandal Was Proof Positive Proposition A Would Limit Donations, Aiming to Cut Big Money's Political Role,* St. Louis Post Dispatch, Oct. 23, 1994, at 1B. I poll my students on the first day of my election law class, and have found that approximately 75% will "agree" or "strongly agree" with the statement, "Too much money is spent on political campaigns."

Nevertheless, Professor Nicholson agrees that spending on campaigns is not excessive and suggests that such an argument is a "non-battle....No thoughtful student of campaign finance will dispute....this point, despite the fact that demagogues may occasionally still argue to the contrary." Nicholson, *supra* note 3, at 473; *see also* Lowenstein, supra note 3, at 350 (arguing that restricting PAC contributions would require replacement source of revenue). However, as Professor Nicholson also notes, "reform proposals designed by Democrats in Congress routinely include overall expenditure limitations." Nicholson, *supra* note 3, at 473. While Nicholson may be convinced that we do not spend too much on campaigns, many reformers are not. *See, e.g.,* Debra Burke, *Twenty Years After the Federal Election Campaign Act Amendments of 1974: Look Who's Running Now,* 99 Dick. L. Rev. 357, 375-76 (1995); Wertheimer & Manes, *supra* note 3, at 1132-33; Kenneth J. Levit, Note, *Campaign Finance Reform and the Return of* Buckley v. Valeo, 103 Yale L.J. 469, 473 (1993) ("[*Buckley*] ignored the role excessive campaign spending plays in compromising the electorate's confidence in the democratic process."); *see also* Sorauf, *supra* note 5, at 1357 ("[A] consensus agenda for mainstream reform... includes...a reduction in the total sums being raised and spent on contemporary campaigns....").

Furthermore, even reformers such as Nicholson tend to favor contribution limits. As Professor Lowenstein has discussed, such limits, set low enough, will have the effect of restricting overall spending. *See* Daniel H. Lowenstein, *A Patternless Mosaic: Campaign Finance and the First Amendment After* Austin, 21 Cap. U. L. Rev. 381, 399-401 (1992). Most reform proposals include contribution limits. And Professor Nicholson herself is ready to accept overall spending limits as part of a reform package. *See* Nicholson, *supra* note 3, at 475.

press constantly reinforces that perception. Candidates "amass war chests" with the help of "special interests" that "pour" their "millions" into campaigns. "Obscene" expenditures "career" out of control or "sky-rocket" upwards.[64] This language notwithstanding, there is actually good cause to believe that we do not spend enough on campaigns.

The assertion that too much money is spent on campaigning essentially begs the question: Compared to what? Compared to yogurt or potato chips? Americans spend more than twice as much money each year on yo-gurt,[65] and two to three times as much on the purchase of potato chips,[66] as they do on political campaigns. In the two-year election cycle culminat-ing in the elections of November 1994, approximately $ 590 million was spent by all congressional general-election candidates combined.[67] Although this set a new record for spending in congressional races, the amount is hardly exorbitant, amounting to roughly $ 3 per eligible voter spent over the two-year period between elections. Total direct campaign spending for all local, state, and federal elections, including congressional elections, over the same period can be reasonably estimated as between $ 1.5 and $ 2.0 billion, or somewhere between $ 7.50 and $ 10 per eligible voter over the two-year cycle.[68] When one considers that this per-voter fig-

---

Thus, less careful reformers and much of the public believe that too much is spent; more thoughtful reformers may not believe that too much is spent, but they see little harm in further restricting spending. Either way, the assumption is incorrect.

64. *See, e.g.,* SORAUF, *supra* note 1, at 26; Wertheimer & Manes, *supra* note 3, at 1132-33.

65. *See* George F. Will, *So We Talk Too Much,* NEWSWEEK, June 28, 1993, at 68, 68 (observing that total cost of 1992 congressional races equaled 40% of what Americans spent on yogurt that year).

66. Clare Ansberry, *The Best Beef Jerky Has Characteristics Few Can Appreciate,* WALL ST. J., Apr. 4, 1995, at A1, A12 (noting annual spending on potato chips in excess of $ 4.5 billion).

67. *Post-election Reports Point to New Records,* POL. FIN. & LOBBY REP., Dec. 28, 1994, at 1, 1 [hereinafter Post-election Reports]. This only includes total spending by vic-torious primary candidates. An additional $ 76 million was spent by losing primary elec-tion candidates. *Id.* at 5.

68. Herbert Alexander and Anthony Corrado estimate total direct spending on all local, state, and federal campaigns for the 1991-92 cycle (not including ballot issues and the presidential campaign) at $ 1.543 billion. DANIEL H. LOWENSTEIN, ELECTION LAW: CASES AND MATERIALS 478 (1995) (citing HERBERT E. ALEXANDER & ANTHONY CORRA-DO, FINANCING THE 1992 ELECTION (1995)). Approximately $ 950 million is spent on party organization and administration and political action committee overhead. *Id.* at 477-78. Spending on congressional races increased by roughly 17% from the 1991-92 to the 1993-94 cycle. *Post-election Reports, supra* note 67, at 1, 5. Applying a similar rate of increase to Alexander and Corrado's figures for state and local races in 1991-92, total

ure is spread over several candidates for which that voter is eligible to cast a ballot, it is hard to suggest that office seekers are spending "obscene" sums attempting to get their messages through to voters.

Comparisons to levels of corporate spending on product advertising help to illustrate that spending on political campaigns is minimal. The sum of the annual advertising budgets of Procter & Gamble and Philip Morris Company, the nation's two largest advertisers, is roughly equal to the amount spent by all federal and state political candidates and parties in a two-year election cycle.[69] The value of such comparisons can be disputed: If one views the problem as the allegedly corrupting effect of campaign money, then the suggestion that it may take less to buy politicians than to sell soap and tobacco provides little comfort. But such numbers are useful to put political spending into perspective when it is the raw levels of spending that are challenged, and to consider the probable effect on political communication of reform measures that would limit spending.[70]

---

direct campaign spending at all levels in 1993-94 would have been approximately $ 1.8 billion.

In recent years, the reform literature has expressed growing concern about "soft money" in campaigns. *See, e.g.,* Wertheimer & Manes, *supra* note 3, at 1144-48 (arguing that "soft money" threatens integrity of presidential and congressional campaigns). In fact, "soft money" is a small part of total spending, approximately $ 83 million in 1991-92, or about 4.5% of the amount of direct spending. Marty Jezer & Ellen Miller, *Money Politics: Campaign Finance and the Subversion of American Democracy,* 8 Notre Dame J. L. Ethics & Pub. Pol'y 467, 489-90 (1994) (citing Joshua Goldstein, Soft Money, Real Dollars: Soft Money in the 1992 Elections 3-4 (1993)). The arguments against soft money are the same as those against direct contributions (though one additional criticism applicable to soft money and not to other types of contributions is the absence of reporting requirements for soft money, *see* Wertheimer & Manes, *supra* note 3, at 1144-45), and therefore do not change the terms of the debate. In fact, soft money actually has several advantages over direct contributions. To the extent reformers are concerned about the potential corrupting effects of campaign contributions, soft money, which is given to the parties, should ameliorate that perceived problem. It allows parties to channel their funds into competitive races and do generic party advertising, which may be beneficial for electoral competition, *cf.* Lowenstein, *supra* note 3, at 354-55 (arguing that generic party advertising has potential to move political system toward responsible party government), and it may increase party discipline by making candidates more reliant on their parties, which many political scientists view as a good thing, *see, e.g.,* Leon D. Epstein, Political Parties in the American Mold 3 (1986) (noting that most observers view parties as "organizationally desirable and probably essential in a democratic nation").

69. Schotland, *supra* note 17, at 444 (using 1987-88 data).

70. Also, one can have a lot of fun with such numbers. For example, Sony Music International will spend some $ 30 million, or about the cost of Michael Huffington's 1994 U.S. Senate campaign, to promote a Michael Jackson CD with the lyrics, "'Jew me, sue

Increased campaign spending translates into a better-informed electorate. Gary Jacobson's extensive studies have shown that "the extent and
content of information [voters]...have has a decisive effect on how they
vote."[71] Voters' understanding of issues increases with the quantity of
campaign information received.[72] In short, spending less on campaigns
will result in less public awareness and understanding of issues.

Accepting the premise that too much money is not being spent in absolute terms, one searches for an explanation as to why the public perception differs from the reality. It may be fairly suggested that the perception
stems from a belief that what money is spent is largely ineffective or even
destructive. In other words, the perceived problem, on closer examination, may not be that too much is spent, but that too little benefit is received in return. In particular, high spending has been linked to many voters' disgust with what is perceived as the relentless negativity of modern,
televised campaign advertisements.[73]

---

me, everybody do me, kick me, Kike me, don't you black or white me.'" *See Sony's States-
manship*, WALL ST. J., June 20, 1995, at A18. Or one can cite the $ 100 million, more
than the cost of a presidential campaign, being spent in 1995 to promote reruns of the situation comedy, "Seinfeld." *See* Roxanne Roberts, *The Remote Controllers; Meet the
Folks Who Keep You Tuned to Their Show*, WASH. POST, June 10, 1995, at B1.

71. GARY C. JACOBSON, MONEY IN CONGRESSIONAL ELECTIONS 31 (1980).

72. Gottlieb, *supra* note 17, at 266; *see also* Wertheimer & Huwa, *supra* note 3, at 58
(noting that greater use of television advertising increases electorate's knowledge about
candidates and issues and stimulates interest in campaign) (citing Charles Atkin & Gary
Heald, *Effects of Political Advertising*, 40 PUB. OPINION Q. 216, 228 (1976)). Kentucky
officials reported a sharp decline in voter turnout and interest in the 1995 gubernatorial
primaries, the first state election after the state passed legislation that reduced campaign
spending in 1994. John Harwood, *Kentucky's New Campaign-Finance Law Limits
Donations as Well as Interest in Governor's Race*, WALL ST. J., Oct. 5, 1995, at A16.
However, turnout in the November 1995 general election was approximately 44%,
about the same as in 1991. Al Cross, *Final Tally Trims Patton's Edge*, COURIER-JOURNAL
(Louisville), Nov. 28, 1995, at 3B.

73. *See, e.g.*, Wertheimer & Manes, *supra* note 3, at 1130-31 (quoting former Senate
Majority Leader George Mitchell on campaign finance reform: "[Americans] see a cam-
paign finance system that places tremendous money demands on those who run...and a
system dominated by negative campaigns.'"); Peter F. May, Note, *State Regulation of
Political Broadcast Advertising: Stemming the Tide of Deceptive Negative Attacks*, 72
B.U. L. REV. 179, 187-89 (1992). This perception may itself be influenced by press reporting and editorials critical of campaign advertising. *See, e.g.*, John Balzar & Doug Conner,
With Foley, Noble Era Will End, L.A. TIMES, Nov. 10, 1994, at A1, A17 (asserting that
negative ads, along with special interest intrusion, constitute "the dark streak of American
campaign politics"); Stuart Elliott, *Ketchum Protests Political Ads*, N.Y. TIMES, Nov. 10,
1994, at D23 (quoting advertising executive as saying negative ads are "political filth that
is not advertising and shouldn't be dignified by being called advertising'"); Charles

However, efforts to limit spending on campaigns-either directly, through spending limits, or indirectly, through contribution limits-bear no relationship to the negativity of the campaign, and may actually cause an increase in unfair, negative campaigning. Less spending only reduces the amount of communication; it does not mitigate any negative tone that the communication might have. This reduction in the flow of information would tend to make well-produced negative advertising more valuable, as candidates will need to get the maximum political mileage from each expenditure, and as a poorly informed electorate may be more susceptible to misleading political advertisements. More perniciously, candidates who have reached a spending limit, or who cannot tap proven supporters to raise additional funds, may be unable to respond to late, unfair, negative assaults.

Moreover, it is a mistake to assume that the elimination of negative campaigning would necessarily serve the public. Negative advertising that is relevant to the issues can increase public awareness in a positive way. Bruce Felknor notes that without negative campaigning aimed at underscoring an opponent's bad side, "any knave or mountebank in the land may lie and steal his or her way into the White House or any other elective office."[74] He thus distinguishes between "fair" and "unfair" campaigning, based on truth and relevance.[75] To suggest that candidates should not point to each other's perceived shortcomings, writes Felknor, is "preposterous."[76]

There are no objective criteria by which to measure whether "too much" is spent on political campaigns. What is spent on campaigns, one might fairly suggest, is the amount that individuals feel it is worthwhile to contribute and that candidates find it is effective to raise and spend. Considering the importance of elections to any democratic society, it is

---

Krauthammer, *Political Suicide*, WASH. POST, Oct. 28, 1994, at A27 (characterizing political advertising as "virulent, scurrilous, wall-to-wall character assassination"); Robin Toner, *Bitter Tone of the "94 Campaign Elicits Worry on Public Debate*, N.Y. TIMES, Nov. 13, 1994, at A1 (discussing negative tone of 1994 campaign). But whether modern, televised campaign advertising is overly negative may simply be a matter of individual voter preference. Negative advertising is popular for a simple reason: It works. Indeed, as Bruce Felknor, former Executive Director of the Fair Campaign Practices Committee, has stated, "without attention-grabbing, cogent, memorable, negative campaigning, almost no challenger can hope to win unless the incumbent has just been found guilty of a heinous crime." BRUCE L. FELKNOR, POLITICAL MISCHIEF: SMEAR, SABOTAGE, AND REFORM IN THE U.S. ELECTIONS 29 (1992).

74. Felknor, *supra* note 73, at 29.
75. *Id.* at 30.
76. *Id.* at 29.

hard to believe that direct expenditures of approximately $ 10 per voter for all local, state, and national campaigns, over a two-year period, constitutes a crisis requiring limitations on spending.

B. Assumption Two: Campaigns Funded with Small Contributions are More Democratic

Within the reform movement lies a deep-rooted belief that democratic political campaigns should be financed by small contributions.[77] This position is motivated by the belief that large contributions corrupt either or both the electoral and legislative systems. Such a belief suggests that a campaign funded through small contributions will in the end lead to less corruption. However, small contributions are often seen as an end in themselves, on the notion that even if money were not corrupting, small contributions epitomize the American belief in self-government and participatory democracy.[78] This notion of the campaign funded through small contributions as the embodiment of representative democracy is unrealistic.

First, this vision appears to be based on an idealized image of democratic politics. As shown in Part II, the burden of financing political campaigns has always fallen on a small minority of the American public. Today, as many as eighteen million Americans make some financial contribution to a political party, candidate, or PAC in a given election cycle.[79] "No other system of campaign funding anywhere in the world enjoys so broad a base of support."[80] Yet this "broad base of support" amounts to only some 10% of the voting-age population.[81] With the exception of the

---

77. *See* Sorauf, *supra* note 5, at 1356.

78. *Id.*

79. SORAUF, *supra* note 1, at 29 (citing data from University of Michigan National Election Study of 1988 election). PACs are widely assailed as the ultimate villains in the reformers' frame of reality. *See, e.g.*, Wertheimer & Huwa, *supra* note 3, at 48-53; Wertheimer & Manes, *supra* note 3, at 1136-40. In fact, PACs are nothing more than an agglomeration of small contributors, many of whom might not contribute to politics absent PAC solicitation. To the extent that reformers truly believe that campaigns should be funded by small contributions, therefore, PACs ought to be viewed as a positive force. *Cf.* LARRY J. SABATO, PAYING FOR ELECTIONS 19–22 (1989) (arguing against limits on PAC donations).

80. SORAUF, *supra* note 1, at 30.

81. *Id.* at 29 (citing data from University of Michigan National Election Study of 1988 election). This figure has been quite stable for three decades. *See generally* Ruth S. Jones, *Contributing as Participation, in* MONEY, ELECTIONS, AND DEMOCRACY 27 (Margaret L. Nugent & John R. Johannes eds., 1990) (observing that typically 10-12% percent of electorate donates to campaigns).

occasional race with a candidate who can whip up an ideological fervor on the fringe of mainstream politics, such as George McGovern or Oliver North, Americans are simply unwilling, individually, to contribute enough money in small amounts to run modern campaigns.[82]

It is a mistake to assume that a broad base of contributors necessarily makes a campaign in some way more representative or more attuned to the popular will. Though the eighteen million who contribute to campaigns constitute a far broader base of financial contributors than existed in the eighteenth and nineteenth centuries, few would argue that this has made the political system more democratic or more responsive.[83] Indeed, it is an article of faith in reformist literature that our system has grown less responsive to popular will in the last century. In fact, however, those candidates who have been best able to raise campaign dollars in small contributions have often been those who were most emphatically out of the mainstream of their time. Barry Goldwater's 1964 presidential campaign, for example, raised $ 5.8 million from 410,000 small contributors, before going down in a landslide defeat.[84] On his way to an even more crushing defeat in 1972, George McGovern raised almost $ 15 million from small donors, at an average of approximately $ 20 per contributor.[85] And if we assume that reliance on numerous small contributions makes a campaign in some way more "democratic," then the most "democratic" campaign of 1994 was the U.S. Senate campaign of Oliver North. North raised approximately $ 20 million, almost entirely from small contributors, and actually outspent his nearest rival by nearly 4 to 1.[86] Yet he still lost to an unpopular opponent plagued by personal scandal.[87] All of these campaigns were among the most prominent extremist candidacies in recent decades. This suggests that the ability to raise large sums in small

---

82. *See* Lowenstein, *supra* note 3, at 348 (citing Gary Jacobson, *Party Organization and Distribution of Congressional Resources: Republicans and Democrats in 1982*, 100 Am. Pol. Sci. Q. 603, 610 (1985-86)).

83. *Cf.* Wertheimer & Manes, *supra* note 3, at 1129-30 (citing polling data indicating public distrust of politicians).

84. Sorauf, *supra* note 1, at 4.

85. *Id.* Segregationist George Wallace was another prominent figure who raised large sums in small amounts: $ 5.8 million in contributions under $ 100 in his 1968 presidential run. *Id.*

86. It is interesting to note that despite his reliance on small donations from a large donor base, North was roundly castigated by many campaign finance reformers for the high cost of his campaign. *See, e.g., High-cost Campaigns*, St. Petersburg Times, Nov. 14, 1994, at 8A; Richard Roeper, *Hofeld War Chest Filled With Lost Opportunity*, Chicago Sun-Times, Nov. 9, 1994, at 9.

87. *See* Michael J. Malbin, *Most GOP Winners Spent Enough Money to Reach Voters*, Pol. Fin. & Lobby Rep., Jan. 11, 1995, at 8, 9.

amounts is a sign of fervent backing from a relatively small minority, rather than a sign of broad public support. At the same time, truly mass-based political movements have historically relied on a relatively small number of large contributors for "seed money," if not for the bulk of their funding.[88]

Campaign finance reform efforts tend to overlook the significant collective action problem that prevents most voters from giving financially to candidates. Even if large contributions were totally banned, thereby increasing the relative importance of small contributions, no single contribution would be likely to have a significant impact on an election.[89] Voters, therefore, still have little rational incentive to make contributions. This collective action problem may be overcome by a radical campaign in which donors are motivated by ideology rather than rational, utility-maximizing calculations. However, in most instances, there will not be sufficient funds available to finance campaigns at a level that informs the electorate unless a resort is made to public funds.[90] Thus, a system of private campaign finance will almost inevitably come to rely on large individual donors who believe that their substantial gift can make a difference, and on interest groups (i.e., PACs) that overcome voter inertia by organizing voters to address particular concerns.[91]

C. Assumption Three: Money Buys Elections

The third assumption of campaign finance reform is that money "buys" elections in some manner incompatible with a functioning democracy.[92] It seems axiomatic that a candidate with little or no money to

---

88. *See* Gottlieb, *supra* note 17, at 220-21; *see also infra* notes 144-46 and accompanying text. Thayer notes how such progressive turn-of-the-century candidates as Woodrow Wilson, Robert LaFollette, William Jennings Bryan, and Hiram Johnson (who was elected on the slogan "Kick the corporations out of politics") were financed by a small number of wealthy supporters. GEORGE THAYER, WHO SHAKES THE MONEY TREE? 54–57 (1973). Ross Perot has recently announced his intention to create a new mass party, which will presumably rely on his millions to get started.

89. *Cf.* Lillian R. BeVier, *Campaign Finance Reform: Specious Arguments, Intractable Dilemmas*, 94 COLUM. L. REV. 1258, 1274 (1994) (noting that "pervasive collective action problems" discourage Americans from following politics closely).

90. *See* Lowenstein, *supra* note 3, at 350.

91. BeVier, *supra* note 89, at 1274-75.

92. Within the reformist literature, there is some disagreement over the importance of this issue. Professor Lowenstein, for one, seems relatively comfortable with large monetary contributions made as part of an "electoral" strategy—that is, with the hope of electing sympathizers to office. *See* Lowenstein, *supra* note 3, at 308-13. His primary concern is with contributors pursuing a "legislative" strategy, i.e., seeking to influence, rather than to elect, a legislator. *See id.; see also* Daniel H. Lowenstein, *Political Bribery and the Inter-*

spend is unlikely to win most races. Furthermore, the candidate who spends more money wins more often than not.[93] But correlation is not the same as cause and effect, and one must be careful not to make too much of such simple numbers. The correlation between spending and victory may stem simply from the desire of donors to contribute to candidates who are likely to win, in which case the ability to win attracts money, rather than the other way around.[94] Similarly, higher levels of campaign contributions to, and spending by, a candidate may merely reflect a level of public support that is later manifested at the polls.[95] Generally speaking, the same attributes that attract voters to a candidate will attract donations, and those that attract donations will attract voters.[96] In other words, the candidate who is able to raise more money would usually win even if that candidate could not spend the added money: The ability to raise money is evidence of political prowess and popularity that would normally translate into votes, regardless of spending.[97]

At the same time, higher spending does not necessarily translate into electoral triumph. As Michael Malbin puts it, "Having money means having the ability to be heard; it does not mean the voters will like what they hear."[98] One need only look at recent elections to prove his point. In the 1994 U.S. House elections, for example, many incumbents won while

---

mediate Theory of Politics, 32 UCLA L. REV. 784, 791-95 (1985). Others seem equally or more concerned with the idea of "buying elections" and with the importance of voter equality. See, e.g., David A. Strauss, Corruption, Equality, and Campaign Finance Reform, 94 COLUM. L. REV. 1369, 1371-82 (1994); Sunstein, supra note 14, at 1392. Reformers whose primary goal is to reduce the allegedly improper influence of contributions on legislative decisionmaking will be less worried about efforts to elect a candidate who agrees, in principle, with the donor. By contrast, reformers who see equality as the fundamental goal of campaign finance reform will be concerned with efforts to "buy" elections. As Professor Lowenstein notes, equality is an issue that appeals to most political liberals but has little appeal to many conservatives, whereas the potentially corrupting influence of money is generally frowned upon by observers of all political stripes. See Lowenstein, supra note 3, at 346.

93. See HERBERT E. ALEXANDER, FINANCING POLITICS: MONEY, ELECTIONS, AND POLITICAL REFORM 20 (3d ed. 1984).

94. See STEPHANIE D. MOUSSALLI, CAMPAIGN FINANCE REFORM: THE CASE FOR DEREGULATION 4 (1990); Gary C. Jacobson, Money in the 1980 and 1982 Congressional Elections, in MONEY AND POLITICS IN THE UNITED STATES: FINANCING ELECTIONS IN THE 1980s, supra note 17, at 38, 57.

95. Moussalli, supra note 94, at 4.

96. See Gary C. Jacobson, The Effects of Campaign Spending in House Elections: New Evidence for Old Arguments, 34 AM. J. POL. SCI. 334, 342-43 (1990).

97. SORAUF, supra note 18, at 161-64.

98. Malbin, supra note 87, at 9.

spending considerably less than their opponents.[99] More pointedly, the thirty-four Republican challengers who defeated Democratic incumbents spent, on average, only two-thirds of the amounts expended by their opponents,[100] and one spent less than one-twentieth as much as did his incumbent opponent.[101] Given the inherent advantages of incumbency, this is powerful evidence that a monetary advantage alone does not mean electoral success.

In support of the assumption that money buys elections, some commentators have recently expressed concern about the "war chest mentality," the tendency of incumbents to amass large campaign funds well in advance of a race in order to scare off challengers.[102] Recent research by economists Philip Hersch and Gerald McDougall has found that a large incumbent war chest does indeed correlate with a lower likelihood of a serious challenge in U.S. House races.[103]

On closer examination, however, the war-chest argument is merely a variation on the basic assumption that money is the primary determinant of who wins office. In the "war chest" version, one candidate, usually the incumbent, has simply raised cash early enough that opponents do not even try to contest for the seat, recognizing that such a quest is unlikely to succeed. But the war-chest argument, like the basic assumption that money buys elections, still does not account for how or why the incumbent is able to raise large sums early in the election cycle. Hersch and McDougall note that a large campaign fund at an early date tends to indicate that the candidate is popular and has other attributes that make a challenger unlikely to succeed.[104] An early accumulation of cash also demonstrates a determination by the candidate to run a hard, competitive campaign. Thus a war chest may serve as a signal to potential challengers that the incumbent is popular and determined, and that a challenge is therefore unlikely to succeed. At the same time, it helps to explain why

---

99. *See Late Money in Key House Races*, POL. FIN. & LOBBY REP., Jan. 11, 1995, at 3, 5-6.

100. Malbin, *supra* note 87, at 9.

101. *Money in House Seat Turnovers*, POL. FIN. & LOBBY REP., Nov. 23, 1994, at 3, 4.

102. *See, e.g.,* Vincent Blasi, *Free Speech and the Widening Gyre of Fund-Raising: Why Campaign Spending Limits May Not Violate the First Amendment After All*, 94 COLUM. L. REV. 1281, 1284–89 (1994).

103. *See* Philip L. Hersch & Gerald S. McDougall, *Campaign War Chests as a Barrier to Entry in Congressional Races*, 32 ECON. INQUIRY 630, 630-37, 640 (1994) (examining U.S. House races during 1988 election cycle). Hersch and McDougall define a war chest as the amount of cash on hand 11 months before the election, a time when challengers must usually decide whether to pursue a campaign. *See id.* at 635.

104. *See id.* at 632.

we might not expect a strong challenge even in the absence of a war chest: Good candidates will not waste energy challenging a popular incumbent.[105]

Further, the Hersch/McDougall study indicates that it is not the size of the war chest, but these other qualities, including the candidate's popularity, that diminish the chances of serious challenge. The average war chest in their study was only $ 159,000, rising to just $ 203,000 in races in which the incumbent eventually ran without serious competition.[106] This second figure barely reaches the lower end of the estimated fund of $ 200,000 to $ 500,000 needed to run a competitive race at the time of the study.[107] Thus, a challenger would normally have expected the incumbent to spend at least the amount of the war chest, and probably more, regardless of whether the candidate had the amount on hand well before the election. Moreover, Gary Jacobson's empirical studies have shown that added incumbent spending yields little or no vote gain at certain levels.[108] Because higher levels of spending would be of little value to the incumbent in any case, any head start gained by amassing a war chest would be of relatively little importance. Thus, challengers are probably not discouraged by the presence of a war chest per se, but by what the early accumulation of campaign funds signifies in terms of tenacity, political ability, and popularity.[109]

The assumption that money buys elections is based on simple correlation: The candidate who spends the most usually wins. However, it would be surprising if this were not the case, as contributions flow naturally to

---

105. Hersch and McDougall suggest that by discouraging monetary expenditures on futile campaigns against popular incumbents, war chests may actually increase efficiency in the use of campaign resources. *See id.* at 634. Of course, this overlooks other benefits that may materialize from even a long-shot challenge, such as public awareness of issues and a voting outlet for the minority of voters dissatisfied with the incumbent. For present purposes, the key fact is that the correlation between larger war chests and less competition does not directly support the thesis that money buys elections, but rather underscores the point that otherwise strong candidates can usually raise large sums of money as well.

106. *Id.* at 635.

107. *See* Gary C. Jacobson, *Enough is Too Much: Money and Competition in House Elections, in* ELECTIONS IN AMERICA 173, 179 (Kay Lehman Schlozman ed., 1987) (estimating that $ 500,000 is needed for challenger to have realistic chance of success in U.S. House campaign in 1986); Larry Sabato, *Real and Imagined Corruption in Campaign Financing, in* ELECTIONS AMERICAN STYLE 155, 169 (A. James Reichley ed., 1987) (suggesting $ 150,000 was "minimum financial base needed to conduct a modern campaign").

108. *See* GARY C. JACOBSON, THE POLITICS OF CONGRESSIONAL ELECTIONS 132 (3d ed. 1992); Jacobson, *supra* note 96, at 349; Jacobson, *supra* note 94, at 61.

109. *See* Sorauf, *supra* note 1, at 178.

those candidates who are popular and are perceived as having a good chance of winning. It seems clear that many candidates win despite spending less than their opponents, and that the correlation between spending and success is not as strong as other indicators, such as the correlation between incumbency and success.[110] The problem, if it exists, is not that some candidates "buy" elections by spending too much, but that other candidates spend too little to reach the mass of voters.[111]

D. Assumption Four: Money is a Corrupting Influence on Candidates

A fundamental tenet of the reform movement is that money has corrupted the legislative process in America.[112] Large numbers of Americans have come to view legislative politics as a money game, in which campaign contributions are the dominant influence on policymaking.[113]

---

110. *Id.* at 175-76, 178.

111. *See id.* at 178-79; *see also* Sabato, *supra* note 107, at 169. For a further discussion of this point, *see infra* notes 148-58 and accompanying text.

112. *See, e.g.,* Lowenstein, *supra* note 3, at 306-35; Wertheimer & Manes, *supra* note 3, at 1126; Wright, *supra* note 4, at 609-10.

113. *See* Wertheimer & Manes, *supra* note 3, at 1129-30 (citing polling data). In *Buckley*, the Supreme Court held that the mere "appearance of corruption" is a constitutionally sufficient justification for infringing on First Amendment rights through campaign finance regulation. Buckley v. Valeo, 424 U.S. 1, 26 (1976) (per curiam). This argument is not particularly persuasive for several reasons.

First, although the importance of appearances is discussed by Wertheimer & Manes, *supra* note 3, at 1130-31, among others, it is not a major argument in the campaign finance reform literature.

Second, the "appearance of corruption" rationale is both unnecessary and dangerous. If the campaign finance system leads to actual corruption, then that may be a constitutionally sufficient justification for the state to infringe on free speech rights, in which case the "appearance of corruption" basis is superfluous. If the campaign system does not lead to actual corruption, then it seems very dangerous to suggest that the mistaken view of some could justify restricting the First Amendment liberties of others. For example, if complete campaign finance reform were insufficient to change the public's erroneous view, would the state then be justified, under a least restrictive means test, in censoring political reporting that wrongly focuses excess attention on money and thus itself creates the "appearance of corruption?" The justification of such restrictions by a belief known to be erroneous is a sharp departure from traditional First Amendment doctrine. Even in the midst of World War II, the Court did not uphold a law requiring a salute of the U.S. flag, *see* West Virginia State Bd. of Educ. v. Barnette, 319 U.S. 624 (1943), even though a refusal to salute the flag might have created an appearance of disunity damaging to the U.S. war effort-surely an important government interest. *See id.* at 640-41. Allowing the "appearance of corruption" to justify government intrusion on First Amendment liberties essentially allows the

In many respects, this would seem to be the most sound of the fundamental reformist assumptions. Experience and human nature tell us that
legislators, like most people, are influenced by money, even when it goes
into their campaign funds rather than directly into their pockets. Many
legislators themselves have complained of the influence of money in the
legislature.[114]

In fact, however, a substantial majority of those who have studied voting patterns on a systematic basis agree that campaign contributions affect
very few votes in the legislature.[115] The primary factors determining a legislator's votes, these studies conclude, are party affiliation, ideology, and
constituent views and needs.[116] Where contributions and voting patterns
intersect, they do so largely because donors contribute to those candidates
who are believed to favor their positions, not the other way around.[117]

These empirical results cut against our intuitions. Yet to accept the
findings of these repeated studies does not require us, in Professor
Nicholson's phrase, "to park [our] common sense at the academy
door."[118] First, people who are attracted to public office generally do have
strong personal views on issues.[119] Second, there are institutional and po-

---

majority to justify the suppression of minority rights through its own propaganda.

Third, one of the themes of this Essay is that money has not "corrupted" the system. I
know of no way to challenge the "appearance of corruption"—others' subjective perceptions that corruption does exist—other than to make the case that their perceptions are
wrong. *Cf.* Gary C. Jacobson, *Campaign Finance and Democratic Control: Comments on
Gottlieb and Lowenstein's Papers,* 18 HOFSTRA L. REV. 369, 377 (1989) ("To the extent
that the argument verges on "[corruption is] there even if we can't see it,' it is not…open
to disconfirmation…"). A person swayed by the arguments in this Essay should not much
care about the "appearance of corruption."

114. *See, e.g.,* Wertheimer & Manes, *supra* note 3, at 1128-40.

115. *See* Moussalli, *supra* note 94, at 6; Sorauf, *supra* note 18, at 316; Janet Grenzke,
PACs and the Congressional Supermarket: The Currency is Complex, 33 AM. J. POL. SCI.
1, 1 (1989); Sabato, *supra* note 107, at 159-62; *cf.* W.P. Welch, *Campaign Contributions
and Legislative Voting: Milk Money and Dairy Price Supports,* 35 W. POL. Q. 478, 479
(1982) ("The influence of contributions is 'small,' at least relative to the influences of constituency, party, and ideology."). *But see* Lowenstein, *supra* note 3, at 313-22 (arguing
that such studies are seriously flawed).

116. Sabato, *supra* note 107, at 160.

117. Moussalli, *supra* note 94, at 5-6.

118. Nicholson, *supra* note 3, at 464.

119. This simple observation is often missed by campaign reformers, even those with
an otherwise skeptical eye. For example, Sanford Levinson found it "scandalous" that 64
Democrats in the House of Representatives voted for a capital gains tax cut in 1989, writing, "I cannot believe [they] would have voted for this bill…if they were not so dependent
on campaign contributions from that sector of the population which is most likely to ben-

litical incentives to support party positions. These can include logistical and financial support,[120] appeals to party unity,[121] pressure regarding committee assignments,[122] and promises of support from party leaders on future issues.[123] Third, large campaign contributors are usually offset by equally well-financed interests that contribute to a different group of candidates. In fact, contributors frequently suffer enormous losses in the legislative process, as funds are spent to promote positions that ultimately fail.[124] Finally, money is not the only political commodity of value. For example, in 1993-94 the National Rifle Association (NRA) contributed nearly $ 2 million to congressional campaigns through its PAC.[125] However, the NRA also has over three million members, "who focus intently, even solely, on NRA issues in their voting."[126] In many congressional districts, the NRA is capable of "shifting vote totals by close to five percent."[127] The NRA's power thus would seem to come more from votes than from dollars. However, to the extent that it comes from dollars, that too is related to votes; i.e., it is the group's large membership that yields

---

efit from the bill." Sanford Levinson, *Electoral Regulation: Some Comments,* 18 HOFS-TRA L. REV. 411, 412 n.5 (1989). Though hotly debated, considerable literature suggests that a reduction in capital gains tax rates would actually increase government revenue. *See, e.g.,* George R. Zodrow, *Economic Analyses of Capital Gains Taxation: Realizations, Revenues, Efficiency and Equity,* 48 TAX L. REV. 419, 429-30 (1993). Perhaps these Democrats believed such arguments, and merely wanted to cut the deficit or raise revenue to fund social programs.

An unwillingness to accept the possibility of legislative defeat (or in this case victory— the capital gains tax cut was defeated) on the merits tends to permeate reformist writing. *See, e.g.,* Wright, *supra* note 4, at 618-19.

120. *See* David Adamany, *Political Finance and the American Political Parties,* 10 HASTINGS CONST. L. Q. 497, 539-41 (1983).

121. *See, e.g.,* Norman J. Ornstein, *The Rising Republican Centrists: Congress's New Power Brokers,* WASH. POST, Nov. 20, 1995, at C3 (noting that in order to achieve even limited goals, pressure for party unity grows as party's legislative strength declines).

122. *See, e.g.,* Richard Reeves, *A Matter of Conscience,* BUFF. NEWS, Mar. 17, 1995, at B3 (discussing Republican pressure on Senator Mark Hatfield to give up his seat as Appropriations Committee chairman after voting against balanced budget amendment to U.S. Constitution).

123. *See, e.g.,* Alan McConagha, *Inside Politics,* WASH. TIMES, Dec. 9, 1993, at A5 (noting that Representative Marjorie Margolies-Mezvinsky cast decididng vote for President Clinton's 1994 budget because President promised to hold conference on entitlements in her district).

124. *See* SORAUF, *supra* note 1, at 165.

125. *The Top PACs of the 1993-94 Election Cycle,* POL. FIN. & LOBBY REP., Apr. 26, 1995, at 3.

126. SORAUF, *supra* note 1, at 166.

127. *Id.*

large amounts of contributions. Groups advocating gun control often complain that the NRA outspends them, but rarely mention that the NRA also outvotes them.[128]

If campaign contributions have any meaningful effect on legislative voting behavior, it is on a limited number of votes, generally related to specialized or narrow issues arousing little public interest.[129] A legislator is unlikely to accept a campaign contribution, which can be used only to attempt to sway voters, in exchange for an unpopular vote, which definitely alienates voters.[130] Therefore, specialized issues provide the best opportunity to trade votes for money.[131] On these issues, prior contributions may provide the contributor with access to the legislator or legislative staff.

---

128. When confronted with a liberal Congress and President in 1993-94, money did not gain the NRA victory over the Brady Bill or the assault weapons ban. However, the election of a new congressional majority in 1994 may result in repeal of both of the aforementioned pieces of legislation.

Of course, the NRA is not a typical group, and is perhaps an unfair example. Professor Lowenstein suggests that many groups lacking the NRA's level of voter support manage to obtain legislative success, suggesting used car dealers, sugar beet growers, and members of the tobacco industry as examples. See DANIEL H. LOWENSTEIN, ELECTION LAW: CASES AND MATERIALS, TEACHER'S MANUAL 116 (1995). Yet these examples are not so persuasive for the reformers' cause as it might seem. Certainly the tobacco industry can call on large numbers of voters throughout the Upper South, and even in parts of southern Ohio, Indiana, and Maryland, which are home to tobacco growers, processors, pickers, packagers, marketers and more. Behind them stand millions of Americans who enjoy smoking. Over 80,000 used car dealers dot the American landscape, employing tens of thousands of workers. Max Gates, FTC Targets Buyer's Guide Violations, AUTOMOTIVE NEWS, Mar. 27, 1995, at 46. Sugar beet growers can be found from Ohio to California and likewise draw on a vast network of employees and suppliers for support. Combined with the domestic corn syrup industry, beet growers provide over 420,000 jobs. David Hendee, Defending the Sugar Program, OMAHA WORLD-HERALD, July 17, 1995, at 1.

For an excellent discussion of the complex yet limited relationship between contributors and legislative voting, see Sorauf, supra note 18, at 307-17.

129. SORAUF, supra note 1, at 166-67; Sabato, supra note 107, at 160. Lowenstein argues that the emphasis on floor votes misses the point; the action may take place elsewhere in the legislative process, such as in committee. See Lowenstein, supra note 3, at 313-29; see also Wertheimer & Manes, supra note 3, at 1140 ("[The payback] may not come in a vote.'" (quoting former Senator Proxmire)). This would seem to be true at some level. But as Gary Jacobson points out, this argument suffers from the weakness of not being open to disconfirmation. See Jacobson, supra note 113, at 377. To the extent we have empirical data, however, it appears that the reformers consistently overstate the influence of money on the legislative process.

130. See Strauss, supra note 92, at 1372-73.

131. See Sabato, supra note 107, at 160.

The contributor may then be able to shape legislation to the extent that such efforts are not incompatible with the dominant legislative motives of ideology, party affiliation and agenda, and constituent views.[132] Whether or not the influence of campaign contributions on these limited issues is good or bad depends on one's views of the resulting legislation. The exclusion of knowledgeable contributors from the legislative process can just as easily lead to poor legislation with unintended consequences as can their inclusion.[133] In any case, it must be stressed that such issues are few.[134]

The motivation for efforts to limit campaign contributions and spending may not be the belief that money sways votes in the legislature, but the fact that many campaign finance reformers are unhappy with the ideologies and voting tendencies of those being elected to office.[135] Campaign finance reformers sometimes seem to envision a world in which career officeholders, freed from the corrupting influence of money, lobbyists, and, it might be said, public opinion, would produce good, wise, and fair legislation. This notion of the philosopher-bureaucrat, popular during the Progressive era, has been largely discredited by modern public choice scholarship as an unattainable and, indeed, undesirable ideal.[136] And al-

---

132. *See id.* at 160-61.

133. *See* Strauss, *supra* note 92, at 1378-79.

134. *See* Sabato, *supra* note 107, at 160. Just how many votes are affected is uncertain. Welch's study of dairy price supports, a relatively specialized issue not usually subject to intense public scrutiny, found that the influence of money was dwarfed by party, ideology, and constituent concerns. *See* Welch, *supra* note 115, at 479.

135. *See* Lowenstein, *supra* note 3, at 346-47; *see also* Wright, *supra* note 4, at 618-19 (citing congressional resistance to numerous "liberal" causes, including a windfall tax on oil companies, government cost controls on hospitals, environmental legislation, regulation of auto dealers, investment credits, and "any other legislation that affects powerful, organized interests," as evidence of need for campaign finance restrictions).

Of course, campaign finance reform, like most issues, does not always divide along traditional liberal/conservative lines. Many prominent conservatives, such as Barry Goldwater, have supported reform efforts, *see* Wertheimer & Manes, *supra* note 3, at 1127, while liberals such as Professor Martin Shapiro have often remained skeptical, *see* Martin Shapiro, *Corruption, Freedom and Equality in Campaign Financing*, 18 HOFSTRA L. REV. 385 (1989). This does not change the basic point that many reformers see the issue in terms of silencing the forces that have defeated cherished legislation. Goldwater, incidentally, would have benefited from limits on contributions, since he, more than most candidates, relied on a large base of small donors. *See supra* text accompanying note 84.

136. *See* Gottlieb, *supra* note 17, at 274-76. For a sampling of work by public choice economists, *see, e.g.*, JAMES M. BUCHANAN & GORDON TULLOCK, THE CALCULUS OF CONSENT (1962); RANDALL G. HOLCOMBE, AN ECONOMIC ANALYSIS OF DEMOCRACY (1985); DWIGHT R. LEE & RICHARD B. MCKENZIE, FAILURE AND PROGRESS (1993); Geoffrey Brennan & James Buchanan, *The Normative Purpose of Economic 'Science': Rediscovery of an Eighteenth Century Method*, 1 INT'L REV. L. & ECON. 155 (1981). The

though campaign finance reformers have long posed as disinterested citizens seeking only good government, in fact they have often targeted certain types of campaign activities, "at least in part because [those activities] are closely tied to political agendas that reformers oppose."[137] They therefore favor regulation that would tilt the electoral process in favor of preferred candidates.[138]

The available evidence simply does not show a meaningful, causal relationship between campaign contributions and legislative voting patterns. While campaign contributions may influence votes in a few limited cases, this would not seem to justify wholesale regulation.

The pressure for campaign finance regulation has been based on assumptions that are, at best, questionable, and, at worst, seriously flawed. Not surprisingly, then, campaign finance reform efforts enacted into law have had negative consequences for our political system.

IV. The Undemocratic Consequences of Campaign Finance Regulation

Campaign finance reform has generally focused on three specific tactics for promoting change: limiting contributions, whether by individuals, corporations, or PACs; limiting campaign spending; and, ultimately, using public funding for campaigns.[139] These reform tactics have several negative consequences, which can be broadly labeled "undemocratic."

---

basic insight of public choice theory as applied to government is that government officials, like private individuals, will attempt to maximize personal worth, whether through power, wealth, or some other benefit. Thus, they must be checked by outside interests. *See, e.g.,* RANDALL G. HOLCOMBE, PUBLIC POLICY AND THE QUALITY OF LIFE 5-6, 18-20 (1995); DWIGHT R. LEE & RICHARD B. MCKENZIE, REGULATING GOVERNMENT 10-13 (1987).

137. BeVier, *supra* note 15, at 1061.

138. Sanford Levinson, *Regulating Campaign Activity: The New Road to Contradiction?*, 83 MICH. L. REV. 939, 945 (1985).

139. *See, e.g.,* Lowenstein, *supra* note 3, at 351-60; Wertheimer & Manes, *supra* note 3, at 1131. A fourth legislative tactic, public disclosure of campaign finance information, was included in FECA and most state legislation regulating campaign finance, and may have even broader support. *See* Sabato, *supra* note 107, at 171. Even many ardent opponents of campaign finance reform accept the benefits of disclosure laws. *See, e.g.,* Moussalli, *supra* note 94, at 20-21. My own view is that disclosure laws raise serious First Amendment questions, and thus are not free from difficulties. *See* Bradley A. Smith, *Congress Shall Make No Law...*, WASH. TIMES, Dec. 29, 1994, at A19. Because disclosure laws do not have the same type of broadly "undemocratic" consequences as the other major tactical goals of the reform movement, this Essay does not address them.

Specifically, campaign finance reform efforts entrench the status quo; make the electoral system less responsive to popular opinion; strengthen the power of select elites; favor wealthy individuals; and limit opportunities for "grassroots" political activity.[140] This part discusses each of these consequences in turn, assuming that any regulation exists within a system of private campaign funding. A discussion of the consequences of public funding follows in Part V.

A. Campaign Finance Reform Entrenches the Status Quo

Campaign finance reform measures, in particular limits on contributions and overall spending,[141] insulate the political system from challenge by outsiders, and hinder the ability of challengers to compete on equal terms with those already in power.

Contribution limits tend to favor incumbents by making it harder for challengers to raise money and thereby make credible runs for office.[142] The lower the contribution limit, the more difficult it becomes for a candi-

---

140. Supporters of heavy campaign finance regulation argue that the failure of the 1974 FECA Amendments, and specifically FECA's contribution and expenditure limits, to solve the alleged evils of the current system is due to the unwarranted constitutional restrictions placed on their efforts by *Buckley v. Valeo*, 424 U.S. 1 (1976) (per curiam). *See, e.g.*, Kirk J. Nahra, *Political Parties and the Campaign Finance Laws: Dilemmas, Concerns and Opportunities*, 56 FORDHAM L. REV. 53, 55 (1991); *see also* John S. Shockley, *Money in Politics: Judicial Roadblocks to Campaign Finance Reform*, 10 HASTINGS CONST. L. Q. 679, 714-15 (1983). This Essay demonstrates, however, that regardless of *Buckley*, the fundamental assumptions of the reform effort are incorrect. The criticisms that follow do not depend on the current constitutional regime: They would apply to FECA as originally enacted, and, to varying degrees, to the various reformist schemes proposed in the post-*Buckley* world. A public policy based on flawed assumptions is unlikely to be successful no matter how enacted.

Furthermore, the Court has not retreated from *Buckley*'s basic holdings, and thus reformist efforts must take the constraints of *Buckley* into account.

141. Limits on campaign contributions are allowed under the *Buckley* framework, have been enacted into federal law, and are included in virtually every reformist-scholar proposal. *See, e.g.*, Lowenstein, *supra* note 3, at 357 (recommending limiting contributions to just $ 100); Nicholson, *supra* note 3, at 471; Jamin Raskin & John Bonifaz, *The Constitutional Imperative and Practical Superiority of Democratically Financed Elections* 94 COLUM. L. REV. 1160, 1191 (1994); Wertheimer & Manes, *supra* note 3, at 1155. Though mandatory limits on overall spending levels are not allowed under *Buckley*, voluntary limits linked to the disbursement of public funds are permitted, *see Buckley*, 424 U.S. at 85-108. For an excellent discussion of the Court's decision on this point, *see* Marlene A. Nicholson, *Political Campaign Expenditure Limitations and the Unconstitutional Condition Doctrine*, 10 HASTINGS CONST. L. Q. 601 (1983).

142. Malbin, *supra* note 87, at 9.

date to raise money quickly from a small number of dedicated supporters. The consequent need to raise campaign cash from a large number of small contributors benefits those candidates who have in place a database of past contributors, an intact campaign organization, and the ability to raise funds on an ongoing basis from PACs.[143] This latter group consists almost entirely of current officeholders. Thus, contribution limits hit political newcomers especially hard because of the difficulties candidates with low name recognition have in raising substantial sums of money from small contributors.

Even well-known public figures challenging the status quo have traditionally relied on a small number of wealthy patrons to fund their campaigns. For example, Theodore Roosevelt's 1912 Bull Moose campaign was funded almost entirely by a handful of wealthy supporters.[144] Senator Eugene McCarthy's 1968 antiwar campaign relied for seed money on a handful of six-figure donors, including Stewart Mott, who gave approximately $ 210,000, and Wall Street banker Jack Dreyfus, Jr., who may have contributed as much as $ 500,000.[145] John Anderson would probably have had more success in his independent campaign for the Presidency in 1980 had his wealthy patron, the ubiquitous Mr. Mott, been able to contribute unlimited amounts to his campaign.[146] And whereas Ross Perot's 1992 campaign was made possible by the Supreme Court's holding in *Buckley* that an individual may spend unlimited sums to advance his own candidacy, the contribution limits upheld in *Buckley* would make it illegal for Perot to bankroll the campaign of a more plausible challenger in 1996, such as Colin Powell or Bill Bradley.[147] Despite recent polls showing strong voter interest in a third-party or independent candidate

---

143. *See* Colloquia, *Constitutional Implications of Campaign Finance Reform*, 8 ADMIN. L.J. AM. U. 161, 169 (1994) (comments of Robert Peck).

144. *See* Thayer, *supra* note 88, at 55.

145. *See* Deposition of Eugene McCarthy, Ex. C at 50, Buckley v. Valeo, 519 F.2d 821 (D.C. Cir. 1975) (No. 75-1061), aff'd in part and rev'd in part, 424 U.S. 1 (1976) (per curiam); Deposition of Stewart R. Mott, Ex. D at P 11, *Buckley*, 519 F.2d 821 (No. 75-1061) [hereinafter Statement of Stewart R. Mott].

146. *See generally* Stewart R. Mott, *Independent Fundraising for an Independent Candidate*, 10 N.Y.U. REV. L. & SOC. CHANGE 135, 138-41 (1981).

147. More recently, millionaire Malcolm S. Forbes, Jr., a political neophyte, declared his intention to seek the Republican presidential nomination in 1996. Forbes indicated that he would not have sought the nomination had former Congressman and Secretary of Housing and Urban Development Jack Kemp decided to run. Martha T. Moore, *Main Goal: Carry Banner of Supply Side Economics*, USA TODAY, Sept. 6, 1995, at 4B. Kemp chose not to run in part because he did not want to engage in fund-raising. Alan Elsner, *Running for the White House Will Take Megabucks This Time*, S.F. CHRON., Feb. 1, 1995, at A9. Were Forbes able to donate to Kemp the $ 25 million he planned to spend

for President in 1996, contribution limits make a serious independent challenge virtually impossible, unless Mr. Perot himself, or someone of comparable wealth, is again the candidate.

Beyond making it harder for challengers to raise cash, contribution limits also tend to decrease overall spending,[148] which further works against challengers. Incumbents begin each campaign with significant advantages in name recognition.[149] They are able to attract press coverage because of their office, and they often receive assistance from their staffs and send constituents postage-free mailings using their franking privilege.[150] Through patronage and constituent favors, they can further add to their support.[151] One way for challengers to offset these advantages is to spend money to make their names and positions known. Those few studies that have attempted to isolate and quantify the effect of campaign spending on votes have found that, once a candidate spends the minimal amount needed to penetrate the public consciousness, additional spending affects a very limited number of votes.[152] However, the positive effect of added spending is significantly greater for challengers than for incumbents.[153] In fact, studies show an inverse relationship between high levels of incumbent spending and incumbent success. Heavy spending by an incumbent

---

on his own campaign, Kemp might have run and would quite likely have been a front-runner for the Republican nomination.

148. Lowenstein, *supra* note 63, at 399-401. This is because a candidate's spending is limited to available funds. By making it harder to raise money, contribution limits will indirectly lower overall spending levels. *Id.*

149. Gottlieb, *supra* note 17, at 224.

150. *Id.*

151. *Id.*

152. *See* JACOBSON, *supra* note 108, at 54.

153. *Id.* at 50, 53; Jacobson, *supra* note 94, at 62-63 (finding that challengers gained approximately 3.5 percentage points for each $ 100,000 spent, while incumbent vote totals actually went down with higher spending). This would appear to be because the incumbents are better known to the constituency at the start of the campaign. The advantages they gain from holding office can be viewed as money already spent in a campaign, and indeed often reflect past campaign spending. *See* John R. Lott, Jr., *Explaining Challengers' Campaign Expenditures: The Importance of Sunk Nontransferable Brand Name*, 17 PUB. FIN. Q. 108 (1989). As such, incumbents will reach a point of diminishing marginal returns sooner than challengers, with better-known and longer-serving incumbents reaching that point sooner than lesser-known and short-term incumbents. Anecdotal evidence from the 1994 elections would seem to support this last point. The three incumbents who lost despite spending at least $ 1 million more than their challengers were three of the best-known, longest-serving incumbents in Congress: Dan Rostenkowski, Thomas Foley, and Jack Brooks. *See Money in House Seat Turnovers*, POL. FIN. & LOBBY REP., Nov. 23, 1994, at 3, 4.

indicates that the incumbent is in electoral trouble and facing a well-financed challenger.[154] Because an incumbent's added spending is likely to have less of an effect on vote totals than the additional spending of a challenger, limits on total campaign spending will hurt challengers more than incumbents. By lowering overall campaign spending, therefore, contribution limits further lock into place the advantages of incumbency and disproportionately harm challengers.

Absolute spending ceilings, whether "mandatory" or "voluntary," have the potential to exacerbate this problem considerably.[155] Set low enough, they may make it impossible for challengers to attain the critical threshold at which they can reach enough voters to run a credible race.[156] Overall spending caps also prevent challengers from ever spending more than incumbents. While spending more than one's opponent is not necessary to win an election,[157] a challenger's ability to outspend an incumbent can help to offset the advantages of incumbency.[158] Efforts to limit spend-

---

154. JACOBSON, *supra* note 108, at 53.

155. Mandatory spending ceilings are not allowed under *Buckley*, but voluntary ceilings created by offering public subsidies to candidates who agree to abide by the ceiling are a common feature of many reform proposals. *See* Nicholson, *supra* note 3, at 473-75; Wertheimer & Manes, *supra* note 3, at 1149-54. Many of these "voluntary" proposals would be prime candidates to be struck down by the Supreme Court as violating the "unconstitutional conditions" doctrine. Typically, they are so punitive toward candidates who do not opt into the system that voluntary limits are, in effect, mandatory. *See, e.g.,* U.S. CONGRESS ASSESSMENT PROJECT, THE HERITAGE FOUNDATION, ADVANTAGE INCUMBENTS: CLINTON'S CAMPAIGN FINANCE PROPOSAL 11 (1993) [hereinafter ADVANTAGE INCUMBENTS] (discussing reform bill proposed by President Clinton in 1993).

156. Incumbent lawmakers will always have powerful personal incentives to set spending caps at a level that disadvantages their challengers. *See, e.g.,* ADVANTAGE INCUMBENTS, *supra* note 155, at 9-10; Lowenstein, *supra* note 3, at 335.

157. *See* discussion *supra* Section III.C.

158. Sabato, *supra* note 107, at 169. Incumbency is already the single best predictor of electoral success. Limits on campaign financing, by handicapping challengers still further, tend to add to political ossification. Though rates of success of incumbents seeking reelection have been consistently above 75% since the turn of the century, these rates have risen to record heights in this era of extensive campaign finance regulation. *See* JOHN H. FUND, TERM LIMITATION: AN IDEA WHOSE TIME HAS COME 5 tbl. 2 (1990). Even in the 1994 elections, which resulted in significant political realignment, 91.4% of congressional incumbents seeking reelection were victorious. *See* Edward Zuckerman, *Money Didn't Matter for Most Challengers Who Won*, POL. FIN. & LOBBY REP., Nov. 23, 1994, at 1, 1. The Republican gains came primarily from the GOP's near sweep of "open" seats, i.e., seats in which the incumbent did not seek reelection. While money can help to "buy" votes, it "buys" far more votes for challengers than for incumbents. This being the case, money is an equalizer in the system, helping challengers to overcome the tremendous advantages of incumbency. Ruy A. Teixeira, *Campaign Reform, Political Competition, and Citi-*

ing, whether mandatory or through incentive-based "voluntary" caps, should therefore not be viewed as benign or neutral.

B. Campaign Finance Reform Promotes Influence Peddling and Reduces Accountability

Limits on contributions increase the incentives for contributors to seek "influence" rather than the election of like-minded legislators, and reduce the effectiveness of legislative-monitoring efforts. We have previously seen that, though the argument is overstated, campaign contributions may affect legislative votes on a limited number of issues.[159] Many reformers have been more concerned about contributors who adopt a "legislative" strategy, attempting to influence legislative votes, than with donors who adopt an "electoral" strategy, aimed at influencing election outcomes.[160] Yet strangely enough, contribution limits, the most popular reform measure, encourage PACs and other monied interests to adopt legislative strategies. This results in the representative system being less responsive to public opinion.

Campaign contributors must weigh the costs and benefits of pursuing an electoral strategy versus a legislative strategy. Money given to a losing challenger is not merely money wasted, it is money spent counterproductively, as it will probably increase the enmity of, and decrease access to, the incumbent. With incumbents winning in excess of 90% of House races, an electoral strategy of supporting challengers has very high risks. Even in close races, so long as a contributor is limited to a maximum contribution of $ 10,000 (or some other amount),[161] the contributor's campaign donation is unlikely to increase significantly the odds of a victory for the challenger. The low-risk alternative is to contribute to incumbents in the hope that a legislative strategy might succeed, at least by minimizing otherwise hostile treatment aimed at the contributor's interests.[162] Thus, because the risk of an electoral strategy is so high, contribution limits tend to lock the rational contributor into a legislative strategy.[163] To the

---

zen Participation, in RETHINKING POLITICAL REFORM: BEYOND SPENDING AND TERM LIMITS 5, 10-11 (Ruy A. Teixeira et al. eds., 1994).

159. *See* discussion *supra* Section III.D.

160. *See supra* note 92.

161. This is the maximum contribution for a PAC making a donation in both the primary and general election under FECA. *See* 2 U.S.C. 441(a) (1988).

162. *See* Lowenstein, *supra* note 3, at 308-13, for a general discussion of the strategy considerations facing donors.

163. It may be worthwhile to consider the proposition that PACs have less of a corrupting influence on incumbent legislators than those legislators have on PACs. *See*

extent, then, that campaign contributions influence legislative voting behavior, campaign finance regulation in the form of contribution limits is likely to make the problem worse.[164]

Professor Lowenstein attempts to get around this problem by setting the contribution threshold at $ 100, a level so low that a legislative strategy would have no real chance of success.[165] This would effectively abolish private funding of political campaigns.[166] As a practical matter, then, public funding would have to take over the system,[167] with the attendant problems I will shortly address. Even if public funding could be successfully implemented, however, squeezing out private money would in other ways make the political system less responsive.

PACs perform a valuable monitoring function in the current campaign regime, a function that would be lost were private funding to be eliminated. It has been suggested that the real issue that the campaign reform movement attempts to address is "shirking," or the tendency of elected officials to betray their public trust in favor of their own or other interests.[168] In most cases, it will not be rational for individuals to devote considerable time to monitoring the performance of elected officials. However, by banding together with others having similar concerns, individuals can perform the monitoring function at a reasonable cost. Interest groups, and the PACs they spawn, thus play an important role in monitoring officeholders' performances so as to prevent shirking.[169] Therefore, measures that would limit or eliminate the role of PACs are likely to reduce legislative monitoring, leading to a legislature ever more isolated from the people.

Strauss, *supra* note 92, at 1380-82 (arguing that incumbent lawmakers may use threat of adverse legislative action to "extort" contributions from political contributors).

164. This does not mean that large contributors, even PACs, never give to challengers. They may gamble that a challenger can be the exception who wins, or they may be motivated purely by ideology. But to the extent they hope to see a difference as a result of their contributions, a legislative strategy will almost always make more sense.

165. *See* Lowenstein, *supra* note 3, at 357. At a maximum contribution of just $ 100, it is hard to see a legislator being swayed by any single contribution. Note, however, that this would make bundling of contributions and independent spending, two other villains in the reformist literature, more valuable.

166. *See* Jacobson, *supra* note 82, at 610-11. It is worth noting that private funding has many advantages: It is easy to administer; it supports traditional American values of volunteerism; it avoids First Amendment problems; and it actively involves millions of Americans in the political process far more than does a government check-off. See Sorauf, *supra* note 5, at 1361.

167. *See* Lowenstein, *supra* note 3, at 350.

168. *See* Jacobson, *supra* note 113, at 370.

169. BeVier, *supra* note 89, at 1273-76.

Finally, there is always the possibility that limiting private contributions will simply increase the value of a more corrupting alternative: outright bribery.[170] It is naive to think that when the government is heavily involved in virtually every aspect of economic life in the country (and quite a few noneconomic spheres as well), people affected by government actions will accept whatever comes without some kind of counterstrategy.[171] In this way, too, contribution limits may make the electoral system less responsive to public opinion and, therefore, less democratic.

C. Campaign Finance Regulation Favors Select Elites

Campaign finance reform is usually sold as a populist means to strengthen the power of "ordinary" citizens against dominant, big-money interests.[172] In fact, campaign finance reform has favored select elites and further isolated individuals from the political process.

There are a great many sources of political influence. These include direct personal attributes, such as speaking and writing ability, good looks, personality, time and energy, and organizational skills, as well as acquired attributes, such as wealth, celebrity, and access to or control of the popular press. In any society, numerous individuals will rise to the top of their professions to become part of an "elite." Both as a prerequisite to their success and as a reward for it, such individuals will have certain abilities that they can use for political ends. For example, Hollywood celebrities, by virtue of their fame, may gain audiences for their political views that they would not otherwise obtain. They may be invited to testify before Congress, despite their lack of any particular expertise,[173] or they may use their celebrity to assist campaigns through appearances at rallies.[174] Similarly, successful academics may write powerful articles that change the way people think about issues. Labor organizers may have at their disposal a vast supply of human resources that they can use to support fa-

---

170. Professor Nicholson is right when she argues that the cost of illegal bribery is so high that most influence seekers and peddlers will not attempt it. *See* Nicholson, *supra* note 3, at 466-68. Nevertheless, influence seekers denied a lawful means to press their case will be more prone to consider unlawful means, and there will always be takers at the right price.

171. BeVier, *supra* note 89, at 1276.

172. Sorauf, *supra* note 5, at 1356.

173. *See, e.g., Celebrity Hearings: Much Show, Little Go*, SAN ANTONIO EXPRESS-NEWS, July 11, 1994, available at 1994 WL 3558496 (noting that Meryl Streep and Steven Spielberg both admitted their lack of relevant knowledge during their testimony before congressional committees).

174. *See* Nina Easton, *Star Trek: Hollywood on the Stump*, L.A. TIMES, Oct. 11, 1988, at 1.

vored candidates. Media editors, reporters, and anchors can shape not only the manner, but also the content, of news reporting. Those with marketing skills can apply their abilities to raise funds or to produce advertising for a candidate or cause. Successful entrepreneurs may amass large sums of money that they can use for political purposes.[175]

The regulation of campaign contributions and spending limits the political employment of immediately available wealth but not any of these other attributes.[176] As an initial matter, there is no serious reason why the successful entrepreneur should not be able to transfer her talents at creating wealth to the political arena, while the successful marketer or political organizer is permitted to do so.[177] There is no a priori reason why a person with a flair for political organizing should be allowed political influence that is denied to the person with a flair for manufacturing.

The common response to this argument is that money can buy other sources of power: It can purchase labor, marketing know-how, media access, even speaking coaches and improved physical appearance.[178] Not only does this response not justify the prejudice against money,[179] however, but it is simply incorrect, insofar as it sees this as a unique feature of money. A winning personality, the ability to forge political alliances, and the time to devote to politics can, like money, be used to gain access to the media, labor, and other prerequisites to political success. Moreover, these skills, like the ability to produce moving television ads or to write effective campaign literature and speeches, are themselves convertible into money. For example, money can be raised through slick direct mail pitches, operation of phone banks, advertisements, speeches at rallies, booths at county fairs, and countless other means. The trick to effective electoral politics is to take the assets with which one begins and to use them to obtain additional assets that one lacks. Money is no different.[180]

---

175. As may most others on this list, especially celebrities.

176. BeVier, *supra* note 89, at 1268.

177. *Id.*

178. DAVID W. ADAMANY & GEORGE E. AGREE, POLITICAL MONEY 3 (1975).

179. *See* BeVier, *supra* note 89, at 1268.

180. As of October 1995, Senator Phil Gramm appeared to be able to convert his fund-raising skills into a substantial campaign fund, but having gone that far, he seemed unable to use those campaign funds to acquire other assets needed in his campaign for President. *See* Paul West, *Pryor's Retirement Heartens "96 GOP Hopefuls,* CHI. SUN-TIMES, Apr. 23, 1995, at 24. Conversely, there are numerous examples of candidates beginning with little money who are able to capitalize on other attributes to raise campaign cash. One example is President Bill Clinton, who began his 1992 presidential campaign with little cash. *See* Jack W. Germond & Jules Witcover, *Money is Tight for the Democratic Six*, 23 NAT'L J. 2984, 2984 (1991).

Once we accept the fact that different individuals control different sources of political power, it becomes apparent that attempts to exclude a particular form of power -money-from politics only strengthen the position of those whose power comes from other, nonmonetary, sources, such as time or media access. For example, though the Supreme Court has allowed states to limit even independent expenditures by nonmedia corporations in candidate races,[181] newspapers, magazines, and TV and radio corporations can spend unlimited sums to promote the election of favored candidates. Thus, Donald Graham, the publisher of the Washington Post, has at his disposal the resources of a media empire to promote his views, free from the campaign finance restrictions to which others are subjected. ABC News anchor Peter Jennings is given a nightly forum on national television in which to express his views.[182]

Media elites are not the only group whose influence is increased by campaign spending and contribution limits. Restricting the flow of money into campaigns also increases the relative importance of in-kind contributions and so favors those who are able to control large blocks of human resources. Limiting contributions and expenditures does not particularly democratize the process, but merely shifts power from those whose primary contribution is money to those whose primary contribution is time, organization, or some other resource-for example, from small business groups to large labor unions. Others who benefit from campaign finance limitations include political middlemen, public relations firms conducting "voter education" programs, lobbyists, PACs such as EMILY's List that "bundle" large numbers of $ 1000 contributions,[183] and political activists.[184] These individuals and groups may or may not be more representative of public opinion than the wealthy philanthropists and industrialists who financed so many past campaigns.

---

181. Austin v. Michigan State Chamber of Commerce, 494 U.S. 652 (1990). For further discussion of media influence, *see* Levinson, *supra* note 119, at 412–13.

182. Surveys have indicated that the views of journalists often differ sharply from those of the public at large. *See* Stanley Meisler, *Public Found to be More Cynical Than Press*, L.A. Times, May 22, 1995, at A11 (noting that only 5% of journalists, versus 39% of the public, describe themselves as politically "conservative"). For an ex-journalist's view of this power, *see* Jonathan Rowe, *The View of You from the Hill*, Colum. Journalism Rev., July 1994, at 47.

183. "Bundling" is a practice in which a PAC solicits its supporters for contributions not only to the PAC itself, but directly to the candidates. The PAC collects those campaign donations, "bundles" them together, and delivers them to the candidate on behalf of the individual donors.

184. *See, e.g., Money in Politics*, 10 Hastings Const. L.Q. 466, 486 (1983) (providing comments of Herbert Alexander).

In theory, it may be possible to limit in-kind contributions in the same manner as monetary contributions.[185] In practice, however, such an effort raises almost insurmountable administrative difficulties and, in the end, would not solve the unequal treatment created by the prejudice against money. Consider, for example, a politically talented, twenty-five-year-old Harvard law student from a privileged background, who chooses to volunteer on a presidential campaign during summer break, passing up a law firm clerkship paying $ 15,000 for the summer. Consider, at the same time, a West Virginia high school dropout who goes to work in a body shop at age seventeen, scrapes together some money to launch his own shop at age twenty-two, opens a second shop two years later, and then at age twenty-five, angered over government policies affecting his business, seeks to promote political change by contributing $ 15,000 to a political campaign. Each individual seeks to forego $ 15,000 in consumption to promote his political beliefs, but only the activities of the Harvard law student are legal.[186] As this simple illustration shows, truly limiting the comparative advantages of in-kind contributions is simply not possible. How, for example, would we limit the ability of Arnold Schwarzenegger to turn his celebrity into Republican votes in any manner compatible with the First Amendment? Could we order Republican media whiz Roger Ailes to divide his time evenly between Democratic and Republican candidates? Prohibit Meryl Streep from giving congressional testimony? Order Jesse Jackson to cease his voter registration campaigns, which are clearly aimed at registering more probable Democratic than Republican voters?[187] The question is whether people will be allowed to convert their varied talents into political influence. Efforts to limit the flow of cash exclude from the process those whose talents do not directly lend them-

---

185. Several proposals to limit in-kind contributions have been made. *See, e.g.,* Carville B. Collins, *Maryland Campaign Finance Law: A Proposal for Reform,* 47 MD. L. REV. 524, 544-46 (1988); Wertheimer & Manes, *supra* note 3, at 1557-58. For a more theoretical discussion of the administrative problems involved with limiting in-kind contributions, *see* Edward B. Foley, *Equal-Dollars-Per-Voter: A Constitutional Principle of Campaign Finance,* 94 COLUM. L. REV. 1204, 1246-49 (1994). Reformist scholars, however, choose almost exclusively to target the influence of money.

186. Looked at from the campaign's point of view, one might argue that the law student's real contribution is only what it would cost the campaign to hire someone else to do the same job. The hypothetical remains the same, of course, if the body shop owner's contribution is merely reduced to this amount.

187. A full discussion of the relationship between money and political equality is beyond the scope of this Essay. For a detailed discussion of the issue, *see* Bradley A. Smith, Money Talks: Speech, Money, and Political Equality (unpublished manuscript in progress, on file with author).

selves to political purposes, thereby increasing the relative power of those whose talents are directly applicable to the political arena.

Moreover, the way in which campaign finance regulation favors certain elites raises First Amendment concerns. Traditional First Amendment jurisprudence requires most speech restrictions to be content-neutral, i.e., not to favor any particular viewpoint.[188] Even those critical of *Buckley v. Valeo* have recognized that content-neutrality is necessary to uphold campaign finance legislation.[189] Many reformers, however, usually political liberals, view campaign finance reform favorably precisely because they assume that the targeted power base of money works mainly to the advantage of their political opponents.[190] Once it is conceded that legislation is intended to hamper the expression of some ideas and not others, it is difficult to assert that the regulation is content-neutral.

Favoring nonmonetary elites is also problematic in light of the reformers' goal of achieving political equality. The targeting of a single source of political power, money, does not necessarily make the system more responsive to the interests of the middle and working classes. It is a serious mistake to assume that all members of any one elite group, be it journalists, academics, celebrities, or business people, think alike. As Professor Lillian BeVier points out, such an assumption rests on a group mentality and, at least where money is concerned, relies on a rather callow and unsubstantiated notion of a society irretrievably divided between some group known as the "rich," all having similar views and interests, and another group, the "poor," who share a different set of common views and interests.[191]

However, to the extent that differing opinions on issues may be generally held within different elites, the ordinary public is best served by allowing for the interplay among those elites, rather than attempting to exclude a single elite.[192] Efforts to ensure "equality" of inputs to the campaign process are less likely to guarantee popular control than is the presence of multiple sources of political power.[193] By decreasing the num-

---

188. Lawrence H. Tribe, American Constitutional Law 12-3, at 798 (2d ed. 1988).

189. *See, e.g.*, Levinson, *supra* note 138, at 943 (describing views of John Rawls).

190. *See supra* note 135 and accompanying text.

191. BeVier, *supra* note 89, at 1268-69.

192. *See generally* Gottlieb, *supra* note 17, at 271-72 (arguing that presence of fewer power bases fosters tendency towards "oligarchy," which can be offset by "multiple sources of power"). At the risk of being accused of gratuitously hauling out the heavy artillery of political discourse, *see also* The Federalist No. 10 (James Madison) (discussing control of faction by interplay).

193. *See* Gottlieb, *supra* note 17, at 271 (citing Power, Inequality and Democratic Politics 7 (Ian Shapiro & Grant Reeher eds., 1988)).

ber of voices in the political debate, a strategy of silencing one source of influence increases the power of groups whose forms of contribution remain unregulated. By creating added instability and a decentralization of power, the interplay of numerous elites may increase opportunities for traditionally less empowered groups to obtain influence.[194]

D. Campaign Finance Limitations Favor Wealthy Candidates

Though campaign finance restrictions aim to reduce the role of money in politics, they have helped to renew the phenomenon of the "millionaire candidate"—with Michael Huffington and Ross Perot as only the most celebrated recent examples.[195] In the *Buckley* decision, the Supreme Court held that Congress could not limit the amount that a candidate could spend on his or her own campaign. Contribution limits, however, force candidates to raise funds from the public only in small amounts. The ability to spend unlimited amounts, coupled with restrictions on raising outside money, favors those candidates who can contribute large sums to their own campaigns from personal assets. A Michael Huffington, Herb Kohl, or Jay Rockefeller becomes a particularly viable candidate precisely because personal wealth provides a direct campaign advantage that cannot be offset by a large contributor to the opposing candidate.[196] These candidates represent an array of views across the political spectrum. The point is not that these "rich" candidates hold uniform views but, more simply, that a system favoring personal wealth in candidates will restrict the number of viable candidates, potentially limiting voter choice. While most reformers have criticized *Buckley* for creating precisely this situa-

---

194. *See id.* at 272.

195. Burke, *supra* note 63, at 357 (noting that over half of U.S. Senators are millionaires).

196. In 1994, Huffington spent approximately $ 24 million of his own fortune to run for the U.S. Senate. *High-cost Campaigns, supra* note 86, at 8A. By September 30, 1994, Kohl had contributed almost $ 4 million to his 1994 reelection effort. Edward Kennedy and Mitt Romney each loaned or contributed $ 2 million to their campaigns for U.S. Senate in Massachusetts. *Senate Candidates Add $ 31.5 Million to Their Own Election Campaigns,* POL. FIN. & LOBBY REP., Oct. 26, 1994, at 1, 3. Physician Bill Frist of Tennessee ($ 3.75 million) was another big spender. *See* Edward Roeder, *Big Money Won the Day Last November,* PLAIN DEALER, Dec. 25, 1994, at 1-C. On the House side, Republican Gene Fontenot ($ 2 million) and Democrat Robert Schuster ($ 1.1 million) provided much of their own campaign financing. Edward Zuckerman, *Money Didn't Matter for Most Challengers Who Won,* POL. FIN. & LOBBY REP., Nov. 23, 1994, at 1, 4.

tion, it seems a mistake to exacerbate the problem through added regulation as long as *Buckley* remains law.

At the same time that contribution limits help independently wealthy candidates, they may harm working-class political interests. Historically, candidates with large constituencies among the poor and the working class have obtained their campaign funds from a small base of wealthy donors.[197] By limiting the ability of wealthy individuals such as Stewart Mott to finance these efforts, regulations may harm working-class constituencies. Supporters of these candidates simply do not have the funds to compete with other constituencies and candidates. As Stephen Gottlieb has pointed out, "candidates with many supporters who can afford to give the legal limit may be relatively unscathed by 'reform' legislation. As a consequence, it appears that national campaign 'reform' legislation has benefitted the wealthy at the expense of the working class."[198]

E. Campaign Finance Regulation Favors Special Interests Over Grassroots Activity

Campaign finance regulation is also undemocratic in that it favors well-organized special interests over grassroots political activity.[199] Limitations on contributions and spending, by definition, require significant regulation of the campaign process, including substantial reporting

---

197. Gottlieb, *supra* note 17, at 220-21.

198. *Id.* at 221 (footnote omitted). It is worth noting that this dynamic would exist, albeit to a lesser extent, even at Lowenstein's suggested $ 100 contribution limit.

199. *See id.* at 225 n.61, and sources cited therein.

Of course, one person's "special interest" is another's "grassroots lobby," and vice versa. By "special interest," I mean a person or group seeking to influence legislation and government policy, usually in pursuit of a narrowly defined economic interest, typically employing professional staff, and usually having a strong, top-down leadership structure. Such a group is usually more concerned with influencing legislative than public opinion. By a "grassroots lobby," I mean a group that tends to operate outside of traditional centers of political leadership, that typically relies more heavily on volunteer help and a decentralized structure, and that is more likely to be ideologically motivated, even if focused on a narrow issue. Such a group would be somewhat more populist and would usually aim not to influence legislative opinion directly so much as to influence public opinion and awareness and make public opinion known to legislators. I recognize that these definitions are far from precise. The point is that campaign finance regulation leads to a professionalization of politics that may alienate more typical voters and hinder local, volunteer, and unorganized or less organized activity. In discussing "grassroots activity" in this section, I refer to political activity other than the giving of money.

requirements as to the amounts spent and the sources of funds. Typically, regulation favors those already familiar with the regulatory machinery and those with the money and sophistication to hire the lawyers, accountants, and lobbyists needed to comply with complex filing requirements.[200] Such regulation will naturally disadvantage newcomers to the political arena, especially those who are themselves less educated or less able to pay for professional services. Efforts to regulate campaigns in favor of small contributors thus have the perverse effect of professionalizing politics and distancing the system from "ordinary" citizens.

Regulation also creates opportunities to gain an advantage over an opponent through use of the regulatory process, and litigation has now become "a major campaign tactic."[201] Again, one can expect such tactics to be used most often by those already familiar with the rules. Indeed, there is some evidence that campaign enforcement actions are disproportionately directed at challengers, who are less likely to have staff familiar with the intricacies of campaign finance regulation.[202]

Perhaps those most likely to run afoul of campaign finance laws, and thus to be vulnerable to legal manipulations aimed at driving them from the political debate, are unaffiliated individuals engaged in true grassroots activities. For example, in 1991, the Los Angeles Times found that sixty-two individuals had violated FECA contribution limits by making total contributions of more than $ 25,000 to candidates in the 1990 elections.[203] As the Times noted, while many of these sixty-two were "successful business people" who "usually have the benefit of expert legal advice on the intricacies of federal election laws," the next largest group of violators consisted of "elderly persons...with little grasp of the federal campaign laws."[204] Threats of prosecution have, in fact, been used in ef-

---

200. *See* Mott, *supra* note 146, at 135.

Although the necessary legal expertise can be bought, the cost will often be higher for candidates and groups with no prior experience. In local races, funds may not be available to counter the expertise gained by incumbents through experience. And, of course, it would seem to cut against the grain of the entire reformist effort to increase the importance of specialized legal skills, not to mention the availability of funds to pay for those skills, in determining who wins a campaign.

201. Moussalli, *supra* note 94, at 9.

202. *See, e.g.*, Amicus Brief of American Civil Liberties Union of Ohio Foundation, Inc. at 12-14, Pestrak v. Ohio Elections Comm'n, 926 F.2d 573 (6th Cir.) (Nos. 88-3131 & 88-3132), *cert. dismissed*, 502 U.S. 1022 (1991) (noting that Ohio Election Code has been enforced almost exclusively against challengers).

203. *See* Sara Fritz & Dwight Morris, *Federal Election Panel Not Enforcing Limit on Campaign Donations*, L.A. TIMES, Sept. 15, 1991, at A1, A8-A9.

204. *Id.* at A1, A8-A9.

forts to silence dissent from those without "the benefit of expert legal advice on the intricacies of federal election laws."[205]

Even sophisticated interest groups have found campaign finance laws to be a substantial hindrance to grassroots campaign activity and voter education efforts. In 1994, for example, both the U.S. Chamber of Commerce and the American Medical Association (AMA) decided not to publish and distribute candidate endorsements to thousands of their dues-paying members, in response to threats of litigation from the Federal Election Commission (FEC). Under FEC regulations, only sixty-three of the Chamber's 220,000 dues-paying members qualified as "members" for the purposes of receiving the organization's political communications. Similarly, the FEC had held that it would be unlawful for the AMA to distribute endorsements to some 44,500 of its dues-paying members. One AMA lawyer noted that, under the circumstances, communicating endorsements to its dues-paying members was not "worth the legal risk."[206]

Campaign finance regulation has been packaged as a means of returning power to "ordinary people." In truth, however, such regulation acts to exclude ordinary people from the political process in a variety of ways: It insulates incumbents from the voting public, in both the electoral and legislative spheres; it increases the ability of certain elites to dominate the debate by eliminating competing voices; it places a renewed premium on personal wealth in political candidates; and it hampers grassroots political activity. These problems are not the result of a poorly designed regulatory structure, but rather the inevitable result of a regulatory structure built on faulty assumptions.[207]

---

205. *Id.* at A9. *In McIntyre v. Ohio Elections Commission*, 115 S. Ct. 1511 (1995), Margaret McIntyre, an Ohio housewife, was fined by the Ohio Elections Commission for the peaceful distribution of truthful campaign literature outside a public meeting. Ms. McIntyre was distributing flyers in opposition to a school tax levy and had signed her brochures simply, "Concerned Parents and Tax Payers." An assistant school superintendent first threatened McIntyre and later brought charges against her for violating an Ohio law prohibiting the distribution of anonymous campaign literature. Only after seven years of litigation was McIntyre exonerated by the Supreme Court. Before the Supreme Court, the State had argued that the Court's failure to uphold such regulation would make *Buckley* unenforceable. *See* Respondent's Brief at 20, *McIntyre*, 115 S. Ct. 1511 (No. 93-986).

206. Edward Zuckerman, *Speechless in D.C.*, POL. FIN. & LOBBY REP., Nov. 9, 1994, at 1, 2. The regulation in question was struck down by the D.C. Circuit approximately one year after the 1994 elections. *See* Chamber of Commerce v. FEC, No. 94-5339, 1995 U.S. App. LEXIS 31925 (D.C. Cir. Nov. 14, 1995).

207. *See supra* Part III.

On Campaign Finance Reform: The Root of All Evil is Deeply Rooted

[Excerpt One]

Daniel Hays Lowenstein

I. Introduction

Alexander Heard, in his great treatise on campaign finance, identifies money as a unique political resource because it can be converted into many other political resources, as need may dictate.[1] This observation is often invoked by reformers when skeptics of campaign finance reform object that there is no justification for regulating the use of money in politics more stringently than other resources, such as celebrity, ownership of or access to the mass communications media, or even personal qualities such as good looks or articulateness.[2] The reformer's response, in Heard's words, is that money "is a universal, transferable unit infinitely more flexible in its uses than the time, or ideas, or talent, or influence, or controlled votes that also constitute contributions to politics."[3]

---

1. ALEXANDER HEARD, THE COSTS OF DEMOCRACY 3 (1960).

2. *See* Levinson, *Regulating Campaign Activity: The New Road to Contradiction?*, (Book Review), 83 MICH.L.REV. 939, 948-52 (1985) (discussing other resources which are unevenly distributed and reviewing ELIZABETH DREW, POLITICS AND MONEY: THE NEW ROAD TO CORRUPTION (1983)).

3. HEARD, *supra* note 1, at 90; *see also* DAVID ADAMANY & GEORGE AGREE, POLITICAL MONEY 3 (1975) (discussing the liquidity and flexibility of money as a political resource). In fact, money can be used to achieve other, less flexible resources:

> [M]oney can buy most non-economic political resources. It can pay canvassers, or skilled campaign managers, or publicists, or researchers. It cannot endow a candidate with intelligence, but it can buy him a brain trust.

> It cannot change his voice or face, but it can hire a make-up man, a voice coach, and a clever film editor. Those with money can buy virtually any of the resources that other citizens give directly. *Id.*

Levinson makes no response to Heard's point. *See* Levinson, *supra* note 2. Many of

The special qualities of money have broader implications than this snippet from the standard debate over campaign finance reform suggests. There is a sense, related to money's peculiar qualities, in which the problem of campaign finance is a very simple one. The payment of money to bias the judgment or sway the loyalty of persons holding positions of public trust is a practice whose condemnation is deeply rooted in our most ancient heritage.[4] This condemnation, together with the recognition that money has the power to tempt men and women to stray not only from their ethical responsibilities, but from their own highest interests, gives rise to that strain in our culture that perceives money as the root of all evil. To the extent that campaign finance practices are corrupt in the traditional sense,[5] a central goal of reform must be to root out and eliminate the practices to the maximum extent practicable.

Of course, in a different sense, the campaign finance problem is an inordinately complex one. The complexity derives from the infinite flexibility that Heard identified as money's distinguishing attribute as a political resource.[6] Because of its flexibility, money is everywhere in our political system, and almost unimaginably diverse in its uses and effects. This means that efforts to regulate the flow of money, whether to root out corruption or for any other purpose, are likely to affect the system and its participants in innumerable ways, large and small, foreseeable and unforeseeable.

The inevitability of unforeseeable effects, the so-called law of unanticipated consequences, has become a rhetorical focal point for opponents of reform.[7] These opponents cite common sense and past experience for the

---

Levinson's examples of anomalies that can result from campaign finance reform are ingenious, but most of them seem to be either overdrawn or of little practical significance. Pointing to inconsistencies in the manner of the law school class discussion is not helpful in discussion of broad reforms unless it can be shown that the inconsistencies have systemic significance. In this sense, I disagree with Levinson that reformers must generate "a coherent and consistent theory" justifying their proposals. *Id.* at 952. A set of reforms that will do more good than harm and that have a chance to get enacted would satisfy me, with or without a theory. Without such reforms, what good is a theory?

4. *See generally* JOHN T. NOONAN, JR., BRIBES (1984) (discussing bribes in a variety of cultures and contexts throughout history). For a criticism of the portion of Noonan's book dealing with campaign finance, *see* Lowenstein, *For God, for Country, or for Me?* 74 CAL.L.REV. 1479, 1500-07 (1986).

5. *See infra* notes 26-154 and accompanying text (analyzing whether campaign finance practices actually are corrupt).

6. *See* HEARD, *supra* note 1, at 90 (discussing the unique characteristics of money).

7. *See, e.g.,* Michael Malbin, *Looking Back at the Future of Campaign Finance Reform, in* MONEY AND POLITICS IN THE UNITED STATES 232, 238-443 (Michael Malbin ed. 1984) [hereinafter MONEY AND POLITICS] (discussing the unintended consequences of proposed campaign finance legislation); Larry Sabato, *Real and Imagined Corruption in*

proposition that campaign finance reforms are likely to have surprising results.[8] If the law of unanticipated consequences is interpreted as an injunction to think through the consequences of reform proposals as best we can, it becomes a benevolent bromide that can go on the shelf between "tell the truth" and "do not forget to brush after every meal." Caution and a degree of skepticism are always appropriate when dealing with questions of far-reaching significance. But this "law" derives its point from the opponents' assumption that the unanticipated consequences of campaign finance reforms are far more likely to be harmful than beneficial. This assumption, which has no basis in logic and has not, to the best of my knowledge, been demonstrated with the empirical rigor these opponents demand that reformers provide for their assumptions, is supposed to create a strong presumption against adoption of new reforms, and to chastise those of us who have had a finger in past reforms.[9]

Such a strong presumption cannot be imposed for two reasons. First, the argument has no stronger force in the field of campaign finance reform than in any other major field of human endeavor, each of which is subject equally to the inscrutability of the future. The law of unanticipated consequences is not an argument against campaign finance reform; it is an argument against any significant departure from the status quo. Second, the status quo itself is subject to the law of unanticipated consequences. Since change is a constant in human affairs, the consequences of a governing arrangement in one portion of the political system (or any

---

Campaign Financing, in ELECTIONS AMERICAN STYLE 155, 164-67 (A. James Reichley ed. 1987) (warning of possible adverse consequences should political action committees' contributions be limited).

8. The consequences were not really unanticipated in some of the past experiences which such opponents cite. In particular, some of the consequences of the 1974 amendments to the Federal Election Campaign Act were warned against by reformers who opposed some provisions but supported the package as a whole in the belief that the benefits would outweigh the drawbacks. *See, e.g.,* Fred Wertheimer, *The PAC Phenomenon in American Politics*, 22 ARIZ.L.REV. 603, 605-06 (1980) (arguing that certain elements of the 1974 amendments to the Federal Election Campaign Act were never truly intended as a "reform").

9. I was one of the drafters of the California Political Reform Act of 1974, *see* CAL. GOV'T CODE §§ 81000-91000 (West 1987), an initiative statute adopted by the California electorate in 1974. In addition, I served as the first appointed chairman of the California Fair Political Practices Commission from 1975-1979. To complete my confession of past sins, I had the pleasure of serving on the National Governing Board of Common Cause from 1979-1985. I continue to be an enthusiastic supporter of Common Cause, though readers of Daniel H. Lowenstein & Jonathan Steinberg, *The Quest for Legislative Districting in the Public Interest: Elusive or Illusory?*, 33 UCLA L. REV. 1 (1985), will attest that my views do not always coincide with those of Common Cause.

other human system of importance) will change drastically as the environment changes, even if the particular governing arrangement is unaltered. The unanticipated consequences of failing to change can be as unpleasant as the unanticipated consequences of changing. (Just ask a dinosaur, if you can find one!) Since the law of unanticipated consequences therefore counsels equally against action and inaction, it would be a guide to complete immobilization if it were taken seriously. Of course, it is not taken seriously. It is nothing but a rhetorical ploy, and one that deserves to be discredited.

The serious problem for reformers is not the unforeseeable consequences of their proposals, but the foreseeable ones. The pervasiveness of money in politics assures that analysis of any far-reaching reform proposal will reveal a diverse array of foreseeable consequences for a host of participants, interests and values in the political system.[10] Generally speaking, the very flexibility and pervasiveness of money make it possible to adjust reform proposals to avoid or minimize foreseeable consequences that are deemed harmful and to promote those deemed beneficial. The problem is that even among those who join in the desire to expunge corrupt campaign finance practices, there is not, and never will be, a consensus on how to evaluate the numerous additional foreseeable effects the reforms will have on politics.

This is the fundamental strategic problem that has frustrated campaign finance reform efforts. Sit most people down individually, and you can devise a reform package that is likely to reduce the corruption in our system and that will be at least acceptable in its other consequences. It is exceedingly difficult, however, to come up with a single package that is agreeable even to a majority, not to mention the near-consensus that our system of checks and balances, combined with divided party government,[11] requires for enactment. Any package will have foreseeable effects on the major parties,[12] on the party system as a whole,[13] on incumbency,[14] on the nature

---

10. For a discussion of the foreseeable consequences of the reforms proposed by this Article, *see infra* notes 258-66 and accompanying text.

11. "Divided party government" refers to the situation in which no single party controls the presidency and both chambers of Congress. *See generally* Lloyd N. Cutler, *Party Government Under the American Constitution*, 134 U. Pa. L. Rev. 25 (1985-86) (discussing the lack of party government and its relation to the decline in party loyalty).

12. *See infra* notes 182-91, 258-61 and accompanying text.

13. *See infra* notes 194-95 and accompanying text (discussing why people choose a given political party); *infra* notes 240-45 and accompanying text (discussing generic party advertising).

14. *See infra* text accompanying notes 263-64.

of election campaigns,[15] and on whole classes of society[16] as well as on a variety of more specific economic and other interests, and on particular officeholders, candidates, and other participants in the system. The consequences of campaign finance reforms cut across a bewildering array of dimensions.

The strategic problem resulting from the pervasive, diverse and manipulable consequences that must attend any serious reform proposal cannot be solved or avoided. It can only be contended with. Part Three of this Article demonstrates the far-reaching effects this strategic problem has had on the way we debate the campaign finance issue.[17] This Part shows that the intertwining of levels of argument, ranging from the most pure public-interest orientation to the level of pure self-interest, is complex, but need not be a cause of extreme confusion or discomfort if things are sorted out properly.

Prior to discussing this strategic problem, a preliminary issue must be considered. As stated earlier, the central problem of campaign finance reform is a simple one to the extent that present practices are corrupting in the traditional sense. Although I believe this premise is accepted by the overwhelming majority of Americans, it has been contested by some scholars.[18] Part Two of this Article explains why I believe these scholars are wrong and lays some of the groundwork for the discussion in Part Three.[19]

Part Four broadly outlines a reform package for legislative general elections.[20] This package consists of a relatively low aggregate limit on the amount of contributions over $100 a candidate may receive from all

---

15. *See infra* text accompanying notes 262-64 (discussing the effect of this Article's proposal on the way challengers and incumbents will conduct campaigns).

16. *See infra* text accompanying notes 257-58 (discussing the effect of this Article's proposal on egalitarians and libertarians).

17. *See infra* notes 153-202 and accompanying text.

18. *See infra* text accompanying notes 28-32.

19. *See infra* notes 26-154 and accompanying text.

20. *See infra* notes 277-86 and accompanying text. Although the discussion in this Article centers on Congress, the proposals and most of the discussion can be easily adaptable to the legislatures of many states. The fact that the proposals apply only to general elections is undeniably a significant defect. As should be clear from the nature of the proposals, they are not adaptable to primary elections.

I do not discuss in this Article the question of minor parties and independent candidates. My preference would be to provide public financing to non-major party candidates only on terms comparable to those contained in the present provisions for the public financing of presidential campaigns. Those who favor more generous treatment of non-major party candidates could easily adapt my proposals to that end.

sources, except certain qualified political action committees (PACs);[21] a separate aggregate limit the same size as the first on the amount a candidate may receive from qualified PACs, which qualify by not accepting contributions over $50;[22] public financing, to be allocated in amounts determined by the partisan leadership of the legislative houses to candidates of their own parties, with the amount provided to each party in each house set at a level high enough to permit the parties to fund a significant number of challenges while allocating enough to permit incumbents to defend themselves against challenge;[23] and a separate public financing fund made available to the partisan house leaders for expenditure on generic advertising, which supports the party as a whole rather than specific party candidates.[24]

Few, if any, parts of this package are new, although some of them have received relatively little attention. The overall configuration may be distinctive. I set forth and defend this package in order to contribute to the ongoing debate, but with no expectation that it will be adopted, nor even more than a tentative commitment to it myself. Elaboration of the package is intended to support the more general theme of this Article by showing that a variety of values and interests, including some that often have been regarded as inexorably in conflict with campaign finance reform, in fact are compatible with serious efforts to reduce corrupt practices.[25]

Campaign finance reform is like a very long menu in a restaurant that requires everyone at the table to order the same meal. There is something on the menu that will satisfy almost any taste. If you do not see what you want, the chef may be able to prepare something special for you. The trouble is that the longer the menu, the harder it is to get everyone to agree on a single selection.

II. The Campaign Finance System is Corrupt

At the outset of his treatise, Alexander Heard recognized that a major dissatisfaction with campaign finance in America was the perception that

---

21. *See infra* text accompanying notes 240-44.
22. *See infra* text accompanying notes 247-48.
23. *See infra* text accompanying notes 216-26.
24. *See infra* text accompanying notes 228-32.
25. *See infra* notes 257-68 and accompanying text (discussing the effect of the proposals suggested by this Article on various interested parties).

candidates' need for money "opened opportunities to swap party and public favors for the cash."[26] Cautious attentiveness to the degree of contributor influence over public decision-making is a pervasive theme in Heard's book. In contrast, Frank Sorauf's recent text, *Money in American Elections*, does not give serious attention to the possibility that campaign contributions might affect public actions, other than through their possible effects on election outcomes, until the 307th of its 384 pages.[27] Sorauf devotes ten pages to the subject and concludes:

> [T]he evidence simply does not support the more extravagant claims about the "buying" of the Congress. Systematic studies indicate at most a modest influence for PAC contributors, a degree of influence usually far less important than the voting constituency, the party, or the values [of] the legislator. Moreover, several other studies suggest that the goals and capacities of most PACs are not congruent with assumptions that they set out to change congressional votes. In fact, both the extent of their influence and the nature of their operations fit much better their own stated goal of access. Finally, the development of PAC pluralism—both in the increase of countervailing PACs and in the wide dispersion of their contributions in small sums—also leads one to a more modest assessment of PAC influence. Such conclusions may serve few demonologies, but they are the only ones that serve the facts as we know them.[28]

---

26. HEARD, *supra* note 1, at 8. The other major dissatisfaction was the unequal resources available to election contestants. *Id.*

27. *See* FRANK SORAUF, MONEY IN AMERICAN ELECTIONS 307-17 (1988). If the appendices and index are included, the book runs to 416 pages.

Although Sorauf's discussion of the influence issue is rather one-sided, this in itself might be stimulating and provocative for students, most of whom probably approach the subject with assumptions contrary to Sorauf's. It is not his treatment of the merits of the issue, but relegation of the issue to peripheral status in a textbook on this subject which is likely to be disorienting for students and, in my opinion, puts the entire treatment of campaign finance out of joint. It is for this reason that, despite its many impressive virtues and its author's unquestioned stature, I cannot regard *Money in American Elections* as an altogether worthy successor to Heard's *The Costs of Democracy*.

A teacher searching for campaign finance texts might also wish to consider *Political Money*, written by David Adamany and George Agree. Though not as seriously dated as Heard's book, parts of *Political Money* are, of course, no longer current. Other portions have survived well, such as the chapter on campaign finance disclosure, *see* ADAMANY & AGREE, *supra* note 3, at 83-115, which probably remains the best treatment of this subject. Although *Political Money* is broadly conceived, its focus is on reform proposals and it does not aspire to the comprehensiveness of Heard's and Sorauf's works.

28. Sorauf, *supra* note 27, at 316.

Similarly skeptical views have been expressed by Michael Malbin.[29] Other scholars, including Gary Jacobson,[30] Larry Sabato,[31] Kay Lehman Schlozman and John Tierney,[32] have reviewed the same literature as Sorauf and Malbin and have given greater credence, in varying degrees, to the claim that special interest contributions influence legislative behavior.

A. Do Contributors Seek Influence?

Let us begin with Sorauf's suggestion that PACs may not even attempt to influence legislative behavior with their contributions.[33] It has been widely recognized that interest groups making campaign contributions might use either or both of two strategies to influence public policy. Under the "electoral" strategy, they make contributions to enhance the chances of victory of candidates who are likely, if they are elected, to pursue the policies the contributors favor.[34] Under the "legislative" strategy, they

---

29. *See* Malbin, *supra* note 7, at 247-52. Malbin concludes as follows:

> [T]he fact that a contributor intends his money to have a certain effect does not mean that it was received in the same spirit, even if the recipient behaves as the contributor might have wished. The world is too complicated to be encapsulated by such simple analysis. Anyone who wants to say something precise about the independent effect of contributions will have to pursue a different line of research from the ones we have seen so far.

Id. at 252.

30. *See* Gary Jacobson, *Parties and PACs in Congressional Elections, in* CONGRESS RECONSIDERED 131, 151-52 (Lawrence Dodd & Bruce Oppenheimer eds. 3d ed. 1985) [hereinafter Jacobson, *Parties and PACs*] (noting that some connection exists between contributions and voting, but warning that "[m]uch more work is needed before we can have a clear idea of how commonly PAC contributions influence congressional behavior.").

31. *See* Sabato, *supra* note 7, at 159-61 (agreeing that "PAC money buys access to congressmen" but rejecting allegations of "vote-buying").

32. *See* KAY LEHMAN SCHLOZMAN & JOHN TIERNEY, ORGANIZED INTERESTS AND AMERICAN DEMOCRACY 253-56 (1986) (evaluating the effect of contributions, noting that the "evidence...gives cause for concern, though not hysteria," and calling for more studies).

33. *See* SORAUF, *supra* note 27, at 316 (stating that "the goals and capacities of most PACs are not congruent with assumptions that they set out to change congressional votes.").

34. *See* SCHLOZMAN & TIERNEY, *supra* note 32, at 206-07 (noting that an assumption often made by interested groups is that the mere election of a like-minded candidate will promote the causes of that organization without any further efforts); W.P. Welch, *Patterns of Contributions: Economic Interest and Ideological Groups, in* POLITICAL FINANCE, 199, 200-01 (Herbert E. Alexander ed. 1979) (explaining this hypothesis in terms of "ideological group contributions").

make contributions to whomever they think is likely to be elected, in the hopes of influencing the likely winner to pursue the favored policies by reason of gratitude, a desire to encourage future donations from the same or additional groups, or similar motivations.[35]

A group pursuing an electoral strategy would make contributions in races where they are likely to be of the greatest electoral value, which means in races regarded as close.[36] It would be irrational, within an electoral strategy, to contribute either to hopeless candidacies or to those assured of victory.[37] Like the electoral strategy, the legislative strategy dictates against contributing to likely losers.[38] Similarly, both strategies call for contributions in close races. It is true that for the legislative strategist such a contribution is risky, since there is no benefit in influencing the policy pursuits of the recipient of the contribution if he or she fails to get elected. This consideration is offset by the possibility of a higher payoff, since the gratitude of a candidate who had a real need for the contribution may be especially great. Furthermore, a close contest may indicate a serious challenge in future elections, in which case the incumbent will be under pressure to retain the favor of contributors.

Where the difference between the two strategies is most likely to reveal itself is in contributions to sure winners. A pure electoral strategist should never make contributions to such candidates, whereas a legislative strategist should do so frequently.[39] In addition, an electoral strategist will always contribute to candidates whose existing policy views are compatible with the group's, or at least substantially more compatible than the views of the candidates' opponents. The relation between the candidate's policy views and the dictates of a legislative strategy are equivocal. Since the legislative strategist is interested in the change that the group's contribution may induce in the candidate's policy views, rather than in the absolute location of those views, there is no reason to expect the legislative strategist to limit contributions to those whose initial views are particularly compatible with those of the group.

---

35. *See* SCHLOZMAN & TIERNEY, *supra* note 32, at 207.

36. *See* Welch, *supra* note 34, at 213 (reaching the conclusion that an "ideological group…will aid candidates in close races.").

37. *See* SCHLOZMAN & TIERNEY, *supra* note 32, at 207 (arguing that the strategy of electing "ideologically congenial candidates" avoids wasting scarce resources on sure winners or sure losers).

38. *See id.*

39. *See id.* (noting that "since the goal is to ensure that officeholders feel compelled to be responsive, organizations active in electoral politics frequently aid certain winners, even candidates running without opposition."); Welch, *supra* note 34, at 213 (arguing that the legislative strategist "will make its largest gifts to likely winners").

According to most scholars who have considered the question, economic interest contributors tend to follow a legislative strategy.[40] They reach this conclusion on either theoretical or empirical grounds. The theoretical basis stems from the collective choice consideration that the benefits of an electoral strategy would be shared with all other groups favored by the candidate's overall policy views whereas a legislative strategy can be more particularized to the narrower goals of the contributor.[41] The empirical basis is an analysis of contributor patterns.[42]

Sorauf based his contrary conclusion on a study by John R. Wright that dealt only with PACs controlled by trade associations.[43] Wright's analysis is unpersuasive, even when limited to the type of PAC he was studying.[44]

---

40. See sources cited *infra* note 42.

41. See generally MANCUR OLSON, THE LOGIC OF COLLECTIVE ACTION (1965).

42. See, e.g., Henry W. Chappell, Jr., *Campaign Contributions and Congressional Voting: A Simultaneous Prohibit-Tobit Model*, 64 REV. ECON. & STATISTICS 77, 82 (1982); Benjamin Ginsberg & John C. Green, *The Best Congress Money Can Buy: Campaign Contributions and Congressional Behavior, in* DO ELECTIONS MATTER? 76, 79-80 (Benjamin Ginsberg & Alan Stone eds. 1986); Welch, *supra* note 34, at 199-213.

43. See SORAUF, *supra* note 27, at 313 n.27 (citing John R. Wright, *PACs, Contributions, and Roll Calls: An Organizational Perspective,* 79 AM. POL. SCI. REV. 400 (1985)).

44. Wright reported that Washington officials of the PACs approved without modification 80 to 90% of the recommendations from locally active PAC members regarding candidates to whom PAC funds should be donated. *See* Wright, *supra* note 43, at 404. Aside from the fact that Wright seems to have relied solely on the PAC officials' word for these figures, he does not say in what percentage of cases such local recommendations were received, nor whether the local members may have consulted with the Washington staffs prior to making recommendations. *See generally id.* However, in the belief that he has demonstrated that trade association PAC contributions are controlled locally rather than coordinated centrally by the lobbying staffs, Wright goes on to conclude that in consequence the contributions will be guided by an electoral strategy rather than by a legislative strategy. *See id.* 405-06. He supports this conclusion by asserting that local PAC members "are much more likely to be familiar with electoral politics of geographic constituencies than with the mechanics of influencing legislation in the Congress." *Id.* at 406. This statement is not at all self-evident, especially since local PAC members have ready access to the Washington staff who presumably are willing and able to give them advice on the Congressional situation, and Wright makes no effort to support his statement empirically. He says that the supposed local domination of contribution decisions will force legislators to curry favor with the local PAC activists rather than with the Washington staff, *see id.* at 406, but his conclusion that this will undermine a legislative strategy is mysterious, since the local PACs presumably share the legislative goals of the Washington staff, and nowadays "grass-roots lobbying" is widely regarded as an especially potent form of lobbying.

Wright tests his theory by considering whether his five PACs were more likely to contribute to a rank-and-file, ideologically compatible incumbent from a competitive district (electoral strategy), or to an influential, ideologically hostile candidate from a secure dis-

The fact that labor union PACs have supported Democrats almost exclusively[45] has been taken as an indication that they are following an electoral strategy, at least partially.[46] There is empirical support for the proposition that some business-oriented PACs also are at least partially driven by an electoral strategy.[47] However, there are several practices commonly engaged in by interest group contributors that are either inconsistent or in tension with the idea that they are engaged in a pure electoral strategy.

---

trict (legislative strategy). See id. at 406-08. Three of his PACs tended to give more to the former type of candidate, while two of them favored the latter. Id. Wright regarded this as confirmation of his theory, but his results are unimpressive, especially in light of the demonstration in the text above that a legislative strategy would lead to contributions to both candidates, whereas any contribution at all to the second type is inconsistent with a pure electoral strategy.

45. See SCHLOZMAN & TIERNEY, supra note 32, at 233 (noting that labor PACs gave an average of $20,200 to Democrats in 1980, but a mere $1,000 to Republicans); SORAUF, supra note 27, at 100 (noting that 94.7% of labor PACs' contributions went to Democratic candidates in 1984 and 92.5% in 1986).

46. See SCHLOZMAN & TIERNEY, supra note 32, at 236-37 (concluding that both labor and corporate PACs also "seek out like-minded candidates who can be trusted to be supportive, even if left to their own devices.").

47. See J. David Gopoian, What Makes PACs Tick? An Analysis of the Allocation Patterns of Economic Interest Groups, 28 AM. J. POL. SCI. 259 (1984). The main thrust of Gopoian's study considers whether certain economic-group PACs pursued broad ideological goals or narrow, particular goals. His conclusion was that they pursued the latter primarily, but among oil industry PACs, there was a substantial element of the former. See id. at 279. Gopoian's research was based on the 1978 House of Representative elections, see id. at 259, and it would be interesting to see whether his results would stand following the later drive by Democrats in the House to increase their share of business-PAC donations in general, and of oil industry contributions in particular. These events are reported in ELIZABETH DREW, POLITICS AND MONEY (1983) and BROOKS JACKSON, HONEST GRAFT: BIG MONEY AND THE AMERICAN POLITICAL PROCESS (1988).

Gopoian also claims that his data show that the PACs he studied were not following a legislative strategy. See Gopoian, supra, at 266. This claim, if valid, would tend to support Sorauf's assertion in his textbook. The claim, however, is based on fallacious assumptions about legislative strategy. Gopoian assumes that a legislative strategist must pursue either "access," calling for disproportionate contributions to sure winners, or "power" over legislators, calling for contributions to candidates in electoral jeopardy. Id. at 264. To the contrary, the legislative strategist is likely to give to any candidate other than a likely loser. Since almost no incumbents fit into this category, it is consistent with a legislative strategy to find no particular correlation between the incumbent's electoral vulnerability and his or her likelihood of receiving a contribution. Such a lack of correlation is exactly what Gopoian found. See Gopoian, supra, at 266-67. Since a pure electoral strategy would call for contributions only to candidates in close elections, Gopoian's data actually undercut rather than support Sorauf's conclusion.

First, although business leaders are not entirely homogeneous in their political views, they are generally imagined to be heavily Republican.[48] Yet, a very substantial percentage of business PAC contributions in House elections has gone to Democrats, who as the majority party are the most crucial targets of a legislative strategy.[49] Reportedly, fifty-five percent of business PAC contributions in 1988 House elections went to Democrats.[50] It is hard to explain these facts if the business PACs are following a pure electoral strategy. Brooks Jackson has given a more plausible explanation:

> The reason that Democrats...received significant support from business and professional PACs was that the donors cared more about particular bills than about any broad philosophy of free-market economics. Vander Jagt [head of the Republican House fund-raising committee] thought businessmen had a moral commitment to fostering free enterprise and minimal government. Coelho [head of the Democratic House fund-raising committee] figured that corporate managers were interested in preserving their companies' short-term, after tax profits. When Republicans talked about being pro-business, they were speaking of freedom from government regulation. When Democrats said they were pro-business, they more often were touting federal subsidies or tax loopholes. Coelho appreciated, as Vander Jagt at first did not, that business PACs gave mostly to open the doors of the lawmakers who controlled the good things the federal government had going.[51]

Second, economic-group PACs commonly give to opposing candidates in the same election.[52] Internal pressures in a PAC can cause this to occur, but often it is a sign of a legislative strategy at work, albeit a rather heavy-handed one.[53]

Third, the practice of contributing to a winner after the election is over is even more heavy-handed and unambiguous as an indicator of a legisla-

---

48. *See* SCHLOZMAN & TIERNEY, *supra* note 32, at 233 (examining the relationship between corporate PACs and Republicans).

49. *See* SORAUF, *supra* note 27, at 100.

50. Charles R. Babcock, *Recipients Mull Campaign-Finance Changes*, WASH. POST, July 23, 1989, at A4.

51. JACKSON, *supra* note 47, at 87.

52. *See* SCHLOZMAN & TIERNEY, *supra* note 32, at 241 (noting that 58% of corporate PACs, 57% of trade association PACs, and 43% of labor PACs had engaged in cross-giving). Alexander Heard, writing in a more benighted age, found that the practice of giving to candidates of both parties had a bad reputation, although only a fraction of such contributions went to opposing candidates in the same election. HEARD, *supra* note 1, at 58-67.

53. *See generally* SCHLOZMAN & TIERNEY, *supra* note 32, at 241-42 (providing an excellent discussion of the cross-giving issue).

tive strategy. Larry Sabato reports that following the 1986 elections in which seven incumbent Republican senators were defeated by Democrats, "there were 150 instances in which a PAC gave to the GOP candidate before the election and then made a contribution to the victorious Democrat after the votes were counted."[54]

In summary, although it would be an overstatement to suggest that economic interests always or nearly always contribute to influence official conduct rather than to influence the outcome of elections, it is probably correct to say that they usually follow this strategy, with the possible and partial exception of labor unions.[55] For the purposes of this Article it is necessary only to put forth a weaker claim, that whether or not it is their predominant strategy, economic-group contributors often are driven by a legislative strategy when they make their contributions. There can be no reasonable denial of that claim.[56]

B. Do Contributors Get Influence?

1. A review of the evidence. — A considerable amount of the money that goes to candidates from economic-group contributors is motivated by a desire to influence the performance of officeholders rather than to influence who is elected.[57] A more controversial issue among academics has been whether the legislative strategy works. Are the legislators influenced by contributions? Several studies have appeared using various econometric methods to explore the relationship between contributions, almost in-

---

54. Sabato, *supra* note 31, at 155; *see also* Daniel H. Lowenstein, *Political Bribery and the Intermediate Theory of Politics*, 32 UCLA L.REV. 784, 827 n.157 (referring to a successful 1982 Democratic candidate for governor of Texas who received 90 post-election contributions in amounts ranging from $10,000 to $50,000 from contributors who had supported his Republican opponent before the election).

55. Oddly, not even Sorauf disagrees with this, except when he is intent on belittling the idea that campaign contributions may have a significant effect on legislative behavior. Sorauf, referring to the legislative strategy, writes: "This is perhaps the dominant strategy for all of the PACs with parent organizations. It is reflected primarily in their overwhelming support for incumbents running for reelection. It is reflected as well in patterns of support for members of the leadership and members of specific committees." SORAUF, *supra* note 27, at 103.

56. Writers skeptical of campaign finance reform usually concede at least this much. In Daniel D. Polsby's cogent formulation: "Evidence that politicians are regularly bought by malefactors of great wealth is hard to come by. But there is plainly an enormous amount of shopping going on." Daniel D. Polsby, Buckley v. Valeo: *The Special Nature of Political Speech*, 1976 SUP. CT. REV. 1, 23.

57. *See supra* note 33-56 and accompanying text.

variably PAC contributions, and congressional roll call votes.[58] Some of these studies have reported no statistically significant relationship between PAC contributions to House members and their votes on bills of interest to the PACs;[59] some have reported unavoidably ambiguous results;[60] some have reported statistically significant but modest effects;[61] and some have reported effects both substantial and statistically significant.[62]

These divergent results may be due to the fact that the researchers were looking at different events. Perhaps contributor influence was present in

---

58. *Compare* John P. Frendreis & Richard W. Waterman, *PAC Contributions and Legislative Behavior: Senate Voting on Trucking Deregulation*, 66 Soc. Sci. Q. 401,410 (1985) (finding that campaign contributions affect legislative votes on certain kinds of issues) *and* W. P. Welch, *Campaign Contributions and Legislative Voting: Milk Money and Dairy Price Supports*, 35 W. Pol. Q. 478, 493 (1982) (finding that "[c]ongressmen who received contributions from the dairy PACs in 1974 were more likely to vote for higher milk price supports in 1975 than congressmen who did not.") *and* Allen Wilhite & John Theilmann, *Labor PAC Contributions and Labor Legislation: A Simultaneous Logit Approach*, 53 Pub. Choice 267, 274 (1978) (concluding that "labor PACs are able to affect legislation.") *with* Chappell, *supra* note 42, at 83 (reporting that it is not possible to conclude contributions have a significant impact on voting) and Janet M. Grenzke, *PACs and the Congressional Supermarket: The Currency is Complex*, 33 Am. J. Pol. Sci. 1, 19 (1989) (concluding that PACs "do not maintain or change House members' voting patterns.").

59. *See, e.g.*, Grenzke, *supra* note 58, at 19-20 (concluding that "[l]imiting PAC contributions will not significantly change the power of these organizations because when they do influence legislators, it is because they can mobilize votes in the district").

60. *See, e.g.*, Chappell, *supra* note 42, at 83 (explaining that "it is probable that [the] rather poor overall explanatory power in the equations explaining contributions leads to imprecision of these estimates in the voting equation.").

61. *See, e.g.*, Welch, *supra* note 58, at 479, 493 (stating that "our results indicate that the influence of contributions is 'small,' at least relative to the influences of constituency, party, and ideology"). Welch concluded that dairy contributions enhanced by 1.5% the probability that a House member would vote for increased milk price supports in 1975. *Id.* at 491. This would translate to about seven members, or a potential swing of fourteen votes.

62. *See, e.g.*, Frendreis & Waterman, *supra* note 58, at 409-11 (arguing that the "impact of contributions is most felt by representatives with neither a strong positive nor a strong negative disposition toward the contributor."); Ginsberg & Green, *supra* note 42, at 80-84 (finding a correlation existed between contributions of an important, interested lobbying group, and the voting of senators considering the 1980 Motor Carrier Act); Willhite & Theilmann, *supra* note 58, at 272-75 (finding that "the tendency of a representative to support labor issues was directly related to the size of the campaign contributions from labor PACs").

some and not in others. The divergent results may also result from differences in methodology.[63] Although this Article will not comment on the
more technical aspects of the controversies that have emerged, a number
of more general observations are offered.

One point that has been made in many of the studies themselves is that
the roll call vote is not necessarily the place where contributor influence is
likely to be strongest.[64] The reason most commonly given is that roll call
votes are the most visible actions of legislators, and therefore are the least
likely settings in which legislators will be willing to prefer the desires of
contributors to those of constituents.[65] Contributor influence might therefore be greater in committees and other less visible roles and settings, such
as agenda-setting, scheduling, and informal negotiation over legislation.[66]
Rather like the fabled inebriate who searched for a lost key at night at the
opposite end of the block from where he dropped it because the light was
better there, most of the econometric studies have ignored these activities,
because they are harder to measure, while acknowledging they may be
more important loci of contributor influence than floor votes.

One study has measured committee action, and found a strong relationship between co-sponsorship by committee members of the Bank
Underwriting Bill, which would have permitted commercial banks to
compete with securities firms, and a surprisingly crude indicator consisting of contributions received from banking interests less contributions received from securities interests.[67] It has long been believed that more lob-

---

63. The methodologies used in studying contributor influence include from a focus on
role call voting on particular bills, *see, e.g.*, Welch, *supra* note 58, at 478-79; on the influence of contributions on a collection of otherwise unrelated bills regarded as important by
the contributors, *see, e.g.*, Wilhite & Theilmann, *supra* note 58, at 274; and on the effectiveness of contributions as a means of gaining access to the representatives themselves,
see, e.g., James F. Herndon, *Access, Record and Competition as Influences or Interest
Groups' Contributions to Congressional Campaigns*, 44 J. POL. 996, 1000 (1982).

64. *See, e.g.*, Ginsberg & Green, *supra* note 42, at 78-79; Grenzke, *supra* note 58, at
3; Welch, *supra* note 58, at 493.

65. *See, e.g.*, Welch, *supra* note 58, at 493.

66. *See, e.g.*, SCHLOZMAN & TIERNEY, *supra* note 32, at 255; Malbin, *supra* note 7, at
248-49; Wright, *supra* note 43, at 400-01 n.3.

67. *See* Jean Reith Schroedel, *Campaign Contributions and Legislative Outcomes*. 39
W. POL. Q. 371 (1986). One strength of this study, relative to many of the others, is that
Schroedel did not limit the contributions considered to PAC contributions. In addition to
PACs, she included contributions from individuals who could be identified with either the
banking or the securities industry. *See id.* at 377 (listing the sources of contributions in the
Schroedel study).

bying is directed to committees than to floor activities,[68] and in the past decade, members of the House of Representatives have increasingly sought membership on committees, such as Energy and Commerce, that affect moneyed interests and therefore generate large amounts of PAC contributions for their members.[69]

It is sometimes suggested that even if contributors obtain heightened influence over committee actions and other less visible activities, matters decided in these settings are of little importance:

> [W]hile contributions may influence who gets the contract to build a particular missile, whether anyone gets the contract and the broad outlines of how much is spent are the more critical decisions for the American public. The latter decisions are generally surrounded by publicity and are decided by roll call votes on the House floor.[70]

This suggestion overlooks the fact that many floor votes are not close, so that in effect, all the crucial decisions regarding much legislation are made in committee or in less formal settings.[71] In many cases, the contributor's objective may be to prevent a bill from ever being brought to the floor.[72] Even with regard to bills that ultimately do face a sharply contested roll call vote, many matters of considerable significance will have been settled in committee.[73] Schlozman and Tierney have noted cogently that "[a]ffecting the details of policies is not merely a trivial form of influence. The world of pressure politics is a world of compromises and half-loaves."[74]

Aside from the likelihood that contributor influence is greater off the floor than on, there are other reasons for believing that statistical analyses of roll call votes may be an infertile field for measuring such influence. The roll call vote of a member may not be what it seems. It is not uncommon for a member to vote one way on the floor when his or her committee or other actions have leaned in the opposite direction.[75]

---

68. *See, e.g.,* John Kingdon, Congressmen's Voting Decisions 72-109 (3d ed. 1989).

69. *See* Jackson, *supra* note 47, at 90.

70. Grenzke, *supra* note 58, at 18 (emphasis in original).

71. *Cf.* Ginsberg & Green, *supra* note 42, at 78 (stressing that roll call voting is not the most important congressional activity).

72. Grenzke, *supra* note 58, at 18 (noting the role of campaign contributions in blocking legislation at the committee level).

73. *See id.* (criticizing PAC studies because "[t]o the extent that PAC contributions help interest groups bury issues in committee, the findings underestimate the impact of money." (citation omitted)).

74. Schlozman & Tierney, *supra* note 32, at 8.

75. *See, e.g.,* Brooks Jackson & Jeffrey H. Birnbaum, *Rep. Matsui is Finding It Hard to Roll Back Break He Gave Utilities,* Wall St. J., July 13, 1989, at A1. The Wall Street

The assumption of the statistical studies of floor votes, and especially of some of the interpretations of these studies, has been that if contributions are an effective lobbying device, a large number of the votes of recipients of contributions should be influenced on each matter of interest to the contributors, and non-recipients of such contributions should be uninfluenced.[76]
This reflects an unrealistic conception of lobbying, which often is not directed at large numbers of the members:

> It may well be true that the average congressman neither is approached by, nor pays much attention to, interest group representatives. But the average congressman is unimportant in a strategic sense. The crucial one is undecided, on the committee, or otherwise in a pivotal position. Such congressmen do receive a good deal of attention.[77]

One reason that interest groups can and do target their lobbying efforts on a few key members is that one of the greatest sources of influence on members' floor votes is the lead of, or advice from other members, especially other members who sit on the committee that heard the bill.[78] If a key member on a particular issue is influenced by campaign contributions, and if that member influences the votes of several others, many of whom may not have received contributions, considerable static will be created for the econometrician who attempts to discern the influence of contributions on the roll call. Nevertheless, the influence may be great. If logrolling exists, the amount of static for the econometrician will increase accordingly.

Another questionable assumption, basic to several of the econometric studies, is that the contribution must precede the floor vote to provide in-

---

Journal reported that Representative Cardiss Collins, who co-sponsored a bill in 1987 to deprive utilities of a tax benefit, received $17,500 in contributions from utility PACs for her 1988 reelection, and declined to co-sponsor similar legislation in 1989. *Id.* at A4. Nevertheless, according to a staff member, she would probably vote for the bill if it reached the floor. *See id.*

Lest I be accused of "suffer[ing] fatally from too simple a model of legislative decision making," SORAUF, *supra* note 27, at 311, I hasten to add that these facts do not prove that Representative Collins was influenced by the contributions she received. They do illustrate, however, that a floor vote is a very incomplete indicator of a legislator's total performance on a matter.

76. *See, e.g.*, Grenzke, *supra* note 58, at 4 (noting that the article's "research conceptualizes the relationship between member's voting behavior on issues and PAC contributions as reciprocal and simultaneous").

77. KINGDON, *supra* note 68, at 164.

78. *Id.* at 72-109.

fluence.[79] To the contrary, a legislator might just as plausibly vote in order to increase the chance of receiving future contributions.[80] Furthermore, as Jacobson has pointed out, the legislator might be influenced even if he or she never receives a contribution, if casting an occasional vote in favor of a generally hostile group might be a means of avoiding that group's strong support for a challenger in the next election.[81]

2. A call for a game-theoretic approach—Another way of thinking about the validity of studies of floor votes as an indicator of influence generated by campaign contributions is to hypothesize a legislative process in which contributors do seek influence, and legislators are willing to be influenced to enhance their prospects of getting increased contributions in the future. As is usual in this sort of exercise, contributors and legislators are assumed to act rationally in pursuit of their objectives,[82] and information is assumed to be costly.[83]

In this hypothetical process, contributors are more concerned with the change they can induce in legislators' performance than with the absolute level of that performance. We can think of any given legislator's performance with respect to a particular contributing group as located on a scale running from zero to one hundred, with a higher score representing performance more beneficial to the group than a lower score. Zero and one hundred are limits that can be approached but not reached, since it would always be possible for a legislator to devote even more energy and ingenuity to assisting or opposing a group's interests. One way of moving up or down the scale is to vote on the floor on one or more bills of interest to the group. Whether these will be large or small moves will depend on the importance of the floor vote to the group, the closeness of the vote and many other factors.

If the political system did not allow for contributions, each legislator's position on the scale would be determined by considerations such as con-

---

79. *But see* Grenzke, *supra* note 58, at 4 (purporting to analyze "whether PAC contributions influence legislator's voting and/or legislator's voting influences PAC contributions"); Welch, *supra* note 58, at 479 (noting that "contributions may be given to reward congressmen for past favors or to ingratiate congressmen who vote their way on future legislation").

80. The truth of this statement is implicit in one PAC manager's comment: "'There is no question that if we went to them time after time and never showed any support for them when they came to us at election time, we'd wear out our welcome pretty fast.'" JACKSON, *supra* note 47, at 89.

81. *See* Jacobson, *Parties and PACs, supra* note 30, at 151-52.

82. *See generally* PETER C. ORDESHOOK, GAME THEORY AND POLITICAL THEORY (1986).

83. *See* KINGDON, *supra* note 68, at 227-41 (analyzing the importance of information in congressmen's decision making).

stituency, ideology and party. The positions determined in this manner will be referred to as the legislators' "natural" positions. The natural position for each legislator, of course, is different. However, since our hypothetical process includes contributions, legislators may depart from their natural positions. Not to put too fine a point on things, a departure from a natural position will be called "cash-motivated."

Movement anywhere along the scale may be as beneficial (or harmful) to the contributing group as movement anywhere else. Suppose Andy, an influential member of the Ways and Means committee who has long been hostile to an industry, is cash-motivated not to offer an obscure amendment to a tax bill that would cost that industry hundreds of millions of dollars.[84] Andy may vote consistently against the industry in committee and on the floor, but this single act of restraint may be of great value to the industry, perhaps enough to raise Andy on the scale from a five to a thirty. Barbara, who sometimes supports the industry and sometimes opposes it, may be cash-motivated to vote on the floor for a bill the industry is sponsoring and that passes by a safe margin. Barbara may move only from 50 to 52 on the scale. If the industry could make a single contribution and knew that its contribution would influence one of these actions, surely it would contribute to Andy.

Certainly, the notion of a scale is artificial, and an interest group might find it difficult to weigh the precise benefits of disparate legislative actions. However, what makes the contributor's strategy difficult is not this problem, but the fact the contributor's goal is not to assess each legislator's present spot on the scale. The goal is to move the legislators up the scale (or prevent them from moving down). Furthermore, contributors operate in an environment of imperfect information. They cannot know whether Andy ever seriously intended to introduce the hostile amendment. Equally significant, they must bear in mind the incentives created by the patterns of their contributions, and recognize that the information of other legislators besides Andy will be limited. If Andy receives a large contribution while Barbara does not, other legislators ignorant of the circumstances may think it is futile to support the group.[85]

---

84. *Cf.* Sara Fritz & Paul Houston, *Amid Scandal and the New Accent on Ethics, Senators Tread Carefully*, L.A. Times, Feb. 11, 1990, at A26. (reporting that one Senator is being investigated for dropping "junk bond legislation opposed by Drexel Burnham Lambert Inc. after receiving $70,000 in political contributions from the firm's executives and clients").

85. A third legislator, Carl, may have a rating of 98, because he cooperates with the industry energetically at virtually every opportunity. Since it would take prohibitive efforts for him to do even more, the industry can expect little or no direct benefit from contributing to him. Furthermore, the nature of Carl's district may be such that he cannot turn against the industry. Welch argued that although interest groups contribute under such

Legislators who wish to maximize their contributions from the group also face a tricky situation. With the understanding that what is important to the group is their cash-motivated movement on the scale rather than their absolute position, their goals will be to make sure contributors are aware of any cash-motivated legislative benefits they provide to the group, and to mislead the contributors into believing they are providing cash-motivated benefits when they are not, either because they are not really providing the benefits, or because they are but it is natural for them to do so. The incentive they have to engage in deception and the contributors' recognition of that incentive greatly increase the difficulty of succeeding in making any genuine, cash-motivated movement on the scale known.[86] Such difficulties are probably a major reason that lobbyists frequently complain that they are the victims of extortion in the campaign finance system.[87]

What can be expected to result from this array of incentives and uncertainties? Technical methods exist for analysis of the problem; unfortunately game theorists have not developed models to predict strategies for making and responding to campaign contributions. Pending their assistance, an untutored guess is that contributors would tend to make contributions to incumbents across the spectrum, since they have an equal interest in moving all incumbents up the scale or keeping them from dropping. There would, however, tend to be an upward tilt. Contributions would get larger as the incumbents' past performance placed them higher on the scale.[88] Legislators would always have an incentive to move higher, thereby serving the contributor's purposes. This method does not discriminate between natural and cash-motivated benefits provided by legislators, but the cost of information may make it impossible to incorporate such discrimination into a general strategy.

If this is the rational contributor strategy, then the rational legislator willing to be influenced would move up the contributor's scale to the

circumstances, they act irrationally in doing so. Welch, *supra* note 58, at 493. Perhaps interest-group contributors know their business better than Welch. The industry must contribute generously to Carl, both to create appropriate incentives for other legislators and to prevent Carl from backsliding, either as a means of extorting contributions or to pursue opportunities to earn contributions from others. Given the costs of information, it is unlikely he will suffer in his district if he slips from 98 to, say, 90.

86. Andy may have devised the tax amendment with the intention of dropping it, purely as a means of moving up on the industry's scale and attracting contributions, or so the industry may suspect. Barbara, after mulling the situation over, may be tempted to move down to 30 for a while, or to make the industry think she may do so.

87. *See* JACKSON, *supra* note 47, at 78-79.

88. Rather than increasing the amounts to candidates higher on the scale, contributors could increase the probability of their receiving a contribution, or these two methods could be combined.

point at which the increased expected contribution equalled the cost, in whatever units of value are salient to the legislator—electoral risk by offending constituents, loss of in-house influence from deserting a party position, loss of expected contributions by virtue of moving down on the scale of contributors with conflicting interests, or conscience.

Contributors might diverge from the basic pattern for various reasons. For example, they might give more to legislators who hold leadership positions or who sit on key committees, since moving them up the scale by a fixed amount would be worth more than moving the average legislator the same amount.[89] More idiosyncratic reasons also could come into play, such as special ties with the legislator, or a plant in the legislator's home district.

Finally, the contributor would give more when there existed a specific reason to believe the legislator had extended cash-motivated benefits. As we have seen, legislators would do what they could to make such actions known to the contributor.[90] A special case of a reward given for benefits rendered would be the explicit deal an agreement to perform a specified legislative service (or refrain from a harmful action) for a specified contribution. Abscam[91] and other scandals tell us that such deals occur.[92] Social scientists, if they refer to such deals at all, are reassuring. "All knowledgeable Capitol Hill observers agree that there are few truly corrupt congressmen," they tell us.[93] They are probably correct—they rely on "knowledgeable observers," after all—but this is another instance of a

---

89. Because this would be the case, contributor demand for influence over the influential members would be high, and would be reflected in the price of moving the influential members. The contributor could therefore expect to have to give more to influential members to move them the same distance as average members. This is consistent with the demand noted above among legislators for membership on committees of importance to major contributors. *See generally* Janet M.Grenzke, *Candidate Attributes and PAC Contributions*, 42 W. POL. Q. 245 (1989) (presenting evidence that when other factors are controlled, interest groups contribute more to legislators in positions of power over legislation of importance to the groups).

90. *See* JACKSON, *supra* note 47, at 98-100 (discussing cases where politicians seemingly "advertised" for PAC contributions); supra note 86 and accompanying text.

91. *See* NOONAN, *supra* note 4, at 604-19 (discussing the ABSCAM scandal in detail).

92. For example, Brooks Jackson reported that on the second day after young Tony Coelho became administrative assistant to Representative B.F. Sisk, a lobbyist asked Coelho for Sisk's support in getting a bill to the floor, and handed Coelho an envelope containing $500. After consulting with the congressman and receiving equivocal instructions, Coelho returned the money, whereupon the lobbyist became indignant. *See* JACKSON, *supra* note 47, at 29-31. This was but a single incident, but the lobbyist's conduct was inexplicable if the incident was an isolated one.

93. Sabato, *supra* note 7, at 162. The reader is invited to contemplate the role of the adverb "truly" in Sabato's sentence.

non-axiomatic proposition being accepted without the rigorous proof that is demanded of campaign finance reformers.

Whether or not the foregoing speculations—on the behavior of rational participants in a legislative process where information is imperfect and influence is both sought after and available—are accurate, there is no reason to believe that in such a system roll call votes would bear particularly great significance. Wherever a legislator is located on a contributor's scale, the contributor's goal is to move the legislator somewhat higher and to avoid the legislator moving somewhat lower.[94] Thus, the area surrounding the legislator's natural location can be regarded as the contributor's potential range of influence for that legislator. Since a roll call vote will fall within a contributor's range of influence for only a fraction of the members of the legislature, measuring influence over roll calls will understate the total influence the contributor is exerting.[95]

This provides another reason for skepticism regarding the econometric studies. When one takes into account all the defects and difficulties inherent in these studies, it becomes increasingly difficult to regard their mixed results as a clean bill of health for the campaign finance system.

C. What Is Meant By Influence?

Ironically, the inability of the econometric studies to answer whether campaign contributions have measurable effects on legislators' actions may result, in part, from the single-mindedness with which they have asked the question. Apparently believing that the extent of such measurable effects is of overriding importance, econometric analysts have attempted to tease out answers from data and mathematical tools ill-suited for the task. These analysts might make greater progress if they conducted a more open-ended inquiry into the dynamics of how campaign contribu-

---

94. *See supra* text accompanying notes 83-85.

95. It may appear that this is merely a restatement of the earlier point that legislators may be more susceptible to influence when they engage in activities less visible than roll call votes. *See supra* notes 70-74 and accompanying text. Actually, the two points are distinct. The earlier discussion suggested that legislators may be more resistant to influence in visible activities than in less visible ones, so that measurement of influence on a visible activity may yield a deceptively low result. *Id.* The present point suggests that even if legislators are equally susceptible to influence in all their activities, roll call votes will not come within the range of influence of many or most legislators for a given contributor or group of contributors. Of course, the two points are not mutually exclusive. To the extent the first point is true, the second is reinforced, as the probability that a roll call vote falls within the range of influence is lowered by reason of the higher cost to the legislator resulting from greater visibility.

tions enter into the legislative process and how they interact with other influences, rules and institutional factors to guide the conduct of individual legislators and the legislature as a whole.[96] They would be well-advised to do so, not only to produce better social science, but because the degree of measurable aggregate influence of campaign contributions over legislative activity does not have the crucial normative significance that they have assumed.

It is commonly observed that any influence over legislative behavior generated by campaign contributions is intertwined with other influences. Michael Malbin, for example, points out that it is "difficult to separate the importance of PAC contributions from the lobbying efforts they are supposedly meant to enhance."[97] Some writers conclude that because it is impossible to be confident that legislative actions favorable to contributors have been caused by contributions, concern over contributions may be minimized.[98] Their premise of intertwining is correct and important, but the conclusion they draw from it is wrong by 180 degrees.

The conclusion is wrong because the question of campaign finance is a question of conflict of interest. A conflict of interest exists when the consequences of a decision made in the course of a relationship of trust are likely to have an effect, not implicit in the trust relationship, on either the interests of a person with whom the decision-maker has a separate rela-

---

96. In doing so, econometric analysts might draw inspiration from Gary Jacobson's work over the past decade on the workings of money in congressional elections. Jacobson began with the narrow but significant insight that to assess the effects of campaign spending, it might be more useful to consider the absolute spending levels of challengers and incumbents than to consider their relative spending levels. *See, e.g.*, Gary Jacobson, *The Effects of Campaign Spending in Congressional Elections*, 72 AM. POL. SCI. REV. 469 (1978). Over the years, Jacobson has constructed a rich, complex, and subtle explanation of how numerous factors interact to form the dynamics of congressional elections. He could not have done this if he had assumed his only task was to isolate and quantify the incremental effects of spending on election outcomes.

97. Malbin, *supra* note 7, at 249; *see also* SORAUF, *supra* note 27, at 310 (stating that "[i]t is…very hard to separate the effects of lobbying and of constituency pressures from the effects of a campaign contribution").

John Kingdon quoted a House member who stated: "A close friend of mine, who's been associated with me for years and is an important campaign contributor, is in the oil business. I had no idea how this bill would affect the oil people until I heard from him." KINGDON, *supra* note 68, at 34. Would the friendship have been sufficient to make this legislator pay such heed without the contributions? If so, why did the member mention the fact that the friend is a contributor? Would the friendship be as close without the contributions? Could the legislator answer these questions with certainty?

98. The quotations from Malbin and Sorauf cited in the previous footnote occur in a context in which they point to this conclusion. *See supra* note 97.

tionship of trust[99] or on the decisionmaker's self-interest.[100] It is the latter situation we are concerned with here.

Often, and in various contexts, we take institutional steps to minimize the occurrence of conflicts of interest, or we disqualify a person from acting when a conflict of interest arises.[101] Why do we do so? Part of the reason, and not necessarily the most important part, is our concern that the individual may deliberately set aside his or her obligations of trust in favor of self-interest. Even if we were sure we could identify all such cases of overt dishonesty, we would continue to regulate conflicts of interest because of the probability that even an honest person's judgment will be impaired when in a position of conflict. Centuries before terms such as "selective perception" were current, it was understood that an individual whose own self-interest is at stake finds it difficult to view a situation dispassionately and objectively.[102] That is why we refer to a person without conflict as "disinterested."

Some people in a conflict situation may be able to act in the position of trust without being the slightest bit moved by the potential effects on self-interest. Others may find that considerations of self-interest are present in their minds but may be able, nonetheless, to struggle through to a conclusion based only on proper considerations. Still other people may be biased in their judgments in situations not conventionally regarded as conflicts of interest.[103] The reason these situations can, and commonly do exist, is that conflict of interest is a concept based on the average person. Sometimes individuals are unusually resistant to being moved by self-interest, sometimes they are unusually susceptible, and sometimes their goals and pref-

---

99. This is the situation Jesus referred to in his famous statement that a servant cannot serve two masters. *Luke* 16:13 An example would be a legislator voting on a bill affecting a charity of which he or she is a board member.

100. It is possible to use the term "conflict of interest" in a context which carries no ethical significance. For example, one could consider whether a quarrel between two nations reflected a genuine conflict of interest. By incorporating the concept of a relationship of trust into my definition, I limit the use of the term to ethically significant situation. *See generally* Austin Scott & W. Fratcher, Scott on Trusts 170 (1987) (stating that the holder of a trust may not place himself in a position where a violation of a duty owed to his beneficiaries would inure to his benefit).

101. *See, e.g.,* Bruce L. Payne, *Devices and Desires: Corruption and Ethical Seriousness, in* Public Duties 175 (Joel Fleishman, Lance Liebman & Marv Moore eds. 1981) (stating that "illegal or irregular acts by public officials, motivated by their own self-interest, are at odds with prevailing conceptions of public interest").

102. *See generally* Noonan, *supra* note 4 (chronologically discussing in detail the 4,000 year history of corruption).

103. *See, e.g.,* Public Utils. Comm'n v. Pollak, 343 U.S. 451, 466 (1952) (disclosing Justice Frankfurter's reason for recusing himself).

erences are sufficiently idiosyncratic that what constitutes self-interest is unusual. Therefore, conflict of interest regulation sometimes disqualifies an individual who is not biased, while at other times it fails to disqualify an individual who is biased. This does not mean that the regulation is faulty. It happens because there is no alternative to regulating on the basis of what we believe are typical human reactions.

What is the significance of the fact that the campaign finance question is a question of conflict of interest? First consider this statement from one of the econometric studies: "It is useful to imagine that the exogenous variables [such as party, ideology and constituency] determine an 'initial position' on the issue for a candidate, and that contributions cause shifts away from that position."[104] As a heuristic device, this is often a useful procedure.[105] As a description of reality it is woefully inadequate because of the intertwining of campaign contributions with other influencing factors.[106] From the beginning of an issue's life, legislators know of past contributions and the possibility of future ones from the interest groups that are affected, just as the legislators know of relevant constituency effects, party positions, various aspects of the merits of the issue and so on.[107] All of these combine in a manner no one fully understands to form an initial predisposition in the legislator.[108] Thereafter, the legislator may receive new information on any or all of these factors. The new information may modify the legislator's initial position, but the information that is received and the manner in which it is processed will themselves be influenced by the initial position.

In reality, then, the influence of campaign contributions is present from the start, and it interacts in the human mind with other influences in an unfathomable but complex dynamic. It affects the "chemistry" or the "mix" of the legislator's deliberations. It may or may not affect the legislator's ultimate actions, but setting aside the most flagrant cases, no one can be sure, perhaps not even the legislator in question. For this reason, to

---

104. Chappell, *supra* note 42, at 78.

105. Treatment of contributions as operating with independent force is implicit in a rational choice framework, which itself is heuristic. This procedure was followed in the foregoing discussion of an assumed legislature in which contributors sought influence and legislators were willing to be influenced. *See supra* text accompanying notes 82-87.

106. *See supra* notes 57-81, 96 and accompanying text (discussing the contributions as one factor intertwining with other factors).

107. *See* Jacobson, *Parties and PACs, supra* note 30, at 151-52 (reviewing the scope of legislators' knowledge).

108. The exposition is simplified by assuming a new issue and an initial predisposition. Many issues, of course, predate current members of the legislature and are likely to survive them, but the point made in the text is not affected by this fact.

say that campaign contributions "taint" the legislative process is to use the language with precision. It is not that the entire legislative process or even a great deal of it is corrupt; rather, it is that the corrupt element is intermingled with the entire process, in a way that cannot be isolated.

The conflicts of interest caused by campaign contributions are illustrated routinely in nearly every daily newspaper. For instance, the following example appeared in the Los Angeles Times while these paragraphs were being written. It is from an article about six Democrats, mostly from the south, on the House Ways and Means Committee.[109] At the time of the article, it was believed that these six members of Congress might swing the committee to report out a reduction in the tax on capital gains, supported by President Bush and the Republicans but opposed by a majority of the Democrats:

> Whatever the outcome, Bush has laid bare a deep split between Democrats' traditional ideology of opposing special treatment for the wealthy and the party's growing dependence on contributions from a host of business special interest groups, particularly real estate developers, that would benefit from the tax cut.

"We've got wealthy Democrats in this country too," said a longtime supporter of a capital gains cut, Beryl Anthony Jr. (D-Ark.), who is a key party fund-raiser as head of the Democratic Congressional Campaign Committee.[110]

A common way of describing this type of situation is to say that there is an "appearance of impropriety." While not exactly wrong, discussion of the campaign finance question in terms of appearances is misleading. It suggests that there is an underlying reality that is either proper or not proper, and if we could only look behind the locked door or, perhaps, into the legislator's head, we would know. Used as a rationale for reform measures, the argument is that the appearance of impropriety is a sufficient justification for reform, because it undermines popular confidence in government. Depending on who is speaking and who is listening, there may be an implied wink to the effect that impropriety is really very unlikely but that some sop must be thrown to the ignorantly suspicious public. Alternatively, the implied wink may suggest that of course there is impropriety, but it would be impolitic to say so directly.[111]

Rather than saying there is an appearance of impropriety in the Democrats' dependence on contributions from interests demanding a cap-

---

109. Tom Redburn, *Six Democrats Backing Capital Gains Tax Cut*, L.A. TIMES, Jul. 25, 1989, at 1.

110. *Id.*

111. *See* Jacobson, *Parties and PACs, supra* note 30, at 152.

ital gains reduction or in similar situations, it is more precise to say that there is a reality of conflict of interest. There was no meeting, behind closed doors or otherwise, not even a moment in a single legislator's mind, in which a decision was made either to succumb to the contributors or not to succumb. The pressure from the contributors is simply part of the mix of considerations out of which a position evolves. At best, one can exercise a judgment as to whether the outcome would have been different if there had been no contributions and no possibility of contributions.[112] Even if the hypothetical outcome would have been the same, however, it does not change the fact that the real outcome results from an actual, tainted process. That is why the question of how much contributions affect legislative outcomes, while surely important, is not normatively crucial.

It may be objected that the conflict of interest argument applies equally to many of the major influences on the legislative process other than campaign contributions. Legislators who are highly responsive to their constituents, for example, most likely act in that manner because they believe it will help them get reelected—a self-interested reason. Legislators who adhere to the party position or the wishes of influential colleagues may do so because they hope for reciprocity in the future, or for advancement within the legislative chamber. They also act out of self-interest.

The fallacy in this objection is its assumption that all considerations of self-interest are equal.[113] No one ever claimed that systems are corrupt

---

112. My own judgment is that campaign contributions probably had little effect in the case of the Democrats and the capital gains cut, despite Representative Anthony's position as head of the DCCC and the statement attributed to him in the Los Angeles Times. *See supra* text accompanying note 110. For one thing, the Democratic leadership has staunchly opposed the capital gains tax cut. Redburn, *supra* note 109, at 12. For another, there are other pressures besides fund-raising needs that push some Democrats to vote with the Republicans. Some apparently are moved by the fact that the tax cut is expected to bring additional revenues in the short term, and thus alleviate the immediate budget deficit problem (at the expense of the long term). *Id.* This response to fiscal problems may be shameful, but it is not corrupt. In addition, timber and farming interests that are important to southern Democratic districts stand to benefit. *Id.*

113. This fallacy runs rampant in Michael Malbin's writing. *See* Malbin, *supra* note 7, at 254-55, 268-69. For example, Malbin describes as his "main point" in one portion of his essay that "[n]either public financing nor strict expenditure limits nor even the complete exclusion of private contributions from the general election can eliminate interest groups from the electoral process." *Id.* at 255. This statement follows several examples, such as the endorsement of President Carter in the 1980 New Hampshire primary by leading chiropractors at the time that the Carter administration changed certain portions of his national health insurance proposal to benefit chiropractors. *Id.* at 254-55. It may be mentioned in passing that Malbin's assumption that the two events were causally connect-

simply because they contain incentives. If this were the case, there would be a conflict of interest any time an employer paid an employee a salary, since the employee who did a good job in hopes of keeping the job or being promoted would be acting corruptly. Such incentives are not conflicts of interest because they are implicit in the relationship of trust, in this case between the employer and employee.

A variety of pressures characterize political life in America. Sorting out which pressures are proper and which are not is difficult.[114] There are, however, some easy cases. Constituency influence is an example. One side of the Burkean debate maintains that while legislators should regard constituent opinions as relevant data for public policy, they should be guided only by their own best judgments.[115] There is no consensus in favor of that position. Accordingly, some degree of responsiveness to constituents' views is at least permissible in legislative positions of trust in this country.

The paradigm case of improper influence is the payment of money to the official for the official's benefit.[116] That is what a campaign contribution is. Indeed, the distinction between a campaign contribution and a payment for the recipient's personal use can be blurred or nonexistent. Nevertheless, there are some differences. Campaign contributions, under current conditions, are more likely to be indispensable to an elected official than personal payments. This makes campaign contributions the more dangerous, though not the more unethical practice. A second difference is that the contributor may be motivated not to influence the recipient but to promote a cause that the recipient represents. In other words, contributors may follow an electoral rather than a legislative strategy. My discussion in this Part is not concerned with contributions to the extent

---

ed is based on anecdotal evidence of the sort he scorns when relied on by reformers as evidence of the effects of campaign contributions. *See id.* at 247-49.

Malbin mistakenly assumes that the goal of campaign finance reform is to eliminate interest groups from elections, as if that were even imaginable. The central goal of campaign finance reform is to eliminate corrupt practices. President Carter's deferral to the chiropractors may not have been an example of the highest statemanship, but it was well within the range of acceptable politics. It is hard to see how a democracy could function if politicians had no incentive to seek the electoral support of constituent groups.

Despite this and other criticisms of Malbin in this Article, his essay is still one of the more penetrating writings one can find in the campaign finance literature.

114. *See generally* Lowenstein, *supra* note 54 (exploring difficulties associated with the efforts of bribery laws to define certain improper pressures on politicians).

115. *See generally* HANNA PITKIN, THE CONCEPT OF REPRESENTATION, 144-240 (1967).

116. To say this is the paradigm case is not necessarily to say it is the worst. For example, threatening officials with violence might be regarded as a worse way of exercising influence than offering them bribes. Incumbents might be especially attracted to this view.

they are so motivated, and I have shown that the set of contributions that are not so motivated is far from being an empty set.[117] Nevertheless, the fact that many contributions are ideological may affect the way people think about all contributions.

Despite differences, it is clear that our culture regards it as inappropriate for public officials to be influenced by campaign contributions. We need not look to Common Cause,[118] Elizabeth Drew, and Brooks Jackson to establish this point. Stronger evidence comes from the scholars with whom I have joined issue in this part. Frank Sorauf,[119] Michael Malbin,[120] and others with similar views would not be at such great pains to characterize the influence of campaign contributions as minimal if they did not believe that it would be wrong if the contributions were influential, or at least that the over-whelming majority of their fellow citizens believe that it would be wrong.

Further confirmation can be found in the fact that a campaign contribution made with the intent to influence official conduct constitutes bribery, as that crime is defined in most American jurisdictions.[121] It is true that the typical special interest bribe in the form of a campaign contribution is very rarely prosecuted.[122] I doubt that this reflects approval of the practice as much as recognition of its pervasiveness, which in turn results from the fact that the receipt of special interest contributions is more or less a practical necessity for most legislators. This necessity may constitute an excellent reason for not prosecuting such routine transactions as bribes, but it does not justify preservation of the system that creates the necessity.

It is a fact of our political culture that although a great variety of the pressures brought to bear on politicians embody forces that are regarded as more or less democratic and therefore legitimate, this is not true of pressure imposed by payments of money to politicians, either for their personal benefit or for campaign use. At best, the existence of such pressures is tolerated as a necessary evil. The evil is necessary within the existing campaign finance system, but the existence of the evil provides a compelling reason for reforming that system.

---

117. *See, e.g., supra* notes 33-56 and accompanying text.

118. Common Cause is a "self-styled people's lobby [which] has mounted a campaign against PACs...." SORAUF, *supra* note 27, at 8. For an explanation of this Author's connection to Common Cause, *see supra* note 9.

119. *See* SORAUF, *supra* note 27, at 326.

120. *See* Malbin, *supra* note 7, at 267-68.

121. *See* Lowenstein, *supra* note 54, at 808-09, 826-28.

122. *See id.* at 789 (noting that "many...of the transactions identified...as definite or likely bribes are engaged in by public officials and those who deal with them on virtually a daily basis, with only the remotest chance of triggering a bribery prosecution.").

D. Anecdotal Evidence and Simple Correlations

In anti-reform writing, and in much of the social science literature on campaign finance regardless of orientation, it is nearly de rigueur to refer in a belittling way to "anecdotal" evidence of the effects of special interest campaign contributions of the sort provided by Elizabeth Drew,[123] Brooks Jackson,[124] and other journalists, and to the simple correlations published from time to time by Common Cause and other groups, matching campaign contributions received with votes rendered on matters of interest to the contributors.[125] I have already shown that the social science research that is offered as an alternative is only slightly informative[126] (a point that is more or less conceded by many of the critics and social scientists, who have admitted the fragmentary and contradictory quality of the results to date) and not as central as has been imagined to the normative question.[127] I shall conclude this Section by explaining briefly why I believe that the anecdotal evidence and simple correlations are persuasive and pertinent, and that therefore the investigative journalists and public interest groups perform a valuable service in bringing information about campaign finance before the public in the manner that they do.[128]

The point about anecdotal evidence, of course, is that it is only anecdotal. Knowing about a specific incident does not tell us how representative that incident is. What is impressive about the anecdotal evidence, however, is how much of it there is. As Larry Sabato has said: "The horror stories about campaign finance seem to flow like a swollen river, week after week, year in and year out."[129] But how horrible are the stories? What do they prove? Let us consider a typical example.

In the Wall Street Journal, Brooks Jackson and Jeffrey H. Birnbaum recently reported on efforts of Representative Bob Matsui to reverse a tax provision that he himself had sponsored in 1986.[130] Utility customers pay fees reflecting anticipated future taxes of the utility companies. The corporate tax rate reduction in 1986 caused these future taxes to be reduced

---

123. DREW, *supra* note 47, at 84-93.

124. JACKSON, *supra* note 47, at 82-94.

125. *See* SORAUF, *supra* note 27, at 308. As usual, Jacobson is more judicious. He writes that such evidence should not be dismissed "out of hand," though it is "hardly conclusive." Jacobson, *Parties and PACs, supra* note 30, at 151.

126. *See supra* notes 57-81 and accompanying text.

127. *See supra* notes 96-122 and accompanying text.

128. Naturally, in defending the genre, I do not defend every specimen of the genre.

129. Sabato, *supra* note 7, at 156.

130. *See* Jackson & Birnbaum, *supra* note 75, at Al.

by a total of $19 billion.[131] In the normal course it would have been up to state regulatory commissions to decide the manner of refunding customers. In 1986, however, Representative Matsui inserted a provision into the tax reform legislation calling for repayment over periods as long as 30 years.[132] This provision attracted little attention at the time, but within a few months after its passage, many legislators, including eventually Matsui, concluded that it was unjustifiable.[133]

Repeal has been strongly resisted by the utility companies and their associations. For example, the U.S. Telephone Association listed defeat of the repeal measure as its most important legislative goal[134] and, according to Jackson and Birnbaum, "brought waves of company executives to Washington" to try to influence representatives from their states.[135] In addition, the utilities and their associations gave more than $5 million in contributions during 1987-88 to individuals who were members of the House in 1989, including $510,000 to members of the Ways and Means Committee, as well as a total of $446,000 in speaking fees to Representatives and Senators in amounts up to $2,000 each.[136] Jackson and Birnbaum quote Representative Matsui as stating: "I have been told a number of times by [House] members whom I have sought as co-sponsors that my bill makes good policy sense but dangerous political sense to them....Rich in honorariums and campaign contributions...[the utility lobbyists'] talk is pretty loud in the halls around here."[137]

A lobbyist for Pacific Telesis was quoted by Jackson and Birnbaum as giving this explanation of the utilities' tactics: "It's the way you do business in this town....We're not trying to buy votes; we're trying to get our point of view across. It takes a long time....And sometimes we need a member's undivided attention."[138]

The Wall Street Journal article contains considerable information regarding the benefits received by certain legislators from the utilities and their developing positions on the repeal bill. For instance, it was reported that:

---

131. *Id.*

132. *Id.*

133. *Id.* at A4.

134. *Id.* at Al, A4.

135. *See id.* at A1.

136. *Id.* at A4.

137. *Id.* at A1.

138. *Id.* at A4. This Section has not addressed the usual claim of the defenders of the campaign finance system that the only thing contributors get for their money is access to legislators. This claim was addressed previously in Lowenstein, *supra* note 54, at 827-28. For an excellent discussion, see SCHLOZMAN & TIERNEY, *supra* note 32, at 164-65.

Democrat Terry Bruce of Illinois co-sponsored the Dorgan [repealer] bill but signed the ["dear colleague"] letter arguing against it. Rep[resentative] Bruce received a $1,000 honorarium from the telephone association on Jan. 28, 1987. He received another $250 honorarium from Edison Electric Institute three days before the letter.

On April 9, he took the highly unusual step of rising on the floor of the House to ask unanimous permission for his name to be removed from sponsorship of the refund bill. The next month he got a $2,000 appearance fee from Illinois Bell, followed, in August, by $1,000 from Pacific Telesis. And before the end of his successful 1988 reelection campaign, he got from the utility PACs $28,158 in political contributions.[139]

The Journal article presents policy arguments for and against the repealer in some detail, and recounts the history of the repeal efforts up to the time the article appeared, and its apparent prospects.[140] Finally, it quotes Representative Matsui on his meetings with utility lobbyists during the period he was beginning to reconsider his position:

I had at least three or four meetings with the utility coalition and asked them to provide me with an analysis about why their position was pro-consumer. Each time, they would say they would try to come up with something, and on the way out someone from the USTA [U.S. Telephone Association] would want to talk to me about fund-raising.... The first time I kind of sloughed it off, the second and third time it got to be a little trying.[141]

What can be said about this article, which is a typical example of the genre? Does it prove that legislators adopted a position solely to receive more contributions and speaking fees from the utilities? No. The article itself provides other factors that could have been influential. Some legislators may have been persuaded by the utilities' substantive arguments and visits by the heads of local telephone companies.[142] Furthermore, the article does not attempt to compare contributions received by those who supported the utilities' position, and by those who opposed it. Similarly, although the article provides considerable information about the amount of utility contributions and other benefits to members during the period of the controversy, it does not indicate whether this constituted an increase over previous periods.[143]

Does the Journal article rely solely on correlations between contributions and legislative votes to arouse suspicions? No. There is additional evidence, both circumstantial and testimonial. First, there is the fact that

139. Jackson & Birnbaum, *supra* note 75, at A4.
140. *See id.*
141. *Id.* (brackets in original).
142. *See id.*
143. *See id.*

whatever the merits of the industry's arguments,[144] and however prestigious the telephone company executives pressed into action as lobbyists, the industry was asking congressmen to intervene over the objection of state officials in matters ordinarily left to the states, in order to permit telephone and electric companies to withhold money belonging to their customers for great lengths of time.[145] On its face, this is not an attractive political position.

Second, there is Matsui's characterization of his colleagues' remarks to the effect that the bill makes "good policy sense but dangerous political sense."[146] In light of the first point, indicating that on its face the bill seemed to make excellent political sense, it is hard to see what these colleagues could have been getting at other than that voting for the bill might offend major contributors. Third, the timing of some of the contributions and other benefits seemed close in some instances to legislative actions supporting the industry, although not enough instances are given to negate the possibility of coincidence. Finally, Matsui's account of his meetings with utility lobbyists described repeated attempts to rely directly on fund-raising as a lobbying tool.[147]

What the Jackson-Birnbaum article and others of its genre do is illustrate and flesh out the validity of the conflict of interest approach. There is no "smoking gun"[148] in this, or in most cases, but neither is there reason for anyone other than a criminal investigator to search for one. The campaign contribution is pervasive. It is present in legislators' talks among themselves, in their meetings with lobbyists and in lobbyists' evaluations of their own tactics and strategies. Contributions come before a legislative issue arises and contemporaneously with the legislative deliberations, and will continue to come after the particular issue is forgotten. Are contributions the only consideration in the legislative deliberations? Of course not. Are they the dominant consideration? Probably not in most cases. But they are always there, and their effects can never be isolated or identified

---

144. For what it is worth, this distinctly non-expert reader found the industry's arguments neither frivolous nor extremely persuasive.

145. *See id.* at A1.

146. *See supra* text accompanying note 137 (quoting Representative Matsui's remarks).

147. *See supra* text accompanying note 144.

148. *See* SORAUF, *supra* note 27, at 309. Sorauf entitled an inset in his section on the influence of contributions on official behavior, "The Search for the Smoking Gun." *See id.* This is a pun based on the fact that the incident Sorauf is analyzing involved legislation affecting the National Rifle Association. *See id.* at 309-10. Nevertheless, casting the issue in these terms is symptomatic of Sorauf's lack of consideration of the conflict of interest problem.

with precision. Anecdotal evidence, because it is contextual and, when presented by the better journalists, conveys the complexity and the ambiguities in the process, enhances our understanding of the campaign finance problem.

Similarly, publication by groups such as Common Cause of correlations between contributions received by legislators from interest groups and their votes on matters of interest to those groups is an entirely legitimate and constructive contribution to the campaign finance debate. Admittedly, the fact that members of Congress received contributions from used car dealers and then voted against a requirement that those dealers disclose known defects to their customers does not prove that they were motivated solely or predominantly or at all by the contributions.[149] It is open to elected members to persuade the public that they are indifferent to contributions. It is open to the used car dealers to explain that their practice is simply to watch and wait for candidates to come along who have an ideology that opposes disclosure of defects to used car buyers.[150]

Publication of such simple correlations is criticized on the ground that they create unfounded implications that legislators are for sale.[151] The correlations also are said to be misleading because, unlike the econometric studies I have already discussed,[152] they make no effort to see whether the votes in question might be explicable without reference to the contributions.

These criticisms are themselves unfounded once it is understood that the allegation need not be that the legislators are for sale, but that they routinely act within a position of conflict of interest. Perhaps it is likely that legislators would have acted in the same manner if the conflict of interest had not been present. That likelihood does not change the fact that, when they did act, the conflict existed. The studies of the public interest groups show the breadth of the conflict of interest problem; the investigative journalists' anecdotal evidence shows its quality.

---

149. *See* SCHLOZMAN & TIERNEY, *supra* note 32, at 163.

150. Another common argument of anti-reform writers is that whatever influence interest group contributors have is offset by the contributions of opposing groups. *See, e.g.*, Malbin, *supra* note 7, at 266-69. Apparently, then, we may assume that used car dealer money was matched by used car buyer money. Given the assurances of the anti-reform writers on this score, *see id.*, I have not deemed it is necessary to search the records of the Federal Election Commission to find out how many used car buyers' PACs there are, or how much they have contributed to congressional campaigns in recent years.

151. It is important to note that the studies and correlations published by public interest groups typically do not focus on individuals, in McCarthyite fashion. Usually they emphasize the defects in the system as a whole.

152. *See supra* notes 57-95 and accompanying text.

The legislative process is not corrupt, but it is tainted with corruption.

Legislators, by and large, are not corrupt. Neither are lobbyists. They are doing what they must to carry out their roles in the system as it presents itself to them. They are not corrupt, though sometimes they are corrupted.

The campaign finance system is corrupt.

Corruption, Equality, and Campaign Finance Reform

David A. Strauss

Why should we want to reform the way political campaigns are financed? Two reasons are customarily given. One objective of reform is to reduce corruption, understood as the implicit exchange of campaign contributions for legislators' votes or other government action. The other objective is to promote equality: people who are willing and able to spend more money, it is said, should not have more influence over who is elected to office.

The Supreme Court's view of these two objectives can be summarized quickly: Corruption is a permissible target of reform legislation; inequality is not. That summary is not quite right, because some of the Court's decisions allow measures that seem to be directed at inequality.[1] But *Buckley v. Valeo*,[2] famously or notoriously, said—and the Court has repeated many times[3] that "the concept that government may restrict the speech of some elements of our society in order to enhance the relative voice of others is wholly foreign to the First Amendment."[4] By contrast, "preventing corruption or the appearance of corruption are the only legitimate and compelling government interests thus far identified for restricting campaign finances."[5] This was one of the principal bases for *Buckley's*

---

1. For example, in *Austin v. Michigan Chamber of Commerce*, 494 U.S. 652 (1990), which upheld a restriction on campaign-related expenditures, the Court asserted that the restriction was concerned with "corruption" but defined "corruption" in a way that made it essentially equivalent to inequality. *See id.* at 660; *see also* Julian N. Eule, *Promoting Speaker Diversity*: Austin *and* Metro Broadcasting, 1990 Sup. Ct. Rev. 105, 109–13.

2. 424 U.S. 1 (1976).

3. *See, e.g.*, Meyer v. Grant, 486 U.S. 414, 426 n.7 (1988); Citizens Against Rent Control v. City of Berkeley, 454 U.S. 290, 295 (1981); First Nat'l Bank v. Bellotti, 435 U.S. 765, 790–91 (1978).

4. 424 U.S. at 48–49.

5. Federal Election Comm'n v. National Conservative Political Action Comm., 470 U.S. 480, 496–97 (1985).

determination to permit restrictions on campaign contributions, which might be corrupting, but not on independent campaign expenditures.[6]

Buckley, of course, has been widely criticized. But many commentators agree with *Buckley* that the concern of campaign finance reform should be the elimination of corruption;[7] some do not even consider the promotion of equality to be worth discussing.[8] And even among those who advocate the promotion of equality, there seems to be little dissent from the proposition that reducing corruption is also an imperative goal.[9]

In fact it is far from clear that campaign finance reform is about the elimination of corruption at all. That is because corruption understood as the implicit or explicit exchange of campaign contributions for official action is a derivative problem. Those who say they are concerned about corruption are actually concerned about two other things: inequality, and the nature of democratic politics. If somehow an appropriate level of equality were achieved, much of the reason to be concerned about corruption would no longer exist. And to the extent the concern about corruption would persist under conditions of equality, it is actually a concern about certain tendencies, inherent in any system of representative government, that are at most only heightened by quid pro quo campaign contributions specifically, the tendency for democratic politics to become a struggle among interest groups.

The true targets of campaign reform, therefore, are inequality and certain potential problems of interest group politics that are endemic to representative government. Efforts to root out implicit quid pro quo "corruption" are justifiable only insofar as they are means to those ends. Reformers who, following the Supreme Court's lead, focus on corruption and ignore inequality either have things backward or are after bigger

---

6. *See* 424 U.S. at 58–59. Another important basis for this distinction is that contributions, because they enlist the efforts of another speaker, are, according to the Court, a less pure form of speech than expenditures. *See, e.g., id.* at 19–22.

7. *See, e.g.,* LARRY J. SABATO, PAYING FOR ELECTIONS: THE CAMPAIGN FINANCE THICKET 6 (1989); Daniel H. Lowenstein, *On Campaign Finance Reform: The Root of All Evil is Deeply Rooted*, 18 HOFSTRA L. REV. 301, 302 (1989).

8. *See, e.g.,* Lowenstein, *supra* note 7; Michael W. McConnell, *Redefine Campaign Finance "Reform,"* CHI. TRIB., June 29, 1993, 1, at 15; DAVID B. MAGLEBY & CANDICE J. NELSON, THE MONEY CHASE 3, 197 (1990); Henry C. Kenski, *Running With and From the PAC*, 22 ARIZ. L. REV. 627, 643–44 (1980).

9. *See, e.g.,* SABATO, *supra* note 7; David Adamany, *PACs and the Democratic Financing of Politics*, 22 ARIZ. L. REV. 569, 570–71 (1980); Joel L. Fleishman & Pope McCorkle, *Level-Up Rather Than Level-Down: Towards a New Theory of Campaign Finance Reform*, 1 J.L. & POL. 211 (1984); J. Skelly Wright, *Money and the Pollution of Politics: Is the First Amendment an Obstacle to Political Equality?*, 82 COLUM. L. REV. 609, 616–20 (1982).

game than they acknowledge: they are concerned with features that may be inherent in the democratic process itself rather than in any system of campaign finance. The task of campaign finance reform is not so much to purify the democratic process as to try to save it from its own worst failings.

In Part I, I will try to show that "corruption" in the system of campaign finance is a concern not for the reasons that true corruption, such as conventional bribery, is a concern, but principally because of inequality and the dangers of interest group politics. I will also discuss the possibility that so-called corruption is objectionable not because of what contributors do to the political system but because of the danger that the contributors themselves will be subjected to coercion.

* * *

I. Corruption as a Derivative Evil

A. Corruption and Inequality

The best way to understand the relationship between corruption and equality is to consider what the corruption problem, so-called, would look like if the inequality problem were solved. Since the inequality problem will never be solved to everyone's satisfaction, this requires a suspension of disbelief. But one might suppose, for example, a scheme that equalizes people's ability to make contributions (and expenditures; for these hypothetical purposes there is no difference) by multiplying contributions by a factor inversely related to the contributor's income.[10] The idea would be that a contribution of, say, one percent of any individual's income would be either supplemented or taxed by the government so that, no matter what the person's income, the same amount would be made available to the candidate. Assume, for the sake of argument, that such a scheme would implement an acceptable notion of equality and that it would be constitutional. (Both assumptions may be incorrect, of course.)

Suppose that in such a world, contributions made to politicians' campaigns were overtly "corrupt" in the sense in which that term is used in discussions of campaign finance reform. That is, individuals (and PACs)

---

10. This notion, analogous to the "district power equalization" proposal for school finance reform, *see* JOHN E. COONS ET AL., PRIVATE WEALTH AND PUBLIC EDUCTION (1970), is discussed in Edward B. Foley, *Equal Dollars Per Voter: A Constitutional Principle of Campaign Finance*, 94 COLUM. L. REV. 1204 (1994).

promised contributions explicitly contingent on a legislator's voting in a certain way; explicitly rewarded legislators for past votes; punished legislators by reducing contributions for legislative actions that the contributors opposed; made contributions during campaigns with the intention of reminding the candidate to whom they contributed of their support and redeeming their "IOU;" and so on. This is the anti-corruption nightmare scenario.

Many of those who see corruption as the central problem treat such a state of affairs as self-evidently unacceptable. Legislators should respond to constituents' wishes, their own judgments of good policy and the public interest, or some mixture of the two. But in a "corrupt" system, legislators respond to those who pay them, and to the amount they are paid. They have sold their office and thus breached their duty to the people.[11]

That is certainly true when the corruption takes the form of standard bribery—a payment that goes into the representative's pocket. But there is a difference between straightforward bribery and corruption, on the one hand, and even the nightmare scenario I described above. Campaign contributions are not, or need not be, the same thing as bribes. Campaign contributions can be spent only on a campaign. They can be spent only in order to gather votes, directly or indirectly. They do not go into the legislator's pocket. Of course, in reality, the line is not always so distinct, and there may be limits on how clearly this line can ever be drawn.[12] But it is at least plausible that we could have a regime in which campaign contributions, by and large, were spent to gather votes and for no other purpose.

That means that these "bribes" have only a certain kind of value to the recipient. In a sense they are like vouchers, redeemable only for a certain purpose. To obtain a bribe, a legislator might deliberately cast a vote that

---

11. *See, e.g.*, Kenski, *supra* note 8, at 643–44; Lowenstein, *supra* note 7, at 305–35.

12. For example, when a candidate is willing to spend her own money on a campaign, contributions may replace the candidate's own money and thereby, in effect, personally enrich her. But this problem will occur only if contributions cause the candidate to end up spending less of her own money than she otherwise would (instead of simply adding the contributions to what she was already planning to spend from her own resources). And contributions replace the candidate's own resources dollar-for-dollar only to the extent that the total expenditures made on the campaign do not exceed the amount the candidate was willing to spend from her own wealth. Suppose, for example, a candidate who would have been willing to spend $ 10,000 of her own money receives contributions of $ 100,000 and decides to spend none of her own money. Only one-tenth of the dollars contributed to her effectively ended up in her pocket, so the $ 100,000 in contributions is not equivalent (in its corrupting effects) to a $ 100,000 bribe. If she decides to spend her own $ 10,000 in addition to the contributed $ 100,000, none of the contributions ends up in her pocket.

she knew would ruin her chances of reelection. But it would be irrational for a legislator to cast such a vote in return for a campaign contribution-since the most the contribution can do is to improve her chances of reelection.

This is an important difference, not a technical point. The conventional form of corruption occurs when elected officials take advantage of their position to enrich themselves. In effect they convert their public office into private wealth. But when the quid pro quo for an official action is not a bribe but a campaign contribution, the official has used the power of her office, not for personal enrichment, but in order to remain in office longer. In a democracy that is not necessarily a bad thing for an official to do. In some circumstances, of course, it is problematic, as I will discuss; but it is not problematic for the same reasons as bribery. Speaking of "corruption" in the context of campaign contributions tends to blur this distinction.

It follows that, leaving inequality aside, promising a campaign contribution to a legislator if she takes a certain side on an issue is in many ways similar to promising to vote for her if she takes that side. The latter practice is not only legitimate but arguably an important feature of democratic government. If equality is secured, then because campaign contributions are valuable only as a means to get votes, rewarding a legislator with a contribution is, in important ways, similar to the unquestionably permissible practice of rewarding her with one's vote. Even assuming there is a direct relationship, so that the more money raised for a campaign, the more votes the candidate will receive, making a campaign contribution is roughly equivalent to delivering a certain number of votes to the legislator-and nothing more.

In other words, each dollar contribution (making relatively crude, but good enough, assumptions) is a fraction of an expected vote. A legislator who receives a contribution has increased her expected number of votes by a certain amount (where "expected number of votes" means the number of votes discounted by the probability of receiving them). This is only approximately correct, both because greater campaign expenditures might not directly translate into more votes and because a contribution to one candidate can be offset by a contribution to another. The important point, however, is that at most a contribution amounts to delivering a certain expected number of votes. The legislator does not get anything more out of the contribution than that.

Considerations of equality aside, therefore, when a milk producers' PAC, for example, threatens to withhold a contribution, it is doing something that is in principle similar to threatening to mobilize milk producers to vote against the legislator in the next election. When it rewards a legislator with a contribution, its behavior is similar in principle to "delivering" the milk producers' vote. If, by hypothesis, everyone has equal power to make contributions, then the making of contributions is arguably just another way of casting votes.

In some respects, in fact, "delivering votes" by means of contributions is superior to delivering them by mobilizing the membership—superior in the sense that it is a better way of aligning officials' actions with popular sentiment. For one thing, a system of contributions mitigates the bundling problem: a voter is likely to approve of some positions a candidate takes and disapprove of others, but she can only vote in favor of or against the candidate's entire package.[13] Contributions can be more discriminating. A contributor can make a legislator's reward depend precisely on the degree to which the legislator has taken positions of which the contributor approves, and the contributor (in a "corrupt" system) can tell the legislator which positions will produce greater contributions. In that way, a system of delivering contributions might better reflect popular sentiment than a system of delivering votes.

Second, and related, contributions allow voters-that is, contributors-to register the intensity of their views. At the ballot box, a voter has a difficult time showing how enthusiastically she supports a candidate. She can vote for or against, or she can abstain. (Sometimes voting for a third party candidate may also be a way of expressing a weak preference for one of the major candidates.) By contrast, a contributor can spend her money in direct proportion to the intensity of her views.

Third, illegal old-fashioned machine practices aside, votes cannot be delivered as reliably as contributions. A legislator knows that even if an organization asks its members to vote against her (and even if there is no bundling problem, because the members do not care about any other issues strongly enough), not all of the members will receive the message, and not all will remember to act on it. A contribution, however, can be given to an intermediary organization and thereby placed under its direct control if the individual contributor so chooses, and so can be reliably "delivered."[14]

It might be objected that this kind of reliability is not a good thing but rather a serious problem. Many contributions are controlled not by individuals but by intermediaries, notably PACs. This important difference, however, has complex implications, and they point in different directions.

---

13. On the bundling problem in voting for candidates, *see, e.g.,* James D. Gwartney & Richard E. Wagner, *Public Choice and the Conduct of Representative Government, in* PUBLIC CHOICE AND CONSTITUTIONAL ECONOMICS 10 (James D. Gwartney & Richard E. Wagner eds., 1988). I am indebted to Julie Roin for discussions of this point.

14. Of course, the contribution does not necessarily translate directly into votes, so to that extent this point must be qualified.

People contribute to PACs (or other intermediary organizations) because they believe the PACs will more effectively further their objectives in the political arena.[15] PACs can take advantage of economies of scale and, perhaps more important, can overcome the problems faced by unorganized individual actors.[16] PACs can acquire information about legislative events that are likely to affect their contributors, approach legislators and convey clear messages, distribute contributions among legislators, and so on. If a "corrupt" system of contributions is similar to a system of voting, then the collective organization of contributions permits people to cast more effective "votes"-contribution-votes that reflect superior information and that are better targeted than votes cast at the ballot box.

Finally, a system in which citizens deliver votes by means of contributions, instead of at the ballot box, is arguably superior because it funds the democratic process. At least in theory (and surely to some degree in practice), campaign contributions will be spent on things that a representative government needs to function well-conveying information and arguments from candidates to citizens. This is not true of conventional bribes, and it does not happen when a citizen simply promises a vote, instead of giving a contribution, to a candidate. No one should be too Panglossian about the level of discourse in political campaigns. But by the same token there is something useful, even commendable, about giving a candidate money so that she can better explain herself to the electorate.

B. Corruption and Democracy

Assuming equality, then, the real problem of "corruption" through campaign contributions is not the problem of conventional corruption; the problem is not that representatives sell their offices and betray the public trust for personal financial gain. In fact, assuming equality, there are substantial arguments that a regime in which official action is exchanged for campaign contributions is superior to one in which it is exchanged for votes. But even in a regime of equality, the anti-corruption nightmare scenario I described above still seems to be a nightmare. What accounts for that intuition?

The answer, I believe, is that even in a regime of equality, the nightmare scenario presents a heightened version of certain problems that are endemic to any representative government. The first problem is that a "corrupt" system of campaign contributions will tie representatives

---

15. *See* Magleby & Nelson, *supra* note 8, at 75–76; Bruce Ackerman, *Crediting the Voters: A New Beginning for Campaign Finance*, AM. PROSPECT, Spring 1993, at 71, 74.

16. The classic statement of these problems is MANCUR OLSON, THE LOGIC OF COLLECTIVE ACTION (2d ed. 1971).

closely to their constituents' wishes. In a sense this is the dark side of reducing bundling problems. To some extent representatives are supposed
to reflect their constituents' wishes. But on any plausible conception of
representative government, elected representatives sometimes should exercise independent judgment.[17] A representative who need only answer at
the ballot box every few years is relatively free to exercise independent
judgment. A representative who must act with an eye toward campaign
contributions, which can be awarded or withheld in precise measure for
specific actions that the representative takes, has much less freedom. She
must pay close attention to her potential contributors' views on each
issue, and she will pay a price each time she defies them.

The point should not be overstated. People can (and no doubt do)
make contributions to representatives because they believe the representative exercises good independent judgment, or because of the representative's position on a range of issues, rather than because of particular positions the representative has taken. Conversely, people sometimes vote for
or against representatives because of the representative's position on particular issues. Campaign contributions do not create the possibility that
representatives will follow instead of lead; that is an unavoidable (and to
some extent desirable) part of any democracy. But because contribution-
votes can be so much better targeted than votes at the ballot box, a system in which contributions are implicitly or explicitly exchanged for official action will accentuate this tendency of representative government.

Second, a system of quid pro quo campaign contributions is likely to
exacerbate the tendency of politics to become a process of accommoda-
tion among groups with particular selfish interests, instead of an effort to
reach the best decisions for society as a whole. This seems likely to occur
for two reasons. First, contributions can be put directly under the control
of interest groups; while interest groups also promise to deliver votes,
they deliver them much less efficiently and reliably. Second, and more sub-
tly, voting at the ballot box rather than through contributions may encourage voters to concern themselves with the public interest, or at least
with a range of issues, rather than with their more narrow group interests.
Again, that is because a voter is forced to express approval or disapproval
of a candidate's entire record, while a contributor has the opportunity to
limit her approval or disapproval to specific actions.[18]

In addition, a voter looking for a PAC to contribute to-an intermediary
that can spend her contribution more effectively than she herself might-

---

17. The classic statement of this view is Edmund Burke, *Speech to the Electors of Bristol, in* 2 THE WORKS OF EDMUND BURKE 89, 95–97 (3d ed. Boston, Little, Brown 1869).

18. The ceremonial aspects of voting-the fact that it is to some degree a self-conscious
act of citizenship-may also contribute to this effect.

may be hard pressed to find a "public interest" PAC. Small groups whose members are intensely interested in an issue have an organizational advantage over larger groups whose members have a more diffuse interest.[19] That makes it more likely that intermediary groups reflect narrow interests. A potential contributor wishing to take advantage of an intermediary, unlike a voter, may have to choose among various groups that represent narrow interests.

Again, however, a "corrupt" system of campaign contributions does not create this problem; it only heightens it. Even if private campaign contributions and expenditures were banned altogether, voters would still sometimes vote according to narrow group interests. This arguable dysfunction of representative government-the degeneration of the process from the pursuit of some conception of the public interest into a conflict among interest groups-seems more likely to occur in a system in which contributions are exchanged for official action. But the problem is endemic to democracy in any form. And again it is not a problem of "corruption" in the sense of outright bribery.

In these ways, campaign contributions might be problematic even if equality were secured. But the problem arises because, in an important sense, allowing "votes" to be cast by means of contributions is only a way of providing a more refined and efficient system of democracy. Contribution-votes allow citizens to do more effectively what they would like to do with their ballot box votes-influence elected representatives to do the things that the voters, perhaps selfishly, most want them to do. The problems of representatives' failure to exercise independent judgment and of special interest fragmentation-if in fact they are problems-are features of representative government that might be heightened, but are not created, by a "corrupt" system of campaign finance.

Still, one might say that the danger of exacerbating these problems is itself sufficient reason, apart from equality, to reform the system of campaign finance. While exchanges of official action for campaign contributions are not corrupt in the sense that bribes are, it might be said, they are corrupt in a more traditional sense. They corrupt the political process by

---

19. *See* OLSON, *supra* note 16, at 53–57; *see also* DENNIS C. MUELLER, PUBLIC CHOICE II: A REVISED EDITION OF PUBLIC CHOICE 308–10 (1989). Certain party or electoral structures might counteract this tendency. For example, in a society with sharply differentiated ideological parties, contributors might be more concerned with advancing the broad range of policies supported by one party. (If there is a strongly ideological pro-business party opposed by an ideological anti-business party, for example, business contributors will be less concerned with specific issues than with maintaining the pro-business party in power.) But in our system there seems to be little to counteract the tendency for groups to coalesce around specific issues.

helping it to degenerate in the ways I have described. Therefore the central goal of the anti-corruption reform agenda-to eliminate implicit quid pro quo exchanges of contributions for government action-should remain intact, although for a different reason.

Unfortunately, the matter is not that simple. The question of how responsive a representative should be to the electorate is notoriously difficult, and it is not clear that the greater responsiveness that comes from allowing contributions will make matters worse. There are both theoretical questions-what mix of responsiveness and independence do we want?-and empirical questions-exactly how much more independence will we get if we reform campaign finance?

Similarly, the question of how far we should go in trying to remedy the interest group character of democratic politics raises extremely difficult theoretical and empirical issues. The problem is not, as some seem to suggest,[20] on the conceptual level of defining a difference between interest group politics and the effort to promote some version of the public good. Plainly there is a difference between a struggle among groups overtly pursuing selfish interests and a deliberative effort to promote the good of the whole, or a just society. The problem comes in practice. Few people admit that they are simply trying to promote their selfish interests instead of seeking the good of society. As a result, without an elaborate and controversial normative theory, it is difficult in practice to distinguish between pernicious interest groups and politically active good citizens.

Compare, to use a common example, civil rights groups and, say, the lobby for agricultural subsidies. Both are well-organized groups. Both purport to be concerned with the good of society and to be trying to implement a vision of social justice, not just promoting their own selfish interests. Of course, we do not have to take the claims of every interest group at its word. Many people hold a normative view according to which some groups (such as the civil rights groups) are trying to promote the public good and others (such as the farm lobby or the gun lobby) are acting out of narrow self-interest. But the examples show how controversial any such theory will be. One side's chief examples of narrow and self-interested groups will be the other side's examples of groups that pursue the public interest. If campaign finance reform is intended to restrict the power of supposedly narrow and pernicious interest groups, while not disadvantaging supposedly public-interested interest groups, then reform necessarily takes on an extremely partisan cast.

This problem might be avoided by saying that the goal of reform should simply be to limit the power of all well-organized intermediary

---

20. For perhaps the best-known discussion, *see* ROBERT A. DAHL, A PREFACE TO DEMOCRATIC THEORY (1956).

groups, without trying to differentiate between good and bad interest groups. Certain systems of public financing would have this effect, for example if they involved the distribution of funds directly from the Treasury, perhaps keyed to a formula that reflected a candidate's popular support. Because the funds would be transferred directly to the candidate-with no opportunity to pass through the hands of intermediary organizations-the influence of those organizations would be reduced.

This, too, unfortunately, is not a perfect solution. That is because the public interest might in the end be better promoted by allowing, rather than dampening, interest group activity. The question is a very complicated one. Intermediary organizations increase the advantages of people with intense preferences, and arguably more intensely felt positions should be accorded more weight in the democratic process. In addition, some positions on certain issues may be less well represented in the public debate than their merits warrant; intermediary organizations, by speaking forcefully for these interests, might improve the quality of public deliberation over what would prevail if intermediaries were discouraged. For many, gay and lesbian groups, or anti-abortion groups, are examples.

In addition, as I noted above, people give to intermediary organizations precisely because they believe those organizations will transmit their views more effectively. If people think their views will be more effectively promoted by contributing to a PAC instead of contributing directly to a candidate, reformers should at least hesitate before concluding that the system would be more democratic if people were denied the chance to do so.[21]

Finally, and related, intermediary organizations are likely to be relatively sophisticated consumers. That is again a principal reason why people trust these organizations with their money: they think it will be better spent by the intermediary. One would expect intermediary organizations to be affected less by political appeals based on slogans and the manipulation of images, and more likely to make sound judgments on matters of substance. This is just a result of the division of labor and the benefits of organization.

The case for reforming campaign finance in order to curb the possibly bad tendencies of democracy is, therefore, a complex and difficult one to

---

21. The German Constitutional Court, for example, has concluded that unrestricted public subsidies of political parties are unconstitutional partly because they are undemocratic: "The parties must remain dependent upon citizen approval and support not only politically but economically and organizationally as well. Public funds thus may not be permitted to liberate individual parties from the risk of failure of their efforts to obtain sufficient support from the voters." 85 BVerfGE 264, 287 (1992), *as quoted in* DAVID P. CURRIE, THE CONSTITUTION OF THE FEDERAL REPUBLIC OF GERMANY (forthcoming 1994) (chapter 4, manuscript at 38 n.155, on file with author).

make. That is not to say it cannot be made. There is no reason (at least in the account I have given so far) to indulge a presumption against reform. It certainly may be the case that there are reforms that can significantly improve the quality of democratic politics by reducing the influence of certain kinds of destructive interest groups. But that task should be undertaken with full awareness both of the objective-the reduction of representatives' responsiveness and of interest group influence, not the elimination of bribery-like corruption-and of the complexities involved.

All of this suggests that the issues raised by campaign finance reform are much larger than many think. The implicit vision of many reformers is that there is, underneath the layers of corruption precipitated by campaign contributions, a well-functioning system of representative government. The job of reform is to strip away the corruption and restore the normal processes. I have suggested, instead, that campaign contributions heighten certain of the characteristic tendencies of representative government. Part of the task of campaign finance reform is to try to determine what kind of representative government we want-which aspects of representative government we want to suppress, which we want to encourage, and at what cost.

C. The Coercion of Contributors

In at least one respect, corruption in campaign finance cannot be reduced to a problem of inequality or interest group politics. In a system in which campaign contributions are freely exchanged for official action, there is a danger that representatives may coerce potential contributors, in effect extorting contributions by the threat that they will act against the contributor's interests. Although some such extortion might be possible if the currency were votes, instead of campaign contribution dollars, votes are cast in secret and can go only to one side; the dangers of extortion are therefore far greater when contributions are allowed. To the extent this danger exists, contributors, instead of being predators as they are in the usual anti-corruption story, become the victims. Instead of the contributor working her will on the representative, who feels obligated to comply with the contributor's request in order to obtain money, the representative forces an unwilling citizen to make a contribution. When extortion of this form occurs, the problems I have already mentioned-inequality and interest group domination-can develop; in addition, there is unfairness to the extorted contributor, and there are possible inefficiencies. The clearest example of extortion of this kind is an elected judge who solicits campaign contributions from the parties to a case before her, or a regulatory official with adjudicative power who solicits the firms she regulates. In these cases an outright ban on contributions seems an appropriate solution. But if extortion can occur in those cases, it will also be at least a theoretical possibility in the case of legislators and other elected representatives. For example, chair of a legislative subcommittee that has jurisdiction over a bill that would help, say, the railroad industry at the expense of the trucking industry, will be in a good position to gain contributions from both industries. The slightest hint on the part of the representative, falling far short of a solicitation that would be independently criminal, might be enough to make the contributors think they had better ante up. Even if the representative has no intention of extorting contributions at all, the contributors might decide to make a contribution in order to protect their interests.

It is of course difficult to determine how frequently extortion or quasi-extortion of this kind occurs. Some of the data-notably the high level of contributions to incumbents with safe seats-suggest that it is quite common.[22] To whatever extent it does occur, it presents the problems I have already canvassed, although in a slightly different and possibly less severe form. If inequality exists, those with more resources will be better able to satisfy the implicitly or explicitly extortionate demand. Well-organized groups will also be better able to satisfy these demands. Oddly, however, in some situations the possibility of extortion might curb the advantage that well-organized groups are thought to have. That is because only a group or individual with an intense interest will be subject to extortion. A diffuse, unorganized group, none of whose members individually has a strong interest in an outcome-consumers of subsidized agricultural products, for example-presents an impossible target for extortion. There is no way for a representative to coerce contributions from them even if she wants to.[23]

In addition to those problems, extortion introduces the independent problem of unfairness to the contributors, or (in the case of firms who pass the costs through) to those who end up paying increased prices to underwrite the contributions. There are also likely to be allocative inefficiencies (because the effective cost of activities that lead to a person's

22. See FRANK J. SORAUF, INSIDE CAMPAIGN FINANCE: MYTHS AND REALITIES 60–97 (1992). For an argument to the effect that extortion of this kind is always a danger in the absence of strict limits on legislative authority, see Fred S. McChesney, *Rent Extraction and Rent Creation in the Economic Theory of Regulation*, 16 J. LEGAL STUD. 101 (1987); see also Jamin Raskin & John Bonifaz, *The Constitutional Imperative and Practical Superiority of Democratically Financed Elections*, 94 COLUM. L. REV. 1160, 1176-77 (1994) (noting inordinate advantages of incumbency in campaign finance).

23. See Einer R. Elhauge, *Does Interest Group Theory Justify More Intrusive Judicial Review?*, 101 YALE L.J. 31, 40 n.36 (1991); Fred S. McChesney, *Rent Extraction and Interest-Group Organization in a Coasean Model of Regulation*, 20 J. LEGAL STUD. 73, 85–89 (1991).

being subject to extortion will be artificially increased). These problems of unfairness and inefficiency would also be an appropriate target of campaign finance reform. Again, however, the problem of corruption is derivative from these problems. In fact, this is nearly the opposite of the way corruption is usually characterized: to the extent extortion is a concern, the goal of campaign finance reform becomes the protection of private moneyed interests from the democratic process instead of vice versa.

Somewhat surprisingly, there is little sentiment for reform on this ground. Most of those interested in campaign finance reform do not identify extortion as an evil.[24] Nor do those groups who are likely targets of extortion call for reform to eliminate it (at least in the United States). Indeed, one would expect to see agreements among rival groups not to give in to implicitly extortionate demands-in effect, a buyers' cartel in the market for political favors. Those groups (such as the railroad and trucking industry trade associations, in the example above) are often well-organized, and they often have repeated dealings with each other, so such an agreement would be relatively easy to enforce. But so far as I know, such agreements are not common. It may be that reaching and enforcing such agreements is in most cases too difficult, or it may be that the intermediary associations who distribute campaign contributions have interests at odds with those for whom they speak; a system in which there were fewer contributions exchanged for government action would be one in which the intermediaries and their employees would be less important.

In any event, this is an independent respect in which corruption, so-called, is a derivative problem. At least some instances of potentially coerced contributions—such as the case of judges or adjudicatory officials-are surely worth trying to eliminate. In other instances the problem may or may not be severe enough to be worth attacking; one would have to know more about the magnitude of the problem and the possible solutions before reaching a firm conclusion. But in any event, we again will not have a good handle on the problem unless we recognize that it is not just an easy-to-condemn matter of officials enriching themselves by selling their offices, but rather a different and more complex issue.

In sum, corruption, in the sense of a system in which campaign contributions are exchanged for specific acts by representatives, is a derivative problem. It is a problem because of inequality, or because it promotes interest group politics, or because it can lead to the coercion of potential contributors. But outside the core case of officials with judicial or quasi-judicial authority, the problem of extortion is complex and its magnitude

---

24. *See* SORAUF, *supra* note 22, at 60–73, 96–97.
* * *

is uncertain. Interest group politics is endemic to democracy, and while a "corrupt" system of campaign finance almost certainly heightens it, the questions whether it is truly a problem and, if so, what should be done to reduce it, are fraught with theoretical and empirical difficulties.

* * *

The Concept of Corruption in Campaign Finance Law

Thomas F. Burke

In *Buckley vs. Valeo*,[1] the Supreme Court put the concept of corruption at the center of campaign finance law. The Court held that only society's interest in preventing "corruption and the appearance of corruption" outweighed the limits on free expression created by restrictions on campaign contributions and expenditures. Other goals, such as equalizing the influence of citizens over elections, limiting the influence of money in electoral politics, or creating more competitive elections, were rejected as insufficiently compelling to justify regulating political speech.[2] The Court's focus on corruption has been reiterated in a series of cases following *Buckley*, which have decided whether various provisions of the Federal Election Campaign Act, or local laws, violate the First Amendment.[3] Barring a major shift in this area of law, corruption is the criterion by which the constitutionality of further reforms in campaign finance regulation will be measured.

The Court's emphasis on "corruption and the appearance of corruption" has stimulated criticism on several fronts. From the left, the Court is criticized for not giving credence to other interests served by campaign finance regulation.[4] From the right comes the criticism that the Court has

---

1. 424 U.S. 1 (1976).

2. *Id.* at 25–27.

3. First National Bank of Boston v. Bellotti, 435 U.S. 765 (1978); Citizens Against Rent Control v. Berkeley, 454 U.S. 290 (1981); California Medical Ass'n v. FEC, 453 U.S. 182 (1981); FEC v. National Right to Work Comm., 459 U.S. 197 (1982); FEC v. National Conservative Political Action Comm., 470 U.S. 480 (1985); FEC v. Massachusetts Citizens For Life, Inc., 479 U.S. 238 (1986); Austin v. Michigan Chamber of Commerce, 494 U.S. 652 (1990); and Colorado Republican Federal Campaign Comm. v. FEC, 116 S. Ct. 2309 (1996).

4. J. Skelly Wright, *Money and the Pollution of Politics: Is the First Amendment an Obstacle to Political Equality?*, 82 COLUM. L. REV. 609 (1982).

been inconsistent in its application of the corruption standard.[5] Others find the problem in the term "corruption" itself. Frank Sorauf argues that while the phrase "has a ring that most Americans will like...its apparent clarity is deceptive, and its origin is at best clouded."[6] Yet whatever its flaws, politicians, activists, judges and even picky academics continually employ the concept of corruption in their claims about the campaign finance system. I hope in this article to give some sense of both the possibilities and the limits of understanding campaign finance as an issue of corruption.

* * *

III. Does Money Corrupt?

I have argued that the Court is on firmest ground when it adopts the "monetary influence" standard of corruption. But what is it about monetary influence—or for that matter *quid pro quo* trading—that is so corrupting? On what basis can we say that public officials who are influenced by contributions are corrupt?[45] Because the Court does not develop

---

5. *See* Antonin Scalia's dissent in *Austin*, 494 U.S. at 679.

6. Frank J. Sorauf, *Caught in a Political Thicket: The Supreme Court and Campaign Finance*, 3 Const. Comm. 97, 103 (1986). *See also* two wide-ranging critiques of the Court's corruption standard: Jonathan Bernstein, *Goo Goo Terror*, 95 Inst. of Governmental Studies Working Paper 22, Institute of Governmental Studies, University of California-Berkeley (1995); and Ron Schmidt, Jr., *Defining Corruption*: Plunkitt *to* Buckley *and Beyond*, 95 Institute of Governmental Studies Working Paper 21, Institute of Governmental Studies, University of California-Berkeley (1995).

* * *

45. A related question is whether campaign contributions actually do influence representatives. The short answer, drawn from a growing body of evidence, is that contributions do influence representatives, but less than many suppose. Political scientists have produced a wealth of studies on this question but are only beginning to answer it. Most of the studies have attempted to measure the influence of PAC contributions on votes on the floor. While the results are mixed, most of the studies find only small effects. Contributions seem to go to representatives already inclined—by ideology or constituency—to support the contributor. But floor voting is only the tip of the iceberg of legislative activity.

There is little investigation of how contributions influence behavior in committee, where most legislating (and deliberating) gets done, though one study found significant effects on legislators' level of activity on behalf of contributors. *See* Richard L. Hall and Frank W. Wayman, *Buying Time: Moneyed Interests and the Mobilization of Bias in Congressional Committees*, 84 Am. Pol. Sci. Rev. 797 (1990). Similarly there is a paucity of research on how contributions influence representatives' willingness to meet with constituents or intervene for them in administrative disputes (like the Keating affair). On the access issue, *see* Laura I. Langbein, *Money and Access: Some Empirical Evidence*, 48 J. of

its own account of what makes an action corrupt, we must go beyond the campaign finance cases to answer these questions.

Daniel Lowenstein argues that the "payment of money to bias the judgment or sway the loyalty of persons holding positions of public trust is a practice whose condemnation is deeply rooted in our most ancient heritage."[46] Lowenstein believes that there is a strong cultural norm in our society that public officials not be influenced by money, in the form of either gifts or campaign contributions. As evidence, Lowenstein cites both the writings of various scholars on the subject, and the law of bribery, which in many jurisdictions makes *quid pro quo* campaign contributions illegal.[47] Thus Lowenstein appeals to the public opinion and legal norms approaches in defining financial influence as corruption. As noted earlier, these are problematic appeals. Lowenstein has no polling data to show that the vast majority of Americans agree with his norm, but even if he did we might still contend that Americans are simply misguided in believing that financial influence is corrupting. Martin Shapiro argues that Lowenstein, by operating as a "cultural anthropologist," might be able to discover a societal norm, but that such a norm cannot be the basis of constitutional law: "There is a cultural norm of racism in our society. Does

---

POL. 1052 (1986). On floor voting, *see* Henry W. Chappell, Jr., *Campaign Contributions and Voting on the Cargo Preference Bill: A Comparison of Simultaneous Models*, 36 PUB. CHOICE 301 (1981); Henry W. Chappell, Jr., *Campaign Contributions and Congressional Voting: A Simultaneous Probit-Tobit Model*, 64 REV. OF ECON. AND STAT. 77–83 (1982); Garey Durden and Jonathan Silberman, *Determining Legislative Preferences on the Minimum Wage: An Economic Approach*, 84 J. OF POL. ECON. 317 (1976); Diana Evans, *PAC Contributions and Roll-Call Voting: Conditional Power in* INTEREST GROUP POLITICS (Allan J. Cigler and Burdett A. Loomis, eds., Cong. Q., 2d ed. 1986). John P. Frendreis and Richard W. Waterman, *PAC Contributions and Legislative Behavior: Senate Voting on Trucking Deregulation*, 66 SOC. SCI. Q. 401 (1986); Janet M. Grenzke, *PACs and the Congressional Supermarket: The Currency is Complex*, 33 AM. J. OF POL. SCI. 1 (1989); JAMES B. KAU AND PAUL H. RUBIN, CONGRESSMEN, CONSTITUENTS AND CONTRIBUTORS: DETERMINANTS OF ROLL CALL VOTING IN THE HOUSE OF REPRESENTATIVES (Martinus Nijhoff, ed., 1982); Jean Reith Schroedel, *Campaign Contributions and Legislative Outcomes* 39 W. POL. Q. 371 (1986); W.P. Welch, *Campaign Contributions and Legislative Voting: Milk Money and Dairy Price Supports*, 35 W. POL. Q. 478 (1982); Allen Wilhite and John Theilmann, *Labor PAC Contributions and Labor Legislation: A Simultaneous Logit Approach*, 53 PUB. CHOICE 267 (1987); John R. Wright, *PACs, Contributions, and Roll Calls: An Organizational Perspective* 79 AM. POL. SCI. REV. 400 (1985); and John R. Wright, *Contributions, Lobbying and Committee Voting in the U.S. House of Representatives*, 84 AM. POL. SCI. REV. 417 (1990).

46. Daniel Hays Lowenstein, *On Campaign Finance Reform: The Root of All Evil is Deeply Rooted*, 18 HOFSTRA L. REV. 301, 302 (1989).

47. *See generally id.*

the existence of such a norm give constitutional legitimacy to racist statutes?"[48] Shapiro maintains that Lowenstein cannot define what is corrupt merely by reference to social norms or legal principles. Even the fact that bribery statutes often cover campaign contributions traded for political favors is not determinative. Only a theoretical argument can answer the question. Everything else is question-begging.[49]

Thus any serious thinking about corruption must move us back to first principles, to fundamental beliefs about government. The debate over the place of corruption in campaign finance ultimately turns on the theoretical foundations of representative democracy.

In several recent articles Dennis Thompson has grounded his approach to legislative ethics in a theory of representation which stresses deliberation. The debate between Thompson and Bruce Cain, another expert on campaign finance, illustrates the deep roots of the controversy over corruption.

Representation and Deliberation

Thompson advances a seemingly simple notion: In a functioning democracy, representatives must deliberate about the public good. Private interests have a legitimate place in a democracy as long as they subject themselves to "the rigors of the democratic process." To get their way, private interests must convincingly articulate public purposes.[50]

Private interests which attempt to bypass this deliberative process are "agents of corruption."[51] They tempt representatives to ignore public pur-

---

48. Martin Shapiro, *Corruption, Freedom and Equality in Campaign Financing*, 18 HOFSTRA L. REV. 385, 387 (1989).

49. *Id.* at 387–94.

50. DENNIS F. THOMPSON, ETHICS IN CONGRESS FROM INDIVIDUAL TO INSTITUTIONAL CORRUPTION 28 (The Brookings Institution 1995). The only alternative is logrolling, but recent research suggests that logrolling is both more difficult and more rare than is commonly supposed. *See* KEITH KREHBIEL, INFORMATION AND LEGISLATIVE ORGANIZATION (U. of Michigan Press, 1991). Of 29 case studies of legislation considered in Congress between 1945 and 1970, Joseph Bessette found only four examples of logrolling. And even in those cases logrolling turned out to be only a small part of the story, with deliberation on the merits also playing an important role. Bessette even argues that the case often held up as the paradigmatic instance of logrolling, the creation of the food stamp program, was more a matter of deliberation. JOSEPH M. BESSETTE, THE MILD VOICE OF REASON: DELIBERATIVE DEMOCRACY AND AMERICAN NATIONAL GOVERNMENT 67–99 (U. of Chicago Press, 1994).

51. THOMPSON, ETHICS IN CONGRESS, *supra* note 50, at 28.

poses and to pay attention to influences "that are clearly irrelevant to any process of deliberation."[52]

What influences are clearly irrelevant? Thompson gives as his primary example personal gain. Personal gain tends to take time and attention away from what should be the job of the legislator and can overwhelm the "unsteady inclination to pursue the public good."[53] Thus bribes, for example, corrupt the deliberative process.

Campaign contributions, Thompson says, are different from bribes because they are a necessary part of the political process. Moreover, Thompson says we should admire those who, within limits, pursue political gain, including campaign contributions.[54] But campaign contributions corrupt deliberative democracy when they influence representatives to change their stands or to refocus their energies.[55] Thus Thompson accepts what I have called the "monetary influence" standard of corruption. For him, campaign contributions that seek to influence elections are vital to the democratic process, but those that seek to influence the representatives' decisions corrupt the process. Thompson shows how a deliberative theory of representation leads to a "monetary influence" standard of corruption.

In a recent article, however, Bruce Cain rejects both deliberative theory and the monetary interest standard. Cain argues that deliberative theory is "excessively restrictive and very naive," and that it is out of step with the philosophical foundations of American government.[56] Further, Cain sug-

---

52. *Id.* at 20. Thompson calls this the independence principle. In his earlier writings Thompson calls it the principle of autonomy; *see* DENNIS F. THOMPSON, POLITICAL ETHICS AND PUBLIC OFFICE 111–16 (Harv. U. Press, 1987). The argument is also outlined in Dennis F. Thompson, *Mediated Corruption: The Case of the Keating Five*, 87 AM. POL. SCI. REV. 369 (1993).

53. THOMPSON, ETHICS IN CONGRESS, *supra* note 50, at 21.

54. *Id.* at 66.

55. *Id.* at 117.

56. Bruce E. Cain, *Moralism and Realism in Campaign Finance Reform*, 1995 U. OF CHI. LEGAL F. 111, 120.

Cain also claims that the deliberative theory "rests on the rationalist's faith that right reasons can be found for actions, and that political discourse will lead to the discovery of commonly acknowledged truth." *Id.* at 120. The first charge is true only in the modest sense that deliberative theory demands that representatives give reasons for their actions and that debate focus on the adequacy of those reasons, *see* the discussion of Cass Sunstein's "republic of reasons," *supra* note 52. As to the second charge, that deliberative theorists naively believe that debate will lead to consensus, nothing in deliberative theory necessitates this belief. If people are completely immune to persuasion, then of course deliberation is futile. But as long as debate is capable of moving people, then the fact of pluralism is quite compatible with deliberative theory. Hanna Pitkin eloquently expresses

gests that Thompson's approach relies on Edmund Burke's trustee notion of representation, which, Cain claims, is not widely accepted.

Instead Cain offers his own "procedural fairness" vision of democracy, drawn from the pluralist tradition in political science. He groups under this label theorists such as Joseph Schumpeter, Anthony Downs, Robert Dahl, and James Madison (or at least, Dahl's rendition of Madison). What these otherwise disparate theorists share, according to Cain, is an approach to politics that is nondeliberative. Each treats democracy as a matter of preference aggregation, and each expects representatives to act as delegates in order to be elected.[57] For proceduralists, Cain seems to conclude, the notion of corruption in campaign finance is simply meaningless. If, after all, politics is simply a matter of counting preferences, campaign contributions can be seen as a kind of vote, a way to signal the direction (and intensity) of one's desires. Money is then just another currency in the counting process, one which advantages some groups and disadvantages others. The only real issue in campaign finance, according to Cain, is how to count fairly and opinions about this will naturally differ depending on which groups one favors.[58]

---

the deliberative view of democracy:

> Political life is not merely the making of arbitrary choices, nor merely the resultant of bargaining between separate, private wants. It is always a combination of bargaining and compromise where there are irresolute and conflicting commitments, and common deliberation about public policy, to which facts and rational arguments are relevant.

HANNA FENICHEL PITKIN, THE CONCEPT OF REPRESENTATION 212 (U. Cal. Press, 1967).

Some versions of republican theory do seem incompatible with pluralism. But as Frank Michelman has argued, republican theory at its best depends on the diversity of views "that citizens bring to the debate of the commonwealth." Michelman seeks to resolve the tension between republicanism and pluralism in his article *Law's Republic*, 97 YALE L.J. 1493, 1504 (1988).

57. Cain, *supra* note 56 at 122. Strictly speaking, the proceduralist representative is not really a delegate but a "rational actor." She is not committed to the norm of following the views of her constituency but simply to saving her own skin—or, as the economists like to say, maximizing her utility—whatever that involves. Normally one of the best ways to get reelected is to follow the opinion of one's constituency, so there is often a happy marriage between the delegate role and rationality, but a divorce is always possible. In a system with uncontrolled campaign contributions, for example, it may be rational for a representative to dismiss the views of a majority of her district when they conflict with the desires of a generous contributor.

58. Cain argues that "By littering the intellectual landscape with irrelevant issues, moralist/idealists obstruct the path to a full, open discussion of the public's views about the proper distribution of power and influence." Cain, *supra* note 56 at 112.

The conflict between Thompson and Cain is so fundamental that it is difficult to arbitrate. Perhaps the best place to start is with Cain's contention that deliberative theory is a "nontraditional conception of American democracy."[59] This is a surprising claim, for as Thompson argues, deliberation was at the center of the Framers' conception of representative government.[60] The *Federalist Papers*, for example, justify many aspects of the Constitution—separation of powers, bicameralism, methods of election, size of legislative bodies—in terms of their effect on the deliberative process. The aim was to replace the excess of passion and "local spirit" that had overtaken state legislators with a concern for "the permanent and aggregate interests of the community," or as the *Federalist Papers* variously puts it, "the good of the whole," "the public weal," "great and national objects," "the great and aggregate interests," the "common interest," the "common good of the society," and the "comprehensive interests of [the] country."[61] Indeed, Madison's famous defense of an extended republic in *Federalist 10* was built on deliberative theory. He argued that such a republic was more likely than other systems of government to refine and enlarge the public views by passing them through the medium of a chosen body of citizens, whose wisdom may best discern the true interest of their country and whose patriotism and love of justice will be least likely to sacrifice it to temporary or partial considerations.[62] Madison was, of course, a subtle thinker who understood the complex interplay of interests and deliberation, so one is likely to oversimplify his views by selective quotation. Yet the deliberative aspects of his thought cannot be denied. Over the past three decades, scholars in law, history and political science have demonstrated the profound influence of republican theory, with its emphasis on deliberation about the public good, on the thought of the Framers, particularly Madison. The historian Gordon Wood concludes that Madison and the Federalists were far from "modern-day pluralists:"

---

59. *Id.* at 120.

60. THOMPSON, ETHICS IN CONGRESS, *supra* note 50 at 19.

61. This point is made by Joseph Bessette in Bessette, *supra* note 50 at 27 (quoting the *Federalist Papers*).

62. THE FEDERALIST NO. 10 (Madison) *in* THE FEDERALIST PAPERS, 77, 82 (Willmoore Kendall and George W. Carey, eds., Arlington House, 1966). Of course Madison was not so naive as to believe that representatives would always deliberate in the public interest, but he thought this ideal would be more closely approached in an extended republic, where factions would have a difficult time gaining control over the government. Daniel Hays Lowenstein, in a review of Cain's paper, also makes the point that Madison was no "proceduralist." Daniel Lowenstein, *Campaign Contributions and Corruption: Comments on Strauss and Cain*, 1995 U. CHI. LEGAL F. 163, 177.

> They still clung to the republican ideal of an autonomous public author-
> ity that was different from the many private interests of the society....
> Nor did they see public policy or the common interest of the national gov-
> ernment emerging naturally from the give-and-take of these clashing pri-
> vate interests....Far, then, from the new national government being a
> mere integrator and harmonizer of the different special interests in the
> society, it would become a "disinterested and dispassionate umpire in dis-
> putes between different passions and interest in the State."[63]

The Framers, in Sum, Embraced Deliberative Theory

The elitism of the Framers, who envisioned rule by a virtuous gentry, soon fell out of favor.[64] But their concern for deliberation has lived on. A long list of studies highlights the continuing importance of deliberation in American democratic theory and practice. As Philip Selznick writes in a recent review, "Deliberative democracy is moving to the forefront of political theory."[65] But attention to deliberation is hardly limited to theorists.

---

63. GORDON S. WOOD, THE RADICALISM OF THE AMERICAN REVOLUTION 253 (Alfred A. Knopf, ed. 1992) (quoting from a letter by Madison to Edmund Randolph, April 8, 1787, *in* PAPERS OF MADISON, IX, 384, 370).

Other historians who trace the influence of republicanism on the Framers include J.G.A. POCOCK, THE MACHIAVELLIAN MOMENT: FLORENTINE POLITICAL THOUGHT AND THE ATLANTIC REPUBLICAN TRADITION 506–52 (Princeton U. Press, 1975); and BERNARD BAILYN, THE IDEOLOGICAL ORIGINS OF THE AMERICAN REVOLUTION 22–54 (Belknap Press, 1967).

Foremost among legal scholars who have embraced republicanism are Cass Sunstein and Frank Michelman. *See* CASS R. SUNSTEIN, THE PARTIAL CONSTITUTION (Harv. U. Press, 1993); and Frank Michelman, *Law's Republic*, 97 YALE L.J. 1493 (1988).

For a particularly forceful analysis of Madison's thinking by a political scientist, *see* James Q. Wilson, *Interests and Deliberation in the American Republic, or, Why James Madison Would Never Have Received the James Madison Award*, 23 POL. SCI. AND POLITICS 4, 561 (1990).

64. Wood documents this process in *The Radicalism of the American Revolution*, *supra* note 63 at 255–305.

65. Selznick, *Defining Democracy Up*, 119 THE PUBLIC INTEREST 106 (1995). There is much literature on deliberative democracy in political theory. For some examples *see* JAMES S. FISHKIN, DEMOCRACY AND DELIBERATION: NEW DIRECTIONS FOR DEMOCRATIC REFORM (Yale U. Press, 1991); Joshua Cohen, *Deliberation and Democratic Legitimacy*, *in* THE GOOD POLITY: NORMATIVE ANALYSIS OF THE STATE 17 (Alan Hamlin and Philip Pettit, eds., Basil Blackwell 1989); John W. Kingdon, *Politicians, Self- Interest, and Ideas*, *in* RECONSIDERING THE DEMOCRATIC PUBLIC 73 (George E. Marcus and Russell L. Hanson, eds., Penn. State U. Press 1993); Amy Gutmann, *The Disharmony of Democracy*, *in* DEMOCRATIC COMMUNITY: NOMOS XXXV, 126–60 (John W. Chapman and Ian

Political scientists have confirmed the central role of deliberation in American government in their study of legislatures, courts, bureaucracies and the presidency. In his recent book on deliberative theory and practice Joseph Bessette cites thirty-three such studies.[66]

A few examples should suffice. Cass Sunstein argues, based on a review of the fundamentals of constitutional jurisprudence, that we live in a "republic of reasons." Courts, he says, will strike down laws based only on "naked preferences," the mere assertion of private power. To act constitutionally, legislators must provide a public-regarding rationale for their policies. It is through the process of deliberation that these rationales are articulated and judged.[67] Martha Derthick and Paul Quirk trace the influence of ideas and deliberation on regulatory reform of the telecommunications, trucking and airline industries in *The Politics of Deregulation*.[68] Richard F. Fenno finds that making "good public policy" through a careful study of issues is the dominant goal of representatives who seek a position on the Education and Labor and Foreign Affairs committees.[69] As Joseph Bessette has suggested, when political scientists actually examine the process of policymaking they find plenty of deliberation going on.[70]

Deliberative theory is untraditional only among some pluralist political scientists, who, beginning with Robert Dahl, have downplayed the republican and deliberative aspects of American government. The tradition from which Cain works starts not with Jefferson, Hamilton, or Madison, but rather with Arthur Bentley, David Truman, and Dahl.[71] The vision of

---

Shaprio, eds., New York U. Press, 1993); and David Miller, *Deliberative Democracy and Social Choice*, 60 POL. STUD. 54–67 (1992).

66. Bessette, *The Mild Voice of Reason, supra* note 50, at 251–52.

67. *See* Sunstein, *The Partial Constitution, supra* note 63, at 17–39.

68. MARTHA DERTHICK AND PAUL J. QUIRK, THE POLITICS OF DEREGULATION 147–206 (The Brookings Institution, 1985).

69. RICHARD F. FENNO, CONGRESSMEN IN COMMITTEES (Little, Brown and Co., 1973). Fenno's classic work on representation in practice is RICHARD F. FENNO, HOME STYLE: HOUSE MEMBERS IN THEIR DISTRICTS (Harper Collins 1978). For an updating of this book *see*, CAMPAIGNING FOR CONGRESS: POLITICIANS AT HOME AND IN WASHINGTON (Jonathan Bernstein, Adrienne Bird Jamieson and Christine Trost, eds., Inst. of Gov't. Studies Press, 1995).

70. *See* Bessette, *Mild Voice of Reason, supra* note 50, at 67–99.

71. The most influential books in this tradition are ROBERT A. DAHL, A PREFACE TO DEMOCRATIC THEORY (U. of Chicago Press, 1956); DAVID B. TRUMAN, THE GOVERNMENTAL PROCESS: POLITICAL INTERESTS AND PUBLIC OPINION (Alfred A. Knopf, ed., 2d ed. 1971); and ARTHUR F. BENTLEY, THE PROCESS OF GOVERNMENT: A STUDY OF SOCIAL PRESSURES (U. of Chicago Press, 1908).

American democracy as preference aggregation[72] is widespread among political scientists and public choice theorists, but outside of these narrow realms it is hard to say how well it resonates. Whatever popular opinion would hold, though, Cain clearly underestimates the centrality of deliberative theory in American political thought and practice.

Cain's argument that Thompson relies on a trustee theory of representation, however, points to a more troubling issue.[73] In fact Thompson at-

---

72. Cass Sunstein claims that what unifies pluralists is the notion that "laws should be understood not as a product of deliberation, but on the contrary as a kind of commodity, subject to the usual forces of supply and demand." SUNSTEIN, THE PARTIAL CONSTITUTION, *supra* note 63 at 24–25. Similarly, Frank Michelman defines pluralism as "the deep mistrust of people's capacities to communicate *persuasively* to one another their diverse normative experiences.…Pluralism, that is, doubts or denies our ability to communicate such material in ways that move each other's views on disputed normative issues towards felt (not merely strategic) agreement without deception, coercion, or other manipulation." Michelman, *supra* note 63 at 1493, 1507.

Whether this is characteristic of all pluralist thought is questionable. Nelson W. Polsby, who has done much to popularize the term "pluralism," maintains that pluralism is often caricatured by critics who argue against its most extravagant formulations. *See* NELSON W. POLSBY, COMMUNITY POWER AND POLITICAL THEORY: A FURHTER LOOK AT PROBLEMS OF EVIDENCE AND INFERENCE (Yale U. Press, 2d ed. 1980). Polsby contends that on the issue of deliberation, pluralism is silent. (Polsby himself values deliberation, as is seen in his CONSEQUENCES OF PARTY REFORM (Oxford U. Press, 1983)).

On this point, as on several others, there appears to be a plurality of pluralisms. Sunstein and Michelman seem to be particularly concerned with public choice approaches to politics, which can be seen as an outgrowth of pluralism but hardly encompass the sum of pluralist thought. In any case, Cain's approach—and the approach of the theorists he relies on, including Dahl—is to see politics as exclusively a matter of preference aggregation.

73. Cain offers no evidence for his contention that the delegate model of representation is more widely accepted than the trustee model. I could locate only a few instances of polling on this question. In 1938, when respondents were asked, "Do you believe that a Congressman should…vote on any question as the majority of his constituents desire, or vote according to his own judgment?" Thirty-seven percent chose the delegate side, 54% the trustee side. (Roper Center Archives, accession number 0175920, survey sponsored by FORTUNE, August 1938.) A more recent survey asked: "When your Representative in Congress votes on an issue, which should be more important—the way voters in your district feel about that issue, or the Representative's own principles and judgment about what is best for the country?" Sixty-eight percent chose the delegate side, 24% the trustee side. (Roper Center Archives, accession number 0192631, survey sponsored by TIME/CNN, Feb. 10, 1993.) It is unclear whether this represents a time trend or a difference in question wording.

The vast majority of Americans probably haven't devoted much time to thinking about the delegate/trustee issue. Those who have often reject the formulation of a strict dichotomy between the two modes. When members of Congress were asked a

tempts to distinguish his approach from the trustee notion. He points out that the views of the constituency and the views of the representative about what is in the public interest are likely on many issues to coincide. Where they do conflict, however, Thompson says that representatives may voice their constituents' views in order to give them a hearing in the deliberative process. As long as the process itself is deliberative, as long as it focuses on the merits of the issue, it does not matter whether the individual representative is delegate or trustee.[74] And this suggests an important difference between trustee/delegate theories of representation and deliberative theory: Where the trustee/delegate dichotomy focuses on the

---

delegate/trustee question, some rejected it as simplistic. "Who dreamed up these stupid questions?" asked one respondent. THOMPSON, POLITICAL ETHICS AND PUBLIC OFFICE, *supra* note 52 at 99. Moreover, John Kingdon finds that the delegate/trustee dichotomy fails to capture the complex ways in which members of Congress think about and perform their jobs. JOHN W. KINGDON, CONGRESSMEN'S VOTING DECISIONS, (U. Michigan Press, 3d ed. 1989).

Hanna Pitkin concludes that the dichotomy, which she prefers to call the "mandate-independence controversy," "poses a logically insoluble puzzle, asking us to choose between two elements that are both involved in the concept of representation." PITKIN, THE CONCEPT OF REPRESENTATION, *supra* note 56, at 165. As Pitkin, Thompson and others have suggested, we might be better off in discussions of representation if we dropped the notion of a dichotomy between trustees and delegates entirely.

74. Thompson is somewhat elusive on this point:

[T]he ideal legislator in a representative system does not pursue the public interest exclusively (whatever it may be). Such a legislator also has an ethical obligation to constituents that must be weighed against the obligation to a broader public. To find the balance between these obligations, even to decide whether they conflict, the legislator must consider the particular political circumstances at the time....Ethical obligations of these kinds are contingent on what is going on in the legislative process as a whole and may differ for different members and vary over time for all members.

ETHICS IN CONGRESS, *supra* note 50, at 70–71. Elsewhere Thompson says that the deliberative principle "is consistent with conceptions of representation ranging from delegate to trustee." The principle requires only that representatives defend their views on public policy "in a public forum—and at the risk of political defeat." *Id.* at 114. Similarly: "[R]eelection or party loyalty could also count as principled reasons, when they are consistent with...legislative deliberation."

POLITICAL ETHICS AND PUBLIC OFFICE, *supra* note 52, at 113–14. Thompson does not specify how far this goes. At some point, presumably, the forces of constituency pressure, reelection anxiety, or party loyalty overwhelm the process of deliberation.

As these passages indicate, Thompson, like many other political theorists, is quite critical of the delegate/trustee dichotomy. *See for example* Dennis F. Thompson, *Representatives in the Welfare State, in* DEMOCRACY AND THE WELFARE STATE 131, 132–36 (Amy Gutmann, ed., Princeton U. Press, 1988).

level of the individual representative, the deliberative theory leads us to look at what is happening to the institution as a whole.

Yet this refinement creates another difficulty, one that Thompson does not address. If in a deliberative democracy representatives can in some circumstances act as delegates for their constituents, why can they not also act as delegates for their contributors?[75] I think the answer is that Thompson allows for only a narrow exception to the basic rule that representatives must deliberate. In giving voice to the views of their constituents, representatives can on some occasions move deliberation forward. But if a significant number of representatives are acting *solely* as delegates, ignoring not only the arguments of others but even their own views, deliberative democracy is imperiled.[76] This corruption of the deliberative process is much more likely when representatives fall under the sway of their contributors. Contributor-influenced representatives are unlikely to be candid about the motivation for their actions; the last thing they want is an open examination of the quality of their reasons and their process of deliberation. Thus where contributor-influenced representatives predominate, legislative deliberation becomes a sham. By contrast, constituent-influenced legislators can acknowledge the pressures on them and, where their own views conflict with those of the constituents, can even deliberate publicly about how the two can be reconciled.[77] Constituent influence can itself become a matter for deliberation in a way that contributor influence never can. Hence contributor influence is much more likely than constituent influence to have a pernicious effect on deliberative democracy.

Deliberative theory, then, provides a grounding for the monetary influence standard of corruption. If politics is nothing more than a market, and politicians nothing more than retailers, then there is no need for deliberation, and no necessary problem with "bribery" through the campaign finance process. That is the vision behind Cain's procedural theory. But if representation involves deliberation about the public good, then contributions that influence representatives are a corruption of the democratic process.

Deliberative theory is well-grounded in American political philosophy and practice. It is an attractive, approachable ideal. Its appeal explains

---

75. This is the crux of David Strauss's argument against the deliberative approach to the concept of corruption. *See* David A. Strauss, *What is the Goal of Campaign Finance Reform?* 1995 U. OF CHI. LEGAL F. 141.

76. Hanna Pitkin goes so far as to say that when representatives act as pure delegates they are no longer doing something that can be called representation. *See* PITKIN, THE CONCEPT OF REPRESENTATION, *supra* note 56, at 210–211.

77. This is a point that Lowenstein makes; *see* Lowenstein, *supra* note 62, at 191.

why, despite criticisms like those voiced by Cain, academic, legal and popular debate about campaign finance continues to revolve around notions of corruption.

IV. The Utility of "Corruption"

I have argued that the concept of corruption can be applied to one of the major problems in campaign finance, the influence that contributors have on the actions of representatives. The monetary influence standard of corruption has been invoked in several Supreme Court cases, but the Court has drifted in its treatment of corruption. At some points the Court characterizes the issue as a matter of vote trading, of *quid pro quos*. At other times, the Court has portrayed the problem as one of "distortion" of public opinion. Nonetheless, I believe the Court has been on firmest ground when it has recognized the issue as one of contributor influence.

Of course this recognition would not by itself determine the constitutionality of any particular regulatory scheme. Indeed it is just one of the factors involved. People may balance the goal of preventing corruption and the First Amendment interests at stake differently even though they recognize the legitimacy of both claims. Still, by focusing on the meaning of corruption I hope I have given some sense of its place in this mix.

Clearly corruption is a limited concept. It cannot encompass all the concerns we have about the campaign finance system.[78] Because so much stress has been put on corruption in campaign finance law, there will always be a temptation to use it more broadly to cover goals that are only partly related—to stretch its meaning, as I believe the Court has done in *Austin. Austin's* proclamation that the political system is corrupted when campaign contributions don't mirror public opinion cannot be maintained. "Corruption" will be drained of meaning if it becomes a mere synonym for "inequality." The concept of corruption has a worthy place in campaign finance law, and if the Court chooses to recognize other interests in campaign regulation it should not tarnish this one.

---

78. Cain complains that Thompson's approach to corruption fails to address many of the key issues in campaign finance, particularly the inequalities created in the election system by disparities in campaign contributions. Cain, *supra* note 56, at 122. But those who embrace corruption as an important concept in campaign finance law need not limit themselves to this one principle. The American campaign finance system is flawed in many respects, and no one principle can capture all of them.

Indeed if Cain had merely argued that too much attention is given to issues of corruption in the popular debate over campaign finance and not enough to other concerns I would be in full agreement.

Free Speech and the Widening Gyre of Fund Raising: Why Campaign Spending Limits May Not Violate the First Amendment After All

Vincent Blasi

I. Introduction

Candidates for office spend too much of their time raising money. This is scarcely a controversial proposition.[1] A major impetus for campaign fi-

1. *See* DAN CLAWSON ET AL., MONEY TALKS: CORPORATE PACS AND POLITICAL INFLUENCE 79, 203–04 (1992); ELIZABETH DREW, POLITICS AND MONEY: THE NEW ROAD TO CORRUPTION 96 (1983); BROOKS JACKSON, HONEST GRAFT: BIG MONEY AND THE AMERICAN POLITICAL PROCESS 69, 91–92, 108 (1990); BURDETT LOOMIS, THE NEW AMERICAN POLITICIAN: AMBITION, ENTREPRENEURSHIP, AND THE CHANGING FACE OF POLITICAL LIFE 195–96 (1988); DAVID B. MAGLEBY & CANDICE J. NELSON, THE MONEY CHASE: CONGRESSIONAL CAMPAIGN FINANCE REFORM 43–45, 197 (1990); FRANK J. SORAUF, INSIDE CAMPAIGN FINANCE: MYTHS AND REALITIES 72–73, 187–88 (1992) [hereinafter SORAUF, INSIDE]; FRANK J. SORAUF, MONEY IN AMERICAN ELECTIONS 183–84 (1988) [hereinafter SORAUF, MONEY]. One (unnamed) Republican senator summarized the problem vividly: "I knew Congress well before I came here, but I did not know the amount of time consumed by fundraising and how that encroaches on your ability to work here. It devours one's time-you spend the two or three years before your re-election fundraising. The other years, you're helping others." PETER LINDSTROM, CENTER FOR RESPONSIVE POLITICS, CONGRESS SPEAKS: A SURVEY OF THE 100TH CONGRESS 80 (1988) [hereinafter CONGRESS SPEAKS]. In his memoir describing life as a member of the House of Representatives, Congressman David Price, a former political science professor, decries "the constant preoccupation with fundraising." *See* DAVID PRICE, THE CONGRESSIONAL EXPERIENCE: A VIEW FROM THE HILL 26 (1992). House majority leader Richard Gephardt, a hugely successful fund-raiser, has noted how time-consuming the process is: "If you have the need to raise three or four hundred thousand dollars, you're

nance reform is the frustration politicians now feel concerning how much time they must devote to courting potential donors, often by methods borrowed from the marketplace that can only be described as demeaning.[2] The situation has gotten worse as electoral merchandising has grown ever more sophisticated and expensive.[3] Herbert Alexander, a student of campaign finance for over thirty years, sketches the disturbing pattern that has developed:

> Throughout the 1980s, as campaign costs escalated, candidates for federal office spent increasing amounts of time in activities related to fund raising. For House members, the pursuit of campaign donations is never-ending. While senators serve six-year terms, many of them are now starting to hold fund-raising events shortly after election and well in advance of reelection, so they can store up enough of a war chest to fend off any serious political opposition. Senators now must raise nearly $ 13,000 each week for their entire six-year terms to amass the average that a winning Senate race costs.[4]

The problem is serious quite apart from the supposition that past and potential donors exert influence over the behavior of representatives far greater than that exerted by constituents who do not make sizable contributions. "Disproportionate influence" is hard to measure, and absent particularly nefarious patterns perhaps is defensible as an inevitable phenomenon in any real world of power. In the effort to criticize the current system of campaign finance on grounds of political favoritism, reformers until recently have failed to emphasize sufficiently how the system harms the candidates themselves.[5] The quality no less than the equity of representation is a concern of constitutional dimension.

---

taking an enormous amount of the members' time just to raise the money." Quoted in DREW, *supra*, at 51.

2. For a description of the bazaars staged by political parties to display their candidates for the inspection of potential contributors, *see* JACKSON, *supra* note 1 at 91–92. Many political action committees require candidate-supplicants to fill out questionnaires pertaining to how they would vote on hypothetical legislative proposals. *See* SARA FRITZ AND DWIGHT MORRIS, GOLD-PLATED POLITICS: RUNNING FOR CONGRESS IN THE 1990S 171 (1992).

3. *See* HERBERT E. ALEXANDER, FINANCING POLITICS: MONEY, ELECTIONS, AND POLITICAL REFORM 78–81 (1992); MAGLEBY & NELSON, *supra* note 1, at 28–34. During the 1977–1978 election cycle, approximately $ 195 million was spent on House and Senate campaigns. Ten years later that figure had increased to $ 459 million. During the 1991–1992 election cycle, $ 678 million was spent, an increase of 52% over the preceding (1989–1990) cycle. *See* Federal Election Commission, Press Release 1 (Mar. 4, 1993) (Report forthcoming) (figures not adjusted for inflation).

4. ALEXANDER, *supra* note 3, at 54 (footnote omitted).

5. During the reform wave of the 1970s, comparatively little mention was made of the time demands of fund-raising. *See* authorities cited *infra* note 15.

A major goal of campaign finance reform is coming to be—and surely ought to be—to protect the time of elected representatives and candidates for office. The quality of representation has to suffer when legislators continually concerned about re-election are not able to spend the greater part of their workday on matters of constituent service, information gathering, political and policy analysis, debating and compromising with fellow representatives, and the public dissemination of views.[6] Likewise, the quality of future representation has to suffer when aspirants for legislative office are not able to spend the bulk of their time learning what questions and problems most trouble voters, formulating positions on major issues, and holding themselves and their views up to public scrutiny. No doubt when candidates spend so much time fund-raising they encounter grievances, in-

---

In contrast, during the recent congressional debates, the need to free candidates from excessive fund-raising obligations was a major theme. *See, e.g.*, 139 Cong. Rec. H10656 (daily ed. Nov. 22, 1993) (remarks of Rep. Gejdenson); *id.* at H10665 (remarks of Rep. Harman); *id.* at H10670 (remarks of Rep. Reed); *id.* at H10671 (remarks of Rep. Hughes); *id.* at H10672 (remarks of Rep. Beilenson); *id.* at H10675 (remarks of Rep. Woolsey); Beth Donovan, *House Takes First Big Step in Overhauling System*, 51 CONG. Q. WKLY. REP. 3246, 3248 (1993) [hereinafter Donovan, *House Takes Step*]; Beth Donovan, *House Will Vote on Limits Nearly $ 1 Million in '96*, 51 CONG. Q. WKLY. REP. 3091, 3091 (1993) [hereinafter Donovan, *House Will Vote*]; Beth Donovan, *Senate Passes Campaign Finance by Gutting Public Funding*, 51 CONG. Q. WKLY. REP. 1534, 1537 (1993) [hereinafter Donovan, *Gutting Public Funding*]; Beth Donovan, *Constitutional Issues Frame Congressional Options*, 51 CONG. Q. WKLY. REP. 437, 437 (1993) [hereinafter Donovan, *Constitutional Issues*]. In addition, recent reform proposals from specialists in campaign finance emphasize how the current system harms candidates by the demands it makes on their time. *See* Magleby & Nelson, *supra* note 1, at 201; Jamin Raskin & John Bonifaz, *The Constitutional Imperative and Practical Superiority of Democratically Financed Elections*, 94 COLUM. L. REV. 1160, 1187–90 (1994); SORAUF, INSIDE, *supra* note 1, at 187–88; Fred Wertheimer & Susan W. Manes, *Campaign Finance Reform: A Key to Restoring the Health of Our Democracy*, 94 COLUM. L. REV. 1126, 1133 (1994).

6. *See* ALEXANDER, *supra* note 3, at 4, 51, 96, 166–67; DREW, *supra* note 1, at 98; LARRY J. SABATO, PAYING FOR ELECTIONS: THE CAMPAIGN FINANCE THICKET 1 (1989). In a survey of members of Congress conducted in 1987, 29.7% of the respondents stated that the demands of campaign fund-raising "significantly" cut into the time they devote to legislative work. When their staff members were asked the same question, 47.5% saw a significant reduction attributable to fund-raising in the time their bosses spent on legislative work. *See Congress Speaks, supra* note 1, at 92. The problem has almost certainly gotten worse in the House since the survey was taken: in 1988 the average House incumbent spent $ 380,000 campaigning for re-election; by 1992, that figure had risen to $ 543,000. *See* LARRY MAKINSON, CENTER FOR RESPONSIVE POLITICS, THE PRICE OF ADMISSION: CAMPAIGN SPENDING IN THE 1992 ELECTIONS 11 (1993) [hereinafter THE PRICE OF ADMISSION]. Spending in Senate elections has held fairly even over the last six years. *See id.* at 10.

formation, and ideas of potential donors that an enlightened representative would want to consider. If the candidate is not substantially free, however, to spend her time considering as well the grievances, information, and ideas of non-donors-in particular her geographic constituents-the process falls short, not just of the ideal but of the constitutional norm.[7] Article One, the Republican Form of Government Clause, and the Seventeenth Amendment guarantee to the People of the United States and of the individual states that they shall be governed by representatives.[8] Legislators and aspirants for legislative office who devote themselves to raising money round-the-clock are not in essence representatives.

Such an extreme way of stating the problem might suggest that I plan to argue that campaign finance reform is a constitutional imperative, judicially enforceable even in the absence of legislation. I can imagine how such a claim could be supported in terms of constitutional theory, but the institutional and remedial problems remain formidable, perhaps prohibitive. More promising is the claim that certain forms of campaign finance legislation can be justified, even against First Amendment challenge, by resort to the constitutionally ordained value of representation. In the debate that continues in the wake of *Buckley v. Valeo*,[9] too much emphasis has been placed on the anticorruption and equalization (or enhancement) rationales for regulating campaign contributions and expenditures.[10] This

---

7. Unless they hold other positions in government, candidates who challenge incumbents do not have official responsibilities that could be discharged were fund-raising a smaller part of effective candidacy. Nevertheless, the process of representation really begins in the campaign itself. That is when future representatives forge their political identities and often when constituents are most actively engaged in expressing their complaints and preferences. Thus, the way nonincumbent candidates allocate their time is a constitutional concern. This does not mean, however, that challengers must be treated exactly the same as incumbents in the matter of campaign finance regulation. *See infra* text accompanying notes 46–47, 49.

8. *See* U.S. Const. art. I, 2; *id.* at art. IV, 4; *id.* at amend. XVII.

9. 424 U.S. 1 (1976) (holding, inter alia, that spending limits on candidates violate the First Amendment).

10. "Enhancement" refers to the policy of facilitating campaign speech by underfinanced candidates even when such support does not eliminate all inequalities of communicative capacity. A particularly good recent development of the enhancement rationale is David Cole, *First Amendment Antitrust: The End of Laissez-Faire in Campaign Finance*, 9 YALE L. & POL'Y REV. 236 (1991). Three important books that explore the relationship between liberty and equality in political and constitutional theory have sections on campaign finance. *See* CHARLES R. BEITZ, POLITICAL EQUALITY: AN ESSAY IN DEMOCRATIC THEORY 192–213 (1989); JOHN RAWLS, POLITICAL LIBERALISM 358–63 (1993); CASS R. SUNSTEIN, DEMOCRACY AND THE PROBLEM OF FREE SPEECH 94–101 (1993). Strong critiques of various egalitarian rationales for campaign finance regulation are Lillian R. BeVi-

emphasis has diverted attention away from the rationale that I believe holds the most promise of answering First Amendment concerns: candidate time protection.

II. Spending Limits, *Buckley*, and the Rise of the War Chest Mentality

If candidate time protection is the objective, the principal regulatory measure must be a limit on the overall amount of money that can be spent in an election campaign. From this perspective, it is a matter of secondary importance what restrictions are placed on the size of contributions to candidates, parties, and political action committees; on the sources of funds collected by candidates; and on "independent" expenditures in support of candidates. Even the availability of public financing of some election expenses, or of a voucher system designed to equalize the opportunity to contribute, pales in significance compared to the need to limit overall spending. Candidates facing or fearing tight races will be preoccupied with fund-raising (or voucher raising) under any system that does not restrict total spending. If candidates are permitted to spend vast amounts of money in pursuit of votes, they will inevitably spend vast amounts of time in pursuit of money. Spending limits are the sine qua non of candidate time protection. The centrality of candidate spending limits was not so apparent when Congress passed its major campaign finance reforms in 1971 and 1974,[11] nor when the Supreme Court in 1976 held several provisions of that legislation unconstitutional, including the mandatory ceilings on overall campaign spending by congressional candidates.[12] At that time, what has come to be known as the war chest mentality had not yet

---

er, *Campaign Finance Reform: Specious Arguments, Intractable Dilemmas*, 94 COLUM L. REV. 1258, 1260–69 (1994), L.A. Powe, Jr., *Mass Speech and the Newer First Amendment*, 1982 SUP. CT. REV. 243. For an argument that the effort to prevent well-financed voices from dominating all others can be justified without resort to egalitarian premises, *see* Julian N. Eule, *Promoting Speaker Diversity:* Austin *and* Metro Broadcasting, 1990 SUP. CT. REV. 105, 111–14.

11. *See* Federal Election Campaign Act Amendments of 1974, Pub. L. No. 93-443, 88 Stat. 1263 (1974); Federal Election Campaign Act of 1971, Pub. L. No. 92-225, 86 Stat. 3 (1972).

12. *See* Buckley v. Valeo, 424 U.S. 1 (1976). For a discussion of how the *Buckley* opinion suffers from the Court's lack of familiarity with the practical dynamics of campaign finance and from the rushed, abstract character of the litigation, *see* Frank J. Sorauf, *Politics, Experience, and the First Amendment: The Case of American Campaign Finance*, 94 COLUM L. REV. 1348, 1349–52 (1994).

seized the Congress. Four years after the *Buckley* decision, however, several House and Senate incumbents were unexpectedly defeated in the 1980 elections. The losers attributed those upsets to massive expenditures by challenger candidates and supportive political action committees in the closing days of the campaign.[13] Ever since, incumbents have lived with the nightmare of a well-financed opponent saturating the media at the eleventh hour and "stealing" an election. No matter how long his tenure, how prominent his position, how favorable the electoral arithmetic in his district, how unimpressive and under-financed his last opponent was, and how hypothetical his next opponent may be, almost every member of Congress feels the need to amass a large war chest, just in case.[14] No package of campaign finance reforms will change substantially how representatives spend their time unless war chests are made unimportant. The best way to make a war chest unimportant is to prohibit the money in it from being spent in the cause of re-election.

One indication of how dramatically the war chest mentality has altered the regulatory landscape is the fact, startling in retrospect, that the Supreme Court in *Buckley* never considered how spending limits might be justified as a means of preventing candidates from spending excessive amounts of time on fund-raising. In 1976, candidate time protection was not seen as a major objective of campaign finance reform. Corruption, disproportionate influence, the fencing out of impecunious candidates, and the alienation of the electorate were the dominant concerns.[15]

---

13. *See* DREW, *supra* note 1, at 20–22; JACKSON, *supra* note 1, at 49–50, 68.

14. *See* ALEXANDER, *supra* note 3, at 78, 97. *See also* MORRIS P. FIORINA, CONGRESS: KEYSTONE OF THE WASHINGTON ESTABLISHMENT 93 (2d ed. 1989) (commenting on the electoral insecurity of congressional incumbents); GARY C. JACOBSON, MONEY IN CONGRESSIONAL ELECTIONS 121–22 (1980) ("Despite the well-known statistics on the reelection rates of incumbent members, they are a surprisingly insecure lot."). In 1980, only three members of Congress had a post-election balance (a "war chest") of greater than $ 250,000. By 1986, 54 had such a post-election balance. *See* Loomis, *supra* note 1, at 189–90. After the 1992 election, 49 representatives had more than $ 250,000 remaining in their campaign coffers. Computation by the author from data reported in THE PRICE OF ADMISSION, *supra* note 6, at 461–70. Of course, many representatives with a low balance immediately after an expensive campaign are able to amass a large war chest during the two years preceding the next election, or at least try hard to do so.

15. This is not to suggest that candidate time diversion went completely unnoticed during that period. The bill passed by the Senate that eventuated in the Federal Election Campaign Act Amendments of 1974 [hereinafter 1974 Act] contained a provision, eliminated in the conference committee, for the public financing of congressional elections. In the Senate committee report, that ill-fated provision was justified partly on the ground that financing expensive campaigns entirely out of private funds "is a great drain on the time and energies of the candidates." S. Rep. No. 689, 93rd Cong. (1974), *reprinted in*

The statutory limits on total campaign spending contained in the 1974 Act were analyzed by the *Buckley* Court in terms of three alternative rationales that have almost nothing to do with the problem of how candidates spend their time. First, spending limits were evaluated as a means of making large contributions less important in election contests so that candidates would have less incentive to find ways to evade the statutory

---

1974 U.S.C.C.A.N. 5587, 5591. The D.C. Circuit's majority opinion in *Buckley* made reference to time diversion, but only in the context of a discussion of the undue influence exerted by special interests free to make contributions of unlimited size. *See* Buckley v. Valeo, 519 F.2d 821, 837–39 (D.C. Cir. 1975). Similarly, the Supreme Court in *Buckley* listed as one of three legitimate justifications for the public financing of presidential elections the need to "free candidates from the rigors of fundraising." 424 U.S. at 91. However, during the public and legislative debates that led to the passage in 1974 of mandatory spending limits for congressional races, and during the *Buckley* litigation which resulted in the invalidation of those limits, candidate time protection was almost wholly ignored as a justification for campaign spending limits. In *Buckley*, the Federal Election Commission's brief in the Supreme Court devoted 15 scattered pages to the various justifications for campaign spending limits without even mentioning the candidate time protection rationale. Brief for Appellees, the Attorney General and the Federal Election Commission at 18–27, 36, 52–54, Buckley v. Valeo, 424 U.S. 1 (1976) (Nos. 75-436 and 75-437). In challenging the constitutionality of spending limits, the excellent brief of the appellants painstakingly criticized several rationales for spending limits but said nothing about the time protection rationale. *See* Brief of the Appellants at 86–104, *id.* A brief submitted by the Attorney General mentioned time protection but devoted to this rationale just one page out of a 30 page discussion of possible justifications for limitations on contributions and expenditures. *See* Brief for the Attorney General as Appellee and for the United States as Amici Curiae at 28–58, *id.* The amicus brief written by Archibald Cox stated in passing that "the pressure upon candidates to raise money from large contributors had become so great as to leave them little time for ordinary citizens." Brief of Senators Hugh Scott and Edward M. Kennedy, Amici Curiae at 45, *id.* No further mention was made of time, while 17 pages were devoted to arguments that spending limits would curb undue influence, restore public confidence in the fairness of elections, and broaden the opportunity to run for office. *See id.* at 34–50. During the period leading up to the 1974 legislation that was invalidated in *Buckley*, the leading legal study supporting spending limits made no mention whatever of the candidate-time-protection rationale. *See* ALBERT J. ROSENTHAL, CITIZEN'S RESEARCH FOUNDATION, FEDERAL REGULATION OF CAMPAIGN FINANCE: SOME CONSTITUTIONAL QUESTIONS 9–10, 32–47 (1971). The leading contemporaneous defender of the *Buckley* Court's holding that spending limits violate the First Amendment ignored (as did the *Buckley* opinion itself) the candidate-time-protection rationale. He concentrated his fire exclusively on the equality justification for spending limits, and emphasized the point that the harm addressed by the equality justification is caused by the communicative impact of speech, which is not true for the harm of candidate time diversion. *See* Daniel D. Polsby, Buckley v. Valeo: *The Special Nature of Political Speech*, 1976 SUP. CT. REV. 1, 24–25.

restrictions on such contributions. The Court rejected this rationale on the ground that vigorous enforcement of the laws prohibiting large contributions to candidates was the better and sufficient way to address the problem.[16] Second, spending limits were assessed as a device to hold down the costs of running for office, thereby removing a major disincentive to many worthy candidacies, particularly those that might challenge uninspiring but entrenched incumbents. The Court responded that "the equalization of permissible campaign expenditures might serve not to equalize the opportunities of all candidates, but to handicap a candidate who lacked substantial name recognition or exposure of his views before the start of a campaign."[17] Third, spending limits were considered as an antidote to "wasteful, excessive, or unwise" spending on campaigns, apparently on the theory that voters might be saturated and perhaps misled or alienated by deluges of campaign advertising. This rationale the Supreme Court found paternalistic in a manner deeply antithetical to the fundamental premises of the First Amendment. It is not, said the Court, a proper function of government to protect voters from hearing too much speech.[18]

Not only did the Court fail to examine the candidate-time-protection rationale, the *Buckley* majority opinion devoted only 4 1/2 of its 144 pages to the issue of campaign spending limits. Before the advent of pervasive war chests and candidate-PAC merchandizing bazaars, candidate time protection was not at the center of either the reform agenda or the constitutional analysis. Accordingly, the issue of campaign spending limits took a back seat to the issues raised by the effort to reduce the influence of wealthy supporters by prohibiting large contributions and independent expenditures.

Now the situation is different. In the congressional debates of 1993, supporters of campaign finance reform emphasized repeatedly that candidate time protection was one of their central objectives.[19] As a result, the search for a constitutionally valid means of establishing campaign spending limits dominated the legislative agenda. A familiar move, upheld in *Buckley* for presidential elections and extended to congressional elections in the bill passed by the House in 1993, is to link a candidate's acceptance of spending limits with his eligibility for public funding.[20] A novel ap-

---

16. *See* 424 U.S. at 56.

17. *Id.* at 56–57.

18. *See id.* at 57.

19. *See supra* note 5.

20. *See* Buckley v. Valeo, 424 U.S. 1, 85–108 (1976); *Campaign Finance Bills Compared*, 52 CONG. Q. WKLY. REP. 262, 262–64 (1994). Nine states have public funding programs. *See* ALEXANDER, *supra* note 3, at 144–46. All but Montana condition public funding on the acceptance of spending limits. *See* SORAUF, MONEY, *supra* note 1, at 275.

proach introduced in the bill passed by the Senate in 1993 is to tax all the campaign contributions received by candidates who decline to abide by prescribed spending limits.[21] On the assumption, derived from *Buckley*, that spending limits cannot be imposed directly, these efforts to induce candidates to accept limits raise a host of interesting issues under the First Amendment.[22] Even the scheme approved in *Buckley* for presidential elections has to trouble First Amendment scholars-critics of *Rust v. Sullivan*,[23] for example- who do not fully embrace the proposition that government funds can be used to purchase the waiver of constitutional rights.[24] Such is the priority attached to spending limits, however, that both the House and Senate chose in 1993 to navigate among these dangerous constitutional shoals. Candidate time protection pursued by means of spending limits is now seen as the centerpiece of campaign finance reform.

In recent congressional deliberations, opposition to campaign spending limits has most often been expressed in terms of constitutional concerns.[25]

---

21. *See* Beth Donovan, *Campaign Finance Provisions*, 51 Cong. Q. Wkly. Rep. 2239, 2239 (1993); Beth Donovan, *Constitutional Doubts Bedevil Hasty Campaign Finance Bill*, 51 Cong. Q. Wkly. Rep. 2215, 2217 (1993) [hereinafter Donovan, *Constitutional Doubts Bedevil*].

22. For a survey of the constitutional objections raised by congressional opponents of the scheme to tax excessive campaign spending, *see* Donovan, *Constitutional Doubts Bedevil, supra* note 21, at 2217; Donovan, *Gutting Public Funding, supra* note 5, at 1539.

23. 500 U.S. 173 (1991) (upholding restrictions on abortion counseling in programs funded by the federal government).

24. For a powerful critique of *Buckley* on this point, *see* Polsby, *supra* note 15, at 26–31. For a thorough discussion, written shortly before *Rust v. Sullivan* was decided, of the question whether public grants can be conditioned on a waiver of the right to engage in abortion counseling within the subsidized program, *see* Alexandra A.E. Shapiro, Note, *Title X, the Abortion Debate, and the First Amendment*, 90 Colum. L. Rev. 1737, 1747–67 (1990). The classic treatment of the unconstitutional conditions doctrine is, of course, William Van Alstyne, *The Demise of the Right-Privilege Distinction in Constitutional Law*, 81 Harv. L. Rev. 1439 (1968). A more recent general examination that is exceptional in its thoroughness and subtlety is Seth F. Kreimer, *Allocational Sanctions: The Problem of Negative Rights in a Positive State*, 132 U. Pa. L. Rev. 1293 (1984).

In his contribution to this symposium, Professor Sunstein, an expert on the issue of unconstitutional conditions, signals his approval of *Buckley's* conclusion that certain campaign finance reforms that cannot be instituted directly by means of prohibition can be achieved indirectly by means of financial incentives. *See* Cass R. Sunstein, *Political Equality and Unintended Consequences*, 94 Colum. L. Rev. 1390, 1411–12 (1994).

25. *See* Donovan, *Constitutional Doubts Bedevil, supra* note 21, at 2217; Donovan, *Gutting Public Funding, supra* note 5, at 1539; Donovan, *Constitutional Issues, supra* note 5, at 434–35.

* * *

There are at least four reasons, however, why the conclusion of the Supreme Court in *Buckley v. Valeo* that limits on overall spending by a campaign violate the First Amendment should not be considered settled law. First, the problem of candidate time diversion is far more serious today than it was in 1976 as a result of dramatic changes in the institutional mechanisms of both fund-raising and campaigning. Second, were new spending limits to be enacted, they would reflect a legislative recognition of both their central importance and their justification as a means of protecting the quality of the relationship between candidates and constituents; the spending limits invalidated in *Buckley* reflected no such legislative judgments. New spending limits would also reflect a legislative calculation not available to the *Buckley* Court regarding what regulations are most efficacious in an environment in which independent expenditures to express views relating to an election cannot be prohibited under the Constitution and in which the constitutionally permissible restrictions on contributions have proved to have significant side effects largely unforeseen twenty years ago. Third, what is today the most commonly voiced and widely acknowledged rationale for overall campaign spending limits —candidate time protection—was never considered when the Court decided *Buckley v. Valeo*. Fourth, as a justification for spending limits, candidate time protection raises a set of First Amendment questions and analogies quite different from those the Court confronted when it reached its conclusion in *Buckley*.

A fresh look at the constitutional issue is in order. If the direct imposition of campaign spending limits does not violate the First Amendment after all, recent legislative efforts to achieve limits indirectly by means of public funding conditions or tax incentives are (1) far less problematic constitutionally and (2) not necessary, given the alternative of direct prohibitions.

* * *

VI. The Quality of Representation as a Constitutional Concern

The candidate-time-protection rationale is notable not only because it does not depend on the communicative impact of speech, but also because it invokes an interest that is itself of constitutional dimension: the quality of representation. One need only read The Federalist Papers and the debates in the House of Representatives preceding the passage of the First Amendment to appreciate how much emphasis the framers of the Constitution and the Bill of Rights gave to the question of representation.[73] They thought long and hard, wrote much, and debated vigorously about how to structure the political system in a way that would encourage certain kinds of persons to seek office and would facilitate certain kinds of relationships between elected officials and their constituents. Indeed, the principal drafter of the First Amendment, James Madison, went so far as to insist that the relevant constituency of members of Congress should be taken to be the nation as a whole rather than the electoral district of each member, in large part because of the quality of representation he thought would follow from that formulation.[74] To a considerable degree, the debates over the Constitution were debates over how best to achieve a high quality of representation.[75]

Candidate time protection is a regulatory rationale that speaks to the quality of representation. If elections are dominated by fund-raising, certain kinds of persons, with certain kinds of skills, priorities, attitudes, and experiences, tend to become elected representatives. Financial "constituencies" become recognizable and compete with geographic constituencies and with Madison's national constituency for the representatives' time and loyalty. How responsive or independent representatives decide to be may depend on the priority they believe they must give to fund-raising. A constitutional system founded on a set of objectives regarding representation must be concerned with how candidates for election spend their time.

These observations are important, but they barely begin to establish the proposition that candidate time protection should be considered a special type of regulatory interest capable of justifying the burdens on speech

* * *

73. Many numbers of The Federalist Papers refer to various facets of representation. Particularly important discussions are in Nos. 10, 52, 56, 57, and 63. On August 15, 1789, the House of Representatives engaged in a lengthy debate over a proposal that constituents be granted the authority to issue binding instructions to their representatives. This discussion occurred during consideration of what became the First Amendment. *See* CREATING THE BILL OF RIGHTS: THE DOCUMENTARY RECORD FROM THE FIRST FEDERAL CONGRESS 151–77 (H. Veit et al. eds., 1991). Representative James Madison led the opposition to the proposal, invoking many of the views regarding representation that he had advanced in The Federalist Papers. *See id.* at 152, 155, 167.

74. *See* SAMUEL H. BEER, TO MAKE A NATION: THE REDISCOVERY OF AMERICAN FEDERALISM 300 (1993).

75. For a synopsis that captures the richness of the debates over representation between the Federalists and the Anti-Federalists, *see* DAVID F. EPSTEIN, THE POLITICAL THEORY OF THE FEDERALIST 147–61 (1984). For a perceptive account, informed by a study of English and colonial antecedents, of the debates over representation surrounding the framing of the Constitution, *see* J.R. POLE, POLITICAL REPRESENTATION IN ENGLAND AND THE ORIGINS OF THE AMERICAN REPUBLIC 353–82 (1966).

that spending limits would entail. The framers of the Constitution were concerned not only with the quality of representation but also with the quality of public debate.[76] And yet the Court in *Buckley* stated in the strongest terms that Congress may not impose campaign spending limits in order to shape the character of public debate: "In the free society ordained by our Constitution it is not the government, but the people—individually as citizens and candidates and collectively as associations and political committees—who must retain control over the quantity and range of debate on public issues in a political campaign."[77] Might not the same be said about who must retain control over the quality of representation?

The *Buckley* opinion does not spell out exactly why the regulatory objective of improving the quality of campaign debate cannot be considered a legitimate basis for spending limits. It is not difficult, however, to supply reasons for the Court's conclusion. Some of those reasons apply also to the regulatory objective of candidate time protection, but some do not.

One reason why legislation designed to improve public debate must be viewed with suspicion is the lack of widely shared norms regarding what should count as an "improvement." Partly because political partisanship so dominates perceptions on this question, and partly because the very concept of "the public debate" is amorphous, one despairs of developing meaningful constitutional standards for evaluating legislative efforts to reform public debate. Lillian BeVier effectively articulates the problem:

> When has the public received "enough" information to satisfy the constitutional value of an "informed public"? At what point does effective participation in political debate become transformed into constitutionally proscribed "undue influence"? Is the average citizen sufficiently "active and alert"? What is the constitutional norm against which "distortions" of election outcomes can be said to occur? Is the concept of political equality compatible with the concept of political freedom, and if not, what does the Constitution say about how the tensions are to be resolved? Does the concept of political equality embrace eliminating the impact of all the ways in which citizens can be differentially effective, or does it only refer to differences traceable to inequalities of wealth? And if only the latter, why only those?[78]

In contrast, the normative landscape regarding the problem of candidate time diversion is not so complicated or controversial. As difficult as the general subject of representation can be, one does not need a sophisticated understanding of either republican theory or modern interest group

---

76. *See* BEER, *supra* note 74, at 270–75.

77. Buckley v. Valeo, 424 U.S. 1, 57 (1976).

78. Lillian R. BeVier, *Money and Politics: A Perspective on the First Amendment and Campaign Finance Reform,* 73 CAL. L. REV. 1045, 1073–74 (1985) (footnotes omitted).

politics to conclude that there is a failure of representation when candidates spend as much time as most of them now do attending to the task of fund-raising. This feature of modern representation should trouble those who favor close constituent control as well as those who favor relative independence for legislators; those who favor an "aristocracy of virtue"[79] as well as those with more populist ideals regarding who should serve; those who conceive of representation as flowing exclusively from geographic constituencies as well as those who see a role for constituencies defined along other lines, be they racial, ethnic, gender, economic, religious, or even ideological.[80] Whatever it is that representatives are supposed to represent, whether parochial interests, the public good of the nation as a whole, or something in between, they cannot discharge that representational function well if their schedules are consumed by the need to spend endless hours raising money and attending to time demands of those who give it.

It might be argued that the modern money chase can be characterized as a system of representation with a certain logic of its own. So long as candidates are required to solicit a large number of donors, as is now the case given that both individual and PAC contributions are subject to highly restrictive caps but overall spending is unrestricted, those who achieve elective office will have had to consider a fairly wide range of grievances and opinions. They will in most cases have had to make a variety of commitments and to have established lines of future communication with many different financial "constituents." We may now have an "extended republic" of multifarious contributors, whose divergent agen-

---

79. This idea was central to Jefferson's view of representation and illustrates how the quality of representation can be important even in the context of egalitarian concerns. Jefferson contrasted the "natural" aristocracy of virtue and wisdom with the "tinsel" or "pseudo" aristocracies of birth and wealth. He thought public education was especially important because it would promote the ascendancy of the natural aristocracy composed of citizens from humble as well as privileged backgrounds, a phenomenon he thought essential to the survival of the democratic form of government. *See* GARRETT W. SHELDON, THE POLITICAL PHILOSOPHY OF THOMAS JEFFERSON 78–82 (1991).

80. An important recent development is the growth of PACs that support candidates who represent racial, gender, or religious perspectives. Particularly influential has been EMILY's List, which supports female candidates. *See* ALEXANDER, *supra* note 3, at 57. Proposals to limit contributions by PACs have occasionally caused concern among legislators who support minority and feminist agendas. *See* Donovan, *Constitutional Doubts Bedevil, supra* note 21, at 2216; Donovan, *Gutting Public Funding, supra* note 5, at 1533; Beth Donovan, *Campaign Finance: Clinton Offers Details of Plan: Big Test is GOP Unity,* 51 CONG. Q. WKLY. REP. 1121, 1121 (1993) [hereinafter Donovan, *Clinton Offers Details*]; Beth Donovan, *Clinton Readies New Proposals: Senate Panel OKs Old Bill,* 51 CONG. Q. WKLY. REP. 646, 646 (1993).

das might cancel each other out somewhat in the manner envisioned by Madison in Federalist No. 10 when he argued for sizable geographic constituencies as a safeguard against domination by concentrated local factions.[81]

This argument ought not to be accepted, even by those who believe that representatives should be little more than conduits for the preferences of their constituents however defined. For even if independence of mind, quality of judgment, and concern for the common good are not important attributes in a representative—a view of representation directly antithetical to Madison's, incidentally[82]-other personal qualities are important, for example the capacity to pursue a legislative agenda (no matter how parochial) energetically, systematically, knowledgeably, and shrewdly. Representatives who must devote huge portions of their time to fund-raising no doubt learn something in the process about the regulatory issues that most concern their financial constituents, but not as much as they could if spending limits curtailed the importance of fund-raising. For those who, more in the spirit of Madison, see representation as a process by which elected officials "refine" and "enlarge" the views of their constituents,[83] the focus on fund-raising is diversionary even when not corrupting. An electoral system that leads most incumbents and challengers to spend large amounts of their time courting donors violates a norm that is important across a broad spectrum of theories of representation: that representatives must have the opportunity and the incentive to serve well the political objectives of the persons they represent, not just their own political objective of getting elected.

The availability of a coherent norm, derived from the constitutional concern for the quality of representation, makes the candidate-time-protection rationale for spending limits less problematic than the quality-of-public-debate rationale that was ruled illegitimate in *Buckley*. Nevertheless,

---

81. Still the best brief discussion of Federalist No. 10 is Douglass Adair, *"That Politics May Be Reduced To a Science": David Hume, James Madison, and the Tenth Federalist,* 20 Huntington Libr. Q. 343 (1957), *reprinted in* Douglass Adair, Fame and the Founding Fathers 93–106 (Trevor Colbourn ed., 1974). For an insightful discussion of whether in democratic theory the making of a campaign contribution should be analogized to other forms of constituent preference assertion, *see* David A. Strauss, *Corruption, Equality, and Campaign Finance Reform,* 94 Colum. L. Rev. 1369, 1375–80 (1994).

82. *See* Isaac Kramnick, Republicanism and Bourgeois Radicalism: Political Ideology in Late Eighteenth-Century England and America 272 (1990); Jennifer Nedelsky, Private Property and the Limits of American Constitutionalism: The Madisonian Framework and Its Legacy 54 (1990); Garry Wills, Explaining America: The Federalist 186 (1981).

83. *See* Wills, *supra* note 82, at 223–37.

the availability of a norm does not put to rest the fear that any legislation governing campaign finance will be overwhelmingly the product of partisan objectives. This concern is one of the reasons to be suspicious of legislative efforts to reshape public debate, and there is no reason to think that efforts to redirect how candidates spend their time are any less infected by self-interested political calculations. To the degree that is true, congressional implementation even of a coherent, widely accepted norm regarding representation would reflect no judgment worthy of respect in the face of a constitutional challenge.

There is much force to this point, but it must be embraced with care lest it prove too much. If the high likelihood of partisan motivation were to invalidate legislation ipso facto, then all campaign finance laws must fall, even the limits on the size of contributions that were upheld in *Buckley*[84] and the prohibition on corporate contributions to candidates that has been on the books since the Tillman Act of 1907.[85] The fear of partisan motivation rather should operate to refute any suggestion that Congress' judgment regarding the validity and importance of its regulatory justification deserves deference from the judiciary.[86] When serious speech interests are adversely affected by campaign finance regulation, as they are in the case of spending limits, it is incumbent on courts to scrutinize closely and evaluate independently the regulatory rationale. When such independent scrutiny is undertaken, the availability of a coherent justificatory norm should be a major factor in the constitutional calculus. For this reason, the First Amendment issue posed by the candidate-time-protection rationale for spending limits is fundamentally different from that posed by the quality-of-public-debate rationale.

The lack of norms and the fear of partisan motivation are not the only reasons why Congress might be denied any authority to improve the quality of public debate. Robert Post argues that the very concept of self-government, the value that many consider to be the foundational justification for the freedom of speech, implies that public discourse be "open-ended" in the sense that government may not seek to structure communication according to any norm, any "specific sense of what is good or valuable."[87]

---

84. *See* Buckley v. Valeo, 424 U.S. 1, 23–36 (1976).

85. Ch. 420, 34 Stat. 864 (1907).

86. For a persuasive argument that deference to the legislative judgment is inappropriate in the context of campaign finance legislation, *see* BeVier, *supra* note 78, at 1074–81. In his contribution to this symposium, Professor Schauer places this issue of deference in the broader context of constitutional and democratic theory. *See* Frederick Schauer, *Judicial Review of the Devices of Democracy,* 94 COLUM. L. REV. 1326 (1994).

87. Robert Post, *Meiklejohn's Mistake: Individual Autonomy and the Reform of Public Discourse,* 64 U. COLO. L. REV. 1109, 1116 (1993).

Public discourse, says Post, must not be regulated by a particular conception of national identity. Rather, that collective identity must remain "perpetually indeterminate."[88] Post himself hedges regarding whether this idea precludes campaign finance laws,[89] but defenders of *Buckley's* rejection of the quality-of-public-debate rationale for spending limits certainly could build on his analysis. Might not the quality of representation, particularly as it relates to how candidates spend their time, similarly be considered so basic to the concept of self-government that Congress lacks all authority to shape it in a purposive manner?

This is a question that goes to the heart of the comparison between the candidate-time-protection rationale and the quality-of-public-debate rationale. Professor Post treats as the linchpin of his case for an unprescribed public discourse the proposition that the "collective identity" of the political community must be left free to develop on its own.[90] How we talk to each other, what speech is disseminated and what speakers are given credence, what informational and ideological environment we inhabit, are factors that profoundly shape our individual and collective identities. How our representatives spend their time may be a crucial determinant of political power but does not seem quite so central to questions of collective identity as is the structure of public discourse. We are not really "constituted" as a community by the time allocations of our representatives the way we are constituted by the form our public debate takes. For one thing, every citizen is shaped by the structure of public discourse: our lives change as it changes, as the modern movement toward shorter units of discourse demonstrates. When representatives spend more and more of their time fund-raising, or when the quality of representation changes in other respects, the consequences can be serious but the collective identity of the community need not be altered. Perhaps the cynicism that can follow from a weakening of representation can be considered identity-destroying, but even in the best of representational worlds ordinary citizens participate very little in determining the time allocations of their elected officials. As a result, few persons are really shaped by, or define themselves or their citizenship according to, how much time politicians spend fund-raising. The widening gyre is pernicious, but its effects are incremental, insidious, and easy for citizens to ignore.

Moreover, we have long since passed beyond the point where how candidates spend their time can be considered open-ended in the sense that Post uses the term. The recent increase in time devoted to fund-raising did not evolve "naturally." Rather, it developed in response to the patchwork

---

88. *Id.* at 1116.

89. *See id.* at 1132–33.

90. *See id.* at 1116.

legislative scheme that was left standing after the selective invalidations of *Buckley v. Valeo*: no limits on overall spending, severe limits on the size of contributions, and no limits on independent expenditures for and against particular candidates. The war chest mentality was born of this regulatory residue. Had the 1974 campaign finance law at issue in *Buckley* either never been passed or been upheld in its entirety, the quest for contributions would look very different.[91] Almost certainly, it would be far less time consuming because either candidates would not seek to raise so much money (if they couldn't spend beyond a set limit) or they could raise it much more efficiently (by means of large contributions). So even if we are constituted as a political community by how our representatives allocate their time, that feature of our collective identity is already the result of prescription at least as much as open-ended evolution.

Professor Post finds the conscious structuring of public discourse to be a violation of the premise of self-government because such a project treats citizens not as autonomous subjects but as heteronomous objects of political prescription.[92] He does not invoke any kind of antipaternalism principle in the strict sense. His argument is not that citizens should be trusted to protect themselves from being unduly influenced by the way public discourse is structured. He argues instead that autonomous citizens must be permitted to create the public discourse, not just be protected from it. However, the holding in *Buckley* that Congress has no authority to try to improve the quality of electoral debate might also be defended on antipaternalism grounds. Because that is true, we must inquire whether the candidate-time-protection rationale offends the antipaternalism principle implicit in the First Amendment.

On several occasions, the Supreme Court has expressed its aversion to the argument that audiences must be protected from being misled, offended, tempted, or conditioned by the communications they receive.[93] The Court has insisted that audiences be trusted to protect themselves from both wily demagogues and importuning boors. One could go so far as to view the First Amendment as a commitment to audience self-help. Reject the message, avert the eyes, put down the book—these are the remedies that must be preferred "if authority is to be reconciled with freedom."[94] If speech during an election campaign is unbalanced, voters can compensate by tuning out the messages of some candidates and seeking

---

91. *See* MAGLEBY & NELSON, *supra* note 1, at 205.

92. *See* Post, *supra* note 87, at 1116.

93. *See* Texas v. Johnson, 491 U.S. 397, 418–20 (1989); Linmark Assoc., Inc. v. Township of Willingboro, 431 U.S. 85, 95–96 (1977); Cohen v. California, 403 U.S. 15, 24–25 (1971).

94. Whitney v. California, 274 U.S. 357, 377 (1927) (Brandeis, J., concurring).

out the messages of others. Whether or not this antipaternalism argument is fully persuasive in the special context of election campaigns, the principle that audiences ought to be trusted whenever possible is both appealing and well recognized in our First Amendment tradition.

The effort to protect candidates from fund-raising demands can be considered paternalistic in one sense: candidates could just refuse to get drawn into the war chest syndrome, or opponents could agree among themselves to hold down spending and thereby free up time from fund-raising. The nature of this paternalism, however, is rather different from that which informs the effort to improve the quality of public debate. Candidate time protection reflects no distrust of audiences and no denigration of the traditional self-help remedies relating to audience response. In fact, one of the major problems with the current system of campaign finance is that voters seldom have a choice between candidates who differ greatly in their devotion to fund-raising: virtually all candidates spend long hours soliciting donors, the candidates who get outspent no less than the candidates who outspend. Candidate time protection may indeed reflect distrust of candidates, but that seems less problematic under the First Amendment than distrust of citizens generally. The principle of self-government embodies, among other things, the precept that the people, the true sovereigns, are more to be trusted than their delegates, those who hold elective office.[95]

Moreover, the "distrust" of candidates reflected in spending limits is not so much a low estimation of their character or judgment as a recognition of a collective action problem they all face. That most candidates would benefit from ending the war chest syndrome does not mean they will agree to cease round-the-clock fund-raising. Unless parties to self-imposed restraints can be assured that rogue candidates will not be able to take advantage of the situation, unilateral forbearance or agreements to cap spending are not likely to occur. In this respect, it is not paternalistic to impose spending limits by law in order to circumvent the collective action problem that partly explains why fund-raising has gotten out of control.

Once again, the candidate-time-protection rationale introduces some important new elements into the constitutional calculus regarding spending limits. With regard to paternalism as well as to the absence of norms and the ideal of citizen control over collective identity, the quality-of-public-debate justification for spending limits proves to be in tension with

---

95. *See* James Madison, *A Memorial and Remonstrance Against Religious Assessments* (1785), in 2 THE WRITINGS OF JAMES MADISON, para. 2, at 185 (Gallard Hunt ed., 1901).

First Amendment values in ways that the candidate-time-protection justification is not.

VII. Efficacy

Even if candidate time protection is a rationale for spending limits that cannot be dismissed as antithetical to the First Amendment in a fundamental way, there remains the question of efficacy. Recall that in *Buckley* only one of the three rationales proffered, improving the quality of public debate, was rejected in principle.[96] The two other rationales reducing the incentive to violate contribution limits and facilitating insurgent candidacies were held to be insufficiently advanced to justify limiting the overall quantity of electoral speech.[97] Can we say that the goal of candidate time protection is better served by spending limits than were these other goals?

One must be extremely circumspect about any claim of reform efficacy in the realm of election practices. The stakes are high and so, consequently, will be the ingenuity devoted to adaptation and evasion.[98] The history of campaign finance regulation is largely a history of reforms that have misfired, often making matters worse.[99] Conservatives who exalt the law of unintended consequences can reap a rich harvest of object lessons in this regulatory domain.[100]

---

96. *See* Buckley v. Valeo, 424 U.S. 1, 55–57 (1976).

97. *See id.*

98. *See* SORAUF, INSIDE, *supra* note 1, at 214.

99. *See* ALEXANDER, *supra* note 3, at 23–46, 161; Jacobson, *supra* note 14, at 163–97; BeVier, *supra* note 78, at 1078–80. Spending limits regarding Senate and House campaigns were, in fact, on the books from 1911 until 1971. However, the levels were unrealistically low and virtually all candidates evaded the limits by establishing numerous campaign committees whose expenditures were not cumulated. The Justice Department declined in effect to enforce the laws limiting spending; no record exists of anyone ever having been prosecuted for violating them. *See* ALEXANDER, *supra* note 3, at 25–26.

100. For example, the limits placed by the 1974 Act on the size of contributions to candidates reduced the role of large donors but also contributed greatly to the fund-raising preoccupation that now consumes the time of candidates. *See* MAGLEBY & NELSON, *supra* note 1, at 205. The restrictions in the 1974 Act on donations to candidates from political parties, together with the Act's parallel legitimation of political action committees, contributed to the weakening of the parties during the last two decades, a development some knowledgeable observers regard as especially lamentable. *See* ALEXANDER, *supra* note 3, at 42; SABATO, *supra* note 6, at 43–50. The legislative effort in 1979 to restore vitality to the parties by encouraging contributions of soft money, *see infra* text accompanying notes 110–113, led to vast amounts of unreported contributions flowing into the campaign finance system, possibly undercutting the heroic attempt in the 1974 Act to

Moreover, several of the most careful and balanced proponents of campaign finance reform question whether spending limits would have a salutary effect.[101] There is reason to doubt, for example, whether the Federal Election Commission and state counterparts would ever be given enough authority and resources to monitor effectively the numerous campaigns that would be covered were spending limits applied to legislative elections.[102] Money that could not be spent by candidates legally sometimes would be spent nonetheless, by means of funneling to various supporters whose ties to the candidate would be kept secret.[103] Apart from fraud of this sort, a regime of spending limits on candidates might enhance the relative effectiveness of genuinely independent expenditures for or against particular candidacies. In the past, many independent expenditures have gone for inflammatory and arguably misleading negative advertising; the notorious "Willie Horton" commercial of the 1988 presidential campaign was produced and disseminated independently of the Bush campaign.[104] Furthermore, candidates subject to spending limits might be tempted in their own advertising to "go negative" earlier or more often on the theory that a negative message can influence voters more quickly, with less repetition or development and thus with less expenditure, than can a positive message.[105]

These are valid concerns, perhaps serious enough to lead one to doubt the efficacy of spending limits as a means to achieve fairer elections or the reduction of influence over politicians stemming from surreptitious forms of large financial support. Critics of spending limits, however, have not addressed their arguments to the specific problem of candidate time diver-

---

reduce the risks of undue influence stemming from large contributions. *See* SORAUF, INSIDE, *supra* note 1, at 149–51. For a rumination on possible unintended consequences of various proposals on the current reform agenda, *see* Cass R. Sunstein, *supra* note 24, at 1400–11.

101. *See* ALEXANDER, *supra* note 3, at 169–70; SABATO, *supra* note 6, at 22–23; SORAUF, INSIDE, *supra* note 1, at 210–14.

102. *See* SORAUF, INSIDE, *supra* note 1, at 213.

103. *Buckley v. Valeo* invalidated limits on expenditures in support of a candidate made by persons or organizations independently of the candidate's campaign. *See* Buckley v. Valeo, 424 U.S. 1, 39–51 (1976). Thus, were a candidate able to siphon money to such ostensibly independent supporters, or even to help them raise money, the expenditures that would result could not be subjected to limits so long as the candidate's connection to those supporters remained concealed. For accounts of how nominally independent supporters can act in tandem with a campaign, *see* DREW, *supra* note 1, at 134–45; JACKSON, *supra* note 1, at 217–18.

104. *See* ALEXANDER, *supra* note 3, at 104.

105. *See id.* at 170.

sion.[106] If altering how candidates spend their time is taken to be a priority for campaign finance reform, spending limits are not so vulnerable to objections grounded in lack of efficacy as is true when other regulatory objectives are emphasized.[107]

The regulatory logic pertaining to time diversion is remarkably simple. The problem is not subtle, as are the problems of undue influence exerted by donors and inequitable electoral competition due to wealth disparities or negative advertising. The time problem is one of degree, so there is room for dispute regarding what state of affairs should be considered satisfactory. But if we can agree that currently most candidates devote quite a bit more time to fund-raising than any tenable theory of representation can justify, even a modest reduction in time spent seeking contributions would represent an improvement. The logic of this reform is not all or nothing: incremental progress is real progress.

Moreover, the logical relationship between spending limits and time directed to fund-raising is relatively direct. If only so much money can be spent, only so much money need be raised. Were spending limits in force, some incentive to build a war chest probably would remain, perhaps as a hedge against a future election cycle when even the limited amount that can be spent might be more difficult to raise. Candidates, however, have many demands on their time. There is little reason to fear that under a regime of spending limits they would attach much priority to raising money they cannot spend.

But would time freed up from fund-raising be spent in ways that serve the quality of representation? Perhaps candidates no longer desperate for donations would spend even less time with ordinary citizens, and less time studying the regulatory issues that concern potential contributors. Perhaps the newly liberated hours would be devoted to leisure, or to forms of self-promotion that benefit neither constituents nor the broader public good. No doubt some candidates would use most of their freed-up time in ways that did not improve the quality of representation, and most candidates

---

106. In their various criticisms of spending limits, neither Alexander, Sabato, nor Sorauf discusses the time-protection rationale as a basis for spending limits. *See* authorities cited *supra* note 101. Alexander and Sorauf both mention that public financing might relieve the time pressure on candidates but do not consider the possible effect in this regard of spending limits independent of public subsidies. *See* ALEXANDER, *supra* note 3, at 70; SORAUF, INSIDE, *supra* note 1, at 212.

107. Misgivings about promoting negative campaigning or otherwise harming the electoral process might lead one to oppose spending limits on policy grounds. Not everyone will view the time problem as the controlling consideration. Such misgivings, however, would not weaken the constitutional defense of spending limits under the candidate-time-protection rationale.

would continue to fall short of the ideal in the matter of time allocation. No one mildly cognizant of human nature should think that spending limits could bring about a direct and complete redistribution of candidate time from fund-raising to representation.

That tidy a consequence is hardly the proper standard of efficacy, however. So long as a significant number of candidates currently are precluded by fund-raising chores from paying as much attention to constituents and legislative business as they would like, there is good reason to believe that spending limits could have a salutary effect on the quality of representation. Many candidates complain that fund-raising has just such a preclusive impact.[108] Even if the time-drain of fund-raising can serve as a scapegoat for shortcomings that have deeper, more personal causes, it seems likely that most candidates would find valuable ways to spend at least some of the extra time they might gain from spending limits. Progress might entail fairly simple changes, such as spending more time in one's home district or attending more legislative sessions, reducing problems of absenteeism that are often attributed to fund-raising demands.[109]

Of course, if spending limits were easily evaded, the regulatory logic would collapse. And it probably is true that, at the margin, spending limits are difficult to enforce, at least when they are not confined to a particular medium that can be monitored systematically. But marginal violations ought not to affect substantially how candidates spend their time. A system of spending limits need not be completely impermeable in order to tame the war chest syndrome. Even if spending limits could be evaded to some degree by accounting legerdemain or fraudulent siphoning to "independent" supporters, candidates indulging in such evasions would still have little incentive to spend long hours raising money that could only be spent with great ingenuity and at considerable risk.

The most serious threat to the efficacy of spending limits may come from the practice of raising what is known as "soft money." Contributions made to state political parties for use in state campaigns are not regulated by federal law. Yet these funds typically are deployed for generic party advertising and get-out-the-vote drives that can benefit all the party's candidates, including those running for federal office.[110] Soft money has become so important that now even presidential candidates devote time to helping their parties raise it.[111] Many states permit individual contributors to give unlimited amounts of soft money, and some allow corporations and labor

---

108. *See supra* notes 1 and 4.

109. *See* CLAWSON ET AL., *supra* note 1, at 89; MAGLEBY & NELSON, *supra* note 1, at 34.

110. *See* SABATO, *supra* note 6, at 64–66.

111. *See* ALEXANDER, *supra* note 3, at 104–05.

unions to do so.[112] Consequently, this type of solicitation by candidates is potentially highly productive. Were federal campaigns to be governed by spending limits, the pursuit of soft money might intensify, with resultant increases in the time candidates allocated to the enterprise. In terms of candidate time protection, soft-money fund-raising is just as problematic as hard-money fund-raising, even though the two categories of solicitation differ in other respects, such as potential links to corruption.

Reform proposals sometimes prohibit efforts by federal candidates to raise soft money for state political parties. The otherwise divergent bills passed by the House and Senate in 1993 both contain this feature.[113] Properly drafted prohibitions of this sort certainly qualify as efficacious in terms of the candidate-time-protection rationale. Spending limits coupled with such restrictions also would seem not to be problematic on grounds of efficacy.

But what if spending limits were imposed without any restrictions on the raising of soft money by candidates? Whether the soft-money phenomenon would be sufficient to undercut the regulatory efficacy of spending limits then would depend on how strictly specified and monitored were the uses to which soft money could be put. If candidates did not stand to gain much for their own campaigns from the money so raised, one doubts that party loyalties (or pressure) would lead to excessive diversion of candidate time to this form of fund-raising. Were that supposition to prove false in actual practice, however, the system of spending limits might well be invalidated for lack of efficacy.

As the preceding discussion illustrates, the case for the regulatory efficacy of spending limits depends rather heavily on the assumption that how candidates spend their time is highly responsive to their calculations of personal electoral advantage. In this realm, one can fairly speculate, habits, affections, and ideals count for less than in many other endeavors that require time allocation judgements. Thus, the primary way to change behavior is to change partisan incentives. It would be a mistake, however, to treat candidates as nothing but rational calculators. One reason to believe that spending limits would reduce the time devoted to fund-raising is that most candidates begrudge the time so spent.[114] Many no doubt enjoy a competitive advantage in a system that rewards solicitation stamina, but almost all would benefit in some ways they value were the money chase to

---

112. *See* Magleby & Nelson, *supra* note 1, at 19.

113. *See* Donovan, *House Will Vote, supra* note 5, at 3093; Donovan, *Campaign Finance Provisions, supra* note 21, at 2241. The Senate Bill also prohibits federal candidates from raising soft money for candidates seeking state office, a practice permitted by the House bill. *See id.*

114. *See* Fiorina, *supra* note 14, at 129; Sorauf, Inside, *supra* note 1, at 72–73.

be brought under control. Efforts to reform behavior are more likely to succeed when most members of the target population have something to gain from the desired reform, even if many of them have still more to lose.

Perhaps the strongest ground for considering spending limits a potentially efficacious way to protect the time of candidates is that the objective itself is a relatively modest one. Proponents of this reform need have no perfectionist ambitions. They need not claim it will create genuinely fair election contests or legislatures that are free from inequities of access or leverage. For spending limits to serve a valuable purpose, all that needs to happen is that candidates for office find themselves able to behave more like politicians and less like mendicants and merchants.

VIII. Overbreadth

One type of candidate who need not beg or trade as much as others is the person who is able to finance a campaign for office out of personal funds. To subject such a candidate to spending limits would be to limit her speech without necessarily altering how she spends her time. Yet a regime of spending limits that exempted self-financed candidates would place an even greater premium on personal wealth as a political credential than is true under our current system, which already seems seriously askew in this respect. Would the imposition of spending limits on self-financed candidates violate the First Amendment for overbreadth? Or would the desire not to disadvantage persons who cannot finance their campaigns out of personal resources justify limiting self-financed candidates to the same levels of spending that bind all other candidates?

Buckley v. Valeo invalidated restrictions on the use of personal wealth in election campaigns.[115] The limits at issue were set at levels much lower than the overall campaign spending limits that were established in the federal statute under review. This feature presented the possibility that a candidate who was being outspent by his opponent (a successful fund-raiser) could be prevented from drawing on his personal wealth to close the gap. The Court observed that such a system of limits "may fail to promote financial equality among candidates,"[116] and also could not be justified as a means to prevent corruption.[117] A spending limit that made no differentiation based on the source of funds would permit wealthy self-financed candidates to close but not create spending gaps, and thus should promote

---

115. *See* Buckley v. Valeo, 424 U.S. 1, 51–54 (1976).

116. *Id.* at 54.

117. *See id.* at 53.

greater "financial equality among candidates" regarding actual expenditures.

In *Buckley*, however, the Court did not rest content with its showing that the limits on the use of personal funds were not narrowly tailored to serve equality and anticorruption values. "Second, and more fundamentally," said the Court, "the First Amendment simply cannot tolerate" a restriction on the use of a candidate's personal funds to speak "on behalf of his own candidacy."[118] Read broadly, this dictum seems to assert that the First Amendment is particularly solicitous of expression made possible by personal wealth.[119] Perhaps that priority can be derived from a robust notion of autonomy or from an amalgam of property and liberty interests that might be read into the First Amendment. The putative right to project one's views as fully as one's private resources allow does have a distinct plausibility in a liberal constitutional tradition built upon the right of private property.

I would argue, however, that in the context of election speech, the claim to use personal wealth without limit is strongest regarding independent expenditures made by individuals who are neither candidates themselves nor surrogates speaking in co-ordination with a candidate's campaign organization. Just as candidates and campaign workers can properly be subjected to reporting requirements in the interest of the smooth and lawful conduct of elections, such persons can be made to forgo at least some opportunities to leverage their private resources. The freedom to conduct a campaign from personal resources is surely a First Amendment interest of considerable weight, but that interest is not so fundamental either to the concept of representative democracy or the concept of limited government that no constraints whatsoever on the use of private wealth by candidates can be justified. After all, candidates cannot purchase votes, even from would-be sellers who, acting with full knowledge and uncoerced will, wish to trade their government-created asset for something they value more. Designation on a ballot is another government-created asset of a character that should preclude those who seek to exploit it from making claims grounded in pristine liberty (as contrasted with claims grounded in the implications of the system of self-government).

How much the use of private wealth by candidates can be limited is a difficult question. There is much to be said for *Buckley's* holding that a can-

---

118. *Id.* at 54.

119. In his close reading of the *Buckley* opinion, Daniel Polsby adopts this construction of the dictum: "the implication is that of all First Amendment rights, the right to stand for public office using one's own money to communicate with the electorate is the most basic of all.... This seems if not obvious, at least an entirely allowable reading of the First Amendment." Polsby, *supra* note 15, at 26.

didate cannot be precluded from using his private wealth to match expenditures by an opponent who is able to draw effectively on other sources. If private wealth can buy quality education and health care, why should it not also buy name recognition or state-of-the-art polling? Additional considerations enter the equation, however, when spending by self-financed candidates is limited not in order to promote equality or protect the electorate from hearing too much speech but rather to make workable an electoral system not dominated by the time-drain of fund-raising. If spending limits can be justified under the First Amendment when imposed on candidates who in their absence would feel the need to devote long hours to fund-raising, permissible also should be the regulatory decision to apply such limits universally so as not to create disparities in the spending opportunities of different candidates.[120] It is true that such universalization would result in the imposition of spending limits on some candidates who would not in any event devote much time to fund-raising, but that fact neither establishes the irrationality of the scheme of coverage nor resolves the overbreadth issue.

* * *

X. Conclusion

I have shown, I believe, that in terms of the traditional canons of First Amendment doctrine, campaign spending limits justified by the objective of candidate time protection should not be presumed to be unconstitutional. Spending limits are content neutral in form and indeterminate in political impact. The time-protection justification does not depend on any concern about the communicative impact of speech. Spending limits address a problem that is central to the system of representation ordained by the Constitution. The regulation of spending is the most efficacious way to alter how candidates spend their time. No comparably effective less drastic means to this goal can be identified. The reasons given in *Buckley v. Valeo* for invalidating spending limits under the First Amendment do not apply to the candidate-time-protection rationale.

I have not shown in this essay that spending limits designed to free candidates from excessive fund-raising can be defended against the full range of First Amendment objections that could be mounted. For example, it might be argued that under the principle of freedom of speech properly

---

120. Congressman Price believes that any regime of spending limits would be undercut were self-financed candidates permitted to spend as much as they could afford while their opponents were constrained by the limits. *See* PRICE, *supra* note 1, at 23, 27.
    * * *

understood it is axiomatic that a candidate has an unqualified individual right to purchase whatever speech she can, using whatever money she can legally raise. This argument would not proceed from the premise of self-government and would not rely on claims regarding the aggregate consequences of the liberty claimed. The focus of such an argument would be on the sphere of individual freedom that is invulnerable to any regulatory rationale, rather than the legitimacy or efficacy of a particular rationale. Other objections to spending limits can be imagined that proceed from elaborate calibrations of consequences, or sensitive calibrations of partisan bias and benefit, or affirmative duties to reform the financing of elections more fundamentally so as better to empower voters or broaden the opportunity to run for office.

Responses to these objections can be imagined that build from the proposition that time freed from fund-raising creates new opportunities for speech—among representatives, for example, or by a candidate to ordinary constituents and vice versa—as well as financial constraints on the capacity to project speech maximally. To the degree that spending limits restore voter confidence in the quality of representation, the gain in citizen engagement can be computed in First Amendment terms. There can be little doubt, moreover, that candidates in the present fund-raising environment frequently hold back on the expression of their views and intentions for fear of alienating some of the many diverse donors they must court.[144] Naturally, candidates would do this to some degree to avoid the wrath of voters even were funding not a concern, but there is reason to fear that the need to keep various donors in line exacerbates the age-old problem of trimming. If so, once again the loss is truly one of free speech. When the conventional reluctance to look beyond one-dimensional notions of quantity in measuring speech effects is overcome, spending limits can be seen to advance First Amendment values in some ways, even while threatening them in other ways.

Whatever may be true on the cutting edge of constitutional argument, the conventional doctrines and principles of the First Amendment are not inhospitable to spending limits so long as they are instituted not to prevent corruption and undue influence, alter the balance of electoral competition, or improve public debate, but to redirect how candidates spend their time. In this respect, the candidate-time-protection rationale can and should move the debate over spending limits beyond *Buckley*.

---

144. *See* JACKSON, *supra* note 1, at 108–09.

The Structure of Government Accountability: Commentary, Back to the Future of the American State, Overruling *Buckley v. Valeo* and Other Madisonian Steps

Peter M. Shane

I. Introduction

It's no secret that we live in a time of profound alienation from government. In one recent tally, seventy percent of Americans polled agreed that the government is "run for the benefit of special interests, not to benefit most Americans."[1] Sixty percent think: "Government leaders are out of touch. They don't know or care about what's going on in the rest of America."[2] Moreover, the American people, having so recently wielded the heavy hammer of electoral accountability on Congress, now do not like their handiwork.[3]

Professor Mashaw doubts that a new spirit of government managerialism will get us out of this mess; the American preoccupation with legality and our distrust of bureaucratic discretion will defeat the managers' en-

---

1. *The Mood on Washington,* AM. ENTERPRISE, Nov.-Dec. 1995, at 106.
2. *Id.*
3. Richard Morin, *Public Sides with Clinton in Fiscal Fight; Poll Indicates Growing Disapproval of Republicans in Congress, Opposition to Proposed Cuts,* WASH. POST, Nov. 21, 1995, at A4; Richard Morin, *Poll Finds Disapproval of GOP's Budget Plans,* WASH. POST, May 16, 1995, at A1; Kevin Phillips, *The Rise and Folly of the GOP; As Voter Disgust Rises, So Do Clinton's Chances,* WASH. POST, Aug. 6, 1995, at C1.
 * * *

thusiasms.[4] Professor Breger, however, foresees "accountability by devolution"; through new technology and the spirit of privatization, the Anti-Federalists will finally have their day, and power will flow out of Washington to the people, who shall increasingly run their affairs through direct democracy.[5]

Whether or not one shares Professor Breger's enthusiasm for his vision, that vision is wishful thinking for two reasons at least as fundamental as the cultural distrust of administrative discretion that Professor Mashaw identifies. First, too many of our national problems transcend the problem-solving capacities of local government. The "Republican Revolutionaries" do not really deny this. It is just that they would nationalize subjects different from those that have heretofore been centrally controlled-such as the terms of products liability law or the capacity of the states to permit abortions.[6] Second, the fact is that a relatively few individuals and economic entities with vast amounts of capital hold much of the real power in this country-the power to distribute resources, to influence elections, to shape popular culture.[7] It is not in the interest of postindustrial capital that all important government decision making reside at local levels.[8] Therefore, over the long run, it will not.

The usual way reformers talk about redressing the imbalance of political power in American society focuses on strategies of material equalization. If accountability follows power, and if power follows money, then, to broaden political accountability, we should redistribute wealth. Indeed, it is hard to doubt that, if more individuals had the wherewithal to affect the electoral process, government officials would be responsive to more people. But I wonder whether it might be possible to try to change the equation significantly. That is, could we have a system in which power follows not money, but something else-for example, knowledge? Could we have a system in which analysis and understanding count more in political decision making than do campaign treasuries? If we are truly to be

---

4. Jerry L. Mashaw, *Reinventing Government and Regulatory Reform: Studies in the Neglect and Abuse of Administrative Law,* 57 U. PITT. L. REV. 405 (1996).

5. Marshall J. Breger, *Government Accountability in the Twenty-First Century,* 57 U. PITT. L. REV. 423 (1996).

6. *E.g.,* H.R. 1833, 104th Cong. (1995) (banning partial birth abortions); S. 939, 104th Cong. (1995) (same); H.R. 956, 104th Cong. (1995) (establishing legal standards and procedures for product liability litigation).

7. *See generally* KEVIN P. PHILLIPS, ARROGANT CAPITAL: WASHINGTON, WALL STREET, AND THE FRUSTRATION OF AMERICAN POLITICS (1994).

8. The classic argument of this position with respect to railroad regulation is GABRIEL KOLKO, THE TRIUMPH OF CONSERVATISM: A REINTERPRETATION OF AMERICAN HISTORY, 1900-1916, at 57-61 (1963).

awash in new information technology, then surely this is a logical goal. But is it realistic?

To ask these questions is not necessarily to suggest a new paradigm.[9] On the contrary, the commitment to a national government in which "the permanent and aggregate interests of the community" are determined through a deliberative process that is free, as much as possible, from the effects "of passion, or of interest," is the starting point of Madisonian constitutionalism.[10] Unfortunately, the original design of our national government's structures and deliberative processes have not fulfilled that commitment. The anomalies in our current governance would call for a paradigm shift if, in fact, the United States has exhausted the achievements of which the Madisonian tradition is capable. But we should not lightly conclude that this has happened. It may be that what the current revolution in information technology makes possible, and what the current level of our national discontent compels, is a maturation of Madisonian government. Before hailing (or decrying) a paradigm shift, we should consider what aspects of current governmental process could be redesigned in order to make more likely the realization of the Madisonian ideal. Only if such reforms are incongruous with Madisonian assumptions would it be necessary to abandon the Madisonian paradigm.

* * *

II. Returning to the Paradigm: Overruling *Buckley v. Valeo*

The preoccupation of social theorists with "paradigms" is rooted in the seminal work of philosopher of science Thomas S. Kuhn.[11] Kuhn's work is an effort to understand how revolutionary shifts occur in what counts as "normal science," that is, "the activity in which scientists inevitably spend almost all their time,... predicated on the assumption that the scientific community knows what the world is like."[12] According to Kuhn, the normal science of any age includes "research firmly based on one or more past scientific achievements," which serve "for a time implicitly to define the legitimate problems and methods of a research field for suc-

---

9. For a discussion of "paradigms," *see infra* notes 11-15 and accompanying text.

10. THE FEDERALIST NO. 10, at 78 (James Madison) (Clinton Rossiter ed., 1961).

11. THOMAS S. KUHN, THE STRUCTURE OF SCIENTIFIC REVOLUTIONS (2d ed. 1970).

12. *Id.* at 5.

ceeding generations of practitioners."[13] At some moments, however, certain scientific work is "sufficiently unprecedented to attract an enduring group of adherents away from competing modes of scientific activity," and "sufficiently open-ended to leave all sorts of problems for the redefined group of practitioners to resolve."[14] Such work, Kuhn argues, serves over time to generate a new "paradigm," or "an entire constellation of beliefs, values, techniques, and so on shared by the members of a given community."[15] In retrospect, the historian can ascertain the existence of a revolution in normal science from a shift in paradigms.

By analogy, one can speak of what counts, in a community, as "normal governance." That is, for every polity, there is a set of beliefs, values, techniques, practices, and behaviors that those subject to authority accept as legitimate to the prevailing system of government. Not all political upheavals embody paradigm shifts, because not all upheavals change prevailing beliefs, values, techniques, practices, and behaviors in Kuhn's sense. On the other hand, the American Revolution certainly did mark a paradigm shift. Thus, to ask now, in Kuhnian terms, whether we are facing a similar paradigm shift in American politics is to pose the question whether the foundational theoretical work for late eighteenth century constitutional development—the Federalist Papers, Locke, Montesquieu, and so on—still defines "the legitimate problems and methods" of constitutional government for us, the citizen-practitioners of American governance. Or, alternatively, is the Madisonian way of doing business losing ground either because it is not up to current challenges, or because more and more people are drawn to unprecedented alternative prescriptions for governance that cannot be reconciled with the Madisonian paradigm?

One testament to the durability of the Madisonian paradigm is how readily important reforms may be undertaken even within the most conventional understandings of proper legal and governmental practice. An ideal place to start would be undoing a major piece of self-inflicted damage, namely, the Supreme Court's holding in *Buckley v. Valeo*[16] that Congress may not regulate direct spending on federal candidate elections. Because inordinate and unequal campaign spending can so distort electoral discourse, it is imperative, at the very least, that our elected representatives be authorized to regulate these abuses. *Buckley* not only invalidated the expenditure limitations enacted in the Federal Election

---

13. *Id.* at 10.
14. *Id.*
15. *Id.* at 175.
16. 424 U.S. 1 (1976).

Campaign Act of 1971 ("FECA"),[17] it virtually eliminated the capacity of legislatures to restrict direct political spending, except as a quid pro quo for the public funding of elections. I believe this damage can be repaired without any shift in conventional assumptions about proper government practice, including the practice of constitutional interpretation.

That is, there is already a "normal" practice with respect to the Supreme Court's abandonment of past constitutional holdings. Such corrections customarily occur upon the Court's reappraisal of a number of factors: "whether the overruled decision was wrong from the start, whether its basis has eroded over time, whether the Court has had difficulty in applying the decision, and whether later decisions are in tension with it."[18] Other considerations have been the "practical workability" of the holding, and whether the holding has become "subject to a kind of reliance that would lend a special hardship to the consequences of overruling."[19] On all relevant counts, *Buckley* looks ripe for overturning.

For immediate purposes, the important holding of *Buckley* was that political contributions to federal candidate elections are, by and large, constitutionally regulable, but that direct expenditures on such elections, by and large, are not. ("Contributions," in general, are distributions of funds for political purposes that are turned over to another party for actual expenditure on a political campaign.[20] "Independent expenditures" are distributions of funds for political purposes controlled by the funder. Thus, for example, if I spend my own money on political ads for a candidate, but coordinate their message with the candidate's campaign manager, I am making a "contribution," not an "independent expenditure," because the candidate is controlling the publicly communicative aspect of my efforts.)[21] The Court regarded restrictions on either activity as involving constraints on political speech itself,[22] but nonetheless upheld a series of statutory limits on political contributions, while overturning those parts of the 1971 FECA that would have limited independent expenditures either by, or on behalf of, a federal candidate.[23]

Why did the Court treat contributions and expenditures differently? First, and most remarkably, the Court dismissed out of hand an obvious

---

17. *Id.* at 143.

18. Philip P. Frickey, *A Further Comment on Stare Decisis and the Overruling of National League of Cities,* 2 CONST. COMMENTARY 341, 342 (1985).

19. Planned Parenthood v. Casey, 505 U.S. 833, 854 (1992).

20. *Buckley,* 424 U.S. at 23 n.24.

21. *See id.* at 46 n.53.

22. *See id.* at 20-21, 39.

23. *Id.* at 58-59.

rationale that would have sustained both sets of regulations: the importance of "equalizing the relative ability of all voters to affect electoral outcomes."[24] That is, the 1971 FECA was based in part on the commonplace notion that the process of truth-testing in the "marketplace of ideas" can be significantly undermined if proponents of some propositions have disproportionate resources to urge their message, and can dominate the marketplace for reasons unrelated to the content of their ideas. The Court simply declared, however, that "the concept that government may restrict the speech of some elements of our society in order to enhance the relative voice of others is wholly foreign to the First Amendment."[25]

Turning to a second rationale for the FECA—namely, limiting the "actuality and appearance of corruption"[26] from big money politics—the Court found this justification to be persuasive in sustaining the regulability of contributions, but not of expenditures.[27] Contributions, the Court reasoned, facilitate corrupt quid pro quo arrangements between candidates and special interests.[28] And "of almost equal concern," Congress could properly worry about "the impact of the appearance of corruption stemming from public awareness of the opportunities for abuse inherent in a regime of large individual financial contributions."[29] Although the Court insisted that any regulation of contributions would have to be closely scrutinized, it concluded that contribution limits involve "little direct restraint on...political communication, for [they permit] the symbolic expression of a support evidenced by a contribution but do not in any way infringe the contributor's freedom to discuss candidates and issues."[30]

By contrast, the Court determined that the "independent advocacy" that is constrained by the regulation of direct expenditures "does not presently appear to pose dangers of real or apparent corruption comparable to those identified with large campaign contributions."[31] And, with regard to a candidate's own independent expenditures, quid pro quo problems do not arise; a candidate cannot bribe himself or herself.[32] Although, hypothetically, some independent expenditures might suggest corruption, the overreaching of the FECA's categorical limits on expenditures was, in

24. *Id.* at 17.
25. *Id.* at 48-49.
26. *Id.* at 26.
27. *Id.* at 51, 58.
28. *Id.* at 26-27.
29. *Id.* at 27.
30. *Id.* at 21.
31. *Id.* at 46.
32. *See id.* at 45.

the Court's judgment, intolerable.[33] The Court reached this conclusion because, unlike the Act's limits on contributions, "the expenditure limitations contained in the Act represented substantial rather than merely theoretical restraints on the quantity and diversity of political speech."[34] Thus,
any system of expenditure limits "heavily burdens core First Amendment
expression."[35]

A great deal may be said in objection to the Court's analysis and conclusion, and, indeed, shortly after *Buckley*, Judge Skelly Wright wrote a
devastating critique of the Supreme Court's equation between the dis-
bursement of funds and actual speech.[36] It might also be observed, on the
face of *Buckley*, that the Court's willingness to second-guess the elective
branches on the political realities of electoral politics was the height of institutional chutzpa. But what is most implausible about the Court's holdings on contributions and expenditures is its pronouncement ipse dixit
that expenditures have communicative value that contributions do not. It
is chiefly on this score that the Court determined that Congress may remedy the appearance of corruption "inherent in a regime of large individual
financial contributions," but society must tolerate the very same problem
as engendered by large individual expenditures.[37]

A number of Justices have agreed that this bifurcated doctrine is anom-
alous, among them, Justices Burger[38] and Blackmun,[39] who would have
overturned the contribution regulations at issue in *Buckley*, and Justices
White[40] and Marshall,[41] who would have upheld the entire regulatory
scheme. More recently, Justice Stevens has explicitly rejected the distinction as having little or no relevance to the regulation of corporate participation in candidate elections-which strongly suggests he might rethink it
altogether.[42]

---

33. *See id.* at 56-57.

34. *Id.* at 19.

35. *Id.* at 48.

36. J. Skelly Wright, *Politics and the Constitution: Is Money Speech?*, 85 YALE L.J.
1001 (1976).

37. *Buckley*, 424 U.S. at 27.

38. *Id.* at 235 (Burger, C.J., concurring in part and dissenting in part).

39. *Id.* at 290 (Blackmun, J., concurring in part and dissenting in part).

40. *Id.* at 257 (White, J., concurring in part and dissenting in part).

41. *Id.* at 286 (Marshall, J., concurring in part and dissenting in part).

42. Austin v. Michigan Chamber of Commerce, 494 U.S. 652, 678 (1990) (Stevens, J.,
concurring). It is notable also that Chief Justice Rehnquist has expressed the view that
stare decisis applies with less force to constitutional opinions that were hotly contested
when decided and questioned by the Justices in subsequent opinions. Payne v. Tennessee,
501 U.S. 808, 827-30 (1991).

It's not hard to see why many Justices find this bifurcated doctrine irregular. From a funder's point of view, there is no difference in communicative value between an expenditure and a contribution. Both communicate exactly as much as the funder chooses to communicate. Furthermore, a contribution may convey a highly articulate message; by bundling my contribution, for example, with those of a host of other environmentalists, I can clearly state to a candidate not only my support, but the issues driving that support. Conversely, an expenditure may communicate nothing but the name of my chosen candidate-for example, if I pay for imprinted balloons carrying my candidate's name.

The Supreme Court's confidence that independent expenditures have lower corruption potential is similarly odd. According to the Court: "The absence of prearrangement and coordination of an expenditure with the candidate...also alleviates the danger that expenditures will be given as a quid pro quo for improper commitments from the candidate."[43] But counterexamples are obvious. For instance, a sufficiently wealthy person could devote millions, without any formal coordination with a candidate, to the independent republication—with the funder's name prominently featured—of the candidate's key sound bites as full-page newspaper ads. The use of such expenditures to purchase improper influence hardly seems fanciful.

To the extent *Buckley* rests on the distinction between contributions and expenditures, it seems clearly wrong. If there are in fact politically salient differences, Congress would be far better able to judge them than would the Court. Moreover, the Court's rejection of "speech equalization" as a permissible rationale for campaign-financing legislation ignores Madisonian wisdom. The Federalist No. 10, perhaps Madison's most profound text, points to the differential capacity to accumulate property as the key source of fractious opinion, which in turn gives rise to the spirit of faction:

> By a faction I understand a number of citizens, whether amounting to a majority or minority of the whole, who are united and actuated by some common impulse of passion, or of interest, adverse to the rights of other citizens, or to the permanent and aggregate interests of the community.[44]

Madison rejects, as means of circumventing factions, either the destruction of liberty or the attempt to equalize all property.[45] Instead, he urges the creation of a republic, rather than a direct democracy, as a way of circumscribing the influences of interest and passion, and he argues for

---

43. *Buckley*, 424 U.S. at 47.
44. THE FEDERALIST NO. 10, at 78 (James Madison) (Clinton Rossiter ed., 1961).
45. *See id.* at 78-79.

structural measures in the new Constitution to ameliorate the force of faction in government, even of a faction embracing an electoral majority.[46] From this standpoint, limiting the capacity of money to buy a disproportionate share of attention and efficacy for some political speech would seem to be a pure Madisonian initiative.

But even if one is unpersuaded by this logic that *Buckley* was so wrong when decided to be disposable for that reason alone, it should also be recognized that the jurisprudence founded on *Buckley* is largely incoherent. There are two issues on which the Court has waffled.

The first, albeit less important, conundrum concerns the questions whether contributions should be entitled to more constitutional protection if they carry an issue-oriented political message, and, conversely, whether expenditures should be entitled to less if they do not. A 1982 case, strongly implying negative answers to these questions, adhered instead to *Buckley*'s seemingly categorical distinction between all contributions, on one hand, and all expenditures, on the other. In *California Medical Ass'n v. Federal Election Commission*, the Court rejected the position that, in a candidate election, contributions ought to be treated more like independent expenditures when made to political action committees ("PACs"), rather than to particular candidates.[47] The California Medical Association had argued to the Court that PAC contributions affiliate their donors more with specific sets of political interests or positions than with particular candidates, and contribution limitations on the PACs themselves curb any concern about corruption.[48] Yet, the Court perceived no diminution in Congress's interest in combatting corruption through contribution limits, even funneled through PACs.[49]

Another line of cases, however, involving contributions and expenditures in referendum campaigns, has followed a different approach. In 1978, in *First National Bank of Boston v. Bellotti*, the Court overturned a Massachusetts statute barring banks and certain other business corporations from contributing funds to referendum campaigns.[50] In 1981, in *Citizens Against Rent Control/Coalition For Fair Housing v. City of Berkeley*, the Court overturned a city ordinance that was adopted through an initiative and referendum that limited political contributions to referendum campaigns.[51] In both cases, the Court reasoned that limitations on contributions in a referendum context could not be sustained because bal-

---

46. *Id.* at 80-84.
47. 453 U.S. 182, 197 (1981).
48. *Id.* at 195-96.
49. *Id.* at 197-99.
50. 435 U.S. 765 (1978).
51. 454 U.S. 290 (1981).

lot propositions, unlike candidates, cannot be "bought" in a corrupt sense, and because a contribution on behalf of a ballot proposition ought to count as a direct exposition of ideas.[52] With a pleasing sort of symmetry, in 1982 the Court in *Federal Election Commission v. National Right to Work Committee* also decided that corporations could be prohibited from using their money in candidate elections for the purpose of encouraging persons who were not members of the corporation to make contributions to a corporate political action committee.[53] Although the Court's reasoning focused chiefly on the permissibility of legislating to avoid corporate abuses—a topic to which we will soon turn—it also seems evident that the unanimous Court was less vigilant in protecting independent expenditures which conveyed no political message but were intended chiefly to facilitate contributions.[54] The net result of this line of cases, however, is a tension between them and *California Medical Ass'n* over the appropriateness of applying the contribution/expenditure dichotomy contextually.

A second tension in the post-*Buckley* case law, however, is more fundamental, and reveals far deeper ambivalences about the supposed illegitimacy of regulating campaign finance practices in order to equalize the force of competing interests' political speech. This tension is embodied in the Court's treatment of the regulation of business corporations.

As noted above, the Court held in the 1978 *Bellotti* case that, in referendum campaigns, the contributions and expenditures of corporations, like those of individuals, are not constitutionally susceptible of regulation.[55] The Court thus explicitly barred the states from treating as a form of corruption the power of corporations to influence referenda disproportionately through their special capacity to amass and deploy private wealth.

Yet, in the 1982 *National Right to Work Committee* decision, a unanimous Court upheld restrictions on the capacity of corporations to solicit contributions to PACs, in part "to ensure that substantial aggregations of wealth amassed by the special advantages which go with the corporate form of organization should not be converted into political "war chests" which could be used to incur political debts from legislators who are aided by the contributions."[56] This is a stunning concession, especially be-

---

52. *Accord* Federal Election Comm'n v. Massachusetts Citizens for Life, Inc., 479 U.S. 238 (1986).

53. 459 U.S. 197 (1982).

54. Oddly, the FECA seems to treat the use of corporate funds to engage in permissible solicitations as itself a form of "contribution," *Id.* at 198 n.1, although solicitation seems plainly to be a form of expenditure.

55. *Belloti,* 435 U.S. at 795.

56. *National Right to Work,* 459 U.S. at 207.

cause the Court so recently had barred states from regulating the corporate conversion of their "substantial aggregations of wealth" into "war chests" that could be used to control referendum campaigns.

But this concession as to Congress's legitimate interests, of course, reaches much further than *Bellotti*. It implies directly that the government regulation of "aggregations of wealth" is permissible where such aggregations are specially facilitated through law. But if that is true, then *Buckley* is untenable. Of course, individual contributors do not benefit from the legal regime of limited liability that makes corporations such effective engines of wealth creation. But inheritance laws, tax shelters, and the general system of legal protection for private property are every bit as significant in terms of conferring legal advantages upon wealthy persons. The Supreme Court has never explained why government need be indifferent to the political war chests of individuals blessed with their legal advantages, while at the same time having extensive power to regulate the war chests of those organizations whose shareholders enjoy limited liability.

National Right to Work Committee proved to be no lark. In 1990, the Court decided in *Austin v. Michigan Chamber of Commerce* that the "compelling governmental interest in preventing corruption supports the restriction of the influence of political war chests funneled through the corporate form."[57] The Court held, in essence, that *Buckley* did not protect corporations other than ideologically oriented non-profit entities from the regulation of direct political expenditures.[58] This conclusion is sound, but Justice Kennedy's dissent, arguing that the *Austin* majority effectively undercuts the foundational logic of *Buckley*, is, on that point, right on the mark.[59] For no persuasive reason, the speech-equalization rationale that the Court in *Buckley* deemed wholly foreign to the First Amendment is not only made permissibly familiar in *Austin*-it becomes compelling enough to survive strict scrutiny.

On top of all this, the passage of time has demonstrated the unwisdom of *Buckley*. Americans' growing alienation from their government must surely defeat by now any hope that five Justices might have entertained in 1974 that the 1971 FECA's contribution limitations would alone restore public confidence that the electoral system was free of the appearance of corruption. What the Court has since held with respect to the potential distortions of corporate wealth in the marketplace of ideas holds no less for wealthy individuals. On this front, it is time to go back to the Madisonian paradigm.

---

57. 494 U.S. 652, 659 (1990) (quoting Federal Election Comm'n v. National Conservative Political Action Comm., 470 U.S. 480, 500-01 (1985)).

58. *Id.* at 661-62.

59. *Id.* at 705-06 (Kennedy, J., dissenting).

* * *

* * *

A few years prior to the end of apartheid, a South African friend of mine said to me, "I know what a just South Africa would look like. I just don't know how to get there." Thanks to James Madison, I believe we also know what kind of political process would win the hearts and minds of the American electorate. We just don't know how to get there. Yet, I cannot help but feel that the distance from "here" to "there" is less daunting for us than it should have been in the mind of any reasonable South African examining the realities of that society a decade ago. Given how far South Africa has traveled in a decade towards the dreams of its people, we are entitled to some hope. In theory, at least, it is plausible that steps consistent with Madisonian values-steps like those I've outlined-might move us significantly to a state of public confidence. Such steps are no more utopian than Professor Breger's anti-federalism. And, if Professor Mashaw's skepticism on reinventing government is well-founded, perhaps we would do better trying to honor the best tradition we have.

Section IV

Alternative Methods of Regulation

Campaign Finance Reform: A Key to Restoring the Health of Our Democracy

[Excerpt Two]

Fred Wertheimer
Susan Weiss Manes

III. The Presidential Public Financing System: A Model for Reform

At the same time that Congress enacted congressional campaign finance reform in 1974, it established a new presidential campaign finance system that provided public financing and set limits on campaign spending.[86] Under the system, candidates who voluntarily agree to abide by spending limits and who raise a threshold amount in contributions are eligible for public matching payments in the presidential primaries.[87] During the general election, major party candidates are eligible for a grant equal to the amount of the spending limit.[88] The system is financed through a voluntary dollar tax checkoff on federal income tax returns.[89]

* * *

86. *See* 2 U.S.C. 441a(b), (c) (1988); Presidential Election Campaign Fund Act, 26 U.S.C. 9001–9013 (1988); Presidential Primary Matching Payment Account Act, 26 U.S.C. 9031–9042 (1988).

87. *See* 26 U.S.C. 9033(b), 9037 (1988).

88. *See* 26 U.S.C. 9004(a)(1) (1988).

89. *See* 26 U.S.C. 6096(a) (1988). In 1993, the dollar income tax checkoff, which finances the presidential system, was increased for the first time since its inception in 1974, to $ 3, in order to offset the impact of inflation over the years and to address the projected

A. Early Success

The initial experience under the presidential system makes clear that a system of public financing and spending limits can be an effective means for curbing special-interest influence in elections, controlling campaign spending, and allowing challengers to compete with incumbents' otherwise overwhelming financial edge. The role and influence of private campaign contributions, so evident in the Watergate scandal, were dramatically curtailed as a result of the 1974 Act during the first decade of the system's existence,[90] and political-influence money at the presidential level became a nonstory. While the media increasingly reported on the impact of campaign contributions on congressional decisions, few tales of campaign contributions influencing presidential decisions surfaced. This helped to restore the integrity and credibility of the presidency in the aftermath of Watergate.

In 1985, the bipartisan Commission on National Elections, headed by Melvin Laird, Secretary of Defense in the Nixon Administration, and Robert Strauss, former chair of the Democratic National Committee, recognized the value and success of the presidential system. The Commission concluded that: "Public financing of presidential elections has clearly proved its worth in opening up the process, reducing undue influence of individuals and groups, and virtually ending corruption in presidential election finance. This major reform of the 1970s should be

---

funding shortfall in the system. *See Congress Increases Tax Check-Off; FEC says '96 Presidential Elections Will Be Fully Funded*, PRESS RELEASE (Fed. Election Comm'n, Washington, D.C.), Aug. 20, 1993. The projected shortfall developed principally because of a structural flaw in the system. While the spending limits-and therefore the amount of public financing provided to candidates under the system-were indexed to inflation in 1974 and had increased by more than 250% by 1992, the dollar tax checkoff which finances the program was not similarly indexed. *See* 2 U.S.C. 441a(c) (1988). Had the dollar tax checkoff been indexed to inflation, the system would not have developed a projected shortfall and in fact would have maintained a surplus. While the increase in the checkoff to $ 3 is projected to restore the solvency of the presidential election campaign fund, the checkoff still needs to be indexed to prevent a shortfall in the future. Over the years, the number of tax returns that designated the checkoff has varied from a high of 28.6% in the years following the Watergate scandal to 17.7% in 1991. *See* FED. ELECTION COMM'N, THE PRESIDENTIAL PUBLIC FUNDING PROGRAM 37 (1993). While opponents of public financing point to this decrease in the percentage of taxpayers who check off as the cause of the potential shortfall, the fact is that if the checkoff had been indexed, there would be no funding problem. *See also infra* text accompanying notes 134–135.

90. David Ignatius, *Return of the Fat Cats*, WASH. POST Nov. 20, 1988, at D5.

continued."[91] Former Senator Paul Laxalt (R-Nev.), who chaired the 1976, 1980, and 1984 presidential campaigns for President Reagan, also praised the presidential system. In discussing the campaign finance problems in Congress, Senator Laxalt said: "'The problem is so bad we ought to start thinking about federal financing' of House and Senate campaigns. 'It was anathema to me...but in my experience with the [Reagan] presidential campaigns, it worked, and it was like a breath of fresh air.'"[92] The presidential public financing system was a historic step in protecting the integrity of the presidency. The presidential system's early record of success bears out the wisdom of its creation, and of its continuing importance today.

All but one of the major party presidential candidates have chosen to participate in the presidential public financing system since it was established in 1974.[93] The presidential system's track record convincingly contradicts the argument that public financing and spending limits are an incumbents' protection system. While there are obvious differences between a nationwide presidential election and local congressional elections, the experience under the presidential public financing system refutes claims that a system of spending limits and public financing entrenches incumbents. In the four general elections under this system involving an incumbent president (1976, 1980, 1984, and 1992), the challenger won three times. This is a reelection rate of only 25%. The first two presidents to run under the presidential public financing system, Gerald Ford and Jimmy Carter, became the first two incumbents to lose a presidential election since President Hoover lost in 1932. In 1992, incumbent President George Bush was defeated by challenger Governor Bill Clinton. This record contrasts sharply with the record under the congressional campaign finance system, where no public funds are available, where spending is unlimited, where incumbents overwhelmingly outraise and outspend their challengers and where reelection rates are better than 90%.

---

91. *Senate Comm. on Rules and Administration*, 102nd Cong. 5 (1991) (Comm'n on Nat'l Elections report quoted in testimony of Fred Wertheimer, President, Common Cause).

92. David S. Broder, *How to Fix Congress—Advice from the Alumni*, WASH. POST, Jan. 6, 1991, at C1 (quoting Sen. Laxalt) (alteration in original).

93. John Connally, a Republican candidate in the 1980 presidential primary elections, is the one major-party presidential candidate who chose not to participate in the public financing system. For a list of all major party presidential candidates who have participated in the public financing system, *see* FED. ELECTION COMM'N, THE PRESIDENTIAL PUBLIC FUNDING PROGRAM, at app. 3 (1993).

Under the presidential public financing system, candidates have been able to run for office without relying on PAC contributions or large individual contributions. As stated above, PAC contributions to congressional candidates have jumped from $ 12.5 million in 1974[94] to $ 173 million in 1992 and now represent nearly half of the contributions raised by House incumbents and more than 30% of the contributions raised by Senate incumbents.[95] In contrast, PAC contributions play a minor role in presidential campaigns, representing less than 1% of the total funds given to presidential candidates in 1992.[96]

B. Soft Money Threatens the Presidential System

While the presidential campaign finance system generally has worked well over the years, a major problem unfolded in the mid-1980s as presidential campaigns used political party "soft money" contributions to inject huge private contributions back into presidential elections. If left unchecked, political party soft money threatens to render meaningless all federal limits on campaign contributions and to destroy the integrity of the presidential campaign finance system.

Soft money contributions circumvent the contributions limits in the following way. First, PACs, corporations, and wealthy individuals make contributions to a candidate's political party. Because these contributions are not made directly to the candidate, they are not subject to the limits under current campaign finance laws. The political party then channels this "soft money" to state political parties, where it is spent to support the presidential campaign by financing activities such as get-out-the-vote drives. Presidential candidates can thereby raise money, through their political parties, that is not subject to the campaign contribution limits.[97]

The use of soft money violates the federal election statute, as well as its fundamental purposes.[98] The law never envisioned allowing publicly fi-

---

94. *See 1974 Congressional Campaign Finances*, PRESS RELEASE (Common Cause, Washington, D.C.), 1976, at viii.

95. *See 1992 House Campaign Financing, supra* note 27, at Chart 1; *1992 Senate Campaign Financing, supra* note 23, at Chart 1.

96. *Fed. Election Comm'n, FEC Presidential Receipts and Disbursements Through December 31, 1992*, PRESS RELEASE (forthcoming) (preliminary draft on file with the *Columbia Law Review*).

97. *See* Helen Dewar, *Stalemate of Survival*, WASH. POST, Aug. 6, 1992, at A1.

98. *See* 2 U.S.C. 431(8)(B)(x)(2), (xii)(2), (9)(B)(viii)(2), (ix)(2) (1988) (All monies spent by state committees on listed activities for federal elections must be paid out of "contributions subject to the limitations and prohibitions of this [FECA] Act [the FECA Act].").

nanced presidential campaigns to solicit millions of dollars in contributions from sources and in amounts banned under federal law. The law also never envisioned allowing state parties to serve as conduits for the injection of such funds to finance a presidential or any other federal election. Nevertheless, the FEC, which is responsible for enforcing federal election law,[99] has failed to act to curb these abuses, despite a 1987 federal court order which found that the FEC's approach failed to reflect the intent of the law.[100] The FEC's initial inaction effectively sent a message that invited presidential campaign organizations to violate the law with impunity. What began as a trickle soon became a flood as presidential campaigns recognized that the use of soft money would not be checked by the FEC.[101]

The presidential campaigns justify their soft money drives by ignoring their legal agreement not to raise or spend private funds in exchange for their receipt of public funding. They and the political party committees that receive the soft money claim that the money is for party building activities, pointing to the 1979 amendments to FECA law that allow state parties to make unlimited expenditures during presidential campaigns on "party building" activities[102] such as voter registration and "get-out-the-vote" drives. The 1979 amendments flatly state, however, that state political parties may not spend any contributions on party building activities in support of a presidential candidate unless the contributions comply with federal limits on the amount and source of allowable contributions.[103] The plain intent of Congress was to ensure that activities that aid presidential candidates are not financed with contributions that are illegal under federal law because they exceed the limits on allowable individual and PAC contributions or because they are from prohibited sources, e.g., corporations and labor unions.

As early as 1984, Common Cause petitioned the FEC to promulgate regulations to address the then-nascent problem of soft money. Two years later, after the FEC voted against taking action to address the use of soft money, Common Cause filed suit in federal district court, seeking to overturn the Commission's denial of the Common Cause petition. In August 1987, the court ordered the FEC to reconsider its denial of the Common Cause petition, holding that the FEC's failure to deal with the soft money

---

99. *See* 2 U.S.C. 437c(b) (1988).

100. *See* Common Cause v. Federal Election Comm'n. 692 F. Supp. 1391, 1395 (D.D.C. 1987) ("FEC's failure to regulate improper or inaccurate allocation between federal and nonfederal funds with respect to these activities was contrary to law....").

101. *See* Thomas B. Edsall, *Is the FEC Undermining Campaign Law?*, WASH. POST, Oct. 20, 1986, at A23.

102. 2 U.S.C. 431 (8)(B)(xii), (9)(B)(ix) (1988).

103. *See* 2 U.S.C. 431(8)(B)(xii)(2), (9)(B)(ix)(2) (1988).

problem "was contrary to law"[104] and criticizing the agency for interpreting the law "in a way that flatly contradicts Congress's express purpose."[105]

When the FEC had still not acted a year later, Common Cause returned to court. The court again rejected the agency's excuses, chastising the FEC for its "laggard" response to its mandate.[106] The court took the unusual step of ordering the agency to report every 90 days on its progress in promulgating soft money rules. The court reasoned that "although lives do not hang in the balance, the climate of concern surrounding soft money threatens the very "corruption and appearance of corruption" by which "the integrity of our system of representative democracy is undermined,' and which the [FECA] was intended to remedy."[107]

It was not until June 1990 that the FEC finally issued a revision of its rules regarding soft money.[108] The new regulations, however, continue to sanction the use of soft money in federal elections.[109] The one significant change is the requirement that national party committees disclose soft money contributions.[110]

While political party soft money first came into significant use in the 1984 election, it erupted as a major campaign finance abuse during the 1988 presidential election when both the Bush and Dukakis campaigns embarked on major soft money fund-raising drives for contributions as

---

104. Common Cause v. Federal Election Comm'n, 692 F. Supp. 1391, 1395 (D.D.C. 1987).

105. *Id.* at 1396; *see* Common Cause v. Federal Election Comm'n, 692 F. Supp. 1397, 1398 (D.D.C. 1988).

106. Common Cause v. Federal Election Comm'n, 692 F. Supp. 1397, 1400 (D.D.C. 1988).

107. *Id.* at 1401 (quoting Buckley v. Valeo, 424 U.S. 1, 25, 26–27 (1976)).

108. *See* Fed. Election Comm'n, 11 C.F.R. 102, 104, 106; Methods of Allocation Between Federal and Non-Federal Accounts; Payments; Reporting; 55 Fed. Reg. 26058 (1990).

109. *See* 11 C.F.R. 106.5106.6 (1993) (specifying new allocation method for expenses between federal and nonfederal candidates and activities by party committees). Under current FEC regulations, political party activities such as get-out-the-vote drives that affect both federal and nonfederal candidates may be financed with a mixture of "hard money" (contributions that comply with federal contribution limits and prohibitions) and "soft money" (contributions that do not comply with federal limits and prohibitions). The mix of hard and soft money is based on the percentage of the activities which political parties "allocate" to federal and nonfederal purposes. This is referred to as "allocation." *See* 11 C.F.R. 106.1(e) (1993).

110. *See* 11 C.F.R. 104.8(c)(1993) (increasing the reporting burden for contributions made to national party committees).

large as $ 100,000 from wealthy individuals and special interests.[111] Even though both campaigns elected to take part in the presidential campaign financing system, pledged to abide by campaign spending limits, and received public campaign funds in exchange, the campaigns and their political parties raised and spent approximately $ 25 million each in soft money contributions outside the system.[112] By the 1992 presidential elections, the soft money system, improperly sanctioned by the FEC, had become entrenched. The Bush and Clinton campaigns and their respective political parties together raised nearly $ 85 million in soft money contributions during the 1991–1992 election cycle-$ 49.6 million for the Republicans and $ 35.3 million for the Democrats.[113] Overall, 69 contributors gave $ 100,000 or more each to the Bush-RNC efforts during the two-year election cycle,[114] and 72 contributors gave $ 100,000 or more each to the Clinton-DNC efforts during the two-year election cycle.[115]

Soft money abuses are undermining congressional campaigns as well. As far back as 1986, Charles Keating, a conservative Republican and former S&L owner now sentenced to prison for his S&L activities, made a soft money contribution of $ 85,000 to a California Democratic Party get-out-the-vote effort to help reelect former Senator Alan Cranston (D-Cal.)-a contribution that Senator Cranston acknowledged as aiding his 1986 Senate re-election.[116] In 1990, the Louisville Courier-Journal disclosed

---

111. *See Fat Cat "Soft Money" Contributors Funnel Millions Into '92 Presidential Campaign; Soft Money Ban Is Essential to Anti-Corruption Legislation*, EDITORIAL MEMORANDUM (Common Cause, Washington, D.C.), Sept. 1992, at 3 (on file with the *Columbia Law Review*).

112. *See id.*

113. *See Soft Money to Republican National Committee & Bush Tops $ 32 Million During 1991–1992 Election Cycle*, COMMON CAUSE NEWS (Common Cause, Washington, D.C.), July 23, 1993, at 12 (on file with the *Columbia Law Review*).

114. *See id.* at 3.

115. *See Soft Money for President Clinton & Democratic National Committee Tops $ 29 Million During 1991–1992 Election Cycle*, COMMON CAUSE NEWS (Common Cause, Washington, D.C.), Mar. 3, 1993, at 2 (on file with the *Columbia Law Review*). It is important to note that these figures represent the soft money contributions reported by the national party committees to the FEC and are not complete soft money totals for the 1992 presidential election. In 1988, for example, a number of soft money contributions raised by the presidential campaigns went directly to the state political party committees. Such contributions are not included in the FEC reports filed by the national party committees.

116. *See* Joe Scott, *The Tip of a Money Scandal?*, SAN DIEGO UNION, July 21, 1989 at B6.

that Mary C. Bingham of Louisville, Kentucky, a known supporter of 1990 Democratic Senatorial candidate Harvey Sloane, contributed approximately $ 250,000 to the Democratic National Committee. Shortly thereafter, the DNC transferred $ 250,000 to the Kentucky Democratic Party. The Kentucky state party in turn spent the money on a television advertising campaign that was created by Sloane's media consultant, used Sloane's campaign slogan, and addressed federal issues.[117] These and other congressional cases vividly illustrate that unless the soft money system is ended, huge soft money contributions will continue to be a dangerous and growing problem for congressional as well as presidential elections.

In 1989, in the 101st Congress, Senator George Mitchell (D-Me.), and Senator David Boren (D-Okla.) introduced comprehensive campaign finance legislation that included strong provisions to end the soft money system.[118] Although the legislation passed the Senate, the bill never emerged from conference with the House.[119] Similar legislation was introduced by Senators Mitchell and Boren in the 102nd Congress. The legislation passed both houses of Congress, but the final conference agreement was vetoed by then-President Bush.[120] In 1993, the bill was reintroduced and passed by the Senate.[121] The House also passed a comprehensive campaign finance reform bill in 1993 that includes provisions to address the soft money problem, although they are significantly weaker than the provisions of the Senate-passed bill.[122]

C. A Flawed Enforcement System

Nowhere is the devastating impact of the Federal Election Commission's failure to enforce the law effectively more clear than in the case of the soft money problem. Unfortunately, the blind eye turned by the FEC to that problem is not an isolated case. Although the FEC has an excellent track record in making campaign finance information available to the public and the media, the agency, on the whole, has not carried out its responsibility

---

117. *See* Robert L. Garrett, *Mary Bingham's $ 250,000 Gift to Democrats Buoyed Sloane,* COURIER J. (Louisville, KY.), Nov. 9, 1990, at 1; Mike Brown, *$ 250,000 Bingham Gift to Democrats Raises Questions About "Soft Money,"* COURIER J. (Louisville, Ky.), Nov. 10, 1990, at 1.

118. *See* S. 137, 101st Cong. (1989).

119. 1990 CONG. Q. ALMANAC 59 (1990).

120. *See* S. 3, 102nd Cong. (1991); 138 CONG. REC. S6478 (daily ed. May 12, 1992) (veto message on S. 3).

121. *See* S. 3, 103rd Cong. (1993).

122. *See* H. R. 3, 103rd Cong. 403 (1993); S. 3, 103rd Cong. 311–314 (1993).

to enforce the law. Dominated by the interests of the political parties and incumbent officeholders, the agency's approach to its enforcement responsibilities has seriously undermined the efficacy of federal election laws.[123]

The performance of the FEC Commissioners has served as a roadblock to effective enforcement. The Commission consists of three Democrats and three Republicans, a structure which too often has resulted in deadlock along partisan lines.[124] The result, as Daniel Swillinger, a former assistant general counsel at the FEC, told The Wall Street Journal, is that "people take the attitude that the commission is never going to get four votes, and so they can do anything they want."[125] As The Washington Post noted, "Politicians on both sides of the aisle take the view that the FEC represents little threat to "innovative' uses of money and fund-raising committees."[126] It is essential to overhaul the FEC and to create a workable enforcement system in order to protect the integrity of the campaign finance laws already in place and to ensure the effectiveness of any new reforms.

* * *

---

123. *See* Andrew P. Buchsbaum, Comment, *Campaign Finance Re- Reform: The Regulation of Independent Political Committees*, 71 Cal. L.Rev. 673, 690 & n.108 (1983).

124. *See id.; see also* 2 U.S.C. 437c (1988).

125. Brooks Jackson, *Off Guard: Election Commission Set Up as a Watchdog, Has Become a Pussycat*, Wall St. J., Oct. 19, 1987, at A1 (quoting Daniel Swillinger).

126. Edsall, *supra* note 101, at A23.

* * *

Political Equality and Unintended Consequences

Cass R. Sunstein

It is a familiar point that government regulation that is amply justified in principle may go terribly wrong in practice. Minimum wage laws, for example, appear to reduce employment.[1] Stringent regulation of new sources of air pollution may aggravate pollution problems, by perpetuating the life of old, especially dirty sources.[2] If government closely monitors the release of information, there may be less information.[3] Unintended consequences of this kind can make regulation futile or even self-defeating.[4] By futile regulation, I mean measures that do not bring about the desired consequences. By self-defeating regulation, I mean measures that actually make things worse from the standpoint of their strongest and most public-spirited advocates. We do not lack examples of both of these phenomena. It is unfortunate but true that current campaign finance laws may well provide more illustrations.

Some campaign finance regulation is amply justified in principle. As we will see, there is no good reason to allow disparities in wealth to be translated into disparities in political power. A well-functioning democracy distinguishes between market processes of purchase and sale on the one hand

---

1. *See* FINIS WELCH, MINIMUM WAGES: ISSUES AND EVIDENCE 34–38 (1978). *But see* Stephen Machin & Alan Manning, *The Effects of Minimum Wages on Wage Dispersion and Employment: Evidence from the U.K. Wages Councils*, 47 INUDS. & LAB. REL. REV. 319 (1994) (concluding that the minimum wage has either no effect or a positive effect on employment).

2. *See* Richard B. Stewart, *Regulation, Innovation, and Administrative Law: A Conceptual Framework*, 69 CAL. L. REV. 1256, 1281–84 (1981).

3. *See* Richard Craswell, *Interpreting Deceptive Advertising*, 65 B.U. L. REV. 657, 678 (1985).

4. *Cf.* ALBERT O. HIRSCHMAN, THE RHETORIC OF REACTION: PERVERSITY, FUTILITY, JEOPARDY 11–12, 43–45 (1991) (citing two arguments: the perversity thesis, which asserts that "the attempt to push society in a certain direction will result in its moving...in the opposite direction," and the futility thesis which asserts that "[any] attempt at change... will be largely surface, facade, cosmetic, [and] hence illusory").

and political processes of voting and reason-giving on the other. Government has a legitimate interest in ensuring not only that political liberties exist as a formal and technical matter, but also that those liberties have real value to the people who have them.[5] The achievement of political equality is an important constitutional goal. Nonetheless, many imaginable campaign finance restrictions would be futile or self-defeating. To take a familiar example, it is now well-known that restrictions on individual expenditures-designed to reduce influence-peddling-can help fuel the use of political action committees (PACs), and thus increase the phenomenon of influence-peddling.[6] This is merely one of a number of possible illustrations.

I can venture no exhaustive account here, and I attempt to describe possibilities rather than certainties. But one of my principal goals is to outline some of the harmful but unintended[7] consequences of campaign finance restrictions. I conclude with some brief notes on what strategies might be most likely to avoid the risk of unintended (or intended but unarticulated) bad consequences. My basic claim here is that we might attempt to avoid rigid command-and-control strategies for restricting expenditures, and experiment with more flexible, incentive-based approaches. In this way the regulation of campaign expenditures might be brought in line with recent innovations in regulatory practice generally.[8]

* * *

---

5. *See, e.g.*, JOHN RAWLS, POLITICAL LIBERALISM 324–31 (1993) ("The first principle of justice [should include] the guarantee...that the worth of the political liberties to all citizens, whatever their social or economic position, [is] approximately equal.").

6. *See infra* text accompanying note 52.

7. Of course some of these effects might be intended.

8. *See, e.g.*, STEPHEN BREYER, REGULATION AND ITS REFORM 156–88 (1982) (describing alternatives to classical regulation); Bruce A. Ackerman & Richard B. Stewart, *Reforming Environmental Law: The Democratic Case for Market Incentives*, 13 COLUM. J. ENVTL. L. 171, 182–83 (1988) (arguing that a reform of environmental regulation relying on market incentives will improve both meaningful democratic debate and regulatory efficiency). For a popular treatment of regulatory innovation, *see* DAVID OSBORNE & TED GAEBLER, REINVENTING GOVERNMENT 15, 301–05 (1992) (suggesting that governments employ a market-based regulatory policy which would operate by incentives rather than by commands).

* * *

II. The Problem of Unintended Consequences

In principle, then, there are good arguments for campaign finance restrictions. Insofar as *Buckley* rejects political equality as a legitimate constitutional goal, it should be overruled. Indeed, the decision probably
ranks among the strongest candidates for overruling of the post-World
War II period. But there are real limits on how much we can learn from
abstract principles alone. Many of the key questions are insistently ones of
policy and fact. Was the system at issue in *Buckley* well-designed? How
might it be improved? What will be the real-world consequences of different plans? Will they fulfill their intended purposes? Will they be self-defeating? Might they impair democratic processes under the guise of promoting them?

My goal here is to offer a brief catalogue of ways in which campaign
finance legislation may prove unhelpful or counterproductive. My particular interest lies in the possibility that campaign finance legislation may
have perverse or unintended consequences. The catalogue bears directly
on a number of proposals now receiving attention in Congress and in the
executive branch. Of course it would be necessary to look at the details in
order to make a final assessment. I am describing possibilities, not certainties, and a good deal of empirical work would be necessary to come to
terms with any of them.

A general point runs throughout the discussion. Although I have criticized what the Court said in *Buckley*, considerable judicial suspicion of
campaign finance limits is justified by a simple point: Congressional support for such limits is especially likely to reflect congressional self-dealing.
Any system of campaign finance limits raises the special spectre of governmental efforts to promote the interests of existing legislators. Indeed, it is
hard to imagine other kinds of legislation posing similarly severe risks. In
these circumstances, we might try to avoid rigid, command-and-control
regulation, which poses special dangers, and move instead toward more
flexible, incentive-based strategies.

A. Unintended Consequences in Particular

1. Campaign Finance Limits May Entrench Incumbents.—
Operating under the rubric of democratic equality, campaign finance
measures may make it hard for challengers to overcome the effects of incumbency. The problem is all the more severe in a period in which it is

TABLE 1
Re-Election Rates
Senate Incumbents, Re-Elected, Defeated, or Retired

Year	Retired	Total seeking re-election	Defeated in primaries	Defeated in general election	Total re-elected	Re-elected as percentage of those seeking re-election
1946	9	30	6	7	17	56.7%
1948	8	25	2	8	15	60.0%
1950	4	32	5	5	22	68.8%
1952	4	31	2	9	20	64.5%
1954	6	32	2	6	24	75.0%
1956	6	39	0	4	25	86.2%
1958	6	28	0	10	18	64.3%
1960	5	29	0	1	28	96.6%
1962	4	35	1	5	29	82.9%
1964	2	33	1	4	28	84.8%
1966	3	32	3	1	28	87.5%
1968	6	28	4	4	20	71.4%
1970	4	31	1	6	24	77.4%
1972	6	27	2	5	20	74.1%
1974	7	27	2	2	23	85.2%
1976	8	25	0	9	16	64.0%
1978	10	25	3	7	15	60.0%
1980	5	29	4	9	16	55.2%
1982	3	30	0	2	28	93.3%
1984	4	29	0	3	26	89.7%
1986	6	28	0	7	21	75.0%
1988	6	27	0	4	23	85.2%
1990		32	0	1	31	96.9%
1992		28	1	4	23	82.1%

extremely difficult for challengers to unseat incumbents. Consider Tables 1[42] and 2[43] (page 272).

The risk of incumbent self-dealing becomes even more troublesome in light of the fact that dissidents or challengers may be able to overcome the advantages of incumbency only by amassing enormous sums of money, either from their own pockets or from numerous or wealthy supporters.[44]

Consider in this regard the candidacy of Ross Perot. The Perot campaign raises many questions, but it is at least notable that large sums of

42. *See* NORMAN J. ORENSTEIN ET AL., VITAL STATISTICS ON CONGRESS 57 (1989-1990) (source for years 1948-88); Statistical Abstract of the U.S. 277 (1993) (source for years 1990-1992).

43. *See* ORENSTEIN *supra* note 42 at 56; Statistical Abstract of the U.S. 277 (1993).

44. *See* FRANK J. SORAUF, MONEY IN AMERICAN ELECTIONS 155–59 (1988).

TABLE 2
Re-Election Rates
House Incumbents, Re-Elected, Retired, or Defeated

Year	Retired	Total seeking re-election	Defeated in primaries	Defeated in general election	Total-re-elected	Re-elected as percentage of those seeking	Re-elected as percentage of House
1948	29	400	15	68	317	79.3%	72.9%
1950	29	400	6	32	362	90.5%	83.2%
1952	42	389	9	26	354	91.0%	81.4%
1954	24	407	6	22	379	93.1%	87.1%
1956	21	411	6	16	389	94.6%	89.4%
1958	33	396	3	37	356	89.9%	81.8%
1960	26	405	5	25	375	92.6%	86.2%
1962	24	402	12	22	368	91.5%	84.6%
1964	33	397	8	45	344	86.6%	79.1%
1966	22	411	8	41	362	88.1%	83.2%
1968	23	409	4	9	396	96.8%	91.0%
1970	29	401	10	12	379	94.5%	87.1%
1972	40	390	12	13	365	93.6%	83.9%
1974	43	391	8	40	343	87.7%	78.9%
1976	47	384	3	13	368	95.8%	84.6%
1978	49	382	5	19	358	93.7%	82.3%
1980	34	398	6	31	361	90.7%	83.0%
1982	40	393	10	29	354	90.1%	81.4%
1984	22	409	3	16	390	95.4%	89.7%
1986	38	393	2	6	385	98.0%	88.5%
1988	23	409	1	6	402	98.3%	92.4%
1990		407	1	15	391	96.1%	89.9%
1992		367	19	24	324	88.3%	74.5%

money proved an indispensable mechanism for enabling an outsider to challenge the mainstream candidates. One lesson seems clear. Campaign finance limits threaten to eliminate one of the few means by which incumbents can be seriously challenged.

There is particular reason to fear self-dealing in some of the proposals now attracting considerable enthusiasm in Congress. For example, incumbent senators tend to have less difficulty in raising money than do members of the House of Representatives. Members of the House are therefore more dependent on PAC contributions. It should be unsurprising that while Senate bills propose a complete ban on multi-candidate PACs,[45] the leading House bill proposes a much less draconian contribution limit of $

---

45. *See* S. 951, 103rd Cong. (1993); S. 7, 103rd Cong. (1993); S. 3, 103rd Cong. (1993).

2,500 per candidate.[46] More generally, the current proposals do nothing to decrease the benefits of incumbency, and they may well increase those benefits.[47]

Whether campaign finance limits in general do entrench incumbents is an empirical question. There is some evidence to the contrary. Usually the largest amounts are spent by incumbents themselves; usually incumbents have an advantage in accumulating enormous sums, often from people who think that they have something to gain from a financial relationship with an officeholder.[48] In these circumstances, one of the particular problems for challengers is that they face special financial barriers by virtue of the ability of incumbents to raise large sums of money. Probably the fairest generalization is that campaign finance limits in general do not entrench incumbents, but that there are important individual cases in which such limits prevent challengers from mounting serious efforts. In any case, any campaign finance reforms should be designed so as to promote more electoral competition.

2.   Limits on Individual Contributions Will Produce More (and More Influential) PACs.—The early regulation of individual contributions had an important unintended consequence: It led directly to the rise of the political action committee. When individuals were banned from contributing to campaigns, there was tremendous pressure to provide a mechanism for aggregating individual contributions. The modern PAC is the result. Consider Tables 3,[49] 4,[50] and 5[51] on pages 275–277.

The post-*Buckley* rise of PACs has a general implication. If individual contributions are controlled while PACs face little or no effective regulation, there could be a large shift of resources in the direction of PACs. Of course a combination of PAC limits and individual contribution limits

---

46. *See* H.R. 3, 103rd Cong. (version 1) (1993).

47. Moreover, it is possible that lesser known challengers would be more likely to raise funds through a more limited number of extremely generous donors. Certain types of campaign finance restrictions could foreclose this avenue to a successful campaign for people without the benefits of incumbency or a major party's backing. *See* Stephen E. Gottlieb, *The Dilemma of Election Campaign Finance Reform*, 18 HOFSTRA L. REV. 213, 221 (1989).

48. *See* Jamin Raskin & John Bonifaz, *The Constitutional Imperative and Practical Superiority of Democratically Financed Elections*, 94 COLUM. L. REV. 1160, 1176–78 (1994).

49. *See* FEC Reports on Financial Activity, Final Report, Party and Non-Party Political Committees (1990).

50. Statistical Abstract of the U.S. 287 (1993).

51. Statistical Abstract of the U.S. 288 (1993).

TABLE 3
PAC Activity
Average PAC Contribution by Type, By Year, By Candidate Type

		Senate Candidate Type							House Candidate Type						
		DI	RI	DC	RC	DO	RO	Total Senate Contribution	DI	RI	DC	RC	DO	RO	Total House Contribution
1978	Corporate	646	754	613	726	591	707	3,616,388	335	328	366	442	428	413	6,158,00
	Labor	2,367	1,576	2,308	1,500	2,184	1,748	2,831,336	848	708	1,099	596	1,174	938	7,462,42
1980	Corporate	871	666	587	972	654	875	7,731,966	446	401	421	529	461	495	12,743,10
	Labor	2,680	2,245	2,164	1,294	2,501	1,508	4,192,159	1,078	751	1,199	727	1,472	507	9,714,30
1982	Corporate														
	Labor														
1984	Corporate	1,122	1,300	793	952	1,127	1,511	14,260,807	626	573	443	626	546	662	24,004,40
	Labor	2,582	2,175	3,253	735	4,069	4,333	5,580,536	1,622	1,319	1,672	1,073	2,012	1,849	20,290,13
1986	Corporate	1,382	1,603	1,306	1,588	1,347	1,834	21,721,324	728	669	606	600	650	718	27,829,83
	Labor	2,949	2,488	4,269	1,194	4,599	2,683	7,908,118	1,759	1,613	2,315	1,211	2,477	1,365	23,104,30
1988	Corporate	1,638	1,753	1,305	1,617	1,535	1,795	21,928,118	861	771	566	730	722	729	32,404,98
	Labor	3,570	2,743	4,469	1,905	3,948	3,165	7,686,772	2,122	1,685	2,667	1,247	3,022	1,994	27,197,18
1990	Corporate	1,764	1,822	1,211	2,256	794	2,034	21,934,718	1,012	885	709	870	943	922	36,153,94
	Labor	3,799	2,671	4,115	1,424	3,632	3,360	6,746,738	2,342	1,714	2,541	1,437	3,180	3,231	27,952,72

D—Democrat, R—Republican, I—Incumbent, C—Challenger, O—Open seat

TABLE 4
Number of Political Action Committees, by Committee Type: 1980 to 1991
[as of December 31, 1992]

COMMITTEE TYPE	1980	1985	1986	1987	1988	1989	1990	1991
Total	2,551	3,992	4,157	4,165	4,268	4,178	4,172	4,094
Corporate	1,206	1,710	1,744	1,775	1,816	1,796	1,795	1,738
Labor	297	388	384	364	354	349	346	338
Trade/membership/health	576	695	745	865	786	777	774	742
Nonconnected	374	1,003	1,077	957	1,115	1,060	1,062	1,083
Cooperative	42	54	56	59	59	59	59	57
Corporation without stock	56	142	151	145	138	137	136	136

could counteract this problem. But limits of this kind create difficulties of their own.[52]

3.　Limits on "Hard Money" Encourage a Shift to "Soft Money."—In the 1980s, the tightening of individual contribution limits—"hard money"—helped increase the amount of "soft money,"[53] consisting of gifts to political parties. It should not be surprising to see that in recent years there has been an enormous increase in fund-raising by political parties, which dispense contributions to various candidates. In 1980, the two parties raised and spent about $ 19 million; in 1984, the amount rose to $ 19.6 million; in 1988, it increased to $ 45 million.[54] Consider Table 6 [55] on page 276.

In some ways the shift from hard to soft money has been a salutary development. It is more difficult for soft money contributors to target particular beneficiaries, and perhaps this reduces the risk of the quid pro quo donation. Reasonable people could believe that soft money poses lower risks to the integrity of the political process while also exemplifying a legitimate form of freedom of speech and association. But the substitution, if it occurs, means that any contribution limits are easily evaded. Candidates

---

52. See *infra* notes 64–65 and accompanying text.

53. Federal law exempts certain state and local activities-like voter registration and grass roots campaign materials—from regulation. Funds for these activities are subject only to state law, which often permits corporate and labor union political contributions. *See* HERBERT E. ALEXANDER, FINANCING POLITICS: MONEY, ELECTIONS, AND POLITICAL REFORM 66–67 (4th ed. 1992).

54. *See id.* at 67.

55. Statistical Abstract of the U.S. 286 (1993).

TABLE 5
Contributions to Congressional Campaigns by Political Action Committee(s) (by Committee) Type: 1979 to 1990

[In millions of dollars. Covers amounts given to candidates in primary, general, run-off, and special elections during the 2-year calendar period indicated.]

Type of Committee	HOUSE OF REPRESENTATIVES						SENATE					
	Total	Democrats	Republicans	Incumbents	Challengers	Open seats(a)	Total	Democrats	Republicans	Incumbents	Challengers	Open seats(a)
1979–80	37.9	20.5	17.2	24.9	7.9	5.1	17.3	8.4	9.0	8.6	6.6	2.1
1981–82	61.1	34.2	26.8	40.8	10.9	9.4	22.6	11.2	11.4	14.3	5.2	3.0
1983–84 total(b)	75.7	46.3	29.3	57.2	11.3	7.2	29.7	14.2	15.6	17.9	6.3	5.4
Corporate	23.4	10.4	13.1	18.8	2.6	2.0	12.0	3.2	8.8	8.8	1.1	2.2
Trade association(c)	20.4	10.5	9.9	16.5	2.1	1.3	6.3	2.7	3.7	4.5	0.9	1.0
Labor	19.8	18.8	1.0	4.9	3.5	12.4	5.0	4.7	0.3	1.6	2.3	1.2
Nonconnected(d)	9.1	4.7	4.4	4.9	2.9	3.0	5.4	3.0	2.4	2.4	2.0	1.0
1985–86, total(b)	87.4	54.7	32.6	65.9	9.1	2.8	45.3	20.2	25.1	23.7	10.2	11.4
Corporate	26.9	12.9	14.0	22.9	1.0	3.6	19.2	4.8	14.4	11.7	2.7	4.9
Trade association(c)	23.4	12.3	11.2	19.3	1.3	2.6	9.5	3.8	5.7	5.7	1.6	2.1
Labor	22.6	21.1	1.6	14.7	4.3	10.0	7.2	6.6	0.6	2.2	3.2	1.9
Nonconnected(d)	11.1	6.6	4.5	6.1	2.4	1.9	7.7	4.2	3.4	3.1	2.4	2.2
1987–88, total(b)	102.2	67.4	34.7	82.2	10.0	2.5	45.7	24.2	21.5	28.7	8.0	9.0
Corporate	31.6	16.3	15.4	28.6	1.1	3.3	18.8	7.2	11.6	12.7	2.4	3.7
Trade association(c)	28.6	16.5	12.0	24.6	1.5	1.9	10.4	4.8	5.6	7.1	1.3	2.0
Labor	28.8	24.8	2.0	18.3	1.5	13.6	7.1	6.5	0.5	3.6	2.2	1.3
Nonconnected(d)	11.4	7.4	3.9	7.3	2.2	3.2	7.8	4.8	3.0	4.2	2.0	1.6
1989–90, total(b)	108.5	72.2	36.2	87.5	7.3	3.6	41.2	20.2	21.0	29.5	8.2	3.5
Corporate	35.4	18.7	16.7	30.8	1.4	4.5	18.0	6.1	11.9	13.0	3.5	1.5
Trade association(c)	32.5	19.3	13.3	27.5	1.4	1.8	10.0	4.2	5.8	7.2	1.8	0.9
Labor	27.6	25.8	1.8	19.8	3.2		6.0	5.6	0.4	3.9	1.7	0.4
Nonconnected(d)	8.5	5.5	2.9	5.5	1.1		5.7	3.5	2.2	4.2	1.1	0.5

(a) Elections in which an incumbent did not seek re-election. (b) Includes other types of political action committees not shown separately. (c) Includes membership organizations and health organizations. (d) Represents "ideological" groups as well as other issue groups not necessarily ideological in nature.

TABLE 6
Political Party Financial Activity, by Major Political Party: 1981 to 1990

[In millions of dollars. Covers financial activity during 2-year calendar period indicated. Some political party financial activities, such as building funds and State and local election spending, are not reported to the source. Also excludes contributions earmarked to Federal candidates through the party organizations, since some of those funds never passed through the committees' accounts.]

Year and Type of Committee	DEMOCRATIC				REPUBLICAN			
	Receipts net (a)	Disbursements net (a)	Contributions to candidates	Monies spent on behalf of party's nominees(b)	Receipts net(a)	Disbursements net(a)	Contributions to candidates	Monies spent on behalf of party's nominees(b)
1981–82	39.3	40.1	1.7	3.3	215.0	214.0	5.6	14.3
1983–84	98.5	97.4	2.6	9.0	297.9	300.8	4.9	20.1
1985–86, total	64.8	65.9	1.7	9.0	255.2		3.4	14.3
National committee	17.2	17.4	(Z)	0.3	83.8	86.7	0.4	(Z)
Senatorial committee	13.4	13.5	0.6	6.1	84.4	83.7	0.6	10.0
Congressional committee	12.3	12.6	0.6	1.5	39.8	40.8	1.7	4.1
Conventions, other national	7.9	8.1	(Z)	–	0.2	0.2	–	–
State and local	14.0	14.3	0.5	1.0	47.0	47.4	0.8	0.3
1987–88, total	135.2	129.1	1.8	17.9	267.1	261.0	3.4	22.7
Senatorial committee	52.3	47.0	0.1	8.1	91.0	89.9	0.3	8.3
Congressional committee	12.5	12.5	0.7	2.4	34.7	33.7	1.6	4.1
Conventions, other national	19.2	19.2	–	–	9.6	9.6	–	–
State and local	35.0	34.1	0.6	1.2	65.9	64.5	0.7	0.1
1989–90, total	85.8	90.9	1.5	8.7	206.3	213.5	2.9	10.7
National committee	9.1	9.1	0.4	2.9	33.2	34.4	0.9	2.8
Senatorial committee	14.5	18.5	0.1	0.1	68.7	70.4	0.3	0.1
Congressional committee	17.5	17.6	0.4	4.5	65.1	67.6	0.7	7.7
Conventions, other national	8.8	9.2	–	–	–	–	–	–
State and local	35.8	36.4	0.5	1.2	39.3	41.1	1.0	0.2

– Represents zero. Z Less than $50,000. (a) Excludes monies transferred between committees. (b) Monies spent in the general election.

know, moreover, the identity of the large contributors to the party, and for this reason soft money can produce risks of corruption as well.

4.   Limits on PACs Lead to an Increase in Individual Expenditures— In the next few years, Congress may well impose limits on PACs, or even eliminate them altogether.[56] If it does so, there will be pressure for more in the way of both individual contributions and individual expenditures.[57] Limits or bans on PAC expenditures will increase the forms of financial help that Congress' original efforts in 1971 were specifically designed to limit. It is ironic but true that new legislation designed to counteract PACs will spur the very activity against which Congress initially sought to guard.

For reasons suggested above,[58] this development, even if ironic, may improve things overall. There is a good argument that PAC contributions are especially harmful to democratic processes, because they are particularly likely to be given with the specific purpose of influencing lawmakers. It is also the case that candidates who receive individual contributions are often unaware of the particular reason for the money, whereas PAC beneficiaries know exactly what reasons underlie any donation. For all these reasons, a shift from PACs to individual expenditures may be desirable.

On the other hand, PACs have some distinctive benefits as well. They provide a method by which individuals may band together in order to exercise political influence. Sometimes they offer a helpful aggregative mechanism of the kind that is plausibly salutary in a democracy. A shift from PACs to individual expenditures may be unfortunate insofar as it diminishes the power of politically concerned people to organize and pool their resources on behalf of their favored causes.

On balance, individual expenditures do seem preferable to PACs, because the most severe threats to the "quid pro quo" and public deliberation come from PAC money. Restrictions on PACs that move people in the direction of individual expenditures and contributions are therefore desirable. My point is only that there is a trade-off between the two.

5.   Limits on PACs Can Hurt Organized Labor and Minority Candidates.—Sometimes minority candidates can succeed only with the help of PACs specifically organized for their particular benefit. For this reason, PAC limits will in some circumstances diminish the power of minority candidates. The Congressional Black Caucus has expressed concerns over campaign finance regulation on this ground.[59] Similar results

---

56. Such measures are called for in the bills referred to *supra* notes 45–46.

57. Of course, some of these problems might be mitigated by a combination of limits on PACs and individual contributions.

58. *See supra* text accompanying notes 23–25.

59. *See* Tim Curran, *Campaign Finance Reform Bill Besieged by Four Separate Democratic Factions*, ROLL CALL, May 17, 1993, at 1, 20.

are possible for PACs organized to benefit women. PAC restrictions may also hurt organized labor. Currently labor PACs spend most of their money on individual candidates, especially incumbent Democrats.[60] By contrast, corporate PACs contribute about equally to Democrats and Republicans,[61] and give substantial sums to the parties rather than to individual candidates. A ban on PACs may therefore diminish the influence of labor unions without materially affecting corporate PACs.[62] Perhaps these effects are good or justified on balance. But many people who favor campaign finance regulation might be disturbed to see this effect.

6.   Limits on PACs May Increase Secret Gifts.—Many current interest groups appear unconcerned about PAC limits, even though their interests would appear to be jeopardized by the proposed limits.[63] Perhaps it will be easy for them to evade any such limits, especially by offering "soft money" and also by assembling large amounts as a result of contributions from unidentifiable sources. We lack detailed evidence on this issue, but there is reason to think that the concern is legitimate. It is possible that limits on PACs will make it harder to identify sources of money without materially decreasing special interest funding. The current proposals do not respond to this risk.

7.   Limits on Both PACs and Contributions Could Hinder Campaign Activity.—Most of the discussion thus far has been based on the assumption that campaign finance reform proposals would limit either PACs or individual contributions. In either case, limitations on one could lead to increased spending through the other. A third option might be to limit both PACs and individual contributions. But this option could quite possibly lead to a number of negative effects. If the limits were successful, campaign activity might be sharply limited as a whole.[64] Any such limit would raise First Amendment problems and perhaps compromise democratic government.[65] Alternatively, resources could be funneled into campaigns through "soft money," secret gifts, or other loopholes in the reforms.

---

60. See JOHN THEILMANN & AL WILHITE, DISCRIMINATION AND CONGRESSIONAL CAMPAIGN CONTRIBUTIONS 93 (1991).

61. See supra Table 3.

62. Of course labor strategies may shift with new campaign finance laws.

63. See Johnathon S. Cohn, Money Talks, Reform Walks, AM. PROSPECT, Fall 1993, at 61, 66.

64. See Gottlieb, supra note 47, at 213, 222 (limits on PACs and individual contributions could drastically reduce campaign activity).

65. See GARY C. JACOBSON, MONEY IN CONGRESSIONAL ELECTIONS 164 (1980) ("If competitive elections are an essential element of democracy—and it would be odd to argue that they are not—the extent of democratic competition depends on candidates' financial resources.").

B. Possible Strategies

What I have said thus far suggests considerable reason for caution about campaign finance proposals. It also suggests that those who design such proposals should be attentive to the risks of futile or self-defeating reform. I do not attempt here to describe a fully adequate regulatory system. But I will outline two possibilities that appear especially promising. Both of them respond to the largely unfortunate American experience with command-and-control regulation in the last generation. Such regulation—consisting of rigid mandates and flat bans—is peculiarly likely to be futile or self-defeating.[66] Mandates and bans invite efforts at circumvention. Because of their rigidity, they tend to have unintended adverse consequences; creative members of regulated classes are likely to come up with substitutes posing equal or greater risks.[67] To say this is not to say that mandates and bans are necessarily inferior to alternatives. But it is to say that we ought to explore approaches that make self-interested adaptation less likely.

1.   Incentives Rather Than Bans.—The *Buckley* Court was unwilling to accept a flat ban on expenditures. But it was quite hospitable to federal financing accompanied by viewpoint-neutral conditions-most notably a promise not to accept private money as a condition for receiving federal dollars.[68] This model of incentives rather than bans has a number of attractions. For one, it survives even the rigid constitutional scrutiny of *Buckley* itself.

The system of incentives-in the form of federal financing accompanied by a promise not to accept private money-responds to the deepest concerns of people who are skeptical of flat bans. Some people argue that the acquisition of private sums can be at least a crude way to register public enthusiasm for a candidate, and to enable dissidents and outsiders to overcome the advantages of incumbency. A system of incentives leaves the private remedy intact. At the same time, such a system can help counteract the distortions built into exclusive reliance on private contributions. It does so by allowing electoral competition from people who are not well-financed.[69]

---

66. *See* Richard B. Stewart, *Reconstitutive Law*, 46 Md. L. Rev. 86, 97–98 (1986); Cass R. Sunstein, *Administrative Substance*, 1991 Duke L.J. 607, 627–31.

67. *See* Ackerman & Stewart, *supra* note 8, at 182; Cass R. Sunstein, *Paradoxes of the Regulatory State*, 57 U. Chi. L. Rev. 407, 413–29 (1990).

68. *See* Buckley v. Valeo, 424 U.S. 1, 85–97 (1976).

69. Because legitimate justifications were at work, the campaign finance system with such strings attached should not be regarded as including an unconstitutional condition. On this point, the *Buckley* Court was quite right. *See id.* at 57 n.65.

To be sure, some people think that full federal funding is the best route for the future.[70] But a system of incentives promoting public financing is more likely to be constitutional. Full federal funding would apparently foreclose private expenditures, in violation of *Buckley*; a system of incentives does not eliminate private expenditures. Such a system allows the private check to continue to exist, a strategy that poses certain risks, but that has benefits as well. Finally, a system of incentives accomplishes many (if not all) of the goals of full public funding. It does this by encouraging candidates not to rely on private funds and by ensuring that people unable to attract money are not placed at a special disadvantage.

A system of incentives could take various forms. Adapting the model upheld in *Buckley*, the government might adopt a system of optional public financing, accompanied by (1) a promise not to accept or to use private money as a condition for receiving public funds and (2) a regime in which public subsidies are provided to help candidates to match all or a stated percentage of the expenditures of their privately financed opponents. Under (2), a candidate could elect to use private resources, but the government would ensure that her opponent would not be at a substantial disadvantage. Of course any such system would raise many questions. We would, for example, have to decide which candidates would qualify for support, and there is a risk that people would be unfairly excluded. We would also have to decide what sorts of disparities would be tolerable between candidates raising substantial private funds and candidates relying on government. I suggest only that it is worthwhile to explore a system in which candidates are encouraged but not required to accept only public funds, on the theory that such a system would be less vulnerable to the various risks that I have described in this essay.

2.   Vouchers.—An alternative approach has been suggested by Bruce Ackerman.[71] Ackerman argues for an innovative voucher system, in which voters would be given a special card—citizen vouchers in the form of red, white, and blue money—to be used to finance political campaigns. Under this system, regular money could not be used at all. Candidates could attract citizen vouchers, but they could not use cash. The goal would be to split the political and economic spheres sharply, so as to ensure that resources accumulated in the economic sphere could not be used for political advantage. Ackerman's approach is therefore closely connected to the goal of preventing economic inequalities—fully acceptable in the American tradition—from becoming political in nature.

Obviously a system of this kind could not be implemented simply. But it might have many advantages. Like any voucher system, such an ap-

---

70. *See, e.g.*, Raskin & Bonifaz, *supra* note 48, at 1189–1203.

71. *See* Bruce A. Ackerman, *Crediting the Voters: A New Beginning for Campaign Finance*, AM. PROSPECT, Spring 1993, at 71.

proach would reduce some of the problems posed by centralized, bureaucratic control of finances and elections. The requirement that candidates use a special kind of "money" could much simplify administration and to some extent make it self-implementing. At the same time, the system would be ideally suited to promoting political equality, and it could do this without threatening to diminish aggregate levels of political discussion.[72] Compared to the approach in *Buckley*, a voucher system would leave candidates and citizens quite free to take and give as they choose; but what would be taken and given would not be ordinary money, and would be understood to have limited functions.

The voucher system would not be perfect. There would be a risk of evasion here as well. It would not be simple to police the boundary between vouchers and ordinary money. Moreover, the line between campaign expenditures and usual political speech—which would be unaffected by the proposal—is not crisp and simple. The flat ban on the use of ordinary money could raise constitutional and policy objections. Perhaps the ban would run afoul of *Buckley*, though I do not think that it should.[73] A voucher system could also create distinctive implementation problems. A bureaucratic apparatus would be necessary to provide the vouchers, to decide on their aggregate amount, and to dispense them in the first instance. A voucher system might not sufficiently promote the goal of political deliberation, for candidates would be highly dependent on private support. But no system is perfect. Because a voucher system would so sharply separate the economic and political spheres, and allow intensities of interest to be reflected in campaigns, it certainly warrants serious consideration.

Conclusion

In principle, there are strong arguments for campaign finance limits, especially if these are taken as part of a general effort to renew the old aspiration of deliberative democracy. In some respects, the Supreme Court's decision in *Buckley* is the modern analogue to *Lochner v. New York,* offering an adventurous interpretation of the Constitution so as to invalidate a redistributive measure having and deserving broad democratic support. The special problem with *Buckley* is that it permits economic inequalities to be translated into political inequalities, and this is hardly a

---

72. This depends on the assumption that the allocation of vouchers would be designed with high levels of aggregate speech in mind.

73. *See supra* text accompanying notes 40–41; *see also* Ackerman, *supra* note 71, at 77–78.

goal of the constitutional structure.[74] Properly designed campaign finance measures ought to be seen as fully compatible with the system of free expression, insofar as those measures promote the goal of ensuring a deliberative democracy among political (though not economic) equals.

There is, however, good reason for the Court and for citizens in general to distrust any campaign finance system enacted by Congress, whose institutional self-interest makes this an especially worrisome area for national legislation. Moreover, the argument from principle does not suggest that any particular system will make things better rather than worse. A number of imaginable systems would be futile or self-defeating, largely because of unintended (or perhaps intended) bad consequences. In this essay, I have tried to identify some of the most important risks.

My general conclusion is that dissatisfaction with *Buckley*, and enthusiasm for the goals of political equality and political deliberation, ought not to deflect attention from some insistently empirical questions about the real-world effects of campaign finance legislation. Any policy reforms will have unanticipated consequences, some of them counter-productive. Private adaptation to public-spirited reform is inevitable. In this context, our task is not merely to debate the theoretical issues, but also to identify the practical risks as systematically as possible, and to favor initiatives that seem most likely to promote their salutary goals.[75]

---

74. I do not suggest that courts should invalidate a system that allows economic inequalities to become political inequalities; assessment of such matters is generally beyond judicial competence. I suggest only that well-designed campaign finance regulations are highly compatible with some defining constitutional commitments.

75. The point suggests the need for public and private monitoring mechanisms, so as to overcome the predictable problems of implementation.

Format Restrictions on Televised Political Advertising: Elevating Political Debate Without Suppressing Free Speech

Timothy J. Moran

The First Amendment...is not the guardian of unregulated talkativeness...
What is essential is not that everyone shall speak, but that everything
worth saying shall be said.[1]

Introduction

Contemporary political advertising presents as apparent dilemma for a
society striving to achieve the twin first amendment goals of robust unin-
hibited debate and informed self-government. Traditional free speech
principles hold that political speech, particularly when made in connection with elections, should be completely free of governmental restraint.
However, many observers contend that the nature of political advertising
impedes self-government by creating advertising that at best lacks substance and at worst obscures and distorts crucial issues.

This Article analyzes current proposals that would elevate political debate by regulating the format of political advertising. It concludes that
proposals to restrict political advertising to a narrow issue-oriented format violate the first amendment because they substantially reduce the
quantity and communicative impact of political speech. However, similar
goals can be achieved by directly subsidizing political advertising-by
vouchers or the award of free air time-and by conditioning the receipt of

---

1. ALEXANDER MEIKLEJOHN, POLITICAL FREEDOM: THE CONSTITUTIONAL POWERS
OF THE PEOPLE 26 (1960).

this benefit on the candidate's agreement to conform to an issue-oriented format of suitable length.

This Article is divided into three parts. Part I summarizes what political and media observers have found about political advertising. It concludes that contemporary advertising does not promote a meaningful discussion of issues and may distort them. However, research indicates that a "talking-heads" format, in which the candidate simply addresses the camera without the benefit of music or additional images, tends to produce more informative and issue-oriented advertising. Part I concludes by summarizing proposals to make advertising more informative and issue oriented.

Part II proposes a constitutional framework for analyzing format restrictions on political advertising. It argues that the extent of infringement on individual autonomy-the individual's interest in advertising in whatever manner she chooses-is largely irrelevant to a proper first amendment analysis. Instead, a restriction should be judged by the degree to which it advances the government's interest in informed and rational political debate without substantially reducing the quantity of speech, decreasing its communicative potential, inhibiting certain views, or creating the opportunity for dangerous governmental interference with political speech. A restriction that advances the government's interest in informed political debate and is narrowly tailored to minimize the above threats to free expression is constitutional.

Part III analyzes in depth four proposals to regulate the form of a candidate's political advertising. One proposal would require that the candidate appear personally in any advertisement that attacks another candidate. A second proposal would require that all advertising conform to a talking-heads format. Part III argues that both of those proposals are unconstitutional because they curtail the airing of a substantial degree of political speech that can provide important information to voters and increase the voters' participation in the political process. A third proposal, strengthening disclosure and identification requirements, probably is constitutional if the requirements are narrowly tailored. However, it is doubtful that this proposal would significantly raise the level of public debate. The most promising proposal is to add issue-oriented advertising to the political marketplace by giving candidates free advertising, through either broadcast vouchers or free air time. Candidates who accepted this benefit would be required to produce advertising that uses a talking-heads format with a minimum length suitable to the development and discussion of issues. Because candidates would remain free to use their own funds to produce advertising of their choice, regardless of whether they accepted the free advertising, this subsidy proposal would not suppress any speech. This proposal is, therefore, constitutional.

* * *

III. The Constitutionality of Proposed Format Restrictions on Political Advertising

Applying the previously discussed criteria to the proposed restrictions yields a limited but adequate opportunity for the government to elevate political debate through format restrictions. Proposals that mandate format restrictions for all advertisements-the personal appearance and the talking-heads requirements-are unconstitutional because they would suppress a significant amount of speech that can be quite effective at communicating ideas and information to voters. Narrowly tailored disclosure requirements are probably constitutional. However, they probably would not improve significantly the level of public debate. Most promising are proposals to provide candidates with free advertising, subject to format restrictions likely to encourage candidates to make issue-oriented advertisements. These proposals would add a particular kind of advertising to the political marketplace without curtailing other modes of expression favored by candidates.

A. Personal Presentation of Negative Advertising

Requiring a candidate to personally present negative campaign advertisements is inconsistent with freedom of expression and illustrates the potential dangers of permitting format restrictions by an incumbent government.[204] Its most obvious flaw is that it is not neutral with respect to the viewpoint of the advertisement. It singles out speech that is critical of a candidate and subjects it to greater restrictions than speech that endorses a candidate. Candidates who engage in such "positive" advertising are free to use whatever media enhancements and third-party spokespersons that they desire, while a negative attack must be made "in person."

The effect of this proposal would be to eliminate the most widely used and most effective negative advertisements because placing the candidate in the advertisement would often blunt the ads' effectiveness or risk backfiring on the sponsoring candidate.[205] Most negative advertising operates

---

* * *

204. Most commentators who have examined the personal presentation requirement have concluded that it is unconstitutional. *E.g.*, Scott M. Matheson, *Federal Legislation to Elevate and Enlighten Political Debate: A Letter and Report to the 102d Congress About Constitutional Policy*, 7 J.L. & POL. 73, 127-29, 132 (1990).

205. *See* MONTAGUE KERN, 30-SECOND POLITICS: POLITICAL ADVERTISING IN THE EIGHTIES 78 (1989).

by associating the opponent with something perceived to be bad in order to create fear, uncertainty, and anxiety about that candidate.[206] Generally the technique used is to impose the picture of the favored candidate only at the end of the advertisement, so that the candidate emerges as the resolution to the fear, uncertainty, or anxiety that is associated with the opponent.[207] If the candidate appears visually in a negative advertisement, she risks being associated with the problem rather than emerging as its solution.[208]

The proposal also would necessarily prevent or greatly impede the use of a number of popular techniques used in negative advertising. These include the use of the candidate's family, the use of an actor or other celebrity, or the use of constituents from the opponent's district to criticize her record.[209] Also impeded would be the use of visual images that may be highly relevant to a pressing issue, such as a war[210] or the need for environmental controls.[211] Significantly, the proposal would impede or eliminate "neutral reporter" advertisements, which employ visuals and an off-screen announcer to compare the opponent's record or positions with those of the favored candidate.[212] Such advertisements, while less frequent now than in the past, can provide valuable information to the voter in a rational manner.[213] Finally, research has shown that the techniques used in current negative political advertising can be quite effective in communi-

---

206. *Id.* at 102-107. This is particularly the case with what Kern calls "hard sell" negative emotional advertising, which employs threatening music, dark colors, and harsh sound effects to create a particularly intense feeling of dread. *Id.*

207. *Id.* at 33. This technique borrows from the "get 'em sick, then get 'em well" theory of commercial advertising, in which a product is presented as the solution to a problem which the consumer is shown to have. *Id.* at 30.

208. *Id.* at 79.

209. *Clean Campaign Act of 1989: Hearings on S. 999 Before the Subcomm. on Communications of the Senate Comm. on Commerce, Science, and Transportation,* 101st Cong. § 22 [hereinafter *1989 Hearings*]. (Statement of Barry Lynn, Legislative Counsel, American Civil Liberties Union).

210. *E.g.,* MICHAEL PFAU & HENRY C. KENSKI, ATTACK POLITICS: STRATEGY AND DEFENSE (1990). (an Eisenhower ad).

211. Dwinell, *Talking Heads Ignores Body and Soul,* CAMPAIGNS & ELECTIONS Jan.-Feb. 1989 (arguing that candidates should be able to demonstrate their stand on environmental issues with images of nature, such as a beach).

212. KERN, *supra* note 205, at 49; Jamieson, *The Evolution of Political Advertising in America, in* NEW PERSPECTIVES ON POLITICAL ADVERTISING 18-19 (Lynda Lee Kaid, Dan Nimmo, Keith R. Sanders eds. 1986).

213. Jamieson, *supra* note 212, at 18-19 ("[N]eutral reporter ads...are rational political ads that offer factual data, invite or stipulate a conclusion, and warrant that conclusion.").

cating information to voters and interesting them in the political process. Voters tend to remember negative advertisements longer than positive ones precisely because the negative advertisements are hard hitting, entertaining, and stylistically interesting.[214] Thus, the effect of a personal presentation of negative campaigning requirement would be to render less effective advertising that is critical of a candidate.

There is no legitimate government interest in suppressing or inhibiting negative advertising. The increasing prevalence of negative advertising[215] has prompted considerable criticism from the popular press and from candidates.[216] From the standpoint of providing information to voters, however, this criticism is probably unjustified. Although negative advertising can be criticized for all the reasons outlined in Part I, there is no indication that negative advertising per se is less informative or provides a less-meaningful discussion of issues than positive advertising. Indeed, because negative advertising often focuses on specific positions or actions of an opponent, negative advertisements may well be more informative than positive advertisements.[217]

Particularly troubling is the fact that negative advertising has traditionally been employed more by challengers than by incumbents.[218] This is because the incumbent can often afford to rest on name identification, while the challenger can best attract attention initially by tarnishing the incumbent's image. Thus, a personal presentation requirement might operate to make it more difficult for challengers to win and to dampen enthusiasm for incumbents.[219] This is intolerable, since first amendment protections are

---

214. PFAU & KENSKI, *supra* note 210, at 2-4.

215. *Id.* at 13-59 (noting a significant growth in negative advertising); MICHAEL L. YOUNG, THE AMERICAN DICTIONARY OF CAMPAIGNS AND ELECTIONS 60-61 (1987) (One out of two candidate advertisements is negative, up from one out of five in 1962, and 80% of advertisements sponsored by independent groups are negative.); Robert Guskind & Jerry Hagstrom, *In the Gutter,* NAT'L J., Nov. 5, 1988, at 2782 (noting increase in negative advertising on state level).

216. *Much Ado About Ads Knocking Candidates,* BROADCASTING, Sept. 16, 1985, at 64.

217. Garramone, Atrim, Pinkleton & Cole, *Effects of Negative Political Advertising on the Political Process,* 34 J. OF BROADCAST AND ELECTRONIC MEDIA 299, 300-01 (1990); Joslyn, *Political Advertising and the Meaning of Elections, in* NEW PERSPECTIVES, *supra* note 212 at 160.

218. PFAU & KENSKI, *supra* note 210, at 13-60. This trend may be changing. Guskind & Hagstrom, *supra* note 215 (noting incumbents are beginning to use negative advertising more at the outset of a campaign).

219. This had led some to charges that the Clean Campaign Act is intended to protect incumbents from challengers and increase their chances of remaining in office. *Clean Campaign Act of 1985: Hearings on S.1310 Before the Subcomm. on Communications*

most necessary for speech that is critical of the status quo and that advocates change.[220] Negative advertising can force a candidate to face certain issues or defend aspects of her record that she would rather avoid. Negative advertising can thus help keep an incumbent accountable for the positions that she has taken and her acts in office. For these reasons, any proposal that would curtail the effectiveness of negative advertising, as would the personal presentation requirement, should be held unconstitutional.

B. Talking Heads

A requirement that all advertisements have a talking-heads format is more evenhanded than the personal presentation requirement but is still constitutionally troubling. The case most pertinent to this proposal is *Zauderer*.[221] In *Zauderer*, the state sought to prohibit the use of pictures in advertising because the use of visual images "creates unacceptable risks that the public will be misled, manipulated, or confused."[222] The state argued that it would be impossible to police deceptive visual advertising on a case-by-case basis

> because the advertiser is skilled in subtle uses of illustrations to play on the emotions of his audience and convey false impressions. Because illustra-

---

of the Senate Comm. on Commerce, Science, and Transportation, 99th Cong. 80, 101, 121 (1985) [hereinafter *1985 hearings*]. (Statements of Terry Dolan, Chairman, National Conservative Political Action Committee, and Robert Heckman, Chairman, Fund for a Conservative Majority).

220. *See* New York Times v. Sullivan, 376 U.S. 254, 270 (1964) ("Debate on public issues...may well involve vehement, caustic, and sometimes unpleasantly sharp attacks on government and public officials."); Vincent Blasi, *The Checking Value in First Amendment Theory*, 1977 AM. B. FOUND. RES. J. 521.

221. 471 U.S. 626. *Zauderer* is part of a line of cases establishing fairly strong first amendment protection for commercial speech but allowing the state to regulate speech that is inherently misleading or that has been used to mislead or deceive consumers. *See* Peel v. Attorney Registration and Disciplinary Comm., 110 S. Ct. 2281, 2287 (1990); *In re* R.M.J., 455 U.S. 191 (1982); Bates v. State Bar of Ariz., 433 U.S. 350 (1977); Virginia Citizens Consumer Council v. Virginia Bd. of Pharmacy, 425 U.S. 748 (1976); *see also* Central Hudson Gas & Elec. Corp. v. Public Service Comm'n, 447 U.S. 557, 566 (1980) (State may not regulate truthful advertising concerning lawful activity unless regulation directly advances a substantial governmental interest and is no more extensive than necessary to serve that interest.). Commercial speech has been defined narrowly to include only speech that does no more than propose a commercial transaction. *See* Bigelow v. Virginia, 421 U.S. 809, 818-21 (1975). Political advertising, therefore, cannot be considered commercial speech, but the analogy is still helpful because if a format restriction would not survive scrutiny under commercial speech doctrine, it would also be unconstitutional under the more rigorous protection accorded political speech.

222. 471 U.S. at 648.

tions may produce their effects by operating on a subconscious level, the State argue[d], it [would] be difficult for the State to point to a particular illustration and prove that it is misleading or manipulative.[223]

The state, therefore, argued that a prophylactic bar of visual advertising was justified.[224] The Court rejected this argument, noting the advertisement in question was not deceptive and the state had presented no evidence that it could not continue to regulate visual advertising on a case-by-case basis for deception, as it already did for other attorney advertisements and as the Federal Trade Commission (FTC) did for visual advertisements.[225]

In an earlier case, however, the Court had suggested that the "special problems of advertising on the electronic broadcast media, will warrant special consideration."[226] Expanding on this suggested distinction, three states have restricted the use of visual images in advertising by attorneys on television, requiring instead a format thought more conducive to conveying information.[227] The courts have upheld such restrictions, reasoning that the unrestricted use of television would probably produce advertisements more likely to appeal to a person's emotions or fears than provide the information necessary to make an intelligent choice regarding the selection of an attorney.[228] In fact, the Supreme Court dismissed an Iowa

---

223. *Id.*

224. *Id.*

225. *Id.* at 648-49.

226. *Bates,* 433 U.S. at 384; *see also Zauderer,* 471 U.S. at 673 n.1 (O'Connor, J. concurring in part, concurring in the judgment in part, and dissenting in part).

227. The Florida Bar: Petition to Amend Rules Regulating the Florida Bar-Advertising Issues, 571 So. 2d 451, 461 (Fla. 1990) (Television advertisements may not contain dramatizations, all information must be articulated by a single voice, and only lawyers who will be providing the advertised services may appear in the ad.); Iowa Code of Professional Responsibility for Lawyers DR 2-101(5) (West 1991) (Television advertisements for attorney services may contain no visual display except printed words articulated by a single nondramatic voice and no background sound.); New Jersey Rules of Professional Conduct rule 7.2(a) (West 1991) (Television advertisements for attorney services may not contain drawings, animation, dramatization, music, or lyrics.); *see also* Baker v. Registered Dentists of Okla., 543 F. Supp. 1177, 1181 (W.D. Okla. 1981) (striking down ban on television advertisements by attorneys but noting misleading nature of medium and suggesting abuses might be better corrected by prohibiting celebrity endorsements).

228. Bishop v. Committee on Professional Ethics, 521 F. Supp. 1219, 1224-25 (S.D. Iowa 1981), *vacated as moot,* 686 F.2d 1278 (8th Cir. 1982); *Florida Bar,* 571 So. 2d at 457-58. Petition of Felmeistler & Isaacs, 518 A.2d 188, 201-02 (N.J. 1986); Committee on Professional Ethics v. Humphrey, 377 N.W.2d 643 (Iowa 1985), *appeal dismissed,* 475 U.S. 1114 (1985), *reh'g denied,* 476 U.S. 1165 (1986).

case upholding the most stringent of these restrictions for want of a substantial federal question,[229] an action that is generally treated as equivalent to a judgment on the merits.[230]

These cases suggest a coherent argument for mandating similar restrictions for political advertising.[231] If the premise of these states' regulations is correct, restricting the use of images and dramatizations will tend to prohibit advertising that primarily exploits emotions or stylistically promotes a candidate, while permitting advertisements that tend to be informational. Certainly, there is at least as strong an interest in encouraging advertising that provides information to voters in an election as to consumers of legal services. Furthermore, televised advertisements arguably are more likely to mislead voters and obfuscate issues than the print advertising protected from regulation by *Zauderer*; while print advertising is fixed in a tangible medium that can be studied and considered, television images are by their nature transient and therefore may be less susceptible to rational consideration.[232]

Finally, a talking-heads requirement appears to be the most narrowly tailored way of prohibiting manipulative and substanceless political advertising. In *Zauderer*, the main reason the Court gave for striking the state's prohibition of pictures was that the state could instead regulate false and deceptive advertising on a case-by-case basis. Such case-by-case adjudication is impossible with respect to political advertising. While commercial advertising can be regulated if it has a tendency to mislead, only intentional or reckless falsity can be regulated if the speech is political. Any more comprehensive case-by-case policing of political advertising would necessarily involve repeated application of indefinite standards, which would disrupt the electoral process and deter campaign speech.

---

229. *Humphrey*, 377 N.W.2d 643, *appeal dismissed*, 475 U.S. 1114 (1985). Prior to this dismissal, the Court had vacated an earlier Iowa Supreme Court decision with the same result for reconsideration in light of *Zauderer*. Committee on Professional Ethics v. Humphrey, 355 N.W.2d 565 (Iowa 1985), *vacated*, 472 U.S. 1004 (1985).

230. Hicks v. Miranda, 422 U.S. 332, 344-45 (1975). However, such a disposition is probably not entitled to the same precedential weight as a decision on the merits. Metromedia, Inc. v. City of San Diego, 453 U.S. 490, 500 (1981). In fact, one commentator has suggested that a dismissal for lack of a substantial federal question is entitled to scarcely more weight than a denial of certiorari. Winnick, Comment, *The Precedential Weight of a Dismissal by the Supreme Court for Want of a Substantial Federal Question: Some Implications of* Hicks v. Miranda, 76 COLUM. L. REV. 508, 511 n.19, 518-19 (1976).

231. *See* Winsbro, Comment, *Misrepresentation in Political Advertising: The Role of Legal Sanctions*, 36 EMORY L.J. 853 (1987) (arguing that a talking- heads requirement for televised political advertisements is constitutional).

232. *See Humphrey*, 377 N.W.2d at 646.

The scope for permissible case-by-case adjudication is so narrow that it could not even prevent misleading and deceptive advertising, much less make advertising more informed. By contrast, a clear, uniform requirement that all advertisements be of a minimum length and contain only a candidate addressing the camera would be unambiguous and easy to administer.

While the case for requiring a talking-heads format for all televised political advertising cannot be lightly dismissed, a close analysis reveals that, whatever its merits for attorney advertising, such a restriction would be intolerable for political advertising because it would sharply curtail the quantity and the communicative impact of political speech. First, it is not clear that a talking-heads requirement would necessarily permit full exposition of the ideas that are most crucial in an election. The idea that a war engaged in by the government is unjust or unwise, or that more environmental controls are needed, can often be expressed more vividly in images than in words.[233] This is so not only because the picture conveys more emotion, but also because it more clearly evokes the reality of war or of pollution than any sterile recitation of statistics.

Second, the advertisements that are common today are chosen because they are effective at attracting the attention of voters and being remembered. Many advertisements convey valuable information to voters. Others may initially attract voters' attention so that they are drawn to follow the election and perhaps investigate the issues and the candidates more closely. While few would dispute that many advertisements do not convey the information voters need, the fact that they convey any information at all or interest voters even minimally is significant.[234] If the advertisements most likely to attract attention are effectively banned, the communicative impact of the relatively dull advertisements that remain may be significantly less.[235] Furthermore, making advertisements less visual will be most likely to prevent advertisements from reaching those who are poor, uneducated, or illiterate, persons who already vote in disproportionate numbers. This same concern has been expressed with respect to attorney advertisements. Thus, the Model Rules and the vast majority of states permit unrestricted television ads on the theory that more

233. *See supra* text accompanying notes 197-99.

234. *Cf. Bates*, 433 U.S. at 374 ("Advertising does not provide a complete foundation on which to select an attorney. But is seems peculiar to deny the consumer, on the ground that the information is incomplete, at least some of the relevant information needed to reach an informed choice.").

235. In *Zauderer*, for example, the attorney's illustrated advertisement generated over 200 inquires while an unillustrated version attracted none. *The Supreme Court-1984 Term, Leading Cases*, 99 HARV. L. REV. 193, 198-99 (1985).

information will reach people who need access to legal services, particularly people of modest income.[236]

Third, there is a possibility that such restrictions would result in significantly fewer political advertisements.[237] Some feel this would be beneficial because it would force candidates to reach the voters in more meaningful ways, such as by public speeches and face-to-face campaigning.[238] However, a regime that could result in significantly less speech has to be regarded with some skepticism. There is some indication, for example, that the increased importance of the broadcast media in political campaigns has made the political parties more democratic, less secret, and more accountable to the public.[239] A significant reduction in the influence of political advertising might well have adverse effects on the participation and influence of the public in election campaigns.

Restricting political advertising to a talking-heads format, therefore, raises significant free speech problems. It could impair the effective communication of important ideas, make advertisements less likely to reach and involve voters, and substantially reduce the overall quantity of political advertising. Such eventualities make a talking-heads restriction on political advertising both unwise and unconstitutional.

C. Disclosure and Identification Requirements

The government's interest in keeping candidates and independent groups accountable for their advertisements can best be served through narrowly tailored disclosure and identification requirements. The government has an interest in voters knowing the source of a communication so they can better judge its message.[240] The Court has generally upheld disclosure requirements that provide valuable information to the public.[241]

A valid concern is that a disclosure requirement might disparage a particular message, communicate to others that they should not give it weight, or give a false impression. In *Riley v. National Federation for the*

---

236. *See* MODEL RULES OF PROFESSIONAL CONDUCT, Rule 7.2 cmt. (1983).

237. EDWIN DIAMOND & STEPHEN BATES, THE SPOT: THE RISE OF POLITICAL ADVERTISING ON TELEVISION 383-84 (rev. ed. 1988).

238. *Id.* at 384-87.

239. *Id.* at 373.

240. *See Messe v. Keene*, 481 U.S. 465, 478 (1987).

241. *Messe*, 481 U.S. 465 (upholding statutory scheme that labeled certain materials produced by a foreign government "political propaganda"); *Zauderer*, 471 U.S. at 650-53 (State could require attorney advertisements to state that clients might be liable for litigation costs, even if their suit was unsuccessful.); Buckley v. Valeo, 424 U.S. 1, 60-84 (1976) (per curiam) (upholding requirement that candidates reveal size and source of contributions).

Blind,[242] the Court struck down a requirement that professional fund raisers, when conducting solicitation drives, disclose at the beginning to every solicitation for a charity the average percentage of gross receipts actually turned over to the charity by the fund raisers for all charitable solicitations conducted in the state in the past year. The Court noted that such a requirement would tend to dissuade potential donors or encourage them to view the fund raisers with suspicion before the fund raiser had a chance to discuss the charity.[243] More importantly, the Court observed, the required disclosure was misleading because it gave the impression that there was something corrupt about using a professional fund raiser or that a charity received no benefit from using a professional fund raiser. Neither was necessarily true, since a professional fund raiser helped a charity in making more people aware of its activities.[244] If the state was concerned with disclosing to donors that some of their donations would go to the fund raiser rather than to the charity, the Court indicated that it could accomplish this by requiring that fund raisers disclose their professional status.[245]

This doctrine indicates that the question of whether a disclosure requirement is constitutional has no talismanic answer. The *Riley* Court suggested one when it stated that "[m]andating speech that a speaker would not otherwise make necessarily alters the content of the speech. [It is] therefore...a content-based regulation of speech."[246] However, this statement is puzzling in light of the almost casual manner in which the Court upheld disclosure requirements in *Buckley, Zauderer*, and *Riley*. The fact that a disclosure is mandated in the context of speech cannot alone make it virtually unconstitutional per se. Rather, the outcomes of the cases suggest that a more fact-based inquiry is appropriate. If a disclosure requirement merely provides pertinent information, it should be upheld. However, if it tends to interfere with the content of the speech in

---

242. 487 U.S. 781 (1988).

243. *Id.* at 799-800.

244. *Id.* at 798-99. Lower courts have similarly struck requirements that a fund raiser disclose the percentage of gross receipts that will be retained by the fund raiser on the ground that the requirements wrongly presume that a charity obtains no benefit from the money it pays to fund raisers. Indiana Voluntary Firemen's Ass'n v. Pearson, 700 F. Supp. 421, 442-44 (S.D. Ind. 1988); People v. French, 762 P.2d 1369, 1374-75 (Colo. 1988). *But see* City of El Paso v. El Paso Jaycees, 758 S.W.2d 789 (Tex. App. 1988) (upholding requirement that fund raiser disclose approximate percentage of funds that will go to fund raiser).

245. *Riley*, 487 U.S. at 799 n.11. At least one court has upheld a state regulation to this effect. *Pearson*, 700 F. Supp. at 442.

246. *Riley*, 487 U.S. at 795.

such a way as to unfairly suggest that its message should be devalued or regarded with skepticism, it is more suspect. A disclosure requirement is not constitutionally troublesome because it intrudes upon the autonomy of the speaker. It is constitutionally troublesome because of the degree to which the requirement hinders the communication of information and ideas to others.

Applying these criteria, the case for more stringent disclosure requirements for advertising sponsored by independent groups is fairly straightforward. The existing identification requirements are quite modest.[247] In practice, independent groups make them so small that advertisements will sometimes be wrongly attributed to a candidate to her detriment.[248] There is also the possibility that an independent group will take advantage of the group's relative anonymity to cover up its biases regarding the issue addressed by the advertisement.[249]

The Court has indicated that at times a group has a first amendment right to remain anonymous when disseminating political messages.[250] However, such decisions rest on the need to protect unpopular groups from persecution.[251] Requiring disclosure of the source of campaign materials serves the important governmental interest of providing pertinent information to voters, while still leaving open the opportunity for persecuted groups anonymously to protest the government's policies or oppressive practices through pamphleteering or other speech not connected with an election.[252] It is not surprising, therefore, that the courts have uniformly upheld the federal identification requirements for campaign advertisements. The courts have reasoned that the peculiar interest in preserving accountability in election campaigns justifies an identifica-

---

247. 2 U.S.C. 441d(a)(3) (1988) (Ad must "clearly state the name of the person who paid for the communication and state that the communication is not authorized by any candidate or candidate's committee.").

248. Mitchell Gaynor, Note, *Curbing Injurious PAC Support Through* 2 U.S.C. § 441d, 35 HASTINGS L.J. 869, 869-70, 874-76 (1984).

249. In Massachusetts, for example, the utilities who control the Seabrook nuclear power plant produced television advertisements advocating nuclear power, under the purported sponsorship of the umbrella organization, the Coalition for Reliable Energy (CRE). Critics charged that the advertisements gave the false impression that CRE was a disinterested grass roots organization. *See Massachusetts Lawsuit Assails Seabrook Ads.* N.Y. TIMES, Mar. 15, 1987, at § 1, 42.

250. Talley v. California, 362 U.S. 60 (1960) (striking state law requiring all handbills to contain name and address of person or group which prepared and distributed it); NAACP v. Alabama, 357 U.S. 449 (1958) (striking down requirement that NAACP disclose names of its members).

251. *Talley,* 362 U.S. at 64-65; *NAACP v. Alabama,* 357 U.S. at 462-63.

252. United States v. Insco, 365 F. Supp. 1308, 1312 (M.D. Fla. 1973).

tion requirement for campaign speech and that, in any case, groups who have access to the television media and can afford to advertise there are not the kind of groups that are so subject to persecution that an absolute right to anonymity is required.[253]

The specific proposals regarding independent advertising still raise constitutional problems. The requirement that the source of the message be broadcast continuously and take up a certain percentage of the screen could blunt the impact of the advertisement and distract the viewer. It also might convey implicitly to the viewer that there was something wrong with an advertisement that was not affiliated with a candidate. The government's interest in disclosing the source of the advertisements could probably be adequately accomplished by requiring a full-screen announcement at the end of the advertisement. Even better, the announcement could inform viewers that further information about the group was available by writing to or calling a specified address or number.[254] These changes would ensure that valuable information is provided to voters, without affecting the substantive content of the advertisements.

The proposed requirement that the candidate appear at the beginning or end of every advertisement raises slightly different concerns. Ensuring that viewers are informed that the candidate is responsible for the advertisement could probably be accomplished by requiring a prominent picture of the candidate with a statement that the candidate or candidate's campaign committee paid for the advertisement.[255] However, the purpose is not to identify the source of the advertising[256] but to link the candidate firmly to the advertisement. Research indicates that in time viewers will tend to disassociate the content of an advertisement from its source.[257] As a result, candidates and advertisers may feel that they are not fully accountable for the advertisements. Advertisers may be more careless about making false and deceptive statements, and candidates may permit such

---

253. *Id.;* United States v. Scott, 195 F. Supp. 440 (D.N.D. 1961).

254. *Cf.* Telco Communication, Inc. v. Carbaugh, 885 F.2d 1225, 1231 (4th Cir. 1989) (upholding statute requiring professional solicitors to disclose in writing that financial statements for the previous fiscal year are available from the state consumer affairs office), *cert. denied,* 110 S. Ct. 1923 (1990).

255. 42 U.S.C. § 441d(a)(1) requires advertisements sponsored by a candidate or a campaign committee to clearly state who paid for the advertisement. However, in practice consultants often attempt to make the reference to advertising sponsorship so fleeting that most viewers might not notice it. *See* S. 521, Campaign Advertising and Disclosure Act of 1991, S. Rep. No. 59, 102d Cong. (1991).

256. Indeed, it appears that voters are likely to assume that every advertisement endorsing a particular candidate is sponsored by the candidate.

257. Pfau & Kenski, *supra* note 210, at xiii.

carelessness by allowing their media advisers to distribute advertisements without personally approving them. Requiring a brief appearance by the candidate, it is thought, will encourage candidates to personally monitor advertisements that will be firmly linked to them. A candidate's campaign generally knows the most about the claims that are made; thus, increased monitoring inside the campaign will make it more likely that the statements in the advertisement will be true.

It is disconcerting that the candidate identification proposal is motivated in part by hostility to negative advertising.[258] However, as long as the candidate would have the option of placing the appearance at the end of the ad, it would not deter negative advertising. Most advertisements usually do refer to the favored candidate at the end after the attack on the opponent, in order to present the candidate as the resolution to the problems and dangers associated with the opponent.[259] Furthermore, the appearance would not affect the content of the advertisement any more than do the present identification requirements. The one thing the candidate would be unable to do would be to focus entirely on her opponent without conjuring up her own image. However, the interest in accountability and in ensuring that voters are reminded of the importance and consequences of their decision—namely that one candidate will take the office and the others will not—would seem to justify a candidate identification requirement.

In sum, disclosure and identification requirements are constitutional so long as they are narrowly tailored either to provide information to voters or to link advertisements to the candidate who authorized them. Proposals that do this, without changing the message or diminishing the effectiveness of the ads, are constitutional. Disclosure and identification requirements, however, will do little to improve the level of public debate during elections. Even if they are completely successful, they will deter, at most, false statements and inform voters as to the interests and motivations of the independent groups participating in the political process. They will not in any way make advertising more likely to address the issues or stimulate rational political debate.

D. Free Advertising Proposals

The proposals most likely to elevate political debate are those providing candidates with free advertising on the condition that the candidates

---

258. Some of the Representatives and Senators who spoke in favor of a bill containing an identification requirement argued that the bill was desirable because it would help stop negative campaigning. *E.g.,* 137 CONG. REC. S480 (daily ed. Jan. 14, 1991) (statement of Sen. Boren); *id.* at S479 (statement of Sen. Mitchell); 136 CONG. REC. H6867 (daily ed. Aug. 3, 1990) (statement of Rep. Penny); *id.* at H6858 (statement of Rep. Price).

259. KERN, *supra* note 205, at 33.

agree to conform to a talking-heads format and agree to create advertisements of a minimum length conducive to a meaningful discussion of issues. Such a proposal would not only make it more likely that issue-oriented advertising would be produced, it also could be structured in a way that would focus public and press scrutiny on free advertisements and away from paid spots. For example, Taylor argues that providing five-minute spots for each candidate alternating each night for the last four weeks of the presidential campaign would generate greater public scrutiny of what the candidate said during the five-minute spot than of the paid advertisements.[260] It would also create some expectation that the candidate would address issues during that time, thereby pressuring the candidate to do so. A successful advertising proposal could therefore change the nature of political debate during elections, although in ways that might cause candidates to prefer that it had stayed the same. This part of the Article analyzes two potential first amendment obstacles to free-advertising proposals: that the free-advertising proposal imposes an unconstitutional condition and that it unduly infringes on the editorial discretion of broadcasters.

1. Unconstitutional Conditions in Free Political Advertising

A free-advertising proposal with a talking-heads format raises an unconstitutional conditions problem because it "offers a benefit on condition that the recipient perform or forgo an activity that a preferred constitutional right normally protects from government interference."[261] In order to obtain the free advertising, a candidate must surrender her discretion as to choice of format. This is a discretion that the government could not restrict directly.

One could rather superficially argue that a free-advertising proposal does not impose an unconstitutional condition because the candidate who chooses not to accept the free advertising loses nothing other than the offered benefits. A free-advertising proposal can thus be termed an offer, rather than a threat.[262] The proposal does not threaten the candidate with the loss of an interest that she already has; it merely offers her a new option, subject to conditions. One might say that the free-advertising proposal involves a nonsubsidy rather than a penalty. Providing free advertising with conditions simply reflects the government's decision to subsidize advertising that follows a certain format and not to subsidize other adver-

---

260. Paul Taylor, See How They Run: Electing the President in an Age of Mediacracy 268-71 (1990).

261. Kathleen Sullivan. *Unconstitutional Conditions*, 102 Harv. L. Rev. 1415, 1421-22 (1989).

262. *See* Kenneth W. Simons, *Offers, Threats, and Unconstitutional Conditions*, 26 San Diego L. Rev. 289, 311 (1989).

tising.[263] The candidate who declines to accept the subsidy is not penalized because she did not face the loss of anything external to the declined benefit.

The Court's recent decision in *Rust v. Sullivan*[264] demonstrates that the Court sometimes succumbs to the temptation to engage in the above analysis and allows the government to restrict even the viewpoint of speech as long as the governmental regulation can be termed a decision not to fund a particular activity. Upon analysis, however, it is apparent that such distinctions among threats and offers and subsidies and penalties are inadequate to distinguish an unconstitutional condition on the acceptance of free advertising from a permissible condition. A requirement that a person who accepts funding from the National Endowment for the Arts (NEA) agree not to produce obscene art, for example, is neither a penalty nor a threat.[265] Neither is a law that subsidizes the speech of all who agree to join the Democratic party.[266] In both cases, the individual is not coerced into losing anything other than the subsidy itself, if they decline to accept it. Yet both are unconstitutional. The former is unconstitutional because it chills protected speech.[267] The latter is unconstitutional because the government is illegitimately using its power to advance the expression of one viewpoint over another.[268] Similarly, it can hardly be imagined that the Court would also approve a regulation that forbade a legal services lawyer from advising a client to file an action for a breach of the warranty of habitability or of other legal rights, even though such a regulation would be analytically difficult to distinguish from the situation in *Rust*.

Whether a condition is constitutional, therefore, should turn not on whether the condition can be termed a decision not to subsidize a particular activity, but on the substantive effect it has on free expression.[269] A

---

263. *See* Lawrence Tribe, American Constitutional Law § 11-5 (2d ed. 1988); Sullivan, *supra* note 261, at 1439-42, 1464-68.

264. 500 U.S. 173 (1991).

265. *See* Bella Lewitzky Dance Found. v. Frohnmayer, 754 F. Supp. 774 (C.D. Cal. 1991).

266. *See* Tribe, *supra* note 263, at § 11-5.

267. *Bella Lewitzky*, 754 F. Supp. at 782-83.

268. Tribe, *supra* note 263, at § 11-5.

269. *See* Cass R. Sunstein, *Is There an Unconstitutional Conditions Doctrine?*, 26 San Diego L. Rev. 337, 338 (1989) (Whether a condition is constitutional should be a function of the constitutional right at issue, not of an independent constitutional conditions doctrine.). The *Rust* decision is therefore incorrect to the extent that it relies on the characterization of the regulation as a government decision not to subsidize abortion counseling. The Court's decision might better be explained either as resting on skepticism that the regulation would significantly affect the ability of a clinic doctor to give frank

free-advertising proposal could certainly have the effect of changing the nature of political debate. Because the advertising spots would be free, candidates would likely elect to use the spots if they thought that the spots would help them in any way. Once guaranteed this free exposure, candidates might find less need for paid advertising and diminish their use of it.[270] Even if a candidate would otherwise choose not to use the free advertising, they might be pressured to use it to avoid being criticized by their opponent or the press for avoiding the issues.

These significant effects are all consistent with free speech. First, the free advertising would probably not reduce the total amount of speech. Indeed, if candidates continue to run paid advertisements in the same manner as before, the total amount of political speech during campaigns would be increased. The only reason that candidates might reduce the number of advertisements that they run would be if they found that the free advertisements were actually so effective at conveying their message that additional advertising was unnecessary. Second, because the restriction requires only a conventional format, it is not biased against the expression of any ideas or viewpoints. Third, requiring a talking-heads format does not require repeated intrusion into the political campaigning process or the application of vague standards that might chill speech or create a potential for arbitrary or discriminatory enforcement. A requirement that free advertising feature the candidate addressing the camera without the presence of other visuals, dramatizations, or music would be easy both to describe and to enforce.

The effect that a free-advertising proposal is most likely to have, if successful, is to give an advantage, as measured against the present state of affairs, to candidates who are best able to articulate and defend convincing policy proposals. This is legitimate since those are among the qualities most valued in a potential leader. It would be improper for the government to prevent candidates from advocating other reasons why they should be elected.[271] However, this proposal would only give candidates

---

advice to a patient or as a *sub silentio* holding that the right to an abortion is so insignificant that it can be substantially regulated and restricted.

270. In economic terms, one could say that the subsidy for one commodity, advertising with restrictions, will reduce demand for unrestricted advertising, a competing commodity. The adverse effect of a subsidy on competition is evidenced by the fact that antitrust law generally prohibits "predatory pricing," or selling a product in competition below cost. III P. Areeda & D. Turner, Antitrust Law 711 (1978). A government subsidy, however, is immune from antitrust liability. *See Bates*, 433 U.S. at 359-63.

271. Monitor Patriot Co. v. Roy, 401 U.S. 265, 275 (1971) ("Given the realities of our political life, it is by no means easy to see what statements about a candidate might be altogether without relevance to his fitness for the office he seeks.").

an opportunity and incentive to engage in a type of advertising that tends not to be employed currently because shorter and more creative advertising is thought to be a more effective use of scarce funds and because broadcasters are reluctant to run longer advertisements. If the voters choose to ignore the free advertising and focus on the attributes and image portrayed in paid advertisements, free advertising will not impede them from doing so. However, if people focus on free advertising and base their decisions on it, free advertising will provide voters with additional information relevant to their choices.

In this way, free advertising is similar to public funding for campaigns, which has been upheld by the courts.[272] Assume that candidate A is able to raise a maximum of $100,000 while candidate B can only raise $50,000. The Court in *Buckley* held that government could not eliminate A's advantage directly by limiting its spending.[273] But it could accomplish much the same end by matching a candidate's expenditure, provided that the candidates spend no more than a certain amount. If the government sets the limit at $50,000 and then provides matching funds of up to $50,000, it eliminates A's financial advantage. Both A and B will each have $100,000. The direct expenditure limit is therefore not invalid because it infringes upon a candidate's right to outspend its opponent, for public funding infringes upon that "right" as well. Rather, the Court's decision to invalidate the limitation can only be justified on the basis that expenditure limits curtail the access of the public to the communication of ideas and information by reducing the overall quantity of speech during election campaigns.[274]

Similarly, the current state of political advertising gives an advantage to the candidates who can afford to produce it and who are best able to use its limitations to convey their message. The government cannot eliminate this advantage directly by requiring all advertisements to conform to a talking-heads format. However, the government can diminish that advantage by subsidizing advertising if candidates employ a talking-heads format. Both free advertising and public funding alter the range of choices

---

272. *Buckley*, 424 U.S. at 57 n.65; Republican Nat'l Comm. v. Federal Election Comm'n, 487 F. Supp. 280 (S.D.N.Y. 1980) (three judge court), *aff'd*, 445 U.S. 955 (1980).

273. *Buckley*, 424 U.S. at 39-59.

274. This analysis suggests that *Buckley* may have been incorrectly decided if it overvalued the importance of maintaining the same high volume of campaign speech and undervalued the improvement in political dialogue that could result as a result of more balanced campaign expenditures. To the extent that the *Buckley* Court hinged its ruling on the fact that the government was restricting or enhancing individual candidates' abilities to convey their message to voters, the decision was flawed because voluntary expenditure limits similarly alter the relative quantity of candidates' speech.

that a candidate would otherwise have. Yet both are permissible because they help to compensate for wealth inequalities between candidates and encourage informative advertising without hampering the communicative impact of ideas and information to the voter.

A free-advertising proposal with a talking-heads condition is constitutional because it advances free expression by providing additional avenues for political debate without curtailing those that already exist. It is important to reiterate that the argument being made here is not that the government can accomplish indirectly, through funding conditions, what it cannot accomplish directly by mandating a talking-heads restriction. Rather the argument is that the two proposals do two very different things. A proposal to mandate a talking-heads format for all advertisements also mandates the kind of political debate that will take place. By contrast, the free-advertising proposal merely gives candidates the opportunity to use an avenue of expression that is not used frequently because of financial constraints and the restrictions sometimes imposed by networks on the length and timing of political advertisements.

Two additional objections to the free-advertising proposal can be raised. One objection is that it would tend to favor candidates who look good on television.[275] A candidate's ability to use television has been important at least since the elections of 1960. It is unlikely that a free-advertising proposal mandating a talking-heads format would significantly exacerbate this phenomenon in a time where sound bites, interviews, press conferences, and candidate debates are commonplace. What it would do is give an advantage to a candidate who was interesting and dynamic in discussing issues and the future of the country. That is preferable to giving an advantage to a candidate who because of superior funding is able to hire better media advisers.

A second objection is that the proposal would tend to coerce candidates to engage in a certain kind of advertising when they would rather not do so. One might be concerned that through this proposal the government would aggrandize the power to affect the nature of election debate that would otherwise be held by a candidate. However, our whole democratic system is premised on the idea that the press and the public will "coerce" the candidate to address their questions and concerns even if the candidate does not want to. Indeed, after the 1988 campaign, many argued that the press needed to become more aggressive about policing the accuracy of the candidates' statements and forcing them to address issues. There is no reason why the government cannot work to achieve these goals as well, as long as it does so in an evenhanded manner that minimizes the dangers posed by government intrusion.

---

275. Dwinell, *supra* note 211.

Thus far, this Article has considered a pure free-advertising and talking-heads proposal in which the advertising is free and the format restriction is conditioned on nothing other than an acceptance or rejection of the paid advertising. Under such a system, the candidate's decision of whether to use the advertising will hinge entirely on the candidate's assessment of whether the format will be helpful in conveying a message and whether the public will listen.

At least two other variations are possible and should be considered. One possibility is that the government would condition other benefits, such as public funding, on advertising that adhered to a particular format. Such a proposal would be constitutionally troublesome because the candidate's decision to use the free advertising would be motivated by external conditions other than the perceived effectiveness of the advertising. The effect of this proposal would be that a particular kind of advertising would be more prevalent simply because the government decided to encourage it. Because the advertising would be free, such a proposal would not cut off other avenues of expression; and because only a talking-heads condition would be mandated, there would be no danger that the restriction would be used to affect the message of the advertising. Therefore, such a proposal might well pass constitutional muster. The proposal is slightly more problematic, however, because it allows the government to alter the nature of political debate based on little more than the government's whim. By contrast, under the pure condition proposal, the effect on political debate is contingent only on the candidate's judgment of what the voters would want to hear.

Even more troublesome would be a proposal that offered a reduced rate on advertising that adhered to a restricted format. Under this proposal, the candidate's decision to spend money on the restricted format would also reduce the amount that the candidate could spend on unrestricted advertising. Therefore, the proposal would have the effect of reducing the number of non-talking-heads advertisements and thus of curtailing an effective avenue of political expression. The candidate's decision to run the cheaper advertisements would not be motivated solely by an assessment of what was most effective, but would also be influenced by financial considerations.

The least troubling free-advertising proposal is one that offers free talking-heads advertising conditioned on nothing other than accepting the advertising itself. Because a candidate's decision to use the free advertising would be influenced by nothing other than the candidate's assessment of what would be politically effective advertising, this type of proposal would provide advertising that the public wants to hear but is not receiving because of monetary constraints, broadcaster pressure for shorter advertisements, or the desire of the candidates to avoid formats that require them to address issues directly. The free-advertising proposal will affect the nature of political debate only if there is a current deficiency in the political marketplace. Other variations on talking-heads conditions are more troublesome because of the possibility that they would alter the nature of political advertising independent of public preferences as expressed through the democratic process.

This Article has argued that a free-advertising proposal should be judged by the extent to which it enhances free expression, rather than by its infringement on a candidate's autonomy. If this is the standard, one might ask, why be content with merely mandating a talking-heads format? Why not go further and require the candidate to discuss issues[276] or to discuss certain issues, such as the environment or crime? It is impossible to consider the complete range of regulations that might be adopted. However, restrictions that go far beyond a talking-heads format plus a fixed minimum-length requirement would probably pose significant dangers of suppression of speech. A requirement that candidates discuss issues during free advertising, for example, would require repeated adjudications-presumably by the Federal Communications Commission (FCC)-to determine whether particular advertisements involved "issues" within the meaning of the legislation. This would delay the airing of certain advertisements, thus interfering with a campaign. Worse, the standard might be interpreted with a bias toward approving advertisements addressing conventional issues. Advertisers might choose to create advertisements that avoid controversial topics to avert a challenge to a particular advertisement. A requirement that candidates discuss certain issues is similarly problematic. At a minimum, someone would have to choose the issues. The government might attempt to prevent the discussion of controversial or embarrassing topics in an attempt to divert public attention from them.

2. Broadcaster Editorial Discretion

A final consideration is the extent to which free-advertising proposals impinge on the editorial discretion of broadcasters. A requirement that broadcasters run advertisements of certain lengths at certain times, as some of the free-advertising proposals require, curtails the broadcasters'

---

276. See Arbogast, *Political Campaign Advertising and The First Amendment: A Structural—Functional Analysis of Proposed Reform*, 23 AKRON L. REV. 209 (1989) (proposing that the government condition the award of the lowest unit rate for political advertising on the candidate's agreement to run one and one-half minute advertisements in which the candidate identifies an issue, states her position on it, and explains why she holds that position).

editorial discretion regarding the choice of programming,[277] and it does so more intrusively than the current reasonable access requirement.[278] However, the editorial discretion of broadcasters, like the individual speech rights of candidates, should be protected only to the extent that it contributes to informed political debate during elections in particular and to free expression values in general.[279] Currently, the exercise of unfettered editorial discretion has resulted in electoral political debate that is carried out largely through short, often substanceless commercials. Nothing in our constitutional system justifies broadcasters being able to curtail public debate in this way simply because they happen to control the airwaves. The first amendment, therefore, permits even intrusive infringements on broadcasters' editorial discretion, as long as such infringements enhance the opportunity for informed public debate during elections without diminishing the free exchange of ideas and information.

The idea that editorial discretion is protected only to the extent that it promotes free expression is fully consistent with Supreme Court precedent. The Court has twice upheld significant restrictions on the editorial discretion of broadcasters on the grounds that such restrictions enhanced the public's access to information and contrasting viewpoints. In *Red Lion Broadcasting Co., v. FCC*,[280] the Court upheld the fairness doctrine, which granted a right of access to persons attacked in a broadcast editorial, on the grounds that it provided listeners and viewers with access to speech from a variety of sources and perspectives. In *CBS v. FCC*,[281] the Court upheld the requirement that broadcasters provide reasonable access to candidates, noting that it helped ensure that the airwaves were used in the public interest.[282]

More importantly, decisions protecting broadcasters' editorial discretion have also evidenced a concern with the impact of this discretion on the flow of information and ideas to society.[283] In *FCC v. League of*

---

277. *See*, Matheson, *supra* note 204, at 123-25.

278. 47 U.S.C. § 312(a)(7) (1988); *see* Kako, Note, *The Right of Reasonable Access for Federal Political Candidates Under Section 312(a)(7) of the Communications Act*, 78 COLUM. L. REV. 1287 (1978).

279. *See* Melvin B. Nimmer, *Introduction-Is Freedom of the Press a Redundancy: What Does It Add to Freedom of Speech?*, 26 HASTINGS L.J. 639, 653-54 (1975) (The press cannot be said to have rights to self-fulfillment or self-expression. Their rights derive from the interests of a self-governing people to hear all possible views bearing upon political decisions.).

280. 395 U.S. 367 (1969).

281. 453 U.S. 367 (1981).

282. *Id.* at 397.

283. 453 U.S. 367. Arguments that *Red Lion* is no longer good law because there is no longer spectrum scarcity do not undermine the claim that the editorial freedom of the broadcaster should be protected only to the extent to which such freedom contributes to

Women Voters,[284] the Court struck down a prohibition on the airing of editorials by public broadcasting stations, noting that editorials were crucial to free expression because they provided the public with ideas, information, and critical judgment.[285] In *CBS v. Democratic National Committee*,[286] the Court affirmed the FCC's refusal to require broadcast licensees to accept all paid political advertisements. In doing so, the Court emphasized that the FCC decision was consistent with providing the public with a balanced presentation of viewpoints, because a first-come, first-served rule would permit those wealthy enough to afford repeated purchases of editorial spots to dominate public debate.[287] Neither *League of Women Voters* nor *CBS* can be explained solely as upholding the right of broadcasters to editorial discretion. Instead, the decisions rest at least partly on the beneficial impact that the editorial discretion would have on the public's access to information and ideas.

In the context of election campaigns, one can determine whether a proposed restriction on the editorial discretion of broadcasters is consistent with free speech by examining the degree to which it diminishes or enhances the role that the broadcast media plays in our system of free expression. Essentially, broadcasters carry out two functions: that of a conduit of information and ideas and that of a critic, analyzing the information provided and critiquing the viewpoints of others.[288]

A free-advertising proposal undermines neither of these functions. Free-advertising proposals actually enhance the media's role as a conduit by providing the public with longer and more issue-oriented advertisements that might otherwise not be aired. Some possible restrictions on editorial discretion could undermine the media's role as a conduit. A contingent access requirement, such as that formerly proposed by Senators

---

free speech. The FCC ultimately abandoned the fairness doctrine, not because it abridged the autonomy of broadcasters, but because the agency felt that the rule undermined free speech by deterring the press from airing personal attacks. In the Matter of Inquiry into Section 73.1910 of the Commissions's Rules and Regulations Concerning the General Fairness Doctrine Obligations of Broadcast Licensees, 102 F.C.C.2d 143, 159 (1985).

284. 468 U.S. 364, *appeal dismissed*, 468 U.S. 1205 (1984).

285. *Id.* at 382.

286. 412 U.S. 94 (1973).

287. *Id.* at 123.

288. For other formulations of the free speech functions served by the press, *see* Jerome A. Barron, *Access to the Press-A New First Amendment Right*, 80 Harv. L. Rev. 1641, 1653-56 (1967) (Free expression requires that media allow expression of ideas that would otherwise not be aired before the public.); Nimmer, *supra* note 279, at 653-58 (The press helps preserve a democratic dialogue by providing information and opposing viewpoints to the public.).

Hollings and Danforth,[289] might dissuade broadcasters from airing advertisements to avoid triggering the access requirements[290] and deter groups from airing the attacks to avoid giving the disfavored candidate free air time.[291] Similarly, restrictions that prevented the media from providing certain information or viewpoints or that displaced a substantial portion of broadcast programming with programming mandated by the government would undermine the media's role as a conduit by curtailing the ideas and information that it provided to the public. Free-advertising proposals do not present this problem because they provide the public with more information relating to election campaigns without significantly reducing the flow of information provided through a broadcaster's regular programming. Even the most ambitious of the free-advertising proposals would only consume a few hours of air time each year.[292] As long as the length was five minutes or less, such advertising could fit in between programs.[293]

Free advertising proposals also do not diminish the media's critical function. The restriction struck down in *League of Women Voters* diminished the critical function by depriving broadcasters of one of their primary tools of critical analysis. The same would be true for any restriction on television's ability to provide news and news analysis. Free-advertising proposals leave the broadcast media completely free to continue its analysis and criticism of the election.

A regulation that diminished the broadcaster's choice of programming to such a degree that the government was in fact determining the nature and content of programming would also threaten the broadcast media's critical function. Such a regulation would give the government the power to control the agenda of public discussion by controlling the nature of ideas and information disseminated to the public. Free advertising does

---

289. S. 999, 101st Cong. § 2 (1989) (A candidate who is attacked by independent advertisements would receive free response time of equal length.). For analysis of this provision, compare Matheson, *supra* note 204, at 129 (arguing provision is unconstitutional) with Clinger, Note, *The Clean Campaign Act of 1985*, 3 J.L. & POL. 727 (1987) (arguing provision is constitutional).

290. Matheson, *supra* note 204, at 129; *see also* Lee C. Bollinger, Jr., *Freedom of the Press and Public Access: Toward a Theory of Partial Regulation of the Mass Media*, 75 MICH. L. REV. 1, 29 (1976).

291. Matheson, *supra* note 204, at 93.

292. LARRY J. SABATO, THE RISE OF POLITICAL CONSULTANTS: NEW WAYS OF WINNING ELECTIONS 31 (1981).

293. An effective free-advertising proposal should probably not require advertisements longer than five minutes because longer advertisements tend to lose their audience. *Id.* at 34.

not raise this concern because the government is only requiring political discussion; it is not dictating the content of that discussion.

Finally, a government regulation that so entangles the media with the government that it gives the government the power to influence the content of broadcast news and programming threatens the critical function of the broadcast media. The most obvious example would be direct censorship. A less obvious example would be a symbiotic regulatory regime in which the government and broadcasters were constantly interacting on a variety of issues. Such a system could make the broadcast media reluctant to threaten the government lest the government retaliate by exercising its regulatory power in a way that injures the media actor.[294] To some extent, this government entanglement in the broadcast industry may already exist. In any case, a free-advertising proposal certainly does not exacerbate it. As previously discussed, a rule that required the broadcast of advertisements of certain length at certain times is easy both to describe and to enforce. It does not require continuing supervision and enforcement by the government.

In sum, the free-advertising proposals do not infringe either the autonomy of candidates or the editorial discretion of broadcasters in ways that diminish free speech values. In fact, they enhance such values by providing voters with potentially valuable, issue-oriented advertising. Therefore, free-advertising proposals are consistent with the first amendment.

Conclusion

It is an interesting paradox of our constitutional system that a society so dedicated to democratic decision making is virtually alone among industrialized democracies in taking no regulatory steps to improve the level of public debate during elections. The apparent premise behind this hands-off approach is that enlightened public debate is best achieved through an absence of government regulation. However, an analysis of both the nature of contemporary political advertising and of free speech principles reveals that this assumption is unrealistic. Government not only can, but it should take affirmative steps to improve the level of public debate during elections. It is irrelevant that such restrictions infringe on the autonomy of candidates and broadcasters. The predominant concern should be to create opportunities for more informed public debate.

That being said, however, one cannot countenance format restrictions on political advertising based on nothing more than a congressional find-

---

294. *See* Bollinger, *supra* note 290, at 29-31.

ing that such restrictions will elevate political debate. The healthy fear we should have that restrictions might be imposed by the government to serve its own ends, as well as the subtle and multifaceted nature of televised communication, mandates a rigorous analysis of proposed format restrictions to determine whether they enhance or diminish free expression. This analysis can be accomplished by examining format restrictions in light of their effect on the communicative impact and quantity of campaign speech, as well as by examining the potential that the restrictions will be used to suppress disfavored ideas.

Applying this analysis to proposed format restrictions reveals that the scope of permissible restrictions is modest. Proposals that restrict the permissible formats for political advertising endanger free speech because they would blunt the impact of advertising that is highly effective at communicating ideas and information to voters. The most promising use of format restrictions is to provide information and discussions to voters that would otherwise not be aired. This can be accomplished by disclosure requirements or, most effectively, by providing free advertising to candidates on the condition that the candidates produce advertising that conforms to an issue-oriented format. In addition, identification requirements can make candidates more accountable for their advertising and thus more careful about its content.

The relative modesty of permissible reforms should not obscure their significance. The free-advertising proposals, if properly structured, may create pressures and expectations that can make campaigns more substantive. Furthermore, the restrictions illustrate that society need not simply accept substance-free campaigns as the inevitable outcome of freedom of speech. By carefully considering the effects of regulation on free speech values, government can fashion regulations that create opportunities for the rational political dialogue that is necessary for the proper functioning of our democratic system of government.

Frankenstein's Monster Hits the Campaign Trail: An Approach to Regulation of Corporate Political Expenditures

Jill E. Fisch

I. Introduction

Since states began to grant corporate charters, the corporate form has been viewed by many with suspicion and distrust. Corporations have been perceived as dangerous because of their size, their ability to concentrate the power to control large amounts of capital in the hands of a few managers, and their influence on the lives of most citizens through control of consumer, investment, and employment markets. This fear of the corporate form, which led Justice Brandeis to describe the industrial corporation as a "Frankenstein monster,"[1] prevailed for many years and caused states to impose limitations on the size,[2] powers,[3] and duration[4] of corporations.

---

1. Louis K. Liggett Co. v. Lee, 288 U.S. 517, 567 (1933) (Brandeis, J., dissenting).

2. Statutes limited corporations to a certain amount of authorized capital. Under the state corporation laws in effect in the mid-1800's, provisions limiting the capital stock of a corporation to $ 100,000 or even less were common. See id. at 550–54 (Brandeis, J., dissenting).

3. Before the adoption of modern corporation statutes, corporate charters were required to contain a statement of the purpose for which the corporation was formed. This purpose provision was generally viewed as a limitation on the corporation's powers; actions by the corporation that were outside the corporation's stated objectives were deemed ultra vires, literally beyond the corporation's power. Stockholders or third parties could attack such actions on the ground that the corporation had acted in an unauthorized manner. For a discussion of the classical ultra vires doctrine, see H. HENN & J. ALEXANDER, LAWS OF CORPORATIONS 184 (3d ed. 1983); Herbert Hovenkamp, *The Classical Corporation in American Legal Thought*, 76 GEO. L.J. 1593, 1662-72 (1988).

In spite of the warnings by Justice Brandeis and others about the corrosive power of the corporate form, corporations gradually gained acceptance and were given increased powers, including the power to own other corporations, the power to make charitable contributions, and the power to invoke the attorney-client privilege. In the 1990's, corporations have become an acceptable business form for the large multinational business, the small shop owner, and the public interest group. That is not to say, however, that the historic fear of the corporate form has disappeared.

The Supreme Court's recent decision in *Austin v. Michigan Chamber of Commerce*[5] serves as a reminder that the "Age of Corporate Mistrust" is not dead. In *Austin*, the Court upheld against first amendment challenge a Michigan law prohibiting corporations from making independent expenditures that support or oppose a candidate for state political office.[6] *Austin* represents a significant cutback on the corporation's right to engage in political speech. Previous Supreme Court decisions established that independent expenditures constitute political speech and that corporate political speech, like that of individuals, is protected by the first amendment.[7] *Austin* rejected neither of those principles, but concluded that the Michigan statute was legitimate because the prohibition on corporate political speech served a compelling state interest: the interest in preventing the "corrosive and distorting effects" of corporate speech on political campaigns.[8]

The amendment of corporation laws to permit general purpose clauses, that is, charter provisions that permit the corporation to engage in any lawful business, has virtually erased the classical ultra vires doctrine. For example, *see* § 102(a)(3) of the Delaware Code:

> It shall be sufficient to state…that the purpose of the corporation is to engage in any lawful act or activity for which corporations may be organized under the General Corporation Law of Delaware, and by such statement all lawful acts and activities shall be within the purposes of the corporation, except for express limitations, if any.

DEL. CODE ANN. tit. 8, § 102(a)(3) (1988). Most states adopted such modern statutes in the mid-1800's. See *Liggett*, 288 U.S. at 555 n.27. In addition, most states have limited the application of the ultra vires doctrine by statute. *See, e.g.*, DEL. CODE ANN. tit. 8, § 124 (1988).

4. In the early 1900's, many states limited the duration of corporation existence to periods from 20 to 50 years. *See Liggett*, 288 U.S. at 555 n.29.

5. 494 U.S. 652 (1990).

6. *Id.* at 1401.

7. *See, e.g.*, First Nat'l Bank v. Bellotti, 435 U.S. 765, 776 (1978); Buckley v. Valeo, 424 U.S. 1, 23 (1976) (per curiam).

8. *Austin*, 494 U.S. at 659–60.

Corporations have historically been subjected to greater restrictions than unincorporated entities. Nevertheless, the Court's willingness to find an evil inherent in speech based simply on the speaker's "corporateness"[9] is troubling.[10] More importantly, the Court decided *Austin* in a vacuum, divorced from any consideration of the special powers and limitations associated with use of the corporate form.[11] In determining that the Michigan statute was "narrowly tailored" to its goal,[12] the Court thus did not find it necessary even to consider whether state corporation law, the traditional method of regulating corporate conduct, might be a more appropriate and less restrictive method of preventing the evils perceived by the Michigan legislature.

* * *

In *Austin*, the Court considered a Michigan statute[133] analogous to FECA.[134] As applied to corporations, the Michigan statute, like its federal counterpart,[135] prohibited corporations from making independent expenditures in support of or in opposition to the election of a candidate for Michigan office. Like FECA, the Michigan statute also allowed corporations to establish separate political funds[136] that could make political expenditures and to support and administer such segregated political funds, but the statute prohibited corporations from spending their own treasury funds, either directly or through the segregated fund, to support or oppose political candidates. Violation of the statute was a felony.[137]

---

9. The evil addressed by regulations such as the Michigan statute appears to be an evil associated with the corporate form, not the political involvement of businesses in general. *Id.* at 699 (Kennedy, J., dissenting).

10. Equally troubling are *Austin's* implications for the first amendment protection of group or associational speech. This issue was a primary subject of Justice Kennedy's dissent in *Austin. See id.* at 695 (Kennedy, J., dissenting).

11. *See infra* notes 226-51 and accompanying text.

12. *Austin*, 494 U.S. at 660–61.

* * *

133. MICH. COMP. LAWS ANN. § 169.254(1) (West 1979).

134. The Michigan statute was modeled after § 441b of FECA. *See Austin*, 110 S. Ct. at 1395 n.1.

135. FECA makes it unlawful for a corporation or labor union "to make a contribution or expenditure in connection with" any federal election. 2 U.S.C. § 441(a) (1988). It defines an "expenditure" as the provision of anything of value "for the purpose of influencing any election for Federal Office." *Id.* at § 431(9)(A)(i).

136. Contributions to the fund may be solicited from the corporation's members, stockholders, officers, directors, and executive and administrative employees. MICH. COMP. LAWS ANN. § 169.255(2)-(3).

137. Section 54(4) currently provides:
A person who knowingly violates this section is guilty of a felony punishable, if the

Although the statute did not apply to media corporations, it did not exempt nonprofit corporations.[138]

The statute was challenged by the Michigan State Chamber of Commerce, a nonprofit corporation whose objectives and purposes include "promoting conditions conducive to economic development, training and educating its members, encouraging the maintenance and observance of ethical business practices, and receiving expenditures and making contributions for political purposes."[139] The Chamber of Commerce wanted to place a paid advertisement in the newspaper in support of a candidate for the Michigan House of Representatives.[140] Although it had a separate political fund, the Chamber of Commerce sought declaratory and injunctive relief that would enable it to pay for the advertisement with general treasury funds.[141]

The Supreme Court did not question the body of case law holding that the expenditures in question, although made by a corporation, constitute protected political speech.[142] Nor did the Court retreat from its previous finding that restrictions on independent expenditures constitute direct burdens on speech;[143] it accepted, without discussion, the premise that the Michigan statute burdened protected political speech.[144] Accordingly, the

---

person is an individual, by a fine of not more than $ 5,000.00 or imprisonment for not more than 3 years, or both, or, if the person is not an individual, by a fine of not more than $ 10,000.00. *Id.* at § 169.254(4).

138. Michigan law excludes from the Act's coverage any "news story, commentary, or editorial in support of or opposition to a candidate" by any "broadcasting station, newspaper, magazine, or other periodical or publication." *Id.* at § 169.206(3)(d).

Although the legitimacy of the media exclusion is beyond the scope of this Article, the role of the institutional press in election contests might easily be described as "corrosive." The press appears to wield considerably more power in the political process than any single commercial corporation. *See Austin*, 494 U.S. at 690–91 (Scalia, J., dissenting).

139. Michigan State Chamber of Commerce v. Austin, 856 F.2d 783, 784-85 (6th Cir. 1988), *rev'd*, 494 U.S. 652 (1990).

140. *Austin*, 494 U.S. at 656.

141. *Austin*, 856 F.2d at 785.

142. *See Austin*, 494 U.S. at 657–58. The Court explained:

> Certainly, the use of funds to support a political candidate is "speech"; independent campaign expenditures constitute "political expression 'at the core of our electoral process and of the First Amendment freedoms.'" The mere fact that the Chamber is a corporation does not remove its speech from the ambit of the First Amendment.

Id. at 657 (quoting Williams v. Rhodes, 393 U.S. 23, 32 (1968), *quoted in* Buckley v. Valeo, 424 U.S. 1, 39 (1976) (per curiam)).

143. *See Buckley*, 424 U.S. at 39.

144. *See Austin*, 494 U.S. at 657–58.

very question that the Court had reserved in *Federal Election Commission v. Massachusetts Citizens for Life, Inc.*[145] was now before it. The Court's precedents required it to apply strict scrutiny to determine whether the regulation of political expenditures by business corporations[146] advanced a compelling state interest and, if so, whether the statute was narrowly tailored to serve that interest.[147]

In support of the regulation, Michigan claimed that the special structure of a corporation justified special regulation.[148] In particular, Michigan noted that state law granted corporations a number of advantages: "limited liability, perpetual life, and favorable treatment of the accumulation and distribution of assets."[149] According to the State, these advantages allowed corporations to "use 'resources amassed in the economic marketplace' to obtain 'an unfair advantage in the political marketplace.'"[150]

The Court accepted this argument.[151] Terming the economic wealth of a business corporation a "'political war chest,'"[152] the Court found that the influence of such war chests was a form of political corruption.[153] The Court noted that this was not the quid pro quo type of corruption[154] recognized in *Buckley v. Valeo*,[155] but rather "the corrosive and distorting effects of immense aggregations of wealth that are accumulated with the

---

145. 479 U.S. 238, 263 (1986) (plurality opinion) ("Regardless of whether that concern is adequate to support application of § 441b to commercial enterprises, a question not before us, that justification does not extend uniformly to all corporations."). *Id.*

146. The Court found that the Chamber of Commerce, although technically a nonprofit corporation, did not come under the narrow *MCFL* exclusion because, inter alia, its membership consisted primarily of business corporations. *See Austin*, 494 U.S. at 664–65; *cf. infra* note 160 (nonprofit corporations do not present much risk of corruption).

147. This standard required the Court to determine whether the prohibition "burdens political speech, and, if so, whether such a burden [was] justified by a compelling state interest." *MCFL*, 479 U.S. at 252 (citing *Buckley*, 424 U.S. at 44-45).

148. *Austin,* 494 U.S. at 658–59.

149. *Id.*

150. *Id.* (quoting *MCFL*, 479 U.S. at 257).

151. *Id.*

152. *Id.* (quoting Federal Election Comm'n v. National Conservative Political Action Comm., 470 U.S. 480, 501 (1985)).

153. *Id.*

154. The Court had previously described the corruption addressed by FECA as "a subversion of the political process [whereby] elected officials are influenced to act contrary to their obligations of office by the prospect of financial gain to themselves or infusions of money into their campaigns. The hallmark of corruption is the financial quid pro quo: dollars for political favors." *NCPAC*, 470 U.S. at 497.

155. 424 U.S. 1, 47 (1976) (per curiam).

help of the corporate form and that have little or no correlation to the public's support for the corporation's political ideas."[156] According to the Court, the prevention of this type of corruption was a sufficiently compelling interest to justify the Michigan statute.[157]

The Court then considered whether the statute was narrowly tailored. First, the Court found that the Michigan statute did not "impose an absolute ban on all forms of corporate political spending" because of the provision that allowed corporations to make expenditures through separate committees.[158] The Court then concluded that the statute was not overbroad as applied to corporations that lacked "vast reservoirs of capital" because those corporations too enjoyed the special advantages of the corporate structure, which gave them the "potential for distorting the political process."[159] After determining that neither the nonprofit status of the Chamber of Commerce[160] nor the statutory exemption of press corporations created constitutional difficulties, the Court upheld the statute.[161]

---

156. *Austin*, 494 U.S. at 660. Commentators had been suggesting for some time that the Court's view of corruption in *First National Bank v. Bellotti*, 435 U.S. 765 (1978), was too narrow and that corporate political spending presented a serious and ascertainable threat to the electoral process. *See, e.g.*, Gary Hart & William Shore, *Corporate Spending on State and Local Referendums:* First National Bank v. Bellotti, 29 CASE W. RES. L. REV. 808, 809–10 (1979). Shockley, *Direct Democracy, Campaign Finance, and the Courts: Can Corruption, Undue Influence, and Declining Voter Confidence Be Found?*, 39 U. MIAMI L. REV. 377, 383-85 (1985).

157. *Austin*, 494 U.S. at 660.

158. *Id* at 660–61.

159. *Id* at 661. The Court never explained how corporations that lack those resources can corrupt the political process. It simply observed that such corporations enjoy the "unique state-conferred corporate structure that facilitates the amassing of large treasuries." *Id*. (emphasis added). *See infra* notes 226-51 and accompanying text.

160. *Austin's* applicability to nonprofit corporations generated a dissent by Justice Kennedy in which he argued that nonprofit corporations in particular presented none of the risks of corruption at which the statute was aimed and that the burden on free speech imposed by applying the Michigan statute to these corporations was substantial. *See Austin*, 494 U.S. at 695–713 (Kennedy, J., dissenting).

Federal law already imposes certain limitations on the political activity of nonprofit corporations. A corporation organized in accordance with 26 U.S.C. § 501(c)(3) (1988) is prohibited from making partisan political expenditures, whereas a corporation organized in accordance with 26 U.S.C. § 501(c)(4) must primarily engage in activities that promote welfare rather than activities such as political campaigning. *See* Rev. Rul. 81-95, 1981-1 C.B. 332. In addition, all political expenditures by a § 501(c) corporation are subject to a special penalty tax. *See* 26 U.S.C. § 527(f).

161. *Austin*, 494 U.S. at 661–69.

State prohibition of independent expenditures by corporations in an election contest does not violate the first amendment.[162]

* * *

B. Is The Regulation Narrowly Tailored?

The Court's decision in *Austin* was based on principles of constitutional rather than corporate law. In considering whether Michigan sufficiently narrowly tailored its regulation, the Court did not find it necessary to consider the attributes of the corporate form. This is a major shortcoming in the *Austin* opinion. One cannot consider regulation of corporate political speech in isolation when, unlike individuals, corporations are subject to a pervasive general system of regulation: state corporation law.[226]

Unlike many less formal groups and associations, such as partnerships, the corporation is created by an affirmative act of the state. A certificate of incorporation must be filed with the Secretary of State before the special attributes of the corporate form are secured. Moreover, the formation of a corporation includes the corporation's explicit agreement to be subject to state corporation law, a body of regulation that may specify a corporation's powers and obligations, set forth certain formal requisites for corporate action, and regulate corporate activities that impact the state. In return for a corporation's agreement to subject itself to this body of regulation, which agreement is evidenced by the act of incorporating under that state's laws, state law gives a corporation certain attributes, including limited liability for the corporation's stockholders, perpetual duration, the capacity to sue and to be sued in the corporate name, free transferability of ownership interests, and treatment as a separate entity for tax purposes.[227]

---

162. *Id.* at 666–68.
* * *

226. Substantial commentary exists on whether and to what extent the system of corporate law functions effectively to monitor management and further the interests of stockholders. *See infra* notes 259-63. This Article is cognizant that the effectiveness of corporate law may be imperfect and suggests not that state corporate law is a panacea, but that it is a fundamental starting point in assessing the validity of statutes addressed to corporate conduct. Because the Court's opinion in *Austin* is bereft of any analysis of the corporate law framework, the Court has failed to conduct the kind of exacting scrutiny that a prohibition on speech mandates.

227. HENN & ALEXANDER, *supra* note 3, §§ 73-76, at 130-38. State corporation law provides the source for corporate creation, yet it typically does not enumerate the full range of rights and powers that a corporation possesses after formation. This principle has its roots in the historic case of *Trustees of Dartmouth College v. Woodward*, 17 U.S. (4

In order to appreciate state regulation of the corporate form, it is necessary to consider two separate aspects of this regulation: the corporation law limitations on corporate conduct and the special benefits of the corporate form. The special benefits of the corporate form are the attributes of "corporateness" upon which the Court justifies its distinctive treatment of

---

Wheat.) 518 (1819), which held that the State of New Hampshire's revocation of a corporate charter violated the contracts clause of article I of the federal Constitution. *Id.* at 712.

Scholars have articulated numerous theories that attempt to describe the corporate entity. These include the "personhood" theory, which views the corporation as a natural entity with an existence and rights separate from its shareholders and other constituencies; the artificial entity theory, which views the corporation as an artificial creation of the state subject to state-imposed limitations; the trust theory, which analogizes the managers of a corporation to trustees and the shareholders to beneficiaries; and the description of a corporation as a nexus of contracts between management, stockholders, employees, and other constituencies. *See, e.g.,* Lewis A. Kornhauser, *The Nexus of Contracts Approach to Corporations: A Comment on Easterbrook and Fischel,* 89 COLUM. L. REV. 1449 (1989) (describing trust theory and nexus of contracts theory); Gregory A. Mark, *The Personification of the Business Corporation in American Law,* 54 U. CHI. L. REV. 1441 (1987) (discussing development of different conceptions of the corporation as association, artificial person, and "organist real person/real entity"). The development of these descriptive theories is not solely an academic exercise. The treatment of the corporation under the law, whether statutory, common, or constitutional, is dependent in large part on its proper characterization. *See* John C. Coffee, Jr., *The Mandatory/Enabling Balance in Corporate Law: An Essay on the Judicial Role,* 89 COLUM. L. REV. 1618 (1989) (implications of the different models for judicial behavior).

For example, courts have struggled for over a century with the question of how properly to characterize a corporation for purposes of the federal Constitution. The Supreme Court first declared the corporation a person for purposes of the fourteenth amendment in *Santa Clara County v. Southern Pacific Railroad,* 118 U.S. 394, 396 (1886). This personhood view of the corporation has enjoyed general acceptance in judicial decisions, and the Court subsequently has held that corporations have protected liberty and property interests under the fourteenth amendment, First Nat'l Bank v. Bellotti, 435 U.S. 765, 778-79 (1978); privacy interests under the fourth amendment, G.M. Leasing Corp. v. United States, 429 U.S. 338, 353 (1977); double jeopardy and due process rights under the fifth amendment, Fong Foo v. United States, 369 U.S. 141, 143 (1962); Noble v. Union River Logging R.R., 147 U.S. 165, 176 (1893); and the right to a jury trial, Ross v. Bernhard, 396 U.S. 531, 543 (1970). Virtually the only constitutional protection that the Court has denied corporations is the fifth amendment privilege against self-incrimination. *See* Bellis v. United States, 417 U.S. 85, 90 (1974); Hale v. Henkel, 201 U.S. 43, 51 (1906). The Court has also denied corporations the privileges of citizens under the privileges and immunities clause. *See* Asbury Hosp. v. Cass County, 326 U.S. 207, 210-11 (1945). For a detailed discussion of the application of Bill of Rights protections to corporations, *see generally* Carl J. Mayer, *Personalizing the Impersonal: Corporations and the Bill of Rights,* 41 HASTINGS L.J. 577 (1990).

corporate political speech.[228] Within these special benefits, the attribute of limited liability traditionally receives the most attention. Commentators have defined limited liability as "the rule that shareholders are not liable for the obligations of the corporation beyond their capital investment."[229] Limited liability is the characteristic primarily responsible for the prevalence of the corporate form among large United States businesses and the characteristic to which commentators have attributed the success of United States business.[230] It permits those wishing to invest in a corporation to limit their exposure to the amount of their investment. For example, an individual can purchase one hundred shares of Exxon stock secure in the knowledge that even if Exxon causes an enormous oil spill which results in millions of dollars of liability, the individual cannot lose more than the amount of his initial investment. Corporations thus allow investors to participate in the earnings of a business without being personally responsible for the consequences of failure, an attribute that makes it easier to raise equity capital through use of the corporate form. Not surprisingly, this attribute makes the corporation the vehicle of choice for many businesses of substantial size.[231]

Although limited liability is a valuable attribute of the corporate form, one should not overestimate its importance. Limited partnerships provide the same shelter for the assets of their passive investors and provide favorable tax treatment as well.[232] Moreover, although limited liability protects the stockholder/investor, it does not shield the conduct of the corporate controllers, such as its officers and directors, from the threat of personal liability.[233] Most importantly, limited liability does not offer any sort of government subsidy to the corporation's business. The corporation itself, as actor, does not share the shield of limited liability and is responsible for

---

228. *See* Fletcher N. Baldwin & Kenneth D. Karpay, *Corporate Political Free Speech: U.S.C.§ 441b and the Superior Rights of Natural Persons*, 14 Pac. L.J. 209, 240 n.218 (1983)(special benefits of the corporate form include "the privilege of limited liability, perpetual existence, use of the corporate name to sue and be sued, and potential tax advantages for shareholders").

229. Philip Blumberg, The Law of Corporate Groups, Substantive Law § 1.02, at 7 (1987).

230. *Id.* at 7-8.

231. For a detailed analysis of the theoretical and economic advantages and disadvantages of limited liability to the business enterprise, *see id.* §§ 4.01-5.02, at 63-101.

232. The State of Michigan, for example, permits investors to limit their liability in the same manner as corporate shareholders through the use of a limited partnership. Mich. Comp. Laws Ann. §§ 449.1108, 449.1301a (West 1989).

233. Limited partners in Michigan, like shareholders, have the right to bring derivative suits. *Id.* at § 449.2001.

the full extent of any debts and obligations it incurs.[234] For corporations with substantial assets, therefore, limited shareholder liability is unlikely to have a substantial impact on corporate decisionmaking.

Nor, upon reexamination, do the other attributes of the corporate form suggest a particularly favored legal status. Corporations do, by virtue of state law, enjoy perpetual life and do not dissolve automatically upon the death of a partner or founder, but businesses that do not operate in the corporate form can achieve the same permanence by contract. Similarly, although corporations often are distinguished from other forms of businesses by the fact that equity interest shares of stock are freely transferable in the corporation, the partnership form can likewise achieve such flexibility through contractual provisions. Indeed, limited partnership interests generally are considered to be securities[235] and often are quoted and traded in much the same manner as stocks.

The ability to sue and to be sued in the corporate name results in judicial recognition of the corporation as an entity. Although useful in that it would be difficult and burdensome for a business with many diverse owners to deal with joinder issues, the class action lawsuit and other procedural devices would enable a corporation to obtain recourse in the courts without this attribute. And of course, judicial recognition of the corporate form does not substantially affect the corporation's ability to function as an economic unit.

Finally, separate taxation of the corporation as an entity can be either a benefit or a detriment to the business organized in the corporate form. Indeed, the Internal Revenue Code recognizes that taxation as a corporation is often a burden for small corporations and provides such businesses with the option of being taxed as a partnership through election of subchapter S status.[236]

Apparently the primary significance of the corporate form is not its special legal attributes; the dichotomy between the corporation and the

---

234. Commentators who wish to present the view of corporations as powerful yet unaccountable frequently ignore this aspect of limited liability. *See, e.g.,* Mayer, *supra* note 227, at 658-59. Professor Mayer states that "corporations enjoy limited liability for industrial accidents such as nuclear power disasters," omitting the explanation that the only individuals shielded from that liability are the stockholders. *Id.* at 658. Neither the employees who negligently cause such accidents to occur, the management whose lax supervision permits the accident, nor the corporation itself receives any special treatment with respect to their liability for the accident, despite the corporate form.

235. *See, e.g.,* People v. Graham, 163 Cal.App.3d 1159, 1164-65, 210 Cal.Rptr. 318, 322 (1985).

236. *See* 26 U.S.C. §§ 1361-1363 (1988).

partnership or alternative business form tends to be overstated. Rather, the distinctive attribute of the corporate form, particularly for large, publicly held corporations, is its organizational structure: the separation in a true corporation of ownership from management.[237] Unlike the partnership or sole proprietorship, the owners of a corporation, the stockholders, are not responsible for managing the corporation; they elect directors who in turn select a corporation's management, its officers. The stockholders' elected agents make the decisions that normally would be made by owners, such as what products to sell, whom to employ, and what type of advertising to purchase.[238] This separation of ownership and responsibility for day-to-day decisions is, in reality, the main attribute distinguishing the large, publicly held corporation from other forms of business.[239]

Because hired agents rather than owners of large corporations carry on corporate management, state corporation law provides limitations on the activities of those agents. The most important of these limitations is the

---

237. Commentators also refer to this attribute as the "separation of ownership and control." Scholars have blamed the separation of ownership and control for many of the evils associated with the corporate form. *See* ADOLF AUGUSTUS BERLE & GARDINER C. MEANS, THE MODERN CORPORATION AND PRIVATE PROPERTY (rev. ed. 1967); RALPH NADER, MARK GREEN, & JOEL SELIGMAN, TAMING THE GIANT CORPORATION (1976); *see also* Hovenkamp, *supra* note 3, at 1684 (discussing implications of the Berle & Means theory and, in particular, the effect that separation of ownership and control has on the presumption that corporations are profit maximizers).

Unlike limited liability, the separation of ownership and control is not an attribute common to all corporations. Corporations with few stockholders, in which the stockholders also participate in the corporation's business as management, directors, and employees, lack this characteristic. Such corporations, known as close corporations, present an organizational structure more nearly analogous to that of an unincorporated business entity, such as a partnership. HENN & ALEXANDER, *supra* note 3, § 257, at 694-97.

238. Fama, *Agency Problems and the Theory of the Firm*, 88 J. POL. ECON. 288 (1980); *see* Oliver Hart, *An Economist's Perspective on the Theory of the Firm*, 89 COLUM. L. REV. 1757, 1758-63 (1989) (discussing principal/agent theory of corporate law and transaction costs imposed by using and monitoring agents).

239. Delegating corporate control to management results in a certain inherent conflict of interest. No matter how responsive management is to the needs of the corporation's stockholders, management views will not reflect those of stockholders on many issues due to fundamental economic differences in their relative positions. For example, management and stockholders are in direct conflict with respect to management compensation, antitakeover charter provisions, and many other areas. For a detailed discussion of the conflict engendered by the separation of ownership and control and a proposed solution, *see* George W. Dent, Jr., *Toward Unifying Ownership and Control in the Public Corporation*, 1989 WIS. L. REV. 881, 886-92.

corporate charter. The charter is often characterized as a contract between the stockholders and management; it is, in essence, the contract for that agency relationship.[240] Through the corporate charter, stockholders can prevent management from taking certain actions, require actions to be subject to stockholder vote, and affect management's accountability to the corporation.[241]

A second, although less significant, limitation is the state corporation law. At one time corporation law was a substantial constraint on corporate activity. Corporations were limited by statute in size and duration. In addition, corporations could engage only in activities that state law authorized. Today, corporation law is generally permissive in nature, providing some minimal constraints by deeming some charter provisions contrary to public policy and by requiring stockholder votes for important corporate activities such as merger or dissolution. State corporation law, however, does impose certain duties upon management: management's fiduciary duty. Both the common law and state corporation law statutes require that management exercise a fiduciary standard of care;[242] that is, management must act in good faith and with that degree of care that an ordinarily prudent person would use under similar circumstances.[243] In addition, statutes specify that in taking action, management must consider the interests of the corporation and its stockholders.[244]

Advocates of a more intrusive system of statutory regulation argue that the contract theory of corporations is inadequate because corporations have an effect on third parties whose rights will not be protected by the contractual charter between stockholders and the company.[245] These advocates suggest that a more rigorous body of state incorporation law is

---

240. *See* HENN & ALEXANDER, *supra* note 3, § 122, at 279-82.

241. For example, statutes such as DEL. CODE ANN. tit. 8, § 102(b)(7) (1988) allow stockholders to release directors from personal liability for violating their duty of care to the corporation.

242. The common law fiduciary duty that corporate management owes to the corporation's stockholders is based on principles of agency law. *See* WILLIAM A. KLEIN & JOHN C. COFFEE, BUSINESS ORGANIZATION AND FINANCE, LEGAL AND ECONOMIC PRINCIPLES 19-37, 118 (4th ed. 1990).

243. *See, e.g.*, N.Y. BUS. CORP. LAW §§ 715(h), 717(a) (McKinney 1986).

244. *See, e.g., id.* at § 717(b) (McKinney Supp. 1990).

245. *See, e.g.*, Jeffrey N. Gordon, *The Mandatory Structure of Corporate Law*, 89 COLUM. L. REV. 1549, 1549-55 (1989); *cf.* Roberta Romano, *Answering the Wrong Question: The Tenuous Case for Mandatory Corporate Laws*, 89 COLUM. L. REV. 1599, 1615-17 (1989) (contract theory of corporation is also inadequate because of the corporation's power to amend its corporate charter).

necessary to guard against perceived corporate "evils." This approach has not gained acceptance in the states, in large part because of the so-called "race for the bottom," a term coined by Professor William Cary[246] to describe state legislatures' proclivity to make their corporation statutes increasingly lax and permissive in an attempt to encourage more corporations to incorporate in the state.[247]

The third limitation on corporate managerial conduct is the common law doctrine of fiduciary duty. The common law and case development both explain and supplement the statutory concept of fiduciary duty. Under the prevailing cases, management has a duty to remain informed, to run the corporation in a prudent manner, and, in so doing, to act in the best interests of the corporation, free from personal motives, self-dealing, and neglect.[248] Management has a duty to act lawfully[249] and an obligation not to enrich itself at the corporation's expense.[250] Such doctrines as fiduciary duty, the duty of loyalty, the duty to act lawfully, and the doctrine of waste have their source in common law limitations on management actions.[251]

What implications does the separation of ownership and control have for the regulation of corporate political speech?

---

246. *See* William L. Cary, *Federalism and Corporate Law: Reflections Upon Delaware,* 83 YALE L.J. 663, 666 (1974). The phenomenon observed by Professor Cary was first described by Justice Brandeis in his dissent in *Louis K. Liggett Co. v. Lee,* 288 U.S. 517, 558-59 (1933), in which he described the competition between states for corporate charters as a race "of laxity." For a description of the development of the term and a compendium of adherents to the principle it reflects, *see* Jonathan R. Macey & Geoffrey P. Miller, *Toward an Interest Group Theory of Delaware Corporate Law,* 65 TEX. L. REV. 469, 469 n.1 (1987).

247. The race for the bottom is generally attributed to interstate competition for corporate franchise taxes. *See* Macey & Miller, *supra* note 246, at 470. The relatively small State of Delaware has, through the attractiveness of its corporation laws, become the state of incorporation for many major United States businesses. *See id.* at 478 (43% of New York Stock Exchange firms are incorporated in Delaware). Delaware pays for 16% of its annual budget through corporate franchise taxes. Melvin Aron Eisenberg, *The Structure of Corporation Law,* 89 COLUM. L. REV. 1461, 1506 n.206 (1989) (citing UNITED STATES DEP'T OF COMMERCE, BUREAU OF THE CENSUS, GOV'T FINANCES — STATE GOV'T FINANCES IN 1987, at 12 (1988)); *see* Cary, *supra* note 246, at 684 ("Perhaps there is no public policy left in Delaware corporate law except the objective of raising revenue.").

248. *See, e.g.,* Joy v. North, 692 F.2d 880, 895 (2d Cir. 1982), *cert. denied,* 460 U.S. 1051 (1983); Smith v. Van Gorkom, 488 A.2d 858, 893 (Del. 1985); Francis v. United Jersey Bank, 87 J.J. 15, 32, 432 A.2d 814, 822 (1981).

249. *E.g.,* Miller v. American Tel. & Tel. Co., 507 F.2d 759, 762 (3d Cir. 1974).

250. *E.g.,* Guth v. Loft, Inc., 23 Del. Ch. 255, 272-73, 5 A.2d 503, 511 (1939).

251. *E.g.,* Bates v. Dresser, 251 U.S 524, 529 (1920).

C. Better Alternatives

The preexistence of a system of corporate regulation suggests that, in order to ascertain whether statutes such as FECA are narrowly tailored to meet the governmental interest involved, the Court should determine if the evils reputedly presented by corporate political speech can be regulated by traditional corporate law. In other words, is an alternative method of regulating corporate political speech equally effective without intruding so deeply on first amendment values?

1. Fiduciary Duty Law

Before endorsing a statutory restriction on corporate political speech, one should understand what restrictions already exist by virtue of common law limitations on management's actions.[252] The common law provides several important restrictions on corporate political speech that the Court seemed to overlook in *Austin*. First, management cannot spend corporate funds on political issues that further its political objectives rather than those of the corporation.[253] Such spending constitutes self-dealing and waste, and the corporation's stockholders have a cause of action in the name of the corporation to recover amounts wrongfully spent.[254] Second, management cannot cause the corporation to engage in

---

252. The common law has been supplemented in name, although probably not in effect, by statutory provisions enacting a standard of due care, *e.g.*, CAL. CORP. CODE § 309(a) (West 1990); N.Y. BUS. CORP. LAW § 717 (McKinney 1990), or setting forth procedures to be followed when a director has a possible conflict of interest, *e.g.*, DEL. CODE ANN. tit. 8, § 144 (1988). Whether these provisions add anything to the common law principles from which they are derived is unclear. *See, e.g.*, Marciano v. Nakash, 535 A.2d 400, 403-04 (Del. 1987).

253. The distinction between spending that furthers the corporation's interests and waste is not always obvious. For a discussion of the legal principles applicable to the doctrine of waste and the inherent difficulty in applying these principles to comparable subjects, such as executive compensation, *see* Cary & Melvin Aron Eisenberg, CORPORATIONS CASES AND MATERIALS 604–32 (6th ed. 1988). Courts generally consider as valid expenditures that further any legitimate corporate objective, even if motivated by personal reasons. The difficulty in distilling from any corporate political spending management's personal motives lends support to Professor Brudney's position that corporate political spending is generally wasteful and therefore that state law may constitutionally restrict it. *See* Victor Brudney, *Business Corporations and Stockholders' Rights Under the First Amendment*, 91 YALE L.J. 235, 256–65 (1981).

254. *See* First Nat'l Bank v. Bellotti, 435 U.S. 765, 795 (1978) ("minority stockholders generally have access to the judicial remedy of a derivative suit to challenge corporate disbursements alleged to have been made for improper corporate purposes or merely to further the personal interests of management").

political speech unless management believes in good faith that such speech will further the corporation's interests. The relationship between the expenditure and the corporation's overall benefit need not be direct; indeed, corporations have long made charitable contributions based on the theory that corporate social responsibility provides an intangible benefit to the corporation, through enhanced reputation or such.[255] Nonetheless, such a relationship must exist; otherwise, courts consider the expenditure a waste of corporate assets and deem it wrongful, rendering management personally liable.[256] Third, management must pursue, as its primary objective, the achievement of corporate profits.[257] Although various statutory amendments have expanded the scope of interests that management may consider in making decisions to include employees, suppliers, and community interests,[258] management that fails to place the needs of the stockholders first[259] will, in the long run, find itself voted out of office.[260]

---

255. *See* CARY & EISENBERG, *supra* note 253, at 115-30 (tracing the development of statutory provisions relating to charitable contributions and examining relation of such contributions to corporate welfare).

256. *See, e.g.*, HENN & ALEXANDER, *supra* note 3, § 234, at 622-23. This is true even if a majority of the stockholders consent to the wasteful action; *see* Brudney, *supra* note 253, at 244 n.40 (citing cases).

257. *See, e.g.*, AMERICAN LAW INST., PRINCIPLES OF CORPORATE GOVERNANCE § 2.01 (Tent. Draft No. 2, 1984) ("A business corporation should have as its objective the conduct of business activities with a view to enhancing corporate profit and shareholder gain....").

258. *E.g.*, N.Y. BUS. CORP. LAW § 717(b) (McKinney 1990); 15 PA. CONS. STAT. § 511(B) (1988).

259. The extent to which corporations consider social policy and choose goals that favor social responsibility at the expense of corporate profits remains an area of debate. *See generally* David L. Engel, *An Approach to Corporate Social Responsibility*, 32 STAN. L. REV. 1, 3-4 (1979) (suggesting that the pursuit of social ends at the expense of corporate profits is socially undesirable, except in certain specified areas); Edwin M. Epstein, *Societal, Managerial, and Legal Perspectives on Corporate Social Responsibility—Product and Process*, 30 HASTINGS L.J. 1287, 1288 (1979) (asserting that "corporate managers [should] take account of the total consequences of their decisions in determining company policies and practices"); Rappaport, *Let's Let Business Be Business*, N.Y. TIMES, Feb. 4, 1990, § 3, at 13, (arguing that corporate participation is an inefficient way to solve social problems and that the corporation's only social responsibility should be to increase its value to "stakeholders").

260. Commentators have termed the mechanism that supposedly aligns the interests of stockholders and management "the market for corporate control." *See* Eisenberg, *supra* note 247, at 1497-99. They claim that this market addresses concerns about management wrongdoing or inefficiency by functioning in such a way that managers who do not perform satisfactorily are replaced. Commentators are divided, however, as to whether the

Two distinct mechanisms, the derivative suit and the stockholder vote, enforce the common law limitations on management conduct. The literature on the effectiveness of both as tools for enforcing compliance with management's duties to the corporation is extensive, and this Article will not review it in detail.[261] Suffice it to say that an ample body of scholarship takes the position that stockholders' tools for disciplining their agents are, in large part, ineffective.[262] The combination of stockholder apathy, inability of small stockholders to communicate and coordinate with one another, lack of access to full information, and procedural hurdles to stockholder derivative suits[263] permits management to undertake many objectionable activities with impunity.

---

market for corporate control actually functions successfully. *See, e.g.,* John C. Coffee, *Regulating the Market for Corporate Control: A Critical Assessment of the Tender Offer's Role in Corporate Governance,* 84 COLUM. L. REV. 1145 (1984); Frank H. Easterbrook & Daniel R. Fischel, *The Proper Role of a Target's Management in Responding to a Tender Offer,* 94 HARV. L. REV. 1161, 1173-82 (1981); Herman, *The Limits of the Market as a Discipline in Corporate Governance,* 9 DEL. J. CORP. L. 530 (1984).

261. For a sampling of the literature addressing the derivative suit, *see* Daniel R. Fischel & Michael Bradley, *The Role of Liability Rules and the Derivative Suit in Corporate Law: A Theoretical and Empirical Analysis,* 71 CORNELL L. REV. 261, 262 n.2 (1986). For scholarship dealing with the effectiveness of shareholder voting and access to the proxy machinery, *see* Patrick J. Ryan, *Rule 14a-8, Institutional Shareholder Proposals, and Corporate Democracy,* 23 GA. L. REV. 97, 99 n.8 (1988).

262. *See, e.g.,* Fischel & Bradley, *supra* note 261, at 292 ("Many analyses of corporate law assume that liability rules enforced by derivative suits play a fundamental role in aligning the interests of managers and investors. We have shown that this widespread assumption is not supported by either the theory of liability rules, the available empirical evidence, or the structure of corporate law."); Daniel R. Fischel, *Organized Exchanges and the Regulation of Dual Class Common Stock,* 54 U. CHI. L. REV. 119, 136 (1987) ("In most cases, the collective action problem faced by dispersed shareholders renders voting relatively ineffective as a monitoring mechanism."); Exchange Act Release No. 34-24623, 52 Fed. Reg. 23,665 (June 22, 1987) (Commission recognizes that the "collective action" limitations on shareholder voting make voting an ineffective tool for shareholders to resist management proposals); *see also* John C. Coffee & Donald E. Schwartz, *The Survival of the Derivative Suit: An Evaluation and a Proposal for Legislative Reform,* 81 COLUM. L. REV. 261, 264-65 (1981) (discussing the impairment of shareholders' mechanisms for enforcing corporate accountability); Frank H. Easterbrook & Daniel R. Fischel, *Voting in Corporate Law,* 26 J.L. & ECON. 395, 395-97 (1983) (comparing assertions that shareholders should take back their lost control over the decisionmaking process with contentions that shareholders do not have the ability to govern); Melvin Aron Eisenberg, *Access to the Corporate Proxy Machinery,* 83 HARV. L. REV. 1489, 1490 (1970) (suggesting that managers rather than shareholders control corporate actions).

263. Procedural hurdles to shareholder derivative suits include the requirements of contemporaneous ownership, a demand on the board, and the posting of security for

These tools would work better if corporate political speech were sufficiently visible. One substantial limitation on a stockholder's ability to discipline his or her managers is the inability to discover what kind of political expenditures the corporation is making and in what amount. A modest addition to the federal securities laws could readily address this problem on the federal level. The Securities Exchange Act of 1934[264] and the Securities Exchange Commission (SEC) rules thereunder[265] require large, publicly held companies to disclose certain information about their annual operations to the SEC and to shareholders.[266] Congress or the SEC could amend the disclosure requirements to mandate specific disclosure of all corporate political expenditures.[267]

Providing a disclosure mechanism within the federal securities laws has several advantages over the current system of regulation. The first advantage is that the disclosure remedy is tied more precisely to the situations in which corporate political speech represents a potential threat. Political speech by small businesses organized as close corporations is not, as we have discussed, materially different from speech by partnerships, sole proprietorships, or other businesses that do not utilize the corporate form.[268] The potential danger in corporate speech comes at the level at which a substantial separation of ownership and management exists. The danger is aggravated at the level of the large, publicly held corporation in which the tools designed to monitor and discipline management function imperfectly. Because the securities laws require disclosure from precisely these corporations, the suggested provision will enable regulation of the poten-

---

expenses. *See* HENN & ALEXANDER, *supra* note 3, §§ 362, 365, at 1058-65, 1069-70.

264. Securities Exchange Act of 1934, 15 U.S.C. §§ 78a-78ll (1988).

265. General Rules and Regulations, Securities Exchange Act of 1934, 17 C.F.R. §§ 240.0-1 to .31-1 (1990).

266. Large, publicly held companies are required to register under § 12 of the Exchange Act. 15 U.S.C. § 78l (1988). Section 13 requires registered issuers to file periodical reports with the SEC. *Id.* at § 78m; *see* 17 C.F.R. §§ 240.13a-1 to -17 (1990). SEC rules prohibit such issuers from soliciting proxies for the election of directors unless the issuer has distributed an annual report to stockholders. *See id.* at § 240.14a-3.

267. This Article takes the position that the required disclosure should include the amount of corporate political expenditures, the medium in which such expenditures were made (such as television or distribution of letters), and the specific candidates to whom the expenditures related. Although disclosure of specific candidates' names may engender adverse publicity for the candidates, it is the most effective way of bringing home to stockholders the nature of the corporate political speech and of enabling stockholders to control speech with which they disagree through the corporate process.

268. Nor is political speech by large corporations different in kind from speech by large unincorporated businesses.

tial harm without burdening small entities that do not present analogous risks.

Second, disclosure will render management more accountable in the area of political expenditures by making corporate political speech more visible to stockholders and the public. Increased visibility will enable market forces governing corporations to function more efficiently. Among these forces is the market for stock prices. If a corporation spends a large amount of money to influence elections, rather than on salaries, research and development, and raw materials, Wall Street is likely to view it with suspicion. The market thus will join with Congress in discouraging expenditures that are not socially valuable. Disclosure and its attendant visibility also are likely to have a direct impact on management conduct. Requiring management to disclose expenditures to stockholders and to the investing public is generally viewed as deterring irresponsible or excessive expenditures; the mere element of accountability improves management performance by discouraging such conduct.

Third, accounting for political expenditures through the federal system of periodic disclosure provides stockholders with information on expenditures in connection with their proxy materials, encouraging stockholders to monitor their corporation's speech more directly by choosing not to re-elect those directors who permit excessive or unpopular political expenditures. Tying disclosure to the federal proxy process results in a system that encourages management's political expenditures to be responsive to stockholder opinion.[269]

2. State Corporation Law Statutes

If a direct statutory restriction on corporate political speech is necessary, the obvious alternative to a regulation like FECA is the alternative indirectly referenced in Justice Rehnquist's dissent in *Bellotti*: state corporation statutes that limit or regulate corporate political speech.[270] As Rehnquist observed, because such statutes are the constitutive instru-

---

269. Increased disclosure may be particularly effective at a time when stockholders are taking an increasingly active role in monitoring and attempting to influence the social policy of their corporations. *See, e.g., Shareholder Activism Replacing Divestment as Social Tool*, METAL WEEK, Apr. 16, 1990, at 3 (describing shareholder resolutions on issues including abortion, pollution, and South Africa); *Staff Acts on Shareholder Proposals on Directors, Stock Buybacks, Charities*, [Jan.-June] SEC. REG. & L. REP. (BNA), at 212-13 (Feb. 15, 1991) (describing various shareholder proposals for spring 1991 annual meetings, including proposals about corporate charitable contributions, election of directors, and director stock ownership).

270. *See* First Nat'l Bank v. Bellotti, 435 U.S. 765, 822-28 (1978) (Rehnquist, J., dissenting).

ments for the artificial entity that is a corporation, limitations on corporate speech in those statutes have an added legitimacy.[271] Although even an outright ban on corporate speech might be legitimate under a state corporation statute, legislatures are unlikely to implement such a ban because modern state corporation laws have failed to serve as significant regulatory tools due to the race to the bottom and the acceptance by state legislators of the lure of flexibility over the sword of Damocles. Expecting states to utilize state corporation law as a check on corporate political speech is thus not reasonable. At best, a statutory provision might require or expressly permit corporate charter provisions to deal with the issue of political expenditures.

3. Charter Provisions

A third way to handle corporate political speech is through the charter as corporate contract. Scholars have recently come to view the corporate contract as a far more potent tool for addressing issues of corporation law and policy.[272] This view is premised on the perception that a corporation is based on consensual relationships between investors, managers, and employees and that the terms of the agreements between these constituencies should govern the corporation. For example, if stockholders decide that they will not hold the directors whom they elect personally liable for breaching their fiduciary duty to the corporation, that decision is within the province of the stockholders and, assuming they make it on an informed basis and without any procedural deficiencies, statutory law should not deem it invalid.[273]

The justification for allowing this freedom of contract is the notion that contractual provisions that are not socially and economically efficient will not endure in a market economy.[274] If it thus turns out that a contractual provision like the one described above harms the corporation by causing directors to act carelessly and irresponsibly, the corporation will be at a competitive disadvantage to similar companies without that provision. The corporation's value, and ultimately its stock price, will suffer. Accordingly, the harmful effect on their investment will discourage stockholders from entering into such contractual provisions.[275]

---

271. *See id.* at 823-25 (Rehnquist, J., dissenting).

272. *See, e.g.,* Frank H. Easterbrook & Daniel R. Fischel, *The Corporate Contract,* 89 COLUM. L. REV. 1416 (1989).

273. *See, e.g.,* DEL. CODE ANN. tit. 8, § 102(b)(7) (1988).

274. *See* Easterbrook & Fischel, *supra* note 272, at 1428-34 (discussing the mechanism by which the terms of corporate governance affect the stock price).

275. *Cf.* Gordon, *supra* note 245, at 1554-85 (arguing that full contractual freedom in corporate law will not necessarily lead to wealth maximization and that some mandatory legal rules are needed to limit corporate behavior).

The contract theory of corporate law suggests an alternative approach to dealing with the perceived problems of corporate political speech. State corporation statutes could require corporations to address the political expenditures issue explicitly in their charters. For example, statutes could permit corporations to engage in political speech only if they have a charter provision that expressly authorizes such speech. The charter provision might limit the total amount the corporation could spend on political speech or the amount spent on any single candidate or issue.[276] In the alternative, the provision might require that all corporate political speech be authorized by stockholder vote. A corporation's management would thus have to submit to the stockholders any proposed expenditure in favor of a political candidate.

Charter provisions offer several advantages over direct regulation of corporate political speech. First, they do not result in state interference with constitutionally protected speech. Any limitations imposed on a corporation's speech are imposed by the corporation itself; they are a decision by the potential speaker not to speak. Second, charter provisions deal specifically with the potential for management abuse. Stockholders who are concerned that management will waste corporate funds on political expenditures can limit such expenditures or require their submission for stockholder approval. Third, charter provisions address the Court's concern in *Austin* that political speech be publicly supported. Stockholders must either approve the political expenditure directly or, by expressly delegating to management the authority to make political expenditures, indirectly.

II. Conclusion

This Article began by recognizing the widespread perception that corporations are evil and that corporate political speech is still viler. Although it questions some of the foundations upon which that perception is based, this Article did not attempt to rebut that view. Nor did it attempt to justify corporate political speech based on the conception of the corporation as person or citizen. Based instead on the premise that corporate political speech, like other political speech, furthers first amendment values such as free trade in the marketplace of ideas, this Article questioned whether an outright prohibition of corporate political speech in connection with candidate elections is justified or necessary. In particular, it asked whether the Supreme Court can legitimately uphold such prohibi-

---

276. The provisions could contain an absolute dollar limitation or a limitation based on a percentage of earnings.

tions without considering the availability of other, less intrusive methods of regulating corporate political speech.

A review of the Court's analysis in *Austin* compels the conclusion that the Court's perception of the potential evil arising from corporate political speech is overstated. Moreover, based on the strict scrutiny with which the Court must examine the prohibition, the potential evil does not justify the ban. Rather, traditional corporation law offers a multitude of less intrusive methods for dealing with the corrosive effect of corporate speech, and the first amendment compels the Court to consider those alternatives.

Clipping Coupons for Democracy: An Egalitarian/Public Choice Defense of Campaign Finance Vouchers

Richard L. Hasen

Introduction

Perhaps nothing is more certain in American society than a cycle of disgust with the political process followed by calls for electoral reform.[1] The moment for reform has arrived yet again. Indeed, widespread public and scholarly disillusionment with the current political process may provide the first opportunity for serious campaign finance reform since Congress passed the post-watergate amendments to the Federal Election Campaign Act (FECA).[2]

Public dissatisfaction with politicians and the political process is at an all-time high. In 1992, three-quarters of all Americans believed that the government was "pretty much run by a few big interests looking out for them-

---

1. Such disgust has become as inevitable as death and taxes. Apparently it was Benjamin Franklin who, in 1789, first commented upon their inevitability. "Our Constitution is in actual operation; everything appears to promise that it will last; but in this world nothing is certain but death and taxes." JOHN BARTLETT, FAMILIAR QUOTATIONS 348 (Emily Morison Beck ed., 15th ed. 1980).

2. Federal Election Campaign Act Amendments of 1974, Pub. L. No. 93-443, 88 Stat. 1263 [hereinafter FECA Amendments].

selves" rather than "for the benefit of all people."[3] By contrast, fewer than one-third of all Americans believed that in 1964.[4] This widespread perception that our political system is corrupt or anti-egalitarian, along with growing concern over Washington "gridlock,"[5] suggests that the American public may be willing to consider radical solutions for political reform.

What else explains both the widespread support for a quirky Texas billionaire perceived as "too rich to be bought," and the rising number of state initiatives aimed at limiting the terms of elected officials[6] and the size of campaign contributions?[7]

Legal scholarship has begun to mirror the public disgust with the current money-driven campaign finance system. Members of the Supreme Court and some legal scholars have been chipping away at the constitutional underpinnings of *Buckley v. Valeo*,[8] the main legal roadblock to fundamental campaign finance reform. In the 1976 *Buckley* decision, the Court upheld the FECA amendments' limits on campaign contributions,[9]

---

3. University of Michigan Center for Political Studies, American National Election Studies 1952–1990, Table 4.13 (unpublished data, on file with author). The actual figure is 76%. *Id.*

4. *Id.* The 1964 figure of 29% rose in each subsequent National Election Survey, with the exception of the 1982 and 1984 surveys. *Id.*

5. Far from distancing themselves from gridlock, some Republicans recently have embraced it. *See* Gloria Borger, *Giving the Voters a False Choice*, U.S. NEWS & WORLD REP., Oct. 24, 1994, at 63 ("So now comes a new political treatise, touted by Republicans everywhere. It is the Good Gridlock Theory of Government, and it is based on an appealing, common-sense calculation: Stopping bad legislation is a good idea.").

6. Before the Supreme Court struck down Congressional term limits passed by state initiative in *U.S. Term Limits, Inc. v. Thornton*, 115 S. Ct. 1842 (1995), supporters of such term limits had prevailed at the polls in 22 states. Linda Greenhouse, *In Term Limits Debate, Justices Take Up a "Very Hard" Case*, N.Y. TIMES, Nov. 30, 1994, at B9.

7. *See* Wade Goodwyn, States Push for Campaign Finance Reform (National Public Radio Morning Edition broadcast, Feb. 13, 1995), transcript available in LEXIS, Nexis Library, Curnws File (noting the success of initiatives limiting campaign contributions in Oregon, Missouri, and Montana, failure of such an initiative in Colorado, and organization in California for such an initiative to be placed on 1996 ballot). A diverse collection of groups has supported these initiatives, including: The Association of Community Organizations for Reform Now (ACORN), the American Association of Retired Persons, Common Cause, the League of Women Voters, and United We Stand America, the organization that grew out of Ross Perot's 1992 presidential campaign.

8. 424 U.S. 1 (1976).

9. *Id.* at 22–35 (upholding a $ 1000 limit on contributions by individuals and groups to candidates and authorized campaign committees); *id.* at 35–36 (upholding a $ 5000 limit on contributions by political action committees); *id.* at 38 (upholding a $ 25,000 limit on total individual contributions during any calendar year).

but struck down its various expenditure limits.[10] However, by 1990, the Court began to voice concern over the "corrosive and distorting effects of immense aggregations of wealth" on American politics, and for the first time it upheld limits on independent campaign expenditures.[11]

Cynicism with the current political climate is understandable. To take one example, consider the case of Brush Wellman, a Cleveland-based mining company.[12] An 1872 mining law, originally intended to encourage homesteading, has allowed companies like Brush Wellman to purchase

---

10. *Id.* at 39–51 (striking down a $ 1000 limit on expenditures relative to a clearly identified candidate); *id.* at 51–54 (striking down a limit on expenditures by candidates from personal or family resources); *id.* at 54–59 (striking down a limit on overall campaign expenditures by candidates seeking nominations for election and election to federal office).

11. Austin v. Michigan State Chamber of Commerce, 494 U.S. 652, 659–60 (1990). An independent expenditure is money spent to support or defeat a clearly defined candidate, which is made "without cooperation or consultation with any candidate, or any authorized committee or agent of such candidate, and which is not made in concert with, or at the request or suggestion of, any candidate, or any authorized committee or agent of such candidate." 2 U.S.C. 431(17) (1994).

Some legal scholars have moved more brazenly, comparing *Buckley* to the infamous case of *Lochner v. New York,* 198 U.S. 45 (1905), and arguing that the Court has no more business preventing legislatures from regulating the political marketplace through campaign finance laws than the Court had preventing the New York legislature from regulating the economic marketplace by limiting the number of hours bakers could work. *See, e.g.,* JOHN RAWLS, POLITICAL LIBERALISM 362 (1993) ("The First Amendment no more enjoins a system of representation according to influence effectively exerted in free political rivalry between unequals than the Fourteenth Amendment enjoins a system of liberty of contract and free competition between unequals in the economy, as the Court thought in the *Lochner* era."); Cass R. Sunstein, *Free Speech Now, in* THE BILL OF RIGHTS IN THE MODERN STATE 255, 291 (Geoffrey R. Stone et al. eds., 1992) ("We should view [*Buckley*] as the modern-day analogue of *Lochner v. New York*: a decision to take the market status quo as just and prepolitical, and to use that decision to invalidate democratic efforts at reform.") (footnote omitted); *see also* Bruce Ackerman, *Crediting the Voters: A New Beginning for Campaign Finance*, 13 AM. PROSPECT 71, 78–79 (1993) (citing repudiation of *Lochner* in defense of campaign finance voucher plan). Perhaps the earliest scholarly effort comparing *Buckley* to the *Lochner* era appears in Note, *The Corporation and the Constitution: Economic Due Process and Corporate Speech*, 90 YALE L.J. 1833, 1855 (1981). One scholar has compared *Buckley* to the infamous case of *Plessy v. Ferguson,* 163 U.S. 537 (1896), arguing that *Buckley* gave rise "to an electoral system in which the rich and the poor are radically separate in power but deemed equal in theory." Jamin B. Raskin, *Challenging the "Wealth Primary,'* THE NATION, Nov. 21, 1994, at 609, 611. To be sure, not all First Amendment scholars accept the *Buckley-Lochner* analogy. *See infra* Part III.D.2, and notes 197–200.

12. *See* Keith Epstein, *Fortune Hidden Under Desert: Cleveland Firm Wants to Buy Land With Rare Ore for $ 26,487*, CLEVELAND PLAIN DEALER, May 22, 1994, at 1A.

publicly owned lands managed by the U.S. Forest Service and Bureau of Land Management for about $ 10 an acre. The Utah land that Brush Wellman will purchase for $ 26,487 contains a rare bertrandite ore that, when processed, could be worth up to $ 15 billion.[13]

Although the Clinton Administration, and particularly Interior Secretary Bruce Babbitt, made overhauling the mining law a major priority,[14] the mining industry prevented passage of a law to place royalties on minerals extracted from these public lands.[15] Brush Wellman, among others, made campaign contributions to key members of Congress in an effort to obtain an exemption from any new mining law. Indeed, in November 1993, two members of Congress who received campaign contributions from Brush Wellman came within 45 votes of exempting the company from the House's proposed legislation requiring higher mining fees and royalties.[16]

If dissatisfaction with the current system provides an opening for true political reform, what type of reform is best? This Article argues for a new system of campaign finance that should appeal to those on the left and the right: a plan for mandatory campaign finance vouchers that supplants, rather than supplements, our current campaign finance system. Under this plan, each voter would have the opportunity to contribute vouchers to candidates or to interest groups in every federal election cycle. The interest groups would use the vouchers to contribute to candidates or to organize independent expenditure campaigns. With limited exceptions, only funds from the voucher system could be spent to support or oppose candidates for elected federal offices.

The voucher plan will replace our plutocratic campaign finance system with a system driven by the intensity of voter support for candidates, causes, and ideologies. The plan does not depend upon utopian hopes that politics can become less self-regarding or more altruistic; instead, it reforms the political market with proper incentives and safeguards that channel self-regarding political behavior to produce fair and efficient political outcomes.

In order to explain how a voucher system will reform the political market to make politics better, this Article turns to public choice theory.[17]

---

13. *Id.*

14. John H. Cushman, Jr., *Congress Drops Efforts to Curb Public-Land Mining*, N.Y. TIMES, Sept. 30, 1994, at A1.

15. *Id.* The bill died in conference. "The House bill would have imposed a royalty of 8 percent on metals, but its negotiators agreed first to 5 percent, then a 4 percent royalty. The Senate's negotiators, on the other hand, agreed to go as high as 3.5 percent, but at that point the Mineral Resources Alliance said that even that figure was too high." *Id.* at A22.

16. Epstein, *supra* note 12, at 14A.

17. Public choice theory is the application of economic methodology to political science. DANIEL A. FARBER & PHILIP P. FRICKEY, LAW & PUBLIC CHOICE 7 (1991) (quoting Dennis C. Mueller, PUBLIC CHOICE II 1 (1989)). Mueller's book is the best technical

Part I briefly reviews the methodology of public choice theory and its positive and normative understandings of the political market. Although public choice theory often has been used to justify anti-democratic and anti-egalitarian political reform,[18] this need not be so. Instead, public choice theory, stripped of its wealth-maximizing orientation, can provide a useful means for assessing the relative strengths of different proposals for egalitarian political reform.

To evaluate democratic reform proposals, I replace normative public choice theory's efficiency criterion with the normative goal of promoting an egalitarian pluralist political market.[19] By a pluralist political market, I mean that (1) political preferences are not distributed randomly across the population, but rather are correlated with membership in groups, such as race, class, gender, and geographical location; and (2) each group's ability to have its political preferences enacted into legislation is a function of the group members' resources, or political capital, relative to other groups. In an egalitarian political market, each person has roughly equal political capital regardless of preexisting disparities in wealth, education, celebrity, ability, or other attributes. Egalitarian pluralism therefore recommends efforts to cure the problem of group under-representation in the political process by redressing inequalities in different groups' political capital.[20]

---

introduction to public choice theory; Farber and Frickey's book is the best non-technical introduction. Like Farber and Frickey, I think it is irrelevant whether the analysis I advance below is characterized properly as an application of public choice theory, interest group theory, social choice theory, or positive political theory. *See* Daniel A. Farber & Philip P. Frickey, *Foreword: Positive Political Theory in the Nineties*, 80 GEO. L. J. 457, 458 n.10 (1992) (recounting how the authors inadvertently became caught in an "academic turf war" between economists and political scientists over the proper meaning of the term "public choice").

18. *See infra* Part I.C.

19. This Article is not intended as a full-scale defense of egalitarian pluralism; in recognition of the law of comparative advantage, I leave that task to others. For a general introduction to and critique of the egalitarian pluralist concept, *see* Joshua Cohen & Joel Rogers, *Secondary Associations and Democratic Governance*, 20 POL. & SOC'Y 393, 411–16 (1992). To be sure, egalitarian pluralism is not the only way to define political equality; indeed, the concept of political equality has been defined in many inconsistent ways. *See generally* CHARLES R. BEITZ, POLITICAL EQUALITY (1989); Rawls, *supra* note 11; AMARTYA SEN, INEQUALITY REEXAMINED (1992); MICHAEL WALZER, SPHERES OF JUSTICE (1983); Ronald Dworkin, *What is Equality? Part 3: The Place of Liberty*, 73 IOWA L. REV. 1 (1987); Ronald Dworkin, *What is Equality? Part 4; Political Equality*, 22 U.S.F. L. REV. 1 (1987); Dennis C. Mueller, et al., *On Equalizing the Distribution of Political Income*, 82 J. POL. ECON. 414 (1974). I discuss criteria for determining whether reform plans meet the goal of egalitarian pluralism *infra* Part III.A.

20. Cohen & Rogers, *supra* note 19, at 412–13.

Part II of this Article uses positive public choice theory to describe the current campaign finance system and presents an egalitarian voucher plan as an alternative. This Part demonstrates that the current political market favors the wealthy and well-organized at the expense of the poor and those who have difficulty organizing for collective action.

Part III describes how a voucher plan would serve egalitarian pluralism by evaluating it under four criteria: egalitarianism, impact on governance, benefits as a preference-aggregation mechanism, and likelihood of enactment.[21] The voucher plan has a number of egalitarian benefits. It minimizes the impact of wealth on the political system and empowers those who currently lack political capital; it is likely to promote a stable transition to a more egalitarian political order and a more chaotic, though fairer, legislative process; its market-orientation registers the intensity of voter preference well; and it is a non-bureaucratic reform plan that has a real chance of being enacted.

Finally, Part IV of this Article uses the four egalitarian pluralist criteria to compare the voucher plan with three other egalitarian pluralist plans: non-voucher public financing of Congressional campaigns, proportional representation, and group-based political solutions. The voucher plan is superior to these plans on a host of grounds. First, in comparison to non-voucher public financing, the voucher plan does a better job of both minimizing the impact of wealth on the political system and of empowering those individuals lacking political capital. It also does a better job of measuring the intensity of voter preferences. Second, the voucher plan is more effective than proportional representation. Although proportional representation measures intensity of voter preferences well, it fails to minimize the impact of disparities in wealth and organizational ability on the political process. In addition, proportional representation may have a negative impact on governance, creating conditions for political instability. Moreover, proportional representation has very little chance of being enacted in the United States any time soon. Finally, the voucher plan is superior to group-based political solutions. Group-based plans raise the level of political capital only for particular "anointed" groups—in the two plans I discuss, these anointed groups are defined either by economic class or group oppression. The anointing process, combined with possible group veto power, undermines basic egalitarian norms. In addition, unlike the relatively stable voucher plan, these group-based plans present a potential for great political instability, which could negate any egalitarian

---

21. I define these criteria *infra* Part III.

* * *

gains that are made. Finally, these group-based plans are unlikely to be enacted in the United States any time soon.

* * *

II. How Mandatory Campaign Finance Vouchers Would Change Current Campaign Finance Laws

* * *

B. The Mechanics of a Campaign Finance Voucher Plan

Generally, campaign finance reform plans either seek to "level-up," by increasing the ability of those shut out of the political system to participate, or to "level-down," by decreasing the ability of those with disproportionate political capital to exercise greater influence over the political system.[87] A voluntary public financing system, which allows candidates either to accept public funds or solicit private contributions, is a classic level-up program; it amplifies the voice of the poor but does not limit the influence of the rich. A law limiting the amount an individual or PAC can contribute to a candidate is a classic level-down program.

Past proposals to use publicly funded vouchers have been of the level-up variety only. For example, in 1967, Senator Lee Metcalf proposed a plan under which taxpayers would receive campaign vouchers from the government, but politicians could accept private money as well.[88]

---

87. *See generally* Joel L. Fleishman & Pope McCorkle, *Level-Up Rather Than Level-Down: Towards a New Theory of Campaign Finance Reform*, 1 J.L. & POL. 211 (1984).

88. Metcalf's plan is described in DAVID W. ADAMANY & GEORGE E. AGREE, POLITICAL MONEY: A STRATEGY FOR CAMPAIGN FINANCING IN AMERICA 189 (1975). Adamany and Agree endorsed a modified level-up voucher plan based upon Metcalf's ideas. *See id.* at 199 (commenting that voucher plan "does not replace all private giving"). Adamany and Agree argued against allowing interest groups to collect the vouchers as intermediaries: "Some reservations about the voucher plan arise from the potential for well-organized groups or powerful institutions to collect certificates from members, employees, and other affiliated persons and then to pass along blocs of vouchers to favored candidates." *Id.* at 189–90. As I explain *infra* notes 127–28, however, this "bundling" by interest groups is an advantage of the voucher plan because it serves important egalitarian pluralist goals.

Schmitter also has proposed a voucher plan for funding political activity which differs

Recently, however, Bruce Ackerman and I independently have proposed publicly financed voucher systems which both level-up and level-down.[89] These voucher plans level-up in the sense that all voters, even those voters who have never made campaign contributions before, are given vouchers to contribute to candidates for federal office. Vouchers facilitate the representation of groups which lack a voice in the current system. But these vouchers also level-down by prohibiting all other sources of campaign money; the rich can no longer exercise greater influence through private contributions and independent expenditures.

Here are the key elements of my voucher plan.[90] The government provides every voter with a voucher for each bi-annual federal election. Each

---

in significant ways from the voucher program here; Schmitter's voucher proposal is level-up, in that Schmitter would put no limit on the ability of the wealthiest and best organized to outspend or outorganize new groups created with vouchers. Philippe C. Schmitter, Corporative Democracy: Oxymoronic? Just Plain Moronic? Or a Promising Way Out of the Present Impasse? 36 (First Draft, 1988) (unpublished manuscript, on file with author) [hereinafter Schmitter, Corporative Democracy]. Schmitter responded to critics who have read his unpublished article in a second unpublished article. Philippe C. Schmitter, Some Second Thoughts about Corporative Democracy: Oxymoronic or Moronic, Promising or Problematic? (Jan. 1991) (unpublished manuscript, on file with author) [hereinafter Schmitter, Second Thoughts]. He also presents a brief published defense of his plan in the symposium on Cohen and Rogers' associative democracy proposal, which I discuss *infra* Part IV.C. *See* Philippe C. Schmitter, *The Irony of Modern Democracy and Efforts to Improve Its Practice*, 20 POL. & SOC'Y 507 (1992) [hereinafter Schmitter, Irony]. Significantly, Schmitter would prevent voucher-funded groups from making contributions to electoral campaigns, political parties, or other associations. Schmitter, Corporative Democracy, *supra* at 59.

89. I proposed a voucher plan originally in my unpublished dissertation. *See* Richard L. Hasen, Beyond the Pursuit of Efficiency: An Enriched Law and Economics Analysis for Constructing Legal Rules, ch.4 (unpublished Ph.D. dissertation, University of California, Los Angeles, on file with author) [hereinafter Hasen, Beyond the Pursuit]. Bruce Ackerman then independently proposed a voucher plan in a short article in the journal American Prospect. *See* Ackerman, *supra* note 11. He has not had occasion to provide a scholarly treatment of his plan. Edward Foley discussed Ackerman's voucher plan in an article arguing for "equal-dollars-per-voter" as a matter of constitutional principle. Edward B. Foley, *Equal-Dollars-Per-Voter: A Constitutional Principle of Campaign Finance*, 94 COLUM. L. REV. 1204, 1208–13 (1994). Smurzynski hinted at a voucher plan in his discussion of campaign finance reforms. Kenneth C. Smurzynski, Note, *Modeling Campaign Contributions: The Market for Access and Its Implications for Regulation,* 80 GEO. L.J. 1891, 1911 (1992) (suggesting that public financing could be done through the "intermediary" of interest groups). This Article is the first published scholarly look at the efficacy and fairness of a post-voucher political system.

90. The plan set forth here differs in certain respects from the ideas of Ackerman and Foley. For example, Ackerman proposes a "pilot program" of voucher financing begin-

voter's voucher has a face value of $ 100, but in order to discourage voters from giving the whole sum to one candidate or group, the value of each donation will be reduced to its square root. A $ 100 donation is reduced to $ 10, while six $ 16 donations are reduced to $ 4 each. Therefore, the voter who gives one big donation only contributes a total of $ 10, but the contributor who makes six different donations could give a total of $ 24, assuming $ 16 is the smallest donation permissible under the voucher plan.[91]

---

ning with a presidential campaign and later extending to congressional elections. Ackerman, *supra* note 11, at 74. The plan discussed here, however, applies to all federal elections. Where there are significant differences between this plan and Ackerman's or Foley's ideas, I describe those differences in the footnotes below.

Regarding the technology for the voucher plan, Ackerman suggests a credit card, called "the Patriot card," for use in these elections. *Id.* at 71. The precise format for disbursing vouchers is unimportant, except that the format must be easy to use, so as not to discriminate against those lacking technical sophistication, and it must contain safeguards to prevent fraudulent use of vouchers.

91. These monetary figures are for illustrative purposes only. The actual amount of the vouchers would depend upon an empirical study of the amount necessary to fund effective campaigns for federal office, and it would have to be large enough so that each person's contribution is meaningful. Perhaps larger amounts would be necessary during presidential election cycles and smaller amounts in other years. Under the square root formula described in detail *infra* Part III.C, the value of the vouchers would be indeterminate before they are allocated by voters; assuming $ 16 is the smallest donation allowable under the voucher plan, a person could donate to six groups the equivalent of $ 4 each (4 being the square root of 16), making the maximum value of the vouchers $ 24. If a person donated her entire set of vouchers to one candidate or group, the voucher's value would be the square root of $ 100, or $ 10. Assuming an initial number of voters at 130 million, *see* Ackerman, *supra* note 11, at 73, the estimated initial cost for the program therefore would be between $ 1.3 billion and $ 3.12 billion, exclusive of enforcement costs. I discuss the political viability of a new $ 3 billion-plus government program *infra* Part III.D.1.

The initial cost of the program likely would go up. I would provide vouchers to all citizens eligible to vote, and not just to registered voters, as Ackerman and Foley advocate. *See* Ackerman, *supra* note 11, at 73; Foley, *supra* note 89, at 1243 n.123. an element of egalitarian pluralism is empowerment, and those with the least political capital in society are most likely to fail to register to vote.

Ackerman advocates a $ 10 voucher to fund only presidential campaigns at a projected cost of $ 1.3 billion. Ackerman, *supra* note 11, at 73. Foley believes Congress should set the total amount to be spent on vouchers as a percentage of the gross domestic product. Foley, *supra* note 89, at 1244. He notes that if the $ 2.7 billion spent for electoral politics in 1988 were divided by the 130 million registered voters, the same amount of overall spending could be reached with $ 20 vouchers. *Id.* at 1243.

I would limit the voucher plan initially to federal elections. Foley argues the constitutional principle of "equal-dollars-per-voter" should apply to state elections as well. Foley,

Voters may donate their voucher dollars either directly to candidates, to licensed interest groups, or to political parties.[92] The groups may serve whatever goals they please, whether ideological or economic. Thus, the NRA, NOW, and other ideological groups will compete for voucher dollars with the Beef Industry Council, the AFL-CIO, and other economic groups.[93]

All campaign contributions and independent expenditures in support of or in opposition to a candidate must be made with voucher dollars. Candidates and elected officials cannot receive any other direct donations, honoraria, soft money benefits, in-kind contributions, or other donations.[94] Elected officials may not be taken to dinner by lobbyists and they may not attend all-expense-paid industry retreats in Maui.[95]

Independent expenditure campaigns must be financed only through collected vouchers; with limited exceptions,[96] no private funds may be used. Individuals like Ross Perot, Herbert Kohl, and Michael Huffington could not bankroll their own campaigns.[97] Corporations (other than li-

---

supra note 89, at 1210 n.16. Moreover, I would allow voters to allocate the $ 100 in vouchers to whatever federal election or licensed interest group they wish. Thus, a New York resident could give her entire $ 100 in vouchers to a candidate for an Ohio Senate seat. But *see id.* at 1254 (suggesting that each voter receive a specific sum of money for each contest in which he is entitled to vote). This right would serve to counteract certain distorting effects of our geographically based electoral system. *See infra* note 130 (discussing cumulative voting, another system aimed to counter the distorting effects of geography).

92. On licensing requirements, *see infra* notes 100–01 and accompanying text. The state would cancel the vouchers of any voter who fails to allocate them in the current election cycle. Foley, in contrast, would allow electoral funds to be saved in accounts from one election cycle to the next, perhaps even earning interest. Foley, *supra* note 89, at 1253 & n.147.

93. Foley would require these organizations to set up separate electoral organizations with separate accounts. *Id.* at 1207–08. At a minimum, separate accounts are required. Schmitter advocates democratic governance of voucher-funded organizations. *See* Schmitter, Second Thoughts, *supra* note 88, at 9. I would leave governance of the interest groups to private agreement, but I would require disclosure of the groups' financial ledgers.

94. A state or national political party may use only vouchers for any activity that might affect the outcome of a federal election. *Cf.* S. 1219, 104th CONG. § 221 (1995) (proposing legislation which would impose a similar limit on the use of soft money).

95. Of course, elected officials still may go to dinner with lobbyists or attend the Maui convention. But they must pay their own way to do so.

96. *See infra* note 107–09 and accompanying text.

97. Ross Perot spent $ 60 million of his own money to mount his independent 1992 presidential campaign. Jamin Raskin & John Bonifaz, *Equal Protection and the Wealth Primary*, 11 YALE L. & POL'Y REV. 273, 329 n.292 (1993). Herbert Kohn used $ 7 million of his own money to run for a Wisconsin Senate seat. *Id.* at 329. Michael Huffington used $ 28 million of his own money to run for a California Senate seat, which, together with his opponent's $ 14 million, easily set a record for amounts spent on a senatorial cam-

censed interest groups) could not donate money to candidates or make independent expenditures for or against a candidate.[98] However, political activity not directly endorsing or opposing a candidate would not be subject to any limits.[99]

Only licensed interest groups could collect voucher dollars from others to run independent expenditure campaigns supporting candidates, and only those groups and the voters themselves could contribute vouchers to candidates. Any voter could register for a license to create an interest group, and the license would be free. An independent federal agency would process license requests. The agency could not turn down a group's licensing request for ideological reasons.

The license-granting agency would be independent of the political branches of government, much like the current Federal Reserve Board. This independence would prevent state officials from manipulating the system for their own benefit.[100] As a consumer watchdog, the agency

---

paign. B. Drummond Ayres Jr., *Feinstein Claims Victory in Senate Race*, N.Y. TIMES, Nov. 19, 1994, at 10.

Although these men may be among the richest politicians, politics is a rich person's game; at least 51 of the 100 Senators of the last Congress were millionaires, compared to one-half of one percent of the general population. *See* Raskin & Bonifaz, *supra*, at 289 (citing *Ten Fun Facts About Congress*, ROLL CALL, Apr. 23, 1992, at 3; *More of Everything: New York Compared with the Nation*, WASH. POST, July 12, 1992, at A11); *see also Just Ask Zoe*, THE NATION, Feb. 15, 1993, at 185 ("Millionaires were 62 percent of Reagan's cabinet, 71 percent of Bush's, and so far, 77 percent of Clinton's.").

Ackerman and Foley agree that candidates should be prohibited from using their own funds. Ackerman, *supra* note 11, at 76; Foley, *supra* note 89, at 1239–41.

98. Current law prohibits corporations from making contributions or expenditures in connection with the election of candidates for federal office. *See* 2 U.S.C. 441b(a) (1994).

99. Foley would include in his plan electoral activities in support of, or in opposition to, a ballot initiative. Foley, *supra* note 89, at 1249. However, as the plan advanced here concerns federal elections only, ballot initiatives are not a serious concern. Under this plan, the occasional drive to enact a constitutional amendment would be open to unlimited funding.

If voucher plans were extended to state elections generally, however, I agree with Foley that ballot initiatives should be covered. Otherwise, those with greater wealth could make an end-run around the legislature through the referendum process, as has happened already in California. *See* Peter Schrag, *California's Elected Anarachy*, HARPER'S MAG., Nov. 1994, at 50, 54. The skills necessary to run a successful initiative campaign have found takers both on the right and on the left: among environmentalists and tobacco prohibitionists on one side, among taxpayer groups on the other, and most emphatically among major industrial and professional groups—the insurance companies, the tobacco companies, the trial lawyers, the doctors—looking to fund special programs, or looking for protection and exemptions from regulation or for advantage against other interests. *Id.*

100. *See* ROBERT A. DAHL, DEMOCRACY AND ITS CRITICS 323 (1989) (discussing the danger posed by allowing the state to regulate political equality). The independent agency

would act to prevent fraud; interest groups could use the vouchers for legitimate organizational expenses, but group officers or employees could not use them for their own personal benefit.[101] The agency's chief mission would be to facilitate disclosure of voucher-collecting activities.

Volunteer time presents a tricky administrative issue for the voucher plan. As a preliminary matter, it should be noted that current law is far from clear as to how volunteer time donated to a candidate's campaign counts toward campaign contribution limits.[102] In *Buckley*, the Court held that a volunteer's expenditures undertaken at the candidate's direction properly could be viewed as contributions to the candidate.[103] Since then, the Court has classified payment of a PAC's administrative expenses by an unincorporated association as a contribution.[104] Lower courts have counted as contributions both post-election loan guarantees[105] and money spent to produce a candidate's television commercials.[106]

---

could prove to be a lightning rod for criticism of the voucher proposal. According to one report, Colorado's recent attempt to enact an initiative limiting campaign contributions was thwarted by the opposition's characterization of the independent commission charged with enforcing the contribution limit as "more government bureaucracy and more government spending." *See* Goodwyn, *supra* note 7 (quoting Rick Bainter, Director of Colorado Common Cause). In fact, the initiative was opposed by big labor and big business not because of the agency, but "primarily because of the limitations on funding for PACs." *Id.* (quoting Becky Brooks, lobbyist for the Colorado Education Association).

101. But salaries must be paid to those who run these groups, raising a host of principal-agency problems. *See infra* note 127 and accompanying text.

102. Under current federal law, independent expenditures are not subject to any limits. *See supra* note 10 and accompanying text.

103. Buckley v. Valeo, 424 U.S. 1, 36–37 (1976).

104. California Medical Ass'n v. FEC, 453 U.S. 182, 198 n.19 (1981).

105. Federal Election Comm'n v. Ted Haley Congressional Comm., 852 F.2d 1111, 1116 (9th Cir. 1988). *See also* Rich Connell & Frederick M. Muir, *Use of Art In Wachs' Campaign Examined*, L.A. TIMES, Feb. 20, 1993, at B1 (discussing the city attorney's determination whether a valuable donated art design is a contribution exceeding the $ 1,000 maximum imposed by city election laws).

106. United States v. Goland, 959 F.2d 1449, 1452 (9th Cir. 1992), *cert. denied*, 113 S. Ct. 1384 (1993). *Goland* presented the difficulty of drawing the line between contributions and independent expenditures. There, the defendant (whose other efforts I discuss *supra* note 79) contended that he wrote, paid for, and produced television commercials for a third party candidate in a U.S. Senate race in order to draw votes away from the Republican candidate thereby aiding the Democratic candidate. *Id.* at 1451–52. The defendant argued that he did not make an excessive "contribution" in favor of the third party candidate but rather made "independent expenditures" in favor of the Democratic candidate. *Id.* at 1452. The Ninth Circuit rejected the argument, noting that under the FECA independent expenditures must be made "without cooperation or consultation with any candidate." *Id.* (citing 2 U.S.C. 431(17); 11 C.F.R. 100.16 (1990)). The court

The post-Watergate FECA amendments exclude from the definition of contribution "the value of services provided without compensation by individuals who volunteer a portion or all of their time on behalf of a candidate or political committee."[107] The voucher plan would take a similar approach, if only to prevent prosecution for de minimis expenditures and an administrative nightmare.

Under the voucher plan, the value of any services volunteered by an individual would not count as a prohibited campaign contribution or expenditure. Thus, if James Carville or Mary Matalin wish to volunteer for their favorite candidate for no compensation, they are free to do so.[108] Nor would a volunteer's travel expenses or other incidental costs (up to $ 200 per candidate per election) incurred in support of or in opposition to a candidate count as a prohibited contribution or expenditure.[109] However, a person could not donate someone else's labor. For example, an employer could not donate her employee's services; such contributions must be paid for with vouchers and thus are limited by that amount.

To better understand these thorny administrability issues, consider three cases: first, a concerned citizen who opposes a particular candidate and wishes to write and distribute a pamphlet explaining why; second, the owner of an advertising agency who wishes to volunteer her time (and that of her employees) by working with the campaign to design political ads; and third, a political commentator for the most influential newspaper in the state, who, without cooperation or consultation with the candidate, writes an op-ed piece endorsing that candidate.

Under the rules of the voucher plan, the would-be pamphleteer can spend all the time she wants writing and creating a pamphlet supporting

---

held that Goland intended to contribute to the third party candidate's campaign, "and it is immaterial to conviction under [the FECA] that he did so in support" of the Democratic candidate. *Id.* The dissent argued that because Goland did not have the "subjective motive" to make a contribution to the third party candidate, his conviction could not stand. *Id.* at 1454–55 (Pregerson, J., dissenting).

107. *Buckley*, 424 U.S. at 36 (quoting the FECA, codified at 8 U.S.C. 591(e) (5) (A)).

108. Of course, they would remain free to write a "kiss-and-tell" book later. *See, e.g.,* MARY MATALIN & JAMES CARVILLE, ALL'S FAIR: LOVE, WAR, & RUNNING FOR PRESIDENT (1994). Campaign volunteers also may take policy-making patronage jobs if their preferred candidate is elected.

109. The candidate must reimburse any expenses incurred by a volunteer over the $ 200 limit that are made in cooperation or consultation with the candidate. The $ 200 limit on incidental costs allows a volunteer to undertake activities like occasional photocopying but prevents the volunteer from making large scale in-kind contributions of goods under the guise of this exception. For example, a director who volunteers her time to make a television commercial for a candidate could not provide thousands of dollars worth of videotapes as an "incidental cost" of making the commercial.

or opposing a candidate.[110] She can also spend up to $ 200 per election cycle on materials to reproduce the pamphlet, incidental to volunteering her time. If she wishes to disseminate the pamphlet further or to produce a glossier version, she has four options: she may (1) register as an interest group and collect vouchers from others; (2) persuade a licensed interest group to spend voucher money on her pamphlets; (3) persuade a candidate to spend voucher money on the pamphlets; or (4) create a bona fide "newsletter" or newspaper that does more than strictly endorse or oppose a candidate.[111]

The advertising executive, like the pamphleteer, may freely volunteer her own time to the candidate's campaign. She may also spend up to $ 200 per election cycle on expenses incidental to producing the ads. However, any additional expenses must be paid for with voucher dollars. Also, she cannot compel her employees to work on the political campaign. Time which paid employees spend working on a candidate's campaign must be paid for with voucher dollars.[112] Of course, if the employees volunteered to work on the campaign, their time would not count as a campaign contribution that must be funded with voucher dollars.

The political commentator writing an op-ed piece endorsing a candidate presents the most difficult administrative issue.[113] For several reasons, I side with Ackerman and against Foley: media endorsements should not be counted.[114] First, there is the administrative nightmare of allocating the correct portion of a newspaper's publishing costs to the production of the op-ed piece. More importantly, newspapers and other news media[115] are a

---

110. There would be no limit upon the right to disseminate political writings that do not specifically support or oppose a candidate.

111. For a discussion of this admittedly large loophole, *see infra* notes 113–17 and accompanying text.

112. Hefty criminal penalties with the real possibility of enforcement would be necessary to prevent employers and unions from coercing employees and union members into "volunteering" their time or signing over their voucher dollars. The anti-coercion provision of the law enacting the voucher plan would include a rebuttable presumption that employees or union members "volunteering" their time or voucher dollars at the "suggestion" of their employer or union were coerced into doing so.

113. It also presents a difficult First Amendment issue. *See infra* notes 175–202 and accompanying text.

114. Ackerman, *supra* note 11, at 75–76; Foley, *supra* note 89, at 1252 & nn. 142–44. However, even Foley would limit the prohibition on newspaper endorsements "to publications that expressly support or oppose a candidate or ballot initiative." *Id.* at 1253.

115. Here, I include television, radio, and the Internet as well. If reining in newspapers is difficult, imagine reining in the decentralized "information superhighway." *See generally* Eugene Volkh, *Cheap Speech and What It Will Do*, 104 YALE L.J. 1805 (1995).

valuable source of information for the public. Newspapers help people overcome collective action problems in acquiring information, a classic public good.[116] The media exception to the voucher plan is the same legitimate "loophole" allowed the pamphleteer discussed in the first hypothetical: she, too, provides information other than the strict endorsement of or opposition to a candidate.

To be sure, volunteer and media exceptions allow a greater voice to the advertising agency owner, the newspaper editorialist,[117] and the attorney who donates her time in support of a candidate, than they do to the janitor or farmer. The latter usually cannot donate services to a political campaign as valuable as those which can be rendered by a professional. However, it is necessary to allow this compromise of pristine egalitarian principles in order to have a workable system. And in any case, it is a small price to pay in order to achieve the overall egalitarian benefits of a voucher plan.[118] The volunteer and media exceptions do not affect the voucher plan's prohibition on significant monetary contributions to a candidate, and they do not allow one person to fund a large-scale independent expenditure campaign.[119] The exceptions present neither the serious danger of corruption, nor do they allow immense aggregations of wealth to distort the electoral system.

In order to assess the desirability of vouchers overall, we must consider what the political market would look like under such a system. The next section uses positive public choice theory to determine how well a voucher-based political system meets egalitarian pluralist goals.

---

116. *See generally* ROBERT COOTER & THOMAS ULEN, LAW AND ECONOMICS 112–116 (1988) (discussing the economics of information).

117. Indeed, Levinson views this inequality as the primary problem with any attempts at campaign reform: why limit what candidates can do when there are no limits on the media? *See* Sanford Levinson, *Electoral Regulation: Some Comments*, 18 HOFSTRA L. REV. 411, 412–13 (1989). I try to provide a rationale for this dichotomy in the text.

118. Even Foley acknowledges "pragmatic" considerations may favor excluding certain activities, like volunteer time, from voucher limits. Foley, *supra* note 89, at 1248. Indeed, pragmatism alone leads me to endorse an exclusion for volunteer time; I disagree with Ackerman that volunteer time should be excluded because citizens who volunteer time are more likely to be acting in "the public interest" than those who donate money. *Compare* Ackerman, *supra* note 11, at 76 ("Volunteers are not in it for the money, and their energies should not be charged against the campaign's budget.") *with* Foley, *supra* note 89 at 1246–47 (criticizing Ackerman's argument). The choice between donating time and money may depend upon one's marginal cost of each. To an unemployed person, for example, it is cheaper to donate time than money, but for a lawyer charging $ 300 an hour, it is cheaper to donate money. This has nothing to do with relative civic virtue.

119. *See supra* note 79 and accompanying text.

III.   The Benefits of a Mandatory Campaign Finance Voucher Plan

Egalitarian pluralism aims to equalize the ability of different individuals to affect the political process. It seeks to have each interest group's influence reflect the number and devotion of its followers, not the group's wealth or ability to organize.[120] This Part uses positive public choice theory to analyze the voucher plan under four egalitarian pluralist criteria:

(1)   Egalitarianism. How well does the proposed plan redistribute political capital from small, cohesive groups to other groups in proportion to their level of support in society?

(2)   Impact on Governance. How stable will the political system be after the redistribution of political capital? Will politicians chosen under the proposed plan be able to govern effectively?

(3)   Benefits as Preference-Aggregation Mechanism. How well does the preference- aggregation mechanism in the proposed plan work at registering intensity of preference? Is it open to strategic voting or manipulation by agenda-setters?

(4)   Likelihood of Enactment. Does the plan have a real chance of being enacted? Is it constitutional?

The first criterion, egalitarianism, is essential to evaluating any system which aims to give every citizen an equal say in the political process. Because egalitarian pluralism is based on the principle that disparities in wealth and ability to organize are not relevant to the individual's right to influence political outcomes, egalitarianism is the first and foremost criterion used to evaluate the proposed voucher plan.

I also evaluate the plan in terms of its impact on governance. Reform of the electoral process is meaningless unless we can expect it to lead to better legislative substance. Governance in the ideal egalitarian pluralist system will reflect the true distribution and weight of all societal interests. It also will be stable; individuals who lose political capital under the reform plan will have neither the power nor a strong incentive to return to the status quo. And finally, it must allow the legislature to make coherent public policy rather than causing it to devolve into a fragmented and ineffectual governing body.

Positive social choice theory suggests inclusion of the third criterion, the benefits of the plan as a preference-aggregation mechanism. As noted earlier,[121] some mechanisms are less open than others to strategic voting

---

120. Cohen & Rogers, *supra* note 19, at 412–13.

121. *See supra* Part I.B.

and agenda setting. Egalitarian pluralism requires that preference aggregation reflect the true distribution and weight of interests in society, not the interests of a few clever manipulators of the system. Moreover, some mechanisms do a better job than others of registering the intensity of individual preferences. A political system should reflect the true distribution and weight of different societal interests by being sensitive to the intensity of individual preferences.

Finally, I include likelihood of enactment as a criterion for evaluating the plan because I believe the window of opportunity for meaningful reform is limited; politicians are under pressure now to reform the political system, and even an ineffective reform plan (like the 1974 FECA amendments that survived *Buckley*) likely will remain in place for a long time. We should pursue proposals with a realistic chance of enactment, rather than proposals that are theoretically sound but politically unacceptable.

As I demonstrate in the rest of this Part and in Part IV, a voucher plan is the best hope for achieving egalitarian pluralism as measured by these four criteria.

A. Egalitarianism

The voucher plan is a perfect method for equalizing political capital to the extent that political capital is coterminous with money spent directly on elections. By providing each citizen with equal resources, the voucher plan guarantees to each an equal fiscal voice in the political process.

However, as explained earlier,[122] political capital is not perfectly correlated with wealth spent to influence elections. An additional key determinant of political capital is organizational ability, which in turn is a function of wealth not spent on elections. Wealthy people tend to be better educated, and education causes individuals to be socialized to participate in the political process despite collective action problems.[123] Moreover, wealthy corporations and individuals have the resources available to organize and often gain enough rents individually that it becomes individually rational to engage in lobbying activities.[124] Both factors indicate that the wealthy face fewer collective action problems organizing for political

---

122. *See supra* Part I.A. *But see* Lillian R. BeVier, *Campaign Finance Reform: Specious Arguments, Intractable Dilemmas*, 94 COLUM. L. REV. 1258, 1262–64 (1994) (disputing, without empirical support, the claim that the political market is stacked against the poor and minorities).

123. *See* Richard L. Hasen, *Voting Without Law?*, 144 U. PA. L. REV. (forthcoming 1996) (manuscript at 21–22, on file with author).

124. This explains the rationality of Brush Wellman's lobbying.

activity.[125] For this reason, financial equalization without organizational equalization will not produce equality of political capital.[126]

By spreading money for use in the political market evenly among all voters, the voucher plan also indirectly redistributes organizational skills. Once each voter has a voucher to spend in the electoral process, and candidates can no longer count on a few large donors to fill their coffers, a new class of political entrepreneurs will emerge who will collect vouchers from voters and deliver them in bundles to the candidates.[127] In the competition

---

125. Hovenkamp, *supra* note 30, at 108–09 ("The well-to-do, as a general rule, are better represented by lobbying organizations than the poor.").

126. Macey, *supra* note 57, at 1680 n.38. Macey opposes campaign finance reforms on these grounds. BeVier similarly argues that "stacking the deck against those "with wealth' inevitably entails stacking it in favor of those with other resources such as time, celebrity status, or a comparative advantage at political, as opposed to private sector, activity." BeVier, *supra* note 122, at 1268. BeVier calls upon those who support equalizing wealth in the political process to "defend these remaining disparities." *Id.* To the contrary, those who support equalizing wealth also should seek to equalize these other factors. The problem, however, is one of administrability. We regulate wealth alone, rather than celebrity status as well, because wealth may be regulated but celebrity status cannot be regulated. Moreover, Levinson points out a key difference between wealth and celebrity status. Although we generally believe there is correlation between one's political ideas and one's wealth, it is plausible to assume that "celebrities' political views are randomly distributed. For every Paul Newman who supports Walter Mandale, there is a Carole King who supports Gary Hart—and a Frank Sinatra who supports Ronald Reagan." Sanford Levinson, *Regulating Campaign Activity: The New Road to Contradiction?*, 83 MICH. L. REV. 939, 949 (1985). Thus, there is a lesser need to regulate use of celebrity status than use of wealth.

127. We should consider from a public choice perspective the motivation for individuals to become entrepreneurs. Although some will be motivated by altruism, many will be motivated by power or money. Because vouchers may be used to pay for interest group organizational support, including for the salaries of group employees, what is to stop the unscrupulous political entrepreneur from setting an extremely high salary for herself? Although this abuse is certainly possible, two factors militate against it. First, the independent agency charged with licensing interest groups will have full access to group books, and it may publicize instances of entrepreneur self-dealing. Second, political entrepreneurs representing competing interest groups will have an incentive to compete for voucher dollars by arguing that a lower percentage of each voucher dollar goes to administrative overhead, including salaries.

Consider the case of the United Way, whose indicted former president made a base salary of $ 390,000 per year. *See* Tim Weiner, *United Way's Ex-Chief Indicted in Theft*, N.Y. TIMES, Sept. 14, 1994, at A12; Evelyn Brody, Institutional Dissonance in the Nonprofit Sector 36–38 (June 30, 1995) (unpublished manuscript, on file with author). After news spread of the ex-president's "lavish living and questionable corporate spending practices," and he was indicted for stealing more than $ 1 million from the organization, confor vouchers, entrepreneurs will have the incentive to motivate and organize communities to use their new political capital; entrepreneurs' reputations will be enhanced by delivering votes to politicians along with voucher dollars. Competition should lead entrepreneurs to represent community interests. In sum, a new class of entrepreneurs will help currently underrepresented groups overcome their collective action problems.[128]

The voucher system will also force politicians to take heed to those voters they have traditionally ignored. A candidate seeks the support of the citizenry in two markets: the market for direct votes in elections and the market for indirect votes in the form of campaign contributions. The politician always has the incentive to look to everyone in the market for direct votes; the voucher system will provide the incentive to explore the entire market for campaign contributions as well. Just as she does in the actual election, the politician will have to pursue contributions from the population at large and all the interest groups that represent the voters.

A voucher system will not fully eliminate inequalities in different groups' organizational abilities, however. First, to the extent the poor have less leisure time, they will be less able to investigate the interest groups seeking their vouchers. Second, to the extent that the poor are less educated, they will be more susceptible to manipulation by interest groups that only purport to represent their interests and less likely to be socialized to overcome collective action problems. Finally, a voucher plan tends to favor already existing interest groups because they will have an organizational headstart in the race to collect voucher dollars.[129] Unfortunately, the poor have the fewest resources to give and face great collective action problems, and thus are poorly represented by the current crop of interest groups.

These problems, however, should dissipate as entrepreneurs create new interest groups to seek vouchers from previously unrepresented groups.

---

tributions to the United Way fell off sharply until United Way cleaned house. Weiner, *supra*, at A12. Similarly, with mandatory full disclosure and incentives to investigate, the voucher-funded interest group market generally should correct abuses of power.

128. One may wonder why voters would bother investigating various groups and candidates seeking vouchers, given the infinitesimal chance of influencing the outcome of an election through the use of vouchers. This argument mirrors public choice arguments made about the so-called paradox of voting: why bother to vote if it is unlikely to make a difference in the outcome of an election? *See* Hasen, *supra* note 123. I predict voucher use will follow voting patterns. To the extent people do not vote, they probably will not be very interested in the voucher plan unless convinced to be interested by political entrepreneurs. To the extent people vote, we can expect them to take the divvying up of voucher dollar seriously.

129. Schmitter, Corporative Democracy, *supra* note 88, at 55.

Also, even if some groups have greater difficulty organizing, their relative strength will increase as the more powerful interest groups lose political capital because of the level-down campaign finance limits imposed by the voucher program.[130]

B. Impact on Governance

In evaluating the voucher plan, it is not enough just to ask whether it will improve voters' opportunities for influencing elected officials. We must also consider the reform's impact on the actual operation of government. Ideally, the legislative process will produce laws reflecting the true distribution and weight of societal interests. Moreover, the law-making process should be politically stable and lead to coherent legislative and executive policies.

Under the voucher plan, legislation will better reflect the true distribution and weight of societal interests. Politician-agents will be responsive to the interest group brokers who bundle voucher dollars for politicians. Like the powerful interest groups of today, voucher-based groups will pressure and cajole politicians into voting for legislation that they support, or else run the risk of losing future campaign contributions. However, instead of securing enormous rents for a few wealthy and well-organized groups, the new groups will provide a reasonable and balanced degree of influence to all of society's interests. The voucher plan will replace our current pluralism, in which some groups are shut out of the political market while others dominate and skew it, with an egalitarian pluralism in which everyone has a more equal voice.

This is not to suggest that politicians will be completely beholden to voucher-backed interest groups. The voucher plan does not limit representatives' choices in voting on bills; it still allows for the Burkean exercise of

---

130. The voucher program does not protect groups that are very small in number or very diffuse in society, because there will not be enough voucher dollars in the system to create incentives for entrepreneurs to protect their interest. Thus, courts should continue to play a major role in protecting "discrete and insular minorities." *See* Bruce A. Ackerman, *Beyond* Carolene Products, 98 HARV. L. REV. 713, 718–22 (1985) (noting tension between pluralist theory and enhanced judicial review for minorities). The voucher plan also leaves the geographical basis of our electoral system untouched; accordingly, additional reforms like cumulative voting or proportional representation might be necessary to overcome these problems. *See* LANI GUINIER, THE TYRANNY OF THE MAJORITY: FUNDAMENTAL FAIRNESS IN REPRESENTATIVE DEMOCRACY 14–16 (1994) (defending cumulative voting); *see also infra* Part IV.B (discussing proportional representation).

independent judgment.[131] While politicians will care about campaign contributions, there is no reason to believe a voucher plan will limit our leaders' discretion any more than the current system does.[132]

Furthermore, although politicians no longer will be dependent on contributions from business interests, they will still seek out the advice and pay attention to the concerns of business. Public officials will always need a smooth, well-functioning economy if they hope to be re-elected.[133] Eliminating private campaign contributions will weaken the inordinate influence of big business, but elected officials will continue to seek advice from industry for the valid purpose of coordinating national, regional, and local economic policy.

The voucher system also will eliminate the extremely large rents that powerful interest groups command under the current system. The plan will lead to a proliferation of interest groups, each seeking to make deals with politicians. The absolute number of groups will increase, given the ease with which new groups can be formed and the incentives political entrepreneurs will have to create new groups. As the absolute number of groups increases, however, their relative power will decrease. Like the move from monopoly to oligopoly to a competitive market, an increase in participants in the political market will deny each existing group some market power. Eventually, each group will be able to extract fewer promises from politicians, who will be able to pick and choose among competing interest groups.[134]

The voucher plan is also likely to preserve political stability. Because adopting the voucher system does not directly change our method of choosing our leaders—unlike proportional representation and group-based political solutions[135]—the politics of tomorrow will echo the politics of today, albeit on a more level playing field. Changes in society will be incremental, not rapid or radical. Vouchers ensure stability because

---

131. Edmund Burke, Speech to the Electors of Bristol (Nov. 3, 1774), *in* 2 THE WORKS OF EDMUND BURKE 89, 95–96 (3d. ed. 1869) (arguing that legislators should exercise independent political judgment rather than simply follow constituents' preferences).

132. For a contrary view, *see* David A. Strauss, *Corruption, Equality, and Campaign Finance Reform*, 94 COLUM. L. REV. 1369, 1375–76 (1994).

133. CHARLES E. LINDBLOM, POLITICS AND MARKETS 134 (1977).

134. If, as I am predicting here, we see healthy competition between interest groups, interest group collusion is unlikely. My argument in the text implicitly assumes that there are no large areas of legislation untouched by current rent-seeking interest groups. To the extent this assumption is false, the over-all amount of rent seeking could increase even though each group would receive a smaller rent on average.

135. *See infra* Parts IV.B-C.

they allow for changes in relative power among groups without a major social upheaval. And as the interests and desires of society evolve, those changes will be reflected through the voucher system's market mechanism at the next election cycle. Thus, if a particular issue raises the ire of many voters, voucher dollars will shift to interest groups dedicated to addressing that issue. The fluidity of the funding mechanism assures more responsive political outcomes.

One could argue that the voucher plan would affect governance adversely by causing politicians to spend greater time collecting smaller amounts of money.[136] No doubt time spent fundraising takes away from a politician's ability to engage in fruitful legislative action. However, the voucher plan allows interest groups to act as brokers and bundle contributions;[137] politicians will inevitably court the larger, more influential groups rather than many small groups or the public at large. Gone will be the frequent trips to California to attend yet another $ 1,000 per plate dinner. Concerns that politicians under a voucher system will spend more time raising money than they do now are overstated.

Another concern is that because the voucher plan will cause the wealthy and well-organized to lose a great deal of political influence with elected officials, they can be expected to shift their battles to more favorable terrain. New targets for the wealthy and well-organized might include state legislatures and state ballot initiatives,[138] administrative rulemaking and adjudicative procedures, and constitutional amendments. However, the voucher-backed Congress would have the upper hand in the last two of these forums and could do much to block the success of any alternative efforts at rent seeking.

The most substantial threat which vouchers pose to political stability and the efficacy of government is their potential to further weaken political parties. Political scientists have identified political parties as serving important stabilizing and legitimating functions. These scholars argue that political parties insure stability by increasing the size of represented constituencies, thereby allowing interest group bargaining to take place within the confines of the party rather than in the legislative bodies themselves, where it is likely to be a free-for-all.[139] Moreover, party discipline

---

136. *E.g.,* Frank J. Sorauf, *Politics, Experience, and the First Amendment: The Case of American Campaign Finance,* 94 COLUM. L. REV. 1348, 1364 (1994).

137. *See supra* text accompanying note 83 (explaining bundling).

138. *See supra* note 99 (discussing whether ballot initiatives should be subject to voucher plan).

139. Michael A. Fitts, *The Vices of Virtue: A Political Party Perspective on Civic Virtue Reforms of the Legislative Process,* 136 U. PA. L. REV.1567, 1612–13 (1988). Lowenstein, another legal scholar highly critical of our current system of campaign

enforced by party leadership within legislatures ensures that politicians are relatively insulated from interest group pressures.[140] Politicians then pass legislation widely supported by parties, who in turn represent large segments of society, thereby legitimating a process of representative government.

In contrast, weak political parties allow special interests to pursue narrow agendas, thereby undermining both stability and legitimacy.[141] Interest groups undermine stability because the party-leadership cannot enforce discipline in passing sensible legislation reached as the result of intra-party compromise, and interest groups undermine legitimacy because political outcomes no longer represent the wishes of a wide spectrum of interests.

Although the voucher plan would weaken political parties, it should not diminish the stability or legitimacy of representative government. Rather than pursuing narrow agendas, the larger (and therefore more influential) of the voucher-financed interest groups no doubt would represent relatively broad interests. They would do so because a broad appeal will be necessary to attract a large number of voucher contributions. Being broadly based, these interest groups should be seen as representing important societal interests, not special interests. Certainly, they would be seen as being no less legitimate than the current two dominant political parties in representing the interests of broad constituencies.[142]

That is not to say that political parties have no role to play under the voucher plan. It may be that political parties would offer economies of scale in a voucher-oriented political market and act as a stabilizing agent in the transition to voucher financing. If political parties continue to serve a useful role under the voucher plan, voters will express their support of parties through their vouchers. But strong political parties do not seem indispensable to effective governance under a voucher plan.[143]

---

finance, has proposed a public financing scheme using the legislative partly leadership as brokers. Daniel H. Lowenstein, *On Campaign Finance Reform: The Root of All Evil is Deeply Rooted*, 18 HOFSTRA L. REV. 301, 351–54 (1989). Adamany and Agree criticized Senator Metcalf's voucher plan because it "ignored the legitimate role of political parties." Adamany & Agree, *supra* note 88, at 191.

140. Fitts, *supra* note 139, at 1628 (describing as "the political science ideal" the Congress of the late nineteenth and early twentieth century, which was characterized by strong party leadership).

141. *See* Morris P. Fiorina, *The Decline of Collective Responsibility in American Politics*, DAEDALUS, Summer 1980, at 25, 40.

142. *See also* Ackerman, *supra* note 11, at 74 (rejecting political party opposition to interest group politics under his voucher plan).

143. Michael Fitts suggests political parties may be strengthened under a voucher plan by mandating that a portion of voucher dollars be allocated to them. *See* Letter to author

Finally, the voucher plan may have a negative impact on governance if it ends up protecting incumbents.[144] Vouchers could benefit incumbents for two reasons: first, campaign contributions follow winners;[145] and second, incumbents generally have greater name recognition than challengers. However, there is no reason to believe that a bias in favor of incumbents will be any worse under a voucher system than it is under the current system of campaign finance. Moreover, the voucher system has several elements that work against incumbents. First, the plan bars the use of the perks of elected office to further electoral goals. Thus the president could not make a campaign trip on Air-Force One without reimbursing the government for the fair market value of a chartered Boeing 747.[146] Also, politicians will be required to disgorge any campaign funds raised before the voucher plan is enacted. Thus, incumbent war chests will not be an obstacle for a challenger entering a race. Finally, some political entrepreneurs probably will capitalize on anti-incumbency feeling by pledging to use voucher dollars donated to them only in support of challengers or to defeat incumbents.[147]

C. Benefits as a Preference-Aggregation Mechanism

A third criterion for determining the merits of the voucher plan is how well it functions as a preference-aggregation mechanism. The principal ad-

---

from Professor Michael A. Fitts 2 (Feb. 13, 1995) (on file with author). I prefer to let political parties argue their virtues in the voucher marketplace.

144. *See* Adamany & Agree, *supra* note 88, at 191.

> [Senator Metcalf's] voucher plan also does not take into account the variability in constituency characteristics or the advantages of incumbency. A number of factors—one-party electoral domination, the unequal strength of the majority and minority party organizations, and the high visibility of the majority party incumbent—are likely to combine, especially in House districts, to produce substantial inequalities in the numbers of vouchers collected by incumbents and challengers.

Id.

145. FRANK J. SORAUF, INSIDE CAMPAIGN FINANCE: MYTHS AND REALITIES 24 (1992).

146. I draw this example from Foley. Foley, *supra* note 89, at 1245. Foley also notes that incumbency problems could be solved through term limits without violating the principle of "equal-dollars-per-voter." *Id.* Whether term limits are desirable given their impact on governance is beyond the scope of this Article.

147. Indeed, the voucher plan could be modified to mandate that a portion of voucher dollars be donated either to candidates who have never before run for elected office or to organizations promising to support such candidates. *See also supra* note 143 (discussing an analogous proposal to bolster political parties' strength).

vantage of the voucher plan under this criterion is that it allows registration of the intensity of preferences.[148] Thus, the plan is more like weighted (or Borda count) voting[149] and cumulative voting[150] than simple majority rule. Under majority voting, each individual has one vote, which cannot be used to express how much the voter likes the candidate or the position she supports.[151] In contrast, mechanisms like the voucher plan allow room to express intensity of preference. In other words, a person does not vote simply AARP> Smith for President> Nature Conservancy, but votes $ 50 for AARP, $ 30 for Smith, and $ 20 for the Nature Conservancy.

Another significant advantage of the voucher plan as an intensity-registering mechanism is that it allows people with strong feelings about particular issues to "plump" all of their support behind a single group or candidate, thereby having greater impact on that issue. In an analogous area, Lani Guinier has argued that the ability to plump through cumulative voting in at-large elections would allow groups previously shut out of the political system to exercise influence more in proportion to their numbers in society.[152]

The possibility of plumping does have a downside, though. Suppose that when the voucher system is enacted, the existing distribution of power among interest groups in far from your ideal. Since you have only $ 100 to give to your preferred groups, you will be tempted to spend all

---

148. *See* Strauss, *supra* note 132, at 1374 ("Contributions allow voters—that is, contributors—to register the intensity of their views....[A] contributor can spend her money in direct proportion to the intensity of her views.").

149. Jean-Charles de Borda first proposed weighted voting in 1781. ALLAN M. FELDMAN, WELFARE ECONOMICS AND SOCIAL CHOICE THEORY 182–83 (1980); Mueller, *supra* note 17, at 133.

150. Under cumulative voting, voters get the same number of votes as there are seats or options to vote for, and they can distribute their votes in any combination to reflect their preferences. Like-minded voters can vote as a solid bloc or, instead, form strategic, cross-racial coalitions to gain mutual benefits. The system is emphatically not racially based; it allows voters to organize themselves on whatever basis they wish.

Guinier, *supra* note 130, at 14–15; *see also* Lani Guinier, *No Two Seats: The Elusive Quest for Political Equality*, 77 VA. L. REV. 1413, 1500 n.297 (1991).

151. Voting in a winner-take-all election is an exceedingly poor way to measure intensity of voter preference. *See* ALBERT O. HIRSCHMAN, SHIFTING INVOLVEMENTS: PRIVATE INTEREST & PUBLIC ACTION 104 (1982) ("The "one man one vote' rule gives everyone a minimum share in public decision-making, but it also sets something of a maximum or ceiling: for example, it does not permit the citizens to register the widely different intensities with which they hold their respective political convictions and opinions.")

152. *See* Guiner, *supra* note 130, at 149.

of your voucher dollars on the single group for which your marginal utility per voucher dollar is highest. For example, you might give all of your money to Smith for President and forsake your interest in social security issues or protecting the environment, so that you could at least hope to make a difference on the issue that is most important to you.

Hylland and Zeckhauser recognized this problem in discussing their own intensity-based preference-aggregation mechanism for determining which public goods society should produce.[153] Their solution applied in this context requires voucher dollars with diminishing marginal returns. This is accomplished by awarding interest groups the square root of the voucher dollars donated to them by voters. For example, a $ 25 voucher donation would be reduced to $ 5, and a $ 16 donation would be reduced to $ 4. The square root approach will lead individuals to spread their votes in proportion to their marginal valuation of the interest groups.[154] This spreading will occur because individuals will have more influence by using the $ 100 in vouchers to make $ 16 donations to six groups (thereby donating a total of $ 24), than by making $ 25 donations to four groups (thereby donating a total of $ 20) or by making a $ 100 donation to one group (thereby donating $ 10).

The square root formula still allows voters to register the intensity of their preferences, but it discourages excessive plumping. In the way, the voucher system will encourage the voter to fund her panoply of interests, not just the most important one. A further benefit of the square root solution is that it does not present strategies for "beating the system;" it will not lead to strategic voting.[155] A disadvantage of the square root formula, however, is that it lacks intuitive appeal to non-economists and accordingly it could undermine the credibility of the voucher plan. The square root solution is a desirable but not a crucial feature of the voucher plan.

As for Arrow's five fairness criteria,[156] the voucher plan, like the Borda count, may violate the "independence of irrelevant alternatives" criterion.[157] But this is equally true of our current system of campaign finance,

---

153. *See* Aanund Hylland & Richard Zeckhauser, Efficient Public Goods Decisions Under an Established Tax System 13–14 (Aug. 1984) (unpublished manuscript, on file with author).

154. *See id.* at 14–17.

155. *See* Mueller, *supra* note 17, at 139; *id.* at 462 (characterizing strategic behavior in the face of the Hylland-Zeckhauser scheme as "both complicated and risky").

156. *See supra* note 40 and accompanying text.

157. Here is how the Borda count may violate Arrow's independence criterion. Suppose two voters are trying to decide between alternative x, y, and z. Under the Borda count, each voter assigns 5 points to her first choice, 4 points to her second choice and 0 points to her third choice:

For instance, suppose person 1 prefers z to x to y, while person 2 prefers y to x to

which also measures intensity of preference in dollars. Rather than compare the voucher plan to some ideal system, we should ask whether there is a better campaign finance reform preference-aggregation mechanism which violates a less objectionable Arrow criterion. I have not found one.[158]

Moreover, it would be a mistake to analyze the voucher plan alone rather than in conjunction with the majority voting that it funds.[159] The voucher plan reduces the risk of cycling in our system of majority voting by limiting the range of realistic electoral choices to those politicians who manage to obtain sufficient voucher funding to run a viable campaign. Majority voting also stabilizes the tumult of the interest group process created by the voucher plan by encouraging voucher dollar spending on candidates likely to obtain a majority vote. In sum, agenda-setting in both markets limits the possibility of Arrovian cycling.

D. Likelihood of Enactment

1. Public Opinion

Congressional support for a true campaign finance reform plan, especially a plan as radical as the voucher plan, is likely to be lukewarm.[160] There are obvious agency problems in letting legislators set their own

---

z.... Now alternative x gets 4 + 4 = 8 points, alternative y gets 1 + 5 = 6 points, and alternative z gets 5+ 1 = 6 points. Therefore, for this preference profile, x is socially preferred to y according to the weighted voting rule.

However, suppose person 1 becomes disillusioned with alternative z, and his preference ordering changes to x over y over z. If the voting is repeated, x gets 5 + 4 = 9 points, y gets 4 + 5 = 9 points, and z gets 1 + 1 = 2 points. Therefore, given this new preference profile, x is socially indifferent to y. Society has become indifferent between x and y, even though neither person has changed his feelings about x and y! Consequently, weighted voting violates the independence requirements.

Feldman, *supra* note 149, at 183; *see also id.* at 199–201 (discussing strategic voting under the Borda count).

158. *See* Jonathan Levin & Barry Nalebuff, *An Introduction to Vote-Counting Schemes*, J. ECON. PERSP., Winter 1995, at 3 ("Arrow...demonstrates that any voting system applied to an unrestricted collection of voter preferences must have some serious defect; we must always choose between flawed alternatives. With conflicting theoretical guidance to help select the least-flawed option, people evaluate a system by its likely effect on the status quo outcome.").

159. *See* Maxwell L. Sterns, *The Misguided Renaissance of Social Choice*, 103 YALE L.J. 1219, 1231–32 (1994).

160. *See* Jonathan R. Macey, *The Missing Element in the Republican Revival*, 97 YALE L.J. 1673, 1680 n.38 (1988) (suggesting that incumbents will pass campaign finance bill "particularly likely to benefit incumbents").

conditions for electoral competition.[161] Therefore, if the voucher plan is to be enacted, it will need widespread public support. The relevant question becomes whether the voucher plan could obtain such support.[162]

Public opinion polls indicate that a majority of Americans oppose public financing of congressional elections.[163] This is no surprise, given the pervasive view that government bureaucracy is inefficient and given the public's antipathy to additional taxes.[164] However, public support has never been measured for the specific voucher plan discussed here, which is a market-based, rather than bureaucracy-based, approach to allocating public funds. Indeed, despite the additional tax burden vouchers would impose, the plan may be especially palatable to those on the right, who already have well-financed organizations in place ready to be funded by vouchers and who have advocated using vouchers in other areas, like edu-

---

161. *See* Richard L. Hansen, *An Enriched Economic Model of Political Patronage and Campaign Contributions: Reformulating Supreme Court Jurisprudence*, 14 Cardozo L. Rev. 1311, 1331 (1993).

162. Public opinion likely will be influenced by the views of currently existing interest groups. For this reason, it is important to gain the support of these groups. Existing groups, at least those that expect to receive support under the voucher plan, should do well in the new system because of their organizational headstart over new groups. Schmitter predicts support for his voucher plan from existing groups who expect to come out as winners. *See* Schmitter, Corporative Democracy, *supra* note 88, at 56. Foley argues the "equal- dollars-per-voters" principle should prevent already-existing interest groups from having an organizational headstart in collecting funds; they would have no funds until voters contributed them. Foley, *supra* note 89, at 1254. This adherence to ideological purity might decrease the chances the voucher plan could be enacted by alienating the very groups whose support may be required for enactment. For this reason, I oppose prohibiting existing interest groups from using their current organizational benefits.

163. For example, a 1994 CBS/New York Times public opinion poll showed 38% of Americans favored public financing and 54% opposed it. *American Political Network, Inc. Poll Update, CBS NY Times: Dole Feels the Health Care Heat, Too*, Sept. 13, 1994, *available in* LEXIS, Nexis Library, Curnws File. But public opinion may depend upon how the question is asked. Indeed, a 1993 poll conducted for Public Citizen, a group that supports public financing of congressional elections, found 72% support for extending public financing to congressional elections, where the proposed reform included campaign spending and contribution limits. Paul D. Wellstone, *True Election Reform*, Christian Sci. Monitor, Mar. 22, 1993, at 18. Senator Mitch McConnell suggested Public Citizen rigged its 1990 poll to produce results showing 58% support for public financing. Robert T. Garrett, *McConnell's Change in Campaign Bill is Killed*, Louisville Courier-Journal, July 31, 1990 at B1, B3.

164. Sorauf explains the lack of serious proposals for full-public funding considered by Congress by reference to such plans' "political unpopularity." Sorauf, *supra* note 136, at 1357 n.36.

cation.[165] Given the public's current disgust with our political system,[166] this may be an opportune moment for those advocating fundamental change in the relationship between money and politics.

A major argument against the voucher plan is that it will lead to an increase in interest group rent seeking, causing a decline in overall social wealth.[167] I have already explained reasons for rejecting Kaldor-Hicks efficiency as the sole criterion applied to creating a good political process.[168] Moreover, the plan probably would not decrease social wealth. As explained above, there is probably a negative correlation, rather than a positive one, between the number of interest groups and the total amount of social wealth lost by rent seeking.[169]

The voucher plan becomes all the more appealing when one considers the tremendous rents that a single group, like Brush Wellman, can command from the government.[170] The cost-effectiveness of a $ 3 billion biannual voucher plan[171] is quite evident in light of just this one $ 15 billion instance of rent seeking, and all the more so when one considers all the other special deals made by those with enormous political capital. As Senator Paul Wellstone has noted, "for a fraction of the estimated $ 500

---

165. Republican Senator Daniel Coats and conservative activist William J. Bennett have advocated school vouchers as part of their 19-bill "Project for American Renewal." Cheryl Wetzstein, *Coats Seeks Taxbreak for Social Welfare Alms*, WASH. TIMES, Sept. 7, 1995, at A5. Of course, the possibility that the voucher plan could strengthen interest groups on the right may lead those on the left to oppose the plan despite its egalitarian benefits.

166. *See supra* notes 2–4 and accompanying text.

167. Richard A. Epstein, *Property, Speech, and the Politics of Distrust, in* THE BILL OF RIGHTS IN THE MODERN STATE 41, *supra* note 11, at 56 [hereinafter Epstein, *Property*]; BeVier, *supra* note 122, at 1265–66.

168. *See supra* Part I.C.

169. *See supra* note 134 and accompanying text.

170. *See supra* notes 12–16 and accompanying text (describing Brush Wellman's rent seeking).

171. *See supra* note 91 (describing costs of voucher plan). The costs easily could surpass $ 3 billion when we consider the possibly high enforcement costs necessary to police the various prohibitions of the voucher program. Even considering extremely high enforcement costs, running into the tens of millions of dollars annually, the voucher program still would be cost effective if it prevents instances of rent seeking like the Brush Wellman example. The political problem arises because enforcement costs are budget items for all to see, while rent-seeking activity is often hidden from public view. Thus, the asymmetric availability of information about the social costs of having or not having a voucher program could affect public attitudes towards it. *See* Richard L. Hasen, Comment, *Efficiency Under Informational Asymmetry: The Effect of Framing on Legal Rules,* 38 UCLA L. REV. 391, 395 (1990) (explaining the "availability" heuristic).

billion it is costing to fix the damage done by savings-and-loan lobbyists who pressed for weakened thrift regulations, we could finance decades of honest, democratic elections."[172]

Some may argue that the voucher plan will enhance the power of "special interests" at the expense of the public interest.[173] This argument is flawed in two respects. First, it compares the voucher plan to some idealized political system rather than to our current system, which is already overrun by interest groups. Second, the argument ignores the important role interest groups play in overcoming collective action problems and monitoring legislative performance. Although individual voters very rarely have adequate incentives to monitor legislative action, interest groups do.[174] Thus, interest groups in and of themselves are not objectionable; interest group competition, when well-regulated to equalize political capital and prevent excessive rent seeking, serves important public interests.

2. Constitutionality

Even if public pressure forced Congress to enact a voucher plan, the plan would be challenged on constitutional grounds. Although just a few years ago the case law seemed hostile to fundamental campaign finance reform, times have changed. Recent Supreme Court decisions and the writings of some legal scholars suggest the voucher plan might pass constitutional muster.

In *Buckley v. Valeo*, the Supreme Court squarely rejected the argument that Congress could limit independent campaign expenditures in an effort to equalize the political influence of different groups in society. "The concept that government may restrict the speech of some elements of our society in order to enhance the relative voice of others is wholly foreign to the First Amendment...."[175] Instead, the *Buckley* Court considered whether Congress' campaign finance regulations could be justified by the government's compelling interest in preventing actual corruption and the

---

172. Wellstone, *supra* note 163, at 18.

173. Recall that earlier campaign finance voucher plans prevented interest groups from collecting the vouchers in order to prevent increased power for such groups. *See supra* note 88.

174. BeVier, *supra* note 122, at 1273–75; *see also* FARBER & FRICKEY, *supra* note 17, at 98 ("Competition between interest groups helps keep the system honest.").

175. Buckley v. Valeo, 424 U.S. 1, 48–49 (1976). The Court failed to consider whether the equalization rationale justified contribution limits because it held such limits were justified to limit the "actuality and appearance of corruption." *Id.* at 25–26; *see infra* note 189.

appearance of corruption.[176] The Court held that limits on campaign contributions "entail only a marginal restriction upon the contributor's ability to engage in free communication."[177] When balanced against the government's compelling interest in preventing corruption, the limits were constitutional. In contrast, limits on independent expenditures "appear to exclude all citizens and groups except candidates, political parties, and the

---

176. *Buckley*, 424 U.S. at 25–29. Indeed, preventing corruption is the only compelling state interest the Court has recognized as justifying a restriction upon campaign contributions. Federal Election Comm'n v. National Conservative Political Action Comm., 470 U.S. 480, 496–97 (1985).

The Court continues to see corruption as the primary basis for campaign finance regulation. Last term, the Supreme Court held that the First Amendment barred an Ohio statute prohibiting the distribution of anonymous campaign literature supporting or opposing a local ballot proposition. McIntyre v. Ohio Elections Comm'n, 63 U.S.L.W. 4279 (1995). In *McIntyre*, the Court carefully distinguished the state's interest in requiring disclosure of the author of a handbill relating to a ballot initiative on the one hand, and the state's interest in requiring disclosure of the source of campaign contributions or independent expenditures in candidate elections on the other:

> Not only is the Ohio statute's infringement on speech more intrusive than the *Buckley* disclosure requirement, but it rests on different and less powerful state interests. The Federal Election Campaign Act of 1971, at issue in *Buckley*, regulates only candidate elections, not referenda or other issue-based ballot measures; and we construed "independent expenditures" to mean only those expenditures that "expressly advocate the election or defeat of a clearly identified candidate." [*Buckley*, 424 U.S.] at 80. In candidate elections, the Government can identify a compelling state interest in avoiding the corruption that might result from campaign expenditures. Disclosure of expenditures lessens the risk that individuals will spend money to support a candidate as a quid pro quo for special treatment after the candidate is in office. Curriers of favor will be deterred by the knowledge that all expenditures will be scrutinized by the Federal Election Commission and by the public for just this sort of abuse. Moreover, the federal Act contains numerous legitimate disclosure requirements for campaign organizations; the similar requirements for independent expenditures serve to ensure that a campaign organization will not seek to evade disclosure by routing its expenditures through individual supporters. *See Buckley*, 424 U.S., at 76. In short, although *Buckley* may permit a more narrowly drawn statute, it surely is not authority for upholding Ohio's open-ended provision.

McIntyre, 63 U.S.L.W. at 4285 (footnotes omitted). But *see id.* at 4293 (Scalia, J., dissenting) (stating that "our primary rationale for upholding" the disclosure provision in *Buckley* "was that it served an "informational interest' by "increasing the fund of information concerning those who support the candidates'," and that the Ohio provision at issue in *McIntyre* "serves the same informational interest" as well as other more important interests) (citing *Buckley*, 424 U.S. at 81).

177. *Buckley*, 424 U.S. at 20–21.

institutional press from any significant use of the most effective modes of communication."[178] But corruption or the appearance of corruption is unlikely with independent expenditures.[179] Accordingly, the Court declared limits on independent expenditures unconstitutional.[180]

Until recently, the Court stuck to the corruption rationale and distinguished between permissible contribution limits and impermissible independent expenditure limits. But in *Austin v. Michigan State Chamber of Commerce*,[181] the Court for the first time upheld government regulation of independent expenditures on what appear to be egalitarian grounds.[182] The law at issue in *Austin* barred corporations, other than media corporations, from using general treasury funds for independent expenditures in state election campaigns.[183] In upholding the law, the Court radically expanded the definition of the kind of "corruption" that can serve as an interest compelling enough to justify restrictions on freedom of speech: "Michigan's regulation aims at a different type of corruption in the political arena: the corrosive and distorting effects of immense aggregations of wealth that are accumulated with the help of the corporate form and that have little or no correlation to the public's support for the corporation's political ideas."[184]

Whether the voucher program will run into First Amendment problems depends upon whether the Supreme Court continues to move in the direction of *Austin* or backs away from it. To be sure, the *Austin* decision limited itself to corporate independent expenditures.[185] But its reasoning applies outside of the corporate context. Indeed, Justice Scalia, dissenting in *Austin*, saw no principled difference between corporate wealth and wealth used for campaign expenditures. "Why is it perfectly all right if

---

178. *Id.* at 19–20 (footnotes omitted).

179. *Id.* at 45–48.

180. *Id.* at 58–59.

181. 494 U.S. 652 (1990).

182. *Id.* at 655, 659–60. The Court hinted at such a distinction in *Federal Election Comm'n v. Massachusetts Citizens for Life, Inc.*, 479 U.S. 238 (1986). For a useful discussion of the relationship between this case and *Austin*, *see* David Cole, *First Amendment Antitrust: The End of Laissez-Faire in Campaign Finance*, 9 YALE L. & POL'Y REV. 261–71 (1991). Ashdown provides a good general overview of *Austin*. *See* Gerald G. Ashdown, *Controlling Campaign Spending and the "New Corruption": Waiting for the Court*, 44 VAND. L. REV. 767 (1991). Justices Scalia and O'Connor have been criticized for their failure to explain their decisions to concur in *Massachusetts Citizens for Life* but to dissent in *Austin*. *See, e.g.,* Daniel H. Lowenstein, A *Patternless Mosaic: Campaign Finance and the First Amendment After* Austin, 21 CAP. U. L. REV. 381, 382 n.3 (1992).

183. *Austin*, 494 U.S. at 654–55, 666–67.

184. *Id.* at 659–60.

185. *Id.* at 676 (Brennan, J., concurring).

advocacy by an individual billionaire is out of proportion with "actual public support' for his positions?"[186]

Justice Scalia is correct. Although the state-sanctioned nature of corporations gives the government an added interest in regulating their activities, the corporate form is irrelevant to whether wealth distorts the political system. Moreover, Justice Scalia is correct that the traditional definition of "corruption" as the political quid pro quo does not include the "corrosive" effects of wealth on the electoral process.[187] Truly independent expenditures[188] in an electoral campaign may allow wealth to distort the political system, but they do not involve a quid pro quo.

But whereas Justice Scalia concludes that the Michigan law cannot pass muster under *Buckley*, I believe the better approach is to acknowledge the logical implications of the Court's reasoning and accept political equality as an interest adequate to justify regulating campaign expenditures.[189] This compelling interest in political equality justifies not only the plan at issue in *Austin*, but also the voucher program proposed here.

Legal scholars already have advanced the argument that egalitarianism should be considered a compelling interest to be weighed against traditional free speech interests.[190] Cass Sunstein, for example, has called for a

---

186. *Id.* at 685 (Scalia, J., dissenting) (finding "entirely irrational" the Court's limitation of its decision to corporate expenditures).

187. Justice Scalia termed this argument by the *Austin* majority, the "New Corruption." *Id.* at 684.

188. Just how "independent" such expenditures usually are is open to serious question. *See* Adam Clymer, *Page By Page, A Chronicle Of Misdeeds*, N.Y. Times, Sept. 8, 1995, at A1, D16 (describing how former Senator Packwood cooperated with supporters making nominally independent expenditures).

189. In *Buckley*, the government asserted that an "ancillary" reason for contribution limits was "to mute the voices of affluent persons and groups in the election process and thereby to equalize the relative ability of all citizens to affect the outcome of elections." Buckley v. Valeo, 424 U.S. 1, 25–26 (1976). The Court did not determine the persuasiveness of this argument, holding instead that contribution limits could be upheld based solely upon the government's compelling interest in preventing the actuality and appearance of corruption. *Id.* at 26. In any case, the Court noted that "contribution limitations alone would not reduce the greater potential voice of affluent persons and well-financed groups, who would remain free to spend unlimited sums directly to promote candidates and policies they favor in an effort to persuade voters." *Id.* at 26 n.26.

190. *E.g.*, Vincent Blasi, *Free Speech and the Widening Gyre of Fund-Raising: Why Campaign Spending Limits May Not Violate the First Amendment After All*, 94 Colum. L. Rev. 1281 (1994). Blasi argues for another compelling interest justifying the enactment of campaign finance reform: candidate time protection. According to Blasi, candidates' preoccupation with fund-raising impedes the quality of representation, thereby invoking constitutional concerns. *Id.* at 1302–09. Blasi believes that his new-found compelling

"New Deal" for free speech, allowing greater government regulation of speech in order to promote certain democratic values.[191] The New Deal for free speech would sound the death knell for *Buckley*, just as the New Deal for property rights spelled the end of the *Lochner* era.[192] This new approach would allow the government to "tone down or amplify particular voices in order to promote speaker diversity."[193]

---

interest in protecting a candidate's time would not preserve a voucher plan against First Amendment attack. "Candidates facing or fearing tight races will be preoccupied with fund-raising (or voucher raising) under any system that does not restrict total spending." *Id.* at 1284. *But see supra* notes 136–37 and accompanying text (arguing that voucher-raising would be less time consuming than fundraising under the current campaign finance system).

191. "In some circumstances, what seems to be government regulation of speech actually might promote free speech, and should not be treated as an abridgement at all.... [Moreover,] what seems to be free speech in markets might, in some selected circumstances, amount to an abridgement of free speech." Sunstein, *supra* note 11, at 267; *see also* Cass R. Sunstein, Democracy and the Problem of Free Speech 93–101 (1993) [hereinafter Sunstein, Democracy] (discussing speech regulation in context of campaign finance reform); Cass R. Sunstein, *Political Equality and Unintended Consequences*, 94 Colum. L. Rev. 1390 (1994) [hereinafter Sunstein, *Political Equality*]. In these two recent works, Sunstein states that "we should look closely at the benefits and risks created by" Ackerman's voucher proposal. Sunstein, Democracy, *supra* at 100; *see* Sunstein, *Political Equality*, *supra* at 1412–13. Although this position is heartening to those who favor voucher plans, Sunstein might ultimately reject the voucher plan because it will promote (albeit on a more equal playing field) the interest group politics Sunstein has criticized in his articles on civic republicanism. *See, e.g.,* Cass R. Sunstein, *Beyond the Republican Revival*, 97 Yale L.J. 1539, 1569–71 (1988) [hereinafter Sunstein, *Republican Revival*]. "On pluralist assumptions it is unclear why laws should not be bought or sold like commodities in a marketplace....But for those who believe in a deliberative function for politics, the marketplace metaphor will be misguided...." *Id.* at 1545. Unlike Sunstein, I do not premise any arguments for reform on the emergence of new civic virtue among either the population at large or legislators.

192. *See supra* note 11 and accompanying text. As Sunstein explains:

The real problem is that *Buckley* removes many difficult issues of campaign finance reform from the democratic process and resolves them through judicial fiat. The Court did not explain why it was constitutionally illegitimate for Congress to say that economic inequalities could not be translated into political inequalities in the form of wide disparities in political expenditures.

Sunstein, Democracy, *supra* note 191, at 98.

193. Julian N. Eule, *Promoting Speaker Diversity*: Austin *and* Metro Broadcasting, 1990 Sup. Ct. Rev. 105, 106. Note that this language parallels the idea of leveling-up and leveling-down. *See supra* note 87 and accompanying text. The voucher plan, by leveling-down and leveling-up, seeks to tone down some voices and amplify others.

Sunstein's New Deal for free speech would allow campaign finance reform plans like the voucher plan to pass constitutional muster if they were narrowly tailored to the goal of achieving egalitarian pluralism.[194] In his discussion of Ackerman's voucher plan, Sunstein notes that it would "promote political equality...without threatening to diminish aggregate levels of political discussion."[195]

Although "aggregate levels" of political discussion will remain constant under a voucher plan, a wealthy individual's ability to promote her views will face limits. Consider the extreme case: an individual with unpopular political ideas is prevented from spending her own money to run for federal office. To the extent that money facilitates speech, the voucher plan will stifle an unpopular political view. Nichol, however, argues persuasively that the current campaign finance system denies a right to speak to the great majority of Americans who could not afford it, a more objectionable result.[196]

Not all First Amendment scholars believe radical campaign finance reform could pass constitutional muster.[197] Kathleen Sullivan, for example, argues against the New Deal for speech movement and in favor of "progressive free speech libertarianism."[198] Sullivan contends that speech is qualitatively different from the goods and services which the government regulates under the New Deal. "Speech might be uniquely privileged as the currency of peaceful political change."[199] Moreover, Sullivan believes

---

194. The voucher plan is narrowly tailored to meet the goal of egalitarian pluralism. Rather than the government preventing speech, the plan gives each individual the opportunity to volunteer unlimited time for or against political candidates, to volunteer unlimited time and donate an unlimited amount of money for or against any other political activity not directly connected with political candidates, and to donate an equal (though limited) amount of voucher money to candidates running for federal office, either with or without an interest group intermediary.

195. SUNSTEIN, DEMOCRACY, *supra* note 191, at 100.

196. *See* Gene R. Nichol, *Money, Equality and the Regulation of Campaign Finance*, 6 CONST. COMMENTARY 319, 324–25 (1989) ("If a $ 1,000 expenditure limit threatens to render a potential $ 10,000 speaker ninety per cent censored, what is the status of a citizen who would like to engage in mass speech but has no money?").

197. *See, e.g.,* Kathleen M. Sullivan, *Free Speech Wars*, 48 SMU L. REV. 203 (1994); BeVier, *supra* note 122, at 1260–69; Charles Fried, *The New First Amendment Jurisprudence: A Threat to Liberty, in* THE BILL OF RIGHTS IN THE MODERN STATE, *supra* note 11, at 225, 228–29.

198. Sullivan, *supra* note 197, at 213. The Sullivan article is based upon a lecture. Sullivan calls her thoughts "the tentative beginnings" of a response to the New Deal for speech movement. *Id.* at 213.

199. *Id.*

there are reasons to "mistrust government regulation of speech more than we mistrust government regulation of markets for goods and services."[200]

The constitutional debate has just begun and the Supreme Court's personnel has changed since both *Buckley* and *Austin*.[201] If the current trend toward the erosion of *Buckley* continues, the Supreme Court should hold the voucher plan constitutional.[202]

* * *

Conclusion

To be sure, a voucher plan along the lines set forth in this Article is no panacea to the problem of unequal distribution of political capital in the political market. Indeed, there can be no perfect solution given the inherent tension in any society as fiercely committed as the United States to both majoritarian democracy and free market capitalism, and given un-

---

200. *Id.* at 214. The three reasons Sullivan suggests are:

First, speech regulation may be more intractably ineffective than other forms of regulation...Second, there may be a greater risk of error when government regulates speech than when it regulates commercial markets....

Third, there might be special dangers in trusting government to change culture even if we trust it to reallocate some aspects of material power.

Id. Note that the voucher plan presents fewer dangers on this score, because allocation of speech is directed by the people through the equalized market mechanism rather than through government fiat.

201. *See* Lowenstein, *supra* note 182, at 383 (noting that given the replacement of Justices Brennan and Marshall with Souter and Thomas, *Austin* may end up as "a temporary aberration in the Court's treatment of the campaign finance issue").

202. Ackerman and Sunstein do not believe *Buckley* would have to be overruled. *See* Ackerman, *supra* note 11, at 77–78; Sunstein, *Political Equality*, *supra* note 191, at 1413. Ackerman's constitutional argument, in part, is that money spent on political campaigns is qualitatively different from the "green" money spent to buy goods and services. Ackerman, *supra* note 11, at 79–80. Although Ackerman's argument might be persuasive if we were writing on a clean slate, I agree with Foley that *Buckley* must be overruled for a voucher plan to be declared constitutional. Foley, *supra* note 89, at 1211–12. It is hard to see how the Court could get around its statement in *Buckley* that "the concept that government may restrict the speech of some elements of our society in order to enhance the relative voice of others is wholly foreign to the First Amendment." Buckley v. Valeo, 424 U.S. 1, 48–49 (1976). Raskin and Bonifaz offer additional arguments for overruling *Buckley*. *See* Raskin & Bonifaz, *supra* note 97, at 320–30.

* * *

equally distributed attributes that bear upon the creation of political capital.[278]

But a commitment to egalitarian pluralism tempered by the realism (and some would say, cynicism) of positive public choice theory leads me to conclude that a voucher plan would be a tremendous improvement over our current campaign finance system. The democratic experiment, especially in a capitalist society, has proven to be exciting and challenging; why not use a market-based approach to promote democratic ideals, allowing intensity of preference rather than the dollars in one's pocket to determine political outcomes?

---

278. *See* Daniel R. Ortiz, *The Engaged and the Inert: Theorizing Political Personality Under the First Amendment*, 81 VA. L. REV. 1, 43 (1995) ("Allowing individuals to parlay their differential economic power into differential political power is in tension with one of the central tenets of democratic theory: the norm of equal political entitlements.").

On Campaign Finance Reform: The Root of All Evil is Deeply Rooted

[Excerpt Two]

Daniel Hays Lowenstein

IV. A Reform Proposal

A. The Problem

A major theme of this Article has been that because of the pervasiveness of money in politics, any regulation that effectively limits conflicts of interest will necessarily affect numerous other interests and values, so that reform proposals inevitably encounter a cross fire of conflicting demands and objections. Over the decade and a half since adoption of the FECA amendments,[202] a particular set of difficulties have come to be regarded as centrally important in both the academic literature and political debate. These are based on the following circumstances, as to which there probably is little serious disagreement:

1. Although American legislative elections retain a significant partisan cast, they have become increasingly candidate-oriented. The identities, records and policy views of legislative candidates are not well known to voters. Nor do most voters do much to seek out such information. Accordingly, to have a chance to win a competitive election, most candidates need to spend large sums of money to get information into the minds of voters.[203]

---

202. Federal Election Campaign Act (FECA) Amendments of 1974, Pub. L. No. 93-443, 88 Stat. 1263 (1974); FECA Amendments of 1976, Pub. L. No. 94-293, 90 Stat. 475 (1976); FECA Amendments of 1979, Pub. L. No. 96-197, 93 Stat. 1339 (1979).

203. *See* Sabato, *supra* note 7, at 158 (reviewing the expenses of campaign communication).

2. By and large, money that Americans acting individually are willing to contribute in small amounts to legislative candidates falls far short of the sums necessary to run a competitive campaign.[204]

3. Under our current system, the only sources of funds available to fill this gap are larger contributions from individuals and funds collected through organizations, most commonly at present through PACs. An unknown but substantial portion of funds from these sources is contributed in accordance with a legislative rather than an electoral strategy, and in this sense may be denominated special interest funds.[205]

4. In the majority of districts, truly competitive elections probably are impossible because of the predominance of one party or the well-entrenched position of the incumbent.[206] Categorization of districts as "safe" or "competitive" is possible, but not according to any fixed or simple criterion. It is a matter of expert judgment, and experts sometimes make mistakes or disagree among themselves.[207]

5. Typically, the effects of campaign spending in a potentially competitive district are not symmetric. Incumbents, by reason of their status and assisted by the substantial subsidies they receive for communication with voters, tend to be better known than their challengers at the beginning of the campaign.[208] Whether for this reason, or because some voters tend to vote for the incumbent in the absence of information suggesting otherwise, or for other reasons, challengers usually need to spend large amounts to have a chance to win. On average, challengers receive a higher percentage of the vote as the amount they spend increases.[209] Incumbent spending has

---

204. *See* Gary Jacobson, *Party Organization and Distribution of Campaign Resources: Republicans and Democrats in 1982,* 100 POL. SCI. Q. 603, 610 (1985–86) [hereinafter Jacobson, *Republicans and Democrats*].

205. *See supra* notes 40-55 and accompanying text.

206. *See* Jacobson, *Republicans and Democrats, supra* note 204, at 610 (reporting that incumbents seeking reelection have a 90% chance of succeeding).

207. Gary Jacobson recently questioned the reliability of political scientists' traditional use of the margin of victory in the previous election as a measure of the competitiveness of a district. *See* Gary Jacobson, *The Marginals Never Vanished: Incumbency and Competition in Elections to the U.S. House of Representatives, 1952-82,* 31 AM. J. POL. SCI. 126 (1987). The measure was defended, by Monica Bauer and John R. Hibbing, *see* Monica Bauer & John R. Hibbing, *Which Incumbents Lose in House Elections: A Response to Jacobson's "The Marginals Never Vanished,"* 33 AM. J. POL. SCI. 262 (1989). However, the dispute is over the reliability of the measure in the aggregate. No one would claim that the previous margin of victory is anything more than a single factor indicating the degree of competition in any given election.

208. *See* Sabato, *supra* note 7, at 157-59.

209. *See* GARY JACOBSON, MONEY IN CONGRESSIONAL ELECTIONS 33-50, 136-62 (1980).

a much smaller effect on the election results on average,[210] but the relatively small number of votes a large amount of spending by the incumbent can influence may mean the difference in a close election.[211]

Given these circumstances, it has been widely supposed that an insoluble conflict exists between the anti-corruption goal of campaign finance reform and the value of maintaining (or restoring) vigorous competition in legislative elections.[212] The dilemma arises from the following elements:

1. To accomplish the anti-corruption goal, candidates' demand for special interest contributions must be reduced drastically. This may take the form of limits on the size of contributions, limits on the aggregate amount of special interest money that may be accepted, or expenditure limits consented to as a condition of accepting public financing.

2. Because small contributions from individuals do not come close to providing the amount needed for competitive campaigns, limits alone, regardless of their form if sufficient to substantially limit the element of corruption in the finance system, would so reduce the flow of funds that challengers, for whom the absolute amounts they can spend are more important than their spending relative to incumbents, would find their hopes of victory seriously impaired.

3. Public financing is proposed to close the gap between what candidates need to spend and what they can raise in "clean" money.[213] As a practical matter, however, the gap is too large for public financing to fill. If a flat amount is given to major-party candidates in each district, most of the money will be wasted on races that have little prospect of being competitive. If public financing is given on a matching basis, raising the private contributions eligible for matching may be difficult. As a result the matching of public funds makes private contributions more valuable, and may, to some extent, subsidize the efforts of contributors following a legislative strategy. The size of the gap and the practical limits on the amount of public financing that can be made available assure that a compromise between the goals of restricting special interest money and permitting competitive races will end up accomplishing neither. In Gary Jacobson's words, "enough" money for a challenger to run a competitive campaign is likely to be "too much" money to be compatible with reform goals.[214]

---

210. *See* Gary Jacobson, *The Effects of Campaign Spending in Congressional Elections,* 72 AM. POL. SCI. REV. 469, 470 (1978).

211. *See* Gary Jacobson, *Enough Is Too Much: Money and Competition in House Elections, in* ELECTIONS IN AMERICA 173 (Kay Lehman Scholzman, ed. 1987) [hereinafter Jacobson, *Enough Is Too Much*].

212. Jacobson's statement of this view is particularly cogent. *See id.* at 175.

213. *See* Sabato, *supra* note 7, at 168-71 (discussing the rationale for public financing).

214. *See* Jacobson, *Enough Is Too Much, supra* note 211, at 192-94.

The dilemma that is assumed to exist turns on the assumption that public funds cannot be allocated to particular races in differing amounts other than through the matching device, which is an imperfect measure of the true competitiveness of an election and which tends to undercut the goals of reform. No one is likely to propose that government officials should make judgments as to which are the competitive races and allocate funds accordingly.

This dilemma can be solved by recognizing that the political parties constitute an excellent conduit for the allocation of public funds. By and large, the parties can be expected to place the funds where they will do the most good. Public financing, then, can provide the greater part of the funds needed in competitive elections, obviating the need for private funds in amounts that come only from special interests. Public financing that is sufficient to fill the gap between what is needed and what can be raised in "clean" money, need not be prohibitively expensive because the parties will avoid wasting money in hopeless districts.[215] The package proposed in this Article is not a cheap one, but it is no Rolls Royce.

The following Section describes the major elements of a reform package built around the political party allocation mechanism. The proposal is sketched in broad outline. Filling in the details will present technical difficulties and, more importantly, fracture whatever support the proposal might be able to generate, as different interests and values are served or disserved by resolving details one way or another.

B. The Proposal

1. Public Financing Allocated by Legislative Party Leadership to Candidates

This is the heart of the proposal. It is important that the money be sufficient to provide most of the needed spending in districts seriously contested. Suppose we assume a House challenger needs $500,000 to run a competitive race.[216] Assume also that serious challengers could be expected to raise at least $100,000 in private funds in light of the regulatory provisions of the proposal. This means that for $20,000,000, a party could fund fifty strongly competitive challenges. A similar amount should

---

215. Some money may be wasted by allocations to incumbents who are safe. *See infra* text accompanying notes 222-24.

216. For the years 1972-84, Jacobson found that challengers who spent $500,000 in 1984 dollars had a 37% chance of winning. *See* Jacobson, *Enough Is Too Much, supra* note 211, at 180 table 2.

be provided for the defense of incumbents and another similar amount should be available for other races.[217] Thus, a crude estimate of the amount that might be made available for allocation under this proposal would be $60,000,000 for each party in the House. Senate elections are held in two-thirds of the states each election year. Allowing for economies of scale in Senate campaigns, a total appropriation of half that for the House, or $30,000,000 for each party, is a similarly crude estimate. Thus, for the two major parties, a cost of $180,000,000 would be involved, or $90,000,000 per fiscal year. In addition, all limits on party participation in federal campaigns, either by contributing privately raised funds to candidates or by direct spending, would be repealed.

The public funds would be allocated by the party leadership in the respective houses rather than by the Democratic and Republican National Committees.[218] This is not essential to the overall thrust of the plan, and some might disagree with this feature out of a desire to centralize party power in a single entity. I favor the Congressional leadership for several reasons. First, although the package's greatest political weakness is that its overall thrust does not benefit incumbents,[219] there is no reason to increase its unpalatibility to incumbents gratuitously. Incumbents cannot be expected to be cheerful about handing considerable influence over their own destinies to any party group, but the pill should be less bitter when the group is directly accountable to the incumbents. Second, the in-house leadership is most directly concerned with the party's prospects in the particular chamber and presumably is most in touch with the ongoing political situation. Furthermore, the leadership has a more direct incentive to seek the use of public funds to win elections and, therefore, is less likely than the party national committees to be distracted by bureaucratic concerns.[220] Third, as Michael Malbin has argued, at least in the case of the party that

---

217. The proposal in this Section does not require the parties to allocate the funds in accordance with this breakdown, which is offered only in rough justification for the amounts suggested. In a bad election year, a party would be likely to allocate more money to the defense of incumbents, and in a good year it could afford to risk allocating more to challengers. *See id.* at 183-84.

218. The leadership would be free to delegate the allocation to any other entity. Presumably they would do so to the respective Senate and Congressional Campaign Committees. However, if intra-party politics resulted in party leadership delegating allocation to the Democratic and Republican National Committees, that would be permissible under the proposal.

219. It is hard to see how any plan could benefit incumbents, and at the same time comply with the demand of many for more competitive elections.

220. *See* Joseph A. Schlesinger, *On the Theory of Party Organization*, 46 J. POL. 369, 393-94 (1984).

controls the White House, giving control to the party national committee could impinge on Congressional independence.[221]

An objection to lodging control in the in-house party leadership could be made on the ground that the result will be that all or most of the money will be allocated to incumbents, many of whom do not need it. Jacobson, while conceding that each incumbent member of a party benefits from the party increasing its membership in the chamber, argues that collective good problems will prevent the incumbents from allocating party funds to challengers.[222] Each incumbent enjoys all the benefit of the enhanced security, however slight, from spending on his or her own campaign, while the benefit of increased party strength is shared with all the other incumbents.[223]

Jacobson's analysis, uncharacteristically, appears to be mistaken. It would be correct if the incumbents had to decide individually whether to give up funds for challengers, but by virtue of the decisions being centralized in the leadership, the incumbents are spared the 'free rider' problem. Each incumbent gives up a particularized benefit with the knowledge that others similarly situated are committed to doing the same. Suppose a party in the House has 200 members, and receives $60,000,000 for allocation. If the money were allocated to incumbents equally, with nothing for challengers, each incumbent would get $300,000. Suppose 150 of the incumbents face no realistic prospect of a serious electoral threat. If these 150 were asked individually to give up $200,000 each for a challenger's fund, Jacobson would be correct that they might be reluctant to comply.[224] However, if the centralized leadership decides to put $200,000 for each of the 150 into a challenger's fund, each gets $30,000,000 worth of collective benefits for a $200,000 individual sacrifice. If the collective good really is a collective good, then by definition, this is a good deal. This is especially so, since the leadership could hold a portion of the public funds in reserve until the late stages of the campaign, to be able to come to the aid of any incumbent facing unanticipated difficulties.

Another possible objection is that the proposal would give rise to "bossism" by giving too much power to the leadership. It is easy to exaggerate the extent to which this would happen. First, the membership has the ultimate ability to unseat the leadership, so that the power relation-

---

221. *See* Malbin, *supra* note 7, at 241-42.

222. *See* Jacobson, *Republicans and Democrats, supra* note 204, at 603-05. Jacobson defines a collective good problem as one that occurs when "rational individual behavior produces inferior collective results." *See id.* at 609.

223. *See id.* at 604.

224. *See id.* (stating that the principal interest of each candidate is winning and that the party's collective interests are secondary).

ship would be a two-way street. Second, the leadership's main concern is always likely to be to elect and reelect party members, so that it may be reluctant to exercise the sanction of withholding funds from recalcitrant members.[225] Furthermore, to the extent strengthening of the party legislative leadership does occur, it may be more good than bad. For many years, observers have been calling for an increase in the cohesiveness and discipline of political parties.[226] Indeed, in a different way, the next portion of the reform package is intended to move in precisely that direction.

2. Public Financing to Legislative Party Leadership for Generic Party Advertising

This portion of the proposal supplements the previous one by promoting competition in Congressional elections, and to that extent helps resolve what has been seen as the insoluble dilemma of campaign finance reform.[227] However, as just indicated, its main rationale is to strengthen the party system, and in that sense it is, admittedly, somewhat gratuitous as a portion of this package.

Generic advertising is advertising urging a vote for candidates of the party generally rather than for a specific candidate. The Republicans used generic advertising in the 1980 and 1982 campaigns, as did the Democrats to a lesser extent, but the practice appears to have declined.[228] To stimulate a revival, each party in each chamber would receive an appropriation, perhaps amounting to $10 million each.[229]

---

225. *See* Gary Jacobson, *Money in the 1980 and 1982 Congressional Elections, in* MONEY AND POLITICS *supra* note 7, at 51 [hereinafter Jacobson, *1980–82 Congressional Elections*]. (stating that "leaders are not about to risk losing congressional seats by withholding support and thereby deliberately weakening their incumbents").

226. For a review of the extensive literature, *see* LEON EPSTEIN, POLITICAL PARTIES IN THE AMERICAN MOLD 3-8 (1986).

227. *See supra* notes 214-15 and accompanying text.

228. *See* SORAUF, *supra* note 27, at 131-32 (describing the Republican's generic advertising campaign in the 1980 election); *see also* Jacobson, *1980-82 Congressional Elections, supra* note 225, at 50 (noting that in the 1982 election, the Republican Party spent $11 million on a national advertising campaign urging voters to "stay the course").

229. If funds were appropriated solely for generic advertising, a more precise definition of the term would be essential. One approach would be to prohibit any candidate's name from being mentioned. This would be unduly restrictive, for the most effective party advertisements might include praise or criticism of the chamber's leaders or of other prominent members. Another possibility would be to prohibit the ad from running in the district of any candidate mentioned. This would be cumbersome and petty. If the Democrats produce an ad praising Speaker Foley, or the Republicans produce one criticizing him, does it make sense to say that it cannot run in the Washington media market including his district? The best statutory definition of generic advertising probably would require that

The hope would be that by assuring a substantial amount of campaign communication focused more on party performance as a whole than on the personal qualities of the candidates, the partisan element in legislative voting might increase and the personal element decrease.[230] If this were to occur, legislative incumbents would have a greater incentive to work for party accomplishment rather than simply for personal positioning and posturing in a manner intended to satisfy constituents who are only slightly attentive.[231] Adoption of the proposal would be nothing more than an experiment, but one that has considerably greater potential for moving the political system in the direction of responsible party government than some of the proposals of the party renewal movement.[232]

3. Aggregate Limit on (Relatively) Unrestricted Contributions

The idea of putting an aggregate limit on the total amount a candidate can receive from special interest sources first attracted prominence when it was incorporated into the Obey-Railsback bill[233] that was approved by the House in 1979, only to be killed by a threat of filibuster in the Senate in 1980.[234] The Obey-Railsback bill applied only to contributions received

---

no more than, say, 25% of the money spent to run the ad be for airing or distribution in a single state. Additional details would need to be worked out, covering, for example, the treatment of media markets covering more than one state.

230. *See generally* BRUCE CAIN, JOHN FEREJOHN & MORRIS FIORINA, THE PERSONAL VOTE: CONSTITUENCY SERVICE AND ELECTORAL INDEPENDENCE 169 (1987) (comparing the present role of incumbency with its role in the 1950s and 1960s when "House elections...[were] party line affairs, buffeted by national effects produced by particular presidential candidates, and administrations").

231. *See generally* DAVID R. MAYHEW, CONGRESS: THE ELECTORAL CONNECTION (1974).

232. *See, e.g.,* Lawson, *How State Laws Undermine Parties, in* ELECTIONS AMERICAN STYLE, *supra* note 7, at 255-60 (suggesting a reduction of state regulation as a way of strengthening the party system). For a leading statement of the constitutional theories underlying many of the party renewal proposals, *see* Stephen E. Gottlieb, *Rebuilding the Right of Association: The Right to Hold a Convention as a Test Case,* 11 HOFSTRA L. REV. 191 (1982). For criticism of some of these theories, *see* Daniel H. Lowenstein, *Constitutional Rights of Major Political Parties: A Skeptical Inquiry,* Paper Delivered at the Annual Meeting of the American Political Science Association (September 1-4, 1988) (on file at *Hofstra Law Review*). For two excellent expositions of some of the concerns that drive both the proposal in this Article, and the party renewal movement, *see* George M. Pomper, *The Decline of the Party in American Elections,* 92 POL. SCI. Q. 21 (1977) *and* Morris Fiorina, *The Decline of Collective Responsibility in American Politics,* 109 DAEDALUS 25 (1980).

233. H.R. 4970, 96th Cong. (1979) (entitled the Campaign Contribution Reform Act of 1979).

234. *See* Malbin, *supra* note 7, at 235.

from PACs.[235] The present aggregate limit applies to all contributions that are not permitted by either of the next two portions of the proposal. $50,000 could be received by a House candidate under this heading.[236]

The purpose of an aggregate limit is to reduce the pressure imposed by contributions. An artificial limit is put on the demand for contributions, while the supply presumably remains constant. The result is that the "price" of the contribution in pressure or influence declines. In ordinary English, the hope is that the candidate will not feel overly indebted to the special interest contributor if there are dozens more lined up outside the door, ready to contribute in case the first contributor becomes dissatisfied. In line with this theory, the goal is to make it as easy as possible for the candidate to get to the limit. Accordingly, there is much to be said for allowing contributions within the aggregate limit from all sources, including corporate and union treasuries, and without limit as to size. However, the conventional antipathy to contributions of very large size or from corporate or union sources suggests that it is most politic to stipulate that within the aggregate limit, the currently existing contribution limits are applicable.[237]

It may be asked why there should be any provision at all for special interest contributions if the objective is to eliminate conflict of interest. The answer is that in the spirit of moderation described in Part Three,[238] competing considerations must be balanced. Here, the relevant consideration is the desire to provide some foothold for the candidate who, for whatever reason, is allocated little or no money by the party leadership.[239] This and the following two portions of the package make it possible, although difficult, to raise enough funds to put on at least a barely credible campaign.

---

235. *See* 125 CONG. REC. 21162 (daily ed. July 27, 1979) (statement of Representative Obey noting that the bill was designed to restrict the role of special interest money); *see also* Malbin, *supra* note 7, at 235 (stating that the purpose of the Obey-Railsback bill was to add new PAC limits to the Federal Election Commission authorization bill).

236. I do not suggest dollar amounts for the aggregate limits for Senate campaigns. Presumably, they would be on a sliding scale, depending on the size of the state. The main point is that the limits should be considerably lower than what an ordinary incumbent would expect to be able to raise in funds subject to the aggregate limit.

237. I believe all the major aspects of the package in this Part are constitutional, but have not attempted to engage in constitutional analysis in this essay. The aggregate limits are probably most susceptible to attack under current doctrine. For a brief and informal analysis of the constitutional considerations applicable to aggregate limits, *see* Daniel H. Lowenstein, *Campaign Finance and the Constitution*, Social Science Working Paper 695, at 7 (California Institute of Technology, Pasadena, California, 1989) (on file at *Hofstra Law Review*).

238. *See supra* notes 153-201 and accompanying text.

239. *See* Jacobson, *Republicans and Democrats, supra* note 204, at 606 (discussing why party leadership would deny funds to candidates).

If we think of legislative elections as party affairs to a large extent, as this package is designed to encourage us to do, then the notion that the party leadership should allocate resources in legislative elections becomes a natural one. But the doctrine of responsible party government never will and probably never should entirely displace the American traditions of progressivism and individualism, which demand that a man or woman have at least a chance of getting elected even if rejected by the party leaders. It is true that independently wealthy candidates able to finance their own campaigns would be some check on the party leaders' monopoly of resources. Progressivism and individualism, however, should not be limited to the upper fraction of the upper one percent. The aggregate limit on special interest contributions is intended to be small enough to minimize pressure from this source, while at least permitting a candidate to raise seed money on which to try to build on the basis of the small individual contributions permitted by the next portion of the package.

4. $100 Limit on Individual Contributions

In addition to the general aggregate limit just discussed, the reform package contains a second aggregate limit for "qualified" PACs, to be described below. Except within these two aggregate limits, no contributions could come from anyone but individuals, and then in amounts not greater than $100.

This suggestion runs against the grain of proposals to increase the current individual contribution limit of $1,000.[240] Often, these proposals are explained as a means to reduce the relative significance of PAC contributions.[241] This approach confuses form with substance. There is nothing about the PAC form that makes PAC contributions any worse than other contributions. The problem is the money contributed in pursuit of a legislative strategy. This can be money from individuals just as easily as money from PACs, especially when contributions of significant size can come from a large number of individuals in the same firm or industry.[242]

---

240. *See, e.g.*, Joel Fleischman & Pope McCorkle, *Level-Up Rather Than Level-Down: Towards a New Theory of Campaign Finance Reform,* 1 J.L. & POL. 211, 288 (1984). (suggesting a $5,000 contribution limit).

241. *See, e.g., id.* (explaining that "[h]igher levels for individual contributions to parties and directly to candidates means that more money will bypass the PAC contribution channel").

242. *See* Sabato, *supra* note 7, at 178 (stating that "the root of the problem in campaign finance is not PACs, it is money").

The rhetorical question is often asked, can a legislator be bought for $1,000?[243] The answer is that such a contribution can exert pressure when it is the largest that can be made and, as we have just seen, it can be multiplied without limit by contributions from others with similar interests. A $100 limit will make it much more difficult to use individual contributions as part of a legislative strategy. The limit also serves the egalitarian goal of reducing, though by no means eliminating, the disparate ability of people of different income levels to influence policy by means of an electoral strategy. It does this with a minimal effect on libertarian values. First, people are free to express themselves by making contributions that always will lend incremental assistance to the campaign.[244] Second, the existence of public funding assures that ample resources will be available for debate where it is most relevant. Third, the outlet of independent expenditures would still be available.

5. Aggregate Limit on Contributions from Qualified PACs

Given the degree to which the public debate over campaign finance has tended to center almost entirely on PACs, it is surprising that there has not been more objection to the fact that PACs have been permitted to contribute $5,000 to candidates[245] whereas individuals have been limited to $1,000.[246] There is a justification for this discrepancy, but it applies only to certain PACs. Individuals who make very small contributions may need to pool their contributions to have any effect. Otherwise, the costs of determining to whom to contribute, and writing a check and sending it might consume a large percentage of the contribution itself. In such instances, pooling, if not a necessity, is at least a great convenience. Those able to make larger contributions are better able to make their contributions as individuals.

There are two major types of PACs that receive their funds in small contributions. The first is composed of labor union PACs. Labor PACs are often in competition with business PACs, whether they are pursuing a legislative or electoral strategy. If there were no provisions permitting extra contributions by PACs whose receipts come from small contributions,

---

243. Of course, the $1,000 figure understates the situation under current law. An individual and spouse can each give a total of $4,000 to a candidate who runs in a primary and general election. *See* Drew, *supra* note 47, at 12.

244. This would not be true under expenditure limits if the campaign had already raised as much as it was allowed to spend.

245. 2 U.S.C. § 441a(a)(2)(A) (1982).

246. *See id.* § 441a(a)(1)(A).

labor would be placed at a disadvantage compared to business. Business and labor would have an equal opportunity to contribute within the basic aggregate limit. Beyond that, individual business managers could give substantial sums collectively in amounts of $100 each. The provision for a separate aggregate limit available only to PACs relying on small contributions is intended at least partially to offset that inequality.

The second type of political action committee relying on small contributions is composed of ideological PACs. These groups ordinarily pursue an electoral strategy, and they provide an additional avenue of expression for individuals who support their goals.[247] They have been subject to criticism,[248] some of which is less applicable to the extent they contribute to candidates rather than make independent expenditures. This proposal would, within limits, permit them to make such contributions.

Specifically, a PAC would qualify by accepting contributions only from individuals, and only in amounts of fifty dollars or less.[249] A candidate could accept contributions from qualified PACs up to $5,000 each, and up to $50,000 in the aggregate. It should be noted that although it is assumed this device would be most convenient for labor and ideological groups, other groups such as businesses and trade associations would be free to employ it as well.

6. Independent Spending

The debate over independent spending has been particularly polarized. Some regard independent spending as an outlet for individual expression and a potential source for introducing new subjects and ideas into a campaign debate.[250] Others see it as an evasion of whatever reform limits are in place that is unfair to the targeted candidate at best, and potentially

---

247. *See generally* Margaret Ann Latus, *Assessing Ideological PACs: From Outrage to Understanding, in* MONEY AND POLITICS, *supra* note 7, at 142 (stating that ideological PACs have electoral objectives because they further "selfless causes," which are considered in the "public interest").

248. *See, e.g.,* Sabato, *supra* note 7, at 174-76 (noting that "the frequent use of negative, even vicious, messages and tactics by independent groups makes any sort of civility in politics much more difficult to achieve").

249. An increased contribution limit for PACs that receive only small contributions has been proposed before. *See, e.g.,* CALIFORNIA COMM'N ON CAMPAIGN FIN., THE NEW GOLD RUSH: FINANCING CALIFORNIA'S LEGISLATIVE CAMPAIGNS 228-29 (1985).

250. *See, e.g.,* Buckley v. Valeo, 424 U.S. 1, 47-48 (1976) (holding that a proposed ceiling on independent expenditures failed to serve any substantive government interest and were therefore unconstitutional under the first amendment).

corrupting at worse.[251] Plainly, independent spending can be any of these, though at the small or medium-sized levels it is more likely to wear its benevolent aspect than at very large levels.

To date most independent spending has been by ideological groups.[252] Although two trade associations have been among the larger independent spenders,[253] by and large independent spending seems to have been engaged in as an electoral rather than a legislative strategic device.[254] This could change if other avenues for a legislative strategy are closed off.

Aside from the question of pressure, when large amounts of independent spending occur on one side of a campaign, it seems unfair to the opposing candidate, especially since independent spending often goes for negative advertising.[255] It is true, as Malbin has pointed out, that independent spending may not help the beneficiary as much as direct spending, and that in some cases it may be of no help at all or even counter-productive.[256] He concludes that it is unfair to the beneficiary for the government to match the independent spending with grants to the opposing candidate.[257]

Although Malbin is correct in his premise that independent spending is not always helpful, his conclusion does not follow. Ordinarily, independent spending will be helpful, at least to some degree. On average, providing offsetting payments to the opposing candidate should be fairer than not doing so.

A final reason for doing something about independent spending is that doing so is one of the major attractions of campaign finance reform for incumbents, whose votes are needed to pass legislation.

For all these reasons, my package matches independent spending, but only above a high threshold. The rough idea should be that independent spending amounting to one or two full page newspaper advertisements throughout the jurisdiction, or a few spot advertisements on television or

---

251. *See, e.g.,* DREW, *supra* note 47, at 134-35.

252. *See generally* Latus, *supra* note 247, at 142-47, 149-50 (discussing ideological PACs and the large independent expenditures among such PACs).

253. *See* SORAUF, *supra* note 27, at 113.

254. *See* Jacobson, *Parties and PACs, supra* note 30, at 140; Latus, *supra* note 247, at 142-63.

255. *See* Jacobson, *Parties and PACs, supra* note 30, at 147-48.

256. *See* Malbin, *supra* note 7, at 239 (stating that "[i]ndependent advertising often forces supposedly favored candidates to spend unwanted time or money dealing with, and sometimes distancing themselves from, positions espoused in the advertisements, just as it forces the attacked opponents to respond").

257. *See id.*

on the radio should not trigger matching payments, but much more than that should. A possible approach would be that in a House race, up to $15,000 would not be matched, from $15,000 to $30,000 the opposing candidate would receive two dollars for every three dollars of independent spending, and above $30,000, the independent spending would be matched dollar for dollar.

This matching proposal should not be offensive to libertarians. Independent spenders would have considerable leeway to disseminate their ideas before matching begins. Even after matching begins, it is hardly a sympathetic ground for objection that speaking has the effect of triggering resources permitting one's opponent to reply.

C. Something for Everyone

The package I have proposed commends itself on three major grounds. First, it drastically reduces the opportunity for contributors to employ a legislative strategy, and thereby reduces the corruption inherent in the campaign finance system. Second, it promotes electoral competition, and does so in an efficient manner by permitting the parties to channel public funds to the districts where they can be used most effectively. Third, it holds forth, if not the promise, at least the potential for shifting our system in the direction of responsible party government by assuring that a significant portion of campaign debate will be cast in partisan terms. This, as a consequence, encourages voters to hold candidates accountable, at least in part, on the basis of party performance.

Consistent with these broad purposes, and in the spirit outlined in Part III, I have attempted to include in the package something for everyone. The following is a brief comment on how the polar positions of each of the major cleavages in the campaign finance debate are affected.

1. Egalitarians. — Several of the major inegalitarian features of the current system are ameliorated. Reducing the individual contribution limit to $100 does not level the playing field much for the poor, but it does for the broad middle class. More importantly, because the proposal reduces private contributions to a more supplemental role, those who cannot or do not contribute may find their relative position improved.

More fundamentally still, party renewal enthusiasts claim that parties in a system of responsible party government will be better able to promote the interests of the poor than in a candidate-oriented system. If so, there could be substantial egalitarian gains. Admittedly, these chickens are a long way from being hatched.

Finally, though perhaps it is not strictly an egalitarian gain, if the narrow interests that employ a legislative strategy in their contributions are losers, dispersed interests such as those of the environment, consumers and small business might be gainers. This too is speculative, for as Heard and others have warned, concentrated wealth finds many avenues for the pursuit of power, and removing one of them, even if that can be done, may not have dramatic effects on overall outcomes.[258]

2. Libertarians.—The only losses for libertarians in this package are the reduction in the individual contribution limit and the new aggregate contribution limits. Except for the most doctrinaire, these losses do not seem severe. For those willing to look beyond form to real consequences, the gains in genuine debate and dialogue resulting from a substantial inflow of money where it can be used most effectively will offset these minor losses. The best news for libertarians is what is not included in the package: spending limits. Those mythical candidates who, in the fantasies of libertarians, can raise massive sums in contributions of one dollar each[259] are free to run their mythical campaigns free of interference from this proposal.

3. Republicans.—If Republicans are serious about their proclaimed desire for campaign reforms that will expand the role of the parties in federal elections,[260] this proposal should make them ecstatic. If this proclaimed goal is simply a front for wanting to enlarge the advantage that superior fund-raising has given them over the Democrats, this plan will not meet their needs. However, they cannot hope to obtain a plan that accomplishes that objective from a Democratic Congress. In the plan proposed here, the equalizing effect of the public funding would dilute the Republican advantage, but this would be offset to some extent by the repeal of limits on party assistance to candidates. Furthermore, as the minority party, the Republicans gain from the assurance of a continuous and generous flow of funds for challenges to incumbents.

4. Democrats.—The Republican advantage in party fund-raising[261] is not eliminated, but the assurance of significant funding for both parties means that the Democrats' absolute disadvantage is much higher on the curve of diminishing returns. The assured money for serious challenges might increase slightly the chances of the Democrats losing their majority in the House. However, compared to other possible changes that could have the same effect, such as a liberalization of party spending without public financing, or an increase in the amounts wealthy contributors can inject into campaigns, this proposal contains an important benefit for Democrats. It was only because the Democrats were the majority party that they were able to increase their share of business PAC contributions

---

258. See HEARD, supra note 1, at 90.

259. See Fleischman & McCorkle, supra note 240, at 279.

260. See Jacobson, Republicans and Democrats, supra note 204, at 624.

261. See id. at 603; supra note 204 & accompanying text.

during the 1980s.[262] If they were to lose their majority, they would face a financial disaster.[263] The proposed plan is a form of disaster insurance for the Democrats.

5. Challengers.—It might seem that some challengers will be better off and some worse off, since some will have access to a major new source of funding, while others will face new restrictions and get none of the new money. However, most challengers who receive little or no money from the party leadership will be the same ones who receive little in large contributions under the present system, and for the same reason, namely, that their cause is nearly hopeless.

The concern here is not really for challengers as a group, but for the public interest in a competitive system. That public interest exists for two reasons, described by Jacobson as "keeping legislators responsive" and "letting voters change the direction of policy by replacing elected officials."[264] Most observers would agree that the first interest is amply satisfied by our present candidate-oriented system. The second goal requires more than a challenger's ability to mount a competitive campaign. So long as campaigns remain candidate-oriented and isolated from other campaigns in other districts, the second goal will not be met, even if several dozen congressional seats change hands every election. The present plan, because it promotes party discipline and encourages campaigns based on party performance rather than on candidate idiosyncracies, holds out a prospect not only of increased competition, but of competition that can fulfill the purpose for which it is touted.

6. Incumbents.—Here's the rub. Most people who are not incumbent legislators believe that increased competition would be desirable under present circumstances. Plainly, any plan that increases competition will be inconvenient for incumbents. In addition, the proposed plan gives decision-making power to the parties over resources that are vital to the incumbents and the parties. Nothing can be done about this, and if these features assure that the plan can never seriously be considered, so be it. However, if these features are not fatal, the plan contains others intended to sweeten the bitter pill for incumbents.

First, the control is in the hands of the party leaders in the chamber, and therefore ultimately in the hands of the incumbents. Second, although the plan assures the funding of numerous serious challenges, it also assures ample resources for the defending incumbents. Although the increased spending is of greater benefit to challengers,[265] the increased

---

262. *See supra* text accompanying notes 49-51.

263. *See, e.g.,* Jacobson, *Parties and PACs, supra* note 28, at 141.

264. *Id.* at 194.

265. *See supra* text accompanying notes 208-09.

spending of incumbents can make a difference.[266] Furthermore, incumbents can expect to defeat even well-funded challengers most of the time. Third, in contrast with public financing plans that assure funding to all challengers, the plan assures incumbents who are not targeted by the opposing party that they will not have to face publicly subsidized opponents who, although they may have little chance to win, can still create a nuisance for the incumbent. Fourth, the plan protects incumbents in the event of a massive influx of hostile independent spending. Finally, by greatly reducing the importance of special interest contributions, the plan relieves incumbents from systematically placing themselves in positions of conflict of interest.

D. Comparison With Other Proposals

Final insight into the nature of the proposal can be gained by comparing it with two competing ideas that have received considerable discussion in recent years.

1. Tax credits. — Prior to the tax reforms of 1986,[267] a tax credit, up to an individual limit of $100, could be taken in an amount equal to fifty percent of any campaign contribution to candidates in federal, state or local elections.[268] Recurrent proposals are heard for restoration of the tax credit, including proposals that the amount of the credit be raised to one hundred percent.[269] The theory is that if people understand that the government will reimburse much or all of a contribution, they will be encouraged to make small contributions, causing candidates to solicit those small contributions, resulting in a significant new source of clean money.

No one knows to what extent tax credits induce increased contributions.[270] One thing that is clear is that tax credits represent an extremely inefficient method of publicly financing election campaigns. We know from current experience that a number of people do make contributions in the absence of tax credits. If tax credits are reinstated, a significant percentage of the lost revenues — possibly almost all of them — will be paid not for new campaign funds but as a gratuitous tax benefit. In short, tax credits are not worth it. In 1984, tax credits totaled $257.4 million.[271]

---

266. *See supra* text accompanying notes 210-11.

267. Tax Reform Act of 1986, Pub. L. No. 99-514, 100 Stat. 2712, §§ 1431-1433 (codified as amended in scattered sections of 26 U.S.C.).

268. 26 U.S.C. § 41 (1982).

269. *See* Richard P. Conlon, *The Declining Role of Individual Contributions in Financing Congressional Campaigns,* 3 J.L. & POL. 467, 470 (1987).

270. *See* SORAUF, *supra* note 27, at 51.

271. SORAUF, *supra* note 27.

This is more than the roughly estimated cost of my proposals—$220 million over a two year cycle, consisting of $180 million for public funds to candidates allocated through the parties and $40 million for generic advertising—without nearly the benefits. While that $257.4 million was lost, the serious problems that gave rise to this Symposium were in full swing.[272]

2. Level-up.—In an article that has attracted considerable attention, Joel Fleischman and Pope McCorkle advocated what they called the "level-up" approach rather than the "level-down" approach they attributed to traditional reformers.[273] By "level-up," they refer to government action that provides resources to those in need, and "level-down" refers to government action that prevents those with extra resources from using them to gain advantage.[274] This idea, like so much that is worthwhile in the campaign finance field, goes back to Alexander Heard, who expressed a preference for "positive action by government" over "the negative restrictions of the past."[275]

Heard's insight was good, and Fleischman and McCorkle show that as a theory, it has many attractive features.[276] But the burden of this Article has been that the campaign finance problem is too deeply rooted, too intertwined with a host of values and interests, to be resolved by any theory that looks at the problem from only one angle. Fleischman and McCorkle provide some unwitting empirical confirmation of this, for their good theory leads them to a bad proposal. The core of their proposal is to provide an amount of public financing in a range of $50,000 to $75,000 to each major party candidate for the House[277] and to increase the contribution limit for individuals from $1,000 to $5,000.[278]

---

272. A 100% tax credit would waste twice as much tax relief for people who would make contributions in the absence of tax incentives. It might induce more contributions than the 50% credit did, but to the extent it succeeded, its cost in lost revenues would soar. It is sometimes proposed to deal with this problem by limiting the credit to those who contribute to federal elections. This would only exacerbate the problem of campaign finance at the state and local levels, where the problem is sometimes at least as serious as in federal elections. Tax credits are a bad idea, but if they are adopted, they ought to be applicable to all federal, state and local elections, including ballot measure elections.

273. *See* Fleischman & McCorkle, *supra* note 240, at 215.

274. *See id.* at 294-95 (explaining how a "level up" framework gives a boost to challengers or otherwise poor candidates, while a "level down" system seeks to cut off the disproportionate participatory influence of the wealthy in the campaign finance process).

275. HEARD, *supra* note 1, at 431.

276. *See* Fleischman & McCorkle, *supra* note 240, at 275-98.

277. *Id.* at 277.

278. *Id.*

The grants they would give are hardly more than tokens compared with what it takes to run a competitive campaign for the House. Their grants would yield a marginal increase in the quantity of campaign debate, but no other benefits.[279] Any increase in competitiveness would be barely noticeable. This is because the greatest share of the money they would give away would go either to safe incumbents with no need for it, or to hopeless challengers. The increase in the individual contribution limit would simply aggravate existing problems of corruption and inequality.

In contrast, by providing for allocation of public funds to the districts where they are needed, the present proposal would be far more effective in increasing competitiveness. It would be a big progressive step rather than a modest regressive step against corruption and inequality. And unlike the Fleishman-McCorkle proposal, it at least aspires to improve competitiveness in a manner that serves the broader needs of the political system, rather than as an end in itself.

---

279. It is also true that their program is cheaper than mine. If the $120,000,000 I proposed in grants to House candidates were divided equally among all major party candidates, each candidate would receive about $138,000. This would buy somewhat more campaign debate and might bring about a noticeable, though slight, increase in the number of competitive campaigns. However, it would still do nothing to alleviate the central problem of conflict of interest created by the campaign finance system, and it would do nothing to move the system in the direction of responsible party government.

Epilogue

Essay on the Constitutionality of Several Frequently Debated Campaign Finance Reform Proposals

Frederick G. Slabach

Critics of the money as speech theory urge the Supreme Court to overturn *Buckley*. Assuming they are unsuccessful, advocates of reforming the current federal campaign finance system must fit their proposals within the traditional confines of strict scrutiny and conditional public financing. What follows are comments on the constitutionality of three frequently proposed campaign finance reforms contained in the McCain-Feingold bill: a ban on "soft money," limits on "issue advocacy," and government benefits conditioned on voluntary spending caps.[1]

---

1. *See* S.25 (version 3), 105 Cong. Among other things, the McCain-Feingold legislation would make the following changes in current law:

    1. Prohibit national political parties and federal candidates from soliciting or accepting soft money and prohibit state political parties from spending soft money for certain federal election activities. *Id*. at § 101. This section also would prohibit national and state political parties from soliciting funds for or contributing funds to not-for-profit entities. *Id*.;

    2. Treat as contributions any expenditure by individuals (including political committees) who coordinate with a candidate or a candidate's agent in broadcasting "issue advertisements" which name or clearly identify political candidates within 60 days of an election regardless of the purpose of such advertisement. *Id*. at § 201. This section also would treat as contributions any expenditures by individuals (including political committees) who coordinate with the candidate or the candidate's party to broadcast issue advertisements which refer to a clearly identified candidate at any time if the purpose is to influence a federal election. *Id*. This section also would expand the definition of express advocacy beyond the "magic words" such as "vote for," "elect," "support," etc. *Id*.;

    3. Condition a political party's ability to make 441a(d) coordinated expenditures contingent upon the party's willingness to forego the ability to make independent expenditures on behalf of the party's candidate. *Id*. at § 204;

A. Ban on Soft Money Contributions for Grass-Roots Activities

"Soft Money" means many things to many people. As it is used in this discussion, soft money is defined as money raised without respect to the source[2] and size limitations[3] of the Federal Election Campaign Act[4] [hereinafter FECA] which is spent on two kinds of campaign related activities: (1) state and local political party grass-roots activities, and (2) issue advocacy that is beneficial to a candidate for federal office. The McCain-Feingold legislation would ban soft money for political party grass-roots activities and prohibit political parties from soliciting soft money.[5]

The term soft money, as it applies to state and local grass-roots activity, first gained general usage in 1979 when new Federal Election Commission [hereinafter FEC] rules redefined "contribution" and "expenditure" to exclude funds to be spent on "grass-roots" political activities by state and local party committees in federal elections. These grassroots activities include distribution of publications listing three or more state and federal candidates by state and local party committees, pins, bumper stickers, brochures, and posters, and voter registration and turnout drives by state or local party organizations on behalf of their party's Presidential ticket. It does not include newspaper or broadcast advertising. [6] In practice these

---

4. Treat as contributions all coordinated expenditures intended to influence the outcome of a federal election regardless of whether it is express advocacy. This section also would vastly expand the definition of "coordination" with a candidate to include, among other things, shared vendors. *Id.* at § 205;

5. Establish a voluntary limit of $50,000 on the use of a candidate's personal funds in exchange for allowing the national parties to make their current coordinated expenditures on behalf of the candidate under § 441a(d). *Id.* at §§ 401–402;

2. FECA source limits include a ban on money from corporate and labor union treasuries. 2 U.S.C. § 441b(1994). The FECA also prohibits contributions by government contractors, *id.* at § 441c, and contributions by foreign nationals, *id.* at § 441e.

3. For example, an individual may give a maximum of $1,000 to a candidate, $5,000 to any political committee other than a candidate committee or the committee of a national political party, $20,000 to a national political party committee in any calendar year, and a maximum of $25,000 in any calendar year to all committees. 2 U.S.C. § 441a (1994).

4. 2 U.S.C. § 431–456 (1994).

5. *See* S. 25 (version 3), 105 Cong., § 101.

6. Congress codified the regulations in amendments to the FECA in 1983. 2 U.S.C. § 431 (8)(B)(v), (x), (xii), 431(9)(B)(iv), (viii), (ix)(1994). The current regulations are found at 11 C.F.R. 100.7(b)(9), (15), (16), (17), 100.8(b)(10), (16), (18)(1997).

funds primarily are raised by the national political parties and distributed to the states based upon the national parties' priorities.[7]

Federal limits on the source and size of the "grass roots" expenditures apply only to the portion of the state or local party committee's funds allocated to federal candidates. The FEC has issued regulations governing the allocation of costs for these "grass-roots" political activities between federal (hard money) and nonfederal (soft money) accounts.[8] The state or local party committees must have enough contributions that meet federal law limitations (hard money) to cover that portion of their expenditures relating to federal candidates. For example, if the state or local party produces a publication listing three state candidates and one federal candidate, the FEC regulations require one-fourth of the production costs be paid from a federal (hard money) account which meets the size and source limits of the FECA, and allows three-fourths of the costs to be paid from a nonfederal (soft money) account.[9] Thus, parties distinguish between "hard money" which is raised and spent within the limits of FECA, and "soft money" which usually is raised by the national parties and distributed to the state and local parties and regulated only by state law.[10]

The McCain-Feingold proposal to ban soft money contributions to the national parties and spent by the state and local parties on grassroots activities appears to present no constitutional problems under the Court's analysis in *Buckley*.[11] Money donated by individuals or other entities to the national parties are clearly contributions, not expenditures under the *Buckley* dichotomy.[12] Although protected by the First Amendment, contributions may be limited if Congress finds it is necessary to avoid the actuality or appearance of corruption of the electoral or governmental processes.[13] Indeed, the statute and regulations under review in *Buckley*

---

7. *See e.g.*, *The Money Trail*, WASH. TIMES, Oct. 10, 1997 at A22 (Democratic National Committee directed $32 million in soft money to twelve battleground states in 1996 Presidential election campaign).

8. 11 C.F.R. 106.5(1997).

9. *See* 11 C.F.R. 106.5(e) (1997).

10. Some states have no limits on the amount an individual can give. *See e.g.* MISS. CODE ANN. § 23-15-801 *et. seq.*

11. The McCain-Feingold legislation would prohibit national political parties from soliciting or accepting soft money and prohibit state and local political parties from spending soft money for certain grass-roots activities during federal elections. S. 25 (version 3), 105 Cong. § 101.

12. Buckley v. Valeo, 424 U.S. 1, 19-23 (1976).

13. *Id.* at 23-38.

did not allow this type of soft money contribution to the national parties if they were spent in coordination with the party's candidates for federal office.[14] One might assume that a return to the statute in existence at the time *Buckley* was decided would not cause the Court constitutional discomfort.

The most recent pronouncement by the Court on the constitutionality of limits on campaign contributions would appear not to change this conclusion. In *Colorado Republican Federal Campaign Committee v. Federal Election Commission*,[15] the Court invalidated the statutory provision which treated all political party expenditures on behalf of a candidate for federal office as "coordinated expenditures" (regardless of whether the contributions were independent in fact) and placed limits on the amount of coordinated expenditures a party could make on behalf of a candidate[16] as applied to independent expenditures by political parties.[17] The FEC argued that coordinated expenditures were essentially contributions from the party to the candidate and could be limited under *Buckley*.[18] No opinion of the Court commanded a majority of the justices. But a majority of the Court treated the advertisements made by the Colorado Republican Party as expenditures which could not be limited by Congress and invalidated the FEC expenditure limits. Three of the four opinions representing eight of the nine justices followed the contribution / expenditure dichotomy established in *Buckley* and reiterated Congress' power to limit contributions but not expenditures. If the Court continues to adhere to *Buckley's* contribution/expenditure dichotomy Congress' power to ban soft money contributions to the national, state and local parties should be upheld.

Justice Breyer's plurality opinion (in which justices O'Connor and Suter joined) stated that a political party, like an individual or political action committee, could make independent expenditures on behalf of candidates for federal office and that these independent expenditures may not be limited under *Buckley*.[19] If such expenditures were in fact coordinated with the candidate, however, they would be contributions and subject to limi-

---

14. The FECA was amended in 1980 to exempt certain grass-roots expenditures from the definition of the Act. Federal election Campaign Act Amendments of 1979 Pub. L. No. 96-187, 93 Stat. 1339.

15. 116 S. Ct. 2309 (1996).

16. 2 U.S.C. § 441a(d)(3).

17. Colorado Republican Fed. Campaign Comm. v. Federal Election Commission, 116 S. Ct. 2309, 2312 (1996).

18. *Id.* at 2314.

19. *Id.* at 2315-16.

tation under the analysis in *Buckley*.[20] Adhering to the *Buckley* contribution / expenditure dichotomy would allow the government to ban soft money. Indeed, Justice Breyer's plurality opinion in *Colorado Republican* specifically noted that if Congress concluded "that the potential for evasion of the individual contribution limits was a serious matter, [it] might decide to change the statute's limitations on contributions to political parties."[21]

Justice Kennedy's concurring opinion argued that the party and its candidates have a practical identity and that all spending by a party, whether independent of a candidate or not, is an expenditure and may not be constitutionally limited under *Buckley*.[22] Justice Kennedy's opinion recognized the *Buckley* dichotomy and reaffirmed Congress' ability to limit contributions, but simply found that when a party spends for its candidate, it spends for itself and Congress may not limit such expenditures.[23] This analysis would also allow Congress to ban soft money contributions to political parties.

Justice Stevens' dissent (in which Justice Ginsburg joined) argued that Congress and the FEC were entitled to deference in determining that it is impossible for a political party to make a truly independent expenditure on behalf of its candidate. Such expenditures, according to Justice Stevens, are contributions to the candidate and may be limited under *Buckley*.[24]

Only Justice Thomas' opinion (in which Justices Rehnquist and Scalia joined in part) argued that the party advertisements were in fact contributions to the party's candidate, but that there was no risk of corruption when the contributor is the party. Therefore, there is no compelling government interest in limiting this contribution and the FEC regulation must fail. In fact, Justice Thomas argued that there is no Constitutional difference between contributions and expenditures and Congress may limit neither.[25] This opinion would cast doubt on Congress' power to ban soft money contributions to the national political parties. If there is no risk of corruption when the party spends money for a candidate, can there be a risk of corruption when a soft money source gives money to the party and then it is spent for a candidate?

---

20. *Id.* at 2317-19.

21. *Id.* at 2316.

22. *Id.* at 2322.

23. *Id.*

24. *Id.* at 2332.

25. *Id.* at 2325-29. (Chief Justice Rehnquist and Justice Scalia did not join this part of Justice Thomas' opinion.)

B. Independent Expenditures and Issue Advocacy

The term "soft money" also has been applied to money raised by the national parties[26] and other entities (such as corporations, labor unions, and 501 (c)(4) corporations)[27] to engage in "issue advocacy." "Issue advocacy" is print and broadcast advertising which does not expressly endorse or oppose the nomination or election of a candidate for federal office. The Supreme Court first differentiated between "issue advocacy" and "express advocacy" of the election or defeat of a candidate in *Buckley* when it interpreted language in a provision of the FECA.[28] The Federal Election Commission then defined express advocacy as those communications that advocate the election or defeat of a clearly identified candidate by using words such as "vote for" or "elect" in conformity with the Supreme Court's opinion in *Buckley*.[29]

---

26. *See, e.g.*, Fred Wertheimer, *Clinton's Subterfuge Is No Technicality*, WASH. POST, Nov. 9, 1997, at C1 (Democratic National Committee raised and spent $45 million on issue advocacy to benefit Clinton Presidential Campaign in 1996); Susan Estrich, *What Everyone's Doing Is Legal*, DENVER POST, Nov. 2, 1997, at I2 (Republican Party raised funds to pay for Dole issue advertisements).

27. *See, e.g.*, Juliet Eilperin and Jim Vande Hei, *Trial Lawyers Are New GOP TV Villain For 1998 Elections*, ROLL CALL, Dec. 11, 1997 (labor unions spent millions on issue advertisements); David Goldstein, *Labor Funds Mean Help, Headaches*, K. C. STAR, Nov. 24, 1997, at A1 (AFL-CIO spent $35 million on issue advertisements in 1996); Peter H. Stone, *Business Strikes Back*, 43 NAT'L J. Oct. 25, 1997, at 2130 (business coalition plan multimillion dollar issue ad campaign to protect Republicans in 1998 elections).

28. There the Court interpreted a section in the FECA which limited expenditures "relative to a clearly identified candidate" to $1,000 per calendar year. The Court was called upon to determine whether the phrase "relative to" was "unconstitutionally vague" before it could proceed to the question of whether such a limitation was an impermissible infringement on free speech. The Court held that the phrase was so indefinite that it failed to "clearly mark the boundary between permissible and impermissible speech." To cure this vagueness problem, the Court held that the phrase must be construed narrowly to "apply only to expenditures for communications that in express terms advocate the election or defeat of a clearly identified candidate for federal office." Buckley v. Valeo, 424 U.S. 1, 42-43 & n. 52 (1976). *See also* Federal Election Commission v. Massachusetts Citizens for Life, 479 U.S. 238, 248-50 (1986)(phrase in 2 U.S.C. § 441b, "in connection with" interpreted narrowly to apply only to express advocacy as articulated in *Buckley*).

29. The *Buckley* opinion defined express advocacy as "'vote for,' 'elect,' 'support,' 'cast your ballot for,' 'Smith for Congress,' 'vote against,' 'defeat,' 'reject.'" 424 U.S. at 44 n. 52. The FEC initially defined the phrase express advocacy in the same terms. The FEC later modified the definition to allow the consideration of external factors to determine whether the communication is so clearly unambiguous that reasonable people could not

If a political party or other entity makes an expenditure that expressly advocates the election or defeat of a clearly identified candidate *and* the entity making the expenditure "coordinates" with the candidate, that expenditure must be treated as a contribution from the entity to the candidate and is subject to the source and size limitations of the FECA.[30] This is known as a "coordinated expenditure." If an entity makes an expenditure that expressly advocates the election or defeat of a clearly identified candidate and does not coordinate with the candidate, it will not be treated as a contribution to the candidate and will not be limited by the size and source limits of the FECA. This is known as an "independent expenditure."[31]

In *Federal Election Commission v. Massachusetts Citizens for Life*,[32] the Court applied the same "express advocacy" definition to the provision of FECA[33] which makes it unlawful for any corporation or labor organization to make contributions or expenditures in connection with a federal election.[34] The Court's definition of "in connection with" means that under current law, corporations and labor unions may use treasury funds to engage in issue advocacy but may not use such funds for "express advocacy" of the election or defeat of a clearly identified candidate for federal office. The identical language ("in connection with") is used in that portion of the current law which regulates spending by political parties.[35] Corporate, union and party funds may be used for issue advocacy regardless of coordination with the candidate since only "express advocacy" is covered by the limiting provisions of the Act.

Money spent for issue advocacy thus also has been termed "soft money" since it need not meet the federal size and source limitations of the FECA.

---

differ as to whether the communication advocates for or against a clearly identified candidate. Magic words were no longer necessary. *See*, 11 C.F.R. § 100.22(b) (1997). This regulation was struck down by the First Circuit Court of Appeals because it is contrary to the FECA as the Supreme Court has interpreted it consistent with the First Amendment and therefore the regulation is beyond the power of the FEC. Maine Right to Life Committee, Inc. v. FEC, 98 F. 3d 1 (1st Cir. 1996)(per curiam).

30. *Buckley*, 424 U.S. at 42-43. Until recently, all expenditures by political parties in connection with the election campaigns of its candidates were conclusively presumed to be coordinated and counted toward the contribution limits contained in the Act. 2 U.S.C. § 441a(d). In 1996, the Supreme Court invalidated this presumption as a violation of the political party's First Amendment right to free speech. *See*, Colorado Republican Federal Campaign Committee v. Federal Election Commission, 116 S. Ct. 2309 (1996).

31. 2 U.S.C. § 441b.

32. 479 U.S. 238 (1986).

33. 2 U.S.C. § 441b.

34. *Massachusetts Citizens for Life*, 479 U.S. at 249.

35. 2 U.S.C. § 441a(d). The language is also contained in the section prohibiting contributions by foreign nationals. 2 U.S.C. 441e.

Groups wishing to influence elections quickly exploited the Court decisions and FEC regulations to create advertisements that were supportive of their candidates without using the magic words "vote for" or "elect."[36] During the 1996 Presidential campaign, many entities made expenditures on "issue advocacy" advertisements that did not expressly advocate the election or defeat of a particular candidate but contained themes supportive of and the name or likeness of a candidate.[37] The Supreme Court recognized this possibility in *Buckley*. "It would naively underestimate the ingenuity and resourcefulness of persons and groups desiring to buy influence to believe that they would have much difficulty devising expenditures that skirted the restrictions on express advocacy of election or defeat but nevertheless benefited the candidate's campaign."[38] Many of these advertisements were created in coordination with the candidate. They were not limited as other coordinated expenditures are because they were not considered express advocacy.

To close that loophole, the McCain-Feingold legislation would treat any advertisement broadcast within sixty (60) days prior to a federal election which contained the name or likeness of a federal candidate to be express advocacy whether or not it contained the magic words. If the expenditure for the advertisement is coordinated with the candidate, it is treated as a contribution and limited by the act to $1,000 for individuals and $5,000 for political action committees. No corporate or labor union treasury money may be used. Thus, within sixty (60) days of an election, soft money could continue to be used for issue advocacy which did not contain the name or likeness of a federal candidate. But, during this time frame, if the name or likeness of a federal candidate is used, the advertisement is a contribution to the candidate and soft money may not be used since the source and size limits of the FECA must be met. The legislation would also create a presumption of coordination with the candidate if a political committee, individual or corporation or labor union coordinated with the candidate's political party in creating an advertisement that refers to the candidate for the purpose of influencing an election.[39]

This issue advocacy portion of the McCain-Feingold legislation raises serious constitutional problems for at least two reasons: the definition of express advocacy may be overbroad based upon *Buckley* and *Massachusetts Citizens for Life*, and the presumption of coordination may run afoul of the Court's recent decision in *Colorado Republican*.

---

36. The Ninth Circuit appears to be the first court to coin the phrase "magic words" as it relates to *Buckley* footnote 52. Federal Election Commission v. Furgatch, 807 F. 2d 857, 862-63 (9th Cir. 1987), *cert. denied* 484 U.S. 850 (1987).

37. *See* notes 26-27, *supra*.

38. *Buckley*, 424 U.S. at 45.

39. S. 25 (version 3), 105 Cong. § 201-205.

1. Defining Express Advocacy—Vagueness or Overbreadth

The Supreme Court has ruled that the FECA restrictions on coordinated expenditures "in connection with" an election campaign must be interpreted narrowly to apply only to express advocacy of a clearly identified candidate.[40] The Court defined express advocacy as words such as "'vote for,' 'elect,' 'support,' 'cast your ballot for,' 'Smith for Congress,' 'vote against,' 'defeat,' 'reject.'"[41] It is unclear whether the Court was applying the concept of vagueness or overbreadth when it arrived at this definition. On the one hand, the *Buckley* Court appears to have defined the statutory phrase "in connection with" narrowly to avoid unconstitutional vagueness. Individuals must know what speech is allowed and what is not.[42] At another point in the *Buckley* opinion, however, the Court referred to this interpretation as being required "[t]o insure that the reach of [the Act] is not impermissible broad."[43] In *Federal Election Commission v. Massachusetts Citizens for Life*,[44] the Court also characterized the *Buckley* decision as applying the overbreadth doctrine implying that a broader definition of express advocacy would have unduly impinged on constitutionally protected speech without a sufficiently compelling governmental interest.[45] If the *Buckley* and *Massachusetts Citizens for Life* definition of express advocacy is compelled by the overbreadth doctrine, Congress may not constitutionally broaden it to include advertisements that merely refer to a candidate. If, however, the Court narrowly defined the Act to avoid a vagueness problem, Congress may define express advocacy as articulated in the McCain-Feingold legislation.

2. Presumption of Coordination Between a Political Party and its Candidate

Whether the definition of express advocacy would be constitutional, the presumption that an expenditure for an advertisement which refers to a candidate is coordinated with the candidate simply because it is coordinated with the candidate's political party would not pass constitutional muster. The Supreme Court's recent decision in *Colorado Republican Federal Campaign Committee v. Federal Election Commission*[46] prohibits the government from creating a conclusive presumption that an advertis-

---

40. *Buckley*, 424 U.S. at 42-43.
41. *Id.* at n. 52.
42. *Id.* at 42-43.
43. *Id.* at 80.
44. 479 U.S. 238 (1986).
45. *Id.* at 248-49.
46. 116 S. Ct. 2309 (1996).

ing expenditure by a political party is coordinated with the party's candidate. Using this analysis, the mere fact that an individual or political committee coordinated a communication with a candidate's political party would not be sufficient to show that the communication was coordinated with the candidate.

Colorado Republican considered a Federal Election Commission regulation with a similar presumption. The rule at issue in that case presumes all political party expenditures on behalf of a candidate for federal office are "coordinated expenditures" (regardless of whether the expenditures were in fact made independent of the party's candidate). The regulation places limits on the amount of coordinated expenditures a party can make on behalf of a candidate. The Colorado Republican Federal Campaign Committee made advertisements critical of the Colorado Democratic Senatorial candidate, Tim Wirth, in the 1986 election. Since the Colorado Republican Party already had assigned its regulated expenditure capacity to the national Republican Party, the expenditure for the advertisement exceeded the limits a party may make "in connection with" the Senate election.

The FEC argued that coordinated expenditures were essentially contributions from the party to the candidate and could be limited under *Buckley*.[47] The Court in *Colorado Republican* rejected this presumption of coordination and this analysis would require invalidation of the McCain-Feingold presumption as well.

Justice Breyer's plurality opinion (in which justices O'Connor and Suter joined) held that Congress could not presume that all expenditures by a political Party on behalf of its candidate are coordinated. A political party, like an individual or political action committee, may make independent expenditures on behalf of candidates for federal office and these independent expenditures may not be limited under *Buckley*.[48] If such expenditures were in fact coordinated with the candidate, however, they would be contributions and subject to limitation under the analysis in *Buckley*.[49] Because the McCain- Feingold legislation *presumes* that all advertisements coordinated with a political party are also coordinated with the party's candidate, it would be invalid under the Breyer plurality opinion. Under the Breyer analysis, if an advertisement containing the name or likeness of a federal candidate were coordinated with a political party but were truly independent of the party's candidate, the cost of that advertisement could not be treated as a contribution and limited under *Buckley*.

---

47. *Id.* at 2314.
48. *Id.* at 2315-16.
49. *Id.* at 2317-19.

The advertisement would be an independent expenditure and the government could not limit it.

Justice Kennedy's concurring opinion (in which Justices Rehnquist and Scalia joined) concluded that all spending by a party, whether independent of a candidate or not, is an expenditure and may not be constitutionally limited under *Buckley*.[50] Using this analysis, the mere fact that an independent expenditure is coordinated with the party would not allow the government to convert the expenditure into a contribution which could be limited.[51]

Justice Thomas' opinion (in which Justices Rehnquist and Scalia joined in part) argued that the party advertisements were in fact contributions to the party's candidate, but that there was no risk of corruption when the contributor is the party. Therefore, there is no compelling government interest in limiting this contribution and the FEC regulation must fail.[52] Using this analysis, the presumption of coordination between the party and the candidate is irrelevant. The presumption is used to convert an independent expenditure which cannot be limited under *Buckley*, into a contribution which can be limited under *Buckley*. If party contributions to its candidates cannot be limited, parties also can coordinate with other entities to make unlimited expenditures for express advocacy.

Only Justice Stevens' dissent (in which Justice Ginsburg joined) in *Colorado Republican* argued that Congress and the FEC were entitled to deference in determining that it is impossible for a political party to make a true independent expenditure. Such expenditures, according to Justice Stevens, are contributions to the candidate and may be limited under *Buckley*.[53] Using this analysis, Congress could enact a presumption that all expenditures coordinated with a party are coordinated with the candidate and therefore subject to limitation as contributions.

Thus, only two members of the Court, Stevens and Ginsburg, appear to support an analysis that would allow Congress to assume that all expenditures coordinated with a candidate's party are coordinated with the candidate and therefore are contributions that can be constitutionally limited. Seven members of the court would find such a limitation unconstitutional.

---

50. *Id.* at 2322.

51. Justice Kennedy's opinion appears to support the proposition that individuals and political action committees, as well as political parties, could make unlimited expenditures on behalf of candidates without regard to whether those expenditures were independent or coordinated with the candidate. This would be a major departure from the *Buckley* analysis. *See, id.* at 2321-23.

52. *Id.* at 2325-29. (Chief Justice Rehnquist and Justice Scalia did not join this part of Justice Thomas' opinion.)

53. *Id.* at 2332.

C. Voluntary Spending Caps Conditioned on Government Benefits/Unconstitutional Conditions

Since *Buckley*, numerous proposals have been introduced to condition various government benefits upon the limitation of certain types of expenditures. For example, Wertheimer and Manes proposed public funding of Congressional campaigns conditioned upon a limit on overall campaign spending. McCain-Feingold proposes to condition the receipt of party contributions on a candidate's willingness to limit the amount of spending from her own private funds.[54] Other proposals would condition free T.V. advertisement time in exchange for limits on total campaign spending.[55]

Footnote 65 of the *Buckley* decision states "Congress may engage in public financing of election campaigns and may condition acceptance of public funds on an agreement by the candidate to abide by specified expenditure limitations. Just as a candidate may voluntarily limit the size of the contributions he chooses to accept, he may decide to forgo private fundraising and accept public funding."[56] Critics of voluntary contribution and expenditure limits tied to the receipt of government benefits have criticized this footnote as a departure from the unconstitutional conditions doctrine.[57]

A federal district court reviewed the issue again in *Republican National Committee v. Federal Election Commission* [hereinafter *RNC*].[58] In this case the Republican National Committee challenged Title H of the FECA which provides full public financing of the campaigns of major party Presidential candidates if they agree not to spend more than the amount of public funds they are entitled to receive from the Presidential Election Campaign Fund and that they will not accept private contributions unless the Fund is unable to distribute the amount candidates are entitled to receive.[59] Plaintiffs in *RNC* claimed that major party Presidential candidates are forced to accept public funding and that condi-

---

54. S. 25 (version 3), 105 Cong. § 401-402.

55. S. 25 (version 1), 105 Cong.

56. *Buckley*, 424 U.S. at 57 n. 65.

57. *See e.g.* Brice M. Clagett & John R. Bolton, *Buckley v. Valeo, Its Aftermath, and Its Prospects: The Constitutionality of government Restraints on Political Campaign Financing*, 29 VAND. L. REV. 1327, 1335 (1976)(public financing conditioned on acceptance of spending limits combined with contribution limits amounts to coerced surrender of First Amendment rights).

58. 487 F. Supp. 280 (S.D.N.Y. 1980) *aff'd*. 445 U.S. 955.

59. *Id.* at 282-83.

tioning acceptance of government benefits on the waiver of First Amendment rights constituted an unconstitutional condition.[60]

Citing footnote 65 from *Buckley*, the Federal District Court for the Southern District of New York held that "the fact that a statute requires an individual to choose between two methods of exercising the same constitutional right does not render the law invalid, provided the statute does not diminish a protected right or, where there is such a diminution, the burden is justified by a compelling state interest."[61] The District Court concluded that public funding did not infringe upon a candidate's First Amendment rights. Even if such conditional government benefit did infringe on those rights, the government had a compelling interest in relieving the candidates of the "burdens of soliciting private contributions and of avoiding unhealthy obligations to private contributors."[62]

While the Supreme Court's summary affirmance of the holding in *RNC* indicates that the government may constitutionally condition public funding of campaigns upon an agreement to limit campaign expenditures, it does not explain the rationale.

The district court in *RNC* reasoned that a choice between two methods of exercising the same constitutional right does not violate the unconstitutional condition doctrine unless choosing the alternative with government benefits diminished the constitutional right. Conditional public financing of political campaigns limits the method of fundraising but does not affect the content or amount (or as stated in *Buckley*, the "quality and quantity") of the candidate's speech. Whether the candidate chooses public financing or private fundraising, she would be able to create and disseminate the same advertisements without change in their content and language.

Likewise, the amount of speech by the candidate will be unaffected. Whether the candidate utilizes public financing or private fundraising, she is free to chose whichever method provides her with the most money for speech. If the candidate believes she may speak more by foregoing public financing and raising private funds, she simply chooses the alternative that allows her to speak more and is not harmed by the rejected offer of public financing. If she believes she will speak more by accepting public financing, her speech is not limited, but augmented, by the public financing offer.

The only argument against conditioning public benefits on expenditure limits may be that it will coerce the candidate to accept public financing

---

60. *Id.* at 283.
61. *Id.* at 284-85
62. *Id.* at 285.

because it will provide the candidate with more money than private fundraising. This is the argument raised by the plaintiffs in *RNC*. But, more money means the opportunity for more speech, not less. The unconstitutional conditions doctrine prohibits a conditional public benefit only if it forces a recipient to reduce the amount of protected activity, not increase it.

This analysis would allow Congress to condition a candidate's ability to receive more generous contributions from political parties upon an agreement to limit the amount of personal funds which may be used in a candidate's campaign. Congress could also condition acceptance of free television time on limiting overall campaign spending. In each case, receipt of the public benefit would not alter the content of the candidate's speech. Nor would acceptance of the public benefit diminish the amount of speech by the candidate. If the candidate believes he can obtain more funds to pay for speech without the public benefit, he may do so.

As the Court noted in *Buckley*, public financing conditioned on expenditure limits does "not abridge, restrict, or censor speech, but rather... use[s] public money to facilitate and enlarge public discussion and participation in the electoral process, goals vital to a self-governing people. Thus [public financing conditioned on expenditure limits] furthers, not abridges, pertinent First Amendment values."[63]

---

63. *Buckley*, 424 U.S. at 92-93.

About the Authors

Lillian R. BeVier is the Henry L. & Grace Doherty Charitable Foundation Professor of Law at the University of Virginia. She is a member of the Board of Trustees of the Atlantic Legal Foundation, the Legal Advisory Board of the Center for Individual Rights and the National Advisory Board of the Independent Women's Forum. Professor BeVier received her J.D. from Stanford Law School. She has published scholarly articles on the subject of constitutional law, the First Amendment, campaign finance regulation, and judicial review. Her article, *Money and Politics: A Perspective on the First Amendment and Campaign Finance Reform*, was first published in 73 CALIF. L. REV. 1045 (1985).

Richard Briffault is the Joseph P. Chamberlain Professor of Legislation, Director of the Legislative Drafting Research Fund, and Vice-Dean of Columbia Law School. His teaching and research have focused on state and local government law, regulation, and the law of the political process. He is the author of a leading treatise on state balanced budget requirements and numerous law review articles. He received his J.D. from Harvard Law School. His article, *Campaign Finance, the Parties and the Court: A Comment on Colorado Republican Federal Campaign Committee v. FEC*, was first published in 14 CONST. COMMENTARY 91 (1997).

Vincent A. Blasi is the Corliss Lamont Professor of Civil Liberties at Columbia University School of Law. He has taught at the University of Texas, Stanford, the University of Michigan, and the University of California, Berkeley. He received his J.D. from the University of Chicago Law School. He edited a book on the jurisprudence of the Burger Court and has published scholarly articles on the First Amendment and other areas of constitutional law. His article, *Free Speech and the Widening Gyre of Fundraising*, was first published in 94 COLUM. L. REV. 128 (1994).

David L. Boren is the President of the University of Oklahoma. He served as Governor of Oklahoma from 1975-79 and as a member of the United States Senate from Oklahoma from 1979 to 1996. Mr. Boren was a Rhodes Scholar and received his J.D. from the University of Oklahoma. In the Senate, Mr. Boren was the primary sponsor of campaign finance reform legislation. During his career in elected office, Mr. Boren refused to accept PAC contributions. He began introducing campaign finance reform legislation in 1985 with former Republican Senator Barry Goldwater. His article, *A Recipe for the Reform of Congress*, was originally published in 21 OKLA. CITY U.L. REV. 1 (1996).

Thomas F. Burke is Assistant Professor of Political Science at Wellesly College. He has been a research fellow at the Brookings Institution and the Institute of Governmental Studies at the University of California-Berkeley. He received his Ph.D. in political science from the University of California-Berkeley. Professor Burke's article, *The Concept of Corruption in Campaign Finance Reform Law,* was first published in 14 CONST. COMMENTARY 127 (1997).

Jill E. Fisch is Professor of Law at Fordham University. She serves as chair of the committee on Corporation Law of the Association of the Bar of the City of New York, on the faculty at the New York City Law Department's Civil Trial Advocacy Workshop, and as a member of the American Law Institute. She received her J.D. from Yale Law School. Professor Fisch has published extensively in the areas of corporate law, securities regulation, and federal courts. Professor Fisch's article, *Frankenstein's Monster Hits the Campaign Trail: An Approach to Regulation of Corporate Political Expenditures*, was first published in 32 WM & MARY L. REV. 587 (1991).

Richard L. Hasen is Associate Professor of Law at Loyola Law School in Los Angeles, California. Prior to joining the law faculty at Loyola, he served as Assistant Professor of Law at Chicago-Kent College of Law, Illinois Institute of Technology. He received his J.D. and Ph.D. in political science from the University of California, Los Angeles. Professor Hasen has published numerous scholarly articles in the area of election law and law and economics. His article, *Clipping Coupons for Democracy: An Egalitarian/Public Choice Defense of Campaign Finance Vouchers*, was first published in 84 CALIF. L. REV. 1 (1996).

Daniel H. Lowenstein is Professor of Law at the University of California, Los Angeles. He serves as a member of the boards of the Shakespeare Society of America and Americans for Nonsmokers Rights and served as a member of the Common Cause National Governing Board. He was the principle draftsperson of the California Political Reform Act of 1974 (Prop. 9) and was Chair of the California Fair Political Practices Commission from 1975 to 1979. Professor Lowenstein received his LL.B.

from Harvard Law School. He has published extensively in the area of election law and is the author of a leading casebook on Election Law. His article, *On Campaign Finance Reform: The Root of All Evil is Deeply Rooted*, was first published in 18 HOFSTRA L. REV. 301 (1989).

Susan Manes retired in 1995 from Common Cause where she served as Vice President for Issues and Legislation. In this position, Ms. Manes formulated and directed Common Cause's legislative efforts on Capital Hill on campaign finance reform and other issues. Prior to joining Common Cause, Ms. Manes was staff director of the United States Senate Democratic Policy Committee. The committee served as the leadership staff to Senate Minority Leader, Robert Byrd (D-WVA). Ms. Manes received her B.A. from Sarah Lawrence College. Her article, co-authored with Fred Wertheimer, *Campaign Finance Reform: A Key to Restoring the Health of our Democracy*, was first published in 94 COLUM. L. REV. 1126 (1994).

Timothy J. Moran is an attorney with the Appellate Section of the U.S. Department of Justice, Civil Rights Division in Washington, D.C. He served as law clerk to the Honorable William Wayne Justice of the United States District Court for the Eastern District of Texas. Mr. Moran received his J.D. from Harvard Law School. His article, *Format Restrictions on Televised Political Advertising: Elevating Political Debate Without Supressing Free Speech*, first appeared in 67 IND. L.J. 663 (1992). The views expressed are those of the author and do not represent the views of the United States Department of Justice.

Peter M. Shane is Dean and Professor of Law at the University of Pittsburg School of Law. He serves as a board member of the Council on Legal Educational Opportunity (CLEO) and was appointed a public member of the Administrative Conference of the United States. He has served as Chair of the Association of American Law Schools Section for the Law School Dean and the sections on Administrative Law and on Remedies. Dean Shane received his law degree from Yale Law School. He has published numerous scholarly articles on constitutional and administrative law topics and is a co-author of two leading casebooks on Administrative Law and Separation of Powers. His article, *Back to the Future of the American State: Overruling Buckley v. Valeo and Other Madisonian Steps*, was first published in 57 U. PITT. L. REV. 443 (1996).

Frederick G. Slabach is the Associate Dean at Whittier Law School. He has served as the Assistant Secretary of Agriculture for Congressional

Relations at the United States Department of Agriculture, Associate Dean at Mississippi College School of Law, Legislative Counsel to the President Pro Tempore of the United States Senate, Administrative Assistant to the Governor of Mississippi and the Executive Director of the Mississippi Democratic Party. He received his J.D. from the University of Mississippi School of Law and his LL.M. from Columbia University School of Law. Dean Slabach has published scholarly articles in the field of voting rights and civil rights. He is also the 1995 recipient of the Elmer B. Staats Public Service Award presented by the Harry S. Truman Scholarship Foundation in Washington, D.C.

Bradley A. Smith is Associate Professor of Law at Capital University Law School in Columbus, Ohio. He is an adjunct scholar of the Cato Institute and serves as a member of the Board of Scholars of the MacKinac Center for Public Policy and the Board of Academic Advisors for the Buckeye Institute for Public Policy Solutions. He received his J.D. from Harvard Law School. Professor Smith has published extensively in the field of campaign finance reform and election law. He has appeared on several national television and radio programs and has testified before committees of the United States House of Representatives and the United States Senate. Professor Smith's article, *Faculty Assumptions and Undemocratic Consequences of Campaign Finance Reform*, was first published in 105 YALE L.J. 1049 (1996).

David A. Strauss is the Harry N. Wyatt Professor of Law at the University of Chicago. He serves as Editor of The Supreme Court Review, has argued several cases before the United States Supreme Court, and authored numerous briefs on the merits in the United States Supreme Court. Professor Stauss received his J.D. from Harvard Law School. He has published numerous scholarly articles in the area of constitutional law, election law and racial discrimination. His article, *Corruption, Equality and Campaign Finance Reform*, was first published in 94 COLUM. L. REV. 1369 (1994).

Cass R. Sunstein is the Karl N. Llewellyn Professor of Jurisprudence at the University of Chicago. He served as law clerk to United States Supreme Court Justice Thurgood Marshall. He is a member of the American Academy of Arts and Sciences, the American Law Institute and serves in leadership positions on the American Bar Association Committee on the Separation of Powers and the section on Administrative Law. Professor Sunstein received his J.D. from Harvard Law School. He is the award winning author of several books and scholarly articles on constitutional law and administrative law. His article, *Political Equality and Unintended Consequences*, was first published in 94 COLUM. L. REV. 1390 (1994).

Fred Wertheimer is the President and Founder of Democracy 21, a non partisan organization working to strengthen and renew American democracy for the 21st century. He served as President and Chief Executive Officer of Common Cause from 1981 to 1995, as a Fellow at the Shorenstein Center on the Press, Politics and Public Policy at Harvard University's Kennedy School of Government, as J. Skelly Wright Fellow and Visiting Lecturer at Yale Law School and as a Fellow at the Institute of Politics at Harvard University. Mr. Wertheimer received his J.D. from Harvard Law School. He is a leading spokesperson on the issues of money in politics, ethics, government accountability, and reform in the political system. He has appeared regularly on network television and radio news and other programs. He has written numerous op-eds and articles for major metropolitan newspapers around the country and has published several scholarly articles on campaign finance reform. His article, co-authored with Susan Manes, *Campaign Finance Reform: A Key to Restoring the Health of Our Democracy*, was originally published in 94 COLUM. L. REV. 1126 (1994).

J. Skelly Wright retired from the United States Court of Appeals for the District of Columbia in 1986. Judge Wright was appointed United States Attorney in New Orleans, Louisiana in 1948 and United States District Judge in New Orleans in 1949. During his tenure on the district court he was a pioneer in desegregating public schools, transportation, parks and sporting events. In 1963, Judge Wright was appointed to the Court of Appeals in D.C., where he authored landmark opinions on racial discrimination, the First Amendment and administrative law. He also wrote law review articles on these subjects. Judge Wright received his law degree from Loyola University School of Law in New Orleans. Judge Wright's racial desegregation opinions were hailed as courageous and visionary by some and traitorous by others, and resulted in a cross burning on his lawn and numerous death threats. When he died in 1988 at the age of 77, the New York Times called him a champion of the poor[1] and the National Law Journal called him a hero.[2] His article, *Politics and the Constitution: Is Money Speech?*, was originally published in 85 YALE L.J. 1001 (1996).

---

1. Margorie Hunter, *Judge J. Skelly Wright, Segregation Foe Dies at 77*, THE NEW YORK TIMES, Aug. 8, 1988, at D10.

2. *A Career of Courage*, THE NATIONAL LAW JOURNAL, Aug. 22, 1998, at 8.

Library of Congress Cataloging-in-Publication Date

The Constitution and campaign finance reform : an anthology / edited
by Frederick G. Slabach.
    p.   cm.
    Includes bibliographical reference.
    ISBN 0-89089-937-1
    1. Campaign funds—Law and legislation—United States.
I. Slabach, Frederick Gilbert, 1956– .
KF4920.C57   1998
342.73'078—dc21   98-15120
                                        CIP